CONFIDENCE AMID CHANGE

David O. McKay at the beginning
of his presidency in 1951, at 77 years of age.

CONFIDENCE AMID CHANGE

The Presidential Diaries of David O. McKay | 1951–1970

Harvard S. Heath, editor

Signature Books | 2019 | Salt Lake City

Dedicated to my wife, Susan,
who understands what dedication means

SIGNATURE LEGACY SERIES

The images reproduced in this book are from the Utah State
Historical Society's Classified, Clifford Bay, Salt Lake Tribune,
and Savage Company Photograph Collections.

FIRST EDITION | 2019

LIBRARY OF CONGRESS CATALOGING-IN-PUBLICATION DATA

Names:	McKay, David O. (David Oman), 1873–1970, author. | Heath, Harvard S., 1945– editor.
Title:	Confidence amid change : the presidential diaries of David O. McKay, 1951–1970 / edited by Harvard S. Heath.
Description:	First edition. | Salt Lake City : Signature Books, 2019. | Includes bibliographical references and index.
Identifiers:	LCCN 2018041922 (print) | LCCN 2018047417 (ebook) | ISBN 9781560853527 (e-book) | ISBN 9781560852698 (hardcover: alk. paper)
Subjects:	LCSH: McKay, David O. (David Oman), 1873–1970—Diaries. | Church of Jesus Christ of Latter-day Saints—Presidents—Diaries. | Mormon Church—Presidents—Diaries. | LCGFT: Diaries.
Classification:	LCC BX8695.M27 (ebook) | LCC BX8695.M27 A3 2019 (print) | DDC 289.3092 [B] —dc23

LC record available at https://lccn.loc.gov/2018041922

CONTENTS

introduction vii

  1 Change, 1951 1

  2 Support, 1952 23

  3 Matters of Politics and Education, 1953 49

  4 Doctrine, the International Church, and More Politics, 1954 . . 87

  5 The South Pacific and Washington DC, 1955 115

  6 Political Perceptions and Misperceptions, 1956 135

  7 Educational and Political Dilemmas, 1957 161

  8 Turmoil and Tragedy, 1958 205

  9 Rebellion, Temples, and Grief, 1959 255

10 Doctrinal Difficulties, 1960 295

11 Seventies, Vacancies, and the Negro, 1961 353

12 Nigeria and Nigerians, Political and
    Polygamous Problems, 1962 403

13 Benson, Difficulties with Birchers,
    and Declining Health, 1963 461

14 Lingering Health and Political Problems, 1964 511

15 A Year of Reorganization and Reiteration, 1965 569

16 Benson and Birchism, 1966 635

17 Grappling with Growth and Changing Contours, 1967 681

18 Predicaments: Policies, Politics, and Succession, 1968 733

19 Continued Difficulties, Despondency, and Death, 1969–70 . . 787

frequently cited sources 825

photographs 833

index 849

Introduction

From their earliest years, members of the Church of Jesus Christ of Latter-day Saints were devoted journal keepers who, like their Puritan forebears, considered it a responsibility to document their role in the Separatist or Restorationist movements.[1] Some of the diaries are personal and introspective, others official in tone. Some only recorded basic diurnal tasks, but either way the diarists give a sense of performing a sacred duty.

This has left us with a diverse treasure trove of records to capture and interpret the Mormon experience at different times and places. With thousands of journals, we see firsthand the evolving story of the LDS Restoration. The diaries of church presidents hold special promise but are not all available for research. Of the nineteenth-century diaries, President Wilford Woodruff's (1807–98) journals have been among the most often cited because of the availability of a typescript of his personal writings for more than thirty years now. Historians have mined it for glimpses of church events spanning seven decades from Ohio in the 1830s to Utah in the 1890s.[2]

Excerpts from the journals of other LDS presidents, as they have become available in the last few years, have been equally valuable in capturing the pulse and tenor of LDS thought through the eyes of Joseph Smith (1805–44), whose diaries were only recently published by the

---

1. Haller, *Rise of Puritanism*, 37–39, 97–100; Allen, *Studies in Mormon History*, 508–24; also Davis Bitton, *Guide to Mormon Diaries and Autobiographies* (Provo: BYU Press, 1977).

2. Laurel Thatcher Ulrich's *A House Full of Females* (New York: Alfred A. Knopf, 2017), recent winner of the David Evans Biography Award, draws heavily on Woodruff's diaries (the name Woodruff elicits 243 hits in the electronic version). For the typescript, see Scott G. Kenney, ed., *Wilford Woodruff's Journals*, 9 vols. (Midvale, UT: Signature Books, 1983–85).

church in three volumes;[3] Brigham Young (1801–77), whose diaries and office journals were scanned a few years ago and made available on the Church History Library website;[4] and daily entries by the secretary to President John Taylor (1808–87).[5]

For the twentieth century, aside from David O. McKay (1873–1970), only the diaries of his immediate predecessor George Albert Smith (1870–1951) are open for investigation. Smith's papers reside at the J. Willard Marriott Library on the University of Utah. Despite their availability, they have not yet been tapped for publication. The papers of President Spencer W. Kimball have been available at the LDS Church History Library for a limited number of preferred researchers, whereas the personal writings of Joseph F. Smith, Heber J. Grant, Joseph Fielding Smith, Harold B. Lee, Ezra Taft Benson, Howard W. Hunter, and Gordon B. Hinckley remain closed.[6] That is among the reasons why publication of the McKay record is important, in that it provides information not otherwise available from twentieth-century LDS presidential diaries for a period of church history that saw significant growth and change.

Content

The breadth of the McKay diaries adds to their significance, in covering the administrative, social, political, and ecclesiastical issues facing the church in the watershed post-war period. No longer is there a preoccupation with polygamy, as there had been for all previous church leaders. McKay is only the second monogamous president, his immediate

---

3. *The Joseph Smith Papers: Journals*, 3 vols (Salt Lake City: Church Historian's Press, 2008–15). A transcript was prepared in 1987 by Scott H. Faulring and published by Signature Books as *An American Prophet's Record: The Diaries and Journals of Joseph Smith*.

4. Brigham Young Office Files, 1832–78, CR 1234 1, LDS Church History Library; the diaries will also be published soon as *Brigham Young, Colonizer of the American West: Diaries and Office Journals, 1832–1871*, edited by George D. Smith, published by Signature Books.

5. Jedediah S. Rogers, ed., *In the President's Office: The Diaries of L. John Nuttall, 1879–1892* (Salt Lake City: Signature Books, 2007).

6. The diaries for a few months of Joseph F. Smith's administration are available online. Occasionally biographers have been given limited access to other presidential collections, and in some instances family members are in possession of copies of documents housed in the church library.

predecessor, George Albert Smith, the first. We can imagine that issues of the twentieth century would have baffled previous leaders.

David O. McKay was the first to break ground in many areas, beginning with his idealization of courtship and marriage, a reflection of his own lifelong love affair with Emma Ray Riggs (1877–1970), providing a model for the rest of the church. McKay's archives at the University of Utah contain thousands of pictures, news accounts, and celebrations of family life. He was also the first president who was not what might be the equivalent of Bostonian blue-bloods, as the obscure grandson of Scottish and Welch immigrants rather than someone with elite connections to earlier church leaders or who had experienced the Midwestern period of LDS history.

Nor should we forget that McKay was the first president since Joseph Smith to be clean-shaven. Yet McKay's roots were in a rural agrarian community in the Wasatch Mountains, while previous leaders had come from urban backgrounds and related vocations. Considering his background, it is ironic that McKay and George Albert Smith were the only two presidents to 1970 who had college degrees. As such, it is understandable that McKay emphasized education in new and powerful ways. He pushed for greater funding of Brigham Young University and other church schools and for professionally trained educators in other areas. He was interested in and concerned about the international membership too. He was the first to consider seriously how policies would affect congregations overseas. Other presidents had travelled abroad and visited the Saints, but none had considered accommodating local programs to foreign needs.

His contacts with national political and cultural leaders involved more than greetings and photo opportunities, illustrated by the times McKay was summoned to the White House, ostensibly to advise Presidents Eisenhower and Johnson on policy matters. He had an ear to the ground at home as well and was anxious to lend a hand or consider another point of view on civic issues.

In his administrative responsibilities, he welcomed innovation, especially in the missionary program and in broadening the reach of the temples, including foreign languages in the ceremonies.[7] He was the first

7. See "David O. Mckay: Prophet, Seer, and Innovator," *Time* magazine, Jan. 1970.

to see temples built outside of the Mormon corridor, even outside of the United States and Canada.

A principal concern in the 1950s–60s was race, and McKay found himself in a quandary when he traveled to South Africa and the South Pacific over how to adjust to the modern world. In the 1960s, some 5,000 Nigerians who had had no prior contact with the church sent letters requesting baptism. The First Presidency discussed what their response should be, considering that the church had not yet extended the priesthood or full temple participation to blacks. His counselors suggested offering them the Aaronic Priesthood, rather than the higher offices of the Melchizedek Priesthood, but McKay could not see it, fearing that this would lead to interracial marriage. In this and other ways, he represented a bridge between the centuries, with one eye one the future and another fixed on the past.

Among the general characteristics of the men McKay surrounded himself with in the church, business, and politics was how many had served in World War II or the Korean Conflict, or for some such as his counselor N. Eldon Tanner, World War I. For those whose birth had placed them between the two wars, they were equally concerned about the aftermath of fascism and the unexpected spread of Communism. Some in the church, along with apostle Ezra Taft Benson, gravitated toward the John Birch Society to search out Communist infiltration in American society generally. McKay's sympathies were with that ultra-conservative wing of the Republican Party, but he kept to the mainstream in adopting policies affecting the church.

That is not to say he was politically aloof, because in 1953 he directed the hiring of seven lobbyists to influence state legislatures in Utah, Idaho, and Wyoming. As his diaries show, he was often on the telephone with LDS politicians in Washington, DC., and he met regularly with two or three close associates in Salt Lake City to discuss strategies for improving the local region. His lunch companions on those occasions were Utah Governor J. Bracken Lee, Salt Lake City Chamber of Commerce director Gus Backman, and later *Salt Lake Tribune* publisher John F. Fitzpatrick.

When it came to theology, McKay was in favor of openness and allowing members the freedom to interpret scripture as best they could.

Some of the other brethren wanted to codify church theology and practice and remove any ambiguity. McKay was similarly wary of the fledgling Correlation Program that aimed to standardize the church's doctrine and activities by requiring every congregation to follow the regulations of a central office, enforced through regional officers. He warned the apostles that they should not let the church be run by a committee—his code for the Correlation Department. Still, he was an advocate for the professionalization of the church in education, finance, construction of chapels, writing of history, and other areas.

Over time he became less able to resist attempts by counselors and apostles to influence him, partly due to his age and partly due to his personality—a desire to avoid conflict. However, this propensity produced confusion that someone with a stronger hand would have avoided. At a time of deep cross-currents in the church and in the world, McKay's motivational style was to cajole, coax, and compromise, with implicit starts and stops as he allowed others to experiment with one program, then discard it for another. Considering that he stood at a divide between the centuries, he did remarkably well. He seemed made for the office. He was comfortable on stage in front of an audience, polished in his delivery, and enjoyed mingling with church members. Occasionally, though, he had to retreat to the family home in Huntsville, Utah, for contemplation and spiritual promptings, instead of having to provide immediate answers to difficulties.

Some readers may suspect that the diaries were the product of McKay's secretary, Clare Middlemiss (1901–83), rather than of the president himself. Since it was an official office record, he avoided the opportunity to confide feelings about his family or the poetry of Robert Burns, as one can infer between the lines. Much of it was dictated to his secretary, and the rest was written by her as she observed his activities and recorded his statements. He has that in common with Joseph Smith, whose diaries were kept by his scribes, and twentieth-century Church Historian Leonard J. Arrington, who dictated entries to secretaries and sometimes relied on them to fill in missing portions.[8]

Some of the content comes in the form of excerpts from the official

---

8. Bergera, *Confessions of a Mormon Historian*, 1:71n9, 157.

minutes of First Presidency and Quorum of the Twelve meetings, word-for-word transcriptions of telephone conversations, and the contents of interviews conducted in the president's office. The result is that readers get a fly-on-the-wall perspective, regardless of which parts were written by McKay or by Middlemiss. The president reviewed and approved the entries in any case. It seems Middlemiss took shorthand notes and compiled the typed diary from those, including her underlining certain words or passages. Perhaps it was done to make it easier to go back and find what McKay had said about a given topic on a given day.

Provenance

The persistence of secretary Middlemiss to ensure the safe keeping and availability of the diaries is a story within a story. McKay had long been a diary keeper. Still, it was not until he employed Middlemiss in 1935 that his diaries took on their complete form. We can see from his missionary diary in Scotland (1897–99), and subsequent attempts to keep a daily journal, how he wanted to chronicle his daily life from an early age but showed more commitment than passion for it.[9] They show an earnest attempt to consistently record the day's events, even if he had little time and the entries varied only from a few lines to one page regardless of how important the day's activities had been.

The diary becomes even more perfunctory when he returns home, so that years are sometimes truncated to the point that they barely capture any of the most important developments in his life. As individuals often do in setting out to maintain a journal beginning in January and discover as March rolls around that they lack the enthusiasm, McKay's entries become sporadic. He continues to struggle with this even after being called as an apostle in 1906 and as a counselor in the First Presidency in 1934.

It was when Middlemiss became his secretary in 1935 that his attentiveness to his diary improved, and it is to her that we owe the finished product, in whatever percentage of encouragement or initiative she devoted to it. The most recent book regarding McKay's life and teachings is dedicated to her memory.[10] McKay mentions that Middlemiss prodded him to be more attentive to his daily record. Whatever

---

9. Stan and Patricia Larson, eds., *What E'er Thou Art, Act Well thy Part: The Missionary Diaries of David O. McKay* (Salt Lake City: Freethinker Press, 1999).

10. Prince and Wright, *David O. McKay*, dedication page, 405–11.

sacrifice this implied, on her part it was a labor of love as she would gather material by day and, according to her nephew, Bob Wright,[11] piece it together at home at night.[12]

I was introduced serendipitously to McKay's diaries in the early 1970s when I joined two other Brigham Young University graduate students in assisting recently released BYU president Ernest L. Wilkinson (1899–1978) to research and write the centennial history of the school. The archives division of the church was struggling to determine how accessible their holdings should be.[13] Leonard J. Arrington (1917–99), the new Church Historian and first non-clerical individual in that position, was as anxious as we were to see that crucial records were available.

The centennial history staff petitioned for access to what we considered to be the most important collections for understanding the history of BYU, but we received a firm rebuff from then-sitting church president Harold B. Lee (1899–1973), who would not entertain any radical departures from existing policies. Wilkinson was perturbed and thought he could persuade the president to make an exception in his case, considering the importance of the project. He finally conceded that it would be impossible to see the documents as long as the existing church president was in office.[14]

Lee passed in December 1973. When we resubmitted our requests, we were surprised to learn that President Spencer W. Kimball (1895–1985), with encouragement from first counselor N. Eldon Tanner (1898–1982),

11. William Robert ("Bob") Wright (1935–2012) was a distinguished attorney in Salt Lake City, an unsuccessful 1980 Republican gubernatorial candidate against Scott M. Matheson, and an LDS Church mission president in the Washington, DC, Mission, 1989–92. He received his undergraduate and law degrees from the University of Utah, served a church mission to Austria, worked for a prominent Utah law firm for nearly thirty years, and became a partner in a law firm in Washington, DC.

12. Prince and Wright, *David O. McKay*, ix–xi, xiv.

13. Among other resources for the controversy regarding accessibility, see Charles P. Adams and Gustive O. Larsen, "A Study of the LDS Church Historian's Office, 1830-1900," *Utah Historical Quarterly* 40 (Fall 1972): 370–89; Davis Bitton, "Ten Years in Camelot: A Memoir," *Dialogue: A Journal of Mormon Thought* 16 (Autumn 1983): 9–33; Leonard J. Arrington, "Personal Reflections on Mormon History," *Sunstone*, July/Aug. 1983; Arrington, "Historian as Entrepreneur: A Personal Essay," *BYU Studies* 17 (Winter 1977): 193–209.

14. There had been some hard feelings between Lee and Wilkinson in the past, and in a staff meeting in the summer of 1973 Wilkinson hinted that things would not change until Lee was out of office.

had agreed to give us access to almost any collection we desired for the duration of the project.[15] The McKay diaries were at the top of our list because we suspected they held notes on the discussions regarding a plan to create regional junior colleges as feeder schools for BYU. While I perused the diary, it struck me that it was an extraordinary document illuminating more than educational policies. It chronicled the rise of the modern church in ways I had not fully appreciated before.

As a young scholar, I supposed the Arrington era of "Camelot" openness would not end and that I would return to scrutinize the diaries in greater detail. That would not happen. As Chaucer said, all good things must end so that better things can happen.[16] In 1982 Arrington was released, the professional historical staff dismantled, and the McKay diaries closed to the public. It was fortuitous that Middlemiss kept a photocopy of the diaries, photocopies of correspondence, scrapbooks, and photographs and bequeathed them to nephew, Bob Wright.[17] Thanks to a gift from him, the collection was added to existing McKay papers at the Special Collections area of the J. Willard Marriott Library, from which I compiled the present abridgment. The diary comprises some 40,000 pages, 88 percent of which (35,000 pages) are from the years McKay was president of the church, 1951–70. Excluding newspaper clippings, agendas and programs, and other things that do not strictly qualify as diary material, the dated entries take up about 15,000 pages, and the amount of material in the current abridged version does not exceed 10 percent of the dated entries.[18]

In view of the scope of the diary, determining what to include was daunting, considering that the full set of dated entries would occupy at least ten volumes. I decided to give preference to history, doctrine, and entries showing the president's administrative style. Sometimes I selected topics to show his home life for variety and to give a sense of his

---

15. For Kimball's views on church history, see Kimball, *Lengthen Your Stride*, 186–90.

16. Or as Sir Thomas Mallory conceived the plot, "Now is this realm wholly mischieved, and the noble fellowship of the Round Table shall be disparpled" (*Le Morte D'Arthur*). The paraphrase of Chaucer is from his *Troilus and Criseyde*.

17. Wright collaborated with Prince on *David O. McKay and the Rise of Modern Mormonism*, in which there is a fuller discussion of the provenance of the diaries (ix–xviii).

18. I am preparing a transcript of the complete diaries for publication by Greg Kofford Books.

personality. I suspect that some of the entries I chose will only prove to be of interest to myself. This compilation is admittedly subjective and does not present a complete portrait of the president. Readers should not assume that the entries I chose are all that is available, because there are many other significant issues, events, and people in the unabridged diaries that would have been included but for the space restriction. That said, this one volume does capture the essence of McKay's faith, temperament, intellect, and character. It will no doubt be useful for researchers looking at important decisions and events. It should also be of more than passing interest to general readers who would probably not be served by more entries about daily routines or administrative minutiae.

Editorial approach

I silently standardized the format of the date lines, closed spaces between paragraphs, and added first-line indents. For typographical errors involving one missing, superfluous, or transposed letter, I silently corrected them, but for anything greater than that (two letters in a word), I placed the correction within brackets. Sometimes I added a footnote to explain what the original spelling or wording was.

When I included only part of a given entry, I supplemented the missing part with ellipsis dots. Readers should be aware that there are gaps between nearly every complete entry but that I chose not to clutter the presentation with ellipses to indicate that, also that whatever ellipses exist are mine, not Middlemiss's. The opposite is true for underlinings, which are hers.

I tried to provide enough information in annotations and bracketed insertions that readers would be able to follow along without difficulty. My intent was not to impose my views, but rather to give contextual information that would illuminate events and identify participants. It is easy for me to check the accuracy of something said in passing or to explain whether a suggestion was carried out or proved successful. I have done so for the sake of historical continuity and reader comprehension, not as a critique of the advisability of a given policy.

Acknowledgments

Thank you to Ardis E. Parshall for producing the initial typescript, the quality of which I can attest to from having proofed it against the photocopies of the original documents. Also to George D. Smith and the Smith–Pettit Foundation and director Gary James Bergera for sponsoring this multi-year project. And to my colleagues at BYU who offered invaluable suggestions—the former library curator James D'Arc, whose long friendship and cogent comments are always appreciated; my doctoral chair Thomas G. Alexander; the late history professor Marvin S. Hill; and others who gave encouragement and criticism. Also to the staff of Signature Books for their design (Jason Francis), hours of fact checking (Ron Priddis), marketing plans (Devery Anderson), and creation of a Kindle version (Greg Jones). There are others too who pitched in: Bryan Buchanan, who proofed the galleys, and David Cramer, who compiled the index. These kinds of projects are always group efforts.

Nor would it have been possible without the assistance of Wayne and Jody Ross, who provided space for my research library and offered support during my son Daniel's bout with cancer and subsequent death. Others offered support in similar ways: Dick and Sharleen Thomas, David and Carolyn Wright, Greg and Jane Cloward, and James and Millie Mitton.

My wife, Susan, has been patient through the vicissitudes and stress that are coincident with this kind of endeavor. The rest of my family has been equally helpful. I could never have been able to navigate the ever-changing computer technologies without the help of my son Nicholas, and he will be happy to know that there will be no more late-night and early-morning emergency calls. I also appreciate the support of my brothers Randy and Shane.

1   Change, 1951

> ... I remember President McKay's sadness, and how ashen his
> face as he felt the full impact of the responsibility that had fallen
> upon him. —Clare Middlemiss, April 5, 1951

April 2, 1951, 10 o'clock. I received word ... that [LDS] President [George
Albert] Smith was in a very serious condition. I went immediately to the
house and was shocked at his appearance. He did not seem to recognize
me—the first time during his sickness. I realized that possibly the end
was not far off. It came as quite a shock to my nervous system, for I
fully sensed then what his passing means. I remained at his bedside until
about 12:30 p.m.[1]

April 4, 1951, 10 a.m. Received a telephone call from Dr. Leroy Kimball, President [George Albert] Smith's personal physician, who reported
that President Smith is failing, and that the end is near—perhaps within
an hour. ...

   Just a few moments after 7 p.m. received a call to come to the bedside of President Smith as the end was drawing near. Arrived there just
a few moments prior to his passing, at 7:27 p.m. President [J. Reuben]
Clark and members of the immediate family were present.

April 5, 1951, 9 a.m. President [J. Reuben] Clark conferred with me relative

---

1. George Albert Smith's diary reads: "Had a relapse this morning. The nurse sent
for the doctor and Arthur [Haycock] came right up, and called President [J. Reuben]
Clark and President McKay who came right away to see me. President Clark was in
Grantsville, and President McKay had been to Huntsville and returned soon after Arthur called." Smith diary, Apr. 2, 1951. See also Pusey, *Builders of the Kingdom*, 344–61.

to statement from the Counselors [in the First Presidency] regarding President [George Albert] Smith's passing.[2]

April 8, 1951, 4:30 p.m. Special council meeting was held in the Salt Lake Temple. Presented to the Twelve [Apostles] the names of my counselors—Elder Stephen L. Richards as First Counselor, and Pres[ident] J. Reuben Clark, Jr. as Second Counselor.[3]

April 10, 1951, 9 a.m. Attended a First Presidency's meeting. From now on a meeting of the President and his counselors will be held every morning at this hour.

April 12, 1951, 10 a.m. to 3:30 p.m. Council meeting. At this meeting I was ordained as President of the Church. Elder Joseph Fielding Smith,[4] President of the Quorum of the Twelve, was voice.

April 14, 1951. Following my morning's work at the office I returned home where I rest[ed] for about an hour, and then [wife] Ray[5] and I went to the

---

2. McKay's personal secretary, Clare Middlemiss, reminisced to some church members, "I remember President McKay's sadness, and how ashen his face as he felt the full impact of the responsibility that had fallen upon him. ... It was a humbling realization for President McKay." Prince and Wright, *David O. McKay*, 3.

3. Spencer W. Kimball was "stunned when [McKay] explained that he had chosen Elder [Stephen L.] Richards first, Pres[ident] [J. Reuben] Clark having served as first counselor for [many] long years to Pres[ident] Heber J.] Grant and Pres[ident] [George Albert] Smith. I looked around and found the other brethren stunned. It was hard to understand. I knew Elder Richards had been a close and lifelong friend but I was not prepared for this. ... Not until we started down the steps of the temple did I come to realize that I was not alone in bewilderment and devastation. All the others of the Twelve seemed to be alike stunned. We had been wholly unprepared for this shock." Kimball diary, Apr. 8, 1951. See also Kimball and Kimball, *Spencer W. Kimball*, 268–69; Quinn, *Elder Statesman*, 145–55.

4. Joseph Fielding Smith, son of church president Joseph F. Smith, was born July 19, 1876, and was ordained an apostle at age thirty–three in April 1910. He became acting president of the Quorum of the Twelve in 1950, a member of the First Presidency fifteen years later, and church president in January 1970. He died a little over two years later in July 1972. He was a prolific writer, known for his conservative approach to doctrine.

5. Emma Ray Riggs was born June 23, 1877, in Salt Lake City. She studied at the University of Utah and Cincinnati Conservatory of Music, and taught school in Ogden. She and David O. McKay married in the Salt Lake temple on January 2, 1901. They were the parents of seven children. She died in November 1970, ten months after her husband.

Villa Theater to see "All About Eve."[6] I did not want to go at first, but Ray insisted that it was a good picture and that I needed a little recreation. I enjoyed the show very much, and it did give me the relaxation that I needed.

April 16, 1951. Eldred [G.] Smith,[7] Patriarch to the Church, then called at the office at my request. Additional space for First Presidency's offices was given consideration. Brother Smith said: "If my room is more convenient for the First Presidency, I shall take another room; anything you want me to do will be all right." I told Brother Smith to get in touch with President Stephen L. Richards, who will probably use his offices. ...

Mrs. Agnes Stuart,[8] General Manager of Auerbach Company called. Said Auerbach Company has made arrangements with the publishers of the book "Family Kingdom" by Samuel Woolley Taylor,[9] to have an autograph party, and to also have a window display of the book. Mrs. Stuart said further that she called Pres[ident] [of the Twelve Apostles] Joseph Fielding Smith and inquired if the Church objected to the book. Pres[ident] Smith told her that the Church <u>did</u> object to the book, and would prefer that Auerbach Company do not conduct the autograph party, nor have the window display; in fact, that he would like to go so far as to ask Auerbach Company not to sell the book. Mrs. Stuart then said that she has found that the De-

---

6. McKay was an enthusiastic patron of Hollywood movies. *All About Eve* focused on an aging star who was gradually overshadowed by a young actress she had taken under her wing. It starred Bette Davis and Anne Baxter and was directed by Joseph Mankiewicz.

7. Eldred Gee Smith (1907–2013) had been Patriarch to the Church since April 1947 and served until October 1979, at which time President Spencer W. Kimball implemented an emeritus status for aging church authorities below the rank of apostle. Kimball chose not to name a replacement for Eldred Gee Smith either, opting to retire the office of church patriarch. See Bates and Smith, *Lost Legacy*.

8. Agnes Lovendahl Stewart (1897–1989) had been manager of Auerbach's department store since 1945. She was born in Salt Lake City, graduated from the University of Utah, earned a master's degree from Columbia University, and worked for Gillham Advertising in Salt Lake City prior to her time with Auerbach's. An article she wrote in 1927 for the church's *Young Woman's Journal.* discussed the complications of being a single LDS woman pursuing a career.

9. Samuel Whittaker Taylor (1907–97) was the son of apostle John Whittaker Taylor and grandson of church president John Taylor. In 1906 his father was dropped from the Council of the Twelve for polygamy, as was apostle Matthias Foss Cowley, when the two came under scrutiny by the US Senate committee investigating fellow apostle and US Senator Reed Smoot. A journalist and historian, Sam wrote biographies of his father, *Family Kingdom*, and grandfather, *The Kingdom or Nothing*, and his fiction was adapted for three Disney movies, *The Absent–Minded Professor, Flubber*, and *Son of Flubber*.

seret Book Store and Z.C.M.I. [department store] are selling the book, and she wondered if there is some misunderstanding. Said she had a card which stated that the Deseret Book Store and Z.C.M.I. recommend the book for reading. Mrs. Stuart was advised that the message would be given to Pres[ident] McKay and that we would call her later.

The secretary [Clare Middlemiss] then called the Deseret Book Store who reported that they had refused to have the autograph party, that they have sent out no cards concerning the book, and that they have no display of the book; that there is one copy of it on the shelf. Z.C.M.I. was also called who reported that they also refused the publishers the autograph party, the window display, and that they had sent out no advertising on it whatsoever; that they have purchased 50 copies and have them on their shelves.

When President McKay was advised of the above, he stated, "You may tell Mrs. Stuart that the church does not approve of the book, but that it is entirely up to the Auerbach Company whether they hold their autograph party or put in a window display on the book." Pres[ident] Clark was also consulted on this matter, and he agreed that we have no jurisdiction over the Auerbach Company; that they of course may do as they choose in the matter.

The secretary then called Mrs. Stuart and gave her the facts regarding the Deseret Book Store and the Z.C.M.I. with respect to this book, and also President McKay's message, and she answered: "We would not want to do anything contrary to the policy of the Church, and we shall not hold the autograph party, nor put in a window display." Mrs. Stuart also explained that the card she has with respect to the Deseret Book Store and Z.C.M.I., was sent directly from the publishers.

April 17, 1951, 7:30 a.m. Conference with President Stephen L. Richards. Reported to him that I had a conference with Patriarch Eldred Smith regarding exchange of offices in order that the First Presidency might have more office space, and that Brother Smith had expressed a willingness to do whatever we wanted him to do. Brother Smith will see President Richards and they will make their plans regarding the exchange of offices. ...

Arthur Haycock [former secretary to church president George Albert

Smith].Told him that we would like him to be an assistant to Brother Joseph Anderson [secretary to the First Presidency] for the present, but that later I will feel free to call on him if I need someone to drive a car for me. I hinted to him that the matter of salary will have to be adjusted by the committee under whose jurisdiction this comes. ...

Elder Albert E. Bowen[10] of the Council of the Twelve—Spoke to him about having him help me in the applications for cancellations of [temple-marriage] sealings, taking it out of the hands of Brother Joseph Anderson, and putting it in the hands of one of the Twelve. Brother Bowen agreed that this is a wise thing to do, and said he would accept "not reluctantly, but freely."

April 19, 1951. As all the brethren were in Council meeting when General Douglas MacArthur gave his speech before a special joint session of Congress this morning, I invited them to a re-broadcast held in the radio room in the basement of the Building. Before leaving for Council meeting I instructed Brother Gordon Hinckley to take a wire recording[11] of the speech so that the brethren could hear it later.

General MacArthur's speech explained his military stand in the Far East, and was occasioned because of his removal as supreme commander at that point by [US] President Harry S. Truman. General MacArthur's speech was magnificent and he proved himself to be a great military leader of broad vision and courage.[12]

April 20, 1951. [Lorin Wheelwright[13] said] he had a solution of the

---

10. Albert Ernest Bowen (1875–1953) was ordained an apostle by Heber J. Grant in April 1937. He had previously been an attorney. His keen intellect is captured in a series of radio addresses later published in book form as *Constancy amid Change*.

11. The earliest voice recorders utilized spools of thin wire rather than reels of magnetic tape and were used mostly for dictation. They could be erased and re-used, the same as later tape recorders.

12. Douglas MacArthur (1880–1964) is considered one of the last American military heroes of the twentieth century, who returned from the Pacific theater of World War II to mixed reviews but not for his speech to Congress that ended with this: "Old soldiers never die; they just fade away. And like the old soldier of that ballad, I now close my military career and just fade away—an old soldier who tried to do his duty as God gave him the light to see that duty. Good-by."

13. Lorin Farrar Wheelwright (1909–87) was co-owner of two prominent Utah businesses, Pioneer Music Company and Wheelwright Press. He had studied at the Juilliard

controversy regarding the land surrounding the [This Is the Place] monument.[14] He said, first, "I wish to tell you I will do anything you say—if you want my land, you may have it." He then suggested that they could purchase his land, and about 30 acres more and set it aside for the beautifying of the monument, and then have the State or the City, or both, make it a restricted district; that no commercial buildings of any kind should be built between the corner of the mouth of the Canyon and the monument, and let buildings be erected east of the 30-acre line.

I answered that I had concluded that I would have nothing to do with it. I am not a member of the Commission; my opinion has not been sought, my judgment has never been asked for. Evidently, they have heard of my opinion that I think it is not necessary to set apart 177 acres merely as a protective measure. However, President [George Albert] Smith was in favor of it, and as his successor I am going to say nothing or do nothing that will counteract his wishes. I refused to accept the Presidency [of the Commission] at the request of the Governor, and recommended that President [J. Reuben] Clark receive the appointment. Whether Pres[ident] Clark has accepted I do not know.

May 2, 1951. Elder Henry D. Moyle called from Florida relative to the purchase of additional land for the Orlando Livestock Co[mpany]. Said they have an opportunity to pick up five thousand acres along the St. John's River, just six miles north of the Melbourne Highway. It is a triangular piece that would bring the property already owned right down to the river. Brother Moyle said he thinks he can get it for $20 an acre which is the price they have been trying to secure it for. I asked Brother Moyle about the chances for drainage, and he answered that this property will come under the flood control protected by the State and Federal Government. I then asked him if Brother [Joseph L.] Wirthlin[15] is of

School of Music and the University of Chicago and received a PhD from Columbia University. In 1967 he was named dean of the BYU College of Fine Arts and Communications.

14. This monument stands at the eastern entrance to the Salt Lake Valley, commemorating Brigham Young's arrival in 1847.

15. Joseph Leopold Wirthlin (1893–1963) was a member of the Presiding Bishopric. He had been in office since 1938 and would become the presiding member of the bishopric in 1952. His son, Joseph B. Wirthlin (1917–2008), would become an apostle in 1986. Another son, Richard B. Wirthlin (1931–2011), would serve a five-year term as a member of the Second Quorum of Seventy.

the same opinion regarding the desirability of the property, and Brother Moyle said that they are both united that it should be purchased. I then told Brother Moyle to go ahead with the purchase.[16]

May 4, 1951. Underwent operation this morning at 9 o'clock. Dr. [Richard P.] Middleton[17] performed a prostatectomy.[18] The operation was successful. Was under opiates all day and night. Mama Ray [wife] sat at my bedside.

May 16, 1951. As it was a beautiful day, I later decided to drive up to Huntsville, thinking that the fresh air would do me good. Spent two or three hours on the farm and the invigorating air up there seemed to benefit me greatly; however, I was very tired when I arrived home—while the trip up there was refreshing to me, I realized that I am not entirely recovered from my recent operation.[19]

May 29, 1951. Bishop [Thorpe B.] Isaacson[20] called to tell President McKay that the new car is ready.[21]

June 22, 1951. Came to the office at 8 o'clock this morning. When I

---

16. This became "one of the Church's investment farms, which operate as taxable commercial ventures. Unlike the Church's welfare farms, which provide food and commodities for bishops' storehouses to help the poor and needy, investment farms and ranches support the Church's mission and principles by serving as a rainy–day fund," according to "Church-affiliated Ranch Balances Agriculture and Conservation in Central Florida," *LDS Newsroom*, www.mormonnewsroom.org, April 2016.

17. Richard P. Middleton (1901–95) was a native of southern Utah who had served an LDS mission and graduated from the University of Utah before receiving a medical degree from Harvard University and becoming chair of the urology department at the University of Utah, then president of the medical staff at LDS Hospital.

18. J. Reuben Clark explained that McKay had his prostate removed to finish an "operation of sometime ago. ... They insist that he have the remainder of the operation done." Clark diary, May 3, 1951.

19. Throughout his presidency, McKay returned frequently to his hometown in the mountains east of Ogden to re-energize himself and enjoy greater peace and tranquility.

20. Henry Thorpe Beal Isaacson (1898–1970) had been a member of the Presiding Bishopric since 1946. In 1961 he would become an Assistant to the Quorum of the Twelve and in 1965 a member of the First Presidency. At this point he was first counselor to Bishop Joseph L. Wirthlin.

21. McKay was legendary for his heavy foot on the accelerator and love of driving his car of choice, a Cadillac.

arrived there I found my secretary and President Ernest Wilkinson[22] of the Brigham Young University waiting for me. Brother Wilkinson discussed with me matters pertaining to the budget of the B.Y.U.

July 9, 1951, 8:30 a.m. President [J. Reuben] Clark assisted me in giving a blessing to <u>Brother Eben R. T. Blomquist</u>[23] pertaining to his work as Chairman of the Committee which will translate the Temple ordinances into foreign languages.

July 17, 1951, 5:30 p.m. [D.] Arthur Haycock, former Secretary to President George Albert Smith, came in to ask me, in behalf of the Smith family, if it would be all right for him to let the Smith Family have the two scrap books that had been compiled by the Assistant secretary during the past two and half years, which contain President Smith's printed speeches and newspaper clippings.

Brother Haycock also asked about the disposition of President Smith's diary.

I told Brother Haycock that so far as the Scrap Books are concerned, they may be kept in custody by the family, as most of the material contained therein have been published and are public information, but so far as the diary is concerned, that should be placed in the custody of the Church.

July 20, 1951, 10:30 to 11:30. Consultation with Harry Clarke.[24] Told him to go on with the Obscene Literature Committee, and to give me a list of the [Christian] ministers on the Committee, also to give me a report of the committee's activity to date.[25]

---

22. Ernest L. Wilkinson (1899–1978) was born in Ogden and received a law degree from Harvard University. Before being appointed BYU president in 1951, he was a Washington, DC, lawyer.

23. Eben Reinhold Thorsten Blomquist (1890–1968), a Swedish emigrant and former president of the Swedish mission, had been prominent in southern California in business and politics representing San Bernardino in the state senate.

24. Harry Clarke was a popular folk singer on KSL radio. His programs, "Songs of Harry Clarke" and "Homespun Hour," were something like Garrison Keillor's later *Prairie Home Companion*. When Clarke's ratings fell after nearly thirty years at KSL (see diary entry for Feb. 6, 1953), he became a "mortuary soloist" and funeral director. "Harry Clarke Joins Staff of Jos. Wm. Taylor Memorial Mortuary," *Salt Lake Tribune*, May 8, 1953.

25. There was concern about pornography, locally and nationally as Congress considered appointing a Select Committee on Offensive and Undesirable Books,

I approved of Brother Clarke's appointing a Treasurer, and to give the other churches a chance to contribute (Brother Clarke remarked that the Catholic Church has made most of the contributions).

I told him also to give me a list of his expenses since President [George Albert] Smith's death.

Brother Clarke denied saying that I should have the Priesthood around me—he said: "I have never said that" (referring to having a man secretary).

August 7, 1951, 12:30. Brother Albert John Elggren was given a blessing under my hands giving him authority to perform sealing ordinances in the Salt Lake Temple, with the exception of second sealings.[26]

August 17, 1951, 11:45 a.m. Left the office for an appointment with Dr. L. E. Viko at his offices in the Intermountain Clinic 699 E. South Temple Street.

My reason for this appointment with Dr. Viko was to have him examine my heart. While attending the [Hill Cumorah] Pageant in Palmyra [New York] last week, I suffered a pain in my chest, and fearing it was my heart, I decided to have a check-up. However, after examining me, Dr. Viko said that my heart, my lungs, and my blood pressure were all in good condition; that the reason for the pain was due to the fact that I had been overworking and was fatigued physically, causing a nerve in the area of my heart to become irritated and thus give acute pain—he said many people mistake this condition for heart trouble. Dr. Viko did, however, again warn me not to work too hard, and advised that I take a day's rest once a week at least.

August 18, 1951. This morning at about 2 o'clock, I had a sudden attack of dizziness and nausea that completely prostrated me. In fact, I have never been so helpless in my life—a six-foot man doesn't like to be knocked out in five minutes of the first round, and that's what happened to me! It was with utmost difficulty that I managed to crawl back to my

Magazines, and Comic Books, which they soon did, the committee's report in 1952 alleging that millions of obscene publications were sold each month in the United States. See the entry for December 6 below for reference to the local task force.

26. Second anointings are the highest temple-related ordinance in the church, but they are considered confidential and are rarely discussed.

bed—Sister McKay [wife] who was sleeping out on the porch, did not at first hear me, but I finally awakened her and when she saw my condition she immediately called for Dr. Leslie White who came right over. He stayed with me through the night, and seeing that my condition was getting worse and that I was much weaker he called for an ambulance and took me to the hospital. Then followed a series of examinations and consultations by several doctors. Dr. White called Dr. L. E. Viko, the heart specialist, who after examination found my heart to be in very good condition, the same as he had found it last Friday when he examined me. Dr. P. C. Bauerlein, a stomach specialist, was then called in. At first they thought there were two probable conditions—one, a rupture in the upper walls of my stomach, or, two, an ulcer that had broken through the lining of the stomach, causing a hemorrhage and violent nausea.

However, after repeated examinations, these conditions were ruled out, and then Dr. Bauerlein concluded that through over-exertion or a moderate infection my balance organ in the inner ear had become slightly deranged which caused the upset.

The doctors administered sedatives and kept me absolutely quiet all day.

September 4, 1951. George Richards Cannon, son of the late Hugh J. Cannon, called at the office and stated that it is the desire of his mother, and other members of the family, that the manuscript his father wrote on President McKay's world tour, should be published. (Pres[ident] McKay when advised of this rather favored the printing of this book as there are many important and inspirational incidents recorded in the manuscript of Brother Cannon.)[27]

September 8, 1951. Later in the afternoon I became pretty well fatigued, so went upstairs to lay down. About an hour later Mama Ray came up and said, "While you were resting, Reverend Arthur W. Moulton,[28] retired Bishop of the Episcopal Church (of 71 South 5th East), called to see

27. See Cannon, *David O. McKay around the World.* The author, Hugh Jenne Cannon (1870–1931), a son of apostle George Q. Cannon, had been a stake president and editor of the church's monthly publication, the *Improvement Era*, and had accompanied McKay on a world tour of the church's foreign missions and stakes.
28. Arthur W. Moulton (1873–1962) was a native of Massachusetts, a graduate of the Hobart Theological Seminary who was ordained an Episcopal priest in 1901.

you.["] She handed me the Reverend's card which gave his address on 5th East, and apartment number, and upon which the Reverend had written (immediately following the apartment number) the words "also 78."

When I read the card I said to Ray: "I must dress and repay the Reverend's visit."

I immediately dressed and drove to the address on the card. I entered the building and climbed to the second floor to "apartment 78" only to find that it was not the Reverend's apartment. I then walked down to the first floor to the Manager's office and was informed by the Manager that the Reverend's apartment was on the fourth floor, so I climbed four flights of stairs to his apartment.

Mrs. Moulton answered the door, and I asked if Reverend Moulton was in. At first she did not recognize me, but invited me in and went to the next room to tell the Reverend that he had a visitor. When he came in and saw me standing there, his face lighted up, and he said: "President McKay—why President McKay! This is the most wonderful thing that has ever happened to me—Why it's wonderful!! Come in, come in—sit down, let me take your hat."

I then said to him: "Reverend Moulton the doctors were probably right when they told me that I should take rest and see no more visitors for the day, and my son was undoubtedly right when he explained to you when you called that I was under doctors orders to see no more visitors for the day, but it is not right for me to let your gracious, considerate call go unheeded, so I am here to pay my respects to you, and to thank you for your consideration in calling at my home today to offer your congratulations and respects on my birthday."

The Reverend was visibly moved and he repeated, "Why I have never had anything so nice happen to me before. Won't you please sit down and visit with me."

I said, "No, thank you. I cannot stay; I must get back home." I then said: "I notice that you wrote on your calling card the words 'also 78.' Is it your birthday today?" He answered, "No, I just wanted you to know that I am also 78 years of age; but how I wish I had the honor of being born on the same day as you!" I then said: "When is your

---

During World War I he was a chaplain in France. In Utah he served as bishop for twenty–six years beginning in 1920.

birthday?" He replied: "May 3," and I exclaimed: "Why that is my father's birthday!" The Reverend remarked: "How wonderful! Now I feel like I am related to you."

As I picked up my hat to leave the Reverend came over to me, put his hands upon my shoulders, bowed his head, and gave me a blessing. I reciprocated by giving him a blessing. He then told me that Bishop Watson of the Episcopalian Church had offered prayers in my behalf in their Sunday morning meeting September 2, 1951 when I was so ill in the hospital. I told Rev[erend] Moulton that the Bishop had sent me a letter to that effect, and that I had sincerely appreciated their thoughtfulness and prayers in my behalf.

Reverend Moulton insisted upon going down the stairs to the door with me. When I remonstrated, he was more determined than ever to go with me. He accompanied me right to my car, and when he saw that there was no one at the wheel, he exclaimed: "What! did you drive the car yourself—didn't any one drive you over here?" I said, "No, I usually drive my car." He then said he appreciated more than ever the effort I had put forth to come to see him to repay his visit.

I left the Reverend feeling satisfied that I had done the right thing by repaying his visit of this afternoon, and that much good would result from the contact we had with each other this day.[29]

September 27, 1951. Reported at Council Meeting that with the approval of my counselors, Sister [Emma Ray] McKay and I left by automobile Saturday morning, September 15 for California. Had a very good rest at Laguna Beach; and said that I did not know of a place along the Pacific Coast that is more restful than this spot that had been selected by President George Albert Smith, the home thereon having been originally built by President David I. Stoddard.[30]

---

29. Perhaps no other single experience in the diaries best captures the essence of McKay's sociability and politeness.

30. Since the turn of the century, church leaders had traveled to the west coast for rest and relaxation, not only to Laguna Beach but also to Monterrey and Oceanside. Presidents Heber J. Grant and George Albert Smith, both of whom had suffered from nervous exhaustion, had found the ocean breezes therapeutic, and liked the decelerated pace. Over the objection of his counselors in 1978, President Kimball ordered the Laguna Beach retreat sold. See Gibbons, *Spencer W. Kimball*, 287.

October 4, 1951, 10 to 2:15 p.m. Council meeting—this was an unusually important meeting inasmuch as the choosing of a new apostle to fill the vacancy in the Twelve, and four new Assistants to the Twelve was undertaken at this time.

I invited all the General Authorities, including the Seventies and the Bishopric to attend this meeting. We dressed in our robes, had prayer circle, and partook of the Sacrament.

Each group was represented as follows:

Council of the Twelve—Elder Joseph Fielding Smith

First Council of 70—by Levi Edgar Young

Assistants to the 12 by Clifford E. Young inasmuch as Marion Romney[31] was asked to open the meeting; Presiding Bishopric by Bishop LeGrand Richards, each of whom spoke of his love and confidence in his brethren, and assured all of his loyalty to the Presiding Authorities, and bore his testimony.

Each of the Presidency then addressed those present, the result being a real spiritual feast.

I then did something which has not heretofore been done: I told each one when he would be called upon to speak at the approaching conference. The brethren were very pleased about this.

All were then excused excepting the members of the Council of the Twelve and the First Presidency who carried on their regular duties.

October 11, 1951, 9 to 9:50. Held the regular First Presidency's meeting. These daily meetings of the First Presidency are proving to be extremely helpful in expediting the work, and we are kept in daily touch with the correspondence and problems that confront us.

October 17, 1951. My son Robert[32] called—said that he was going to be faced with some questions tonight that would be hard to answer without advice from me. A young man in Robert's Ward who has been suffering

---

31. Marion George Romney (1897–1988), the first Assistant to the Quorum of the Twelve in 1941, was chosen at this meeting to become a member of the Quorum of the Twelve. He would later serve as a counselor to two LDS presidents.

32. Robert Riggs McKay (1920–) was the McKays' youngest child. He owned the small but successful McKay Jewelry Company store on Main Street in downtown Salt Lake City.

with cancer, and to whom I administered sometime ago, has just passed away, and the father and members of the family, converts to the Church, do not feel resigned to his having been taken after having been administered to. Robert said a number of the young people will no doubt face him with the answer to this seeming tragedy.

I told Robert that it is our right to ask the Lord to bless the sick, for he has said that if there be any sick among us to call in the Elders. However, the Lord does not always answer our prayers affirmatively; sometimes the answer comes negatively. If we always had an affirmative answer, there would be no death at all. Sometime the power of faith is not sufficient to overcome the law of nature, but it is always our right to ask for a restoration to health, or to rebuke the disease, or whatever it is, and leave the rest for the operation of faith.

October 20, 1951, Washington DC. Through the kindness of Senator [R–Utah] Arthur V. Watkins,[33] an appointment with the Argentine Ambassador (Dr. Hipolito J. Paz) was put forward from Tuesday, Oct[ober] 23, 11:30 a.m. to Sunday at 2:30 p.m.

October 21, 1951, Washington, DC. Our conversation with Dr. Paz was satisfactory in every respect. Brother [L. Pierce] Brady did excellent work in translating, although the Ambassador speaks very good English, so the important part of the interview was in English. Later, at his [Paz's] request, we submitted our application in writing which was to secure three-year visas for each of our [proselytizing] missionaries to Argentina. Our written application was delivered in person by Brother Brady on Monday, the following day. Senator Watkins also wrote a letter of endorsement and recommendation.

November 1, 1951. [Speaking with M. Lynn Bennion,[34]] I said: "I will tell you what I have said about the United Nations: I think it was unthinkable

---

33. Arthur Vivian Watkins (1886–1973) was elected in 1946 and served two terms. His most notable legacy was his prosecution of the overly zealous anti–Communist Joseph McCarthy (R–WI). See Watkins, *Enough Rope.*
34. Milton Lindsay Bennion (1902–98) would spend twenty-three years as superintendent of the Salt Lake City School District, beginning in 1945. Prior to that, he had supervised the church's seminary program for high school-age students.

for Christian nations not to insert the word 'God' when the United Nations charter was drawn up, [an omission made] simply out of consideration for the feelings of atheistic nations. I think it was cowardly, and, furthermore, when the matter came up before the United Nations Assembly, they rejected offering prayer again, and decided they would have a one-minute, silent prayer, so that each could pray in his own way—this is cowardly!! You can quote me on that, but so far as the Church is concerned, it has not taken a stand for or against it."[35]

November 7, 1951, Los Angeles, California. I took occasion to look into the matter of the report that Warner Brothers [film studio] were going to make a moving picture of Juanita Brooks' story of the "Mountain Meadow Massacre."[36]

I contacted <u>Mrs. Mildred Gagon</u>, former secretary of the California Mission, who is now a lawyer and has an official position with the film world. She felt that the best approach would be through the director to whom this particular work had been assigned, and the following day she reported that she had met this young man who is now writing the script, and whose parents were members of the Church. He agreed with Sister Gagon that the script should not be completed after she told him that the First Presidency of the Church were opposed to its production.[37] Mrs. Brooks talked with President [Stephen L.] Richards about the matter and she has also said that it will not be filmed.[38]

---

35. Although there was no official stand, the views of the First Presidency were known. Clark was an isolationist who opposed the United Nations, as well as NATO. He stood, and remained, apart from the more internationalist viewpoints of McKay and Richards. For more, see Quinn, *Elder Statesman*, 311–13.

36. Juanita Leone Leavitt Brooks (1898–1989) was born in northeastern Nevada, studied at BYU and Columbia University, and taught English at Dixie College in St. George, thirty miles from where the tragedy occurred that she researched and saw published by University of Oklahoma Press in 1950. See Brooks, *Mountain Meadows Massacre*; Peterson, *Juanita Brooks: Mormon Woman Historian*.

37. President Clark also interceded, according to his diary entries for November 8, 13. See Quinn, *Elder Statesman*, 220.

38. The church engaged in other efforts to keep films from reaching theaters if the church felt the portrayals would damage the church's image. See Heath, *In The World*, 587, 686; Nelson, "Antagonism to Acceptance," 58–69. In 2007 a treatment of the massacre had a limited run in theaters under the title *September Dawn*, starring Jon Voight.

November 19, 1951, 11:35 to 12. Brother Wilford Wood[39] reported misunderstandings existing between him and Bishop Thorpe Isaacson in relation to church historic properties purchased for the Church. Also reported that the Isaac Hale home,[40] under the orders of George Q. Morris,[41] is in process of being torn down.

Told Brother Wood that I would call President Morris and ascertain just what is being done.

November 20, 1951. President George Q. Morris—called him at New York City and inquired regarding the status of the Isaac Hale property. Said the barn had blown down, and the house is in process of being torn down, according to letter from the First Presidency [to do] at "their own expense and for what they can get for the material." I then asked regarding the foundation, and Brother Morris said that it is intact; that he has instructed them not to touch that part of the house, that part of the house in its original state, but that the house itself was burned down and another one built. I instructed Brother Morris to see if the first story of the house could be saved, and he said he would see about it. I said that he should call someone and find out just how far they have gone, and if they haven't yet torn the first story down to let it stand and perhaps we can rebuild on that.

November 22, 1951. The family gathered at Lawrence's [David Lawrence McKay][42] for Thanksgiving dinner. Immediately after the dinner, Ray [Emma Ray McKay], the boys and I left for the U[niversity] of U[tah] Stadium to see the football game between Utah's Redskins and Idaho University—the U of U were the victors—the score being 40–19.[43]

---

39. Wilford C. Wood (1893–1968) was a dealer in fur coats, and on the side purchased Mormon historic documents, artifacts, and sites that were of significance to LDS history. He sold some of the documents he found to the church and stored the rest in his own private museum in Bountiful, Utah.

40. This was the childhood home of Joseph Smith's wife, Emma Hale Smith.

41. George Quayle Morris (1874–1962) was one of the newly called Assistants to the Quorum of the Twelve, who would be called to the Twelve three years later. His association with McKay extended back to their years as students at the University of Utah.

42. David Lawrence McKay (1901–93), the oldest child, had a law degree from Harvard University. He would later serve as the general church Sunday school superintendent, a position his father had held in the 1920s.

43. McKay played football (right guard) for the University of Utah in the late 1890s.

It was a beautiful day for the game—the sun shining in a clear blue sky; the air crisp and cold. I had on my fur coat, so did not feel the cold, but Ray felt the cold, and laughingly remarked: "You'll never get me to come to another game!"

After the game we went home where we remained all afternoon. After resting for a short time, I went to the basement to fix the soft-water apparatus. I worked with it for some little time, and then decided to leave it until we returned from the theatre, Ray and I having previously made arrangements to go to a Movie. However, I was sorry I did not stay with the job until I had completed it, for when we returned from the Theatre, I found three rooms of the basement flooded with water—consequently, I spent the rest of the evening mopping up water!!

November 30, 1951. At this [First Presidency] meeting there was read to the First Presidency a letter from Pres[ident] Stayner Richards[44] of the British Mission recommending the purchase of a property consisting of 4 3/4 acres with home and barns in Carshalton, near Crydon, near London, on which to erect a Temple. In discussing this matter Presidents [Stephen L.] Richards and [J. Reuben] Clark were unanimously in favor of erecting a temple in Europe, and felt that Great Britain should have the first temple in Europe.[45]

December 5, 1951, 8:50 a.m. Elder Wilford Wood, at my invitation, came in to our First Presidency's meeting to discuss matters pertaining to restoring Liberty Jail [in Missouri]. The brethren of the Presidency were unanimously agreed that the Liberty Jail [where Joseph Smith was incarcerated] should be restored, and that the upper room in the Jail should be used as a reception hall. The caretaker should have his quarters next door. It was felt that an architect should be appointed to work on the plans for restoration.

---

44. Stayner Richards (1885–1953) had been serving as president of the British Mission for two years when he was called as an Assistant to the Quorum of the Twelve in October 1951, and he continued as mission president for another year. His previous occupation had been as a real estate developer.

45. As it turned out, the Swiss temple in the suburbs of Bern would be the first European temple dedicated in September 1955. In 1952, McKay would travel to Europe to evaluate the temple sites. The property in England consisted of thirty-two acres about twenty-five miles south of London, and construction began in August 1953. The temple would be dedicated in September 1958.

December 6, 1951, 9 a.m. Went into the First Presidency's meeting. Some of the items considered at the meeting are as follows:

1. Approved the reorganization of the Missionary Committee, the whole missionary program to be handled under one committee. This would include Stake Missionary Work, the Mission Literature work, the Mission Home, the Indian Missionary Work, etc.

2. Decided to let Harry Clarke carry on with his work connected with obscene literature.

December 7, 1951, 9 to 10:30. First Presidency's meeting—Among important items considered were: (1) Upon the invitation of the First Presidency, the brethren of the First Council of Seventy—with the exception of Oscar A. Kirkham,[46] who was out of the city—called, and President [Stephen L.] Richards, at my request, explained to them the First Presidency's decision, which had been approved by the council of the Twelve, to reorganize the missionary set-up in the Church. The brethren of the Seventy individually and collectively approved the plan as presented.

(2) The question of reorganization of the Historian's Office was considered.

December 10, 1951, 9 to 11 a.m. First Presidency's meeting. At this meeting the following matters were considered:

1. Read and approved the Christmas message prepared by President [Stephen L.] Richards. ...

December 11, 1951, 9 to 10:00. First Presidency's meeting. The following items were among those considered:

(1) Gave further consideration to the invitation received by me to attend a Conference of Religious leaders in Washington, D.C. Read to my counselors the program as submitted, which seemed to provide little or no opportunity for discussion. I have concluded that I should not attend this conference, as I feel that very little if anything would be accomplished by my attending. (Invitation came from Robert Lovett, [US] Secretary of Defense).

---

46. Oscar Ammon Kirkham (1880–1958) was perhaps best known for having overseen the recreational activities of the church's young men in the YMMIA and Boy Scout programs. He was sustained to the First Council of Seventy in October 1941.

(2) Consideration was given to the advisability of adopting Social Security for Church teachers—also for Church employees. It was decided to take this matter up tomorrow when President [J. Reuben] Clark will be present.

December 12, 1951, 9 to 10:30. First Presidency's meeting, at which the following are a few of the most important items considered:

1. Decided to appoint a committee consisting of Delbert Stapley,[47] Joseph L. Wirthlin, to look into the matter of Social Security for Church employees, with Franklin L. West[48] to assist in connection with Social Security for the Church school teachers. The Presidency were unanimously in favor of this program. Bishop Thorpe B. Isaacson was also asked to serve on this committee at the request of President McKay.

December 14, 1951, First Presidency meeting. The brethren felt that a committee should be appointed from among the advisors to the auxiliaries, whose duty it will be to stabilize the courses of study, particularly for the missions. This to be a progressive course of study.

December 17, 1951, 8 a.m. Elder Delbert Stapley came in—he brought up three questions—

1. Relating to the allowances [salaries and benefits] given the General Authorities—if they are only living allowances, why should they pay income tax on them? I answered that they should not pay any more than the Mission Presidents whom we have instructed not to pay income tax. The government objected to their not paying but finally after an appeal to Washington [DC] it was decided that Presidencies of Missions need not pay taxes since they are not paid salaries, but that they should pay income tax on what they spend from their allowance for food and clothing. However, this was such a small amount that they have said nothing about it, so our Mission Presidents do not pay an income tax.

---

47. Delbert Leon Stapley (1896–1978) had been ordained an apostle by George Albert Smith in October 1950. He was previously in charge of the family's hardware business in Mesa, Arizona, where he was stake president.

48. Franklin Lorenzo West (1885–1966) was Commissioner of Church Education. He had previously taught physics at Utah Agricultural College (Utah State University) with a PhD from the University of Chicago.

I said further that the same thing should prevail with members of the Twelve who receive only a living allowance, but rather than bring the question up again, we have suggested that they add that to their yearly report when they make out their income tax statement. ...

President McKay reported that Senator [Arthur V.] Watkins would like to meet the First Presidency and get their views on the matter of the appointment of a representative of the U.S. to the Vatican in Rome. The brethren felt that President McKay might properly tell the Senator we are not going to criticize him for opposing such an appointment.

December 24, 1951. ... Went over to Z.C.M.I. to do some last-minute Christmas shopping. What should have taken me only a few moments took me three hours!! As I entered the office I said to my secretary—"Never again! I have been interviewing persons who stopped me on the street instead of doing my shopping." She told me that just a few moments before I returned to the office Brother Henry D. Moyle[49] was telling her that I should never try to go alone into the crowds without a body guard.

December 27, 1951. Elders Harold B. Lee[50] and Henry D. Moyle ... called at the office—they reported what they have done in the Salt Lake area regarding the coming election, urging Democrats and Republicans to put out good men on both tickets.

I commended them for the good work they are doing, and suggested that they give the same advice in other areas.

December 28, 1951, First Presidency meeting. We gave consideration, also,

49. Henry Dinwoodey Moyle (1889–1963) had been ordained an apostle by George Albert Smith in April 1947 and would later become a counselor to McKay following the death of Stephen L. Richards in 1959. Moyle had a law degree from Harvard University, had studied mining engineering at the University of Utah and in Germany (University of Freiberg), and during World War II directed the US Petroleum Industries Council. He became United States Attorney for Utah and taught law at the University of Utah.

50. Harold Bingham Lee (1899–1973) was ordained an apostle by Heber J. Grant in April 1941, served as a counselor to church president Joseph Fielding Smith (1970–72), and became president of the church on July 7, 1972. He was heavily involved in the Church Welfare Program from its inception in 1936 while serving as president of the Pioneer Stake in Salt Lake City.

to the suggestion by the Relief Society Presidency that the First Presidency write something regarding the "Family Hour." Felt if anything were said it should be to the effect that there should be <u>at least</u> one evening a week for the family. Questioned the wisdom of saying anything from which the implication might be drawn that only one night a week should be devoted to the family.

We also discussed the wisdom of reorganizing the Historian's Office.

2 Support, 1952

I wish to say, Brethren [of the Twelve], I have never sensed more keenly the need of your support, and I wish to express gratitude for your ... loyalty to the office. I sense the need of it more than I have ever sensed it before. —February 21, 1952

January 3, 1952, 9 a.m. to 10 a.m. Attended the regular First Presidency meeting. At this meeting reported that after consultation with Bishop [LeGrand] Richards, Brother Rulon Tingey and Frank[lin] West, also with local government people, authorization was given for our school teachers to make application for <u>Social Security</u> as of December 31, 1951. It was decided, however, to do nothing for the present and to seek further advice regarding the securing of Social Security for Church employees. It is called Federal Old Age Benefit.[1] ...

At the meeting of the First Presidency this morning, I said that I felt if we decide to build a Temple in Great Britain, we should build one at the same time in Switzerland, it being probably the safest country in Europe, and more accessible than England to most of the other European countries. Pres[ident] [J. Reuben] Clark agreed with this feeling.

January 4, 1952, 9 to 10:30 a.m. First Presidency meeting. At this meeting

---

1. The church's abhorrence of government programs had a long history. President Heber J. Grant had argued against welfare and government intervention, feeling it was the church's and its members' duty to take care of their own. This tradition was still well ensconced in J. Reuben Clark's personal philosophy. There had been disagreement between McKay and Clark on a number of issues, including this one. See Quinn, *Elder Statesman*, 396, 423

the following was considered. ... I reported on the present status of <u>Federal Old Age Pension for Church employees</u>, that the [LDS] Department of Education had been authorized to take this; that Brother [Henry D.] Moyle feels we can carry our own plan of a similar nature, into which the Department of Education employees could come later. Bro[ther] Moyle is to work it out and report to us.

January 7, 1952, 9 to 10:45 a.m. Held regular meeting with my counselors. I had read to the brethren a report submitted by Brady, Clawson, and Hess Management Consultants, giving an analysis of the proposed reorganization of [church businesses] Zion's Securities Company and Clayton Investment Company. Among other changes they recommend that both companies be brought under one management, and that one Board of Directors, with the same personnel, serve for both corporations. It was decided to call a meeting of the two Boards for Wednesday, January 9, 11:00 a.m. and present to them this decision, and unite the two boards. It was felt that Brothers Willard R. Smith and Herbert A. Snow should be taken on to the Zion's Securities Board.

It was also decided that at the stockholders meeting of Zion's Savings Bank & Trust company tomorrow, January 8, Wendell Smoot will be sustained as Executive Vice-President. Willard R. Smith will be retained on the Board and also as a vice-president, his special work to be loans and mortgages. It was felt that Stephen L. Richards should be First Vice-President, J. Reuben Clark, Jr., Second Vice-President, and Willard R. Smith, third Vice-President. Virgil A. Smith to be added to the Board of Directors.

January 8, 1952. "We [Harry Clarke's anti-pornography committee] have found on the most reliable authority that the lewd literature which is becoming more and more vicious as time goes on is being produced, handled, and distributed by the Ku Klux Klan. Radio commentator Drew Pearson[2] partially exposed the whole mess Sunday night. He made the most unusual attack on Governor [Herman] Talma[d]ge of Georgia, and there is about to become a nation-wide battle over this illicit traffic. The

---

2. Drew Pearson (1897–1969) was a syndicated newspaper columnist and radio personality in Washington, DC. His understudy, Jack Anderson, was an LDS journalist who had worked at the church-owned *Deseret News*.

organization and their representatives here in Salt Lake City are busy. We are ready to give these people more assistance than probably any other State in the Union.

"As you undoubtedly know, General Agent of the FBI, Jay Newman,[3] is transferred as of January 1 to El Paso, Texas. This is a decided loss to those of us who are engaged in this work. The whole committee are trying to make another contact confidentially and quietly at the FBI office. This is considered most confidential.

"May I proceed along with my friends engaged in the same work to establish a treasury [to] which our Church may be asked to make a reasonably small contribution?"...

After reading the above, President McKay said to tell Brother Clarke to go ahead on the matter referred to in the last paragraph.

January 11, 1952. Elder [Delbert L.] Stapley then brought up the subject of increased salaries for [church] employees. It was decided that all should receive an 8½ per cent increase—the same as has been given to the teachers of seminaries and institutes, and Department of Education offices. That the 1½ per cent withheld from the proposed 10% increase for security or pension plan would apply on whatever plan was decided upon later—whether a Church program or otherwise.

Elder Stapley said that the increase could not be held off any longer as most every one knew about it. I said that I had heard the other day that it was spoken of on the street, so there is nothing left to do but to go ahead with the 8½ percent increase right straight through.

January 23, 1952, 8:30 a.m. I held a meeting with James E. Ellison of the Layton Sugar Company, and Mr. Heath of the Holly Sugar Company, at which we considered the advisability of taking steps to eliminate one of the three [sugar] beet factories running between Davis County [Utah] and Preston, Idaho.

---

3. Actually, Jay C. Newman (1899–1986) was retiring from the FBI. He had been in charge of the Salt Lake City field office and had accepted the position of commissioner of the Utah Department of Public Safety, overseeing the Highway Patrol and Bureau of Criminal Identification. Newman was known for having been wounded in 1934 in a shootout in Wisconsin with Baby Face Nelson of the John Dillinger Gang. He was also the onetime LDS bishop of the San Francisco ward in the 1920s.

Mr. Heath reported that Mr. Benning, Manager of the Amalgamated Sugar company, had said that he, Mr. Benning, would either sell the Amalgamated factory at Lewiston [Idaho], or buy the Holly Factory at Preston, Idaho. Brother James E. Ellison, Manager of the Layton Sugar Company, reiterated the need of the Layton Sugar Factory [Utah] to have all the beets now grown in the Ogden area which are being established by the Amalgamated up to Lewiston.

It was a very profitable conference, but no conclusive action was taken pending further negotiations between the Holly and the Amalgamated Sugar Company.

Later: Called on Mr. [Douglas] Scalley of the Utah Idaho Sugar Company at his offices and reported to him the results of the conference with James E. Ellison and Mr. Heath. Mr. Heath had already reported to Mr. Scalley the former's conference with Mr. Benning. Mr. Scalley was favorable to the removal from that northern area one or the other factory, and said: "Anything that I can do, not only on this transaction, but for anything else, you let me know!"

Immediately after my conference with James E. Ellison and Mr. Heath, I went in to my First Presidency's meeting where I reported the interview with these two brethren. I stated that the Layton Sugar Company must have more acreage, that the Amalgamated as well as the Holly must also have more acreage, as there are three sugar factories between Davis Co[unty] and Preston, Idaho. I reported that from reports of the conference between Mr. Benning of the Amalgamated Sugar Company, and Mr. Heath of the Holly Company, it would seem that Mr. Heath wants to buy rather than sell. The Amalgamated cannot exist without the Ogden area. It would be to Layton's interests for Holly to remain in the Preston area, leaving the Ogden area to Layton.[4]

January 24, 1952, 8:15. Elders Harold B. Lee, and Marion Romney of the Council of the Twelve, and Elders Walter Stover and Carl Buehner[5]

---

4. Church involvement in the sugar beet industry began in the late nineteenth century. See Arrington, *Beet Sugar in the West*; Godfrey, *Religion, Politics, and Sugar*.

5. Carl William Buehner (1898–1974) would be called as second counselor to the Presiding Bishop at the upcoming April general conference. Born in Germany, he graduated from the Illinois Institute of Technology and founded the Buehner Block Company

of the [Church] Welfare Office called and recommended that the Welfare purchase the property in Murray [Utah] presently owned by the Woollen Mills company that is now manufacturing the "Jack Frost" blankets. This factory to be used by the Welfare for the purpose of reprocessing wool, making mattresses, manufacturing cloth, making overalls, etc. It is just what is needed by the Welfare. They stated that all the machinery goes with the building.

The property has been appraised by Brother Barker of the Church Welfare, also by others who estimate its value at twice its price offered to the Church Welfare.

Later Brother Lee and Brother Romney came to the First Presidency's meeting at 9 a.m., at my request, and explained again the conditions and purposes for which the Welfare would use the factory, and we all agreed that the purchase should be made at approximately $175,000.

Brother Stover made the statement that if the Church does not need the factory, he would take it at once.

February 14, 1952, 8 a.m. Met by appointment Elder Delbert L. Stapley, Bishop Thorpe B. Isaacson, and Brother George Jarvis of the Finance Department. Matters pertaining to pension plan for Church employees were discussed. They presented a suggestive program for the employees. After listening to the items presented, I expressed concern (1) regarding cost of program to the Church, (2) over the fact that if any member chose to leave the Church's employ before retirement age, he or she would have no credit in any other security organization. (3) Said that I preferred to have the insured make a contribution, which is in reality a saving. Raised the question that if we did take a 1½% contribution from the insured if this would make it necessary for the government or the state to investigate our books. (4) I also questioned whether we could carry our own insurance which is now carried by the Lincoln Life.[6]

---

in Utah, a source of pre-cast concrete and stone building materials. He was president of Beehive Bank and three companies dealing in animal furs, fertilizer, and lumber.

6. Lincoln National Life Insurance Company had been Thorpe B. Isaacson's employer prior to his call to the Presiding Bishopric, and he remained active as senior partner in the firm, which carried his name (Thorpe B. Isaacson Agency) and employed his son Richard. "Dinner Tonight Honors Isaacson, Salt Lake Agency," *Salt Lake Tribune,* July 17, 1963.

February 20, 1952, First Presidency meeting. I called attention to a grow-ing tendency in the Church to feel that no member of the Church should hold the sacrament [trays] while he himself partakes of it; further, that it is a breach of proper procedure to partake of it with the left hand.

The Brethren felt we should keep away from formalities and leave it to the custom or development of the custom. They felt that while the partaking of the sacrament is a covenant [and] that it is the custom to use the right hand in making covenants, failure so to do would not vitiate the covenant.

February 21, 1952, 10 a.m. to 2:30 p.m. Attended regular Council meet-ing in the Salt Lake Temple. At this meeting I was impressed to say the following to the brethren: When this responsibility of Presidency came upon me, I said to the people: Never before have I so fully realized the force and significance of the commandment of the Lord that the "three Presiding High Priests" of the Church shall be "upheld by the confidence, faith and prayer of the Church." With the united support of the people and divine inspiration given to those appointed and sustained as leaders, no power on earth can destroy the influence or prevent the progress of the Lord's work. Now, with the clear sense of the great responsibility that comes with the office of President, I sense more keenly than ever the sig-nificance of the support from those two sources. In my association with the Twelve and the Presidency, I have always felt the power of fellowship and the spirit of true brotherhood. I felt it when I sat next to Brother Jo-seph [Fielding Smith] in the Council, Brother [Orson F.] Whitney, and Brother [George F.] Richards, with whom I had a closer association be-cause our beginning was so close. Now I sense more clearly than ever, and wish to express here in your presence, my appreciation and gratitude for the support of those two noble men associated with me in the Presidency, President Richards and President Clark. Their loyalty, their devotion and concern, the work which they carry, are more outstanding than any in the Church realize[;] but you Brethren, I know perceive more clearly than anybody else. I love them and hereby express in your presence my appre-ciation and gratitude for their support.

I wish to say, Brethren, I have never sensed more keenly the need of your support, and I wish to express gratitude for your loyalty, for your subordinating any personal hesitation to your loyalty to the office. I sense the need of it more than I have ever sensed it before. I thought that while we are here in the [Prayer] Circle I wanted to say "Thank you" for your loyalty, your willingness to carry your responsibilities as representatives of the Presidency, and also appreciation of your ability as leaders to inspire the membership of the Church and to establish confidence in the church, in the hearts of non-members and others whom you meet. I just wanted to say thank you and God bless you!

President Joseph F[ielding] Smith responded by saying: "We unitedly give you our full support and our faith and prayers."

February 27, 1952, 8 a.m. Met by appointment <u>Brother L. Pierce Brady</u>. I discussed with him three matters: First, regarding the advisability of following up our visit to the Argentina Ambassador at Washington [DC] regarding our desire to obtain permanent visas for Elders [missionaries] who enter Argentina. At present we are able to get only three to six visas.

Since Ambassador [Hipólito J.] Paz, upon whom we called sometime ago, has moved, we concluded yesterday morning that probably it would be well to have Senator [Arthur V.] Watkins call on the newly appointed Ambassador from Argentina.

February 29, 1952. ... <u>President Joseph Fielding Smith</u> of the Council of the Twelve came in to my private office. He asked for approval of the assignment of offices to the various members of the Twelve and Assistants to the Twelve on the second Floor of the Church Office Building. I ventured the comment that the Twelve have too many secretaries, and that less detail work should be carried on in the offices, and more visiting should be done out in the field. President Smith agreed with me.

March 12, 1952. <u>Bishop [Thorpe B.] Isaacson</u> said that he heard something today that grieved him very much, and that is that a brother told him today that he [Isaacson] is using his position in the Presiding Bishopric to further his insurance business. "President McKay," said Bishop Isaacson, "I haven't turned a finger over to get business through the Church—some has come through our insurance of employees, but I didn't ask for it, and I shall give it all up rather than embarrass you brethren.["]

29

I told Bishop Isaacson to pay no attention to the matter; to go along and do his duty as he sees it.

April 1, 1952, 10 to 12:45 p.m. Was convened in meeting of the Expenditures Committee—it was a very important meeting, and many decisions to make. When I returned to my office, I was pretty tired, and so admitted to my secretary.

April 5, 1952. Following the meeting I met at my office Presidents [Stephen L.] Richards and [J. Reuben] Clark. After which I called Joseph L. Wirthlin to my office. I told Brother Wirthlin we had decided to call him to the position of Presiding Bishop of the Church, and that I was speaking to him tonight in confidence so that he might have time to think of his counselors as the matter had not yet come before the Twelve, and the matter must have their approval. Bishop Wirthlin said that he would report his decision first thing in the morning.

April 10, 1952, 10 a.m. Attended Council meeting. At this meeting I gave the charge to Elder LeGrand Richards,[7] newly sustained Apostle of the Church. It was forty-six years ago yesterday that Elder Richards' father—Elder George F. Richards[8]—sat for the first time in council in the Temple and received his charge, and it was a mellowing feeling to welcome his son into this same group.

The brethren of the First Presidency and the Quorum of the Twelve then unitedly laid their hands upon the head of <u>Brother LeGrand Richards and ordained him an Apostle and set him apart as a member of the Council of the Twelve</u>. I was voice in this ordination.

---

7. LeGrand Richards (1886–1983) attended the Salt Lake Business College for a year, served a mission to the Netherlands, and on his return he was hired by the Presiding Bishop's Office. On getting married he took a job in Oregon with the Portland Cement Company. When he returned to Utah, he launched a successful real estate business, which he expanded to southern California. His book, *A Marvelous Work and a Wonder*, became a primer for prospective LDS missionaries.

8. George Franklin Richards (1861–1950) was ordained an apostle the same day as McKay on April 9, 1906. Since his ordination took place first, he was considered next in line in seniority after apostle George Albert Smith, who became church president. However, Richards passed away eight months before Smith, leaving McKay in the senior position in the quorum.

April 17, 1952, with First Presidency and Twelve. President McKay said that for years it has been recommended that the branches in Great Britain and Europe be strengthened, but that members of the Church in those lands when they get the spirit of the gospel realize the importance of temple work and notwithstanding some of them held good positions, they have given those positions up and have come here in order to go through the temple. While [British Mission] President Stayner Richards was in the City at the time of the death of his son last Fall, he consulted the Presidency and among other recommendations, asked if it would not be an opportune time to build a temple in Great Britain. The Brethren of the First Presidency considered it carefully and prayerfully and have now come to the conclusion that if we build a temple in Great Britain we should at the same time build one in Switzerland. ... It is not contemplated than an expensive edifice would be erected but that temples be built that would accommodate the people under a new plan whereby temple ceremonies can be presented in one room without moving from one room to another, utilizing modern inventions. Therefore it is thought that one room might be used and the scenery changed as needed and seats adjusted to accommodate the situation. It is felt that such a building could be erected and adequately equipped for about the cost of one of our present meeting houses, namely, two hundred to two hundred fifty thousand dollars.

Elder [John A.] Widtsoe[9] expressed his gratitude, as did several others of the Brethren, that the First Presidency have such a move in contemplation, stating that the people in Great Britain and foreign-speaking missions are dreaming of a time when a temple will be erected in Europe.

Elder Widtsoe moved that investigation be made, having in mind the erection of a temple in Great Britain and another on the Continent preferably in Switzerland. Motion was seconded by Brother Ezra T[aft] Benson[10] and unanimously approved.

---

9. John Andreas Widtsoe (1872–1952) was a Norwegian convert who advocated and maintained strong ties with European Saints. He married a granddaughter of Brigham Young, Leah Dunford, and was ordained an apostle in 1921 by President Heber J. Grant. He graduated from Harvard and received a doctorate from the University of Göttingen in Germany. After teaching at Utah State Agricultural College and BYU, he became president of USAC and later president of the University of Utah. As an apostle, he also served as Church Commissioner of Education from 1921. See Widtsoe, *In a Sunlit Land*; Parrish, *John A. Widtsoe*.

10. Ezra Taft Benson (1899–1994) was ordained to the apostleship at the same time

April 18, 1952, 7:30 a.m. Met by appointment Gus Backman[11] of the [Salt Lake] Chamber of Commerce. He reported the serious flood situation.[12] Said if it rains during the latter part of May and in June, the water might rise a 1000 feet more a second, and they cannot handle it. Otherwise, they have it in hand, and they think they can handle it without calling upon the government.

He also discussed matters pertaining to the civil defense program.[13] Said he would like permission to consult the President of the Relief Society. I told him that would be all right.

Brother Backman also reported that they have organized the fire department, the police department, and state patrol, so that in a few moments in case of an emergency, they would know what to do. He indicated that they would like to use the Church organizations.

Later, when I reported the purpose of Gus Backman's visit to the First

as Spencer W. Kimball, October 7, 1943, the order of ordination placing him right behind Kimball in seniority, so that he became church president at Kimball's death in November 1985. He had been a stake president in Boise, Idaho, and Washington, DC, and had been involved in the church's relief effort in Europe after World War II. He was born on a farm in Idaho, but went to school in Utah (BYU), Iowa (Iowa State University), and California (University of California–Berkeley) and became executive secretary of the National Council of Farmer Cooperatives in 1939. His agrarian background so impressed US President Dwight D. Eisenhower that he nominated the apostle for Secretary of Agriculture—a post Benson kept through both Eisenhower administrations, 1953–61.

11. Gustave Pollard Backman (1891–1972) had worked in the Backman family business, went to law school, and was an assistant manager at one of the church's ZCMI department stores to 1930 when he was hired as executive secretary of the Salt Lake Chamber of Commerce. Over the years he became instrumental in making the chamber a powerful entity, as he began meeting often to informally discuss issues affecting the city with President McKay and *Salt Lake Tribune* publisher John F. Fitzpatrick in what came to be called a triumvirate representing three major cultural components of the city: Mormon, nominal Mormon (Backman), and non-Mormon (Fitzpatrick). Prince and Wright, *David O. McKay*, 333; Alexander and Allen, *Mormons and Gentiles*, 14, 263, 268, 294–95.

12. Flooding is rare in the Salt Lake Valley, but it happens, most recently in 1983 when the lake rose eight feet and downtown streets were converted into a watercourse for City Creek, which normally flows below the city. Temporary wooden bridges had to be built across the creek, and the banks of the Jordan River and its tributaries (Big Cottonwood, Emigration, Little Cottonwood, Mill Creek, Parleys, and Red Butte Creeks) had to be fortified, while the Jordan was given additional levies and dikes. In the wake of mudslides, hundreds of people were displaced and two died. Sillitoe, *History of Salt Lake County*, 214–15, 291–95.

13. Civil defense programs were *de rigueur* throughout the 1950s–60s because of fear of nuclear attack. Preparation at the state and local level included the construction of bomb shelters. Halberstam, *The Fifties*.

Presidency, we came to the conclusion that we should not permit this organization to use our church organizations, but could, however, use individuals.

Later I telephoned to Sister [Belle S.] Spafford[14] and told her that Brother Backman would call on her; that she should listen to his plan which I think, is to utilize the Relief Society in case of an emergency. Advised her to accept whatever he would like as a citizen, but to be careful not to involve the Church without receiving approval.

Sister Spafford said that she had received letters from the civil defense committee and had attended some of their meetings at the State Capitol. She had, however, acted only as a citizen and had not involved the Church in any way.

April 28, 1952, First Presidency meeting. We discussed the matter of sending Ricks College [now BYU–Idaho] faculty members to visit stake conferences in the areas of the college. Reported to me that it had been decided to ask Pres[ident] [Ernest L.] Wilkinson of the B.Y.U. not to send faculty members into that area [to recruit students]. Pres[ident] Wilkinson has been asked to send us a list of all the students coming from the stakes in that area to the B.Y.U., and suggested that the same thing be asked of the Ricks College.

I reported meeting with Seminary and Institute teachers and students in Tempe, Arizona. The feeling was expressed by non-member teachers in Arizona and also some of our institute teachers, that it is unnecessary to send boys and girls away from home when they have such a good opportunity for religious education in connection with their college.

The brethren favored leaving the matter to the individual choice of the parents where they send their boys and girls. There was serious consideration as to whether they should call off the visits of the B.Y.U. teachers at Stake Conferences.[15]

---

14. Marion Isabelle Sims Smith Spafford (1895–1982) was a counselor to Amy Brown Lyman from 1942 to 1945, then Relief Society president herself from 1945 to 1974. She had been editor of the *Relief Society Magazine* for eight years beginning in 1937. In 1968 she became president of the National Council of Women, in a line of succession harking back to Susan B. Anthony and Elizabeth Cady Stanton.

15. This issue will be probed further as Wilkinson proposes the purchase or construction of colleges throughout the western states as feeder schools for BYU. See, for instance, the proposals of Dec. 18, 1953, to acquire the existing junior colleges in Ephraim, Ogden, and St. George; Jan. 4, 1958, to build a school in Salt Lake County;

May 9, 1952. Bishop Joseph L. Wirthlin, and his counselors, Brothers Thorpe B. Isaacson and Carl Buehner, called at the office—they discussed several matters pertaining to …

3. Statistics showing a great increase in the number of adult men not holding the Melchizedek Priesthood, notwithstanding the thousands that have been reclaimed. They attribute that increase to the number of young men who went to war[16] while they still held the Aaronic Priesthood; soon they were classed among the adult members not holding the Melchizedek Priesthood. The Bishopric recommend the advisability of ordaining worthy young men elders at the age of 18, before they go into the army—instead of 19. The brethren at the First Presidency's meeting today could see no objection and did see some advantages.

May 15, 1952, 9 to 9:50 a.m. Was convened in First Presidency's meeting. … The following were also considered:

1. Letters addressed to me and signed by Richard R. Lyman dated May 10, 1952 and one with an April date, were read.

The one of May 10 expressed regret, remorse, and sorrow for his transgression, and stated that he would like to make restitution and be admitted back into the Church. This matter will be presented at the Council meeting this morning.[17]

May 23, 1952, 7:15 a.m. While I was dictating letters to the dictaphone Milton Hunter[18] of the First Council of the Seventies knocked on the

---

March 31, 1958, to purchase land in southern California for a school; and Oct. 31, 1958, to move Ricks College to Idaho Falls.

16. This refers not only to military personnel participating in the ongoing Korean War but to those who fell through the cracks in the eleven years since World War II. The intent was to have every adult male ordained an elder in order to participate in the management of the church at the local level.

17. The former apostle Richard Roswell Lyman (1870–1963) had been excommunicated in 1943 after being in the Quorum of the Twelve for a quarter century. Prior to his call to be an apostle, he had received degrees in engineering from the University of Michigan, University of Chicago, and Cornell University. His wife, Amy Brown Lyman, was the church-wide Relief Society president. His father, Francis M. Lyman, had been president of the Quorum of the Twelve, and his grandfather, Amasa M. Lyman, had been in the Quorum of the Twelve. See Quinn, *Elder Statesman*, 251–53, 518; Kimball and Kimball, *Spencer W. Kimball*, 208–10; Bergera, "Transgression in the Latter-day Saint Community," 173–207.

18. Milton Reed Hunter (1902–75) was sustained to the First Council of the Seventy

door of my private office. He wishes to see me about his publishing another book. He would like to publish a book containing excerpts from speeches of the First Presidency. I told Brother Hunter to send a letter explaining just what he has in mind and that I should be pleased to present the matter at the next meeting of the First Presidency.[19]

Later, Brother Hunter was advised by letter that it was the opinion of the First Presidency that the book should not be published.

May 26, 1952, 9 to 10:30 a.m. First Presidency's meeting. The following items were a few among many matters discussed at this meeting: ...

3. Milton R. Hunter is compiling messages of the First Presidencies of the Church, and wishes to publish them in book form. The Presidency decided against this, they feeling that the messages were given at the time to fit a special condition perhaps, and that it would not be proper to publish them apart from their settings, or an understanding of why the messages were given. ...

5. It was agreed that nothing should be said at this time regarding the purpose of my trip to Europe; that nothing should be said until after the [temple] sites have been secured. ...

3:30 p.m. Meeting with the Personnel Committee[:] Under the [retirement] plan [for church employees] submitted yesterday, the committee [Delbert L. Stapley, Joseph L. Wirthlin, and Thorpe B. Isaacson] corrected those two items, having each employee contribute half and the church the other half, and including a clause that any one who contributes would have the amount contributed returned when and if they leave the Church's employ, thus giving them a reserve to apply on some other insurance.

The brethren had also associated with their proposed plan the Church Welfare Plan. I said: "That should be eliminated entirely; this proposed plan of insurance has nothing whatever to do with the Welfare

---

in April 1945. His dissertation at the University of California–Berkeley was on the colonizing efforts of Brigham Young. Hunter became a prodigious writer on Mesoamerican archaeology and possible parallels to Book of Mormon themes.

19. A decade later BYU professor James R. Clark (a nephew of J. Reuben Clark) published a six-volume work through Bookcraft entitled *Messages of the First Presidency*. Apostle Harold B. Lee objected to its publication, but a search of the records showed that the First Presidency had approved it in advance. Arrington, *Confessions of a Mormon Historian*, 1:378.

Plan; this is the case of insurance between the employer and employee."
The brethren asked for time to reconsider the plan.

There is this advantage of the Church plan over the Government Social Security; No one needs to retire at 65 years of age; the employee can
continue to work so long as he wishes and increase his retirement fund.

I then reiterated that they should eliminate the Welfare Plan with
regard to this retirement plan for church employees.

Brother Stapley said he had not thought that out clearly. I said: "If you
have in mind giving the employees any welfare products or produce as part
of their compensation, that is out entirely; this is something beyond that
plan. If the allowance is not sufficient after retirement, then the member
of the Church will be treated just like any other member of the Church."

May 27, 1952, 12:30 p.m. Brother Franklin Murdock[20] came in to say
that he had just this moment received word that the Government had
reinstated air flights to Europe so that the original schedule can now be
followed.[21] Sister [Emma Ray] McKay, who was in the office at the time,
received this news with a little concern as she is not too eager to fly.

July 30, 1952, 11:30 a.m.[22] Bishop [Thorpe B.] Isaacson of the Presiding
Bishopric came in for advice regarding the acceptance of chairmanship of
the B[oar]d of Trustees, Utah Agricultural College. Said that at a meeting
held July 27 he was unanimously re-elected as chairman. He said that he
did not attend this meeting for two reasons: first, it was impossible for him
to be present because of conflicting appointments, and, second, he wanted
the Board of Trustees to have complete freedom in electing whomever they
felt inclined to choose for their chairman. Said he had expressed to many
of the board members that he did not feel that he should continue with the

---

20. Franklin J. Murdock (1902–86), president of the Highland Stake in Salt Lake
City and a member of the Church Missionary Committee, owned the travel agency that
arranged transportation for church authorities and missionaries.

21. Aviation fuel was being rationed due to an oil workers strike. The government's
concern was that dwindling reserves could compromise the country's defense capabilities. "Oil Strike Forces New Slash on US, Foreign Airlines," *Salt Lake Tribune*, May 12,
1952; "Oil Case Hearing Today before Wage Stabilization Board," *Paris News* (Texas),
May 12, 1952.

22. McKay was recently returned from a two-month visit to Europe where he
announced construction of the Swiss temple and visited the other European missions.

work as the chairmanship has been very heavy and controversial; and that they [Isaacson insurance company] have been under great pressure with law suits and have been somewhat unpleasant in many respects. He has served on the Board of Trustees for ten years. Said he would be grateful for my counsel, as he is desirous of doing the right thing.

After considering the matter with Bishop Isaacson I told him to go ahead and accept the Chairmanship.

August 5, 1952, 8:30 a.m. At his request, met Elder John Longden,[23] Assistant to the Twelve, who stated that he has an offer from the National Electric Products Company of Pittsburg to accept a good position, lucrative as well as dignified, and that they will give him this position with the understanding that his first duty will be to the Church, including two visits to missions a year, taking two or three weeks at a time. Of course, he would not be able to take a two-weeks' vacation in addition to the time spent touring the missions.

I told Brother Longden to accept this position. He said that he had seen President [J. Reuben] Clark, Jr. who had already given his consent. ...

2 p.m. Returned to the office where I met by appointment at his request Elder Ezra T. Benson. I told him that the First Presidency had approved of his accepting the Chairmanship of the American Institute of Cooperation,[24] but they wished me to state to him that they would oppose anything that would interfere with individual liberty. Brother Benson said, "So should I." In accepting this Chairmanship, however, Brother Benson understands that his first duty is to the Council of the Twelve.

The matter of Brother Benson's accepting membership on the advisory Board of Consultants of the Division of Agriculture and Natural Resources was left for further consideration, Brother Benson having given additional information regarding that.

---

23. Sustained as an Assistant to the Quorum of Twelve Apostles in October 1951, John Longden (1898–1969) was originally from Lancashire, England, where he was born to LDS parents. He graduated from the University of Utah and worked at the Salt Lake branch of Westinghouse Electric Supply Company. He was also known for his musical ability, as a violinist. "Formal Opening of Quarters Set by Electric Firm," *Salt Lake Tribune*, Oct. 3, 1935.

24. The American Institute of Cooperation was based in Washington, DC. Its purpose was to advise farm cooperatives and keep them in touch with the programs of the agricultural schools.

August 6, 1952. I told the Presiding Bishopric that negroes[25] should not be invited to speak in sacrament meetings in and at Firesides.

August 7, 1952, 8:30 a.m. Met by appointment at his request <u>Marriner Eccles</u>[26] who is a candidate on the Republican ticket for the United States Senate. Wanted to know if the Church would be against him in the campaign. I answered that the Church takes no stand whatever in politics; that there are members of the Church who are Democrats, and members who are Republicans, and that I personally am going to treat each group fairly.

August 18, 1952. I concurred in the decision previously made by Presidents [Stephen L.] Richards and [J. Reuben] Clark that returned servicemen might be called on [proselytizing] missions for a shorter period than two years, so that they may return in time to go to school under the G.I. Bill.

August 22, 1952, 8:30 a.m. Met by appointment, at his request, [the Democrat] Heber Bennion, [Utah] Secretary of State. He said he had heard that the Church favors [Salt Lake City] Mayor Earl Glade[27] for [Utah] Governor and favored the Republicans.

I told him that the church takes no stand whatever in politics—there are Democrats in the Church, there are Republicans in the Church, and I am President of the Church, and so far as I am personally concerned, I am going to treat each group in fairness.[28]

---

25. LDS policy prevented black males of African descent from receiving ordination to the priesthood. For a discussion of this, see Prince and Wright, *David O. McKay*, 60–105.

26. Marriner Stoddard Eccles (1890–1977) and brother George co-founded First Security Bank in Salt Lake City, and Marriner went on to become chair of the US Federal Reserve Board in the 1930s–40s. Their father, David, a pioneer business entrepreneur, was a longtime friend of the McKay family. Eccles lost his 1952 bid for the US Senate to incumbent Republican Senator Arthur V. Watkins. For Eccles's memoir, see *Beckoning Frontiers*.

27. Earl J. Glade (1885–1966) was a pioneer in radio broadcasting at KSL radio (formerly KZN radio) as its general manager for over twenty years. In 1944 he became mayor of Salt Lake City and served three terms.

28. The issue of church–state relations has a long history in Utah. Since the state's founding, partisans have raged on both sides, pitting dissenters against the host culture. First was the non-LDS Liberal Party that challenged the LDS-run People's Party. After Utah statehood in 1896 and the acceptance of mainstream American politics, including

I then told Mr. Bennion that I had heard he had made the remark at a social function that he would like to have the salary made by the officials of the Church, especially that of the President.

Mr. Bennion answered: "Yes, that is one time when silence would have been golden." He then said: "I did tell Bishop [Thorpe B.] Isaacson that the Church Authorities got more than the State officials received, and he, Bishop Isaacson, denied that." Mr. Bennion said further that he is sorry that he made that remark and that he understands now that the General Authorities are given an allowance sufficient to pay their living expenses. I said: "That is true, and those of us who have positions and business companies, of course, have that amount augmented by the salaries paid, but that has nothing to do with the Church allowance." Mr. Bennion expressed sorrow for having made the statement, and has no criticism whatever of the meager amount allowed the General Authorities who devote all their time to the Church.

September 3, 1952. <u>First Presidency's Meeting</u> ... At this meeting we agreed that the Deseret News should print no further street editions under the masthead "News-Telegram,"[29] and so notified Elder Mark E. Petersen.[30]

September 25, 1952, 8:50 a.m. Milton R. Hunter of the First Council of Seventy called at the office of the First Presidency at their invitation. The activities of Thomas Ferguson[31] in Idaho Falls in raising funds for an expedition to South America were discussed with Brother Hunter who had

the Democratic and Republican Parties, perceptions of LDS influence persisted, not only in state politics but also in city and county affairs, despite assurances to the contrary by the First Presidency.

29. The *Deseret News* purchased the *Salt Lake Telegram* in 1952 with the intent to eliminate its afternoon competition. The *Telegram*, like the *Deseret News*, was an afternoon paper, owned by the *Salt Lake Tribune*, a morning newspaper. For some time thereafter, the church-owned paper's masthead read *Deseret News–Telegram*.

30. Mark Edward Petersen (1900–84) had been general manager of the *Deseret News* since 1941. In 1944 he was invited into the Quorum of the Twelve. Shortly after returning from his mission to Nova Scotia, he was hired by the newspaper as the music and religion reporter. He eventually authored the unsigned editorials in the Church News section. See Thomas S. Monson, "Mark E. Petersen," *Ensign*, Mar. 1984; Barton, *Mark E. Petersen*, 24, 61–62, 65.

31. Thomas Stuart Ferguson (1915–83) was a proponent of searching for archaeological evidence to support the Book of Mormon, his interests dovetailing with the work of Milton R. Hunter as they co-authored a book in 1950 titled *Ancient America and the*

taken Mr. Ferguson to the Idaho Falls Stake Conference and invited him to speak. I told Brother Hunter that I did not think it a proper thing to let this man go to quarterly conferences and foster an organization that is not sanctioned by the Church. Brother Hunter was requested to get in touch with Pres[ident] [William J.] O'Bryant of the Idaho Falls Stake by telephone and explain to him that this is a private enterprise and that he [Hunter] had no intention of giving any official sanction to it, also to write to Pres[ident] O'Bryant in explanation of the matter and give the First Presidency a copy of what he says to Pres[ident] O'Bryant.

September 26, 1952, 9 to 10:30. Attended regular First Presidency's meeting. I reported that [BYU] President Ernest L. Wilkinson wants a non-member of the Church for his teaching staff at the B.Y.U. Registration is taking place today for this particular course in question. I called Pres[ident] Wilkinson while we were in meeting and said it was my understanding that if we get this man, he will replace one of our present faculty members who is now teaching in a higher department, and he [LDS professor] would be taken from the higher department to teach history. I said the Presidency look with disfavor on the bringing in of a non-member under this arrangement. Pres[ident] Wilkinson said he thinks now that he can get a man from Cornell [University], a Church member, to take this position.[32]

September 30, 1952, 8:30 a.m. I met by appointment at his request, Harold W. Bentley, Director of the Extension Division, University of Utah, who called to discuss with me the Extension Division's program problems, particularly with respect to the appearance of William Warfield[33]—the negro singer—in the S[alt] L[ake] Tabernacle sometime in March [1953].

Book of Mormon. After years of study, Ferguson became disillusioned and no longer believed there was evidence to be found. See Larson, *Quest for the Gold Plates.*

32. The official policy was to hire qualified LDS applicants unless none were available. See, for instance, Wilkinson, *Brigham Young University.*, 425n73; Bergera and Priddis, *Brigham Young University*, 10, 28n56, 64.

33. William Caesar Warfield (1920–2002) would soon leave for Europe under the sponsorship of the US State Department to take a lead role in the touring production of *Porgy and Bess.* He had a degree from the Eastman School of Music in Rochester, New York, and would later become a music professor himself at the University of Illinois–Urbana. In 1959 he would be featured in a recording of the *Messiah* with the Philadelphia Orchestra and Mormon Tabernacle Choir.

Later, I took this matter up with my counselors, and it was decided that inasmuch as we had permitted Marian Anderson, a negro singer, [to] appear in a concert in the Tabernacle, there should be no objection to Mr. Warfield's appearance, unless he be guilty of subversive activity. I so notified Mr. Bentley by telephone. It was suggested to him that he get in touch with Bishop [Thorpe B.] Isaacson for further suggestions relative to this matter.

From 9 until 11 a.m. was engaged in the regular First Presidency's meeting. Among other items discussed, I reported the visit of Professor Bentley of the U[niversity] of U[tah] with reference to the appearance of W[illia]m Warfield on the U[niversity] of U[tah]'s Master Minds and Artists series, March 12, 1952. The brethren understood that Bishop Isaacson was to talk to the people at the University in charge of these programs, telling them that they should not contract for colored artists to appear in the Tabernacle. In discussing the problem the Brethren had some question in their minds as to whether there was any real objection to permitting such performances.

October 5, 1952. In view of the coming [national] election, and in order to refute false statements that are being made regarding the views of the General Authorities pertaining to the candidates of the political parties, I made a definite statement that the Church of Jesus Christ of Latter-day Saints and its leaders are non-partisan and favor neither political party or candidate during the forthcoming election.

October 6, 1952, breakfast with US President Harry S. Truman. I had a very pleasant thirty minutes or so with the President,[34] during which time, I saw the better Truman, and got a glimpse of his better nature— the cockiness was gone. He referred to the fact that this is his last official tour before retiring, saying, "When I get through with this, it is my last." He then told me what he wanted to do; viz. to spend his time instructing the youth of America in loyalty and American ideals. He mentioned some other men whom he would like to have join him in this project.

---

34. Harry S. Truman (1884–1972), thirty-third president of the United States, was not endorsed by McKay in 1948. A staunch Republican, McKay had preferred Dewey. From this short meeting, McKay came away with greater respect and appreciation for Truman.

I commended him for this desire, and told him that I think that is just what we need. I then gave him a few of my ideas on the subject, emphasizing the freedom of the individual; that must be maintained at all cost.

October 14, 1952, 9 a.m. to 10 a.m. First Presidency's meeting. ... We also considered a letter in which the question is asked regarding the attitude of the Church toward the new revised edition of the Bible. The decision was reached that we have taken no stand regarding the first revised edition, nor have we regarding the latest [revision]; they must stand on their merit; that we use the King James' translation.[35]

It was decided at this meeting to take $5,000 of Israel bonds, with the understanding that our subscription is not to be used in any way to indicate the Church is endorsing the issue as to its financial worthiness. This is done merely to show our sympathy with the effort being made to establish the Jews in their homeland.[36]

October 25, 1952. Left early this morning for Huntsville. Upon arrival at the farm found many duties to take care of, so I was busy until late afternoon. I did one job that I had not intended to do, but when I noticed so many branches of trees scattered around on the ground, I decided to rake them into a pile and burn them. Of course, when one starts a job of this kind, one usually stays with it until it is finished. Consequently, I worked too long and hard. Later, at home, [son] Llewelyn noticed that I had a little difficulty in getting out of my chair, and remarked, "So, Daddy, you have been working too hard upon the farm!" and I had to confess that I had overdone.

October 27, 1952, 8 a.m. to 10 a.m. Met by appointment at his request Mr. Clinton Vernon, Attorney General, State of Utah. Mr. Vernon[,] [a Democrat,] said that word has gone out—evidently from two General Authorities (whose names he would not repeat)[—]to Presidents of

---

35. By saying the church uses the King James translation, McKay meant to convey that the KJV is the church's officially recognized version. See D. Kelly Ogden, "Bible: King James Version," in Ludlow, *Encyclopedia of Mormonism*, 1:109; Barlow, *Mormons and the Bible*, especially the chapter on the KJV.

36. The United Nations resolution creating the state of Israel was five years old. About 200,000 immigrants to Israel were still living in refugee tent cities.

Stakes to defeat him in his attempt to be re-elected as Attorney General of the State of Utah. He has specific instances where one of the General Authorities—Alma Sonne[37]—allegedly stated to Presidencies and High Councilmen that he, (Clinton D. Vernon), is an apostate; secondly, that he is in favor of taxing Church property, and thirdly, that he is in sympathy with the "cultists" [polygamists] at Short Creek. "These accusations," declared Mr. Vernon, "are absolute falsehoods." ...

I called up President William Critchlow[38] of the South Ogden Stake, and suggested that he get in touch with Clinton Vernon and hear the latter's side of the question.

November 5, 1952. We were all thrilled with the News [of the election returns]. In my opinion, it is the greatest thing that has happened in a hundred years for our country.[39]

November 10, 1952, 5 p.m. Sister [Emma Ray] McKay and I attended the 5 o'clock [Salt Lake] Temple session. In keeping with a promise made many years ago to <u>Mrs. Mabel Moody</u> Mills (a friend whom I met in 1897 at the University of Utah) to do the Temple work for her father— Dr. Henry L. Moody whom I also met at the University, and for whom I had the highest regard, <u>I did the endowment work for Dr. Moody</u>. Although an agnostic when I knew him at the University, I always admired Dr. Moody as an outstanding, cultured gentleman.

---

37. Alma Sonne (1884–1977) had been an Assistant to the Quorum of the Twelve since April 1941. In another twenty-four years he would be placed in the First Quorum of Seventy. Meanwhile, he continued to serve as president of Logan First National Bank and president of the Utah Bankers Association. While still serving in his church office in 1968, he would help found the Pioneer Bank of Logan.

38. In six years McKay would set apart William James Critchlow Jr.(1892–1968) as an Assistant to the Quorum of Twelve. In 1952 Critchlow was a divisional manager at Utah Power and Light Company in Ogden and president of the church's South Ogden Stake.

39. Although McKay wanted the church to be neutral in politics, he was personally partisan when it came to Republicans. Most of the high-ranking church leaders had disliked the Democratic hegemony of Franklin D. Roosevelt's four terms as US president and longed for a change. Eisenhower seemed to satisfy that political longing. J. Bracken Lee was another story. As a libertarian, some of his political and economic views were welcome, other traits were not as endearing. For a biography of Lee, see Lythgoe, *Let 'Em Holler*.

November 14, 1952, 8 a.m. Met by appointment Bishops [Joseph L.] Wirthlin and [Thorpe B.] Isaacson of the Presiding Bishopric who discussed among other things the Aaronic Priesthood handbook.

I could not see the wisdom of the handbook being curtailed to such an extent as is proposed by the Melchizedek Priesthood Committee; the recommendation of the Melchizedek Priesthood Committee frustrates their plan [for an Aaronic Priesthood handbook] entirely. If they were to follow the instructions of the Melchizedek Priesthood Committee the handbook would be reduced to 17 pages. The Ward Teaching handbook has also been held up. I later reported at the First Presidency's meeting that I had read the handbook and considered it excellent.

Pres[ident] [J. Reuben] Clark said he thought the fundamental thing is the problem as to who is the head of the Aaronic Priesthood—the First Presidency or the Twelve. Pres[ident] Clark agreed with me that the Twelve represent the First Presidency in the organization of the Church, but there are two different Priesthoods, that the President of the Church is the head of the Melchizedek and also the Aaronic, but the Twelve are not.

November 20, 1952. When I arrived home this evening I received a long distance telephone call from Senator Arthur V. Watkins who thanked me for the letter of congratulation that I had sent him, and then told me that Elder Ezra Taft Benson is being considered by General [Dwight D.] Eisenhower for the position of [US] Secretary of Agriculture, and wondered if he would be permitted to accept the position should it be offered to him. I said yes that I thought he would be permitted to accept.

November 24, 1952. Was very much pleased to read in this morning's paper that President-elect Dwight D. Eisenhower had chosen Elder Ezra Taft Benson as Secretary of Agriculture.[40]

November 28, 1952. Setting apart Bro[ther] Ezra T. Benson and blessing [him] in his responsibilities as Secretary of Agriculture of the U.S.[41]

---

40. This particular entry is in McKay's own handwriting.

41. For an account of his tumultuous years as secretary, see Benson's book, *Cross Fire*; Schapsmeier and Schapsmeier, *Ezra Taft Benson and the Politics of Agriculture*. Benson was the second LDS Secretary of Agriculture, the first having been William M.

December 3, 1952, 9 to 11 a.m.. Was engaged in the regular First Presidency's meeting. Among some items considered were:

1. Report given that the Committee on <u>Social Security for church employees</u> is ready to report on a Church plan. I said that I had come to the conclusion that the Church offers a better plan for all except the young girls, that if they do not get married and change their employment they lose out. President [Stephen L.] Richards wondered if the Church should undertake such an obligation if Federal Social Security is reasonably good. I said I thought we should hear the Committee again.

2. I reported that <u>Francis W. Kirkham</u> recommends that Dr. Harvey Fletcher[42] or Dr. Henry Eyring[43] be commissioned by the Church to write a book on the place of science and religion in human life. The brethren felt that there are so many fundamental advances being made in science that it was questionable wisdom to have a book of that kind. I said that I had heard very fine reports of the good work Dr. Eyring is doing with young people in fireside and group meetings.

December 4, 1952, 10 to 2:30 p.m. Was in Council meeting at the temple. With reference to Temple District meetings [solemn assemblies][44] I stated that the strength that comes from prayer and the consciousness

---

Jardine, an Idaho native appointed by Calvin Coolidge in 1925. Jardine later became president of Kansas State University.

42. Harvey Fletcher (1884–1981) was one of Mormonism's most distinguished scientists. A Provo native, he obtained his undergraduate degree from BYU and a PhD in physics from the University of Chicago. He worked at the premier research laboratory in the country, Bell Laboratories, in the areas of stereophonic sound, acoustics, and emerging telephone technology, then taught electrical engineering at Columbia University until accepting the invitation to oversee research at BYU in 1952 and to occupy the position of first dean of the new BYU College of Engineering in 1958.

43. Henry Eyring (1901–81) was, if not the most prominent LDS scientist of the twentieth century, one of the few in the uppermost tier. Born in Mexico, he fled with his family to Arizona during the Pancho Villa raids. He graduated from the University of Arizona and, with a PhD in chemistry, from the University of California–Berkeley, and while teaching at the University of Wisconsin, Princeton, and the University of Utah, he made substantial contributions to his field. He became dean of the graduate school at the University of Utah. His brother-in-law was apostle, and later president, Spencer W. Kimball. Eventually he did produce two books dealing with religion: *The Faith of a Scientist*, published by Bookcraft in 1967, and *Reflections of a Scientist*, published by Deseret Book in 1983.

44. For solemn assemblies, see Richard E. Turley Jr.'s entry in Ludlow, *Encyclopedia of Mormonism*, 3:390–91.

of having the united support of one another enrich the soul and give us encouragement to carry on; that it is a great blessing to meet and renew our covenants by partaking of the sacrament and getting a clear insight into the spirit of each other's soul. What a blessing it would be if this soul enrichment, with its uplifting influence could be felt by all the Priesthood throughout the Church. To a degree we can accomplish it—it is within our power to meet a large majority of the leaders of the Church in quorums, in wards, and in stakes.

With that end in view, a few years ago the presidents of our Temples were authorized to prepare the upper room, the assembly room in each temple. Now those rooms are in pretty good shape, physically, seats are supplied, and it is deemed advisable that we hold temple district meetings inviting the leaders in the district—wards, stakes and quorums—to meet to the full capacity of the room in the Temple and hold such services, adapted to the occasion, as we have held in the temple here. It is proposed that we hold such a meeting first in the St. George Temple, the time to be determined later, as soon after the first of the year as might be deemed advisable. That will be followed, occasionally, by similar meetings in other districts. At these meetings, matters can be discussed, matters which cannot appropriately be taken up in public. The brethren all signified their approval of this proposal.[45]

December 12, 1952. I called <u>Eldred Smith, Patriarch to the Church</u>, and told him that <u>Elder Spencer Kimball and Bishop LeGrand Richards</u> have been appointed to a committee to <u>read patriarchal blessings given</u> by him.[46]

---

45. Also discussed, according to Henry D. Moyle, was a topic that made it "a rather important meeting—altered the pattern of the [temple] garment, by adding an insertion of lace on the ladies garments." Moyle diary, Dec. 4, 1952.

46. Early the next month, Kimball and Richards wrote to McKay and counselors: "We do have some suggestions that might improve the blessings. The opening and closing of his blessings are almost invariably the same. ... We realize this could be overcome if Elder Smith would frequently spend an hour in the library reading the blessings of various patriarchs from Joseph Smith, Sr. down to the present, and from those blessings he would get many ideas as to expressions and the coverage of blessings." J. Reuben Clark replied: "We think you might ... wisely suggest to him that he read some of the blessings of some of the earlier brethren in order to familiarize himself with the work of the early patriarchs of the Church." Kimball and Richards to First Presidency, Jan. 9, 1953; Clark to Smith, Jan. 12, 1953, typed excerpts in Quinn Papers.

December 24, 1952. The First Presidency met with the Executive Committee of the Board of Education—Joseph Fielding Smith, Harold B. Lee, Marion G. Romney, Adam S. Bennion,[47] and Franklin L. West—I said that the First Presidency had learned from one or two sources, seminary teachers and others, that they are [under the impression they are] not to use any books that we have in the libraries [and to rely exclusively on the lesson manual].

Pres[ident] Smith said the Committee had given instructions against the use of certain books and some of these books were considered before the Board several years ago. After some discussion it was decided that the correspondence that has gone out to Seminary teachers on this matter should be examined and if erroneous impressions are going out, as they seem to be, they should be corrected.

---

47. In four months Adam Samuel Bennion (1886–1958) would be called to the apostleship. He had degrees in education from the University of Utah, Columbia University, and the University of California–Berkeley and had alternately taught high school, worked in an administrative capacity at Utah Power and Light, and was director of the Denver and Rio Grande Railroad. As LDS Commissioner of Education in the 1920s, he premiered the first college-level Institute of Religion classes for LDS students.

3 Matters of Politics and Education, 1953

The city [Washington, DC] was engulfed in a dense fog. ... I remarked ... [that this] is typical of the fog that has been hanging
over Washington politically for twenty years. Some in the group
didn't smile. —January 19, 1953

January 13, 1953, 11:30 a.m. Bishop Thorpe B. Isaacson reported difficulties that are now becoming acute among members of the Board of
Trustees of the Utah Agricultural College at Logan, Utah.

I told Bishop Isaacson that I would consult Brother [Ezra Taft]
Benson and see if [College] President [Louis L.] Madsen's[1] services are
not needed by the [federal] Government, if, as Dr. Harris says, President
Madsen is the best agricultural research man in the United States. So I
am to have a letter to take back with me to Washington [DC], and it may
be that future action may be determined by our conversation.

January 14, 1953, 8 a.m. Met by appointment Brother Henry D. Moyle
and Harold B. Lee, concerning political matters.[2] In Wyoming an effort

---

1. Utah State Agricultural College (now Utah State University) President Louis
Linden Madsen (1907–86) would be released and accept a position at Washington State
University as dean of the School of Agriculture. He was from Utah and had a PhD from
Cornell but had locked horns with the USAC board over recruitment of international
students, especially from Iran, and accommodating them with scholarships and help with
English. Students protested Madsen's removal from office, 700 of them demonstrating on
the steps of the Utah capitol. See Parson, "Encyclopedic History of Utah State University."

2. Mormon leaders have always believed it is inherently incumbent to take a
strong political stand on issues they consider moral. Examples have been Prohibition,
liquor by the drink, gambling, the Equal Rights Amendment, the proposed MX missile
installation in Utah, and same-sex marriage.

is being made to pass a law legalizing gambling and permitting the placing of slot machines in public places. [Former] Governor [Leslie A.]
Miller has appealed to [LDS] Bishop Don P. Fowler of Cheyenne, suggesting that the bishops ask their members to write to the legislature
protesting against it. The brethren were agreed that this is the kind of
case where we can express our views. It was decided when I reported that
matter at the meeting of the First Presidency to call the Stake Presidents
in Wyoming by phone asking them to request their bishops to be active
in protesting against it.

The brethren further recommend that we have a man at the Legislature
in Wyoming, ... instructing the Stake Presidents to get in touch with him.

In Idaho the Governor [Leonard B. Jordan] wants to pass a law
against gambling. It was felt that Brother Merrill in Pocatello, Brother
Z. Reed Millar[3] in Boise, and Brother Albert Choules[4] of the Idaho Falls
Temple might meet with Brothers Lee and Moyle and receive instructions, and then let Brother Choules work with the legislators.

In Utah someone is needed to watch things in the legislature, and
Rendell Mabey has been suggested.[5]

January 19, 1953. We arrived in Washington, D.C. the forenoon of
January 19 (for [Dwight D.] Eisenhower's inauguration). The city was
enveloped in a dense fog. ... I remarked to Sister McKay and my friends:
"This fog is typical of the fog that has been hanging over Washington

---

3. Zenith Reed Millar (1896–1984) was a prominent attorney in Boise who succeeded Ezra Taft Benson as president of the Boise Stake.

4. Albert Choules (1876–1966) was five years old when his Mormon family emigrated from England to the United States. After attending BYU he became a clerk in a
men's clothing store, later moving to Driggs, Idaho, to manage a store there. McKay had
him released from the Idaho Falls temple so he could devote his time fully to lobbying the
legislature. His son of the same name became a member of the First Quorum of Seventy.

5. According to Henry D. Moyle, there was an "8 am meeting with Pres[ident]
McKay and Harold B. Lee on political and legislative matters in Utah, Idaho and Wy-
oming. Bro[ther] Lee and I spent [the] balance of [the] morning contacting Bro[ther]
Boyak in Wyoming [and] Bro[thers] Millar[,] Merrill[,] and Charles in Idaho—[and]
Bro[thers] Vernon Romney, Harold Wilkinson[,] and Fred Finlayson in Utah as legislative contacts in the three states. Also [stake] pres[ident] [Lorenzo E.] Ellgren in Salt
Lake. Also had a conference with Richard Bird and Welby Young of Heber on the legislative apportionment bill—to keep cit[ie]s from controlling Legislation to detriment of
small com[mun]ities." Moyle diary, Jan. 14, 1953, typed excerpt in Quinn Papers.

politically for twenty years." Some in the group didn't smile—evidently they were Democrats and sympathetic with the Roosevelt–Truman administration. It seemed to me, however, an apt comparison. ...

That evening Ray and I attended the Inaugural Festival of Dwight David Eisenhower as the 34th President of the United States. ...

Tuesday morning we ... [had a] police escort to the Inaugural Ceremonies ... the most impressive feature was <u>President Dwight D. Eisenhower's introductory remarks followed by his prayer appealing for the guidance of a Divine Providence that he might be able to serve the people of this country.</u> ... I was deeply impressed with his sincerity as manifest in this appeal to the Lord for guidance. ...

<u>The fog of yesterday had vanished, and the sunshine[,] [which] seemed as a manifestation of divine approval for the day[,] was clear and cloudless, as President Eisenhower's thoughts and opinions seemed to be.</u>

... We were driven to our hotel where we dressed for dinner given to us by President and Mrs. J. Willard [Marriott] at the Country Club.[6] ...

Following the dinner we were driven to the Armory ... [for] the Inaugural Ball. We noticed ladies and gentlemen in full evening dress coming out of their cars and walking from a half-a-mile to a mile to get to the Hall. Finally we had to do the same, and therefore, did not arrive at the [hall] until 11:15 p.m. ... We left the Ball room at 12:30 a.m. ... arriving at our hotel at 2:00 a.m.

February 2, 1953, 10:30 to 11:30. Listened by way of the Radio to <u>President Dwight D. Eisenhower's State of the Union address</u>. It was a clear-cut

---

6. J. Willard Marriott (1900–85) was stepson-in-law of apostle–Senator Reed Smoot. Vocationally, he began with root beer stands and Hot Shoppes in Washington, DC, in the 1920s, and by the time of his death he was founder of one of the largest hotel chains and recreational properties in the world. Of this particular event, Marriott's biographer wrote: "Before the ball, they gave a small dinner party for 36 at the Columbia Country Club. Bill and Allie were proud of their guest list. ... Secretary of Agriculture and Mrs. Benson, whom they've known for years, Secretary of the Treasury Ivy Baker Priest (Piute County, Utah native) and her husband; the David O. McKays, the [Edgar and Laura] Brossards (former long-time U.S. Tariff Commissioner and Cache valley native), the Stewarts and even Mother Alice Smoot (second wife of deceased Senator Reed Smoot and mother-in-law to Marriott). The women wore mink jackets and 'Mamie' [Eisenhower] bangs, the men ... wore white tie and tails, white scarfs with their tailored Chesterfields, and silk top hats" O'Brien, *Marriott*, 220–21.

American speech, giving broad, general outlines of his foreign and domestic progr[a]ms, and revealed an Executive who is capable of doing something about the many serious problems now confronting the country.

February 5, 1953, 9 to 9:40. Attended the regular First Presidency's meeting. Among other matters considered, we discussed the Utah State Agricultural College situation. Pres[ident] [J. Reuben] Clark mentioned a conversation he had had with Harold B. Lee and suggested that I talk with Bro[ther] Lee. Appointment made with Brother Lee for later in the day. ...

Returned to the office at 3:30 p.m. at which time I had a conference with <u>Harold B. Lee</u>. He reported a very critical attitude among Stake Presidents in Cache Valley towards the action of the Board of Trustees of the <u>Utah State Agricultural College</u> in dismissing the Dean of Men, Joseph N. Symans.[7] He thought the Governor would release the entire board and appoint a new one, and probably appoint a new President of the College. I listened to Brother Lee, but made no comment, however. I decided at once to see Bishop [Thorpe B.] Isaacson, and followed that to call on the Governor and find out just what his plans are. Accordingly, made arrangements to meet Bishop Isaacson and Governor [J. Bracken] Lee tomorrow morning.[8]

February 6, 1953, 10:30 to 11 a.m. I had a conference with Bishop [Thorpe B.] Isaacson on Utah Agricultural matters. Without saying anything to him, following my conference with him, I made an appointment with Governor [J. Bracken] Lee. ...

---

7. This is Joseph N. Symons (1905-94), dean of students and former sociology professor who had been voted "most popular professor" by the students. He was born in Idaho and had a PhD from the University of Chicago. After being fired at USU, he would find employment as dean of the College of Social Sciences at BYU.

8. It is unclear if McKay knew the extent of Isaacson's involvement with Lee. Isaacson had taken upon himself to visit the governor, acting as if he spoke for the church on a number of issues, whether he was speaking for himself or in behalf of J. Reuben Clark Jr. (Lythgoe, *Let 'em Holler*, 91–101). Isaacson was chair of the board of directors of the agricultural college. "The Board," he wrote in reply to an inquiry from the student newspaper, "does not feel required to account for or give reasons for actions taken ... in accordance with the authority and duties imposed on it by law to manage the [school's] affairs." Parson, "Encyclopedic History."

12 Noon. Called on <u>Governor J. Bracken Lee</u> at his office at the State Capitol. I told him that it was not my intention or desire to interfere in any way with his plans regarding the <u>Utah Agricultural</u> College. Governor Lee replied: "Oh, yes, it is your business; I appreciate your coming up."

So, after a very agreeable conversation regarding conditions at the College, I came away with the feeling that the Governor would reappoint the Board and then throw the responsibility on the Board to arrange satisfactory appointments in the faculty, including the President, so that harmony would again exist. ...

[Harry Clarke called, and Clare Middlemiss reported that] after twenty-eight years, he had been partially terminated from KSL. He gave his last radio program this morning, but will continue to receive a salary until he finds another job.

He feels that this all stems back to President [J. Reuben] Clark. He knows that President McKay does not agree with several things that have been done at the station. ...

He will now go to [Catholic] Bishop [Duane G.] Hunt and ask for help in finding work. He has many fine friends among Catholic business men. This does not mean he is leaving the Church; in fact, he may be able to do the Church much good. He will probably have to leave Salt Lake City, but will keep in touch.

KSL has been wrenched to the staff. Many top men are leaving, one by one. Brother [Ivor] Sharp is fine, but he has no control. He is surrounded by people who are mitigating against the staff. ...

Harry is terribly shaken up. President Clark is to blame. Either he has no control, or the people delegated by him are not competent. Harry's radio program has been replaced by a program of the Edwards Coffee Company. In his last broadcast this morning, KSL inserted an ad for Kool cigarettes. He has asked them to wait until he was out of it, but they refused. He did not think the Church would ever stand for anything like that.

February 7, 1953. <u>President Louis L. Madsen</u> of the Utah State Agricultural College called at the office at 9 o'clock this morning. We had a confidential consultation for over an hour, during which I inferred that one of the most, if not, the most contributing factor to the misunderstanding between the Board and the President of the board and faculty is the Executive Secretary—Russell B. Bernston.[9]

February 16, 1953. Representative [Sulvanus J.] Postma of Logan came in at 2:30 p.m. in the interest of the U[tah] S[tate] A[gricultural] C[ollege]. Said he sat through the Board of Trustees meeting last Saturday, and he is afraid that unless some action is taken at once, President [Louis L.] Madsen will not last through the next board meeting. Two weeks ago, in a meeting with the Governor, the Governor was for keeping Pres[ident] Madsen, but the other day he said he had polled every member of the board of Trustees, and every one of them felt Pres[ident] Madsen would have to go. [LDS] Bishop Postma [of Logan] would like to bring in Secretary of State Lamont Toronto, and Representative Simeon Dunn of Hyrum [Utah], both of whom have sat through board meetings and meetings with the Governor, to discuss the matter with Pres[ident] McKay. They feel they can exert enough control in the Senate that if Pres[ident] Madsen can be saved until July, they can control the appointments to the Board of Trustees, eight of which will be made at that time.

February 17, 1953. Meeting of President David O. McKay with Representatives S[ulvanus] J. (Vean) Postma of Logan and Simeon Dunn of Hyrum and Secretary of State Lamont F. Toronto, February 17, 1953, in regard to the Utah State Agricultural College.

POSTMA: The people of Cache Valley and Logan are very concerned about the welfare of the Agricultural College. The majority want to support President [Louis L.] Madsen. He is capable of handling the job. We feel it would do the College serious damage if he were removed. We know that removing Dean [of Students Joseph N.] Symons was a preliminary step to get President Madsen out. Groups have met with Governor [J. Bracken] Lee on various occasions to urge him that President Madsen is capable of doing the job, but he has not had an adequate opportunity to show that he can do the job. The Governor concurred with us that board member [George D.] Preston[10] perhaps was the cause

---

9. The university president, Louis Madsen, had recommended that the board dismiss Bernston, their secretary/treasurer. Parson, "Encyclopedic History."

10. George D. Preston (1897–1965) was in the Marine Corps in World War I and in World War II commanded a field artillery regiment of the Utah National Guard in

of a lot of the difficulty and ought to be removed. He has two more years to go in his term. The Governor himself initiated the proposal and asked our opinion as to a means of removing Preston or whether to request the entire board to resign. We felt that Preston would not of himself resign. In all the meetings, the Governor has preferred that as a solution. We thought he was going to go through with that, but in the meeting a week ago with the board, a reversal of opinion was taken, and, we understand, out of that board meeting came a united opinion from the Governor and the Board of Trustees that President Madsen must go. We people in Cache Valley want to go about this in a consistent manner. We realize that you met with the Governor and assume that you took a position in the matter. We want to support you and do the right thing, and that is why we are here, to learn your thinking in the matter, if you have assumed a position. A good many people in Logan called me Sunday and said, We understand President McKay visited with the Governor, and whatever his judgment is, we want to go along with him.

PRES[IDENT] MCKAY: My only attitude with the Governor was that it is none of my business, but I think President Madsen must not be hurt, and there should be no reflection on Brother Madsen in this matter. I think that he should be given a reappointment and let him and the board work this out for his own interest and the interest of the school. That is my position. I think he will not be dismissed. I do not know, but I think he and the board should work this out, whatever difficulties there are. … Governor Lee thinks President Madsen is not an executive, and there has been some talk that Brother Madsen does not like that type of work. … How do the people in Logan know I had a conference with the Governor?

POSTMA: Professor L. R. Humphreys was working in the board room next door. As he came out, he said he saw you. …

PRES[IDENT] MCKAY: This should not go out of this committee. Have you heard, as I heard authoritatively, that this man Preston, whom I do not know, has changed his attitude, that he came here two weeks ago or three weeks ago and acknowledged, to use his phrase, "I have been a

---

the invasion of the Marshall Islands, for which he was given a Bronze Star. He received a law degree from the University of Pennsylvania. When he returned to Utah and opened a private practice, it was not long before he was appointed to be a Logan City judge, and in 1932 he was elected Cache County Attorney.

damn fool in fighting the Church in this matter." He said, "We need the Church up here. We need the Church influence here." He said, "I hope the time will never come when we will not have a prominent Church man at the head of the board; and the head of this school should be a Latter-day Saint."

DUNN: George (Preston) has good blood. He is a son of Bishop W[illiam] B. Preston. He went through World War I ...

PRES[IDENT] McKAY: I think that he is not going to be asked to resign; neither will the board be asked to resign. The board, as presently constituted, are appointees of the Governor. Why should he ask his own appointees to resign? I do not think he will do it. I think he will fill the vacancies. The new board will have the job of appointing a new president. I think they should appoint President Madsen ... It appears to me that Preston will be put back; Brother Isaacson will be put back; Mrs. [Fern B.] Ercanbrack will be put back, some of these others will be reappointed, and that board will then function just as it is. The board should reappoint President Madsen as president of that College. He should be given a new executive secretary. I made that remark, and he said he could work with that secretary. He should call him in, if he is President Madsen's choice. I thought a good deal of him when I was up there on the board.

TORONTO: He [Preston] is a good public-relations man.

PRES[IDENT] McKAY: Yes, but he has not sustained Brother Madsen. ... Thank you, brethren. Let us keep public agitation down until we can talk to members of the board, and save Brother Madsen and the school.

* * *

Called Brother [Mark E.] Petersen and asked him if he is acquainted with the proposal to establish in Salt Lake City an <u>Educational TV channel</u>. He answered that he had read about it in the newspaper, and that one day David Wilson from Ogden came in and asked him to serve on a committee.

I then explained to Brother Petersen that they had asked me to be chairman of the Committee, but we thought it unwise for me to act in this capacity, and that I had suggested we ask him to represent us on that committee. I said that we must do something to utilize this force for educational improvement in our home—that we invite the tobacco and whiskey advertisements right into our home—but are doing very little to bring through the television the worthwhile, educational features into our homes. ...

Also told Brother Petersen that I had had a talk with Gus Backman who had opposed the establishment of the channel at first, because he felt that the State Teaching Association was using the issue for propaganda purposes. Now that he knows the leading educational institutions of the State—the B.Y.U.—the U[niversity] of U[tah]—A[gricultural] C[ollege] [of] U[tah] are heading it, and favoring it, threw a different light on it and took it out of the propaganda field. ...

Brother Petersen then said that he will be delighted to work on this committee, and at my suggestion will be pleased to get in touch with [Utah State] Senators [Clifton G.] Kerr and [Alonzo F.] Hopkins to ask for their interest in the project. ...

February 18, 1953, 8:45 a.m. Telephoned to <u>President Stephen L. Richards</u> at his apartment where he is still confined with a heart ailment. He reported that he is feeling much better; however, said the doctors advise that he not put forth any strenuous effort as yet. I warned Pres[ident] Richards to make no effort to attend meetings, or to climb any stairs.

I then talked to him regarding the sending of a letter to <u>Queen Juliana of Holland</u> expressing our sympathy for her subjects in the Netherlands who have been subjected to the terrible ravages of the North Sea.[11] With this letter it is proposed that we <u>send a check for $10,560 (40,000 guilders)</u> to aid in their rehabilitation with the statement to her also that we have placed at the disposal of the Queen's Relief Committee[,] who may appeal to our Mission President in Holland—Brother [Donovan] Van Dam[,] a supply of quilts and blankets, and he will be glad to cooperate with the committee in the distribution of these quilts and blankets for the immediate comfort of those who have suffered from this disaster. President Richards heartily approved of doing this. ...

10:15 a.m. <u>Elder Marion Romney</u> of the Council of the Twelve called at the office in response to a request I made of him on the 16th;

---

11. The flooding at the end of January and first week of February resulted in over 1,800 deaths in Holland and more than 700 deaths in neighboring countries. The water reached a depth of eighteen feet in some areas.

viz., that Brother Romney and <u>Cornelius Zappey</u>,[12] former President to the Holland Mission, look over the correspondence sent by President Van Dam of the Netherlands Mission concerning relief for the disaster victims in Holland, and make their recommendations concerning the assistance we may extend to the flood victims.

Brother Romney reported that through President Van Dam the saints in Holland are making contributions to assist the destitute, though not many of our people are suffering or are in need.

He further reported that there are available from Church Welfare supplies here in Salt Lake 800 quilts valued at $6 each and 200 blankets valued at $6 each could be sent to the Netherlands Mission. Bro[ther] Romney thinks these would be the most helpful assistance we can give at the present time.[13]

March 2, 1953. <u>President Stephen L. Richards</u> called by telephone from his apartment pertaining to a letter addressed to Pres[ident] R. Scott Zimmerman of the Western Canadian Mission, Edmonton, Alberta, Canada, prepared by Pres[ident] [J. Reuben] Clark under date of January 9, 1953, and said, "It is very difficult for me to harmonize my feelings with the stand taken." (The letter pertains to the acceptance by the people in Canada of gratuities of one sort and another granted by the Canadian government, and was sent to President Richards with the request that he read it and give us his opinion of the same.)[14]

President Richards further said: "I just feel that we do not have to do things like that when we can leave the people to act for themselves and while we cannot individually approve of everything governments do. I

---

12. Cornelius Zappey (1894–1955), who was born in Rotterdam, Holland, was president of the Dutch Mission at the conclusion of World War II. As such, he oversaw the church's relief efforts in that country, for which he was awarded a Medal Of Gratefulness by the Minister of Foreign Affairs. McKay was so impressed with his work and with the post-war Dutch Saints that he commented, "[This] is one the greatest acts of true Christian conduct ever brought to my attention." Van Orden, *Building Zion*, 159, 168.

13. McKay sent a letter to Queen Juliana on February 20, 1953, expressing sympathy for the Dutch people. He enclosed a bank draft for $10,560 as a contribution and noted the availability of blankets at the church's Netherlands Mission headquarters. Under this date in the diary is a reply from the queen's private secretary dated March 10, 1953, acknowledging the church's contribution.

14. Clark and McKay differed significantly over such issues. See Quinn, *Elder Stateman*, 131–79. The particular issue in question in this entry is discussed on page 159.

think the policy as outlined in the letter would lead us to take objection to what governments all over the world are doing. We, the Church, are world-wide, and it makes so many people feel that they are not in good standing because they are not fully following the counsel of our brethren."

I answered: "That is true, and they do not like to go against our counsel and as you say, when they do, they feel they are out of harmony."

Brother Richards then said: "We cannot regulate the affairs of all governments, and I wonder if the time has not come when we can say that we express no official view; that we leave it to the people for determination themselves."

I remarked at this point that "We believe in being subject to kings, presidents, rulers and in obeying, honoring, and sustaining the law."

President Richards stated that "there is nothing in the law (Canadian) that prevents us from teaching family solidarity, and from advocating those high principles in our Gospel, but when it comes to interfering with the policies of the government, I doubt that it is our function."

I expressed appreciation to Pres[ident] Richards for his views, and he answered that is the way he honestly feels about the matter.

I then told Pres[ident] Richards that he has our love and blessings, and that I hoped this interruption would not in any way disturb him. He said that it had not; that he had been sitting up a little today, and feels that he is getting better. Said the doctor had let his nurse go today, which is a good sign. I warned him not to get too eager; that rest is the greatest specific [medicine] at this time; that he must take it without any worry. Pres[ident] Richards then said that he thought he had followed the doctor's orders to the letter, and that he had walked only half a block the other day when he had that slight heart attack, and couldn't get back to the apartment without great distress. ...

Brother Lawrence B. Johnson of Randolph, Utah, called from the [Utah] State Capitol where he is engaged with sessions of the Legislature. He conversed with me about— ...

(2) Discussed matters pertaining to the U[tah] S[tate] A[gricultural] C[ollege] Board—the assignment of new members to the Board, and the retirement from the Board of Bishop [Thorpe B.] Isaacson. I said confidentially that if the Governor will reappoint the Board and let the Board and the President work out the difficulties for the present, that nobody

will be hurt and the school will be benefitted. Further, that Brother Isaacson's health is not good, and that he will have to resign after he has straightened out things at the College.

Brother Johnson mentioned the stories that have come out about Bishop Isaacson, and I stated that there is absolutely no truth in them; that I had received letters making apologies for what has been said. I stated that Bishop Isaacson is a fine executive, and that for the present I have in mind the good of the school—it is a good school and must not be permitted to deteriorate.

Bro[ther] Johnson said he would hate to have anything happen to President [Louis L.] Madsen this year. I said that sometime during the year they could probably work things out. Brother Johnson said that just now it would be tragic for Pres[ident] Madsen to leave—felt that if he had a different Board it would be better for him. Mentioned that Bishop Isaacson has two more years on the Board if he cares to remain.

(3) Bro[ther] Johnson then brought up the Appropriations Bill now before the Legislature. I said that I think everything should be done to maintain our schools. Bro[ther] Johnson wondered if I should call Orval Adams[15] and ask him to get in touch with the Governor regarding the allotment to our schools. I said that I had refrained from entering into this—that it is a matter for the State to decide. ...

Governor J. Bracken Lee called—said that he had a "little brain storm" and wanted my advice regarding it. He then said regarding the situation at the Utah Agricultural College—"I am wondering if it would be beneficial to do something like this: Put Thorpe Isaacson on the university of Utah Board, and Dr. Adam S. Bennion on the Utah Agricultural College Board."

I stated that I had suggested to Bishop Isaacson that he had better ask to be released from the Board at the USAC because of his health; and that I thought it would be a good move for him; that when he gets back and can get matters moving along smoothly at the College, he could resign. His health is not good and he should get off that Board.

---

15. Orval W. Adams (1884–1968) had been vice president of Utah National Bank, part of the First Security Company. In 1925 her was recruited by the church for the position of president of Zions Bank. Later he became chair of the Church Finance Committee.

The Governor then said that he thought that could be done without injuring him at all.

I further stated: "Now, I believe that if you appoint him at the U[niversity] of U[tah] you would have to release him from that Board because of his health; otherwise it would be a good move."

The Governor then said that he wished to smooth things out without injuring or hurting any one.

I told him that we appreciate his consideration. It was agreed that I should think about the Governor's proposal and then call him later giving him my advice in the matter.

March 3, 1953, 8 a.m. I telephoned to <u>Governor J. Bracken Lee</u> in response to his request that I give thought to the advisability of appointing <u>Bishop Thorpe Isaacson</u> a member of the Board of Regents of the University of Utah, and <u>Dr. Adam S. Bennion</u> as a member of the Board of Trustees of the U[tah] S[tate] A[gricultural] C[ollege]

I said that inasmuch as Brother Isaacson is one of the four oldest on the Board of Trustees of the College that I think it would be better for him to remain there and with the new appointees on the Board help to settle the difficulties that are now rampant between the Board, the president, and the faculty of the U.S.A.C.

I remarked further that as Brother Isaacson's health is not very good, it may be necessary in a few months for Brother Isaacson to request a release from the Board of Trustees.

The Governor stated that he had no desire whatever to get rid of Bishop Isaacson because, he, the Governor, considers the Bishop one of the ablest men interested in the welfare of the College.

March 9, 1953, summary of telephone conversation with president of University of Utah. The second thing that President [A. Ray] Olpin[16] was concerned about was a visit from [BYU] President [Ernest L.] Wilkinson and Adam S. Bennion where President Wilkinson served notice that

---

16. Albert Ray Olpin (1898–1983) grew up in Utah Valley and graduated from BYU in physics. After receiving a PhD from Columbia University, he worked for Bell Laboratories and became director of research at Ohio State University until he was named president of the University of Utah in 1946. See Peterson, *Years of Promise*.

he has offered Dr. Virginia Cutler a position at the BYU.[17] President Olpin said this was just like a "stick of dynamite" because the Home Economics House was built with Dr. Cutler in mind and Sterling Sill[18] has contacted some 800 people to raise money for the building,—the whole thing has been built around Dr. Cutler and her plans and it is quite a shock to lose her after all the work and plans.

President Olpin said that President Wilkinson's excuse for offering Dr. Cutler the position was that they couldn't find a person and the L.D.S. girls at the BYU need the guidance which Dr. Cutler could give. President Olpin said that the U of U is made up primarily of LDS girls also.

President Wilkinson has been trying for 2 years unofficially to get Dr. Cutler. He has been in and out of her office half a dozen times to talk to her. She has turned him down several times.

President Olpin said that President Wilkinson claimed that he had come with Dr. Bennion with the full approval of the Board to try to get her. President McKay said that was not a fact. He said that, "I had opposed all the time his going to the University and taking any teacher without the approval of the President, and finally we said that this matter be left entirely to Mrs. Cutler and if she wishes to go we shall approve, and Dr. Bennion, as a member of this Board, and also a member of the University Board of Regents, should accompany President Wilkinson and they together should see Dr. Olpin and the matter be left entirely with Dr. Cutler."

Dr. Olpin said, "I would not in any way stand in her way; I had no indication of her desire to go; she has told me how much she has resisted offers before."

---

17. This was an on-going problem between the two presidents. Both were protective of their respective turfs. Wilkinson was in the process of building BYU to surpass the two state institutions and was not averse to seeking some of their faculty. Such incidents placed McKay in a bind, wanting to support his alma mater and at the same time wishing to assist in every way the growth of the church university. In the end, Cutler stayed in Salt Lake City, although she would later be persuaded to accept the position at BYU of dean of the college.

18. Sterling Welling Sill (1903–94) was a graduate of the University of Utah who became an executive with New York Life Insurance Company. A year later, in April 1954, he would be called to be an Assistant to the Quorum of the Twelve Apostles. Then in 1976 he would become a member of the First Quorum of the Seventy; two years later he would receive emeritus status. He was a popular speaker and author of more than thirty motivational books.

Dr. Olpin said that Dr. Bennion came and said, "President Olpin, I am here because the Board suggested that I come; I suppose it is because I am a member of both Boards. President Wilkinson is qualified to speak for himself." This is the only statement made by Dr. Bennion.

Dr. Olpin then remarked that Dr. Cutler is under the impression that Dr. Bennion thinks she should go.

President McKay then said, "Will you please tell her that you have it directly from the President of the Board of Trustees of the BYU that there is no desire on the part of the Board to influence her in the least— that if she has any feeling of obligation to the U of U (and she should have) she is perfectly free to remain where she is—that there is no co-ercion whatever from a religious standpoint—it is left entirely with her. And furthermore, even if she decided to go to the BYU, she should not go without consulting Dr. Olpin."

Dr. Olpin said that they had consulted him, but they did not ask for his objections, that he had plenty of objections to raise. ... Dr. Olpin said that he feels the BYU should be happy in having LDS people in other schools; that "Ernest" has the desire to make the BYU the biggest University in the world.

President McKay said that it will be a very discouraging condition and very detrimental if we let the sentiment go throughout the State that the U[niversity] of U[tah] is a non-member school—that in reality the U of U is our School as much as any other school, and LDS people are supporting it. ...

President Olpin said that President Wilkinson is ambitious, effi-cient and dynamic. He has found difficulty in getting teachers who were right for the school. He has two or three of the faculty upset all the time, talking informally to them.

President McKay said that the U of U is an LDS Institution. Presi-dent McKay asked if he had made himself clear. He said he feels that Dr. Cutler owes obligation to Brother Sill [for funding her program]. There isn't another man who would have done the same thing. He went on with his work after being released from the Board of Regents and he did the work without financial help from the State. President McKay said there would be no disfavor in the eyes of the President and the Board if she decided to stay at the U of U.

March 10, 1953. <u>Governor J. Bracken Lee</u> called to ask my opinion about appointing Matthew Cowley[19] as a member of the University of Utah Board of Regents. I answered that although we are working him pretty hard, he will be a good man on the Board of Regents—that he is a man of good judgment—dependable, intelligent, and forthright.

March 12, 1953, 8:30 a.m. <u>Elders Harold B. Lee and Henry D. Moyle</u> called on me this morning and reviewed what has been going on up at the [Utah] Legislature, and asked if we would like them to continue to guide things for the next election, keeping the brethren informed. I told them yes. They asked if they might have a meeting during Conference with men whom they have heretofore contacted. I said yes, but thought they should not attend it.[20] They thought probably they could coach Pres[ident] [Lorenzo E.] Elggren[21] and Brother [Marion G.] Romney.[22] They felt we should start right now to get good men at the Primaries in both parties—Republicans and Democrats. In regard to the City here, told them to let Colonel [Elmer G.] Thomas go on with his committee as a restraining influence and that they should decide now on some good men to take positions in the City Commission.

8:45 to 9:15. <u>Dr. Ernest L. Wilkinson</u> came in to report that the Legislature had passed the bill for educational television, but that there is evidence that the Governor will veto it. He appealed to me to go and see the Governor, but he would not do so as he did not want to place himself in the position of being turned down. There is assurance from Washington,

---

19. Matthew Cowley (1897–1953) was ordained an apostle five years after the death of his father, the former apostle Matthias Cowley (1858–1940), in an ordinance performed in October 1945 by George Albert Smith. In 1938 Cowley returned to New Zealand as the mission president. His education included degrees from the University of Utah and George Washington University law school.

20. The decision for them to keep a low profile was based on the fact that they were both apostles, Moyle a member of the First Presidency.

21. The president of the Liberty Stake, Albert Lewis Elggren (1902–84), became involved in 1953 in a bill the governor ultimately vetoed, which would have prevented the purchase of groceries or clothing on Sundays. Elggren inherited his father's wholesale food company. In another year he would be called to preside over the Western States Mission, headquartered in Denver. Merrill and Cannon, "Ox in the Mire?" 167–73.

22. This junior member of the Quorum of the Twelve had a degree in political science from the University of Utah and had won election in 1934 to the Utah House of Representatives as a Democrat. He had also been a Salt Lake City prosecuting attorney.

however, that the limit for getting this TV channel will not be June 1, 1953. Brother Wilkinson said that he would see the Governor about it.

Later Dr. Wilkinson came back to report his conversation with the Governor—said that he is determined to veto the bill.

I stated that I think it is not wise for me to try to bring undue influence, or to try to influence the Governor against his own personal convictions regarding the bill.

9:15 to 9:30 a.m. Patriarch Eldred Smith called at the office. Said he does not know where he is at, that he is receiving letters asking why he does not call the patriarchs together and have a meeting. I explained that such a meeting is being called for Conference time, and that it will be under the direction of the Twelve, at which time they will be given instructions. He said he could not understand why he is not the presiding patriarch. I said that is explained in a letter from the Twelve, that his is not an administrative office. The patriarch mentioned that he is told not to give any blessings other than patriarchal blessings here, and yet when he is in the stakes [it does not make sense that] the Brethren will not permit him to do any setting apart or ordaining, but if anybody wants a special blessing they invite him to give it. Later, at our regular meeting the Brethren of the Presidency felt there was no reason why he should not assist in setting apart high councilmen or high priests quorum presidents but that he should not ordain bishops or presidents of stakes.

I told the Patriarch that I would continue the discussion with him, at some later time before Conference.

March 20, 1953. Sterling Sill called me early this morning regarding Virginia Cutler of the Home Economics Department of the U[niversity] of U[tah]. Brother Sill had told Miss Cutler to see me and I told Bishop Sill that I did not wish to see her, that this is a matter she must decide. Pres[ident] [Ernest L.] Wilkinson would like to have her at the B.Y.U.

March 23, 1953. During my absence from the office Mrs. Minerva Teichert[23] of Idaho left several colored slides of paintings she had done of

---

23. Arguably the first Mormon woman artist of any note, Minerva Kohlhepp Teichert (1889–1976) emerged from rural Wyoming and Idaho to attend the Art Institute of Chicago and the Art Students' League in New York City. She may have been overly

<u>Book of Mormon subjects</u>, (which she is planning to have <u>published in book form</u>,) for approval of the First Presidency. She is especially seeking approval of two paintings of Christ which she would like to include in the collection.

Later, upon viewing the two slides containing pictures of Christ, I expressed disapproval of the halo Mrs. Teichert has so pronouncedly placed around the head of Christ—I think this should be modified.

March 27, 1953. Following the meeting I had a confidential talk with Commissioner [Franklin L.] West on the proposed reorganization of the Church School educational system. He thought it was a wise thing to do; however, it was evident that he believes that the controlling body under the Board of Education should be the Commissioner and his associates rather than under the Brigham Young University. However, he expressed a willingness to cooperate in whatever the authorities deemed best.

March 31, 1953. In the late afternoon, President [J. Reuben] Clark and I made another trip to the Buehner Cement Company where we definitely decided upon the color of the blocks to be used on the front of the Los Angeles Temple. We chose the gold color rather than the pink which we had previously considered.[24]

April 1, 1953, First Presidency's meeting. Among items considered were: …

(2) I mentioned that at the meeting to be held in the Temple tomorrow, Thursday, of all the General Authorities at 9:00, I had requested the <u>brethren of the Twelve</u> to be prepared to <u>submit their suggestions for a successor to Elder John A. Widtsoe</u>.[25] …

---

cautious in seeking the church's approval because her younger sister, Annalee Skarin, had been excommunicated a year earlier for promoting spiritualism. Their grandfather was the infamous ruffian William ("Wild Bill") Hickman. For more on Skarin, see McKay diary, June 6, 1955.

24. The outside facade of the temple consists of panels of concrete and crushed quartz that give a slightly off-white sheen. As part of the modernist look that was the brainchild of Salt Lake City architect Edward O. Anderson, it was thought that the color pink would match the style of the neighborhood, where for instance the Beverly Hills Hotel had been painted pink in 1948. Ultimately a more subtle tan was decided upon.

25. Widtsoe died in November 1952. Counselor Henry D. Moyle "suggested Wendell Mendenhall, Henry Eyring[,] [or] George L. Nelson" as a replacement. Mendenhall was a wealthy California rancher and president of the San Joaquin Stake, who would soon be brought in to run the Church Building Department. Henry Eyring was

(4) Considered a <u>proposed elevation for the Swiss Temple and the new plan, which provides that instead of going from room to room, the [decorative elements of the] creation room and the world room will be thrown on a [movie] screen</u>, so that the people will remain in their seats, and then go through the veil into the Celestial room. The brethren were enthusiastic about this new arrangement. …

April 7, 1953, 10 to 11:30 a.m., First Presidency's meeting. <u>President Stephen L. Richards</u> met with us for the first time since he was taken ill several weeks ago. We expressed our great joy in having him with us, and President Richards expressed his appreciation of being able to be with us again, and also his appreciation of the Conference.

We discussed somewhat the condition of Brother Albert E. Bowen and his desire that he should not linger indefinitely.[26]

<u>President [J. Willard] Marriott of the Washington [DC] Stake</u> called in the office of the First Presidency and discussed the matter of the <u>Archaeological Foundation and Tom Ferguson</u>.[27] Told of his long acquaintance with Brother [Thomas Stuart] Ferguson and his interest in the Church and particularly his interest in Book of Mormon archaeology. He mentioned that <u>Dr. [Wells] Jakeman</u>[28] of the B.Y.U. is also interested with him in this work and that <u>Dr. [Alfred V.] Kidder,</u>[29] <u>head of the Archaeological Department of Carnegie Institute is interested</u> (he

dean of the University of Utah graduate school and a member of the Sunday School board. Nelson was an attorney, a member of the *Deseret News* board, and president of the Monument Park Stake. Moyle diary, April 2, 1953.

26. Elder Bowen, an apostle, would die three months later.

27. See entry for Sept. 25, 1952, for more on Ferguson and the New World Archaeological Foundation.

28. Max Wells Jakeman (1910–98) wrote his dissertation at the University of California–Berkeley on the archaeology of the Yucatan. At BYU, where he was hired in 1946, he popularized so-called Book of Mormon archaeology in the classroom, in lectures, and through publications of the University Archaeological Society (later Society for Early Historic Archaeology). See, for instance, his influential 1953 article, "An Unusual Tree of Life Sculpture from Ancient Central America," *Bulletin of the University Archaeological Society*, no. 4. He joined the board of directors of the New World Archaeological Foundation as well.

29. When Alfred Vincent Kidder (1885–1963) was studying at Harvard, he found summer work in the Four Corners area with a team of University of Utah archaeologists, thereby becoming acquainted with Mormons and with the Southwest. He became a research associate at the Carnegie Institution in 1927 and remained to 1950.

is a non-member); he is about to retire and is willing to spend all his time working on the development of this thing. Brother Marriott felt that the book by Brother Ferguson and Milton R. Hunter has more information in connection with the archaeology of the Book of Mormon than anything we have.[30] Dr. Kidder thought they had brought together a wonderful compilation of material. Brother Ferguson would like to show the Brethren some pictures, to be thrown on a screen, of things they have found, the thought being whether the Brethren would feel that it is sufficiently important to assist in the financing. The Presidency agreed to spend the time to see the pictures Thursday morning next at 8 o'clock.

April 9, 1953, 8 o'clock. Presidents [Stephen L] Richards, [J. Reuben] Clark, members of the Council of the Twelve, and I witnessed slide pictures of archaeological discoveries in Central America, as presented by Thomas Ferguson, and in connection therewith he made an appeal for the Church to help their association financially.

April 14, 1953, 9 to 10 a.m. Was engaged in the meeting of the First Presidency ... Discussed the picture slides of archaeological artifacts presented by Thomas Ferguson and his appeal that the church help his organization—New World Archaeological Foundation—by contributing $15,000 for this year and $30,000 a year for the next four years. The brethren decided to make the $15,000.00 contribution this year, but to give no further commitment. The brethren did not want to obligate the Church to finance this enterprise. It was also the feeling that such contribution should be made through someone else and that the Church should not be shown in the transaction. ...

I had a short interview with Bishop [Thorpe B.] Isaacson on U[tah] S[tate] A[gricultural] C[ollege] matters.

For the next two hours—from 3 to 5 p.m.—met by appointment at his request President Louis L. Madsen of the U.S.A.C. During the last hour of the consultation Mrs. Madsen was present.

President Madsen said that he had received definite word that the Board of Trustees had notified him that he would not be reappointed as

---

30. *Ancient America and the Book of Mormon* was privately published in 1950 by Ferguson and Hunter, with a foreword by apostle John A. Widtsoe.

President of the Utah State Agricultural College, and for the next hour he discussed matters pertaining to it. Later, when Mrs. Madsen came in she evidently heard for the first time that her husband would not be re-appointed. She blamed it on the "ten percent of Anti-Mormons who are breaking the hearts of people—discharging them without reason," etc. etc. There then ensued such a tirade as I have not heard for a long time from any woman. She was entirely misinformed and misjudged people without restraint. President Madsen remained quiet during her tirade.

I said "President Madsen, I have information that two positions are open to you—(1) in the government service as a research worker in the Agricultural Department, and the other as head of the agricultural department at the U.S.A.C. in Logan."

He said he would decide later—did not mention resigning. Thought he would wait until he was dismissed from the College.

George Albert Smith, Jr.[31] called at the office re:.position at the U.S.A.C.

Bishop Isaacson came in again about U.S.A.C. matters.

April 16, 1953, meeting of First Presidency and Council of the Twelve. Expressed the feeling that the family ties are fundamental, that the family is the foundation of society. Stated that the First Presidency have suggested to the auxiliary organizations that in choosing members of the General Boards women should be chosen whose family ties will not interfere and that frequently the First Presidency refuse to approve sisters whose names have been submitted because those recommended were rearing young families.

April 22, 1953; Laguna Beach, California. Received telephone call from my secretary Clare [Middlemiss] who advised me of important matters that had come up during my absence, and also from Brother Henry D. Moyle who reported to me in substance his findings with reference to

---

31. George Albert Smith Jr. (1905–69) was a son of the church president by that name. From 1934 to his death thirty-five years later in 1969, Smith Jr. taught at the Harvard School of Business, when not being honored as a visiting professor at Stanford, the University of Hawaii, Yale, or the Institut pour l'Etude des Méthodes de Direction de l'Entreprise in Lausanne, Switzerland. He was also a consultant to the US Commerce Secretary. During World War II, he had been assistant director of the Special Navy Supply Corps.

"Cinerama."[32] It was decided with the approval of the brethren that in the event it is considered necessary to give a report to Mr. Lowell Thomas with reference to the proposals he has made to the Church concerning investment in "Cinerama" that our reply should be in the negative, for the following reasons: First, because of the highly speculative nature of the investment; second, because nothing definite appears at the present time as to collateral advantages that we might secure from our identification with the project; and, thirdly, that the publicity which should be attached to our investment would not be good for the Church nor well received by our members.

Later I telephoned President [Stephen L.] Richards and said that I had been thinking the matter over and that I should be pleased to have the brethren close the matter with Mr. Thomas and thank him for the opportunity, and say it was felt we should not invest in "Cinerama" and make a final conclusion of it.

May 11, 1953. Bishop [Thorpe B.] Isaacson called for advice regarding the Board of the Dee Hospital.[33] Said the Board has not been using Welfare coal—they have always used the coal from the Dee family, the price of which has been below cost. The Board feels that the Dee family should not be hurt by our refusing to use their coal, but the request has come that church Welfare coal be used.

I said in this instance it would be better to say that we feel it inadvisable to make any change for the present.

Bishop Isaacson, referring to the U[tah] S[tate] A[gricultural] C[ollege]

---

32. Cinerama referred to a wide-screen technology and surround sound that utilized three projectors, a curved screen, and a seven-channel audio system. It looked auspicious but was actually ahead of its time due to distortions in the images and problems with synchronization. In 1952 the documentary *This Is Cinerama* had the Tabernacle Choir singing "America the Beautiful" in the background during the finale. As impressive as the technology was, the church decided not to invest in it.

33. The Dee Hospital in Ogden was dear to McKay's heart. In 1969 when the old hospital was demolished and a new building erected, it was named after McKay because, in part, the original founder, Annie Taylor Dee (1852–1934), had gifted the hospital to the LDS Church in 1915. When a second building was added in 1978, the medical complex was renamed the McKay–Dee Hospital. Thomas Duncombe Dee (1844–1905), the founder's husband, was David Eccles's business partner in founding the Ogden Sugar Company (now Amalgamated Sugar), Ogden Savings Bank (later acquired by Wells Fargo), and Utah Construction Company (now Utah International).

trouble, [said] that he had a fine meeting with Brother Adam S. Bennion who is conducting the investigation, and who is under terrific pressure because of this investigation. Bishop Isaacson said Pres[ident] [Louis L.] Madsen has caused a lot of trouble, and is afraid that Pres[ident] Madsen will suffer because of it. Bishop Isaacson said he fought for hours at Board meetings for Pres[ident] Madsen and that he pleaded with him not to have any bitterness. Said he is of the opinion that if Pres[ident] Madsen had followed counsel all the trouble would have been avoided.

May 15, 1953, 11:30 a.m. Bishop Thorpe B. Isaacson—Discussed matters pertaining to Harry Clarke and Ralph Richards. ...

Later in the afternoon I had another conference with Bishop Isaacson—reported meeting he had had with Ralph Richards and Harry Clarke. (Rumors and gossip must cease). ...

Arthur Watkins called from Washington, D.C.—said he is Chairman of the Immigration Committee, and that the president has asked Congress to pass a special immigration bill to allow 240,000 people to come into this country over the course of two years—110,000 Germans or people of German origin from behind the Iron curtain, or those who have escaped from the Iron curtain,—20,000 Dutch people—20,000 Greeks, and 75,000 Italians. Said that he spent an hour with President [Dwight D.] Eisenhower on this matter. The President thinks if we allow these people to come to this country, it will be an example to the South American countries and will greatly aid in the war against Communism. The President promises that he will not repeat the request nor will he repeat the promise regarding this matter which was left him from the other administration.

Senator Watkins said that it is a pretty hard thing for him to do, but he is doing it because of his faith in the President. I remarked that I thought he should go along with the President.

The Senator then said that he is going to fight this foreign spending, but he believes that 240,000 people brought here over a period of two years will not hurt us, that they will be screened very closely and only the best will be allowed to come in. Said that some of the Italians are very fine people, but they will have to be especially careful in allowing only those who are worthy to enter this country—they will all be submitted to very close screening, and if they enter under false pretenses, they will be deported immediately.

I told Senator Watkins that I did not feel too well about the Italians, but that I did feel all right about the Dutch and the Germans. All of them should, of course, be examined closely before entering.

May 19, 1953. ... Bishop [Thorpe B.] Isaacson called to say that he had just learned that the Investigation Committee of the U[tah] S[tate] A[gricultural] C[ollege] matter is going to recommend that three of the members of the Board of Trustees resign—Bishop Isaacson, [attorney] Arthur Woolley,[34] and Dr. [George D.] Preston.[35] This is a most unwise suggestion. I tried to get Brother [Adam S.] Bennion by telephone but failed to reach him.

May 20, 1953. While in this meeting was called to the telephone in my private office. Governor J. Bracken Lee was on the line. Said he had called to express to me his great confidence in Bishop Thorpe B. Isaacson, Ch[ai]r[man] of the Board of Trustees of the U[tah] S[tate] A[gricultural] C[ollege]. Said he had associated with him for years on the Board, and that there is no man for whom he has greater respect, and in whom he has greater confidence. Said he would like to see him go through with his assignment on the Board—at any rate until July. The Governor then said "There is only one man who can get him to do that, and that is you, President McKay. I wish you would express to him my confidence in him and get him not to resign as Chairman of the Board of Trustees and to take charge of the Commencement Exercises at the College."

I thanked the Governor and told him that I would do what I could with Bishop Isaacson.

Later I had a talk with Bishop Isaacson, and he read me his letter of

---

34. Arthur Snow Woolley (1889–1962) came from the small town of Pipe Spring, Arizona, twenty miles southwest of Kanab, Utah, a grandson of apostle Erastus Snow and son of Edwin D. Woolley. His father led the Deseret Telegraph Company and ZCMI. The son was an attorney and political operative who became chair of the Weber County Republican central committee.

35. The board of trustees recommended firing USAC President Louis L. Madsen, but at the last minute appointed a committee to study the issue, to see if there was a consensus with the board. Apparently not. See "U.S.A.C. Minutes Released," *Ogden Standard–Examiner*, May 14, 1953.

resignation as Chairman of the Board of Trustees of the U.S.A.C. He has fully decided to go through with his resignation and will present it to the Board next Saturday—is convinced this is the best thing for him to do.

I then said: "I think so, too, first because I promised Sister Isaacson that I would urge you to do so; and secondly, I think you should resign because of your health. Immediately following your resignation you should take a rest, go on a vacation, and be absolutely free from any worry or anxiety due either to the college or to the Church."

Bishop Isaacson answered that he would do that provided the report of the Committee would give no implication that he is doing it under duress.

Later in the day (5 p.m.) at his request, I met Dr. Adam S. Bennion who let me read the report of the U.S.A.C. Investigating Committee. I think it is much better than the one he submitted yesterday.

June 2, 1953, Chicago. Just before we arrived in Chicago, we heard part of the ceremonies of the crowning of Queen Elizabeth the II. I heard enough to convince me that the Coronation was a sacred ceremony.

June 15, 1953. Dr. Edward R. McKay[36] called—came in to see how I am feeling. Pleaded with me to cut down my strenuous activity. He said, "Father, the least you can do is to take Mondays away from the office—after you have been under the stress of speaking appointments on Sundays, to take a rest on Monday will do you more good than anything you can do." He then turned to my secretary, Clare [Middlemiss], who was present during the conversation and said: "Will you please see that Father does not make appointments for Mondays." I promised Edward that I would try and do better.

June 23, 1953, 7:45 a.m. Met by appointment [*Salt Lake Tribune* publisher] John F. Fitzpatrick and [Chamber of Commerce president] Gus Backman. They came in to talk about civic matters—the calling of a special session of the Legislature, etc., and then spent some time reminiscing about Utah

---

36. The church president's fourth son, Edward Riggs McKay (1915–2008), received his medical degree from Temple University in Philadelphia and thereafter practiced proctology in Salt Lake City. During World War II he had been in the navy medical corps.

Centennial days when they served on the Utah Centennial Commission of which I was Chairman.[37] Had a delightful visit with these men.

June 25, 1953, summary of telephone conversation. It was also stated by Senator [Arthur V.] Watkins to President McKay that a "red hot telegram" had been received from [Utah] Governor [J. Bracken] Lee that day regarding the appointment of an extra Judge for Utah. Governor Lee indicated that as an economy measure another Judge should not be appointed. Senator Watkins feels that Governor Lee's economy measure was defeated with the appointment of Judge [Willis] Ritter.[38] Another Judge should be appointed according to Senator Watkins. Senator Watkins asked President McKay if he backed him up in his decision. President McKay assured the Senator that he was back of him 100% with regards to the matter.

June 26, 1953. The regular First Presidency's meeting continued—President Joseph Fielding Smith, Harold B. Lee, Henry D. Moyle, Marion G. Romney and Dr. Ernest L. Wilkinson, President of the B.Y.U.[,] [who] met with us to discuss the new church educational system. They presented a chart, suggesting that the designation of the University of Deseret be given to the entire Church School System. Brother Wilkinson read a statement, a copy of which he gave to each of the Brethren, explaining the meaning and history of the word "Deseret."[39] The Committee felt that historically, religiously and traditionally, it was the best name they could find. It was explained that the Brigham Young University would be under the direction of the University of Deseret. (They at first suggested

---

37. Their friendship grew out of this commission work during the late 1940s as the state planned its centennial celebration. McKay was chair, and Fitzpatrick was a member of the executive committee.

38. Watkins opposed the appointment in 1950 of Willis W. Ritter (1899–1978) to the federal bench. Now the senator apparently wanted to limit the judge's impact by diluting his work load. Ritter had studied at the University of Chicago and taught at the University of Utah. Known for his liberal views, he was also somewhat erratic in his personal life. Tom Harvey, "Antics, Rulings of Irreverent Judge Propel … Exposé," *Salt Lake Tribune*, Sept. 2, 2007.

39. This vision of Wilkinson's was to unify the entire school network with new nomenclature. He felt the old term Church Educational System meant nothing to non-members. He wanted BYU to be the hub in the organizational structure. Other names besides Deseret were considered: Joseph Smith University and Latter-day Saints University.

Brigham Young Campus, but withdrew that suggestion.) For the time being the President of the Brigham Young University would also be the President of the University of Deseret, having under his charge the entire Church School System.

The chart suggests that there be a vice-president in charge of religious education, under whom there would be the heads of religious education departments of the Brigham Young University, principals of 119 Latter-day Saint seminaries, heads of religious educational departments at junior colleges, and Directors of our 16 L.D.S. Institutes.

There would be a vice-president of finances and business administration, and he would have direction over this phase of the work for the Brigham Young University, the L.D.S. Institutes, the L.D.S. Seminaries and Junior Colleges.

There would be an executive assistant to the President, who would have no authority except that which is delegated to him by the President, and would assist him mainly in maintaining high standards of teaching in these various units.

The Brethren discussed at considerable length the matter of the name that should be given to this Church Educational System. The thought was expressed that perhaps it should be called the Brigham Young University, but some of the Brethren felt, particularly Brother Lee, that it should not be given the name of any one President. The thought was also expressed that if, for instance, we should call the Institute at Logan near the Agricultural College, or at the University of Utah, or in other places where universities are established, the Brigham Young University Institute it might cause some friction.

Pres[ident] Wilkinson was asked to check into the question of who would sign certificates of graduation, also to look into the Articles of Incorporation of the Brigham Young University and other like questions.

The Brethren agreed that we should move ahead right away with this new program. The Committee were asked to make their recommendations to the Board this morning. ...

Telephone Calls

1. Bishop [Thorpe B.] Isaacson reported that he had received a telephone message from Elder Alma Sonne who is in the East regarding the

U[tah] S[tate] A[gricultural] C[ollege] situation. Said that it is rumored that <u>President [Louis L.] Madsen</u> is to be employed at the B.Y.U. and that he will bring with him 200 students from the U.S.A.C. The people in Logan are asking Alma Sonne to contact the First Presidency so that this will not be done.

Note from minutes of First Presidency's meeting regarding this matter: ["]The brethren of the Presidency discussed the attitude they should take regarding Brother Louis L. Madsen's going to the B.Y.U. It was decided to suggest to President Wilkinson that the matter be not brought up in the Board meeting. The Brethren thought that if Brother Madsen were to go to the B.Y.U. it might be interpreted by the people in Logan as an effort on our part to get the Agricultural College dissenters to go to the B.Y.U. President McKay mentioned that someone had phoned or wired stating that a group of citizens from Logan wanted an interview with the First Presidency, protesting Brother Madsen's appointment to the B.Y.U. <u>The Brethren did not feel they should meet the Committee.</u>"

June 30, 1953, First Presidency's meeting. I reported that I had asked Brother [Delbert L.] Stapley to find out how many <u>husbands and wives we have employed</u>. Pres[ident] [J. Reuben] Clark suggested, and the brethren concurred, that we lay down a rule that in the future we shall not employ married women,[40] and that we leave the present largely undisturbed.

July 1, 1953, First Presidency's meeting. I said that I did not feel right about presenting to the [Church] Board of Education tomorrow morning the recommendation that we <u>substitute for the Church Board</u> of Education the term University of Deseret. We were ready, it was agreed, to present the <u>unification plan</u>, that we include under one heading the <u>Brigham Young University, the Ricks College, the institutes and the seminaries</u>, this to be placed under <u>Dr. Ernest Wilkinson</u>. [But] it was agreed that no change would be made in the nomenclature and if it was decided

---

40. In 1966 BYU English instructor Colleen Keyes Whitley was fired for getting married—as one example of how the policy was enforced. She differed from others in that, with the support of her department chair and dean, she challenged her dismissal and was ultimately retained. Seth Lewis, "Women Faculty No Longer a Rare Commodity," *Daily Universe*, Apr. 11, 2001.

to make a change that could be done later. Pres[ident] Wilkinson will be asked to submit the plan and personnel to the Board.

July 8, 1953, 1 p.m. Elder Adam S. Bennion called at the office with [a] statement making [an] announcement of the unification of educational institutions of the Church. Brother Bennion had prepared the announcement at the request of the First Presidency and brought it to me for my perusal and approval.

August 26, 1953, First Presidency's meeting.[41] Among other things the following were given attention: …

(2) In talking with [US] Senator [Wallace F.] Bennett [R–Utah], I reported that I had received word that Senator [Arthur V.] Watkins was going to Europe in the interest of the new immigration program and he wondered if he could do anything to immigrate our people from there. I said I failed to contact Senator Watkins but that <u>we should like our people to remain in Europe and build</u> up strong branches, particularly now that we are taking temples to them. Many of them have good positions there. They can now remain there, build up the branches, receive their endowments and have their temple work taken care of there, both for themselves and their dead. Senator Bennett said that so far as Germany is concerned and the countries the Nazis overran, many of them have a record which would make them ineligible for emigration, if they were in any way identified with the Nazis.

Senator Bennett mentioned that we have a number of our Church people in responsible jobs in Washington and they are outstanding people. He mentioned among others the good work that Congressman [Douglas R.] Stringfellow [R–Utah][42] is doing.

---

41. From July 30 to August 19, McKay was traveling in Europe.

42. Douglas R. Stringfellow (1922–66) was elected to the US House of Representatives as a Republican in 1952, over Democrat Ernest R. McKay (no relation). What subsequently occurred was one of the more bizarre political stories in Utah history. He was elected on the wave of anti-Communism and as a war hero, with stories of daring exploits behind German lines, acts of bravery and espionage, and subsequent war injuries that made him a political darling and sought-after youth speaker for church and civic groups. But in 1954 his political career began to unravel as the elections approached and research into his stories, the ever-probing questions concerning his service record, revealed that he had accomplished less than he had claimed. LDS Church officials and

September 10, 1953, First Presidency's meeting. Among matters discussed at this meeting were the following:

(1) Priesthood quorum organizations and activities as submitted by the General Priesthood Committee. The brethren did not feel to approve certain recommendations by the Priesthood Committee for the handbook, as they felt that in a very short time they might all be subject to reconsideration and possible change. President McKay said he had been concerned about what seemed to him to be a lack of discernment on the part of some of the Brethren between quorum work and <u>what he would designate as ecclesiastical</u> work, that the quorum <u>is a distinct organization by revelation</u>, and it does not function ecclesiastically only as an aid and furnishing capable officers to function when called upon by the Stake Presidency. We have assigned very important functions to other groups: teaching, recreation, and everything that might be incorporated in the quorum unit to strengthen its organization we have given to others. President Richards said he would like the opportunity of expanding these thoughts some time and had been waiting to get this <u>insurance business for the Priesthood under way</u> ...

<u>President McKay said he had faith in men, that we have a great potential power in the Adult Aaronic Priesthood</u>, men like Dr. [Sterling M.] McMurrin.[43] He thought we <u>should have the strongest men to preside over the quorums</u>, that strong men generally are not content to be molded in a certain cast.

---

the Republican Party pressured him to resign, and on the eve of the 1954 congressional elections he stood before television cameras and gave a tearful apology for having embellished his record. See Prince and Wright, *David O. McKay*, 343–49; Jonas, *Story of a Political Hoax*, 1966.

43. Sterling Moss McMurrin (1914–96) was a long-time friend of McKay. Their friendship was ironic, considering that McMurrin was an intellectual who viewed religion, and Mormonism in particular, in an unorthodox manner. With a PhD. in philosophy, he taught in Utah and California and became dean at the University of Utah, with a leave to serve under President John F. Kennedy as the US Commissioner of Education. McKay felt, despite McMurrin's sometimes critical view of church policies, that the scholar was nevertheless an asset who should be made to feel welcome. Others were not so tolerant, and apostles Harold B. Lee and Joseph Fielding Smith urged excommunication. Upon hearing this, McKay informed McMurrin that if a church court were convened, he would be the first witness for the defense. This quashed any further attempts to take church action against him. See McMurrin and Newell, *Matters of Conscience*, 188–89, 195–99.

September 23, 1953. Dr. Edward R. McKay called regarding "contraceptives and the Church's stand toward their use."

I told him that "the Church cannot countenance contraceptives— marriage is for the purpose of having children and rearing a family. If a couple make modifications of this, the responsibility is theirs—they do not have the Church's sanction in the use of contraceptives, and the delaying of having children."

October 2, 1953, First Presidency's meeting. 1. President McKay mentioned he had consulted Brother Richard L. Evans[44] and he had accepted the appointment as a member of the Council of the Twelve. He expressed his inadequacy and unworthiness. He wanted to know about his work on the radio, and President McKay told him wisdom would dictate that he have somebody else in training for that. President McKay advised that he get someone who could take his place when a call from the Twelve required him to go somewhere. He had nobody in mind.

October 8, 1953, 10 to 2 p.m. Regular Council meeting was held. At this meeting I ordained Brother Richard L. Evans an Apostle, and set him apart as a member of the Twelve. I then gave him the charge.

(At this meeting, President McKay made the following statement to the Brethren: "While we are in the [prayer] circle, may I express to you my gratitude for the loyal support and love that these two devoted counselors give to the President. I assure you there is unity in the Quorum of the First Presidency. With all my soul I ask the Lord to continue to bless them, and to you members of the Twelve I should like to express appreciation and gratitude for the loyalty you give to the First Presidency. With all my heart I say God bless you and continue to attend you.")

October 19, 1953, 9 a.m. Elder Hugh B. Brown,[45] new Assistant to the

44. Richard Louis Evans (1906–71) had been sustained a member of the First Council of Seventy in October 1938. Best known as the long-time voice of the Sunday program, "Music and the Spoken Word," broadcast from Temple Square along with the Tabernacle Choir, his four decades on the air endeared millions of church members and non-members alike, who enjoyed his famously melodious speaking voice and words of wisdom. He died at age sixty-five from a viral infection.

45. Hugh Brown Brown (1883–1975) was ordained to the apostleship five years later in April 1958. In October 1961, he would be sustained as second counselor in the First

Twelve, who just arrived from Canada, called at the office. Consulted with him for 30 minutes about his new responsibilities. ...

During our conversation Brother Brown said that Friday night before he received the call from me he was seized by something the like of which he had never had before that seemed to be crushing his very life out of him, that he and his wife spent a good part of the night in prayer, with the result that some peace came to him Saturday morning [October 3]; that he worked through the day, Saturday, and was relaxing in a warm bath when the telephone call came from me, and that with the call came a rejuvenation of his whole spirit;[46] that he has accepted it with a complete consecration, the like of which he has never before been prepared to do. He then said that he would appreciate being set apart for his duties at the first opportunity. This was arranged for the following day.

October 29, 1953, First Presidency's meeting. It was felt that a committee should be appointed to begin preparations for the sound and pictures of the temple ceremonies to be presented in the new Temples.[47] I suggested the following for membership on the committee: Joseph Fielding Smith, Richard L. Evans, Gordon B. Hinckley, [and architect] Edward O. Anderson.

November 5, 1953, 9 to 9:50 a.m. The regular meeting of the First Presidency was held. At this meeting, we decided to release the following from the Church Literature and Publications Committee: Joseph Fielding Smith, Chairman, Harold B. Lee, and Marion Romney.

The following were appointed to take their place: Spencer W. Kimball, Chairman[;] Adam S. Bennion[;] Thomas C. Romney.

November 24, 1953. I reported at the meeting of the First Presidency this morning that members of the Legislature are concerned about what their

---

Presidency, and in October 1963 as first counselor. When McKay died in January 1970, he was released from the church presidency. He had practiced law in Canada before being called to Utah, and during World War I he had been an officer with a reserve cavalry unit.

46. For more on this experience, see Campbell and Poll, *Hugh B. Brown*, 218–19; Firmage, *Abundant Life*, 112–13.

47. Up to this point, the dramatic portion of the liturgy was acted out in live performances. As early as 1927, with the advent of motion pictures, when the issue of using film in the temples was broached, it was summarily rejected. See Buerger, *Mysteries of Godliness*, 166.

attitude shall be toward the proposed amendment to the State Constitution whereby there would be one senator from each county. It is reported
that Brother [Harold B.] Lee and Brother [Henry D.] Moyle have advocated that principle[,] saying that the Church is back of it, and there
seems to be a division of opinion among the legislators. The Brethren
were agreed that the Church should not take a position on the question,
that it is the responsibility of the legislature to make the decision, and if
there are any who feel we have taken a position they should be corrected.[48]

December 7, 1953. Dr. [Henry] Aldous Dixon[49] of the U[tah] S[tate]
A[gricultural] C[ollege], Logan, called—said that pressure has been
brought upon him to make a statement that the Church will take the
Junior Colleges over if the State decides to release them.[50]

I told Dr. Dixon that the Church would not make a statement;
that the church's attitude is that if the Legislature votes to abandon the
schools, then the church would stand ready to take them back in keeping

---

48. Reapportionment was one of the more volatile issues in twentieth-century
Utah. The state constitution mandated the redrawing of districts according to population
every ten years after each census, but nothing had been done since 1940. When Governor
J. Bracken Lee sought to address this, a firestorm broke out. The population had continued a trend of gravitating toward urban counties, away from the sparsely populated areas.
Rural legislators demanded one senator per county despite the inequity of 274,000 people in Salt Lake County and only 364 in Daggett County, for instance. The *Deseret News*
argued vociferously for the "one county, one senator" approach, with some LDS leaders
jumping into the fray on the rural side. Elder Harold B. Lee, a member of the church's
"political committee," said the amendment mirrored the intent of the "inspired" US Constitution. McKay's counselor Henry D. Moyle, also on the political committee, was more
blunt: "Brethren, don't you realize that if this proposal is passed[,] the Church will control twenty-six of twenty-nine senators?" When passage seemed all but assured, McKay
intervened to take the church out of the discussion, which became moot a few years later
through a judicial reversal in *Petoskey v. Rampton*. See Decker, "The LDS Church and
Utah Politics," in Sells, *God and Country*, 109–12 (Moyle quotation on p. 110).

49. Henry Aldous Dixon (1890–1967) was appointed president of the Utah State
Agricultural College (Utah State University) in the wake of Louis L. Madsen's release.
He was previously president of Weber College, as well as a member of the LDS Sun-
day School board. A long-time friend of McKay, he had been McKay's first choice for
president of BYU, rather than Ernest L. Wilkinson. Dixon had degrees from BYU, the
University of Chicago, and USC.

50. At the time the church turned over its academies to the state (Snow in 1932,
Dixie and Weber in 1933), the stipulation was that if Utah ever ceased to operate them
they would revert back to the church. Governor Lee introduced a bill in 1951 to do
expressly that. It was passed by the legislature and signed by Lee, but the transfer never
occurred because a referendum was put to the electorate and defeated.

with the promise made when the Church presented them to the State[,] that when the State decided they no longer wanted these schools, the church would take them back.

I said further that we do not want them to go against their own judgment. However, if their decision is to turn them back, then the Church will take them over.

Dr. Dixon said it would not hurt the U.S.A.C. to run the Junior College at Ogden, and then have the Church take care of the other two. However, I said I felt that if the Church took any one of them, they should take them all.[51]

December 16, 1953, 9 a.m., First Presidency's meeting. Took the time this morning to <u>read telegrams that had been received from people in Ogden</u>—perhaps 25 or 30—<u>expressing opposition to the Church's taking over the Weber College[52] from the State.</u> [In response,] the Brethren reiterated their stand as previously expressed that they had said they would take the three schools—Weber, Snow, and Dixie,—if and when the State ceases to operate them as State Institutions, and operate them as Church schools. There was some discussion as to whether, in view of the fact that there is so much sentiment expressed against the church's taking over the Weber College, it might not be well to make it known that the <u>First Presidency will feel all right if this matter goes over to the regular sessions of the Legislature.</u> It was felt, however, that we should first tell the Governor. The question was raised whether or not, in view of the fact that the Governor has gone forward with the knowledge, since our announcement that we would take over and operate the schools if the State gave them up—and this is part of his general plan of trying to save money—he would not feel that we have gone back on him. It was

---

51. In the nineteenth century, there were thirty-three church-run academies in Canada, Mexico, and seven states throughout the U.S. Only eight survived, and not all under church jurisdiction: Academia Juárez in Mexico, Brigham Young University in Provo and Rexburg, Dixie State University in St. George, Eastern Arizona Junior College in Thatcher, LDS Business College in Salt Lake City, Snow College in Ephraim (Utah), and Weber State University in Ogden. The academies typically had grammar school–, high school–, and college-level classes. Harold R. Laycock, "Academies," in Ludlow, *Encyclopedia of Mormonism.*

52. McKay had been principal of Weber Academy from 1902 until his church call in 1906, so it was special to him.

finally decided to ask Brother Lee to call on the Governor and have a confidential talk with him, telling him that this seems to be creating a great deal of trouble, that we are interested as we assume he is, in the peace of the community, and it would be satisfactory with us if it was postponed until the regular legislative session. Brother [Harold B.] Lee came down[stairs] to the office at the First Presidency's invitation.[53] ...

I called Frank Browning[54] of Ogden in response to a telegram I received from him regarding the Weber College situation. I wanted to let him know exactly where the Church stood. I stated to Mr. Browning that we would abide by the conditions in the deed to the state and if and when the state ceases to take the responsibility of the colleges as state institutions, then we stand ready to take them, and we will continue them as colleges under the Church school program. We are not urging it. ...

Mr. Browning suggested that I make a statement. But I informed him that I did not think it wise for the Church to interfere with politics.

Mr. Browning stated that the Church could take over Snow and Dixie College now and let the Weber College stand until the next session of the legislature. However, I indicated to him that I felt that the decision should be made on the three colleges together.

December 17, 1953. Frank M. Browning of Ogden called at 8:15 this morning. I had a half hour's conversation with him concerning the matter that is now under discussion and debate regarding the State's returning to the Church the Weber College.

Mr. Browning seems to be opposed to putting this question to the people. He wanted me to say that I am opposed to this procedure, but I said that I did not share his concern that if this question is submitted to the people it will cause strife. Mr. Browning favors having the question of whether or not the Junior Colleges should be turned back to the Church delayed until the

---

53. The First Presidency's offices were on the main floor of the Church Administration Building. Above them were the apostles and presidency of the seventy on the second floor, the Church Historian's office on the third floor, the Genealogical Society of Utah on the fourth floor, and records storage above that.

54. Frank Milton Browning (1897–1969) was one of Weber College's major benefactors. His father co-invented the Colt .45 pistol, Winchester rifle, and Browning machine gun. Frank was a World War II veteran, founder in 1952 of the Bank of Utah, a member of the board of the Federal Reserve Bank of San Francisco, and would win election to the Utah State Senate in 1958 and serve for twelve years.

next Legislature. I said that my answer as to that is that the responsibility of this question lies with the Legislature, and that my attitude is just as I have said to the Committee who called on us last evening—that if they want to submit the question to the people that is all right.

... Following my conversation with Mr. Browning, I called Senator Kerr up at the State Capitol, and told him that I had been in touch with a group in Ogden this morning—that they are very much concerned about the Weber College question being put to the people for decision. Told him that I wanted him to know that there is no change in my attitude as expressed last evening to the group who called on us.

Senator Kerr said that Senator Hafen has investigated the matter and finds that it is illegal to submit the question to the people on the bill that has been introduced; this can be done only by constitutional amendment.

I said that the Ogden People did not want it to go through, but that my opinion stands where it was last evening.

December 18, 1953, First Presidency's meeting. A brief article prepared by Dr. Preston Robinson, General Manager of the Deseret News, was presented. It was regarding the Church's taking over the junior colleges in Ogden, Ephraim, and St. George. The statement was approved by the brethren with a slight change.

December 21, 1953. President Ernest L. Wilkinson called—said the Ogden Chamber of Commerce is holding a meeting today at noon to decide whether or not they should start a suit against the State of Utah because of the Legislature's decision to return Weber College to the Church. Said that David J. Wilson, Howard J. Huggins and Frank Browning are taking an active interest in this matter.

Pres[ident] Wilkinson suggested that it might be well for Pres[ident] McKay to have a talk with these men since they are good members of the Church. ...

When this note was handed to President McKay, he said as to the first mentioned subject, he would not enter into the matter ...

December 28, 1953. Called Ira Huggins regarding the Weber College situation. ...

I then told Mr. Huggins that I am leaving tomorrow at 6 a.m. for an extended trip,[55] and that I am concerned about the school situation in Ogden. I said that this matter has been thrown into our lap, so to speak, and that we have not sought it.

Brother Huggins said that the Governor had said that we have, but that he did not believe it, and believed us 100%.

I told Brother Huggins that to this extent I am responsible—When the bill was introduced to discontinue Snow and Dixie and return them to the State, I stated to my associates, that it was not fair, that the Church had given the State three colleges with the stipulation that when the State ceases to use them as State institutions, the property given to the State would revert back to the Church—that if they are going to cease operating any of these colleges, then they should return the three that were given to them, and that is why later (and I did not speak to the Governor at any time) the Weber College was included.

Great pressure came upon me to say that the Church would not take the Colleges back. I made the statement to [Catholic] Bishop [Duane G.] Hunt and to others that when and if the State ceased to operate these Colleges, the Church, according to stipulation, would receive the property back, and furthermore, that it would continue to operate them as church institutions. I made that statement to Bishop Hunt before this matter came up to the Legislature, and to others because Bishop Hunt called on me and asked "What are you going to do with the property if it comes back to you?" I answered that the schools would be operated as church institutions. He said: "If that is the case, I shall take no more steps to get the property." This was before any of this situation comes up.

I then said that the brethren of the General Authorities had voted unanimously to sustain me in the statement that if and when the State discontinued these institutions as state institutions, that we would take them back according to the stipulations in the deed, and furthermore, that we would operate them as church institutions.

Mr. Huggins then talked about the controversies that have arisen in Ogden—how the people are taking sides, etc.

I told him that up to this time an official statement has not been made by the Church.

---

55. McKay was preparing to travel to South Africa.

Mr. Huggins then said that there is a statement coming from Senators Hopkins and Kerr that they were told "pretty well where to vote on this thing." Frank Browning said that after he talked to me, he called Hopkins and Kerr and they both said that they felt they had been told that they should support the bill.

I answered that I questioned very much that those men would say a thing like that—that nobody was bound from this office, and that these brethren were told to do what they thought best, because the responsibility rested upon the Legislature, and that is where the Church stands.[56]

---

56. For more, see Wilkinson diary, Dec. 28, 1953.

4 Doctrine, the International Church, and More Politics, 1954

I told Dr. [Richard D.] Poll [regarding Joseph Fielding Smith's
Man, His Origin and Destiny] that the Church has not approved
of the book, and that so far as evolution is concerned, the Church
has not made any ruling regarding it. —December 29, 1954

January 17, 1954, in Capetown, South Africa.[1] As I stand before you [LDS
missionaries] this morning I feel that I am facing a great responsibility.

For several years the Coloured question in South Africa has been
called to the attention of the First Presidency. We have manuscripts, page
after page, written on it.

I believe there is a misunderstanding regarding the attitude of the
Presidency. I felt it before I became President and since the responsibility
of presiding has become heavier I have sensed it more keenly. To observe
conditions as they are was one of the reasons that I wished to take this trip.

[Quoting from LDS scripture:] ["]Pharaoh signifies king by Royal
blood. Now this king of Egypt was a descendant from the loins of Ham
and was a partaker of the blood of the Canaanites by birth. From this
descent sprang all the Egyptians, and thus the blood of the Canaanites
was preserved in the land. The land of Egypt being first discovered by a
woman, who was the daughter of Ham, and the daughter of Egyptus,
which in the Chaldean signifies Egypt which signifies that which is forbidden. When this woman discovered the land it was under water, who

---

1. From January 2 to mid-March 1954, McKay traveled to South Africa and South
America to meet and counsel with local members, missionaries, and government officials.

afterward settled her sons in it, and thus, from Ham, sprang that race which preserved the curse in the land. Now the first government of Egypt was established by Pharaoh, the Eldest son of Egyptus the daughter of Ham, and it was after the manner of the Government of Ham which was patriarchal. Pharaoh, being a righteous man, established his kingdom and judged his people wisely and just[ly] all his days, seeking earnestly to imitate that order established by the fathers in the first generations, in the days of the First Patriarchal reign, even in the reign of Adam and also of Noah, his father who blessed him with the blessings of the earth, and with the blessings of wisdom, but cursed him as pertaining to the Priesthood. Now Pharaoh, being of that lineage by which he could not have the right of the Priesthood, notwithstanding the Pharaohs would fain claim it from Noah, through Ham, therefore my father was led away by their idolatry.["]—[Book of] Abraham, Chapter 1, Verses 20–27.

Now there's a nobleman [the Egyptian pharaoh], righteous, fair in his judgment, seeking earnestly to guide the people according to the Priesthood which was given to Adam,—[a] man who seems to have been worthy in every respect not only in regard to <u>nobility of character</u> but also in regard to ability in leadership, but he could not <u>receive the Priesthood</u>.

Such is the order regarding his descendants of the Church today. In Hawaii, in Brazil, in the Southern States, in other Missions and Stakes, there are worthy men, able men in the Church, who are deprived of the Priesthood because of their lineage.

Now I think there is an explanation for this racial discrimination, dating back to the pre-existent state, but modern sociologists will not accept it, and they are writing appealing to us to lift the ban upon the Negro race, and adopt racial equality in the Church.

I first met this problem in Hawaii in 1921. A worthy man had married a Polynesian woman. She was faithful in the Church. They had a large family everyone of whom was active and worthy. My sympathies were so aroused that I wrote home to President [Heber J.] Grant asking if he would please make an exception so we could ordain that man to the Priesthood. He wrote back saying, "David, I am as sympathetic as you are, but until the Lord gives us a revelation regarding that matter, we shall have to maintain the policy of the Church." I sat down and talked to the brother explaining frankly the reasons for such seeming discrimination and gave him the assurance that some day he will receive <u>every blessing to which he is entitled</u>; for the Lord is just, and no Respector of persons.

That man has remained true to the Church and so have his wife and children.

Well until the Lord gives us another revelation changing this practice established anciently and adopted in our day we will follow that policy. It is true in the days of the Prophet Joseph [Smith] one of Negro blood received the Priesthood. Another in the days of President Brigham Young received it and went through the Temple. These are authenticated facts but exceptions.

At present, I repeat, until a new revelation comes, the Church will observe the policy of withholding the Priesthood from men of Negro ancestry. Therefore, wherever you find evidence of a Negro strain in a individual, please explain to him that the blessing of membership including the partaking of the sacrament and the renewing of His covenant weekly, is his.

Now I am impressed that there are worthy men in the South Africa Mission who are being deprived of the Priesthood simply because they are unable to trace their genealogy out of this country. I am impressed that an injustice is being done to them. Why should every man be required to prove that his lineage is free from Negro strain especially when there is no evidence of his having negro blood in his veins? I should rather[,] much rather, make a mistake in one case and if it be found out afterwards suspend his activity in the Priesthood than to deprive 10 worthy men of the Priesthood.

There is a misunderstanding regarding the application of your genealogical work, President Duncan.[2] You have page after page I notice of genealogical records in which men cannot trace their genealogy out of the country yet who show no trace whatever of the Negro blood. Why should they be deprived of the Priesthood? Nobody knows whether their ancestry goes back to a White slave or a Black slave. And so, if a man is worthy, is faithful in the Church and lives up to the principles of the Gospel, who has no outward evidence of a Negro strain,

2. Leroy Hardy Duncan (1906–84) was president of the South African Mission from 1952 to 1957, the mission he had served in as a young missionary a quarter century earlier, from 1926 to 1929. He was born in Centerville, Utah, owned a wholesale fruit and produce business, and was president of the Davis Stake for seven years beginning in 1945.

even though he might not be able to trace his genealogy out of the country, the President of the Mission is hereby authorised to confer upon him the Priesthood.

Now this does not mean that you proclaim this ruling or give it too much publicity because it might multiply your difficulties. There are those in the Church here who I am sure are not entitled to receive the Priesthood. But, I am, also sure, after talking with the President and observing other leaders—able leaders—that there are others who are unjustly deprived of the privilege of receiving the Priesthood.

We are assured that the time will come when the Negro will receive every blessing to which he is entitled, including the Priesthood. I mention this merely to help you to explain to some who are probably discouraged and feel that you are showing favoritism.

From now on here in Africa you may treat people just the same as we treat them in South Carolina or in Washington or in New York or in Salt Lake City, or in the Hawaiian Islands. Unless there is evidence of Negro blood you need not compel a man to prove that he has none in his veins.

However, as a precautionary measure all cases of ordinations to the Priesthood, Aaronic and Melchizedek, should be referred to the Mission President.

January 19, 1954, writing from Capetown, South Africa.[3]
Last Sunday afternoon we held a special meeting with the presidency of the mission and the missionaries and presented to them our impressions regarding the perplexing colour questions and the problems involved therein. After careful observation and sincere prayer, I felt impressed to modify the present policy of compelling every man to prove by tracing his genealogy that he has no trace in his blood of negro ancestry. If the present policy were continued for another twenty five years, it is doubtful whether the Church would have sufficient men to carry on the work of the branches, and worthy, capable men, as worthy of the priesthood as any other members of the Church, would be deprived of the blessings of the priesthood.

I am sure that the modification of the plan as set forth in the enclosed

---

3. He was writing to his counselors Stephen L. Richards and J. Reuben Clark.

manuscript will result in renewed impetus and encouragement in the branches here in the South Africa mission. I will explain to you in detail when I meet you again in council.

February 25, 1954, First Presidency and Council of Twelve. President McKay presented the following recommendation: He said that he had already reported to the First Presidency that we should modify our <u>attitude towards the colored people in the Union of South Africa, and that that would apply to Brazil also.</u> He said that he found that in the Union of South Africa no man can hold the priesthood who cannot trace his genealogy out of South Africa, and he felt sure that there are a dozen or more men who are fully worthy of the priesthood who are deprived of it. In Rhodesia a brother who has the responsibility of the branch and organized the branch cannot hold the priesthood because he cannot trace his genealogy out of the country, and so they have to keep two elders there, 1900 miles away from headquarters, and they are out in the woods and in the mines, and yet that man is as worthy of the priesthood, President McKay thought, as anybody, and there are a score of others in the same condition. He said there is a young man who is a professor in the university, who is working for his doctor's degree, and is an instructor in the university at Capetown who cannot trace his genealogy out of the country, and so he does not have the priesthood. There is another young man in Johannesburg the same way.

President McKay said he called the elders together, with <u>President [Leroy H.] Duncan, and after due consultation, suggested this:</u>

That until the Lord gives us another revelation changing this practice[4] ... President McKay said that was his recommendation.

<u>President Richards said that he thought it was a marvelous, inspired statement, as it was reported to the First Presidency in writing before President McKay returned home. He moved that the Council support the statement of President McKay with reference to this matter of tracing the ancestry of South Africans in order to be eligible for the priesthood. LeGrand Richards seconded the motion.</u> The motion was unanimously approved.

---

4. He repeats the remarks he made to the missionaries in Capetown, omitted here.

March 17, 1954. While at Laguna Beach [California], President Stephen L. Richards called me from Salt Lake City. He called attention to two matters: ...

(2) <u>Disturbing report that came to the First Presidency at their meeting with the Presiding Bishopric as to the Girls' Home at the Beehive House</u>.[5] The Police have apparently made some observations and discovered girls out late at night entertaining boys out on the balcony, and in cars parked in front of the home.

<u>Sister Florence Smith</u>,[6] the matron, says that these girls, in a measure, were beyond her control, and would not conform to the regulations she had made. She seems to wonder if the home can be kept as it should be under existing conditions.

I stated that the girls who are giving trouble should be dismissed and turned over to Brother Clayton who is working for the Church with wayward young people.

President Richards stated that the Bishopric who reported these conditions were in full accord in thinking the Beehive House should be discontinued as a place for a girls' home, and make it a point of historic interest.

I answered: "What are we going to do with these girls who are coming to Salt Lake City?"

President Richards answered: "We shall have to try to get them placed in suitable boarding houses without the Church taking the responsibility of their conduct."

I then stated: "We are facing a grave question there. Please hold this matter up until I get back."

---

5. From 1920 to about 1959, the church's YWMIA (Young Women's Mutual Improvement Association) rented rooms in the Beehive House (so named for its stylized cupola) to single young women working as secretaries in nearby offices. It was originally Brigham Young's house, and from 1901 to 1918 it was the official residence of church president Joseph F. Smith, where he initially lived with his four wives.

6. In the next decade the house would be renovated by YWMIA President Florence Smith Jacobsen (1913–2017), a granddaughter of Joseph F. Smith. If this is the same Florence Smith, she would not have been living at the house (perhaps the reason for the problem), because she had her own family to look after. In 1955 her husband, civil engineer Theodore C. Jacobsen, would be called as president of the Eastern States Mission. On their return and her calling as general president of the YWMIA, the Beehive House would become her full responsibility.

The brethren felt that we should not let the Church get into bad repute through the action of these girls. I mentioned the trouble up in the hospital with a girl from Randolph [Utah]—she is now turning to the Catholics. I then stated again that this matter should be held up until my return.

I said that I was quite surprised at the easy regulations under which the girls live at the Beehive House—that they are not required to be in until 12 o'clock on week nights, and on Friday and Saturday nights they may be out until 1:30 a.m. I stated that I think those hours are ridiculous. These matters will all have to be investigated.

In answer to President Richards' question as to Sister [Emma Ray] McKay and my health, I reported that Sister McKay is better, and that we are getting a little rest. Reported that we had a delightful drive down to Laguna Beach. Also had a good night's rest last night.

April 22, 1954, 4 p.m. Elder Mark E. Petersen called to ask if it would be all right to let the Bookcraft Company publish President [J. Reuben] Clark's conference address in a pamphlet which they will offer for sale to the public. I told Brother Petersen if that is agreeable to President Clark, and if the people want to buy a sermon that they can get free of charge in the Deseret News, the Improvement Era, and the Conference pamphlet, that it was all right with me.[7]

May 12, 1954, 8:25 a.m. [BYU] President Ernest L. Wilkinson presented correspondence with Governor [J. Bracken] Lee on the Junior College Situation. The Brethren then read and gave consideration to two suggested letters that had been prepared by President Ernest L. Wilkinson. One of these letters was a letter addressed to the First Presidency by Governor Lee asking certain questions in regard to the attitude of the Church with reference to taking over the Junior Colleges, how they would be operated, etc.

The other letter was a suggested answer to three questions by the First Presidency in a letter addressed to the Governor.

---

7. Clark's theme was that modern translations vitiated fundamental doctrines of the church. He rejected the argument that the KJV, in emphasizing "beauty" and "elegance" of language, was therefore less accurate.

The Brethren felt that there should be some modifications in the letters. They decided to look over the copies that had been left with them.

At the invitation of the First Presidency President Wilkinson met with the First Presidency and made certain explanations regarding these letters. He explained that it was necessary to submit both letters to the Governor so that he would know what the questions and answers would be.

May 21, 1954, 9 a.m. <u>Dr. Ernest L. Wilkinson of the Brigham Young University reported to the First Presidency a conference he had had</u> with the Governor yesterday. Said the Governor had approved the <u>drafts of letters</u> that were submitted to him except that he suggests that in the First Presidency's answer they do not repeat the questions but just give the answers. The Governor inquired if we would have any objection to including a question regarding general vocational training, and President Wilkinson felt we could answer that in the affirmative. It was decided to make the final writing of the letters as indicated, and President Wilkinson was asked to go forward at once.

President Wilkinson also called attention to the athletic program of the B.Y.U. Dr. Wilkinson said that he is going to talk with the chairman of the [Western] Athletic Conference to see if it is not possible to maintain higher educational standards. He said he had already given instructions that unless the athletes occupy the full-time [academic schedule] that other students devote to the work he would not give them jobs. The Brethren told Brother Wilkinson to go ahead and in the meantime try to get a reorganization in the Conference.[8]

President Wilkinson said that he had been asked to recommend someone to go to Hawaii to take charge of the junior college to be established there.[9] He mentioned for this position Reuben Law, Dean of the

---

8. Discontent with the Mountain States Conference (the "Skyline Eight," as the teams along the continental divide were called) resulted in the founding of the Western Athletic Conference in 1962, including BYU, New Mexico, Utah, Wyoming, and two schools in Arizona that had not been in the MSC, and the loss of three schools in Colorado and one in Montana.

9. President McKay would preside over the groundbreaking on February 12, 1955. At first students met in military quonset huts. The first permanent building was completed at the end of 1958.

College of Education at the B.Y.U. He also mentioned Dr. Leon Winsor[10] who at present is at Cornell [University].

Referring to the Ricks College situation, President Wilkinson said, in answer to a question as to how many of the students are graduating with the intention of teaching school, that 66% will obtain teaching jobs. He said that these teachers when they graduate, are qualified and have made a good record; that the B.Y.U. students are certified in exactly the same way.

Further in regard to the Ricks College, he said that the enrollment has been about constant over the years. They have about 25 more students now than they had five years ago. His own feeling is that if we continue the College in Rexburg we shall not have many more students and if we make it a two-year college the number will be reduced. In five years they have graduated 540 students from a four-year course.[11]

President Wilkinson left the meeting at 10:15 a.m., and we continued our regular First Presidency's meeting.[12]

Further mention was made of <u>paintings of the Savior</u>. The Brethren felt that all <u>pictures of the Savior</u> that we use should be pictures of him in connection with his ministry and not any representation of him after his resurrection.

May 28, 1954, 9 to 11 a.m. First Presidency's regular morning meeting was held. Among matters considered were: (1) *Painting of the Savior.*

The Brethren viewed the picture of the Savior as painted by Mrs. Lane of California. The brethren thought highly of it, their only criticism being that they thought the rays above the head should be subdued. They felt that in the event they purchased it, they should have permission to make copies of it.

June 3, 1954. President McKay made the following observation, at the Council meeting today:

---

10. Andrew Leon Winsor (1890–1965) was dean of students at Cornell, where he received his PhD and taught in the Department of Rural Education. He was from St. George and had studied at Weber College before studying in New York.

11. The last four-year graduating class was in 1956. The policy to change the school to a two-year program left President John L. Clarke feeling blindsided. Hemming, "Ricks College," 62.

12. For Wilkinson's account, see his diary, May 21, 1954.

"It is more apparent than ever, becoming more apparent each day, that two great organized forces, the purpose of which is to undermine the high principles of the Restored Gospel, are operating. One is Communism, which is moving aggressively over the face of the earth, fundamentally prompted by disbelief in the existence of God, a rejection of the life of Jesus Christ as the Savior of the world, and is against the Church. The other is the Catholic Church, which is showing more clearly than ever before that they are determined to counteract the influence of the Church in this western country.

"Illustrative of the Communistic influence is the recent dismissal of a great scientist,[13] not that he is a Communist, but that he is risky, a pretty weak dismissal of a man in such a high position, who has threatened the safety of our Republic.

"And then the farce that is going on now in Washington between [Senator Joseph] McCarthy and the Army. Undoubtedly, the Communistic influence is being exerted there to lessen the influence of men who would ferret out the enemies in the high places of our government.[14]

"More than ever the responsibility is ours to appeal to our people to be loyal and true to the reality of the restoration of the Gospel, which discloses the reality of our Father in Heaven, the relationship of his Son to the Father, 'This is my Beloved Son,' and the principles of the everlasting Gospel as restored. May God's influence and guidance be yours, members of the Twelve, and ours as the First Presidency, to discharge our duties in accordance with his mind and will, I fervently pray in the name of Jesus Christ. Amen."

Catholic Advertisement in Wall Street Journal

At the request of President McKay, there was then read for the information of the Brethren a Catholic Church advertisement which appeared in the "Wall Street Journal" Tuesday, May 25, 1954, entitled "Will You Help the Latter-day Saints," and containing a picture of the proposed

---

13. McKay was referring to J. Robert Oppenheimer (1904–67), co-developer of the atomic bomb (therefore "a great scientist"). Like other intellectuals of his day, Oppenheimer had flirted with communism, but lost interest. He also came to oppose the hydrogen bomb, which is how he lost his security clearance.

14. McKay had long been a foe of Communism. His recent trip to Europe in 1952 had only underscored his position. See Prince and Wright, *David O. McKay*, 279–322; Quinn, *Extensions of Power*, 67–115.

abbey to be built in Huntsville [Utah]. The article is an appeal for funds to help build the abbey in their campaign to convert Latter-day Saints. In this connection President McKay referred to a conversation he had with [Salt Lake City] Bishop [Duane G.] Hunt of the Catholic Church a few years ago regarding the missionary pamphlet that the Church had published, at which time Bishop Hunt said that missionary work did not mean that they had in mind the conversion of the people of Utah, but the paying of the expenses of the mission of the Catholic Church.[15]

Wilford Woodruff Handkerchief

A letter from Joseph J. Daynes[16] together with the silk handkerchief enclosed therewith was given attention. The handkerchief is the one that was given by the Prophet Joseph Smith to [apostle] Wilford Woodruff at the time of the founding of Nauvoo [Illinois] when there was much illness among the people, which handkerchief the Prophet told President Woodruff to place upon the faces of two little children who were sick and they would be made well. This handkerchief has been in President Woodruff's family ever since that time. The Brethren signed a letter of acknowledgment and thanks to Brother Daynes.

June 11, 1954, First Presidency meeting. President [J. Reuben] Clark mentioned the critical situation so far as the possibility of war is concerned. Thought we should have this in mind. He raised the question as to what would be done in protecting our mission presidents and missionaries. I said that so far as the Temples in Europe are concerned the work there would be suspended in case of war and we should have to evacuate the missionaries. It was mentioned that we could have instructions given as to what should be done in case of an emergency, but they felt that if we just hinted that we were concerned it would go through the Church like a prairie fire.[17]

---

15. McKay harbored ambivalent views on Catholicism. Despite some long and cherished relationships with prominent Catholics, he was unsettled by the tenets, policies, and practices. See Prince and Topping, "Turbulent Coexistence," 142–63.

16. Joseph John Daynes Jr. (1873–1963) was a son-in-law of Wilford Woodruff and formerly the general manager of Clayton Music Company in Salt Lake City, a stake president, and president of the Western States Mission in Denver. His father was a Tabernacle organist.

17. Clark's fears were predicated on his long history with wars, diplomacy, and international unrest. Compared to McKay, he was highly pacifistic and outspoken in denouncing warmongering (Quinn, *Elder Statesman*, 312–15). Despite the fact that the

Homes for Old Folks

Discussed the matter of homes for our old folks. I expressed myself as favoring having homes for our old people in their own environment. I feel that the expense would be nominal, that there are widows who could take care of such houses and that would be their living. Some of the old folks would have their expenses paid by their own folks, and where they had to be paid for by the Church, it would be cases that the Church has to take care of anyway. The charge would be sufficient only to take care of the operating costs.

June 24, 1954. Henry Smith, Deseret News Church Reporter, called by telephone to see whether or not the paper should carry a story regarding the missionaries who were located in Guatemala. He asked me if the Church is going to move the missionaries out of Guatemala. The anti-Communists are fighting the Communists in Guatemala in an attempt to overthrow the Communistic government. I stated that the latest word was that we had received a cable from Elder Gordon M. Romney, President of the Central American Mission located at Guatemala, suggesting that we move the missionaries to El Salvador. The Presidency sent a cable in reply approving the removal of the Elders to El Salvador or to Panama. I favored Panama because the United States troops are there. Mission headquarters are not being moved for the time being. El Salvador and Panama are still part of the same mission.[18]

July 1, 1954, 10:00 a.m. to 2:15 p.m. Council Meeting ... the last meeting prior to the summer vacation. Note: At this meeting, among other things, President McKay made the following statement:

"Never before, I think, has the Church been [in] a more suitable attitude [position] before the world to render effectively the message of

---

Korean War had concluded with an armistice the previous July and Stalin had died in March 1953, Cold War Europe was still volatile. Anxiety was heightened by the paranoia of Communism brought on by McCarthyism. The concern for missionaries hearkened back to the late 1930s when some of them had to find ingenious and discreet ways to escape Nazi Germany.

18. McKay had visited Guatemala in February, four months before a CIA-backed invasion of that country toppled the democratically elected government of Jacobo Árbenz. The redistribution to peasants of uncultivated land owned by the United Fruit Company was what had rankled the U.S.

the restoration of the Gospel. The Christian sects sense their inadequacy to represent our Lord and Savior. In fact they are not recognizing him as the Savior of the world. The General Authorities of this Church have a responsibility of declaring to the world the divine Sonship of our Lord and Savior Jesus Christ. No other body in the world has the testimony, has the responsibility that we possess. It is mighty but the Lord is with us, and as long as he is with us, he will guide us."

July 9, 1954, 8:30 a.m. Elder Joy Dunyan[19] of the [Church] Department of Education came in by appointment at his request. He reported that Brother Harold B. Lee had asked them to write a paper giving their estimate of value of Joseph Fielding Smith's new book on "Man."[20]

I said that I was of the opinion that Brother Lee had no right to do this, but that I would look into the matter and find out more about it.

I asked Brother Dunyon to ask Brother Lee whether or not this book has been authorized by the [Reading] Committee; that he was to do this on his own and was not to quote me—that it is his responsibility to find out whether or not it is approved. If the book has not been approved, then it should not be used as a text book, or considered in the class, more than any other private book.[21] ...

First Presidency's meeting

Among items considered were the following: (1) Requirements for

---

19. Joy Fitzgerald Dunyon (1910–80) supervised the church's seminaries and institutes and was soon to be president of the Central British Mission. He was being pressured by apostle Joseph Fielding Smith to approve Smith's recent publication as a textbook for the Church Education System, but the book was meeting with resistance on all sides because of its anti-science bias. Dunyon had begun working for the church shortly after his graduation from the University of Utah. His wife would later be called to the presidency of the children's Primary Association.

20. Joseph Fielding Smith's book, *Man: His Origin and Destiny*, had just been released by Deseret Book.

21. Smith's book had opened a Pandora's box on the subject of organic evolution. Three decades earlier, in an acrimonious debate with B. H. Roberts, Smith had laid out the issues of man, the creation, and evolution for church authorities, and the result was a call to cease discussion of the subject. For a summary of McKay's views, see Prince and Wright, *David O. McKay*, 45–49. McKay was not the only member of the First Presidency with concerns, as Quinn points out that Clark and Smith had engaged in a running disagreement over evolution for decades. Clark warned the same group of educators addressed a few days earlier by Smith that some of the brethren speak "out of turn" on issues and ideas for which no revelation had been given. Quinn, *Elder Statesman*, 216–17.

Temple Recommends—Considered a letter from President Haven Barlow of the North Davis [Utah] Stake in which he asks about issuing temple recommends to non-tithe payers. I explained that people who go to the temple should be full tithe payers and should observe the Word of Wisdom; that as a matter of fact, it is a question of their faith. Men who have a testimony of the Gospel and believe it should contribute to it and if they fail to keep their promise to observe these commandments the Bishop has a right to withhold the recommend, not wholly on the failure to pay tithing but because of their lack of faith in the Gospel. Their failure to pay tithing would indicate their lack of faith in the Gospel.

July 26, 1954, 10 a.m. At his request met by appointment Alexander Schreiner[22] who reported that he is to receive his Ph.D. in music from the University of Utah. A story is to be written up about it for the newspapers, and Brother Schreiner would like to know if now is a good chance for him to announce that he is the Senior organist.

I told Brother Schreiner that I would let him know tomorrow morning after I had presented [it] to the First Presidency for their action.

July 29, 1954. Telephoned to Alexander Schreiner and told him that he may go ahead with the announcement in the paper regarding his appointment as first organist, or head organist.

(Note by Secretary [Clare Middlemiss]: When I called Brother Schreiner, he wondered if he could use the term "chief" organist instead of senior or head organist. Said President McKay had used that term when he had his consultation with him in the office a few days ago. I suggested that the word "chief" would probably mean the same thing, but thought he might talk to President [Stephen L.] Richards about it, with whom

---

22. Alexander Schreiner (1901–87) was a Nuremberg, Germany, native of exceptional musical ability. In the current LDS hymnal are several of his compositions: "God Loved Us So He Sent His Son," "Holy Temples on Mount Zion." "In Memory of the Crucified," "Truth Eternal," and "While of These Emblems We Partake." His desire for additional recognition had a long history. As early as 1926, he had petitioned the First Presidency for the title of Chief Organist, stating that his training and experience "qualify me to fill this place." He added that the "title, I realize, won't improve my playing[,] but I am sure that it will make it seem better to the audiences." His request was not approved. See Quinn, *Elder Statesman*, 370–72.

President McKay had discussed the matter. J. Reuben Clark was in the East on business when this consultation occurred on July 27.)²³

August 18, 1954, 7:45 a.m. Met by appointment <u>Elder Adam S. Bennion</u> of the Council of the Twelve. He reported that the Committee in charge of <u>the Utah Educational Association,</u> all but two of whom are members of the Church, <u>have asked what their attitude should be in the coming convention toward the proposition of turning over Weber and other Junior Colleges</u> to the Church. I told him that I thought they should use their own judgment; that the attitude of the Church is plainly stated in the First Presidency's public statement, which is that we are receptive if and when the State ceases to conduct these schools as state institutions; that we will accept them in accordance with our agreement and, furthermore, that we will make good schools of them; that everyone should vote just as he wishes to vote. When I presented this later at the meeting of the First Presidency President [Stephen L.] Richards agreed whole heartedly with me. It was felt that if we campaigned for the schools and succeeded in getting them we would have the antagonism of the non-members.

9 to 1:30 am.—Attended the First Presidency's meeting. Among items considered were:

1. The number of letters that I had received from seminary and institute teachers regarding <u>President Joseph Fielding Smith's book, "Man, His Origin and Destiny."</u> The Brethren were agreed that inasmuch as this <u>book has not been passed upon by the Church that it could not be used as a study course in the seminaries and institutes.</u> They felt that the matter therein discussed is really not essential to the advancement of the cardinal principles of the Church.²⁴

August 26, 1954. Returned to the office and met by appointment <u>Mr. L[orenzo] F. Pett²⁵, General Manager, of the Kennecott Copper</u>

23. This was fortunate for Schreiner since Clark was not an admirer, but rather a Frank Asper votary. After Clark's death and Asper's retirement, Schreiner was elevated to Chief Organist. Quinn, 372.

24. This decision did not deter Smith from telling Church Education System employees, "I hope you take [accept] what I'm saying, because if you don't you have no business in the church school system." Bradford, *Lowell L. Bennion*, 131–36, esp. 132.

25. Lorenzo Fern Pett (1893–1964) was an LDS Church member, originally

<u>Corporation</u> regarding the 10-day-old strike which has idled 11,000 Kennecott workers in Utah, Nevada, Arizona and New Mexico. He explained some features of the strike at the Kennecott Copper Company. A good many of our people are involved. One point that he made was that the Company granted the appeal of the Union for more protection in a welfare way [benefits], and then the Union came back saying, "We will not accept that, but we demand a certain increase in the daily wage," and the Company granted that and came to an understanding. The Union came back a third time, and said, "No, we want a modification. We would like to have a consultation," so the Company said, "All right, you may present that at 8 o'clock tomorrow morning." That was this morning. They promised to do it, and at 8 o'clock this morning they were not there and did not fill their appointment, all of which, according to Mr. Pett, indicates that there is a very determined effort on the part of somebody beyond the local unions to extend this strike, making it a political issue, rather than a local one.

In answer to my question, Mr. Pett said, "It has the marks of the Communists, acting through the Electrical Union." He said that his reason for tal[k]ing with me is that they would like me to be informed of the facts. He said the local people are eager to settle the strike, but there is a very bitter organization backing some of the radicals in this area. (Mr. [J. Parnell] Caulfield [a Kennecott executive] accompanied Mr. Pett in this consultation.)[26]

August 30, 1954. On August 30 by appointment at 8:45 in the morning met Frank M. Browning [Bank of Utah chairman]; W. M. Anderson [Ogden City employee]; A. L. Glas[s]man, [*Ogden Standard Examiner* publisher]; Ernest H. B[a]lch, President of the Ogden Chamber of Commerce; Ira A. Huggins [Utah Senate president]; and Brigham H. Robinson [Weber College Campaign chairman]. They called in regard to the question of the proposed transfer of the Junior Colleges from the state to the Church. President McKay spent three hours with them, told

---

from Brigham City, who graduated from the University of Utah in civil engineering and was hired by Kennecott Copper in 1922. He became general manager of the Utah division in 1952.

26. McKay supported right-to-work laws, which meant the right for workers to be hired without having to join a union as a condition of employment.

them that the Church is not making an aggressive campaign to have these schools turned back; that the deed of transfer when the Church gave the Schools to the state, states that if and when the state ceases to operate the Junior Colleges for educational purposes, the property reverts to the Church, and we stand ready to receive them, and when they do come back, we will maintain them as Junior Colleges. President McKay told them that further than that we were not saying anything, that it would not be wise for us to do so, because if the people do turn them back to us we do not want "you men" (referring to the committee who were present) and others, to say that we used undue influence to get them back. We would rather say that you gave them back, and we want you to help us now in our Church school system.

Mr. Glasman asked President McKay: "Do you want them back?"

President McKay answered him: "Supposing I said that I do want them back, that I am in favor of this referendum, and you publish that in your paper, what would that do? That would be undue influence in your favor. We are not going to use undue influence in our favor, nor in yours."

He then said that our people are saying that if members of the Church vote against turning these schools back to the Church, they are not good members of the Church and will be dealt with. President McKay answered that no member of the Church, General Authority or otherwise, will be dealt with if he votes his own convictions. That is what we want him to do.

President McKay said that Ira Huggins was the most virulent in his attack on the bill and when asked to give an example he said that only recently in one of the wards a young returned missionary got up and said that Pres. Ernest Wilkinson had put five dollars in his hand and told him to go up there and put in a good word for the BYU and the Junior College. President McKay answered that he would see Ernest Wilkinson and ask him about it. He said that fortunately when he got out of the meeting Ernest Wilkinson was in the office waiting, and he faced him with this matter, and he said that that is a mis-statement; that he had not given any missionary five dollars, nor asked him to do what was reported. President McKay said that he then dictated a letter to Ira Huggins, and asked him to please give him the name of the missionary and the ward in which he spoke.

September 13, 1954, 8:30 a.m. Met by appointment at their request the following [LDS] Seminary Supervisors and teachers: Elders Joy Dunyan, Lowell L. Bennion, Edgar T. Lyon, and George Boyd.[27]

They said that they were concerned about what their attitude should be regarding the recent work of President Joseph Fielding Smith on "Man: His Origin and Destiny."

I told them that book should be treated as merely the views of one man; that it does not set forth the views of the Church, and should not be prescribed as a text book, but merely as the views of one man. It is true that one man is President of the Twelve, and makes it more or less authoritative, but it is no more to be take[n] as the word of the Church than any other unauthorized book.[28]

September 22, 1954. Later signed numerous letters, following which I received a call from Eldred G. Smith, Patriarch to the Church. He called regarding his position as Patriarch to the Church.[29]

---

27. Bennion, Lyon, and Boyd all taught LDS Institute classes adjacent to the University of Utah. Boyd's response to this meeting was more emotional: "When we left he [McKay] said, 'You go ahead and teach the way you've been teaching (we had outlined for him our way of handling the subject of science and religion), and if you have any trouble you come to me.' We learned during the interview that President McKay was very much disturbed himself over the publication of the book. I recall a statement he made. He said, 'We have known what Joseph Fielding Smith has thought on this subject for years. The sad part is, now it's in print.'" Prince and Wright, *David O. McKay*, 47–48.

28. In mid-November at the University of Utah, a meeting of the Mormon Seminar (also called the Swearing Elders) was attended by apostle Mark E. Petersen and Seventies leaders Milton R. Hunter and Bruce R. McConkie. Llewelyn R. McKay, a professor of German and the church president's son, allegedly said, "I've talked to my father about the book, and he doesn't like it. He does not agree with it. He would like it to be known that this book doesn't represent the Church's position and that it must not be used for teaching any religious classes." McMurrin and Newell, *Matters of Conscience*, 183–84.

29. A month later, during a meeting of the First Presidency, "it was reported that President [Stephen L.] Richards and President [J. Reuben] Clark had had a conference with Eldred at the request of President McKay. He [Smith] feels that he should have more recognition. ... The thought was expressed that perhaps Brother Smith might ... participate in ordinations and settings apart; that when he goes to the [stake] conferences he should go with one of the other brethren; that in ordaining or setting apart officers he should not do it except under the request and appointment of the one who is there under appointment, which includes the Assistants to the Twelve." First Presidency minutes, Oct. 22, 1954, typed excerpt in Quinn Papers.

September 28, 1954. Henry D. Moyle of the Council of the Twelve called me by telephone regarding the meeting to be held by District Stake Presidents at which time a discussion will be held relative to the distribution of pamphlets concerning the Junior College situation and the Reapportionment. I told him that the Stake Presidents are not to make a campaign that Gen[era]'l Authorities are in favor of the Church's taking over the Junior Colleges, nor that they are in favor of the Reapportionment plan—also that they are not to quote the General Authorities on either issue.

October 4, 1954. President ElRay L. Christiansen[30] of the Salt Lake Temple called by telephone. He stated that a Brother Howells [Barton J. Howell], a good Church member of the North 18th Ward, had informed him that a Mr. William Cagle had brought a microfilm record to him of a book published in 1931 in New York.[31] This film reveals all of our temple ceremonies, almost word for word. Mr. Cagle, who is working with Dean Henry Eyring at the University of Utah in the Chemistry Department, desired Brother Howells, who owns a printing establishment in the City,[32] to print about five copies from this microfilm. Brother Howells felt that his loyalty to the Church would not permit him to publish this material, and he wondered if the man would go somewhere else to have it printed.[33]

---

30. Elray L. Christiansen (1897–1975) was an Assistant to the Quorum of the Twelve. He was a native of Sanpete County who graduated from Utah State Agricultural College and worked for the Forest Service, although he also taught school and played cello in the Utah Symphony Orchestra prior to his church employment. He was president of the Salt Lake Temple for ten years beginning in 1954.

31. This refers to William M. Paden's *Temple Mormonism: Its Evolution, Ritual and Meaning*, published by A. J. Montgomery, a bureau chief with the *New York Herald*. Paden had been pastor of the First Presbyterian Church in Salt Lake City and a prime mover in the Salt Lake City Ministerial Association in opposing apostle Reed Smoot's election to the US Senate, 1904–07.

32. Barton J. Howell (1917–98) was completing a PhD in physics at the University of Utah, but must have had a print shop nearby. A few years after graduating, he would go on to work for NASA, then find employment with the Sperry Corporation (now UNISYS). The University of Utah chemistry professor was Frederic William Cagle Jr. (1924–88), who received his PhD from the University of Illinois.

33. The temple ceremony had been published without authorization on a number of occasions going back to the early days of the church. See Buerger, *Mysteries of Godliness*, 203–27.

President Christiansen was wondering if some influence could be used on this Mr. Cagle, who is not a member of the Church, not to print this material. He thought possibly Dean Eyring could use some influence on Mr. Cagle.

Pres[ident] McKay told President Christiansen to meet with the First Presidency at 8:50 a.m. tomorrow morning regarding this matter. President Christiansen will bring the material he has available with him at this time and the Presidency will work out some plan.

October 6, 1954. The Brethren reconsidered a question pertaining to hypnotism. It was decided to answer the sister who inquired about it that we look with disfavor upon anyone's subjecting his mind to the control of another, that at present we are not advised as to the medical significance of it.

October 13, 1954. Met at 8:00 am. with [US Congressional] Representative Douglas R. Stringfellow and Secretary of Agriculture, Ezra Taft Benson regarding a serious accusation [about Stringfellow's résumé].[34]

3:15 p.m. Appointment with Mr. Milton L. Weilenmann, State Democratic Chairman, regarding the Representative Douglas R. Stringfellow case.

4:45 p.m. Appointment with Representative Douglas R. Stringfellow, Spencer Kimball, Jr., and Mr. Milton L. Weilenmann regarding the accusation against Rep. Stringfellow.

I called by telephone <u>Representative Douglas R. Stringfellow</u>. I stated that we thought it was a good thing when we had had a conference this morning that he and Brother Weilenmann, State Democratic Chairman, meet and talk this matter over. Representative Stringfellow stated that he was leaving at 8 a.m. the next morning on a plane to go to Missouri to give a speech. He said he would have to meet with Mr. Weilenmann this afternoon. The Representative stated that he would be at the Salt Lake City Airport until Senator [Arthur V.] Watkins arrived on a plane, but he felt that he would be free by 4:30 p.m. and that he could meet anywhere it was convenient. It was arranged for him to meet Mr. Weilenmann at my office at 4:45 p.m.

---

34. See the note under August 26, 1953, for discussion of Stringfellow's fall from political grace.

October 14, 1954. I called <u>Elder Ezra Taft Benson</u> in Washington, D.C. I told Brother Benson that I thought he would like to know the outcome of the conference I had had last evening with <u>Representative Douglas R. Stringfellow</u>, Mr. Milton L. Weilenmann, and Spencer Kimball, Jr. Mr. Weilenmann had called Spencer Kimball, Jr. to [ask him to] accompany him and to listen in on the interview. Both Apostle Benson and I agreed with Representative Stringfellow that it was unfair to have Brother Kimball present during the interview.

I told Brother Benson that the conference the evening before had not brought forth any more facts than the conference we had had with him yesterday morning. Representative Stringfellow stated that if the news was made public, he would answer it. I told Brother Benson that the news had already been released in an Army paper in Washington. Brother Benson said that he would probably see this paper.

<u>Dr. O. Preston Robinson of the Deseret News</u> called and asked me about the <u>Douglas R. Stringfellow</u> matter. Dr. Robinson stated that they had had information on this matter since April and that they were running a story in the paper to-night. Dr. Robinson also stated that they had a letter from Representative Stringfellow which he had written to them last May. They had permission from the Representative to run this letter in the paper tomorrow evening. I said that I would withhold consent for the present. Dr. Robinson asked if he had approval to go ahead and dig out what information they could. I indicated that it would be all right for them to go ahead and obtain information in their capacity as a newspaper.

October 15, 1954, 3:00 p.m. I returned to the office to see Senator Arthur V. Watkins regarding the Douglas R. Stringfellow case.

5:15 p.m. Appointment with Dean Henry Eyring, of the University of Utah. Brother Barton J. Howell who operates a business in this city of microfilming manuscripts had received an order for five copies of a manuscript that it is understood is in the Harvard University, which manuscript gives almost word for word, corrected in some places, our temple ceremonies complete. Professor William Cagle of the University of Utah had given the order. Brother Howell's attention was called to it by one of his employees who is a member of the Church, and when Brother Howell learned the nature of this manuscript, he brought the five copies to President ElRay L. Christiansen, who brought them to the First Presidency. Professor Cagle works in Dean Eyring's department at the University of Utah.

At the suggestion of the Brethren I got in touch with Dr. Eyring on this matter. Dr. Eyring said that he felt sure that Professor Cagle would be glad to do anything we wished him to do in regard to this matter; that he is well read on Mormon literature, has made a study of all of Orson Pratt's works; and at Dr. Eyring's suggestion, I promised to meet Professor Cagle.

October 16, 1954, 8:30 am. I met with Dr. Henry Eyring and Professor William Cagle of the University of Utah. ... Professor Cagle said he would do whatever we asked. He mentioned that he had found the manuscript, and that he had had a microfilm made of it.

I explained to him that it was a sacred matter to us, and we would rather not have it publicized and distributed, particularly in this area. Professor Cagle readily agreed to give us the film, from which these copies were taken, and we have the five copies in our possession.

I was very favorably impressed with Dr. Cagle; he claims to be a great admirer of Orson Pratt, and knows our Church history very well. Dr. Eyring thinks he is about converted to the Church. His attitude and that of Dr. Eyring were very cooperative.

2 p.m. At their request by telephone I met in my private office Senators Arthur V. Watkins and Wallace F. Bennett who disclosed that during the conference with Representative Douglas R. Stringfellow in Ogden, the latter had finally confessed to them that his claim to an oversea flight on a secret mission had no basis in fact.

The three of us considered how best Congressman Stringfellow could make his confession to the public. We concluded that he should do this before the C[entral] I[ntelligence] A[gency] in Washington [which] made public the fact that there is nothing in the record of the CIA to substantiate his claim that he ever flew across the sea on a secret mission.

We further considered that arrangements be made to have Congressman Stringfellow appear on the Radio and Television tonight if possible.

About 2:15 p.m. Milton L. Weilenmann, State Chairman of the Democratic Party, telephoned me saying that he had just received word from their correspondent in Washington that the CIA could find no record of the secret mission claimed by Congressman Stringfellow.

October 20, 1954, 8:50 a.m. Appointment with Barton J. Howell. ... Brother Howell operates a business in this city of microfilming manuscripts. He brought to our attention the manuscript which Professor William Cagle wanted published. This manuscript gives almost word for word, corrected in some places, our temple ceremonies complete. During my discussion with brother Howell I learned that several universities have copies of these ceremonies in their libraries, and that there is also such a copy in the University of Utah Library. ...

First Presidency's Meeting
At the meeting this morning I mentioned that I had received a telegram from the Chairman of the Republican party, stating that the committee had accepted Congressman Stringfellow's resignation, and that [Utah State Agricultural College] President H. Aldous Dixon had accepted the nomination.[35] I immediately dictated a reply commending the Committee's action, and wishing "success to President Dixon."

Dr. O. Preston Robinson, Manager of the Deseret News, called by Telephone. He stated that they had two statements regarding the Junior College issue, one for and the other against. They would like to run them both in the paper in order that people may see both sides of the issue.

I told Dr. Robinson that I thought this would be a good idea. Dr. Robinson stated that they would be run in the paper on Saturday on the editorial page, special section for special reports.

October 21, 1954, 10:00 a.m Council Meeting. At this meeting President McKay made the following report on the Douglas R. Stringfellow case:
President McKay reported that since our meeting a week ago he spent a good deal of time with the men who have been closely associated with the Congressman Douglas R. Stringfellow affair. His attention was first called to the matter by Brother Lynn Richards [son of Stephen L. Richards], who felt that it was of such great importance that we should

---

35. Even though the election was only half a month away, Dixon, a Republican, beat the Democratic candidate and former US Congressman Walter K. Granger by seven percentage points.

know about it. Later, Brother [Milton L.] Weilenmann, chairman of the [Utah] Democratic party, sought an interview and gave President McKay the papers which had been secured regarding the case. Subsequently, President McKay and Brother [Ezra Taft] Benson interviewed Brother Stringfellow, who maintained that while he had taken poetic license, as he called it, that he had given the facts as they had been reported in the papers and on television. He maintained that these facts would be supported by the Washington records. President McKay said he was very much grieved when later Senators [Arthur V.] Watkins and [Wallace F.] Bennett called at the office and reported that Brother Stringfellow had admitted that his reported trip overseas on a special mission was a hoax. They also stated that he and his wife would like to come and see President McKay and make amends. Pres[ident] McKay said that he would see him after he had made public confession. The President received a telegram from Brother Stringfellow while the President was in Los Angeles, saying that he and his wife would like to make amends, but President McKay had not yet made an appointment with him.

November 3, 1954. Later I called by telephone President Stephen L. Richards [regarding BYU carillon bells] who did not look upon the matter with favor but he said he would go with me if I approve of it. He said he had submitted the matter to President [J. Reuben] Clark who President Richards thought did not have much objection to it. Later, when I consulted President Clark, I learned that he did not remember that President Richards had presented it to him, and he, President Clark, was not very enthusiastic about it, but said he would go along with the Executive Committee if the latter recommends it.

I presented the matter to the First Presidency and Council of the Twelve at their meeting held November 4, and after a brief discussion, they voted to approve of the uniting of the [student] classes to present this gift of carillons to the Brigham Young University.

November 4, 1954, in conversation with Richard L. Evans. He [Evans] then discussed the matter of <u>choosing a writer for an authoritative History of the Church</u>. Elder Evans has requests from <u>Eastern publishers for this book</u> and they would like one of our members to write it. Elder

Evans suggests Professor [W. Cleon] Skousen[36] of the B.Y.U. as one who would be able to do this.

November 12, 1954. Mr. Myron L. Boardman, Vice President of the Prentice-Hall, Inc. 70 Fifth Avenue, New York, called at the office at 9 a.m. He called with reference to the preparation and publication of a book pertaining to the history of political and religious doctrine and philosophy of the Church. He expressed the desire for a prominent Churchman to write this book, without cost to the Church. I think they rather favor having Elder Richard L. Evans doing this work for them.[37] I introduced Mr. Boardman to President [J. Reuben] Clark who sat in on the conference.

December 16, 1954, First Presidency and Council of Twelve meeting. President McKay reported that on January 2, 1955, accompanied by Sister [Emma Ray] McKay and Brother Franklin J. Murdock, he expects to leave for San Francisco, and from there will fly to the Fiji Islands; that he will take a boat from Suva to Nukualfa, Tonga, visit the school there, and then continue on by boat to Haapai and Vavau in the Islands, and then over to Samoa, visit the School there, and dedicate the buildings that are waiting to be dedicated; that he will then fly from Samoa to Tahiti, and attend to some matters there which need attention. From Tahiti he will return to Suva by plane, and from Suva back to Samoa, and finish whatever work may be necessary there while waiting for the boat. From Samoa the party will go to New Zealand, the special object of the visit there being to look over the situation regarding the school that is being erected there, and to see if some reduction cannot be made in

---

36. Willard Cleon Skousen (1913–2006)) was a prolific writer of Mormon theology, Mormon views on government and politics, communism, and the U.S. Constitution, representing the far right wing of the Mormon political spectrum. He was trained as a lawyer and worked for J. Edgar Hoover's FBI, served as Salt Lake City's police chief until he was fired by Mayor J. Bracken Lee, and taught at BYU before creating the conservative Freeman Institute.

37. The project never materialized. Evans's previous writing of history was limited to *A Century of "Mormonism" in Great Britain*, self-published in 1937. He had published five inspirational books through Harper and Brothers and would see another dozen such books published. Ten year later Boardman would leave Prentice-Hall to run the Foundation for Christian Living, founded by televangelist Norman Vincent Peale.

the proposed estimate cost. (President McKay feels that he can save the Church a half million dollars by this proposed visit.)

President McKay mentioned that President Wendell B. Mendenhall[38] had presented to him the matter of a certain purchase which he proposed be made in connection with the school in New Zealand. Brother Mendenhall said he was going down there in person, and President McKay suggested that he arrange his visit so that he could meet him on the grounds, and they could look over the whole situation together.

The President further stated that he considered it wise to visit Australia while he is in that area, so the party will fly over there and hold meetings with some of the Saints. They will fly back to Hawaii and then home.

December 29, 1954, in conversation with Richard D. Poll.[39] I told Dr. Poll that the Church has not approved of the book [*Man: His Origin and Destiny*] by Joseph Fielding Smith]; and that so far as evolution is concerned, the Church has not made any ruling regarding it, and that no man has been authorized to speak for the Church on it.

December 30, 1954. Called [BYU] President Ernest L. Wilkinson to tell him that I should like him to give a leave of absence to Dr. William F. Edwards[40] in order that he might come to Church Headquarters in Salt Lake and make an overall study of our central accounting system, including our Building Department; that before we go further with the present system, I should like to have expert opinion regarding it, and should like to know just where we are. President Wilkinson agreed to the leave of absence for Dr. Edwards. They will both come in tomorrow for a personal conference on this matter.

---

38. Wendell B. Mendenhall (1907–78) would become the church's building department director in July 1955 on the unexpected death of his predecessor. Mendenhall had informally assisted the church in previous building projects in New Zealand. The property McKay was interested in was a proposed temple site.

39. Richard D. Poll (1918–94) was a BYU professor of history, a prolific author, and popular speaker, who was destined to become vice-president of Western Illinois University.

40. The BYU dean of the College of Business, William F. Edwards (1906–89), was a long-time associate of Wilkinson, having served with him in the Queens Ward bishopric in New York City, where Edwards had been working as an investment banker. Edwards went on to become president of the LDS stake in that area. In 1957 the First Presidency would hire him as its financial secretary.

December 31, 1954, 10:30 a.m. Met by appointment at my request President Ernest L. Wilkinson, President of the B.Y.U., and Dr. William F. Edwards called by appointment at my request.

I stated to them that the First Presidency would like to have Brother Edwards, who is an expert economist, make a special, confidential study of our system of central accounting of receipt and disbursements of church funds and make a report to the First Presidency of recommendations, if any, of improving the present system.[41]

Brother Edwards stated that the job is too big for any one man, and that he would like to have the assistance of two expert accountants. To that we agreed, and I promised to get in touch with President Wayne E. Mayhew[42] in the Berkeley Stake Presidency, and Dr. Clyde Randall, head of the accounting department at the University of Utah. ...

Following the conference with President Wilkinson and Dr. Edwards I had a brief consultation with <u>Brother George Jarvis of the Central Accounting Department</u>, and told him that there is a great responsibility connected with the financial department of the Church, and that we should be sure that the centralized system now presently operating is best for the Church. Brother Jarvis then tried to point out some of the troubles which they have encountered. I then told Brother Jarvis that we are having experts examine the overall system in order that we might know where we stand in this department.

---

41. One of Edwards's recommendations was that church leaders retire from corporate boards, which was slowly implemented over the course of several years.

42. Wayne Elijah Mayhew (1897–1973) was born in Giles, Utah, a town of less than 200 (now a ghost town). He graduated from BYU to become a CPA in Ogden and then San Francisco. He endowed the Vera Hinckley Mayhew writing contest at BYU, in honor of his wife, who was also a BYU graduate.

5   The South Pacific and Washington DC, 1955

> Just before we took our seats, President Eisenhower came up to me and said, "President McKay, your seat is just opposite mine, and before we take our seats, I should like to have you say grace.
> —May 9, 1955

January 8, 1955, Fiji. A telephone call came to the office for President McKay from the <u>Leper Colony</u> just about two miles out of the city [of Suva]. It was a request for him to come and visit a member of the Church who had seen him when she was a little girl and he was visiting Samoa thirty-four years before on his first visit to the South Pacific Missions [as an apostle].[1] We took a taxi and went in search of this lady. Her name was <u>Mrs. Sally Skipps</u> and she was the daughter of the Samoan Family by <u>name of Tooya</u>. The taxi took us up the mountain side to a group of cottages, and we located the Sister in Charge.[2] She greeted us and said that she would send for Mrs. Skipps. It was learned from this Sister in Charge that she had spent thirty years as a nurse in this colony. She was of French extraction and spoke English very fluently. Her assistant was there, and she went down to one of the cottages to find the lady who had made the request. After a few moments the word came that she could not walk very far so the <u>President suggested that we go to her cottage</u>. This was a beautiful tropical spot with all kinds of shrubbery in all the hues of the rainbow

---

1. The previous visit to Samoa was during McKay's world tour of 1921 with Hugh Cannon. See note for September 4, 1951.
2. This was a hostel for the medical staff, mostly nuns, who cared for leprosy patients on the nearby island of Makogai, seventy miles from Suva.

growing so profusely. As we walked along a small corridor we came to an open door and there sat a middle-aged Samoan lady with tears in her eyes patiently waiting to see President and Sister McKay. She spoke very good English and seemed overjoyed to greet her visitors. <u>She explained that she had been listening to her little radio set and yesterday morning it had announced that President McKay of the Mormon Church had landed at the [Nadi] airport.[3] Now he was standing at her door typical of a great kind [man] to heed the request of this troubled heart.</u> Here was an answer to her prayer that she would get to see the Prophet. Prayer is a great blessing to all and especially those who have faith and can find comfort and solace in the exercise of their faith. She had a kind face and a humble heart and seemed so grateful for the visit, and for the blessing she received. She was soon to go back to her family in New Zealand. She waved good-bye and we climbed into the taxi and we discovered the Sister in Charge giving the taxi man the cost of the trip out from Suva which this good member was willing to pay just to have the Prophet come to her door.[4]

February 17, 1955, Salt Lake City, First Presidency and apostles. President McKay said he would make some recommendations to the council this morning. ...

3. Samoa is in good condition. Brother Howard Stone[5] has his feet on the ground. He is keeping things up very well.

4. Was very much disappointed at the plan suggested for our Mapusaga School [near the capital Pago Pago] in American Samoa.[6] Told them the plans would have to be re-drawn.

---

3. The president and his companions were delayed by a hurricane or they would not have traveled 100 miles on the Queen's Highway from Nadi to Suva, where they unexpectedly found a branch of the church. Overcome by the reception they received, McKay declared on the spot that from that time forward, Fijian men would be allowed ordination into the LDS priesthood despite their dark skin color. Jacob and Lesuma, "History of the Church ... in Fiji," online at rsc.byu.edu.

4. McKay's forty-five-day tour extended from January 2 (his and his wife's wedding anniversary) through February 15 and covered 45,000 miles. They visited Hawaii, Fiji, Tonga, Samoa, New Zealand, and Australia.

5. Mission president Howard Burnell Stone (1908–68) was a banker by profession, who hailed from Spanish Fork, Utah. As a young man, he had been a missionary to Samoa and had acted as principal of the school in Sauniatu. Later he would direct the Polynesian Cultural Center in Hawaii.

6. The church had operated a primary school in Mapusaga since 1903; the high

5. We have 650 students enrolled in Samoa.[7] The young man in charge [at Sauniatu] is not an executive but is a nice young man. President McKay recommended that they close the sides of the classrooms. They are around a patio and all the sides facing the patio are open. It is all right from a ventilation standpoint but not from an educational standpoint. They can see everybody that goes by. He recommends that they make each individual classroom an entity and put in a door so that they can lock the door. It will not cost very much. They will still have plenty of ventilation.[8]

6. In Fiji, we have not heretofore done any missionary work. Brother C. G. Smith, a local man, thinks the people have no negroid blood, but the Indians from India are crowding in there and they outnumber the Fijians now. Met 25 members of the Church there. Sunday afternoon had 48 at Suva at the meeting. Governor Garby advises if we are going to get any property there we should do it now in Suva. Had a very interesting conversation with him. He said there is no opposition there, that our elders wanted the privilege of securing property down on the Bay. He said they could not do that, that that belongs to the Government, and that which they chose on the other side also belongs to the Government. He advised that we get freehold property and get it right away. Suva is booming, and President McKay recommended to President Stone that while he is there visiting he look around and make a recommendation. Thought the race problem would be no worse than in South Africa or Brazil.

7. New Zealand. … They have a beautiful rock fence [at the church school in Hamilton] extending all along the main highway. It is a credit. They have had to crush the rock, make their own bricks; they have had to dry their own lumber, season it and haul it from the mill. They have had to hard-surface their own roads. It is not open yet. They have had as high as 80 Maoris contributing two years of their time, supporting themselves or their

---

school that was now under consideration was finished in 1960 and remained in operation until 1974, which is when the government built its own school nearby. "United States Territory: American Samoa," Church News section, *Deseret News*, Jan. 1, 2009.

7. The church had a dozen schools, most of them with significantly less than 100 students. Some of the classes were held in open-air, thatched-roof pavilions called *fales*.

8. Ironically, the school honored McKay's 1955 visit by constructing a *fale* "supported by beams of indigenous wood" carved with "gospel-themed images" and a wooden bust of McKay—and no walls. Jason Swensen, "Samoa's Eden," Church News section, *Deseret News*, Oct. 14, 2005.

parents supporting them, sending them food, and they have had to build houses to accommodate them. They have houses for the married people and houses for the single men, and that is where the expense has been going. These will all be used as dormitories and places for the faculty. ...

President McKay said that the Tahitian Islanders will probably have some difficulty getting to a temple in New Zealand under the present means of transportation, but it will be much nearer than to Hawaii. Eliminating Tahiti, there are Tonga, Samoa, Niue, all of New Zealand and all of Australia. He felt that in a few years there would be 50,000 of our people there. Most all the Tongans and Samoans and the people in Niue can take the [merchant ship] Tofua[9] for a very few pounds at most. Found that many of the people are spending their life's savings to go to Laie and some are selling their property. Thought that such a temple would not cost more than $400,000.

President McKay said our people have no reason for leaving New Zealand and Australia; our men are holding leading positions in Government and other places; that we can have an influence in those countries far beyond anything we have had before. He mentioned that in a meeting held at the Bay of Plenty [New Zealand] there were present a member of Parliament, the Superintendent of Schools, the Chairman of the County Commissioners, all speaking words of praise. The member of Parliament said: "You have done more for our Maori people here than all the other churches put together."

New Zealand Mission and Construction of Temple There

He said that he found the New Zealand Mission was not in very good condition from a missionary standpoint (he met with the missionaries in every country that he visited). President [Sidney J.] Ottley[10] was not going to hold a meeting with the missionaries, and President McKay told him that he must have one, and in that missionary meeting some

---

9. The *Tofua* was a passenger and cargo ship that moved people and goods around Polynesia, stopping every four weeks at the island of Niue, 370 miles northeast of Tonga. It also stopped at Auckland, Apia, Pago Pago, Suva, and Vava'u. McLintock, *Encyclopedia of New Zealand*, s.v. Niue.

10. Sidney J. Ottley (1890–1982) was from South Cottonwood, near Big Cottonwood Canyon in Salt Lake County. When he returned from his mission to New Zealand in the early part of the twentieth century, he farmed and did carpentry until he was called as mission president in 1951.

disclosures were made that were very disheartening.[11] President McKay felt that perhaps these matters would have come to light if the Brethren of the General Authorities had interviewed some of the missionaries when they came home, and he wondered whether we are not losing something by leaving that personal interview to the stake authorities.

President McKay said that some of the people down there are giving their life savings to pay their way to Laie or to Canada or to Salt Lake City in order to go to the temple. Some are selling their property and everything that they have in order to get the blessings of the temple. The President felt that it will be but a short time before there are 50,000 members of the Church in Australia, New Zealand, Tonga, Samoa, and Nuway [Niue], and with the present transportation all the Tongans and the Samoans can go to New Zealand with the expenditure of but a few shillings, and use their own money in taking passage on the Tofua [steamship]. They take their own food with them and sleep on the deck of the ship. The Australians are also willing to go over to New Zealand. Some are leaving Australia to go to Canada instead of building up the branches where they are. Our people are building a school at Hamilton, New Zealand, where they have their own rock crusher, their own sawmill, etc. They are seasoning their lumber. They have workmen putting in the doors and window sashes. They have their trucks, and they have permission from the Government to run their trucks.

We have a beautiful site available for a temple near Hamilton with plenty of acreage, and with a school established, the teachers, many of them, can be temple workers. President McKay recommended that we build a temple such as we contemplate in Bern, Switzerland, near Hamilton, within three quarters of a mile at most of the present school site.

The prospects for missionary work in Australia, New Zealand, and in the Islands are very favorable. The Governor–General, Superintendents of Schools, and leaders in Governmental affairs in these countries are all favorable. The President said that had they been members of the Church

---

11. Further on in his report, the president complains that the missionaries were only spending four hours a day proselytizing, indicating a lack of leadership. There had also been some violence against missionaries. On the island of Niue, people had thrown rocks at the missionaries, and when one cut his feet on coral trying to escape and had to seek hospital care in New Zealand, he left his companion behind alone on the island. Carol Gill, "Preaching Gospel on Remote Isle," Church News section, *Deseret News*, Oct. 24, 2003.

they could not have been more cordial. He held meetings all the way down to Wellington. A large meeting was held at the place which Captain Cook called the Bay of Plenty.

A woman afflicted with leprosy heard that they had arrived at Suva, and a nurse called up and wanted to know if the President would come down and administer to her, she being a member of the Church who remembered President McKay from 34 years ago. President McKay administered to her; and also to a woman who was brought in on a cot to the meeting, but otherwise he thought it would not be wise to administer to the sick. He told them, however, that if they would give him a list of their names that on this day in the temple in the meeting of the Presidency and the Twelve they would be remembered in the prayers of the Brethren. President McKay asked the Brethren to fulfill that promise in their prayer at the altar this morning. He said the people will no doubt be praying at the same time.

President McKay said that he had made a brief summary of his recent tour of the South Pacific Missions with a view of curtailing time; that he would present merely some suggestions which he would call problems, rather than recommendations, so that they would be on record for consideration. He said that it is marvelous how close these missions are to us under the present means of transportation; that the Lord has opened up the way for His interests in all the world to be looked after by those who he called to look after them.

The President said that in a [first-class] compartment of the [Pan American] plane called the President, they were riding in a plane that weighed 145,800 pounds, not counting the passengers; and it would be 15,000 to 17,000 feet in the air, looking over that broad expanse of ocean or clouds, depending upon the condition. There was no sight of land between San Francisco and Honolulu, although you do get a sight of land between Honolulu and Auckland,—the New Hebrides and some of the other Islands in the distance,—but they do not amount to much. President McKay said it was a source of wonderment to him how so much weight, plus passengers and crew, can fly through the air at 300 miles per hour with a feeling of perfect safety; that in invention and discovery, particularly in unleashing forces heretofore unseen and unknown, man has entered the realm of the Creator. Unless such progress in science is accompanied by advancement in character, spirituality, and true brotherhood, the future safety of the human family is mighty precarious. With all those mighty forces in hand, without a counter-balancing belief and confidence in a Creator, and more confidence in fellow-men, we can suffer greatly.

Problems

President McKay mentioned these problems in Samoa. In addition to the new plans for the school at Mapusaga, Brother Adams's translations are not being used.[12] President McKay said he was convinced after meeting with Brother Stone and a young capable leader in Samoa that there is something wrong with these translations.

Tahiti

Needs

1. French speaking missionary or missionaries.

a. Possibility of establishing a school. ...

2. Better understanding regarding disposition and management of [church-owned] Paraita sailing vessel].[13]

New Zealand

The President said that missionary conditions in New Zealand are deplorable. President Ottley has been released, and the First Presidency will have a consultation with [the new president,] Brother [Ariel S.] Ballif[14] about matters before he goes there. Brother Mendenhall, following the meeting with the missionaries, followed up some suggestions that were made. President McKay said he thought things would carry on until President Ballif goes down there. The missionaries, he said, are spending only four hours a day, according to their reports.

---

12. The mission president in the 1920s, John Q. Adams (1882–1971), originally from Centerville, Utah, may have tried his hand at translating the Pearl of Great Price and Doctrine and Covenants, which would not be authorized for publication until 1944 and 1963. The Samoan Book of Mormon was published sixty years earlier in 1903.

13. The *Paraita* was a sailing vessel the missionaries in Tahiti purchased in Los Angeles and sailed back to the islands under the direction of a hired captain. The ship was used to shuttle members and missionaries to meetings. In 1959 it sank in port in Laie after transporting members to the Hawaiian temple. Perrin, "Seasons of Faith," online at rsc.byu.edu.

14. Ariel S. Ballif (1901–95) was a BYU professor of sociology and dean of students for one year, his PhD from the University of Southern California. He and his wife had served a mission to New Zealand, where he was installed as principal of the church-owned Maori Agricultural College. In 1960 he became mayor of Provo.

<u>Australia</u>

President McKay presented the problem as to whether or not Australia should be divided into two missions. He mentioned the main cities along the Coast, starting at Brisbane in the north, with 600,000 population; Sydney, with 2,000,000 in the city, and 3,000,000 in the area there. Then you fly 1500 miles to Melbourne, which is a city of half a million people. It is 615 miles from Melbourne to Adelaide, with 600,000 people; 1600 miles over to Perth, another city of 400,000; with Tasmania across the strait from Melbourne, North of Brisbane, near which President McKay laid the cornerstone for a new meeting house, in Ipswich. He said we have a list of 8 or 10 cities, with 50,000 to 200,000 population each.

Friday, Saturday, and Sunday were spent in Oahu. On Friday broke ground for the Church College of Hawaii at Laie. Had a remarkable experience there in regard to the weather. Had the official recognition of members and non-members alike.

<u>At the suggestion of Elder Richard L. Evans, Council expressed appreciation, amazement and gratitude at what the President was able to do in this significant journey.</u>

President McKay, in answer, said that he recognized the overruling Providence, first in regard to their health; that it was significant that Sister McKay and he had made that trip, taking boats, seaplanes, airplanes, being entertained at various places, going without the necessary sleep, and had returned home without any illness or distress. He said that the prayers of the Brethren were literally answered in their behalf.

He further said that not once did any of their planned meetings or entertainments have to be dispensed with because of storm, though when they were in Suva at the hotel it rained 4 inches in one night, and it also rained in other places. He said there was probably an exception in the open air reception at Laie when the Hawaiians, the Samoans, the Japanese, and a few Tahitians had an open air entertainment, it rained when they drove up there in the automobile. They went through the entertainment, however, without a drop of rain, until the finale. The Relief Society had made their presentations, and the little children came and made their presentation, and it started to rain. As a finale, they sang: "We Thank Thee O God for a Prophet" in each of those languages, and then sang it in English. It started to rain and the crowd of several thousand broke up, but they went through the program.

March 10, 1955. The First Presidency had a visit from Brother Thomas S. Ferguson of Oakland yesterday, a man who is very much interested in Book of Mormon discoveries. The Presidency were very favorably impressed by him, were profoundly impressed with his enthusiasm and also with his knowledge. He is well acquainted with archaeologists and the discoveries they have made down in Mexico and Central America. He has a great deal of enthusiasm for and a sound testimony of the Book of Mormon. The Presidency are considering very seriously encouraging him financially in further research work. He has organized a Board of Directors on which there are archaeologists, some non-members as well as members, and the First Presidency feel that they would be justified in encouraging him in the work he is attempting to do.[15]

On March 15, 1955 Brother Ernest A. Strong,[16] called at President McKay's office (at President McKay's request) and he was asked by President McKay to work with Brother Ferguson in this archeological work. On March 16, 1955 [a] telephone call was made at President McKay's request to Brother Ferguson … informing him of the appointment of Brother Strong to help in his work on Book of Mormon discoveries.

March 12, 1955. President McKay said that the First Presidency cautioned Brother [Thomas Stuart] Ferguson against making extravagant statements regarding their discoveries.

May 5, 1955. Today at <u>Council meeting</u> President McKay made the following significant statement:

"President McKay referred to the recent showing of 'Day of Triumph',

---

15. See the note for September 25, 1952. J. Reuben Clark recorded: "In the course of the interview the feeling was expressed (I fathered an expression of the idea) that all of these agencies should be brought together under one head so that we could know what was being done and be sure that these various archaeological enterprises were not working at cross-purposes" (Clark diary, Mar. 12, 1955).

16. Ernest Albert Strong Jr. (1916–90), of Springville, Utah, was on the original board of the New World Archeology Foundation (1952). He and Nicholas Groesbeck Morgan (1884–1971), an attorney, provided most of the funding. Strong was a general contractor and a stake president.

a new film[17] portraying the life of the Savior. Some of the Brethren had seen the presentation, and thought it was well done, and that there was nothing objectionable to it. President McKay stated that he felt sure that all the Brethren more and more felt the responsibility that is ours to up-hold the divine Sonship of our Lord and Savior; that no other Church now is doing that. He said: 'This is the Church of Jesus Christ, and it is our obligation to preach to the world that he is the Son of God, our Redeemer and Savior, not just a great teacher, but in reality the Son of our Father in Heaven, and the Redeemer of the world; that he has broken the bonds of death and brought the resurrection, and through him and obedience to this Gospel we will gain eternal exaltation in his Kingdom.' President McKay concluded by saying: 'May the Lord give us that power, and increase our ability so to represent Him to the world, I pray in the name of Jesus Christ, Amen.'"

May 6, 1955, 9 a.m. Henry D. Moyle met with the First Presidency. He gave a report of his interview with the Attorney General ([Louis H.] Callister) and Ward Holbrook of the State Welfare Commission regarding plans for enforcing the law pertaining to polygamy.

May 9, 1955, Washington, DC. We arrived in Washington, D.C. over the Baltimore & Ohio at 8:40 this morning, and were met at the [train] station by our grandson, Russell M. Blood,[18] President J. Willard Marriott of the Washington Stake, Sister Ezra Taft Benson [Flora], Union Pacific officials, and newspaper reporters.

President Marriott had reserved a suite of rooms at the Hotel Shoreham, one of the leading hotels. When we arrived there we found a beautiful bouquet of carnations, sent with the compliments of the Management, and two dozen long-stemmed red roses from President and

---

17. *Day of Triumph* had just been released. Starring Lee Cobb and Joanne Dru, it portrayed Christ as seen by the apostle Andrew and a fictional character Zadok, leader of an underground Zealot group. The paragraph appears in the diary in quote marks because it was excerpted from the minutes.

18. The parents of Russell McKay Blood (1930–2015) were Louise McKay Blood, daughter of David and Emma Ray McKay, and Russell Blood, son of the late Utah governor Henry H. Blood. Russell worked for the National Security Agency in Arlington, Virginia.

Sister J. Willard Marriott. Later we received a basket of delicious fruit from a Mr. Hamilton, who has just been elected President of the National Retailers Association. He saw me as I passed through the lobby of the Hotel, recognized me, and then sent this lovely fruit to us. I tried to contact him personally two or three times but was unsuccessful, so contented myself by putting a note of thanks under his door at the Hotel.

Monday Evening—Dinner at the White House as guest of President Dwight D. Eisenhower.[19]

At 7:30 p.m. Brother Ezra Taft Benson (U.S. Secretary of Agriculture) called for me at the Shoreham Hotel, and we drove to the White House where we were received very graciously by President Eisenhower who was then meeting his guests as they arrived, twenty of whom had been especially invited by President Eisenhower.

As I greeted President Eisenhower, I expressed appreciation of the honor extended, and he said: "It is an honor to have you with us." A little later, he said to us all—"The way we do it here is for each of you to introduce yourselves and get acquainted." So we stood around as a group and had general conversation with each other as the servants passed the refreshments. The waiter served me with tomato juice. There was no excessive drinking on the part of anyone—it was just a social hour with appetizers—hors d'oeuvres, tomato juice, ginger ale, and bourbon for those who wanted it.

When the guests had all arrived, President Eisenhower said: "I should like to take you up to my private suite." We accompanied him to a particular room where he had displayed all his souvenirs and presents from countries from all over the world. Among them was a jewel-studded Scimitar (a saber used chiefly by Arabs and Persians) from one of the Far East countries—it was set with a large diamond and other precious jewels. President Eisenhower happened to be by my side while I was examining it, and he said to me, "Now these jewels are not first class; they are genuine, but not the very best—that diamond is large but the cut is not of the very best." However, the jewels were brilliant and beautiful to see.

---

19. McKay was a periodic guest at the White House during his presidency and was held in high esteem by Eisenhower, who on one occasion reportedly stated that he "considered President McKay the greatest spiritual leader in the world." On another occasion, he reportedly commented to Secretary Benson that McKay "was the life of the party." Prince and Wright, *David O. McKay*, 351.

After a very pleasant fifteen or twenty minutes in this room, President Eisenhower said: "Now I should like you to go up into the 'Abraham Lincoln Room.'" In that room there stands the bed which was made especially for President Lincoln who was a very tall man—an old fashioned bed with a large, beautifully carved headboard. There was no canopy as is common with so many old-fashioned beds.

As we approached the window in this bedroom, President Eisenhower said: "This is where President Lincoln signed the emancipation proclamation."

Following a very interesting few minutes in this room, President Eisenhower said: "Now we shall go to the Blue Room for our dinner."

As we came through the hallway, a secretary approached with the plan of the table and the place where each would sit. As I came, he said: "President McKay, your place is just opposite the President's." (This seat, directly across from the President of the United States is the honor seat).

Just before we took our seats, President Eisenhower came up to me and said: "President McKay, Your seat is just opposite mine, and just before we take our seats, I should like to have you say grace."

Following grace, President Eisenhower sat down, and after all were seated he said: "At each one's plate there is a knife especially prepared for this occasion, but there is an old saying that you mustn't give a piece of cutlery as a present unless the one to whom you give the present gives something in return, so you will find that a penny has been attached to the note with the knife, and you may give that penny back to me. I was afraid each of you would not have a penny, so I have given that to you." So each of us passed a penny to President Eisenhower.

Then dinner was served, and the usual dinner conversation ensued.

The gentleman on my left (whose name I do not remember) immediately asked just what my ideas are regarding a sentence I used in offering grace pertaining to the freedom of the individual—this sentence evidently intrigued him. Three-fourths of my conversation was with him on the doctrine of the necessity of individual effort in securing happiness in this life. I told him of our doctrine of free agency, etc.

From 7:30 p.m. to 10:30 p.m, the President entertained us with his experiences as a General and his acquaintance with such men as Sir Winston Churchill, General Patton, and other international characters. He also commented on national and foreign policies, and the guests asked questions regarding the government and the effect of certain policies on the future. I asked about Formosa [Taiwan] and the effect of cessation of hostilities. President Eisenhower discussed these matters with us, all of which, of course, is not to be quoted because this was just a social evening.

President Eisenhower proved himself not only a genial, but a brilliant host, and he seemed to be at his very best this evening.

As the time wore on, I was a little concerned for fear the President would become tired, but he seemed interested, and did not want us to go. It was 11:20 p.m. before he arose and said: "Now, President McKay, I will escort you to the door," and then he said to the others, "If you will all come to the door I will say good-night." I was the first one to whom he said good-night, saying, "It was very gracious of you to come this long distance, President McKay, and I appreciate it. Remember me to your associates out there."

And thus ended one of the most inspiring evenings I have spent, not only because of the brilliance of our host, and the courtesies he extended to me throughout the evening, but aside from all that, just to be present in the White House is an inspiration! As one contemplates that from the days of [George] Washington to the present time, the power to shape the destiny of the world has rested with the President of the United States, his soul is full of emotion. I appreciated, as never before, that Washington, D.C. is the capital of the greatest country in the world, and to be there in the White House as one of the honored guests of the President of the United States was thrilling, and an experience of a lifetime.

June 6, 1955. President Claudi[o]us Bowman[20] of the Mexican Mission called from Mexico at noon today: He reported that one of his missionaries has been affected by Annalee Skarin's book "Ye Are Gods".[21]

20. Claudious Bowman (1890–1958), was born in southern Utah, raised in the Mexican colonies, attended high school in Provo, and returned to Colonia Dublán to run a grist mill and farm and become president of the Chihuahua Bank. He was president of the Colonia Juárez Stake for twenty years prior to his 1853 calling as mission president. He died in Mexico City in an accident after a church meeting.

21. Annalee Skarin (1899–1988) was one of the more interesting Mormon cult figures of the twentieth century. Born to farming parents in American Falls, Idaho, she became obsessed with revelatory processes and wrote a number of books that had Mormon theology and doctrine as their baseline. Her initial work was *Ye Are Gods*, and it

This woman was excommunicated from the Church sometime ago, and the Elder is questioning the right of the General Authorities to cut her off from the Church. He is thoroughly convinced that the doctrine she teaches is inspired and direct from Heaven. The elder ... says he accepts her book with all his heart—that it comes from God. Brother Bowman said that he had been laboring with him for two days and has had no influence whatsoever on him. [The elder's] home is in Provo. He was educated for the ministry of another Church, and is a convert to our Church. His father is a minister, and he is the only member of his family who has joined the Church.

I told Brother Bowman that it is a serious thing to excommunicate a person; that I will look up [the elder's] record here in the office—that in the meantime he should work another 24 hours with the Elder to see if he can make him see the error of his ways. Brother Bowman said the Elder has not taught his doctrine to any one else in the mission field; that he has been fair in that respect.

I then instructed Brother Bowman not to excommunicate this young man, but if he insists upon following his present course, he will have to give him a dishonorable release and send him home.

Later, I called Gordon Hinckley of the Missionary Office,[22] and together we went over [the elder's] record. A telegram will be sent to President Bowman to extend a dishonorable release to [the elder] and instruct him to report to his Ward and Stake authorities, and to the Priesthood quorum that is supporting him in the mission field.

---

was something of a sensation, especially along the Wasatch Front. People formed study groups to discuss it. In the spring of 1952, while she was visiting friends in Salt Lake City and speaking at church meetings and firesides, she was ushered into an office in a ward house and met by apostle Mark E. Petersen, who asked her to recant and repent, informing her that her so-called inspiration was not from the Lord. She rejected his request and was excommunicated shortly thereafter, opting to continue writing and publishing. She eventually proclaimed that she would be "translated" (changed from mortality to immortality) and disappeared, which added to her mystique. Samuel W. Taylor, "The Puzzle Of Annalee Skarin: Was She Translated Correctly," *Sunstone*, Apr. 1991, 42–46; Hilton, *Descent Into Madness*. See also the note for the entry dated March 23, 1953.

22. Hinckley explained that in the Missionary Department, "I would get to work first thing in the morning, and before I could get my hat off the phone would be ringing. All day long, and half the night my phone rang with calls from all over the world. When missionaries were physically sick, homesick, seasick, or love sick, I got the call." Dew, *Go Forward with Faith*, 153.

June 20, 1955, 8 a.m. Met by appointment at his request <u>President Noble Waite of the South Los Angeles Stake</u>.

Brother Waite wanted advice as to whether he should accept the Vice Presidency of the Brigham Young University, in charge of collecting funds for the Brigham Young University. He has received an invitation from President Ernest Wilkinson to serve as the Vice President, and Brother Waite wanted to know whether this is a Call.

I told Brother Waite that it is not a call, that he can use his own judgment as to whether or not he accepts.

Brother Waite then said that he thinks he will not accept the appointment.[23]

June 23, 1955, 2 p.m. to 3 p.m. Immediately following council meeting went up to the 5th Floor of the Temple where all the General Authorities viewed the <u>Swiss Temple Ceremony films</u>.

June 29, 1955, 8:30 a.m. The First Presidency met with <u>Brother William F. Edwards</u> regarding his investigations of the Central Accounting System of the Church, particularly with reference to the plan he has worked out to save time in the presentation of Church expenditures at the meetings held each Tuesday morning.

July 18, 1955, 7:30 a.m. Met Dr. Edward R. McKay and [cardiologist] Dr. L[ouis] E. Viko and had a thorough physical examination, which disclosed the fact that I had had an attack of pleurisy [inflammation of lungs]. They reported that my heart action is good, blood pressure excellent, and I felt better than I had for a week.

July 29, 1955, 8:30 a.m. Consultation with <u>Dr. William F. Edwards</u> regarding his study of office space on Fourth Floor—salaries of employees—recommended a re-examination of general salary levels, especially

---

23. William Noble Waite (1898–1965) would later accept the position of BYU fund raiser, but for the moment he was content to continue as principal of the Huntington Park High School in greater Los Angeles and as president of the South Los Angeles Stake. He and his wife, June, both born in Nevada, would later preside over the North Scotland Mission.

a consideration of salaries in relationship to responsibility and quality of work. Church Purchasing Department—should be [a] change in procedure—examples of inefficiency that could be corrected—hospital orders—equipment purchased for schools—Warehouse could reduce inventory—Church purchasing department functions—dyna[m]ics of Church growth—were among items discussed.

August 3, 1955, 7:30 a.m. Met by appointment at his request Gus Backman of the [Salt Lake City] Chamber of Commerce. He presented problems connected with the new site for the pioneer relics [artifacts] as proposed by the Sons of the Utah Pioneers. Brother Backman feels that the "This is the Place Monument" site would be a much more appropriate place for the memorial to the Pioneers, and furthermore it was originally planned that this site should be used for this purpose.

August 5, 1955, 8 a.m. Met by appointment Gus Backman regarding the establishment of a Pioneer Village. Brother Backman favors the use of the "This is the Place" monument site. The Sons of the Utah Pioneers would like to use the Sugarhouse Prison site for this purpose.[24]

August 10, 1955, 8 o'clock p.m. I went to the Union Pacific Station to bid farewell to members of the [Mormon] Tabernacle choir as they depart on their historic tour of the European countries. Never in the history of the Union Pacific has there been such a large crowd of people gather at this station—it is estimated that there were 5000 relatives and friends there to bid adieu to the Choir members.[25]

---

24. The monument was completed in 1947. Twelve years later work began on Heritage Village, consisting of fifty houses and commercial buildings. Some were historical structures that were moved to the location and others were replicas. It was turned into a living museum on 450 acres adjacent to the monument. Although it is now run by an independent non-profit foundation, it continues to receive some funding from the Utah Division of Parks and Recreation. Brett Prettyman, "Privatized This Is the Place Park Still Relying on State Cash," *Salt Lake Tribune*, Aug. 22, 2011.

25. McKay accompanied the choir to Europe for, among other engagements, the groundbreaking of the London temple on August 27 and the dedication of the Swiss temple beginning on Sunday, September 11, in ten services over a space of five days that were held in eight different languages: English, French, German, Danish, Dutch, Finnish, Norwegian, and Swedish.

September 29, 1955, 9 a.m. Called a special meeting of the First Presidency and Council of the Twelve in the Salt Lake Temple. Special talks were given by one or two of the brethren, and then I addressed the brethren regarding their sacred calling and the coming 126th Semi-Annual Conference of the Church. A very faith-promoting inspirational meeting was held.

October 23, 1955, 8:15 p.m. Ray [Emma Ray McKay] and I attended the United Nations meeting held in the Salt Lake Tabernacle at which [US] Ambassador [to the United Nations] [Henry Cabot] Lodge[26] was the guest speaker. He gave a very good talk on Peace which was carried on national radio and television hook-ups. There was really nothing new in his remarks about the United Nations. He thinks it is a means of forming public opinion. It is impossible for the population of Nations to meet together, but the United Nations furnishes an opportunity for the leaders of Nations to meet and they go back and shape the opinions of their constituents. Sister McKay brought up the point—"Yes, but they go back and lie." I answered that that was true about the Communist leaders, but the others go back and present the truth as far as they can. The question is whether the good they do is worth the expense of this large organization. However, I believe that it is a step in the right direction.[27]

November 1, 1955, Los Angeles. At the conclusion of our luncheon, we went over to the Paramount Studios at the request of Brother Arnold Friberg,[28] for a sitting for a painting to be placed in the Los Angeles Temple.

26. Henry Cabot Lodge (1903–85) was from a prominent Massachusetts political family. Three years previously he had lost his senate seat (1937–44, 1947–53) to another powerful Massachusetts family scion, John F. Kennedy. He was Eisenhower's campaign manager; and after Lodge's defeat, Eisenhower appointed him US Ambassador to the United Nations.

27. The church hierarchy was ambivalent about the United Nations. McKay's counselor J. Reuben Clark Jr., who had been the US ambassador to Mexico, had a dim view of foreign entanglements, international organizations, and the dilution of American sovereignty. He and the apostle–US senator Reed Smoot opposed the League of Nations following World War I. Clark did concede that the church had "avoided taking any stand pro or con on the United Nations because our people were on both sides of the question." Quinn, *Elder Statesman*, 312.

28. Arnold Friberg (1913–2010) was Mormonism's most famous painter. In the early 1950s, he was commissioned to paint twelve Book of Mormon scenes for the *Children's Friend*, and these paintings were reproduced in paperback editions of the Book of Mormon. He was born in Arizona to Scandinavian parents, studied in New York and

Upon our arrival at the studio a group of people consisting of Ora Pate Stewart, Brother Frederick S. Williams, Brother Wiberg and others, presented a proposition to remodel our Bureau of Information at the temple to provide a place in which to exhibit relics taken from the ruins of South and Central America, as evidences of the divine authenticity of the Book of Mormon. They have evidence of steel manufacture which the scientists estimate was between 100 B.C. and 100 A.D. They have evidences of the use of copper, and also evidences that there were buffaloes and elephants here during that ancient time. I told them to write their proposition to the First Presidency and that it would be passed upon later.

November 11, 1955, 7:30 a.m. By appointment called at Dr. L[ouis] E. Viko's office. He gave me a thorough examination, including a cardiogram and x-ray tests. He showed marked concern and told me that I had been "slipping" so far as my heart is concerned; that I have been doing too much. He gave me some definite advice—first, that I must "slow down"—I am to cut out night work and reduce to a minimum the strenuous handshaking after meetings. And then he said: "Now I know it is hard for you to say No, and that you will not consider your own welfare, but I am giving this advice in order that you might prolong your usefulness to your Church."

I appreciated this advice coming from a Catholic doctor who has proved himself to be a loyal friend.

December 22, 1955, 9 a.m. to 11 a.m. A special meeting of the Twelve was held in the First Presidency's office. The regular Council meeting is adjourned until January 15. At this special meeting the Church Budget for 1956 was considered and acted upon.

December 26, 1955. I am grateful for the greetings and letters from all parts of the Church telling of appreciation for what the Brethren of the General Authorities are doing and what the Church is accomplishing at the present time. To me it has been one of the most gratifying Christmas

Chicago, and opened a studio in San Francisco before teaching at the University of Utah and then moving to Hollywood to prepare storyboard art for film magnate Cecil B. DeMille's *The Ten Commandments*.

<u>vacations of my life</u>, and one which has <u>increased my sense of respon-sibility of Presidency</u> and deep gratitude for the association with the Brethren of the General Authorities and their wives. <u>No greater group of men and women</u>, and men and women of more nobility of soul and more willingness to sacrifice and to give all they have to the work of the Lord can be found in the world than the group with whom we are associated among the General Authorities.

6 Political Perceptions and Misperceptions, 1956

President McKay indicated that persons holding responsible positions in the Church should not use their title in connection with such [political] recommendations, but may do so as a citizen of the community. —July 20, 1956

January 13, 1956, 8:30 a.m. Met President Alonzo F. Hopkin[1] (President of the Woodruff Stake [Rich County, Utah]) by appointment at his request.

He wanted to know if there would be any objection on the part of the First Presidency if he accepted the nomination to run for [Utah] Governor on the Democratic ticket.

I told him that he had every right to exercise his rights as a citizen and that there would be no objection on the part of the First Presidency if he accepted such nomination.

January 16, 1956, Los Angeles. Following the tour [of the Los Angeles temple with Cecil B. De Mille[2] and entourage], the group expressed

---

1. Alonzo Francis Hopkin (1900–61) was a rancher with "the longest record of service in the history of the Utah State Legislature," serving as a Democrat twenty-six years beginning in 1935. In 1960 he lost his bid for the governorship. "Death Closes Service of Sen. Hopkin," *Salt Lake Tribune*, Dec. 16, 1961.

2. Cecil Blount DeMille (1881–1959) founded what became Paramount Pictures with Samuel Goldwyn and Jesse Lasky. He released his first feature film in 1914. Thirty-eight years later he won an Academy Award for Best Picture for *The Greatest Show on Earth*. Six of his movies had religious themes, reflecting at minimum his upbringing by a devout Episcopalian father (Cecil was not himself a church-goer) and Jewish

themselves as being very much interested. Mr. deMille said, among other things, "Well, President McKay, in building this great Temple, you have made the motion picture 'The Ten Commandments' seem insignificant." He was impressed with every feature. When we said goodbye, he said, "I shall never forget this experience; to have the privilege of going through with you personally was a great favor." In reply, I said to the group: "I esteem it a privilege to take Mr. deMille and his companions through this Temple, and I want you to know that I esteem Mr. deMille as a true nobleman; a great soul." Sister [Emma Ray] McKay afterwards said that when I said that, Mr. deMille dropped his head and tears came to his eyes.

I was very much thrilled with this tour of the Temple, and I think much good was accomplished by this visit.

January 26, 1956. ... I called Brother Harold B. Lee's attention to the excellent work that was done three years ago by the Committee appointed to get the citizenry of the State of Utah out to the conventions held for both [political] parties. I asked Brother Lee if we could do the same thing this year, because word has been received that certain forces inimical to the present administration are heavily at work. Brother Lee said there is not much time left to do anything because the meetings are to be held soon. I said the first meeting is to be held in Provo, on Monday [January 30]. Brother Lee said that we have not appointed a chairman to succeed Brother Junius Jackson who succeeded Brother A. Lewis Elggren. Now, both of these men are on missions. I asked Brother Lee to get on the telephone and call the stake presidents and have them call their bishops, and the bishops could get in touch with the members of their wards and urge them to attend the mass meetings on both tickets. No one could criticize us for taking this step.

February 3, 1956, First Presidency meeting. ... I explained that it was my understanding regarding plural marriage that the having of more than one wife is not a principle but a <u>practice</u>. The principle of the eternity of

---

mother. In 1920 he helped found the first airline offering commercial passenger service, Mercury Aviation, in Los Angeles. When he spoke at a BYU devotional in 1957, he turned to President McKay on the stand and paraphrased the apostle Paul to King Agrippa, "Almost thou persuadest me to be a Mormon" (appreciation to James D'Arc for this anecdote).

the marriage covenant revealed to the Prophet [Joseph Smith] and all the blessings pertaining to that may be obtained by a man with one wife.[3]

February 4, 1956. In accordance with previous arrangements, <u>went to the LDS hospital</u> for a <u>physical check-up</u>. I have been having trouble with excessive amounts of gas, and the doctors decided that they would ascertain the cause of it, so they had me come to the hospital for examinations.

I remained at the hospital all day. The doctors were unable to find anything organically wrong, but they think some of my trouble is due to eating too hurriedly in order to get to meetings and appointments, too much worry and pressure, and from not resting enough.

February 12, 1956, Ogden. I was not satisfied with my participation in the [dedicatory] services [for the Ogden Tabernacle]. I called on the following to speak—Thomas E. McKay, Bishop Joseph L. Wirthlin, Elder Henry D. Moyle, and President Stephen L. Richards. During all this time we were on the air. After these brethren had spoken, I had only twenty-five minutes to deliver the dedicatory address and prayer. I did not get my message over, I fear. In the interest of time, I was compelled to cut down the dedicatory prayer, and so, all in all, I was very much dissatisfied with my part.

February 29, 1956, First Presidency meeting. A discussion came up regarding a book that is being prepared for publication by Cla[i]re Wilcox telling of a dialogue between Joseph Smith and Willard Richards regarding the taking of other wives and urging that the matter be concealed.[4]

---

3. For an interesting corroborative argument, see Eugene England's "On Fidelity, Polygamy, and Celestial Marriage," in the winter 1987 issue of *Dialogue: A Journal of Mormon Thought*. McKay's declaration offered a tempered view of plural marriage as espoused by nineteenth-century church leaders.

4. This biography, *Intimate Disciple: A Portrait of Willard Richards, Apostle to Joseph Smith—Cousin to Brigham Young*, was to be published the next year (1957) by the University of Utah Press. Three decades later Richard H. Cracroft, BYU dean of Humanities, would recommended it to LDS readers in "Seeking 'the Good, the Pure, the Elevating,'" *Ensign*, July 1981. Cracroft would also recommend Noall's *Surely the Night* about Utah pioneers. Claire Augusta Wilcox Noall (1892–1971) graduated from the University of Utah in journalism and was also the author of *Guardians of the Hearth*, a book about pioneer midwives.

President [Stephen L] Richards says that the author is a relative of his[5] and he thought we should resist the publication of such material. In this connection President McKay gave the following:

Statement by President McKay on polygamy: President McKay stated that his understanding of the revelation given to the Prophet Joseph Smith, contained in the 132nd Section of the Doctrine and Covenants is as follows: That the revelation was regarding the eternity of the marriage covenant; it was not on polygamy. And the Lord revealed to the Prophet that a man who conforms to that revelation, that is, who enters into the eternity of the marriage covenant, received every blessing pertaining to the salvation and exaltation of man. No blessing is withheld. The part of the revelation pertaining to the marriage covenant pertains only to one man and one wife; and then, after the Prophet received it, he asked the Lord what about Abraham, Isaac and Jacob, who had more wives than one. And then follows the answer of the Lord that, if a man marry another wife and she is given to him as this wife is given to him, he does not sin, but he does not get a higher glory. There are one or two verses which will lead one to think that this refers to the plurality of marriage.

Plural marriage as a practice is not a principle. We have not abrogated the principle of the marriage covenant and we never will, and the practice of plural marriage is contrary to the law of the Church and the law of the land. President Richards said he agreed with this understanding one hundred per cent.

President McKay said that some of our people taught it as a principle, which was not correct.

March 2, 1956, 5 p.m. At my Request, Brother A. Hamer Reiser[6] came in. I informed Brother Reiser that I should like him to work in the office of the First Presidency to assist in the heavy load of correspondence

---

5. Richards seems to be referring to the subject of the book, Willard Richards his grandfather.

6. Albert Hamer Reiser (1897–1981) had recently been president of the British Mission and would soon be called as president of the Sugarhouse Stake in Salt Lake City. He was previously a store manager for Deseret Book, but had been secretary to the superintendency of the Sunday School Union and had occasionally filled in as an assistant to McKay on trips.

and other duties of the office. He was delighted and accepted the position wholeheartedly.

March 6, 1956, 11:30 a.m. Met by appointment at his request <u>President Ernest L. Wilkinson of the B.Y.U.</u> The following items were discussed: …

2. President Wilkinson <u>reported that he is being urged to run for Governor</u>. I suggested that he had better not encourage this suggestion as he is needed where he is with the B.Y.U., especially at the present.[7] …

12:15 p.m. <u>Elder Delbert L. Stapley</u> and <u>Elder Adam S. Bennion</u> then came in, and we considered: …

2. The advisability of <u>appointing a General Committee</u> to <u>correlate the courses of study</u> given <u>by the Quorums and auxiliaries of the Church</u>. I told them that both are meritorious, and that they might make their recommendations and have it come before the Presidency and the Council.

March 23, 1956, First Presidency meeting.[8] Comments by President McKay on Economic Conditions: President McKay voiced the sentiment that, if <u>present trends continue</u>, there will not be anything left for stockholders of corporations, that labor and taxes are consuming everything these institutions can make. <u>He feared that the support the Government is giving to labor unions is leading to a condition where there will be nothing for stockholders.</u>

March 25, 1956. Spend most of the day considering 25 or 30 petitions for cancellation of temple sealings. It always gives me a depressing feeling to delve into these letters giving the reasons for the breaking up of homes and the requests for cancellations of their temple sealings. I feel that some of our brethren ought never to have been permitted to go through the temple.

---

7. Wilkinson had long sought to throw his hat into some political arena. In 1964 he would unsuccessfully run for the US Senate against incumbent Utah Democrat Frank E. (Ted) Moss (Bergera, "Sad and Expensive Experience," 304–24; "Strange Phenomena," 89–115). In the end, George D. Clyde was elected governor (127,000 votes), defeating the Democrat L. C. "Rennie" Romney (111,000 votes) and independent incumbent J. Bracken Lee (94,000 votes).

8. From March 9–19, McKay was in Los Angeles presiding over the dedication services for the Los Angeles temple.

March 27, 1956, 8:30 a.m. Met by appointment <u>Mr. Harold Fabian</u>[9] who called previously for an audience with me. He had been appointed Chairman of the Committee assigned the duty of establishing a City Park on the old penitentiary area [Sugarhouse]. He wanted to have my opinion of the project that has been suggested that the <u>penitentiary area be made a cultural and inspirational park patterned after the Golden Gate Park in San Francisco for the use of the public.</u>

I told Mr. Fabian that I favored this plan suggested—that it is an excellent idea, and one which I prefer to the plan to turn the area into an original pioneer town as suggested by the <u>Utah Sons of Pioneers</u>—that I think their plan (the Utah Sons of Pioneers) could very well be carried out on the site of the "This is the Place Monument."

I suggested that Mr. Fabian call me later by telephone—that in the meantime I would talk this matter over with my counselors.

<u>Later:</u> Mr. Fabian called the office by telephone, and I told him that I had discussed our conversation with the brethren and they gave their approval for him to go ahead with the suggestion to be carried out on the site of the penitentiary area.

April 2, 1956. I telephoned to <u>Dr. O. Preston Robinson,</u>[10] <u>General Manager of the Deser[e]t News this morning</u>. He had submitted a suggestive editorial on the problem of [racial inequality, calling for gradual] <u>desegregation.</u>[11] I told him that I had no objection to the editorial's being printed as it now stands with the exception of the reference to segregation in the

<hr>

9. Harold Pegram Fabian (1885–1975) was a local attorney (Fabian and Clendenin) and prominent conservationist who, with John D. Rockefeller Jr., laid the groundwork for creating the Grand Teton National Park in Wyoming and the Jackson Hole Land Trust protecting 24,000 acres adjacent to the park. He was born in Salt Lake City and graduated from Yale (BA) and Harvard (LL.B). In 1959 he would become director of Utah State Parks and Recreation.

10. Oliver Preston Robinson (1903–90) was born in Farmington, about twenty miles north of Salt Lake City. He studied at BYU, received a PhD in marketing from New York University, and spent semesters abroad at Grenoble Alps University and Ludwig Maximilian University of Munich. He was general manager of the *Deseret News* from 1952 to 1964, then president of the British Mission. His wife, Christine Hinckley, was a sister of future apostle and church president Gordon B. Hinckley.

11. The editorial was headlined "Extremism Is Never the Answer." Coming on the heels of the US Supreme Court finding of 1954 that "separate educational facilities [are] … inherently unequal" (*Brown v. Board of Education of Topeka*, overturning the 1896 *Plessy v. Ferguson* doctrine of "separate but equal"), the *Deseret News* editorialized on

school system. I said that there is a different problem attached to this subject; for instance there may be district where the negro is in the majority; that there might be three or four white children. Inasmuch as the negro child is two or three grades below the white child of the same age, it would not be fair to force the few white children to attend—furthermore, the negro really prefers to attend a school for the colored people. I therefore instructed Dr. Robinson to leave the reference to the school room out of the editorial.

April 14, 1956, Los Angeles. The [first endowment] session [in the new Los Angeles temple] was very well conducted, and for the first time in the history of the Church the old-style presentation of the endowment ceremony was given by tape-recording rather than by persons enacting the different parts. It proved conclusively to us that the ceremony can be done very impressively, and that this manner of presentation will probably be used in all the Temples.

May 3, 1956. With many Church problems crowding my mind, I was unable to sleep after 3 o'clock this morning. I was up and dressed at 4 a.m. Came to the office at 6 a.m.[12]

May 31, 1956, 8:15 a.m. Met by appointment at his request Mr. John Wallace of Walker Bank Co.[13] We had a consultation on matters, one of which relates to Westminster College, of which Mr. Wallace is Chairman

---

April 3 that "once the inevitability of desegregation is generally accepted, the extremism on both sides can be lessened." See Garraty, *Quarrels*; Peterson, "Blindside," 4–20.

12. McKay often found sleep difficult in the early morning hours and used the time to go to his office or to the temple to ponder issues and pray. See Prince and Wright, *David O. McKay*, 39.

13. John McChrystal Wallace (1888–1973) graduated from the University of Utah and received an MBA from Harvard. At the end of World War I, he became a civilian aide to the US Secretary of the Army, having served in that branch of the military during the war. When he returned to Utah, he entered into banking and then politics as a member of the Utah State Senate; he was appointed mayor of Salt Lake City in February 1938 when his predecessor was being investigated for receiving bribes from gambling halls and brothels, for which Mayor E. B. Erwin was nevertheless later exonerated. "Mayor Erwin Resigns"; "John Wallace Named Mayor"; "Jury Returns Verdict," *Salt Lake Telegram*, Feb. 7, 19; Oct. 1, 1938.

of the Board. <u>They need some financial help.</u>[14] The Church has given them substantial assistance in the past, and will probably have to give them help again. I suggested to Mr. Wallace as he left that he take up a labor with our Baptist minister in the city. The other members of the ministerial association are rather cooperative, but the Baptist minister is very antagonistic. Mr. Wallace said he would take up a labor with him.

June 5, 1956, 8:30 a.m. to 10:30 a.m. <u>Courtesy call from Dr. Aziz S. Atiya,[15] President of the Institute of Coptic Studies, Cairo, Egypt.</u>

Dr. Atiya who gave the U[niversity] of U[tah] Commencement Address last evening, and Dr. A. Ray Olpin, according to appointment at Dr. Atiya's request, met me promptly at 8:30 o'clock as agreed following the commencement exercises last evening. I called President [J. Reuben] Clark in to meet Dr. Atiya.

Then followed <u>one of the most interesting conversations that we have ever had</u> with a visitor from a foreign country.

Dr. Atiya possesses a noble soul. He loves truth; he has sufficient courage and strength to accept it, and abide by it as he understands it. He is President of the Institute of Coptic Studies, Cairo, Egypt, and a member of the Coptic Christian Church, which he says was organized by St. Mark in the year 61 A.D. I asked Dr. Atiya if they believed that the young man who went into the Garden of Gethsemane on the night of Christ's betrayal with only a linen cloth about him, is the same John Mark[16] as founded the Church in Africa. He answered: "I am not a theologian, and I think I will not express a thought on that."

14. Westminster College dates back to 1875, the same year Brigham Young Academy (BYU) was founded. Originally known as the Presbyterian Preparatory School, it was owned and run by the Presbyterian Church until 1974. Continuing successfully as an independent college, in 2015 it was rated one of the best few hundred colleges in the country by the *Princeton Review*.

15. Aziz Suryal Atiya (1898–1988) studied in Europe, taught Coptic studies in Germany and Egypt, and in June 1956 was between engagements as a visiting professor at the University of Michigan and Columbia University. Three years later the University of Utah would hire him, and he would come to author twenty books and create the university's Middle East Center. He is most remembered for recovering in 1966 the papyri Joseph Smith used in 1835 to produce the Book of Abraham. Atiya helped arrange for the artifacts to be transferred from the archives of the Metropolitan Museum of Art in New York City to the LDS Church.

16. The New Testament twice refers to "John, whose surname was Mark" (Acts 12:12; 15:37).

Dr. Atiya speaks seven languages. President Clark asked him to give some sentences in the Coptic language, and he replied that he could read it, but he does not speak it very well. He gave the beginning of the Lord's Prayer in the Coptic language.

We anticipated having a twenty or thirty-minutes consultation, but it lasted one hour and a half! It was one of the most profitable and interesting conferences that we have ever had.

Dr. Atiya extended to me a cordial invitation to come to Cairo, either officially or personally, and he assured me a warm welcome.

I was very deeply impressed by Dr. Atiya—he is an outstanding man. His address at the University of Utah Commencement Exercises was excellent—he spoke distinctly and sincerely. He is a very learned man.

June 11, 1956, 8:15 a.m. Mr. Kilmer of the Maico Hearing Aid company came in. Decided to have the hearing aid fitted into glasses instead of wearing cord in my ear. (President McKay has a little difficulty in hearing certain persons whose voices are rather high in tone. One or two members of the Council speak too low for him, so he decided to get a hearing aid in order that he would not miss important matters being discussed at that meeting in particular—note by C[lare] M[iddlemiss])

June 14, 1956, First Presidency meeting. I reported a decision I made earlier this morning in the case of a woman who had married out of the church, and who had given birth to three children. Her first husband died. For the benefit of the children, she had consented to their adoption by a bishop and his wife, a childless couple. The Bishop avers that the children were given to them, not only for legal adoption, but also to be sealed to them for eternity. The mother of the children later married a member of the Church in the temple and bore the second husband children. She now wants the children by the first husband sealed to her and the second husband.

I stated that the sealing of the children to the bishop will not be annulled, and that the choice be left to the children to be made when they reach their majority.

July 3, 1956. President McKay made the statement this morning that he believes that civilization is just now beginning to enter into the spiritual realm; that with the discovery of the atomic energy, a whole new world has been opened up to man. Man is living more in the animal realm, true, he has houses with all the modern comforts, clean linen, beautiful clothing, and other luxuries, but, after all, he is pretty much animal.

Said that from the time he was a small child, he realized that there is a spiritual realm to which we may be responsive. As a young boy when he was exceedingly frightened at night, he got out of bed, and on his knees prayed to his Heavenly Father for protection. In answer to his prayer, he heard a voice distinctly say "Be not afraid; nothing will harm you." "This incident is as clear in my mind today as it was the night that it happened."

July 11, 1956. ... Bishop [Thorpe B.] Isaacson telephoned to say that he had been in touch with the [couple's] Bishop [who threatened to excommunicate the couple for inactivity] and told him that we have "90,000 inactive men in the Church whom we are trying through patience and loving kindness trying to bring back into activity—that he had no grounds for excommunicating these people."

July 20, 1956. At the meeting of the First Presidency and Presiding Bishopric this morning a letter was read by President McKay which was sent to him by a Provo City Councilman, indicating that the Stake Presidency and High Council of the East Provo Stake had gone on record [in a letter to a third party], recommending the candidacy of a certain individual for a political position. An objection was raised by the individual to whom the letter was written.

President McKay indicated that persons holding responsible positions in the Church should not use their title in connection with such recommendations, but may do so as a citizen of the community.

July 27, 1956, 8:45 a.m. Howard Barker and Harold W. Burton of the Church Building Committee called at the office. They submitted plans they have drawn up for the replica of the Salt Lake Theatre[17] which is to be built on the University of Utah campus.

---

17. The original Salt Lake Theatre, dubbed the "Cathedral of the West," was finished in 1861 on the north corner of State Street and First South. The $100,000 cost

After looking at these plans, we decided that there are a few changes that must be made. The plans are to be drawn up not as the Salt Lake Theatre was when it was torn down, but as it was when it was first built.

The architects are suggesting an enlargement, but <u>I suggested that they keep the cost to about a million and a half dollars</u>, even though we might have to reduce the seating capacity to 150 or 200 people.[18] However, we shall await for the return of Dr. Lowell Lees[19] from Europe before making a final decision in this matter.

We then held a <u>short discussion regarding the naming of the building</u>. We decided that <u>we shall call it The Salt Lake Memorial Theatre</u>.

August 20, 1956. Pres[ident] J. Reuben Clark, Jr. called me by telephone and stated that he was having difficulty with his side. The doctor has advised him to stay at home for a few days in order that this condition may clear up. President Clark asked me if it was all right with me if he remained at home for the next few days. He also asked how I was getting along. I told him I was in first rate condition. Pres[ident] Clark then said that he was asking for truth.[20] I told him that I was giving him the truth. I told him that I had had an upset stomach which had left me a little weak. I told him that I had seen the doctors Friday. They went over me. They could find nothing wrong, but they gave me a good lecture.

September 4, 1956. Honorable Ezra Taft Benson, United States Secretary

---

was supplemented by the sale of surplus army equipment left behind by Johnston's Army after the Utah War. One observer commented, "The building is itself a rare triumph of art and enterprise [and] it ranks ... in elegance of structure and finish, along with the opera houses and academies of music of Boston, New York, Philadelphia, Chicago, and Cincinnati." The theater was demolished in 1928. Arrington, *Great Basin Kingdom*, 211–13.

18. The structure that was ultimately built in 1961 (the centennial of the theater it replaced), named the Pioneer Memorial Theatre, seats 1,000 people in the main hall and 350 at a basement-level stage. It was funded by the Kennecott Copper Company, LDS Church, and Utah Legislature.

19. Charles Lowell Lees (1904–73) was chair of the Speech and Theatre Arts Department for twenty-one years beginning in 1943. He had graduated from the University of Utah, Northwestern University, and University of Wisconsin. In 1964 he left Utah to produce plays at the Pasadena Playhouse in California, afterward becoming a department chair at Rutgers University and then returning to Utah in 1971.

20. McKay had experienced bouts of illness during the years they had served as counselors under Presidents Grant and Smith. Hence President Clark's desire to know the "truth" about his condition. Clark thought the president had always pushed himself too hard.

of Agriculture, called me by telephone from Washington, D.C. Brother Benson stated that he had received a telegram from Senator Arthur V. Watkins asking him for a [campaign] statement regarding George Dewey Clyde[21] as to his ability as an administrator, and also to confirm a statement that Mr. Clyde had been offered a position in Washington, but that he had declined stating that he could better serve the people of his State by working on the upper Colorado River project. He also wanted Brother Benson to confirm that he knew Mr. Clyde, and that he is a Republican.

Brother Benson stated that he had called Brother Harold B. Lee today, and told him that he had drafted a wire giving a factual statement regarding the background of Mr. Clyde without endorsing him for any political office. Brother Lee and Brother Benson had concluded that they should get my judgment as to whether or not the sending of this draft would reflect upon the Church. Brother Benson was told that the letter which had been sent out by the Bishops had apparently boomeranged, but those who have been critical feel that it may do more good than harm.

Brother Benson said that George Dewey Clyde was employed in the Department [of Agriculture] and he could send a factual wire to Arthur V. Watkins simply indicating that he knew him, and then give the record so far as the department is concerned. Brother Benson stated that he had a draft of the wire before him and he would read it to me. Brother Benson desires to do the thing that is best for the Church. Brother Benson also stated that generally speaking he has refrained from subjecting himself in these Primary elections.

I told Brother Benson that I could see no objection to his sending a wire giving information about any person without casting any reflection on the Church. Brother Benson then read to me the draft of the wire he had prepared. ... Brother Benson then asked me if I thought there would be an unfavorable reaction from Senator [Wallace F.] Bennett about his above statement in connection with Senator Watkins. I told him that it was the truth, and I could not see how it could reflect in any way upon Senator Bennett.

---

21. George Dewey Clyde (1898–1972) would soon become governor (see note 7 above). He had been dean of the College of Engineering and Technology at Utah State Agricultural College and chief engineer for the US Soil Conservation Service, a division of the US Department of Agriculture.

Brother Benson stated that he would go ahead and send this reply to Senator Watkins. He stated that he would not make any reference to our conversation. I advised Brother Benson to send this reply to Senator Watkins as a straight reply. He can then use it as he pleases.

Brother Benson asked if this would do more harm than good, and I told him that I can't see how it could.

September 7, 1956. The purpose of their visit,[22] was to discuss <u>Ezra Taft Benson's telegram</u> giving a recommendation of <u>George Dewey Clyde</u>. They are not in favor of Benson's having done so. I told them that I have nothing to do with the matter, that if Orval Adams wishes to call Brother Benson and talk the issue over with him, he is perfectly free to do so. …

Bishop Thorpe B. Isaacson called me by telephone and stated that Governor [J. Bracken] Lee was terribly upset because he had heard that Brother Ezra Taft Benson had sent at Senator Arthur V. Watkins' request a telegram concerning his knowledge of the experience and background of George D. Clyde, Republican gubernatorial nominee for Governor. He had heard also that they are going to use the telegram in their po-litical campaign. Bishop Isaacson stated that he hated to see Brother Benson get mixed up in this thing. Bishop Isaacson and Bishop [Joseph L.] Wirthlin had been asked to go on television, but they had refused. Bishop Isaacson said that he had not seen the telegram which Brother Benson had sent, but the Governor's office told him what they heard of its contents. He also stated that the Governor's office had wanted to talk to me, but they had called Bishop Isaacson when they could not get in touch with me. Bishop Isaacson felt that Senator Watkins should not bring Brother Benson in on this deal. Bishop Isaacson said that they are going to try and get Brother Benson to send a telegram endorsing the character of Governor J. Bracken Lee. … Bishop Isaacson stated that the Governor's Office wanted to talk to me. He feels that if this telegram is used it will hurt Brother Benson and hurt the Church.

Bishop Isaacson stated that D[avid] A. Skeen is one of the master

---

22. The supporters of Governor J. Bracken Lee who came to complain to McKay about church interference in the election included the chair of the LDS Church Finance Committee Orval W. Adams, a prominent local attorney Clifford L. Ashton, and future CEO of Zions Bank Roy W. Simmons.

minds of this Clyde campaign. I asked him what he is the master mind of. Bishop Isaacson said that he is the man that made that deal with Bishop [LeGrand] Richards, and that he has caused a lot of trouble.[23] I told him that I could see how it would in view of the stationery he used. Bishop Isaacson said that they had wanted him to see Brother Richards about this letter, but he had refused to enter into it. Bishop Isaacson feels that when a Church Authority signs his name to something, it is used, and that is what they are going to do with the Benson telegram. He feels that the telegram is going to be broadcast over the state. I told Bishop Isaacson that Brother Benson has a right to send a telegram giving the facts concerning an individual. Bishop Isaacson said that he feels that it is going to do Benson a grave injustice. It will do Watkins and Clyde good. He stated again that the Governor is disturbed about it.

I told Bishop Isaacson that I would get in touch with Senator Watkins before calling the Governor's Office. ...

[Speaking with Arthur V. Watkins:] Senator Watkins stated that he had sent a wire to the Secretary of Agriculture [Ezra Taft Benson] asking him about Clyde's work in the Department of Agriculture, and if he had a knowledge about his background. Some had tried to say that Clyde is not a Republican. He knew that Brother Benson had known him as a Republican and had known him since school days. He stated that Brother Benson was not urging anyone to vote for Clyde, but he merely gives his record as a good administrator. Senator Watkins felt that Brother Benson discussed this move with the White House before he sent the wire. ...

Senator Watkins felt that Brother Benson would be very embarrassed to send any endorsement of Governor [J. Bracken] Lee.

I told Senator Watkins that this was a free country and Brother Benson could send the wire if he desired. ... I told Senator Watkins that this was a matter between him and Brother Benson, <u>and the Church has nothing to do with it.</u>

I told Senator Watkins that I had been asked to call the Governor's office but that I had wanted to talk to him first.[24] ...

---

23. Isaacson himself had lobbied Governor Lee to appoint apostle LeGrand Richards to the Utah State Board of Trustees, and apparently an endorsement was considered a proper reciprocal gesture of thanks. See Lythgoe, "Special Relationship," 80–81.

24. This incident is omitted from Benson's autobiographical *Cross Fire* and from the biography by Sheri L. Dew. However, J. Bracken Lee's biographer, Dennis L. Lythgoe,

September 10, 1956, 2:30 p.m. Left for <u>Huntsville</u>. The road is now paved right up to the gate of my farm. Upon arrival at the gate I got out of the car, walked over to the gate and <u>called to my horse "Sonny Boy"</u> who was out in the pasture with his head turned away from me. When I called, he picked up his head, turned around and started toward me with all the other horses in the field following him. I had several lumps of sugar in my pocket, and as the horses came up to me I gave each a lump of sugar. Then "Sonny Boy" came over and stood patiently waiting for me to put the halter and bridle on him. <u>I took a thirty-minute ride on "Sonny Boy."</u> Even on the highway with cars whizzing by he was in perfect form and did everything I wanted him to do—<u>I think he is now perfectly trained, and I am delighted with him!</u>[25]

October 23, 1956. Came out of the meeting to meet <u>His Excellency Manlio Brosio, Italian Ambassador to the United States</u> who is a guest of the US Department of Commerce. He was accompanied by the <u>Honorable Fortunato Anselmo, [a US citizen serving as] Italian [Vice] Consul in Salt Lake City</u>, and <u>William A. Lang, local man and President of the [Utah] World Trade Association</u>. Also <u>Mr. Jos[eph] Jerry Jeremy, District Manager, US Department of Commerce, Salt Lake City, Utah</u>.

At the conclusion of a very pleasant visit, Mr. Anselmo suggested that I <u>autograph a Book of Mormon for Ambassador Brosio</u>. I told them that we do not have an Italian copy of the Book of Mormon, but that I should be very pleased to inscribe an English copy.

His Excellency, Ambassador Brosio, <u>asked if the Church had any organizations in Italy</u>, and I answered that we did not. He then said, "While we are Catholic, there are other Protestants over there and <u>we would be pleased to help you organize</u>."

I told him that we would be glad to take advantage of that suggestion.

The Ambassador extended to me an invitation to call on him whenever I am in Washington.

<u>I think we should take steps to get the legal right to go into Italy</u>

---

found that the Benson telegram played a significant role in Lee's loss and added to the confusion and controversy of the 1956 race. See Lythgoe, *Let 'Em Holler,* 205–08.

25. Few things were dearer to his heart than a good horse. See McKay, *Home Memories,* 126–32.

before the Catholics know we are there. I felt that my interview with the Ambassador resulted in much good.[26] ...

4:30 p.m. Senator Arthur V. Watkins called at the office. He is very much worked up over the falsehoods he claims Governor J. Bracken Lee has been circulating, and has decide to speak over the radio tomorrow night at 6:30 and at 10 p.m. over television, answering Governor Lee. Senator Watkins said that he is almost prompted to sue the Governor for libel. The Senator seems quite secure in his feelings that Lee's actions will not defeat the Republican candidate. I expressed concern over the "split" Governor Lee had caused in the Republican party by running as an independent.[27]

October 25, 1956, 7:30 to 8:30. Had a consultation with John F. Fitzpatrick and Gus Backman who presented some statistics regarding polls that had been made on the election, and discussed civic developments, etc.

October 26, 1956, 10 to 11 a.m. Governor J. Bracken Lee called at the office by appointment at his request.

He said he would like to "bare his heart to me" and give his reasons for running as an independent candidate for the governorship.

He told at length the history of the Primary election and instances in which he thought he had been misrepresented, but his reasons for coming out as an independent he has already stated in public. ... He said he thinks the issue now is between him and [George Dewey] Clyde and not between [L. C.] Romney and him as I fear.

I told the Governor that I had supported him as Governor; admired his integrity, and especially his honesty in keeping his word. I cited an instance wherein he had kept his promise to me on a civic matter. "But," I said, "I was deeply grieved when you impugned the integrity and honesty

---

26. The church dedicated Italy for missionary work in 1850. By 1852 the Book of Mormon had been translated into Italian. The initial limited success soon evaporated, however, and in 1854 the mission closed. Roughly seventy converts immigrated to Utah that year. It was not until 1965 that missionaries in Switzerland and Germany were drawn down to form a new Italian Mission after a hundred-year hiatus. A new translation of the Book of Mormon was published the year before and then redone again in 1995.

27. The third candidate ended up hurting the Democratic aspirant, Lorenzo C. "Rennie" Romney. See footnote for March 6, 1956.

of President [Dwight D.] Eisenhower as reported in the press when you made a public appearance in New York."

Governor Lee said the press misrepresented him on that occasion; that he did not in his heart ever impugn President Eisenhower's integrity.

I told Governor Lee that I thought he could not be elected as Governor. I did not give him any encouragement, as I am sorry he has taken the stand he has.

Governor Lee assured me of his confidence in me, because, he said: "You are not a politician, but a Churchman."

We parted good friends, and later in the day he sent me the following letter, with clippings enclosed relating to his attack upon President Eisenhower.

While in the meeting was called to the telephone to answer a courtesy call from Ex-President Harry S. Truman. Mr. Truman explained that he had had a very busy schedule during his stay in Utah, and that at the moment he was at the Airport and would board the plane for the East within a few moments. Said he just wanted to call to say hello and to extend his best wishes and greetings; that he remembered with pleasure our most pleasant visit on the train between Salt Lake and Provo when he spoke at the Brigham Young University a year or so ago.[28]

October 31, 1956, 8:30 a.m. Met by appointment at her request Joan Lee, daughter of Governor J. Bracken Lee. She wanted to know if the rumor is true that the Church is sending out a letter asking people to vote against her Father. She said her father had received word that that is what is taking place.

I told her that she may tell her father that there is no truth whatever in this rumor; the Church has sent out letters urging people to get out and vote for the man of their choice, but no instructions whatever have been given as to how to vote.

---

28. Truman had been invited to speak October 6, 1952, as part of Wilkinson's program to have both parties represented that year. The US president referenced his grandfather, Solomon Young, who had run wagon trains from Independence, Missouri, to Salt Lake City in the 1860s. "Harry S. Truman, item 281—address at Brigham Young University," *The American Presidency Project*, www.presidency.ucsb.edu; cf. Will Bagley, "Rut Nuts Study Opening of the West," *Salt Lake Tribune*, Aug. 20, 2000.

November 5, 1956. Although the day was to have been free from appointments, I was in meeting most of the day with my counselors—Presidents [Stephen L.] Richards and [J. Reuben] Clark, <u>listening to reports by Dr. William F. Edwards</u>, economist on the <u>Church Welfare set-up</u> and <u>the condition of our Banks</u>.

November 6, 1956, 8:45 a.m. The First Presidency met with Wendell B. Mendenhall, Building Committee Chairman, Brother Harold W. Burton, and Brother Howard Barker regarding (1) <u>Genealogical Storage Vault and archives building</u> ...

I called Dr. William F. Edwards at B.Y.U. and told him that we felt it would be a good thing if he would give to the three Presidents of our banks the facts connected with the present small earning power of these institutions.

Dr. Edwards stated that the men were acquainted with the figures as they had secured the figures for him.

I asked Doctor Edwards if these men realize how little they have made at the banks. Dr. Edwards said that it might be a very good thing to let them see the final charts, etc. he had worked out.

I told Dr. Edwards that he gave a very impressive picture on this phase of the work and that I wanted him to know that I appreciated his work. Dr. Edwards told me that he felt the Brethren here were entitled to the best assistance.

I asked Dr. Edwards about compensation for the work he has been doing for the Church. Dr. Edwards said that he had incurred expenses that he had charged against the Church in the amount of $1,000.00 for the two years that he had been making the Church survey. He felt that this was all that he is entitled to. I told Dr. Edwards that I would see him again on this matter as I should prefer it not being this way, because his services have been invaluable to the Church.

It was decided that Dr. Edwards would be in Salt Lake the following Thursday, November 8th. He stated that he would have the bank figures with him, and would be available on Thursday at 3:30 p.m.

November 7, 1956. A <u>Mrs. LeRoy Goodwin, of Ely, Nevada</u> called at the office. She brought with her a clipping from a Nevada paper showing a picture of President McKay and quoting from him on Unions, etc. This had been used as a political ad in the Nevada papers. Mrs. Goodwin thought that President McKay should be advised of this. She was informed that Pres[ident] McKay had not given permission for his name and picture to be used. He was unaware of this until a day or two before the election when someone sent him a copy of the ad.

Mrs. Goodwin was informed by the secretary that President McKay had had nothing whatever to do with this propaganda used by these political people.

November 8, 1956, 3:30 p.m. to 6:30 p.m. Dr. W[illia]m F. Edwards reported to the First Presidency his investigation of our Financial Organizations and the Welfare organization, etc. Brother Edwards has done a masterful job, he and his associates, and the Presidency expressed to him their deep appreciation for his services. He has asked no financial remuneration for his labors, although he spent hours, days, and weeks in this work.

Yesterday, at the First Presidency's suggestion Brother Edwards met with the managers of our three banks and presented to them the detail of recommendations which he gave to the First Presidency. He later reported that his meeting with these brethren was in every way satisfactory.

November 9, 1956, 8 a.m. Met by appointment at his request Mr. John M. Wallace[,] president of Walker Bank]. He very sincerely pointed out the advantages of the church's becoming associated with the Trans-American Banking Corporation[29] with which the Walker Bank has [just] merged. This is a three or four billion dollar organization. One of the advantages is that Church influence would dominate these Western States in this financial world. I appreciated Mr. Wallace's frank and sincere interest. ...

11 a.m.– Bishop Thorpe Isaacson of the Presiding Bishopric reported

---

29. The Transamerica Corporation, a holding company for banks and insurance companies, acquired Walker Bank in February 1956, three months before Congress passed an antitrust law preventing such purchases. Transamerica soon had to divest itself of the Bank of America, and in 1958 the remaining banks in the conglomerate were separated into a new corporation called Firstamerica, which later operated its banks under the name First Interstate. See Arrington, "Banking and Finance in Utah," 30; "Transamerica Corporation," *Encyclopedia Britannica*.

to <u>me a remark that had been made</u> concerning his <u>political support of a</u> <u>certain candidate</u>. Bishop Isaacson said there is not a word of truth in the statement that has been made.

November 14, 1956, 3:30 p.m. <u>Conference with Dr. William F. Edwards.</u> Dr. Edwards has just <u>completed the investigation of our financial organi-</u> <u>zations</u>, and has made his reports to the First Presidency. I told him that we now express our appreciation of his labors, and that he and his asso-ciates are <u>released from their assignment with the gratitude, appreciation,</u> <u>and commendation of the First Presidency</u>.

I said to him: "It is now our duty to put all of your recommendations into effect—the reorganizations to be made, etc." I then said, "Brother Edwards, if I were you, and you were I, and you desired to place me in a position in the Church where your recommendations could be most ef-fectively adopted for the good of the Church, where would you put me?"

Dr. Edwards answered: "I usually try to answer your questions, Brother McKay, but I cannot give an answer to that."

I said: "I want you to be confidential with me now and help me work this out."

We then spent an hour going over some of the Church's problems.

November 16, 1956, 8:15 a.m. Received a <u>courtesy call</u> from <u>Gover-</u> <u>nor-elect George Dewey Clyde</u>. I was <u>impressed</u> with Brother Clyde's <u>sincerity, solidity, and with his desire to do the right thing as Governor</u> <u>of the State</u>. ...

3:30 p.m.—Senator <u>Arthur V. Watkins</u> called at the office. He re-ported that he is going to Hawaii on a mission for the government, because it seems that <u>the Community influence down there is becoming</u> <u>a source of worry and threatening to control the political situation there</u>. The committees of Congress are going down there to investigate.

We also discussed the <u>matter of the site for the new Federal Build-</u> <u>ing</u> here in Salt Lake City. Three sites are under consideration—one on North Temple—one in town, and one at Ft. Douglas. Senator Watkins said "Let's hold the matter off for further consideration."

November 22, 1956, Chicago. While at [daughter] Lou Jean's I received a telephone call from Elder Harold B. Lee, who was enroute to a [stake] Conference appointment. He said that he had received an invitation from the Union Pacific Railroad to act as a member of the Board of Directors of that Company, and he wanted to know if it were agreeable to me for him to accept. I gave my approval of his acceptance of this appointment. I later called by long distance President J. Reuben Clark, who said that Brother Lee had spoken to him about the matter before his departure, and that he had given his approval of this appointment, and suggested that he call me.

November 23, 1956. At the Railroad Station, according to previous arrangements, I met Brother David M. Kennedy,[30] first counselor in the Chicago Stake Presidency, Vice-President of the Continental Illinois National Bank & Trust Company, one of the six largest banks in the United States.

I discussed with Brother Kennedy (1) Church Bank matters, including the advisability of the Church banks joining Trans-American Banking Corporation through the Walker Bank. Brother Kennedy, who is a nationally recognized authority on banking, does not favor the Church's making such a merger. He thinks our better opportunity would be to keep our banks independent of these larger companies.

(2) Brother Kennedy does favor our merging the three church banks—First National, Zion's Savings Bank & Trust Company, and Utah Savings & Trust.

(3) He does not favor selling to [Utah Savings & Trust president] Herbert Snow the Church stock in the Utah Savings & Trust Company. "By doing so," said he, "it makes it possible for Herbert Snow to resell to the merger and double his money."

(4) Brother Kennedy informed me confidentially that he had just been offered the position of President of the Continental Illinois National

---

30. David Matthew Kennedy (1906–96) was born in Randolph, Utah, and died in Salt Lake City. He began his education at church-owned Weber College, then earned master's and law degrees from the Stonier Graduate School of Banking at Rutgers University and George Washington University. He worked with the Federal Reserve for fifteen years to 1945. From 1969 to 1971 he was the US Secretary of the Treasury under the Nixon administration. At the time of this entry, he was CEO of the Continental Illinois Bank. See Hickman, *David Matthew Kennedy*.

Bank & Trust Company of Chicago, and he said that at the meeting the next day he was going to tell the Board he would accept the position.

December 3, 1956, 10 a.m. <u>Called Dr. O. Preston Robinson</u> into my office and expressed to him my great displeasure at <u>the leading editorial which appeared in the Deseret News last Saturday, finding fault with the President of the United States</u>. I stated to him that there was not one constructive suggestion in the editorial.

December 4, 1956. I called Elder Mark E. Petersen by telephone. He had just returned from attending a stake conference in California. Brother Petersen asked me about my trip to Florida, and I told him that I had had a great trip; that it was interesting and successful in every way.

I then told Elder Petersen that when I returned home Saturday night, my attention was called to the leading editorial in the Deseret News. Brother Petersen stated that he had not seen this editorial as yet. I told Brother Petersen that I should like to talk to him about it, that I had called Dr. O. Preston Robinson in to my office yesterday and had talked to him about it. In my conversation with Dr. Robinson I told him that the editorial was unfit for the Deseret News.

Brother Petersen inquired as to the subject of the editorial, and I told him that it was an editorial criticizing the President of the United States. He stated that he was amazed. I told him that I was greatly grieved, and that this is the last thing we ought to be doing. I also stated that there is not one constructive thought in the whole editorial.

Brother Petersen stated that in a [board of directors] meeting recently, Frank Browning had mentioned that some little criticism ought to be made. However, Brother Petersen had not taken it seriously as so little was said about it. He was surprised that anyone else had taken it so seriously, and I answered that it was a very unfortunate leading editorial.

I stated to Brother Petersen that my thought in calling him was to see that Dr. Robinson submits these editorials to the committee before publishing. Brother Petersen stated that the Committee meets regularly, and that he is supposed to submit them to the Committee before publishing. However, they have not submitted every editorial, but that they should submit all important editorials.

I said that I thought I should let him know what had happened, and Brother Petersen said that he would talk to Dr. Robinson.

I mentioned further that the President of the United States would be grieved if he read this editorial and it is possible that somebody will send it to him. I stated that maybe we should send a note to the President, however, that I would leave the matter in his hands.

December 6, 1956. Pres[ident] A. Ray Olpin of the University of Utah called by telephone. He said that he was upset over the article which had appeared yesterday morning in the Salt Lake Tribune regarding the building of a replica of the Old Salt Lake Theatre on the University of Utah campus.[31] Pres[ident] Olpin stated that he had called several people Wednesday evening regarding this matter, and he had felt sure that the story had been "killed."

Pres[ident] Olpin stated that they had been instructed to get the individual signatures of the Regents on this request for a deficit appropriation. They also were to get the individual signatures of the members of the Board of Examiners. Therefore, they wrote a letter explaining this matter and Mr. Morgan, Vice-President of the University of Utah and Pres[ident] Olpin personally carried the letter to every Regent in this area and got telegrams from the Regents out of the area with the exception of [Utah Secretary of State] LaMont Toronto who is also a member of the Board of Examiners. They talked to him, and he said he would sign it if they brought it up to him.

At the suggestion of Governor [J. Bracken] Lee the signing of this paper had been timed so that it would not go to the official meeting of the Board. They had all agreed to this. Then the publicity was to be released properly. Pres[ident] Olpin said that yesterday he had talked to the Attorney General and told him that if they acted on this appropriation, it would

---

31. The student newspaper weighed in the next day, arguing that the new theatre should have a modern design in keeping with the "progressive ideas" of the state's pioneer ancestors, and that it it should not be a replica of the former downtown theatre. (Ultimately a replica is what was built.) Continuing, the editorial argued that the theater should not be controlled by the LDS Church. What surprised people, and McKay had wanted to keep confidential, was that the church was committing $1 million toward construction against the state's half million. "The Salt Lake Theatre Heritage: A Hard Decision to Make," *Daily Utah Chronicle*, Jan. 7, 1957.

be kept confidential until such time as everything was in order, and then the proper thing was for the Church to make the announcement in the Church Section. The Attorney General had agreed with Pres[ident] Olpin. … Pres[ident] Olpin received a call from Mr. Joe Fitzpatrick who covers the news for the Capitol Building for the Tribune. Joe Fitzpatrick began to ask Pres[ident] Olpin some pointed questions. Pres[ident] Olpin asked him where he was getting this information, and he stated that he knew all about it. He stated that he had seen the letter on file in the Secretary of State's office. I said that that did not authorize anyone to look over such papers. Pres[ident] Olpin then called Mr. Toronto at his home. Mr. Toronto stated that any papers addressed to the Board of Examiners were considered public papers as far as he was concerned. Pres[ident] Olpin told him that this would be the worst thing that could happen and told him that it would have to be stopped. Pres[ident] Olpin then called John Fitz-patrick, father of Joe Fitzpatrick. … He also told him that he would not be surprised if the people who had offered to make contributions would withdraw them if this was published at this time. Mr. Fitzpatrick then stated that he would do what he could to see that this article would not be published if the Deseret News did not publish it. …

I told Dr. Olpin that the matter had been very embarrassing to me. I had not seen the newspaper article myself, but when I went to my meeting this morning, one of my counselors called my attention to it. I told Dr. Olpin that I had not taken my associates into my confidence on this matter until I knew where we stood. …

Dr. Olpin said that the Deseret News intended to run a picture of the Old Salt Lake Theatre. I told Dr. Olpin now that the whole story would be out. I also stated to him that our position may change regarding the collect-ing of the million and a half dollars. Dr. Olpin said that that is what he told these people last night and that he had spent the majority of his life getting people to cooperate on matters, and that this publicity is the very worst thing that could be done in connection with a large project of this type.

I told Dr. Olpin that we would now see what develops, and then we would know what to do. …

I told Dr. Olpin that this whole announcement is a blunder. A mis-take can be rectified, but a blunder cannot. Dr. Olpin apologized. I told him that he was not responsible.

December 12, 1956, 8:30 a.m. By appointment at his request met Brother Charles Atkinson,[32] retired athletic coach of the Brigham Young University. He came in to state his grievances at being replaced as coach at the B.Y.U. After listening to his story, I advised him to see President [Ernest L.] Wilkinson.

Proposed Purchase of Land Near Swiss Temple

At the request of President McKay, Elder Gordon B. Hinckley explained the proposal of [Swiss Temple] President [Samuel E.] Bringhurst that additional land near the Temple in Switzerland be purchased in order to control its future use and to protect the area from encroachment by commercial and industrial uses. Brother Hinckley said that a part of the forest land, privately owned, a lot 150 x 305 feet, across the street west from the Temple President's home, and a vacant lot 130 x 202 feet, across the street south from the Temple President's home, together totaling 1.65 acres, can be purchased for $42,500. It is estimated that the timber on the forest land can be sold off and a part of the investment recovered.

After consideration, it was agreed that President Bringhurst be authorized to negotiate for the purchase of the two pieces and that, if they are obtained, restrictions upon their use be imposed by covenant, and that they may then be sold subject to the restrictive covenants, which will protect the Temple property from adverse development of these pieces of land.

December 21, 1956. The proposal, now seemingly widely favored by groups of business men in Salt Lake City, Ogden and Provo, that the site for the new Federal Building in Salt Lake City be the block between Main and State Streets, from North Temple northward, was considered. The interests of Zion's Securities[33] and the presentation of Manager

---

32. Charles "Chick" Atkinson (1918–62) had been BYU's head football coach since 1949. Arriving in Provo from Pocatello, Idaho, where he had been a high school coach, he improved the program somewhat but over an eight-year period amassed a win–loss record of 18–49. Although the public statements said he had resigned, he had actually been fired. In looking for a replacement, Wilkinson felt pressured to expand the search to include non-Mormons, which ended in Harold Kopp being hired. Bergera and Priddis, *Brigham Young University*, 277.

33. Since 1922 the church-owned Zions Securities Corporation had accumulated property and leased it commercially as a for-profit real estate entity. See Quinn, *Wealth and Corporate Power*, 75–76, 84, 87, 112–13, 138, 446.

Peirce Brady were considered. The effect of the project upon property in the general area and with relation to the future needs of the Church for land was reviewed. After discussion, it was agreed that the position of Zion's Securities favoring the project be sustained.

7   Educational and Political Dilemmas, 1957

Because justified or not, thousands of people, young and old, will [otherwise] be imbued with the thought that the assurance given by the First Presidency ... was not kept. ... Once confidence is lost, the foundation of society begins to crumble. —July 11, 1957

January 8, 1957, 8:00 a.m. to 8:20 a.m. Viewed the <u>Los Angeles Temple film</u>. This film was shown by KSL in the Projection Room, Church Office Building. I decided that some changes should be made in this film, and arranged for an appointment Monday morning, January 14, 1957, at 8:00 a.m., to have this film taken again. ...

I called Elder Harold B. Lee by telephone and stated that a request had come asking that one of the General Authorities give the opening prayer of the [Utah] Legislature when it opens Monday. I asked Brother Lee if he would take care of this matter for us. He said that he would be pleased to do anything we desired. I mentioned to him that I think it is appropriate, and we appreciate their asking for a member of the brethren to do this duty. He asked me regarding the time, etc., and I told him that we would contact the Legislature and have them get in touch with him.

Brother Lee then said that he understood that Clare [Middlemiss], my secretary, is in the hospital, but that it is his understanding that she is making some improvement. I told him that I did not know about it until I returned from my trip out of town. I also mentioned that Clare had been ill when I left for my trip and that I thought we should send her to a clinic somewhere. I also stated that she has been working too hard and that she is an excellent secretary.

January 14, 1957, 7:15 a.m. to 8:00 a.m. Met with <u>Mr. Gus Backman</u> at his request regarding civic matters.

<u>Mr. Backman told me confidentially about the attitude of some of our non-Mormon friends here in the city</u> who are rather jealous, apparently, about the fact that nearly all of our civic matters in the city and in the state and in the nation are now controlled by members of the Church,—our city government particularly under the police force, our state government, the Governor and a majority of the legislature, and nationally, all of our senators and representatives are members of the Church. Some who are not sympathetic with us are spreading the rumor that we are trying to push Mormonism down their throats, that the Chief of Police [W. Cleon Skousen] is a little too energetic in enforcing the law in clubs and other places.

I told Brother Backman that certainly he would not wish us to tell the police to ease up on the enforcement of law. Brother Backman said, "No, you could not do that." I asked Brother Backman to use his influence to assure them that the Mormons are not going to try to force our religion on anyone, but we are just simply wanting to obey the law and do our duty. I felt that perhaps we can influence some of our Gentile friends to satisfy some of those who are jealous and assure them that we are not going to take advantage of our position.

January 26, 1957, 10:30 a.m. to 11:15 a.m. At his request I had an appointment with <u>President Ernest L. Wilkinson.</u> I feel that President Wilkinson is jumping into the responsibilities of his office too readily and too energetically. I told Pres[ident] Wilkinson that I fear he might have a setback if he is not careful.[1]

January 27, 1957. During the afternoon Sister [Emma Ray] McKay and I drove to Ogden and <u>paid our respects to Sister David Eccles (Ellen Stoddard Eccles) on her ninetieth birthday.</u>[2] Brother Eccles has been

---

1. Wilkinson had suffered a heart attack on October 6, 1956, and had not reported back to his office until January.

2. Ellen E. Stoddard (1867–1957) was a month away from her death on February 25, 1957. As a seventeen-year-old girl in 1885, she married thirty-five-year-old David Eccles, making her the second of three wives in a polygamous family. Her new husband was a business partner of her father, George E. Stoddard. For more on the Eccles family, see footnote at August 7, 1952.

dead forty-four years, and his widow has reared all of their family. They have had only one death in the entire family, and that was a grandchild. All their nine children are alive. I was pleased to see Royal Eccles there, representing the other family.[3] I met Howard Stoddard,[4] a nephew, who flew out especially to pay his tribute. While George Eccles was helping me on with my coat, he commented, "Well, I think we children had better pay more attention to the Word of Wisdom than we have done." I said, "Yes, I thought so too." There was considerable odor of liquor there. Sister Eccles and the boys were very courteous and considerate.

February 7, 1957, meeting of First Presidency and Twelve. During Council Meeting this morning I made reference to the uprising at the penitentiary at the Point of the Mountain last night, in which some of our L.D.S. boys were held as hostages, they having been there playing basketball with the inmates at the time the uprising occurred. I asked the Brethren if they thought it was a good thing for our boys in Priesthood quorums and auxiliaries, or even members of the Church, to go to the penitentiary to participate in games with the prisoners.

The Brethren of the Council were agreed that it was not a good practice. President Joseph Fielding Smith mentioned that the Twelve had considered the matter this morning, and had anticipated bringing it to the attention of this Council. President Smith moved, which motion was seconded and unanimously approved, that we go on record as being opposed to our boys going to the penitentiary to play basketball with the inmates there.

February 8, 1957, 8:30 to 9:00 a.m. The First Presidency met with [Salt Lake City Police] Chief Cleon Skousen.[5]

3. Royal Eccles (1884–1963) was born to David Eccles and Bertha Marie Jensen (1857–1935), David's first wife. Royal served in Germany for the LDS Church and went to school at the University of Michigan, earning a law degree there, and practiced law in Ogden. He died of a heart attack on a South American cruise off the coast of Chile.

4. As the title of Richard D. Poll's biography notes (*Howard J. Stoddard: Founder of the Michigan State Bank*, Michigan State University Press, 1980), Stoddard (1922–95) founded a prominent Midwestern bank. His sister Ellen was David Eccles's second wife.

5. After spending sixteen years with the FBI and four at BYU as an assistant professor of speech, Skousen became police chief in 1955, appointed by Mayor Adiel F. Stewart. It came about because of an increase in crime in Salt Lake City and public sentiment that a law-and-order man like Skousen would do something about it.

February 11, 1957, 8:30 a.m. Met by appointment at his request [Salt Lake City] <u>Mayor Adiel Stewart</u>.[6] He wanted to know if the city fathers are moving along the right line in [how they are] <u>trying to clean up the city of lawbreakers, especially with regard to the dispensing of liquor through private lockers</u> by some of the [private] clubs here in the city.

I told Mayor Stewart that we not only approve but consider it their duty to enforce the law. I further said that I think <u>Chief Cleon Skousen is the best Chief of Police we have had for many a day</u>, and that he is doing what he thinks is right, and that he (Mayor Stewart) should uphold him in what he is trying to do.

February 15, 1957. Some man who would not give his name and who sounded like a <u>Jew called at 1:15 p.m.</u> He said: "Tell President McKay that the 'Professor' called, and if <u>he and his stooges do not keep out of other peoples' business there is going to be trouble—buying up railroads,</u> mining companies, etc."

I [Clare Middlemiss] answered: "The church has not bought up railroads, mining companies, etc."

"Oh, yes; they have, and if they don't stop there will be trouble."

The secretary answered: "You are insulting to say the least" and hung up the receiver.

February 19, 1957, in conversation with Stephen L Richards. President Richards stated that he had something to report to me. He had attended Church at Logandale[7] Sunday upon invitation of the people, and while there he learned that the members of the Church had just finished one of these "store strikes," and had tried to live for two weeks on the supplies they had on hand, not buying anything from the store.

I asked President Richards how this had affected the little store

---

6. Adiel Fitzgerald Stewart (1897–1960) was beginning the first of four terms as mayor, having acquired previous government experience as chair of the Salt Lake County Commission. He was part-owner of Stewart Coal Company, Stewart Brothers Sand and Gravel Products, and Acme Lime Products, as well as president of Cinder Block Inc. and Plateau Gas and Oil Company. In the area of church activity he was president of the Salt Lake Temple View Stake and a board member for the *Deseret News*.

7. Logandale, Nevada, is halfway between St. George and Las Vegas in the Moapa Valley, which was settled by Mormons in 1864.

in that locality, and he answered that the store did not sell much for two weeks. Then President Richards went on to say further that he had learned that the members of the Church in Las Vegas are just about to go on a "store strike," and live for a period of two weeks without buying anything from the store. I told President Richards to tell the people at this place not to do it. These projects have gone to the extreme, and have been carried too far. President Richards felt that the Welfare Committee should send out instructions pertaining to this, that the people in the stakes have apparently gotten this idea from some of the Welfare Committee visitors at the Stake Conferences. He felt that it would be better for the General Welfare Committee to send out instructions. He said it is his feeling that these visitors had gone to the [stake] Conferences with such enthusiasm that the people had obtained these ideas from them.

I said that I feel that the rumors which have been circulated about the revelation I had supposedly had has also contributed to this situation. Pres[ident] Richards said that this is all stimulating to a feeling that the end of things is very near.[8]

February 20, 1957, 7:30 a.m. Met by appointment at their request Mess[ieu]rs Gus P. Backman and John F. Fitzpatrick.

We considered some pending bills before the State Legislature in the light of which would be of the greatest benefit to the State of Utah. Also considered affairs pertaining to our municipalities.

March 5, 1957, in conversation with Ernest L. Wilkinson. President Wilkinson said that there are rumors that he is going to have some difficulty before the [Utah] Legislature with regard to the Eminent Domain bill.[9] He feels that he might need my help and, if necessary, would like me to

---

8. This sentiment grew out of the paranoia McKay describes here, that the apocalypse was at hand and precautions and practice runs were needed. This was but one of many manifestations of how some in the church interpreted the dangers of the Cold War era. Some bishops and stake presidents named individual families during church services and asked them to live off of their home storage, without shopping for a week, to ascertain their preparedness.

9. Post-war growth in education made the expansion of college campuses necessary. Wilkinson led the charge in lobbying for eminent domain, earning him the sobriquet Julius Seizure.

write a letter to Senator Orval Hafen.[10] If he needs my help, President Wilkinson will make a draft of the type of letter he wishes and get it to me. He feels that the bill will come up tomorrow.

I told President Wilkinson that I had tried to keep away from all this business, but it has been impossible. <u>I mentioned to him further that I had heard a report that the Church, and especially the President of the Church, are being accused of every ill that has come to the Legislature.</u> I indicated to President Wilkinson that if he could get by without a letter from me it would be wiser. He said that if he found out during the day that B.Y.U. is in grave danger of losing out, he will deliver to me or to my secretary a draft of a letter which would be suitable for me to send to Senator Hafen of the Senate.

March 21, 1957. Approved of the purchase of a <u>copy machine</u> for the office of the First Presidency, including my own personal office. This machine miraculously will make a copy in 3 seconds of any letter, document, newspaper clipping, etc. I am sure it will prove of great assistance in expediting the work of the two offices.

April 7, 1957, excerpt from minutes of First Presidency and Twelve meeting, January 31, 1957. Consideration was given to a memorandum from the Twelve calling attention to an action of this Council taken some time ago to the effect that when ordaining boys or men to the office of deacon, the Aaronic Priesthood should first be conferred, and then the person should be ordained to the specific office in the priesthood; that when ordaining brethren to the office of elder, the same procedure should be followed—namely, that the Melchizedek Priesthood should be conferred upon the person, and then that he should be ordained to the specific office in the Melchizedek Priesthood. The Brethren mention that apparently no instruction has gone to the temples in regard to this matter.

President McKay said that at the time of the April General Conference [April 7] there will be held a meeting of the presidents of temples at which time this information will be given them.

---

10. Orval Hafen (1903–64) was an attorney in St. George, who in two years would become president of the Utah State Senate. His son Bruce C. Hafen would become president of Ricks College (BYU–Idaho) and a member of the First Quorum of Seventy.

The Brethren then raised the question as to how aggressive they should be in making the change.

The President said that the information might be conveyed by the Brethren of the General Authorities when they attend quarterly conferences, and that they should set the example when performing ordinations themselves.

April 8, 1957, 9 a.m. Presided at a very important meeting held in the Board Room on the Main Floor of the Church Offices with the following: Presidents Stephen L. Richards and J. Reuben Clark, Jr.; President Ernest L. Wilkinson of the Brigham Young University; Dr. John L. Clarke,[11] President of Ricks College, Rexburg [Idaho]; and the following Stake Presidents ...

This meeting was held in the interest of the future of Ricks College with emphasis on the advisability of moving the College from Rexburg to Idaho Falls.

President Wilkinson presented facts relating to this very important problem, and each of the Stake Presidents present expressed their opinions and viewpoints about the matter.[12]

No decision was reached on this problem. The meeting commenced at 10 a.m. and did not conclude until 2:10 p.m.[13]

April 9, 1957. President Ernest L. Wilkinson called by telephone and

---

11. John L. Clarke (1905–91) was born in American Fork, Utah, and after his mission to Great Britain and master's degree from BYU in political science, he taught in the church's Seminary and Institute programs until 1944, when he became president of Ricks College under Franklin L. West, Church Commissioner of Education. Clarke retired in 1971.

12. Wilkinson dictated a lengthy account of this meeting in his diary (see entry for April 8, 1957). According to his sanguine report, the stake presidents all gave candid views and McKay therefore cautioned confidentially of all those present. The only sour note, according to Wilkinson, came from Rexburg Stake president Delbert Taylor. After the meeting Taylor wrote to the First Presidency opining about the unfairness of the situation, since Wilkinson had been given adequate time to arrange his facts and prepare his presentation, while the Rexburg supporters felt the matter had been sprung on them, and they had had no time to prepare a coherent response. See Hemming, "Ricks College," 66.

13. This fateful gathering set in motion a series of conflicts, ill will, and intense partisan feelings that quickly turned bitter. The issue had been swirling around the Church Education System as early as 1954, always championed by Wilkinson, the arch villain in the controversy, according to Rexburg residents.

asked whether or not I had any instructions for him since my meeting with the First Presidency this morning.

I asked President Wilkinson if he had said anything to any of the brethren about looking for a building site up there, and he stated that he had mentioned the matter to President Cecil E. Hart[14] of the South Idaho Falls Stake. I stated that we were all agreed that we should take immediate action to secure a building site. President Wilkinson then said that he had also talked to a Delbert Groberg.[15] President Hart had recommended him as a good member of the Church and an excellent real estate man. Mr. Groberg will look around for a suitable site without disclosing anything.

I told President Wilkinson that President Stephen L. Richards is acquainted with a prominent banker in the Idaho Falls area. I also stated that it is my understanding that Mr. Gadsby of the Utah Power and Light Co[mpany] is a member of the Governing Board of the Atomic Energy Plant [National Reactor Testing Station]. President Wilkinson said that Mr. Gadsby is an expert in that particular field. Then I mentioned further that President Stephen L. Richards has been instructed to get in touch with George Gadsby and ask him to confidentially contact this banker and see what they can do for us. President Wilkinson felt that if the information gets out on this matter that we will have to pay more for the property. ...

I further informed President Wilkinson that I had instructed President Delbert G. Taylor[16] not to take up the petition he had in mind.

---

14. Cecil Elmo Hart (1896–1987) was born in Moscow, Idaho, served a mission to France, and became president of church-owned Idaho Radio Corporation in Idaho Falls. He was a stake president for eighteen years. In the 1960s he became president the French Mission, and in the early 1970s he was president of the Idaho Falls temple.

15. Delbert Valentine Groberg (1906–2004), who was born on Valentines Day, was raised by an uncle and aunt after his parents died when he was three. He graduated from BYU and became a real estate appraiser and founder of a title company in Idaho Falls. In the late 1970s he became president of the Idaho Falls temple. His son John H. Groberg was ordained a member of the First Quorum of Seventy.

16. Delbert Guy Taylor (1894–1977) was the vociferous Rexburg stake president who, having just returned from overseeing the Eastern States Mission, took up the gauntlet in opposing Wilkinson on closing the church's college in Rexburg. As a young man he had attended Ricks College and Utah State Agricultural College. After filling a mission, he had raised sheep for a while, but eventually established a small empire of car dealerships throughout Idaho, headquartered at Taylor Chevrolet Company on College Avenue in Rexburg.

President Wilkinson said that President Taylor has been critical of him for some years on the theory that President Wilkinson has been doing a lot more for the "Y" than for Ricks College.[17]

I said that I knew the situation and that I also knew President Taylor. I told him that we would work along these lines and that we hoped to get their contributions and get some land up there. I thanked President Wilkinson for [telephone] calling.

April 10, 1957, 8:30 a.m. Elder Jay A. Quealy, Jr.[18], President of the Honolulu Stake, Honolulu. Called at the office. We discussed matters pertaining to the restoring of Joseph F. Smith[19] to activity which will have to await the outcome of my talking with other people involved in this case.

April 11, 1957, 2:15 p.m. Met by appointment at her request Mrs. Thorpe B. Isaacson. She came to seek my advice regarding whether or not she should take a trip to Europe with a lady friend. I told her that this is a decision for her and her husband to decide; however, that if Bishop Isaacson approves, I could see no reason why she should not go.

April 16, 1957. I called Dr. O. Preston Robinson regarding the two highway projects in Salt Lake City, the widening of the 7th East Street and the new Freeway planned in the West part of the city. …

I told Dr. Robinson that I think a favorable comment from the Deseret News on the highway problem at this time would be a good thing. Dr. Robinson said that he would look into the matter. …

---

17. Wilkinson was Commissioner of Church Education as well as president of BYU.

18. Jay Ambrose Quealy (1919–92) later served as president of the Hong Kong Mission. Born in San Francisco and a graduate of Stanford University, he came to own several businesses, including Hawaii Air Conditioning and Hawaii Hotel and Restaurant Supply. In his spare time, he enjoyed outrigger canoes and yacht racing.

19. Released over sexual orientation (see the entry for July 10, 1957), Joseph F. Smith (1899–1964)—not to be confused with the church president of that name—had served as Presiding Patriarch only four years, 1942–46. He was otherwise a speech and drama professor at the University of Utah. After being released from his ecclesiastical office, he and his family (he had a wife and seven children) moved away from Utah, and he became chair of the Department of Speech at the University of Hawaii. He had earlier served a mission there. See Bates and Smith, *Lost Legacy*, 173–200. Middlemiss incorrectly identified him here and elsewhere as Joseph F. Smith III. Although he was a grandson of Joseph F. Smith, his father's name was Hyrum M. Smith.

<u>I repeated again to Dr. Robinson that I thought it would be a good thing for the Deseret News to help this project along by printing something favorable.</u>

April 18, 1957. Brother [Richard L.] Evans then said that he was making reservations, tourist class, for his <u>trip to Europe</u> to fulfill his Rotary assignment and that of the Church in Switzerland. However, I <u>advised him to go first class</u>—that it would be better for the Church and for the Rotary Club for him to travel in safety and comfort. ...

I called Elder Delbert G. Taylor, President of the Rexburg Stake and told him that I was very much disappointed last evening to learn that the Rexburg Radio had broadcast the fact that discussions had been held regarding the transfer of Ricks College from Rexburg to Idaho Falls.

President Taylor said that he was greatly disappointed also—that he had given instructions to his counselors and others concerned not to give anything out. However, when he returned from Butte, Montana at 7:30 last evening, he found out that the news had been given over the Radio.

Brother Taylor then read the statement that was made over the Radio which mentioned that an emergency meeting of the Board had been called to discuss the report that Ricks College may be moved to Idaho Falls—that the Chamber of Commerce is being called into the matter to see what they can do about the matter, etc.

I mentioned that it seems that publicity is being given to the entire affair which is a violation of the instructions that had been given. President Taylor said he did not know how the news leaked out, nor from whence it had emanated; that he had instructed the brethren to keep it quiet.

I said that if the decision be made to move the College, then the property around Idaho Falls will rise to outlandish prices.

Brother Taylor stated that the brethren up there would still like to have the meeting in Salt Lake, Tuesday, April 23rd, as planned. I said that an announcement also had been given over the radio this morning that there would be a meeting of the Rexburg Presidency and others with the General Authorities next Tuesday. Brother Taylor said that he had talked to the other two stake presidencies and invited Brother [Cecil E.] Hart,

President of Ricks [John L. Clarke], and Dr. [Howard E.] Salisbury[20] to attend the meeting in Salt Lake. It was decided that the meeting should be conducted as planned next Tuesday.[21]

April 25, 1957. Mr. Ste[ph]en M. Meikle, President of Idaho Bank of Commerce at Rexburg, Idaho called me by telephone. He is also a member of the High Council in that Stake.

Mr. Meikle said he just wanted to tell me the situation regarding business conditions in Rexburg since the announcement was made that investigation is being made regarding the removal of Ricks College from Rexburg, Idaho to Idaho Falls. He stated that a few years ago [in 1954] there was some unrest in this area regarding Ricks College. However, the people were content when a telegram was received under my signature which was sent to [Grover Hemming, president of] the 84th Quorum of Seventies [in Rexburg]. The telegram read as follows: "Rest assured there will be no change in Ricks College." (This telegram, however, referred to the change from a four-year to a two-year college and had nothing to do with the move to Idaho Falls.)[22] At that time the members of the community went forward and made a lot of commitments.

Recently when the Ricks College matter came up again it was indicated that the people were not making enough progress in Rexburg in building the town up. The bank as a business institution went out and made a survey to see if the community was lagging somewhere in their plans. The following facts were revealed: In the last five years 217 new homes have been built at a value of $4,181,000, 82 new businesses have

---

20. Howard Earl Salisbury (1911–77) was chair of the Fine Arts and Humanities Department at Ricks College. Originally from Springville, Utah, he had been in the navy during World War II and had graduated from BYU. In 1977 he helped draft a pamphlet, *Prologue*, that defended homosexuals, and that apparently ended his career at the church school. See, for instance, Della Dale Smith–Pistelli, "About Howard Earl Salisbury," *Geni: A MyHeritage Company*, www.geni.com.

21. Two days earlier the Church Board of Education "authorized and approved the transfer of Ricks College from Rexburg to Idaho Falls at such time as the Administration shall deem best after a meeting with the Stake Presidencies of Ricks College" (copy of minutes in editor's possession).

22. When rumors circulated again about an impending relocation, there was renewed interest in McKay's 1954 telegram, which would haunt the decision-making process and become a central theme at the Church Board of Education discussion on May 26, 1957. Hemming, "Ricks College," 70.

been built at a value of $3,975,000. This values together around eight million dollars. Many of the homes were built with the idea that they would accommodate students. Business in this area has been thrown into quite a condition since the announcement regarding the possible removal of Ricks College from Rexburg to Idaho Falls. The people have planned on making their payments on their homes with the extra money they receive from renting to college students. Mr. Meikle stated that a number of cancellations have been made on loans for homes, etc. since the news has been received regarding the transfer of the college.

Mr. Meikle said that he wondered if I was aware of these conditions in Rexburg. He also mentioned that in his position in the bank and stake he is charged with a great deal of responsibility and is in a position to know the business conditions, etc. in that area. Mr. Meikle stated further that they are trying to meet this situation as bravely and fairly as possible, but they are interested in this matter in a business and financial way, and wanted me to have this information in mind when a decision is made.

I thanked him for calling.

April 27, 1957. This morning at 8:30 I met by appointment at their request <u>Dr. C. Lowell Lees</u> and <u>Mr. Lee Flint</u> of the Kennecott Copper Company <u>pertaining to matters associated with the building of the Salt Lake Memorial Theatre.</u> We decided that the $500,000 appropriated by the State had been mated by the $600,000 raised by Kennecott Copper Company and the Church, and <u>that now we could proceed to have architectural plans drawn for the Salt Lake Memorial Theatre. ...</u>

<u>Following our discussion the three of us went up to the University of Utah campus, and chose the site preferred of the three sites set aside upon which it may be built.</u>

<u>We decided that the next step will be to prepare the plans, economizing in every way in the erection of this building.</u>[23]

April 29, 1957. Bishop Joseph L. Wirthlin called me by telephone and asked me the Church's position on the following question: He stated that he had been asked to-day if it would be proper for L.D.S. girls to purchase

---

23. For more on this, see Hodson, *Crisis on Campus*, 186–222.

crosses to wear. It is Bishop Wirthlin's understanding that there is a company downtown which is pushing the selling of these crosses to girls.

I told Bishop Wirthlin that this is purely Catholic and Latter-day Saint girls should not purchase and wear them. I stated further that this was a Catholic form of worship. They use images, crosses, etc. Our worship should be in our hearts.

Bishop Wirthlin said that this had been his opinion, but he felt that he should check with me before making a statement.

April 30, 1957, 11:45 a.m. Met by appointment at their request President Delbert G. Taylor of the Rexburg Stake, Bishop [Howard E.] Salisbury of Ricks College, and Mr. S[teven] M. Meikle, President of the Idaho Bank of Commerce, Rexburg, Idaho.[24]

These men presented reasons for retaining Ricks College in Rexburg. They have six reasons which they presented in a convincing manner.

May 8, 1957. This morning we left Cedar City [Utah] at 5:30 o'clock, and I drove directly to Salt Lake arriving there at 10:15 a.m.

An interesting incident happened when we stopped at Cedar City yesterday afternoon. Three boys about 10 years of age came running over to the gas station and said, "Hello President McKay." I greeted them and then asked them how they knew that I was there at the gas station, and they answered: "Oh, the Bishop told us that he saw you, so we came over to say hello to you."

Nothing pleases me more than to have these children come around—to shake their hands, and to partake of their sincere spirit is always a joy to me.

May 9, 1957. President Jay A. Quealy, Jr. of the Honolulu Stake telephoned from Honolulu.

Said that Joseph F. Smith's son's farewell is this coming Sunday night. The missionary son is requsting that his father speak at the farewell. President Quealy asked if he could give Brother Smith permission to speak on this occasion.

---

24. See also Wilkinson diary, Apr. 28, 1957.

I answered that I suppose there is nothing we can do but let him speak—so permission was granted.

May 17, 1957, 8:30 a.m. This morning my counselors—Presidents [Stephen L.] Richards and [J. Reuben] Clark—viewed the M.I.A. film, "How Near to the Angels"[25] which was shown in the Church Office Projection Room.

We decided that the film is very excellent, but it was my judgment that it would be better not to use it for showing in the Missions of the Church as it will only intensify the problem that our young girls are now facing with relation to meeting young men who are worthy to take them to the Temple. There is a question in our minds whether it is best for them to go through life unmarried rather than marry outside of the Church as we feel there are many good men in the world that they could marry with the possibility that they may bring them into the Church later.

May 18, 1957, at 8:30. This morning, I met by appointment President Ernest L. Wilkinson, of the Brigham Young University. He gave review of meetings and actions taken recently regarding the proposed removal of Ricks College from Rexburg to Idaho Falls.

He presented the exaggerated statements of the Rexburg people regarding Rexburg, and pointed out wherein they had exaggerated facts.

After considering all matters, and realizing that the Executive Committee and the Church Board of Education had now referred the entire matter to the President of the Church, I decided to make a trip to Rexburg to personally investigate the whole matter, I invited President Wilkinson to go with me. It was decided that we shall leave next Tuesday morning at 6 o'clock. …

Following a morning of consultations, and work at the office, I returned home where I had lunch and then left for Huntsville. Had quite a time all afternoon working on the farm—ran the mowing machine, cutting the grass which had grown very high during the rains of the past few

---

25. This was one of the first movies produced by the BYU Motion Picture Studio, founded in 1953 under former Disney animator Wetzel Orson Whitaker. The plot of *How Near to the Angels* centered on a teenage girl's attempt to choose a husband from a limited number of LDS boys who were worthy to be married in the temple. It ran forty minutes and was available in black-and-white and color.

days. One <u>thing, I found that I am not as young as I used to be—work</u> <u>on the farm is more tiring to me than it formerly was, so I suppose I shall</u> <u>have to admit that "old age" is taking over.</u>

May 19, 1957. <u>Spent several hours in the [Salt Lake] Temple this morn-</u> <u>ing in meditation, study, and planning for the Church.</u>

May 21, 1957, 6 a.m. Left Salt Lake City for Rexburg, Idaho in company with Ernest L. Wilkinson, President of the Brigham Young University. We were driven by Brother Allan Acomb of the Purchasing Department of the Church.

We arrived in Idaho Falls at 9:30 a.m., where we met by appointment Elder Cecil E. Hart, President of the South Idaho Falls Stake. Pres[ident] Hart took us to inspect some sites that might be used for the Ricks College providing it be moved to Idaho Falls.

Following the inspection of property, the three of us drove to Rexburg where we very much surprised the President of the College, (Elder John L. Clarke).

While we were in the hallway someone telephoned the Radio station and Chamber of Commerce. The Secretary of the Chamber of Commerce extended an invitation for me to attend their luncheon meeting and speak to them, but I sent word to him that we were at the college for a routine checkup of the buildings and would, therefore, not be able to accept his invitation.

Within a few moments of our arrival at the College, President Delbert G. Taylor, President of the Rexburg Stake and his counselors appeared on the scene,[26] they having received a telephone message that I was at the college, so he and his counselors accompanied us on our inspection tour. We also met the Mayor of Rexburg and the faculty members of the College.

I went to Rexburg having in mind three things:

(1) Whether the buildings, if vacated, would be left standing as ghosts to irritate the people who would be disappointed because of the removal of the school.

(2) Whether the claim of those who wanted to keep the College at

26. See also Wilkinson diary, May 21, 1957.

Rexburg be true that very few new buildings, if any, would be needed, and that there would be no expense in keeping them.

(3) Whether the great expense of moving the College would be justifiable.

Therefore, with these three things in mind we inspected each of the buildings—we climbed upstairs and downstairs in building after building. As soon as the students found out we were visiting in their buildings they came out and wanted to shake hands and have pictures taken—some groups gathered together and sang "We Thank Thee O God for a Prophet" and other songs of greeting.

We spent 5 and one-half hours in inspecting these buildings! I was worried about President Wilkinson's climbing the stairways as he has just gotten over a serious heart attack. However, he seemed to take it all right.

My first observation convinced me that one building for which $45,000 has been appropriated is not worth that amount of expenditure, and that after the $45,000 had been expended it would still be of little value.

The Administration Building, which is well constructed, would probably be of little use unless the local School Board could use it, a probability which is even now being considered. Besides this, the Library is located on the top floor of the building, a very unwise situation, which proves the necessity of the erection of a new building for the Library.

There is also need of a new cafeteria building and a new dormitory for the boys. A new chemistry and physics building is needed—part of the present quarters for the student of these subjects is still in one of the discarded army barracks.

The new Recreation and Assembly Building which has just been completed at a cost of nearly $700,000, is a beautiful structure. This building would not stand as a ghost building and would be used by the Stake as an Assembly Hall.

Much to my surprise, it would be less expensive to have the College in Idaho Falls than in Rexburg.[27] Arrived home at 7:45 p.m.!

Although this was one of the busiest days of my life—having

---

27. He seems to mean that all things being equal—absent the existing infrastructure in Rexburg—it would cost less to build and maintain a school in Idaho Falls. A few days later (see the entry for July 11), he clarifies that "it is not worth the cost to move Ricks College to Idaho Falls."

travelled 400 miles and then spent 6 hours in inspecting the buildings and consulting with those concerned about the College—I felt it was one of the most worthwhile and profitable trips I have ever taken!

May 22, 1957, 3:45 to 4:45 p.m. Eldred G. Smith, Patriarch to the Church, called at the office and gave his side of what seems to him to have been a censure given to him by Elders Spencer Kimball and LeGrand Richards.

He then took a great deal of time referring to unpleasant conditions existing in his office. He said that inasmuch as Sister Timmons was employed as a secretary in the office of the Patriarch before he (Brother Smith) was ordained as Patriarch to the Church, she still "assumes" the right to make his appointments. I answered: "Well, haven't you asked her to make your appointments, and to keep a record of them?" He admitted that that was the case.

I further said to Brother Smith: "That spirit should not exist in any office in the Church, and you should plan the affairs of your office so that there should be complete harmony and good will."

Brother Smith said that he had another matter about which he wished to talk to me, but inasmuch as an hour's time had gone by, and that I had an appointment, I told him that he would have to see me at some future time. ...

Bishop Joseph L. Wirthlin called by telephone and stated that a question had come up regarding baptisms. He reported that we are not using the [Salt Lake] Tabernacle font for this purpose now, but we are sending the people to Churches which have fonts in the various wards in the area.

Bishop Wirthlin then asked if we should permit people to perform baptisms in private swimming pools to avoid their traveling distances to some of the fonts in our buildings. I told Bishop Wirthlin that I felt that we should not permit this; that if this practice is permitted, we shall have no way of knowing what extremes might develop in this regard.

I instructed Bishop Wirthlin to inform the people that we do not look with favor on this practice. Baptismal fonts in our buildings have been dedicated for this purpose, and public swimming pools should not be used for this purpose.

I mentioned to Bishop Wirthlin further that it would not hurt any-one to travel a distance for baptism. It would be worth it, and they would remember it. I said to him that I had to walk a half mile to Spring Creek [north of Huntsville] when I was baptized, and I have never forgotten it.

June 1, 1957, at 7:30. This morning left from the Hotel Utah [for Rexburg] in company with Elder Marion G. Romney[28] and Ernest Wilkinson, with Allan Acomb acting as chauffeur for the party.

We arrived at Idaho Falls at 11:30, took lunch at the Bonneville Hotel. We then proceeded to Rexburg, Idaho where we arrived just in time for the meeting at 1:30 p.m.

All 15 Stake Presidents and six specially invited civic leaders from Rexburg were present ...

Brother Howard E. Salisbury representing the group at Rexburg, presented their case for keeping the college at Rexburg. He took some two hours to do so. He stated that the issue is "Ricks College" and pref-aced his argument primarily on the fact that the Brethren should "not remove the ancient landmark which their fathers have set," and that Ricks College could not be moved without shattering its history and traditions. He had figures to show that Rexburg is "not stagnant." To prove this he showed bank deposits, postal savings deposits, and many other things.

At the conclusion of his remarks I called on President Ernest L. Wilkinson, President of the Brigham Young University, to give his side of the question. He went through some 32 charts showing that in 1888, when Ricks College was founded, there were six times as many Mor-mons in Idaho Falls, whereas today there are three times [that] many Mormons in Idaho Falls. He said that over a substantial period of years, the cost of a college at Rexburg for the same number of students would be higher, because in Rexburg the Church would be obligated to build a number of dormitories. President Wilkinson took three hours presenting the facts he had gathered concerning the Ricks College.

Mayor Fred Smith of Rexburg made rather a violent attack on

---

28. Romney had attended Ricks College in 1917–18 and was a star athlete, and his father had been the school president for thirteen years, 1917–30. Because of that, lo-cals assumed Romney would side with them. But when it came down to it, he supported the move. Hemming, "Ricks College," 73.

President Wilkinson, accusing him of being concerned with the financial set-up rather than with "saving souls." Following the Mayor's remarks I arose and defended President Wilkinson and answered the accusations of the Mayor. I said that I had been very concerned over the accusations made by Rexburg people against those of Idaho Falls, and said that according to the records of the Church, members in Idaho Falls were just as faithful as those in Rexburg. (Before going to Rexburg, we had looked at the tithing records, and found that each of the stakes in Idaho Falls were paying more than either of the stakes in Rexburg.)[29]

The meeting came to an end at about 6:30. It was agreed by everyone that no one would give publicity to what happened at the meeting. President Taylor of the Rexburg Stake himself proposed that nothing be said and that he would say nothing.

I asked each person present at the meeting to personally write me as to his views of what should be done about Ricks College. As to the Stake Presidents, I authorized them to consult with their counselors.

Near Accident on Way Home

On the way home between Idaho Falls and Pocatello, as we were traveling south, a woman driver of a car coming north, attempted to pass some other cars going north by driving around them on the left, but she could not get ahead of them, and instead of putting on her brakes and getting behind them in her right lane of traffic, at the last moment turned to the left and shot right out in front of us. It was a miracle it was not a head-on collision. Brother Acomb, our chauffeur, was very cool and managed the car so that we drove between the car driven by the woman and the on-coming traffic which was in proper position. We were all driving around 60 miles per hour, and we could have had a serious collision had it not been averted. So sure was Elder Romney, who was riding with us, that we were going to get it, that he remarked, as he saw the car coming toward us, "THIS IS IT!" We all commented several times during the trip home that it was providential that we had had no accident. We were all thankful that we pulled out of that serious situation.

We arrived in Salt Lake City about 12:30 p.m., after eating at Maddox [Ranch House Restaurant] in Brigham City.

---

29. See Wilkinson diary, June 1, 1957.

No decision as yet has been made regarding the moving of Ricks College to Idaho Falls, but I think the people of Rexburg themselves are now ready to accept a decision.

We all agreed that it was a very beneficial trip.

June 13, 1957, 7:45 a.m. <u>Dr. Lowell Bennion, Director of the University of Utah Institute of Religion</u> called at the office. He came in the interest of <u>Paul Anderson and Joyce Marshall</u>, a young couple who wish to be married in the Temple, but the young lady has been unable to obtain a recommend as it is rumored that she has negro blood in her veins. Miss Marshall's family live in Fillmore, Utah, and a rumor has persisted in this town for years to the effect that the grandmother and the great-grand-mother were colored people. However, there is no evidence to prove this. The family has contacted former missionaries and others who knew the family and were well acquainted with them, and they deny all this, and say they knew the family to be white and that they have no colored char-acteristics whatsoever. There is no evidence of negro blood in the parents, grand-parents, or great-grandmother who had blue eyes and blond hair.

<u>Later telephoned</u> to <u>Elder Marion G. Romney</u> of the Council of the Twelve at Chicago, California, <u>Brother Arthur Brown, formerly President of the Millard Stake</u> where the Marshall family lives, who were visiting in Lynwood, California, <u>Dr. Lowell L. Bennion, Brother Paul Anderson at Fillmore, Utah</u>, bridegroom, and <u>Brother Olpin, President of the Millard Stake</u>, regarding the case referred to above by Dr. Bennion. ...

I called President Ray D. Olpin of the Millard Stake at Fillmore, Utah, and he later reached me in the evening at my home, and I discussed with him the matters of a recommend for the young couple—Paul Anderson and Joyce Marshall. Since there is no absolute proof of Negro blood, I am going to give Miss Marshall the benefit of doubt. "All that you have (Pres-ident Olpin) and that the others have is hearsay. So if they are otherwise worthy, you may inform the Bishop to issue a recommend to this young couple." President Olpin answered, "Oh, thank you, because they are wor-thy! We haven't any better people than the Marshall family in the ward."

June 28, 1957. Arose at 4 a.m. Could not sleep—many problems to solve. ...
<u>9:45 to 10:15 a.m.</u> ... the First Presidency went over dozens of letters

on Ricks College for and against the removal of Ricks College to Idaho Falls. The letters were turned over to [p]resident Richards for his perusal and information.[30]

July 10, 1957, 8:45 a.m.
Case of Joseph F. Smith III
Bishop Lowell Christensen of the Waikiki Ward, Honolulu Stake, called at the office. He asked if Joseph F. Smith III may be given responsibility and assignment in the Ward. Since no official action to excommunicate or disfellowship Brother Smith had ever been taken, and in view of the steadfast faithfulness of his wife and children, and the punishment Brother Smith has suffered; and that he has confessed, asked to be forgiven, and has forsaken his sins, the duty to forgive him was recognized. I presented this matter at our meeting of the First Presidency this morning, and it was agreed that Bishop Christensen be so informed.

Later, when Bishop Christensen returned to the office, I told him of our decision this morning—that Brother Smith is to be forgiven and that he may now be given responsibility in the Ward.[31]

July 11, 1957, 9 to 11 a.m. First Presidency's meeting was held. Most of the time of this meeting was devoted to a discussion on the Ricks college. During the meeting I received a telephone call from President Stephen L. Richards (having put in the call before coming to the meeting) and I presented to him, as I also presented to President [J. Reuben] Clark, my conclusion that it is not worth the cost to move Ricks College to Idaho Falls;[32] that the plan proposed by President [Ernest L.] Wilkinson at the latest meeting of the Board to make Ricks College a part of the Brigham Young University has merit; that the school will grow where it is and that the support of the people of the area will be given and the honor of the General Authorities of the Church in their minds will be preserved.

---

30. See also Wilkinson diary, June 28, 1957.

31. See entries for Apr. 10, Dec. 9, 1957; Apr. 13, 1958.

32. Richards's tone, evident in the transcript of the telephone conversation included in the diary but omitted here, suggests that he felt the decision was premature, and from Wilkinson's diary (July 11, 21, 1957; April 10, 1958) it appears that the reversal ruffled McKay's other counselor too. Contrast McKay's statement in Quinn, *Elder Statesman,* 163; Hemming, "Ricks College," 74–76.

Pres[ident] Richards phoned me from Bellingham, Washington, where he was visiting his son. ...

President Richards agreed to the announcement being made[,] that it is decided by the Executive Committee and the First Presidency that Ricks College will not be moved to Idaho Falls. President Richards thought it would be well to call Mr. D. F. Richards[33] of Idaho Falls and give the announcement first to him. It was agreed that the Executive Committee of the Brigham Young University be asked to meet with the First Presidency at 11 o'clock today to present this decision to them, and to make the suggestion that the announcement be released, as intended earlier, through the newspaper and radio station in Idaho Falls.[34] ...

At 4:30 p.m. I received an unexpected call from <u>Delbert G. Taylor, President of the Rexburg Stake, his counselor, Walter F. Ririe, S. M. Meikle, Sr., member of the Stake High Council and Mr. Art Porter who had piloted the group by airplane from Rexburg to Salt Lake City</u>.

<u>I told them that the decision had been made this morning that Ricks College would not be moved from Rexburg</u>. They were overjoyed with the news, and said that they had not heard the news before they left Rexburg.

I told them that I was happy about the decision, and felt that the right decision had been made.[35]

Note: Patriarch to the Church—Duties of

The following was considered at the meeting of the First Presidency this morning:

---

33. D. F. Richards (1890–1969) was president of the American National Bank of Idaho Falls and director of the Salt Lake City branch of the Federal Reserve Bank of San Francisco.

34. This turnabout shocked Wilkinson. He later complained to Church Historian Leonard Arrington that "before [McKay] made his final decision against moving Ricks College ... a group of his old-time friends from Rexburg, with whom I understand he had hunted in his early days, called on him at his home, bringing pheasants and other wild game which President McKay very much liked. The next day or so he announced his decision not to remove Ricks College. These personal relations were very strong with him. ... I was told later by one of the Authorities that had I gone ahead and dug the basement in Idaho Falls, the decision would not have been reversed" (Wilkinson to Arrington, Dec. 14, 1974, copy in my possession).

35. McKay stated to the Church Board of Education this same day, "Because, justified or not, thousands of people, young and old, will [otherwise] be imbued with the thought that the assurance given by the First Presidency ... was not kept. ... Once confidence is lost, the foundation of society begins to crumble."

The report of Elders Spencer W. Kimball and LeGrand Richards on their interviews with Patriarch Eldred G. Smith was read.[36]

President McKay stated that the Patriarch to the Church is under the direction of the First Presidency; he is appointed by the First Presidency and approved by the other General Authorities of the Church and sustained by them; that he is ordained and set apart by the First Presidency to be Patriarch to the Church; and that it is his duty to be in his office ready to respond to any application, during reasonable hours each day, of any worthy member of the Church for a patriarchal blessing. Formerly when transportation was not so good as it is today the patriarch traveled around the Church giving blessings. The patriarch today should be in his office every day at regular hours whether he receive any calls or not and should be there when people come. He is not under the direction of the Twelve, except as the Twelve may be authorized to visit or give instructions by appointment of the First Presidency. A blessing given by a stake patriarch is a stake patriarch's blessing, and not a blessing of the Patriarch to the Church.

President McKay reported that the Patriarch had come for an interview during which he informed President McKay that he felt that he (the Patriarch) had been neglected by the First Presidency, in not having been invited to the weekly meetings and to sit by the First Presidency. President McKay explained to him that the weekly meetings of the First Presidency and the Council of the Twelve deal with secular and spiritual matters relative to the administration of the stakes, wards, and missions,

36. Kimball's and Richards's report, dated June 20, 1957, recommended: "I. We believe that the people of the Church, particularly those from the missions, are entitled to service from the Patriarch and generally at their convenience. II. We believe that he should give blessings to all who come to him and not send them to Stake Patriarchs except in [the] most unusual situations; at least until the load is heavier. III. If the arbitrary age of twelve is not correct, we believe he should be instructed and that where people come without recommends, they might be obtained[,] something like [how] temple recommends are given under similar circumstances. IV. Try as hard as we can, we seem to be unable to mention his work or make the slightest suggestion without his keen resentment. We are willing to continue as you indicated 'until further notice' but you may feel that someone else could deal with him without his belligerency. V. We believe if he were to receive definite instruction from the First Presidency as to what he should do, it might help him to get settled down to his work. VI. We believe that the small amount of time he is giving is partly responsible for the spirit he possesses and if he were expected to serve devotedly as do others of the brethren that he might catch the spirit and be happy." Typed excerpt in Quinn Papers, Yale University.

and that the Patriarch's work is to give blessings and is not administrative. President McKay told him that the matter would be considered with the First Presidency.

President McKay also reported that the Patriarch said that he had not been consulted in the selection of his secretary and that he resents the attitude of his secretary.

July 18, 1957, 10:45 a.m. Brother Spencer W. Kimball of the Council of the Twelve came in and explained to me the circumstances under which he had a throat operation by Dr. Hayes Martin, eminent cancer specialist in New York in January 1957. ...

Now, since one cord of his throat is still raw after four months, Dr. Leland Cowan, a specialist of this city, is urging that Brother Kimball return to New York and let Dr. Martin, cancer specialist, look at his throat again. If Dr. Martin is alarmed he may wish to operate again which would further extend Brother Kimball's incapacity.

Brother Kimball then said that his work in the Church is more important to him than his life; that he does not fear death, but he dreads the loss of his voice permanently more than anything as it will make it impossible for him to carry on his church work. Said that to lose permanently his voice seems to him to be death, or worse than death.

For these reasons Brother Kimball seeks my advice as to whether or not he should return to New York for further treatment with a possibility of losing his voice, or should he use his voice and expend it, making it last as long as it will.

I told Brother Kimball that if he feels that he has faith enough to be healed, that we shall join him in that faith, and ask the Lord to heal him, but he must ever keep in mind the fundamental principle that the Lord expects us to use the wisdom he gives us, and do all we can first. Then, when we have done everything, and used every means at our command, we have a right to seek his help.

Now, the wisdom of the doctors suggest that he have another examination, and probably an operation. I said that I think he should take their advice, go back to New York, and be examined by this specialist. If he recommends an operation, and that operation deprives Brother Kimball of his voice, he has lost only one means of expression; he still has all his other faculties and can serve the Lord for many years. I referred to Helen Keller who had no voice, no eyesight, and no hearing, yet she became one of the greatest women of the world, and is still rendering service to humanity at an advanced age.

So my advice to Brother Kimball is that he take the advice of his doctors.[37] ...

Miss Barnett called and would like to know if it is all right for a returned missionary who is now serving as a stake missionary (she has been through the Temple and wears garments) to appear on a float in the "Days of 47" Parade in a bathing suit. The float will feature "Fashions for Tall Girls". She had called Elder [Delbert L.] Stapley and he had referred her to President McKay's office. Miss Barnett would like to know the stand or opinion of the church in this case.

President McKay instructed his secretary to tell Miss Barnett that it would be better and more appropriate if she would let somebody else appear in the bathing suit, and she appear in one of the other costumes or fashions for tall girls. Miss Barnett was appreciative of the advice, and said she could easily comply with the suggestions and appear in another costume.

July 26, 1957, 8:25 a.m. Brother Hugh B. Brown called at the office and reported that he had had an interview with the parents of a prospective missionary. It has been disclosed that the young man in question has had an affair with a girl from the Northwest; she is pregnant. The parents of the girl and parents of the boy have made a settlement—they do not want to marry; the father of the boy has agreed to pay all the hospital expenses and let it go at that.

It was later learned that the girl has made arrangements to adopt the baby out—she does not want to keep it.

My first reaction to this case was that the boy and girl owe the unborn child something, and that is a legitimate birth and name. Whether the boy and the girl want to marry and whether or not the parents want it, this couple should marry and give the child a name.[38]

---

37. See Kimball and Kimball, *Spencer W. Kimball*, 263–65, 301–12. Kimball first encountered problems with his throat in 1950. After being given a healing blessing, it temporarily resolved itself, and its recrudescence in December 1956 worried him to distraction.

38. Until recently (2014) the church advised unwed pregnant women to consider giving the child up for adoption to Mormon parents through LDS Family Services.

In consultation with the young man's father I learned that the girl, the young man, nor the parents of the girl and the young man, want such an arrangement as I suggested. It was therefore decided that the girl should go ahead with her adoption plans.

August 20, 1957. At the First Presidency's meeting this morning, the inquiry of the General Superintendency of the Sunday School about office space for Director J. Spencer Cornwall[39] of the Tabernacle Choir under the plan for reassignment of rooms in the [Church Administration] Building at 50 North Main Street was presented.

I stated that Brother Cornwall is writing a book entitled "One Hundred Years of the Choir." The manuscript is being considered in the light of the title. I stated that of several recommendations submitted for a successor to Brother Cornwall, Brother Waite of the Brigham Young University is most favored, though he is now away for two years working on a scholarship. After consideration, it was agreed that Director Cornwall be released and be given a pension, and that <u>Richard P. Condie[40] be appointed to succeed him as director</u> of the Tabernacle Choir, and that the understanding with him be that <u>the appointment is limited</u>.

August 22, 1957. The following statement was made by President McKay at Council meeting held in the Salt Lake Temple today—the first meeting since the adjournment for the summer months:

President McKay said that he had been thinking today how blessed we are as leaders of the Church compared with what the early Apostles had to endure under the circumstances under which they labored, and expressed appreciation of this opportunity of meeting with the Brethren

---

39. Joseph Spencer Cornwall (1888–1983) was born in Millcreek, Salt Lake County. As he conducted the choir for twenty-three years (1935–57), he slowly transformed it from a local choir to a national treasure that performed at US inaugurations and on world tours. He received his education at Northwestern University and was superintendent of music for Salt Lake City Schools before directing the choir.

40. Richard P. Condie (1898–1985), of Springville, Utah, studied at BYU and the New England Conservatory of Music. He performed in operas as a tenor for several years in Europe. Back home again in Utah, he taught at the McCune School of Music, Utah State University, and BYU. He became Assistant Choir Director in 1937 and was promoted to senior director twenty years later, remaining in that position to his retirement in 1974.

in Council Meeting again. In that early day the word Christian was a term of reproach. They were separated by some scores of miles, and in some cases hundreds of miles, with very scanty means of transportation. He mentioned that we have just been listening now to the reports of work that the Brethren have done during the vacation, which was made possible because of the means of transportation, telephone, radio, and the means we have at hand of keeping the Saints in harmony with the tenets of the Church, instead of introducing false ideas. He commended the Brethren for having touched so many members of the Church even during their vacations, and expressed appreciation for the means of transportation and communication that the Lord has given us in this day.

August 23, 1957, 8:30 this morning. Salt Lake City] Mayor Adiel F. Stewart and Commissioner [Grant] Burbidge met me by appointment at their request. They wanted to know if the Church had any views on the Home Rule[41] plan for city government, stating that they do not want to do anything that would be contrary to the ideals of the Church.

I answered, "Since you as members of the committee are promoting the idea I suggest that you get the necessary number of petitioners, and put the question on the ballot next November."

They answered "that is a good suggestion."

At 11:20 this morning Brother Earl J. Glade came in on the same question as the Mayor asked regarding Home Rule. He asked what his attitude should be on the Home Rule issue as suggested by the committee headed by Mr. [Joseph] Rosenblatt.

I told Brother Glade the same thing that I told Mayor Stewart and Commissioner Burbidge—that it is a self-constituted committee and that they should take the responsibility of getting the question on the ballot next November. Brother Glade answered—"Well, that is a sensible solution."

---

41. The concept of municipal home rule was that the city would have the last say on anything pertaining to the city, and the state legislature would have control only over issues of statewide jurisdiction. As two historians wrote, "Realizing that actual political power rested with the Backman, McKay, Fitzpatrick triumvirate, they [home-rule proponents] argued that the commission seemed to address problems raised by the business community, property owners, and supporters of strict morality. Labor seemed unrepresented in the town, as did other interest groups such as women and those concerned with urban planning." Alexander and Allen, *Mormons and Gentiles*, 268–70).

Confidentially he gave me an insight into conditions that have led us to this committee's organization—conditions very enlightening, which confirm the wisdom of letting the committee carry the responsibility of getting the question on the ballot.

September 3, 1957, at 8:15 a.m., Washington, DC. I tried to get in contact with Mr. [James C.] Hagerty, the White House Press Secretary, but was informed that he was in conference with President [Dwight D.] Eisenhower preparatory to his press interview. With the assistance of several secretaries I finally got in touch with Mr. Stevens, the appointment secretary. As soon as President Eisenhower learned that I desired a conference, he granted my request immediately and scheduled an appointment at 11:30 this morning.

The interview was entirely successful and satisfactory. The President shows the marks of the weighty responsibility which he carries. I was deeply impressed by the remark he made with reference to the responsibility of his office. He said that he could not carry it without "aid from On High." I took occasion to tell him that we are thankful that we have a man in the Presidential chair who believes in and appeals to that Higher Power.

Following the conference with the President, we drove over to the office of the Secretary of Agriculture, Ezra Taft Benson, and as my visit to the President deeply concerned Brother Benson, I told the latter what we had in mind. ... that it must be clearly understood that Brother Benson's first duty is to discharge faithfully his duties as Secretary of Agriculture and to do nothing that would weaken the President in carrying out Government policies.

However, if any change is contemplated in his office, we should like to be informed before the October conference.

At the First Presidency's meeting on September 5, 1957, President McKay reported the following on his visit to President Eisenhower:

President McKay reported conferring with President Eisenhower at 11:30 a.m. Tuesday September 3, 1957 on which occasion the proposed reorganization of the Y.M.M.I.A. was explained to President Eisenhower, including the plan of the First Presidency to use Ezra Taft Benson, if he can be spared from the Government. President Eisenhower stated that after the first four years Secretary Benson told the President that he could have his resignation at any time, and the President responded that he would be pleased to have him remain, but that he was free to follow his own wishes. He paid tribute to Ezra Taft Benson saying, "There is no more honest man than Ezra." President Eisenhower said that there is one man who can take Ezra Taft Benson's place, if he (The President) can get him, and then said the matter of leaving the Cabinet is "for Ezra to decide." After the interview, President McKay talked with Brother Benson and informed him, repeating that the responsibility for making the decision is entirely his. President McKay also informed Brother Benson, "We want you to be loyal to your position here, loyal to the government and to the President, but if he can spare you, we would like to use you, and if not, we will do something else."[42]

September 12, 1957. This evening Elder Ezra Taft Benson called me from Washington, D.C. and reported that President [Dwight D.] Eisenhower would like him to stay in the Cabinet for at least a year. I advised him to stay and assured him that the First Presidency would arrange its affairs accordingly. I also told Brother Benson that if President Eisenhower wants him to stay longer that he should give him the assurance that he will stay.

September 15, 1957, 8 a.m. I went to the [Salt Lake] Tabernacle to meet with the members of the Choir just before they went on the air for their weekly broadcast, with regard to the change of directorship of the Choir [from J. Spencer Cornwall to assistant director Richard P. Condie]. At this time I gave the following message to the Choir members.

The Officers and Members of the Choir:

I have no baton in my hand but I have come with a message to the officers and members of the Choir. For over two years the First Presidency has had under consideration the advisability of making a change in the directorship of the Choir, but it was thought advisable that Brother Spencer Cornwall should have the responsibility and the honor

---

42. Benson favored agribusiness over small farmers. "Get big, or get out of farming," he said to family farmers, resulting in heckling and egg throwing when he gave speeches in the hinterland. As he became a political liability, McKay told Eisenhower that he would call Benson home if need be. Clair Barrus, "Ezra Taft Benson Chronology: Secretary of Agriculture," available at *Worlds without End: A Mormon Studies Roundtable*, www.withoutend.org. For Benson's account of this, see *Crossfire*, 259–60.

of directing the now famous European tour made by this organization. It was a climax to many years of great service, not only to the Choir, but to the Church.

Last week, Brother Cornwall was interviewed for the purpose of ascertaining his feelings regarding the most appropriate time to make a change. He answered, "As of now." In accordance with this expressed desire, the First Presidency sent him notice of his honorable release Saturday, September 14th.

I should like to say this in tribute to this great leader: The contribution that the Choir has made under J. Spencer Cornwall's direction to the promotion of good will for the Church, both nationally and internationally, cannot adequately be measured. Brother Cornwall has reason for deep, abiding satisfaction for the highly important part he has played in bringing a reputation for culture, and refinement to the Church that could scarcely be brought about in any other way.[43]

He is acclaimed by thousands the world over for his skillful, artistic conducting of our Choir. His 22 years of devoted service as director of this renowned organization will forever stand as a monument to him in the annals of music in the history of the Church.

Elder Richard P. Condie, assistant chorister, has been chosen as leader of the Choir.

As a matter of information you will be interested to know that prior to the leadership of Brother Evan Stephens there were seven leaders of the Choir. I will not take time this morning to read their names nor the tenure of service of each. Evan Stephens took charge in 1890 and served for 26 years. Anthony Lund served from 1916 to 1935. Brother Cornwall has served from 1935 to 1957—the second longest term in the history of the Choir.

This information leads us to say leaders may come, leaders may go, but the Choir continues constantly. We trust that you will give unstinted service in the future as you have in the past, show your loyalty and unselfishness to the Church as well as to the Choir.

Every effort will be put forth to sustain Brother Condie, his [potential] assistant who may yet be chosen, the officers of the Choir, and you

---

43. Cornwall was less than elated to be released. Hicks, *Mormonism and Music*, 163. See also the entry for October 7 below.

faithful members. Yours is a great mission, none greater in the musical world today than the position and service now held and rendered by this renowned group.

We love Brother Cornwall. He goes out with honors, and we propose to let all that honor continue with him as it will in future history.

God bless the new leader and every member and officer of this institution that it may continue to exert its influences not only upon the Church but upon the nation and nations of the world. I leave you my blessing. We felt that you should have this information today and know conditions as they are. The fact that the change might seem somewhat precipitous is now explained by the fact that Brother Cornwall preferred immediate action.

September 26, 1957, meeting of First Presidency and Twelve. President McKay announced that the First Presidency had been in touch with the Superintendent of Salt Lake City Schools, M. Lynn Bennion; and the office of the State Superintendent of Schools, Brother E. Allen Bateman being out of town, regarding the possibility of their closing school about the time we will hold our October General conference. It was thought we would be in a very embarrassing position if our membership were to come here from distant places in the United States, Canada, and Mexico, if the schools were closed because of the flu epidemic [and the guests were put at risk of contact with those children]. The superintendent of city schools said that they have had consultation with the State Board of Health, and have concluded that probably they can control it better by continuing the schools than by turning the students out on the streets. The state superintendency had come to the same conclusion, and they thought that if any schools were closed that it would be sectioned. They called up later this morning and said they thought they probably would continue schools during the epidemic, although in some places it seems to be quite severe.

Thinking it wise to do so, the First Presidency got in touch directly with the Board of Health, and after some effort this morning, talked personally with Dr. Joseph P. Kesler, who said it is somewhat different to hold Conference than to hold school, because people would come from areas where the flu is not yet prevalent, and even from other countries.

He said that in Canada the flu is in the eastern part, but not in the western part, so far as they know.

The First Presidency asked Dr. Kesler to take the matter up with his associates as to the wisdom of cancelling the Conference. He is evidently one of our own members, and he said he would take it up with his associates on the Board, and call us here at the Temple so that the Brethren might consider the matter this morning.

President McKay had just received a telephone call from Dr. Kesler, and in substance he said that first, though this outbreak of flu is not virulent flu, the reports show that it is the Asian flu, and there is no antidote yet found for it that will be fully effective in all cases. They have proved also that where people congregate in buses or in [meetings] there is a higher percentage of cases than where they do not. He thought it would [most likely] be a source of spreading the disease if Conference were held; that those who have been exposed to it will undoubtedly come down with the disease while they are in Salt Lake City. In cases where they take it and are at home, they can be properly cared for. It has not as yet been fatal, but where people are in hotels or rooming houses it might be a different thing. Then too, if they are exposed to it while here, they will probably come down with the disease on their return home, either in cars, or on trains or planes. He said they hesitate to suggest or recommend that Conference be postponed because of the spiritual value of the Conference, but that they are united in the thought that it would be beneficial to the people and would lessen the spreading of the disease if we saw fit to postpone the conference at this time. He said he would submit a letter containing the reasons for their conclusion. President McKay asked that he do this.

President McKay said that in case the Brethren decide to cancel the Conference, we will have to be very careful in making the announcement as we do not want to add to the uneasiness and apprehension of the people regarding it. President McKay told Dr. Kesler that should an announcement be made, he thought a statement should be included in the announcement to the effect that after consultation with the State Department of Health it had been decided to make this move, and Dr. Kesler thought that should be done. The President said if there is going to be any postponement of the Conference, it would have to be decided today as far as we are concerned, because people will be on their way. Some of the sisters are no doubt already on their way from the mission fields.

Several of the Brethren commented about the matter. Elder Marion G. Romney mentioned that inasmuch as we have sought advice from the State Health Department in regard to the matter, it would be difficult to go contrary to their advice.

Elder Adam S. Bennion mentioned that perhaps much of the purpose of the Conference might be achieved if the Brethren of the Presidency would give a broadcast over the radio to go into the homes of the people on the recommendation that they remain at home. It would not leave them wholly without a spiritual message.

President Stephen L. Richards mentioned that there had been 35 of the missionaries in the Mission Home who had been sick with the flu last week, but all but four of them have now gone to their fields of labor, we having cautioned the doctors not to let them go if there were any hazard to their health. President Richards also said that if the Conference were held, and any serious consequences should ensue and come to the attention of the people, it would be felt that we took an unnecessary hazard.

Elder Mark E. Petersen felt that if the Conference were cancelled, we might consider holding the Priesthood Meeting Saturday evening with no one in the Tabernacle except the First Presidency who would give their messages to all the Priesthood in their respective places.

President Joseph Fielding Smith commented that he did not think we should do anything contrary to the advice of the medical authorities.

President Richards asked President McKay how he felt about it, and he responded that if we contributed in any way to the spread of the flu, which is designated now as the Asian flu, and one life were lost, he thought that holding the Conference would not be worth it, because we can hold Conference again when there is no flu. He further said that if Dr. Kesler states in the letter he is going to write what he said over the telephone, we could not very well hold the Conference because we would be going against the recommendation of the Board of Health. It was Dr. Kesler's own suggestion that he would put it in writing.

Elder George Q. Morris moved that the Conference be cancelled. Motion seconded by Elder Mark E. Petersen.

President McKay added the further comment that Dr. Kesler had said that where the people remain at home they can take care of themselves, but where they are in strange beds in hotels and motels they have a different situation.

President Richards commented that even if deaths did not result it would be a serious thing for our people to lose hours and weeks of gainful employment.

President McKay said: "Now, Brethren, we must be united on this and feel all right about it. I believe it will be the wise thing to do."

The motion already made by Brother Morris and seconded by Brother Petersen was unanimously approved.[44]

October 1, 1957. Telephone conversation with Ezra Taft Benson from Washington, D.C. regarding world tour to include Hawaii, Japan, the Far East, and near East, and finally Rome, Italy where about November 11 to 15, he will be the representative of the government of the United States at an international meeting. He will be one of the scheduled speakers.

The American Ambassador has suggested to him that a meeting with the Pope be arranged.

Later, the Presidency decided that if he could avoid such a meeting without embarrassment, "we would prefer that he do so."

October 2, 1957. … Telephone conversation with Elder Ezra Taft Benson. (<u>Brother Benson was contacted in Portsmouth, New Hampshire</u>). …

President McKay: Regarding the matter we were discussing yesterday, we are all united in the feeling that if you can in honor, and without embarrassment, avoid that conference [with the pope] it would be well for you to do it.

Brother Benson: All right. I think I can.

President McKay: Was it the Ambassador?

Brother Benson: The American Ambassador to Italy.

President McKay: Yes. I see.

Brother Benson: He is the one who has proposed it. But I think I can avoid it, President McKay, because I am going to be in Rome for a

---

44. See "Flu Cancels 128th LDS Conference," *Deseret News and Salt Lake Telegram,* Sept. 27, 1957.

very short time. I have to make an important address for a World Agricultural Congress, and I think the shortness of my stay can probably be used as a reason for not doing so.

President McKay: We have in mind particularly the effect upon our own people.

Brother Benson: Yes. That is the thing that concerned me too.

President McKay: And the dignity that you would have to give to such a conference,.

Brother Benson: Yes, that is right.

President McKay: And really they have everything to gain and nothing to lose, and we have everything to lose and nothing to gain.

Brother Benson: I am in full harmony with that feeling.

President McKay: Well that is good. We are glad of that. We all feel that it would be pretty embarrassing to you, and we are helping you out of what might prove to be a conference that will reflect upon our Church.

Brother Benson: Well, I think it could be embarrassing both to me and to the Church.[45]

October 6, 1957. This morning at 10 o'clock, I met with Elder Richard L. Evans and Brother Gordon B. Hinckley in the Salt Lake Temple where we spent two and a half hours studying the presentation of the temple ceremonies as now given in the temple at Switzerland, and as it will be given in New Zealand and in London. I feel that it was a two-hour period very well spent, and that so development in connection therewith will be presented to the Temple Committee before it is installed.

I have spent several Sunday mornings in the Temple studying the ceremonies, the magnificence and the significance of which (referring to the endowment) are seldom, if ever, really comprehended by our young folks when they first go through the Temple. I think the ceremony can be presented more effectively, but before any changes are made they will be presented to the members of the Temple Committee.

---

45. Two years previous on a similar speaking tour, Benson wrote, "our charming U.S. Ambassador [Mrs.] Clare Boothe Luce took us in charge, arranged an official visit with high men in the Italian government and a tour of St. Peters and other parts of Rome" (Benson, *Cross Fire*, 263). She was a playwright, her husband the publisher of *Time* magazine, *Sports Illustrated*, and other periodicals.

October 7, 1957, 7:30 this morning. Met by appointment at his request, Allen Cornwall, son of Spencer Cornwall. He asked for an explanation as to why his father had been released.

I replied "because it is the most opportune time after 20 years' service for him to receive his honorable release—it has come just at the height of his success."

Brother Cornwall then went on to say that he and his folks could not understand why their father at the height of his success should be released especially when the 20 years' experience would add to his capability as a director.

I answered: "That is a matter of opinion, and in consideration of Spencer Cornwall's 'glory' now is the most opportune time for him to step out and let somebody else carry the responsibility of directorship."

I then asked him if he had seen his father's reply to the First Presidency, and he said, "Yes, my father told me about it."

I stated that his father is in accord with the action taken, and is glad that the release has come in view of the changes that must be made in the personnel of the choir, he feeling that he is too close to them to extend a release to the different members.

Brother Cornwall left apparently pretty well satisfied. He, at least, expressed himself that way.

October 10, 1957. In Council meeting this morning I referred to the attempted expansion in Huntsville by the Catholics; that they had purchased some additional property on the west, and price seems to be no question to them. I reported that it is difficult for me to understand why they now want to buy 303 acres of good property over in what is called "the middle field," which is a mile and a half or two miles from their present property. The bishop of the ward in Huntsville is considering obtaining this property. I mentioned this just to let the Brethren know what the Catholics are trying to do there. Sometime ago they tried to buy the Bingham property just a short distance from their present holdings for the purpose of establishing a nunnery, and it may be that is the purpose they have in mind in trying to get this property in the middle field. I hope to purchase 50 acres of the land for myself in order to help the Bishop secure possession of the property. I said "The Catholic

Church is against us, and wherever they can prevent our growth they are going to do it."

October 20, 1957. When I entered the front gate of the [Salt Lake] Temple this morning, I found that it was unlocked, and I was surprised to see a man, a woman, and two others accompanying them walking around the gates there. When I came out of the Temple, I spoke to the gentleman at the gate regarding these people, and the man said he thought they were going through the gate that leads to the Tabernacle to attend a Quarterly [stake] Conference.

I told the man that the gate should be closed always, and the gate should be locked. He said that no one had ever told him that before.

November 12, 1957, 8:30 a.m. Received a <u>courtesy call</u> from <u>Senator John Kennedy of Massachusetts</u>. He was accompanied by Milton Weilenmann, local Democratic leader who says John Kennedy is the next Democratic presidential candidate.

Mr. Kennedy is a member of the Catholic Church. I enjoyed my visit with him, although not too much impressed with him as a leader. ...

<u>Meeting of President McKay and Senator John Kennedy of Massachusetts, as reported by Joseph Lundstrom of the Deseret News, who was present at the conference.</u>

They greeted each other. President McKay said, "You are younger than I thought."

Senator Kennedy answered that there were a number of younger senators now, since the War. He mentioned Senator [Frank] Church of Idaho as an example.

President McKay said he saw by the papers that 4,000 Democrats turned out for his speech the night before.

Senator Kennedy answered that it was a very enthusiastic crowd.

President McKay said, "The Republicans must have been in hiding," and everyone had a good laugh.

President McKay pointed out some of the oddities of the wood panels in the room, then everyone sat down at the table in the First Presidency's Board Room. President McKay explained briefly the setup of the Church, with a First Presidency of three men and Council of Twelve.

The two men then discussed the outlook for peace. "We are making too much of this science thing,"[46] President McKay said.

Senator Kennedy agreed, although it was not to be underemphasized. "Prospects for economic development of Russia are far more serious for the United States than the race for missiles," he said.

President McKay then asked him his views on the breakup of Russia. "Would the system break up first, or would it have to come to a clash of arms? [Nikita] Khrushchev has now the same position as [Joseph] Stalin. Can he hold it?"

Senator Kennedy answered that it would not much matter whether it was Khrushchev or someone else. The Russian policy of pushing outward through the use of the Communist Party would continue. As for Communism breaking up, it did not seem likely, since there was no alternate system to replace the Communists. While Khrushchev might go, the policy of increasing their power will continue. Communism represents a counterattraction to the poverties suffered by the peoples of Africa, Asia and the Far East.

President McKay said he could not see how the system could continue to last. "They are fundamentally wrong. Free agency is inherent in every individual. Rule by force has been fought against by men throughout history."

Senator Kennedy: "Yes they have the power to continue. Their prospects for the immediate future are bright."

President McKay: "I have hoped for 20 years that they would break up, and I do not see how they can last. It is just wicked to dominate men that way."

Senator Kennedy asked if there were Church members living in Russia.

President McKay answered that there were some in East Germany and in other Communist dominated countries in Europe. He mentioned the Russian journalists who came through Salt Lake City two years ago and told how he had questioned them regarding freedom of worship in Russia and eastern Germany. The Russians maintained they had freedom of worship, but when President McKay cited a case in eastern Germany and Czechoslovakia where Church members had been denied the Book of Mormon, the Russians answered, "Well, that is their country, not ours."

---

46. This was in reference to the October 4 Soviet launching of Sputnik, the first satellite to orbit the earth.

"It is just wrong. There is no freedom and people will rise against it, but I hope we can avert war," said President McKay.

"It will be interesting to see if Islam and Communism can make any adjustment in the Middle East," commented Senator Kennedy.

"They will break sooner or later. It is a fundamental principle of civilization that men will be free. They cannot oppose these principles of God. Man will be free," said President McKay. "They cannot crush their people always," he added.

Senator Kennedy answered: "Your statement that men will be free is one we should take to all the world."

He mentioned that a very serious threat to the free world would be the death of Nehru of India. If he should die and India were to turn Communistic, it would have a tremendous and profound effect on the peoples of Asia and Africa, and would form a China and India block which could be very dangerous.

The meeting then broke up …

November 19, 1957, telephone conversation with apostle/Senator Ezra Taft Benson.

Bro[ther] Benson: … And in Amman [Jordan] I also had a half hour visit with the King, who is a very young man, just turned twenty-three.

Pres[ident] McKay: Well!

Bro[ther] Benson: But a noble character, I believe. He has a tough job. I talked to him about the Church, and I promised to send him a copy of the Book of Mormon and other literature.

Pres[ident] McKay: That is good!

Bro[ther] Benson: That is pretty much a Moslem country, as you know, but he seems to be a fine character. Then the next Sunday, we were in Spain. That is a week ago last Sunday. … On the trip, I met with several of the leaders of nations including some of the heads of State in Israel where we spent a couple of days. I had an hour-long visit with Mr. Ben Gurion,[47] the President of Israel.

47. David Ben–Gurion [David Gruen] (1886–1973) was born in Plonsk, Poland, and immigrated to Palestine in 1906. As he studied law, he helped found the Labor Unity Party in Palestine in 1919, and in 1948 became prime minister of the new Israeli state, remaining in office until 1953, and serving again as prime minister from 1955 to 1963.

Pres[ident] McKay: He is a pretty fine man, is he not?

Bro[ther] Benson: He seems to be a noble soul, President McKay. He was in the hospital. You know that he met with an accident. A fanatic threw a bomb into their Parliament and Ben-Gurion had his left foot injured. He was in the hospital, and I was the first nonmember of his family to visit him. While I was there, he invited in the press and the photographers, and so our visit got a lot of publicity, because it is the first the outside world has heard about him since he went in. But he seems to be a fine character. I reviewed with him our interest in the Jewish people, the visit of Orson Hyde to Palestine, and the dedication of that land for the return of the Jews, and our faith in the prophecies of the Old Testament, and he was very much interested. I am planning to send him a copy of the Book of Mormon.

Pres[ident] McKay: That will be a historic meeting.

Bro[ther] Benson: Yes. I told him some day we would like to establish a mission there. ... He said they did not look with too much favor on active proselyting among the Hebrew peoples, but he felt sure we would be welcome there as any other Christian groups have been. They are doing wonderful things in Palestine. ... There is one other thing I would like to get your judgment on, and I think I know what it will be. About a month ago, Secretary [John Foster] Dulles[48] and [Henry] Cabot Lodge (Cabot Lodge is our Ambassador to United Nations, as you know) approached me and asked whether or not I would be interested in a long-time appointment as the United States Representative on the Economic and Social Council of United Nations. I personally have no particular interest in it, President McKay, but I did not want to give them an answer until I had at least mentioned it to you.

Pres[ident] McKay: I think that you had better give them a negative answer.

Bro[ther] Benson: I think so, too. When this job is over, I know where I would like to be.

Pres[ident] McKay: Yes.

Bro[ther] Benson: And I hope it is where you want me to be.

---

48. John Foster Dulles (1888–1959) was Eisenhower's Secretary of State from 1953 until he resigned shortly before his death from cancer in 1959. He was known for opposing communism and engaging in diplomatic brinkmanship.

Pres[ident] McKay: I think you had better not accept that appointment.

December 9, 1957. [Honolulu Stake] Pres[ident] [Jay] Quealy [Jr.] came in regarding the <u>reactivation of [the deposed church patriarch] Joseph F. Smith</u>. I told Pres[ident] Quealy that no formal action was taken when he was disfellowshipped and that I think we should take no formal action on his participation. Joseph F. Smith has a son on a mission, and Joseph F. Smith has recently confessed to his wife and wrote a full confession to the First Presidency. Now his youngest son is participating in Church activity.

I told Pres[ident] Quealy that we would go this far—that he [Quealy] might use Joseph F. Smith as he (Pres[ident] Quealy) thinks best under the circumstances. That, however, is as far as I felt to go in the matter.

December 12, 1957, meeting of First Presidency and Twelve. President Joseph Fielding Smith said that he had received a letter marked personal in which the statement is made that someone had reported to the writer that President McKay had given consent that the temple endowment work be performed for a negro who is dead, and that therefore we were doing work for negroes in the temple.

I related the following facts for the information of the Brethren, and said that I felt sure that I had previously brought this matter to the Council.

A negro woman had called at the office some few years ago, she having her residency in Ogden. I stated that I think she said she was a Methodist; that her church could not do anything for her husband who was dead, and that before he died he wanted to join our Church; that inasmuch as our Church is the only Church that can do baptismal work for him, and he had requested that she see that his baptism was attended to if he did not recover from his illness, she wanted to have it done.

I told her that that could be done. She explained that she knew that he could not receive the Priesthood. She said that the Ward teachers would do the work for him. I said that the thought came to me as to whether they could be baptized for him, and the matter was discussed in Council later. I gave consent for the Ward teacher to be baptized for this negro lady's husband.

Now the report comes that the temple work was done for that negro, and therefore he was ordained an Elder. The facts are that the ward teachers were authorized to do baptism work for a colored man who had become converted but died before baptism could be performed, and there is no truth to the statement that he was ordained an Elder or permitted to have his endowments. ...

I have something to say to you [counselors] personally as we approach the Holidays and close the year's work. First, I wish to express appreciation and deep appreciation particularly during the last few months as we have sat together in counsel considering weighty problems that affect the Church, not only presently but in the future. [To the Twelve:] My heart has been filled with consolation, and I may say pride and admiration, for their wise counsel. There is a freedom in our council which is unlimited. I am sure they feel free to express their opinions, as they should, and under the inspiration of their callings they contribute to decisions which I am sure are approved of our Father in Heaven. I do not know what other Presidents of the Church have had in their counselors; undoubtedly they have had inspirational help. They have, but I shall say this: that no other President has had greater strength in counselors who exercise greater wisdom than these two Brethren who complete the Presidency of the Church.

I should like to say a word of our love for the Brethren of the Twelve. As fathers, you know of the pride that comes to you when you hear of a son's achievement and a daughter's success. As I awoke this morning I felt that same way for each of you. Letters come reporting your work, your success, and I think I can express my feeling in no other way than to say that I have that same pride and satisfaction when I hear of the success of each of you, as I do for my own sons and daughters.

We appreciate your loyalty and have pride in your success as you go among the people and exert an influence only extended to those who are true representatives of our Lord and Savior, Jesus Christ, which you are.

God bless you during these Christmas Holidays and the years to come, I say with all my heart, in the name of Jesus Christ, Amen.

December 13, 1957. Brother [Orval] Adams <u>offered the suggestion that the Church carry a balance of ten million in the bank</u> for at least a year. We have reduced that balance from 10 million down to seven million, but Brother

Adams pleads for 10 million for the general service the Banks renders the Church in advances to banks in sending money to our foreign missions, etc.

December 18, 1957. Following the meeting, <u>Dr. [A. Ray] Olpin[,] [president of the University of Utah][,] remained and asked for a personal interview. He expressed his regret that the First Presidency saw fit to send him a letter remonstrating against the address given by Dr. W[illia]m Mulder</u> at the annual Fred J. Reynolds Memorial.[49]

Dr. Olpin said that we have a misconception of the address given on that occasion, because it really was a credit to the church rather than casting [a negative] reflection upon it.

December 26, 1957, 8:30 a.m. President Ernest L. Wilkinson of the B.Y.U. came in, and we took up the following points: (1) The advisability of the Brigham Young University professors attending Quarterly [stake] Conferences.

I said that we have looked with disfavor upon their doing so, but will be pleased to have President Wilkinson present the matter to the First Presidency at a meeting to be held January 16, 1958 at 8:30 a.m.

(2) President Wilkinson asked if the suggestive letter to the Stake Presidents and counselors may also be sent to the Mission Presidencies. I told him Yes.

(3) President Wilkinson would like to receive an answer to the letter requesting his opening of a special confidential account a draft of which letter I have handed to President Stephen L. Richards.

(4) President Wilkinson wanted to know if President Hanks could go to Europe with a group of B.Y.U. students through Europe. I told him to bring this matter up at the meeting to be held January 16;

(5) President Wilkinson wanted to know if the $40,000 which the

---

49. William Mulder (1915–2008) ran the Institute of American Studies at the University of Utah. In 1957 he delivered the distinguished faculty lecture, "The Mormons in American History," about how the church reflected the time and place of its founding. His parents emigrated from Holland when he was a boy. He studied English at the University of Utah and received a PhD in history from Harvard. During World War II he was stationed in Okinawa with the US Naval Reserve. In 1957 his dissertation, *Homeward to Zion: The Mormon Migration from Scandinavia*, was published. The following year Alfred A. Knopf published *Among the Mormons: Historic Accounts by Contemporary Observers*, which he co-edited. See Mulder, "Mormons in American History," 60–77.

B.Y.U. has put in its budget for theatrical productions might remain in the budget. I told him that we would consider this matter when he meets with the First Presidency.

(6) President Wilkinson brought up the question of establishing Junior Colleges throughout the Church. This matter was considered at length. President Wilkinson has an appointment with the Governor today on this matter, and no action will be taken until he reports to me the results of his conference with the Governor.[50]

---

50. Wilkinson met with Clyde, who was initially reluctant but gradually became "enthusiastic," according to Wilkinson's diary, Dec. 6, 1957.

8   Turmoil and Tragedy, 1958

Some of them, particularly Dr. Murland F. Rigby, said how much they had prayed about the matter, and Dr. Rigby made the statement that the prayers had all led [them] along the opposite direction from [our decision]—at least, that was the inference—and President Clark interposed, "You know, we prayed about it too." —November 15, 1958

January 3, 1958, 7:30 a.m. ... I gave them [church–affiliated attorneys][1] my permission to go ahead and try to get Dr. Ernest L. Wilkinson appointed to the [US] Supreme Court at the first vacancy that might occur.

January 4, 1958. This morning I had a conference with Dr. Ernest L. Wilkinson who reported his visit with [Utah] Governor George Dewey Clyde about the building of Junior Colleges here in Salt Lake County.

He said that the Governor said that what is proposed by the State is the erection of a Trades Junior College, but that he, the Governor, sees no objection to the building of a Church Junior College if the Church thinks one is needed here.

After the above discussion, we took up the question of Dr. Wilkinson's seeking an appointment to the Supreme Court of the United States. An important phase of such an appointment would be the favorable

---

1. The delegation in McKay's office included Albert R. Bowen (1905–1993), whose law firm represented the LDS Church; John S. Boyden (1906–1980), an attorney and life insurance executive who had run for Utah governor; and Vernon B. Romney (1924–2013), the Assistant Utah Attorney General and church-appointed lobbyist (see footnote at Jan. 14, 1953).

consideration by Senator [Arthur V.] Watkins who, President Wilkinson thinks, is not in favor of such an appointment.

Brother Wilkinson also mentioned the request that had been made for him to seek the nomination for [US] Senator in opposition to Senator Watkins. I said, "Well I shall tell you this much, and only this much: That if they do nominate you for Senatorship, we shall give you a leave of absence from your present position while you run, and let you have your freedom to do as you wish, and you will not lose your position as President of the Brigham Young University."[2]

January 8, 1958, 12 to 12:40 p.m. Elder Lawrence McKay of the General Superintendency of the Sunday School Union, and Lorin Wheelwright, Sunday School Board, came in and asked for an advance of $75,000 to finance the production and publication of a book on the Distinctive Features of Mormonism, the book to be richly illustrated with colored reproductions of the masters. The advance, it is proposed, will be returned from the sales of the book.

I presented this proposal to the brethren of the First Presidency at our meeting, January 9, and it was decided to reserve the matter for further consideration.

January 17, 1958. It is interesting to note that when [McKay's younger brother] Thomas E. [McKay][3] was 11 years of age, he was given a patriarchal blessing by Patriarch John Smith who said in that blessing: "It is the will of the Lord, and thy privilege, that you become a mighty man in Israel and live to the age of eighty and three." Thomas E. died in his eighty-third year.

January 23, 1958, meeting of First Presidency and Twelve. President McKay

---

2. A similar promise was given to Wilkinson six years later when he did run for the US Senate against the incumbent Democrat, Frank E. Moss.

3. David O. McKay's younger brother, Thomas Evans McKay (1875–1958), passed away three days earlier. Superintendent of the Weber County School District, a member of the Utah House of Representatives, Assistant to the Quorum of the Twelve, and past president of the Swiss Mission, Thomas was also the father of Fawn McKay Brodie, author of the controversial *No Man Knows My History: The Life of Joseph Smith*, published in 1945.

said that President [Stephen L.] Richards had related to the brethren in the Expenditures Committee meeting some of his personal experiences in regard to the closing of the Salt Lake Theatre, something which President McKay said was entirely new to him, and he asked President Richards to relate this same thing to the Brethren of the Council for their information.

President Richards said that the matter had come up in connection with the question of an appropriation for the replica of the Salt Lake Theatre to be built on the University campus, and he had remarked that he remembered that when the matter of disposing of the Theatre was under discussion he knew that President [Heber J.] Grant and most of the Brethren were anxious to retain the old Theatre if it were possible to do so.[4] President Richards asked President Grant on one occasion if he might go to the Mayor of Salt Lake City and ask if they would consider taking the property over, thus avoiding taxes because the Theatre had been losing money for a long time and it was no doubt difficult to pay the taxes, let alone any dividends to the stockholders. President Grant said that would be all right. President Richards called on Clarence Neslen, who was then the mayor, and he looked with favor upon some plan to retain it, but he said, "Of course we haven't any money. Some very great concessions would have to be made to the city before we could acquire the property," and there would have to be a considerable reduction in price. President Richards asked the Mayor if it would be all right for him (President Richards) to speak to one or two of the Commissioners, and he did speak to a couple of them, although he did not now remember who they were, and they were pretty much of the opinion that the city might look with favor upon the project if concessions might be made that were sufficient so that the city could meet the financial obligation.

President Grant tried to get the stockholders, or at least some of them, to make a concession in order that an acceptable proposal might be made to the city, but he afterwards reported that it was not feasible, that it could not be done. President Richards said he remembered in that connection that one of the large stockholders by the name of Wrathall would not make any concession under the price that they were to receive

---

4. Partial ownership of the theater had been sold to investors, but President Grant and the LDS Church were still majority stockholders. When the theater was ultimately sold to Mountain States Telephone in 1928, it was demolished that same year.

on the offer from the Mountain States Telephone Company to purchase the property. President Richards thought that President Grant was of a disposition that he would have been willing to accept for the Church a considerable reduction on its major portion of the stockholdings, but other stockholders would not consent and seemed to insist that the Corporation of the Salt Lake Theatre accept the offer which had been made by the Mountain States Telephone Company for that property without making any concessions, and there the matters died because they could not make a proposition to Salt Lake City that the city could meet.

January 30, 1958, 2:30. This afternoon, I received at my office <u>Bishop John O. Hughes of Mendon, Utah, Bishop Staley Brewer, Ogden, Utah, and Robert H. Stewart, President of the Wellsville Mountain Area Project Corporation, Brigham City, Utah.</u>

These men came in by request contained in the letter dated January 13, 1958, in regard to the problems of watershed protection, and the relationship of livestock men to the National Forest Range Problems, and particularly with reference to the talk given by President J. Reuben Clark, Jr. at the Utah Cattlemen's Association on December 13, 1957.

They stated that after the disastrous floods in Wellsville, they organized a company known as the Wellsville Area Corporation, the purpose of which was to <u>replant the devastated area caused by over grazing</u>. On their own initiative, they collected sufficient funds to replant grass and trees in that area.

Now they are deeply concerned over the speech given by President Clark before the Cattlemen's Association, December 13, 1957, in which he took exception to the Government's restricting the number of cattle on grazing areas.

These men were particularly fearful that President Clark was representing the church in what he said although he declared in his opening statement that he was not representing the Church, but speaking for himself.

I assured these brethren that the Church was in favor of conservation of our mountain areas. They specifically asked if some such statement could be made in the public press to that effect. I told them that we would take the matter under advisement and see what can be done. In the meantime, they were authorized to correct that erroneous opinion publicly and privately.

February 4, 1958, 8:45 a.m. By appointment at his request Brother Wilford C. Wood came in. He had with him some pictures and materials which he would like to print in a book. The materials covered events connected with the organization and early history of the Church, including uncut sheets of the first edition of the Book of Mormon.

I did not have time to go over all this material, but from a cursory glance told him that I could see no reason why he should not publish these materials in book form.

Later I received a letter from Dr. O. Preston Robinson, General Manager of the Deseret News Publishing Company who stated that Brother Wood had come to him stating that he had had a chat with me, and that I could see no reason why the material he has should not be published. Brother Robinson then said: "We have agreed to handle the printing of his book which, incidentally, I believe should have wide interest throughout the Church."

I answered Dr. Robinson's letter and told him that it is understood that Brother Wood alone is responsible for the printing of this book— that I had glanced through some of the pictures which he proposes to print with a copy of the first edition of the Book of Mormon, but that for these and whatever else is printed in the book Dr. Robinson and Brother Wood will be responsible, that it is not a Church publication.[5]

February 6, 1958, 8 a.m. Elder Harold B. Lee of the Council of the Twelve came in to inform me that Elder Adam S. Bennion suffered a severe cerebral hemorrhage last evening while eating his dinner. Brother Bennion had been at the office all day—several people had seen him on the street at noon, and he cheerfully greeted them and from all appearances was in the best of health.

This news came as a great shock to me.

---

5. This was published as *Joseph Smith Begins His Work: Book of Mormon 1830 First Edition, Reproduced from Uncut Sheets.* It was printed in 1958 by the Deseret News Press (Wilford C. Wood, publisher), with a companion volume four years later on the Doctrine and Covenants.

At 4 p.m. I left the office and drove up to the L.D.S. Hospital to see Dr. Adam S. Bennion of the Council of the Twelve who was stricken last evening with a cerebral hemorrhage. I was thankful that he knew me, could talk, and move both of his legs. His left arm seems to be paralyzed. I administered to Brother Bennion and left my blessing with him.

Following my visit with Brother Bennion, I called on Wendell Smoot [of Zions Bank] who has recently been operated upon.

As I came out of his room, a man approached me and asked if I should call on his wife who is confined in the hospital. She is a cousin to the Callister girls who are our neighbors.

I then walked down the hall and visited [Assistant Church Historian] Preston Nibley who has been operated upon for hernia.

After my visit with him, I learned that David W. Evans, the advertising man, and a brother to Elder Richard L. Evans was in the hospital, so I visited with him for a few moments.

Just as I had completed all of the above visits, a nurse stopped me in the hall and asked me if I would call on her mother, Mrs. Ann Morris. She said she was in her home just a half a block up the hill from the hospital. She said her mother is facing an operation and needs encouragement. So I responded to this request, and walked up the hill to their home.

Then the mother of a missionary asked me to go to the room of her son (Elder Cecil Briggs)[6] who is dying of cancer, and administer to him. I acquiesced to her request and administered to Elder Briggs, following which he asked his father and mother to leave the room while he talked to me. He questioned me as to why he had to suffer such a dreadful affliction. I talked to him for about an hour, explaining, among other things, that the sufferings of this world are a part of our mortal existence, that this life is so brief compared to the eternities to come. ... I commended Brother Briggs for his firm testimony of the Gospel, and told him to put his trust in the Lord and have faith and rest assured that He will adjust all things for his good. (On Tuesday, February 11, 1958, I learned that this young man had gone to his eternal reward.)

---

6. Cecil Joseph Briggs (1934–58) was twenty-three and hailed from Nephi, Utah. He had attended BYU for a year and served a mission to the Southern states. "Nephi Man Dies in Salt Lake," *Provo Daily Herald*, Feb. 13, 1958.

I was very weary when I arrived home at 6:15 p.m., having been engaged every minute since 6:30 this morning in consultations, meetings, etc.

February 20, 1958, 7:30 a.m. Dr. L. E. Viko gave me a physical examination today. He said that I am in good condition; that my blood pressure is a little high, but nothing to worry about. Dr. Viko talked about my trip to New Zealand this coming April, and asked that I furnish him with a copy of my itinerary so that he could glance at it and see if the schedule is to[o] heavy.

In keeping with my promise, I sent Dr. Viko a copy of my itinerary along with a letter of appreciation and thanks to him.

February 23, 1958. Spent the day going over thirty-three petitions for cancellation of Temple [marriage] sealings! Two or three petitions I rejected their appeals for cancellation. As I have said before, going over and studying these cases is a gloomy task. ...

This evening Elder Ezra Taft Benson called, and told me about the visit to him of Congressmen who intimated to him that he (Brother Benson) has become the scapegoat for the recent near-defeat of Republican senators. A delegation of Republicans will wait on the President today (so they have declared) with the intention of having Brother Benson resign.

Brother Benson said he would get in touch with the President before they do, but this week will decide whether or not he (Brother Benson) will resign or continue on.[7] They are now in session on that important question, and Brother Benson asked to have his name put on the prayer roll at the Temple. (Note: Later, Clare [Middlemiss] called the Temple and put Brother Benson's name on the prayer roll.)

March 3, 1958. Bishop Joseph L. Wirthlin called and said that sometime ago President Ernest L. Wilkinson of the Brigham Young University wanted to know whether or not he could have information about how much tithing the members of the faculty are paying, and that I had suggested that he should not have this information. Now President Wilkinson wants to know if they pay full or part tithing, and he sent the names of all of them.

---

7. See Benson, *Cross Fire*, 279–90.

I told Bishop Wirthlin that President Wilkinson need not know amounts, but that he could be furnished information about whether or not they pay part or full tithing.[8]

March 31, 1958. At a conference with President Ernest L. Wilkinson this morning, I approved of the motion made at a meeting of the Board of Trustees of the B.Y.U. and Board of Education held Friday, March 28, 1958, authorizing "the purchase of property in the San Fernando Valley [California] (137 acres) at an approximate cost of $1,250,000 for use as a future junior college site."

This land is reasonably priced in comparison with other land in the same area. While the average cost will be $9,500 per acre (it could have been purchased for around $7000 two years ago) other property own-ers[,] for land not as conveniently located, are asking $15,000.

All indications are that by the year 1975 there will be over 10,000 Mormon students of college age in this area. By the year 2000 this num-ber will have increased to 30,500. It will of course be impossible to take care of these students at the BYU or in various institutes of the Church.[9]

April 1, 1958, 4:30 p.m. Conference with Dr. Lowell L. Bennion[,] [LDS Institute director, University of Utah]. Asked him to give a talk at the general priesthood meeting next Saturday evening. I told him that I disapproved of the custom among young men and women, when attend-ing dances, to dance all evening with the partner who accompanied them to the dance. I asked Dr. Bennion to discourage this practice in his talk, and also to bring up any other problems concerning youth he thought wise and proper.

April 3, 1958, 2:15 to 2:25 p.m. Elder Harold B. Lee came to my office at my request, and I discussed with him the presentation at the General

---

8. The issue of tithe-payers and church employment was first raised during the Great Depression when salaries were cut and church-employed teachers were told they were required to be full tithe-payers. Wilkinson, *Brigham Young University*, 2:218, 385.

9. These comments came on the heels of the February 28, 1958, meeting of the BYU Board of Trustees, at which Wilkinson projected a church population of 950,000 in Southern California. The trustees voted unanimously in favor of purchasing at least 100 acres of land.

Priesthood meeting next Saturday evening of the moral standards campaign of the Church. It was decided that Brother Mark E. Petersen
would make this presentation.[10]

April 7, 1958, 6:30 p.m. In Company with Sister [Emma Ray] McKay
attended the General Authorities semi-annual banquet and social held in
the Relief Society Building.

At this social a film of Nauvoo which has been prepared under the
auspices of KSL Radio Station, Dr. LeRoy Kimball, and others was
shown to the General Authorities. It is reported that President Richard
C. Stratford of the Northern States Mission, Pres[ident] Junius M. Jackson of the New England Mission, and others are interested in having the
film shown in Nauvoo and the missions.

I have some reservations as to the value of the picture from a propaganda or missionary standpoint. In the picture emphasis is given to
the liberality of the Nauvoo Charter, favorable mention is made of the
Nauvoo Legion, but not much is said as to why the Legion was required
to lay down its arms, and the inference to any stranger might be that
they were guilty of something serious; that the impression is given that
Nauvoo is a ghost town,[11] [that] the houses are still there, [and] the saints
were driven out, but not enough emphasis is given to the fact that the
Prophet [Joseph Smith] and Patriarch [Hyrum Smith] were martyrs. I
feel that the history of Nauvoo and our banishment therefrom is given in
a way that does not reflect as favorably as it should upon the Church or
our Prophets who were martyrs.

April 9, 1958. Telephone conversation between President McKay and
President Ernest L. Wilkinson of Brigham Young University.[12]

---

10. Petersen explained that the church would be producing audio recordings of famous people addressing "character-building and faith-promoting" themes, and that the
church would continue distributing posters to be displayed in local church classrooms and
hallways showing people in moral conundrums, with the caption, "Be honest with yourself." *One Hundred Twenty-eighth Annual Conference of the Church*, April 4–6, 1958, 87–88.

11. The population of Nauvoo remained fairly constant at a little over 1,000 residents throughout the twentieth century.

12. McKay was calling two days before leaving for Hamilton, New Zealand, for
the temple dedication.

President McKay: What did you understand about what I told you, and what was your request regarding the Senate?

President Wilkinson: You told me that you wanted me to think it over, and you wanted to see me before you left.

President McKay: No. You asked if you could have what? Was it that if you should decide to run could you have a leave of absence during the election? Did I understand it right?

President Wilkinson: Yes, that was the question. You say you answered it in writing?

President McKay: Then what did I tell you?

President Wilkinson: You said you would be inclined to say "No," but you would talk it over with your Counselors.

President McKay: Just now, you mean?

President Wilkinson: When I saw you a week ago Monday. You said you would see me before you left.

President McKay: I have talked it over with them, and they look with disfavor upon your getting a leave-of-absence. If you run, it makes your present position secondary to the Senate.

President Wilkinson: What do you think? You are telling me what they think.

President McKay: I think it would make your present position secondary to the Senatorship.

President Wilkinson: Knowing that you are going to be away six weeks, I want to know what your views are if some situation arises …

President McKay: I am afraid that if you enter into this campaign (although it is your right and privilege to do so), it is going to make it more difficult for the present incumbent [Senator Arthur V. Watkins]. As you know, I am afraid this is a Democratic year.[13] I should feel better if you would not run.

President Wilkinson: I have always followed your advice in the past.

President McKay: You are in such a responsible position now, and we have our school—the greatest in the country. I feel that for you to get out and try that, and especially if you did not get it, it would lessen your

13. McKay's political radar was prescient. Watkins would lose to Democratic challenger Frank E. Moss, 113,000 to 101,000, with independent J. Bracken Lee seriously eroding the Republican's chances by garnering 77,000 votes.

dignity. I should rather you would not run this year. But I should like you to run for the other office (the U.S. Supreme Court). There is no chance on the other; tell them you are not going to run.

President Wilkinson: Well, if that is your judgment, as well as the judgment of your Counselors, that means a lot to me.

President McKay: Personally, if you wanted to make the run within the Party, and then received the nomination, I am in favor of giving you a leave-of-absence after you have the nomination, but my Counselors are not. They think if you did that we ought to release you. I shall not think that at all. In view of that, I think it would be best not to do it. If you did not make it, it would hurt you. I would not stand for that. In view of the doubt as to the outcome this year, I believe if I were you I would not do it. I joined with the others in saying that we would not give you a leave-of-absence because if people hear of it in the meantime, then that means that the Presidency are against Watkins. You would have to let the people know that you were given a leave-of-absence.

President Wilkinson: Well, I should not want to put you in that position up there.

President McKay: That is what they would do.

President Wilkinson: I should not want to put anyone up there in a position like that. If any change in the situation develops while you are away, whom should I see?

President McKay: Well, you had better see the two Counselors. I would see them both together.

President Wilkinson: Thanks very much.[14]

April 11, 1958. Telephone conversation with President Ernest L. Wilkinson, B.Y.U.

---

14. The following day, Wilkinson, notwithstanding McKay's counsel, paid visits to Hugh B. Brown (just four days previously made a member of the Quorum of Twelve) and J. Reuben Clark to seek their advice. Brown had unsuccessfully sought the nomination of the Democratic Party for the US Senate in 1928 (William H. King was the two-term incumbent Democratic Senator). Brown informed Wilkinson he was much happier in church service than he would have been in politics, and besides, he felt the incumbent Republican Senator Arthur V. Watkins was going to lose. Clark, also a loser in seeking a senatorial nomination against Ernest Bamberger in 1922, told Wilkinson that he "thanked the Lord for his not being elected." Wilkinson said that on his return he discussed the option with his wife that he would not to run, and Alice "was very happy about that decision" Wilkinson diary, Apr. 10, 1958.

President Wilkinson: Hello, President McKay. I shall only take a minute of your time. You were kind enough to call me day before yesterday. You caught me in someone else's office, and I thought that perhaps my conversation did not sound intelligible.

President McKay: I surmised it.

President Wilkinson: May I just say very quickly that unless there is a complete change in the situation, I am not going to run for the U.S. Senate. I should say very frankly, however, that I am making that decision, not only because of your advice, but because I really think that probably I can do more good here than if I am elected to the Senate. I have come to that conclusion after praying and long thought, and I am being a little presumptuous in thinking I should have a good chance for the Senate. The Democratic State Chairman and others in the State tell me I can easily win over [the Republican incumbent, Arthur V.] Watkins. I am not doing it because I think I would be defeated.

President McKay: Well, I appreciate what you say.

President Wilkinson: Of course, on the other hand I know of the vi[c]i[ssi]tudes and the uncertainties of politics. No one can be sure of anything.

President McKay: You have a right in your position to make a decision to be a candidate in that party for the nomination, but I can see that if the announcement is made that you have permission to have a furlough during your campaign, it will be an implication that the presidency is supporting you over Watkins. Already it came back to us, yesterday or the day before, but you have that right.

President Wilkinson: What came back to you?

President McKay: That the First Presidency would give you a furlough to make your campaign for the Senatorship.

President Wilkinson: I do not know how that could get back to you. The First Presidency never said that, and I never mentioned it to a soul. I got a report that Senator Watkins said that I have a paid agent throughout the State for my candidacy. I have talked to no one but those who have come here.

President McKay: What I said now came through that source.

President Wilkinson: It makes me just indignant. I have not gone out for a number of reasons. While I have been on the job I have not gone out and done that. There is not a single word of truth in it. People have come here, and I have given them no encouragement of any kind.

President McKay: That is not the first time that an untruth has come from that source.

President Wilkinson: I am just ornery enough that I should like to do something about it.

President McKay: That is your right.

President Wilkinson: I cannot keep people from going out and misrepresenting, but I want you to know, and if you get an opportunity in the future, you will correct it, because there is not one single bit of truth in it. That reminds me of one other thing. With respect to the Supreme Court matter, there is no opening at present, but having been in Washington as long as I was I know that the time to get an appointment of that kind is not after a vacancy is filled.

President McKay: I have said to my associates that I should like to have you on that Supreme Court.

President Wilkinson: There are two Supreme Court members eligible for retirement very soon. The Senator can get commitments in advance. Maybe in view of this untruth that has been said about me the Senator would not be at all friendly.

President McKay: I am going to tell you right now in confidence that I mentioned that to the Senator the other day. He is not favorable because of so many appointments from Utah, not because of any feeling against you, but because there are so many judgeships from Utah.

President Wilkinson: That is senseless.

President McKay: I spoke to both senators and told them that we should like to have you.

President Wilkinson: What was the viewpoint of the other Senator.

President McKay: He did not say anything.

President Wilkinson: Well, frankly, I think that is just an excuse.

President McKay: I want to tell you that Gus Backman called me up and stated that he wanted you.

President Wilkinson: I did not know that Gus knew anything about it. I just want you to know that I haven't done any talking. I could not prevent people from coming here to try to get to see me. I do resent those untruths.

President McKay: I shall see you when I come back. We are leaving now. Good-bye.

May 13, 1958.[15] President Stephen L. Richards called me by telephone and stated that he is "flat on his back" with arthritis and is unable to stand on his feet. He, therefore, stated that he would be unable to come to the meeting this morning. I expressed my concern over his illness, and said that inasmuch as we have several important decisions to make, that we would hold the meeting in President Richards' home if it would not contribute to his illness. President Richards assured me that it would not bother him and urged that we come over to his apartment for the meeting.

June 3, 1958, excerpts William F. Edwards's report. I met with President McKay Tuesday morning about 12:15 until 2:00 subject to a brief interruption. We cleared a number of important matters.

1. 1957 Annual Report, in Brief

This was the first opportunity to review with President McKay the 1957 Annual Report that was prepared in March. It was President McKay's desire that we go through the report together and then a copy was left with him [and] for each member of the Presidency. I shall highlight most briefly the significant information:

a. There has been an excess of ordinary income over all budget expenditures each year since prior to 1951, the excess for 1957 amounting to $6,128,000, and for the 7 years 1951 through 1957 the cumulative excess has been $46,816,000.

b. The report contained a summary of cash flow, there being substantial net demands for funds in carrying out the programs of the Church beyond those reflected in the budget as now presented. On a cash basis, there has also been an excess each year since prior to 1951. The excess for 1957 amounted to $2,558,000 and the cumulative total for the 7 years 1951 through 1957 amounting to $41,431,000.

c. The Church has made substantial investments in Orlando [Florida] Livestock Company, Zions Securities Corporation, and other Church-related companies totaling $24,480,000 during the 7 years 1951

---

15. McKay was on his New Zealand trip from April 11 to May 10, 1958.

through 1957. After these investments, there has been a surplus every year except 1957 when there was a cash deficit of $6,064,000. The cumulative surplus after net investment totaled $16,952,000 for the 7 years 1951 through 1957.

d. As of December 31, 1957, total of cash liquid reserve amounted to $100,427,000. As of that date, there were funds held by the Corporation of the President for others in the amount of $4,941,000 and there were unspent appropriations totaling $23,982,000, making total obligated funds of $28,923,000. After subtracting these obligated funds, there remained net cash liquid reserves of $71,504,000. In addition, there were net working funds with missions, temples, etc., totaling $2,742,000. This gives a total net cash liquid reserve and working funds and funds in foreign missions of $74,247,000.

e. The report includes an analysis of the maturity dates of the commercial paper and U.S. Government Securities of the reserve investment account as of March 31, 1958. The cost value of the account was $90,939,000 and the market value of the account was $92,292,000. The report showed that the portfolio is currently yielding at the annual rate of about $2,400,000. However, income for 1958 will be less because of the decrease in interest rates and the resultant lower yield on new purchases and the expected withdrawals during the year to finance authorized expenditures.

f. The report also included the review of 10 significant improvements in financial procedures during 1957.

2. Record of Contributions

I informed President McKay of the work we are now doing on procedures to develop equal control and equally good records over contributions of the Saints in all of the foreign missions comparable to that now in effect for the Saints in wards and North American Branches. President McKay expressed his strong approval of such a program. Our plan is to have the procedures developed and to initiate them at the time the auditors visit the various foreign missions.

3. 1957 Audit of the Corporation of the President

I reviewed with President McKay briefly the conclusion of the auditors and introduced him to the extensive report submitted to my office by the auditors. This is probably the first genuine detailed audit that has been made of the financial records of the Corporation of the President, excluding the Confidential Books. All questions raised in the Audit Report will be thoroughly investigated by my department and the Church Financial Department. We are able to assure the President that, subject to a number of adjustments yet to be made, the books are in order. ...

6. Legal Department

Previously I had made a thorough study of the Legal Department at the request of the First Presidency. I informed President McKay, or rather I brought President McKay up to date on the new procedures now being followed by which the Legal Department prepares and signs most of their own letters. This relieves the First Presidency of a minimum of 50 to 100 letters per week. At the request of President [Stephen L.] Richards and President [J. Reuben] Clark, I review the mail of the Legal Department and President McKay indicated his desire that I continue to do this, at least for the present.

We then discussed the heavy backlog of pending work of the Legal Department. I have reviewed this very carefully and I am entirely satisfied that the Legal Department needs one additional lawyer, one "Clerk" Assistant, and the necessary additional secretarial assistance. The employment of these additional people was anticipated in the 1958 budget. A question was raised as to whether the Legal Department was efficient and as to why it should need the additional staff. I pointed out to President McKay that during the past four years alone there have been created as many new wards as the growth during the administration of President Heber J. Grant from 1918 to 1945. Each new ward increases the responsibility of the Legal Department as well as the Church Financial Department and other areas. President McKay gave his approval to the recommended increase in staff of the Legal Department and authorized me to convey the information to Brother Snyder. ...

8. We presented a report showing 1958 income. Tithing contributions through April are averaging about 9% ahead of a year ago. Other income will be increased considerably because of the larger earnings on the investment of reserves. It now appears that the income for 1958 will be in the area of $2½ to $3 million more than estimated in the budget.

9. Advances to Wards and Stakes

President McKay again expressed his concern over the large increase in the number of advances. I expressed a desire to see a quarterly report on the status of the advances that would keep us informed[,] as we are informed as members of the Executive Committee[,] on the condition of the loans of Beneficial Life. President McKay expressed a strong desire that such a report be prepared and that the summary of the report be brought to the Committee on Expenditures. I shall report this to the Building Committee.

Z.C.M.I.

In view of the importance of the recommendation of the Executive Committee of Z.C.M.I. that the Company remain in the Wholesale Business, I felt it was important to meet with President McKay as Chairman of the Board before the matter went to the Board for their consideration. I pointed out to President McKay that in contrast to the 1957 deficit of $52,200 the management estimates that there will be earnings of $100,000 for 1958, at least $200,000 for 1959 and by 1961 earnings should be up to $400,000. Concurrent with the improvement of earnings, the management estimates that it will be able to reduce the average investment in accounts receivable inventories from $44,785,000 for 1957 to $4,255,000 for 1958 and $4,100,000 for 1959.

June 6, 1958, 11 a.m. I received in the office of the First Presidency Jack Dempsey,[16] former heavyweight champion of the world. Mr. George Florey of Chicago, a business associate of Jack Dempsey's, Bishop Thorpe B. Isaacson, Brother Don Mack Dalton, former President of the South African Mission and childhood friend of Jack Dempsey, and representatives of the Ogden Standard Examiner and Chamber of Commerce, accompanied him.

As I greeted Jack Dempsey, shook his hand and looked into his eyes, I said: "I have waited a long, long time for this—I have wanted to meet

---

16. William Harrison "Jack" Dempsey (1895–1983), dubbed the "Manassa Mauler" for his birthplace in an LDS settlement of that name in Colorado, spent some of his teenage years in Provo, and it was there that he first developed a reputation under the nickname Kid Blackie. In 1919, at age twenty-four, he won the heavyweight championship by defeating Jess Willard. After boxing another eight years, then managing a casino in Mexico, in 1935 he opened a successful restaurant in New York City.

you ever since I heard of you as a young man and later when you climbed to fame as the world champion. I congratulate you on your achievements!"

I then told him that I wanted to tell him an experience that I had had when I was in Scotland as a young man on my first mission. I had become discouraged and homesick one day. Among other things, a Scotchwoman had said to me as I handed her a tract: "Ye better gae hame; ye canna hae any o' poor lassies!" Well I did not want any of their lassies; I had left a sweet one at home, but it made me discouraged to think of the ill-will which these people had toward the Mormons. What misconceived notions they had of our purpose among them! I had just left school, and I loved school and loved young people, and then to go over there and feel their antipathy and prejudice gave me the blues. Furthermore, it was Spring, and as I looked out over the beautiful fields of green, I could see men plowing, getting ready[17] to do their Spring planting. Having come from a farm in a beautiful valley in Huntsville, these scenes made me truly homesick.

I was with Peter G. Johnston, one of the truest friends in all the world. He was from Idaho, and experienced—a wealthy man, and a lover of all things beautiful. I was fortunate to have his companionship. We had been assigned to Stirling, that historic town of which we read in the "Lady of the Lake" where James Fitz James won the championship, and James of Scotland had his dogs and his orchards to keep.[18] Well, I was very interested in these things. We had just been on a tour of old Stirling Castle, and it was afternoon when we left that historic site and started out east of town; that is, around the castle over the playground where James Fitz James and Douglas had their contests. As we were coming back into town, I saw on my right an unfinished dwelling, over the front door of which was a stone on which there was some carving. That was most unusual, so I said to Elder Johnston: "I'm going to see what that is." I was half way up the graveled walk when there came to my eyesight a striking motto carved in stone—it read "WHATE'ER THOU

---

17. The diary has "getting *reading* to do their Spring planting."
18. Stirling Castle was the royal residence of King James V, who in Walter Scott's epic poem "Lady of the Lake" participates in a deer hunt while dressed in disguise as James Fitz-James. His horse collapses from exhaustion and dies, and after being stranded on the shore of Lake Katrine, a young woman, Ellen Douglas, rows across the lake to rescue him. Her father, it turns out, is on a list of suspected enemies of the king.

ART, ACT WELL THY PART." I repeated it to Elder Johnston as we walked in to town to find a place for our lodgings before we began our work. As we walked toward our destination, I thought about this motto "Whate'er Thou Art, Act Well Thy Part," and took it as a direct message to me, and I said to myself, or the Spirit said to me, "You are a member of the Church of Jesus Christ of Latter-day Saints; more than that—you are here in the Mission Field as a representative of the Church, and you are to act well your part as a missionary, and you should get into the work with all your heart."

I then said to Jack Dempsey: "I congratulate you as a man who has acted well your part—one who has brought honor to your profession. More than that—you have been a true son to your parents. I know of your having purchased a home on South Temple for your mother. There is something to a man who will be good to his mother. You have been fair in your dealings with men."

Then we began to tell stories of our lives to one another—Jack Dempsey was interested in the fact that I had been a member of the first football team of the University of Utah.

Following our conversation pictures were taken. ...

11:30 a.m.—Received in the office of the First Presidency, Mr. Stanley Tracy, former Assistant to the Honorable J. Edgar Hoover, Director of the United States Federal Bureau of Information.[19] Had an interesting hour's conversation with Mr. Tracy. He discussed with me the following:

(1) J. Edgar Hoover's latest book. Later, Mr. Hoover sent Pres[ident] McKay an autographed copy of his book "Masters of Deceit."

(2) The surprising attitude of the United States Supreme Court in favoring Communism. He referred to Chief Justice [Earl] Warren[20] of California who is particularly in favor of Communism it seems. I stated that I was never so surprised in my life at Chief Justice Warren's making a

---

19. One writer called Tracy "the prim, humorless assistant director in charge of the identification division." Kahn, *Reader of Gentlemen's Mail*, 217.

20. Earl Warren (1891–1974) was the Republican governor of California for ten years and Chief Justice of the US Supreme Court from 1953 to 1969. His legal philosophy was evident in two prominent cases, *Brown v. Board of Education of Topeka*, outlawing school segregation, and *Miranda v. Arizona*, requiring that criminal suspects be informed of their rights. He would later chair the federal commission that investigated the assassination of President John F. Kennedy.

decision favoring the Communists, and Mr. Tracy answered that he, too, was greatly surprised.

We talked further about Mr. Warren's attitude and agreed that he is not a profound thinker, but more of a politician. We also talked about wiretapping, and Warren's condemning Hoover, and saying that he is violating the law in using this means of keeping close watch on the Communists. I stated that I am in sympathy with Hoover in this regard, and think that sometimes it is necessary.

I told Mr. Tracy that I look upon Communism as an enemy whose sole purpose is destruction of Capitalism and our form of government, and that the use of wire-tapping is justifiable in the preservation of our government.

I enjoyed my conference with Mr. Tracy and invited him to call again when next in the city.

June 19, 1958. President McKay unexpectedly arrived at the office this morning. His eye still bandaged,[21] and the stitches still in, he had decided to hold a meeting of the First Presidency at the apartment of President Stephen L. Richards who is confined there with an illness. ...

President McKay showed signs of having been through a great deal during his operation and confinement in the hospital. It is apparent that the operation has been a great shock to his system but he is nevertheless cheerful and very patient about it all.

June 26, 1958, 9:30 a.m. Although my eye is not yet healed, I came down to the office this morning with the full intention of attending Council meeting, the last to be held before the summer vacation. However, President [J. Reuben] Clark came into my office, and persuaded me not to go to the Temple to attend meeting. After counseling with him, I decided that it was the better part of wisdom not to go. The bandage from my eye has just been taken off, and the stitches only recently removed. Consequently, following a short consultation with my secretary Clare [Middlemiss], had Allan Acomb drive me back home.

---

21. On June 9 he had surgery at LDS Hospital for a cataract in his right eye.

July 8, 1958. Conference with Brother Hugh B. Brown who explained that he had been invited to give the keynote address at the Democratic State Nominating Convention next Saturday at the Rainbow Randevu,[22] and asked if it would be in keeping with the policy of the Church and his office as a Apostle to accept the invitation.

I said that since some think we are one-sided in politics (having a member of the Twelve as Secretary of Agriculture during a Republican administration)[23] it might be a good thing for him to accept this assignment and let the members of the Church know that both political sides are represented in the Church.

July 9, 1958. Note by Secretary[:] Today, noting a worried look on the President's face, and noting a loss of about 30 pounds since eye surgery, during trip to New Zealand, etc., I said: "President McKay, unbeknown to most people, you have had a hard life, haven't you—seven children— the sending of four sons on a mission, having been an apostle of the Church since young manhood, very little conveniences during the most of your life, etc. etc." The President related some of his financial hardships, as well as the trials of illness, etc. and then said in a serious tone of voice, "Yes, I have had a hard life; it hasn't been easy, but I would not have an easy life; I wouldn't have it any other way."

July 14, 1958. I met, according to my call, all the General Authorities of the Church who are in the city at 9 o'clock this morning. President [J. Reuben] Clark, who was not feeling very well, asked to be excused from this meeting. President [Stephen L.] Richards is absent in Yellowstone.

The following is a brief account of what was discussed at this meeting:

1. To let the Brethren know how the First Presidency stands regarding the proposed site for the new Federal building on North Temple [in Salt Lake City]; that they should understand that the First Presidency are united in favoring the North Temple site for the Federal Building. I

---

22. The Rainbow Randevu was a large dance hall in Salt Lake City on Main Street where the Little America Hotel is now located. It featured live bands and sometimes political speeches to crowds of 1,500. In 1959 it changed its name to the Terrace Ballroom.

23. This would not be the only occasion when Brown would serve as counterpoint to Benson in the political arena. See Quinn, *Extensions*, 66–115.

then read to them a quotation from the First Presidency's letter to Senator [Arthur V.] Watkins soliciting his aid in the matter.

2. I told the Brethren that it is not a question of right or wrong as in grammatical construction, but that it is question of right or wrong as in rhetoric when a statement may be better or worse, but the main point is that we should as General Authorities be united.

The Brethren left the room 100% united on the question.[24]

July 19, 1958, 9 a.m. Met by appointment at his request Dr. and Mrs. O. Preston Robinson[,] [general manager of the *Deseret News* and wife, Christine].[25] We held a discussion regarding the Middle East crisis, and the sending of armed forces by the United States and Great Britain to Lebanon.[26] Dr. Robinson repeated the story of his personal visit to President Gamal Abdal Nasser[27] when he traveled to the Middle East a year or two ago, and of his (President Nasser's) negative attitude toward Communism; that he was not in favor of the Communists. Dr. Robinson thinks if the United States had helped Nasser with money for the dam, he would not have turned to the Communists.

I asked Dr. Robinson if he really felt that President Nasser was sincere—that a real Communist will lie, steal, or go to any length in order to carry out the fundamental idea of Marx which was this: That negotiation with the Capitalists is of no use and the only way to deal with them is to exterminate them, and to be ruthless in achieving that end. I said you do not know but what Nasser was deceiving you. Dr. Robison said, "No, I

---

24. See the entry for December 21, 1956, for the church's interest in the location.

25. Robinson's wife, Christine Hinckley (1908–91), was a sister of apostle Gordon B. Hinckley. As a member of the general board of the Relief Society, she was the one who wrote the monthly visiting teaching messages for all the women of the church. She was also an interior decorator. Among her accomplishments was creating the historical decor for restored homes in Nauvoo, Illinois. In Utah she was volunteered as president of the Travelers Aid Society.

26. The United States had just sent 14,000 soldiers/sailors to Lebanon to defend the government from possible incursion by Egypt and Syria over control of the Gaza Strip and Suez Canal.

27. Gamal Abdel Nasser (1918–70) had become disillusioned with King Farouk's leadership during the Arab–Israeli War of 1948 and led a coup in 1952, overthrowing the king. Four years later he assumed the presidency and nationalized the Suez Canal, provoking Anglo–French intervention. After Egypt's military debacle in the six-day Arab–Israeli War of 1967, he was discredited and resigned. He died three years later.

think not, because they have outlawed Communism in Egypt, and only recently have executed two men because they were communists."

I said to Dr. Robinson, "Without saying anything to anybody, excepting to Elder Mark E. Petersen who is Chairman of the Executive Committee of the Deseret News, I think it would be worthwhile for you to go back and meet Ezra Taft Benson and tell him what you have told me. Let nobody get the idea that you are presuming to 'steady the ship of state', but that you may have something which will reveal a side of Nasser which [Secretary of State John Foster] Dulles has not revealed to the President. You go to Mark Petersen, without disclosing the fact that we have had a conversation, present to him your ideas, and if he, as Chairman of the Executive Committee of the Deseret News, thinks it is worthwhile, you may go at once, and I shall make arrangements for you to have a conference with Brother Benson, and it is up to him after that."

While they were still in my office, I got in touch with <u>Brother Benson by telephone</u> and told him what I had told the Robinsons. I told him that I thought it was worth while for Dr. Robinson to have a conference with him, and Brother Benson expressed himself as feeling the same way. Brother Benson said he would arrange for a meeting with President [Dwight D.] Eisenhower.

Later in the day Brother Robinson called me at home and reported that he had seen Brother Mark E. Petersen who agreed that it would be worth while for Brother Robinson to go back and meet Brother Benson Monday morning and get that side of the question at least to President Eisenhower through Brother Benson. Evidently, following our telephone message to Brother Benson, he went to the White House and told President Eisenhower of our conference ...

July 23, 1958. Notes of Conference with Dr. W[illia]m. F. Edwards written by Dr. Edwards.

I met with President McKay Wednesday morning, July 23, at 10:30 for about 25 minutes. The following items were cleared:

1. President [Ernest L.] Wilkinson had requested approval for the B.Y.U. to loan $300,000 as a first mortgage in connection with property given the University by Mr. George L. Barrett of Los Angeles, and also in connection with a business transaction of a former partner of Mr. Barrett.

The proposal is that the former partner would pay the University $62,250 for a property with 175 ft. frontage and this property, together with an adjoining property with 425 ft. frontage owned by the former partner, would be used as a building lot for a structure to cost approximately $400,000. The proposed building and the land are appraised at $580,000. This would be a 12 year, first mortgage bearing interest at 6%. President Wilkinson and his staff will be responsible for the management of the loan. The funds would be provided out of surpluses in the Auxiliary Enterprises of B.Y.U. President Wilkinson also points out that this would be a favor to Mr. Barrett and that he would greatly appreciate this favor. It might be added that Mr. Barrett originally conveyed property to the University having a value of around $400,000. By successive conveyances, he has now conveyed properties which have an aggregate value of around $1,000,000. The making of this loan was approved by President McKay and I was asked to notify President Wilkinson.

2. Return Fares of Missionaries

In the past it has been the practice to refer to the First Presidency for signature a statement prepared by Brother [Franklin J.] Murdock authorizing the Church to pay for the return fare of missionaries being honorably released. Naturally there are many of these documents to be signed. This seems to be an entirely unnecessary procedure and actually an inefficient and unwise procedure. I pointed out to President McKay that it would be more effective if the travel invoice was referred to Brother Gordon Hinckley's Office to have them check to verify that the missionary is being released and that this is the only ticket purchased for him. With their confirmation to this effect, the established policy of the Church would mean that the bill should be honored. Therefore, the matter could be referred directly to Brother Rulon Tingey, disbursement officer. President McKay approved of this procedure as entirely desirable. He asked that we contact Brother Joseph Anderson and Hamer Reiser to be certain that they would notify Gordon Hinckley's Office of any missionary being released dishonorably so that return fare tickets would not be purchased for such missionaries.

3. Payment of Secretaries for Patriarchal Blessings

The Patriarchs of the Church pay up to $1 per blessing for a secretary.

Much of the work is done without payment. The Patriarchs prepare statements requesting that the secretary be paid and this statement has been referred to the First Presidency for signature. This is another instance where this places a burden upon the First Presidency that does not seem warranted. So long as the statement submitted by the Patriarch is in order, there is nothing to do but to pay it in accordance with established policy. President McKay approved of all such documents being referred to Rulon Tingey and he will process them for payment.

July 30, 1958. <u>Dr. O. Preston Robinson's report on visit to President [Dwight D.] Eisenhower[:]</u> On July 30, 1958, I [Robinson] made a brief report to President McKay on the visit Sister Robinson and I, in company with Secretary and Sister [Ezra Taft] Benson, had with President Eisenhower in Washington [DC] on the morning of July 21st between 11:45 and 12:30 noon. I told President McKay of the cordial way in which President Eisenhower received us and reported his expression of best wishes which he asked us to convey to President McKay.

At the outset of our interview, President Eisenhower said he was most interested in receiving our views on the critical Middle East situation and indicated that often religious people were able to get information which others could not obtain.

I told President Eisenhower briefly about our meetings with Middle East leaders, particularly President Gamel Abd[e]l Nasser, in 1954 and again in October 1957. The President was most interested in our impressions of Mr. Nasser and in our opinions as to his objectives. I emphasized my convictions that Arab nationalism is a powerful force to which we should be sympathetic and that the Moslem people, including President Nasser, fear and resist Communism. They have accepted help from the Soviets only after attempting and failing to obtain help from Western nations. Due to recent and present political domination by Western nations in the area and because of the West's extensive economic interests, the Arabs are suspicious of Western intentions and fear the Americans are attempting to replace the British and the French in control of the area. This fear, plus the creation and existence of Israel, are the chief reasons why anti-Western feeling runs so deep in the Middle East. For an Arab to be pro-West in that area now is almost treasonable.

Despite this anti-West sentiment, there is a deep reservoir of respect and admiration for Western and particularly for American ways of life and for the American form of government. This reservoir needs to be tapped in order to reverse the present drift which is leading this area ever closer to Communist domination.

I reported to President Eisenhower that President Nasser had told us that his country and other Arab countries would resist to the bitter end outside domination from any source. However, he told us, if they must be dominated, they would rather be dominated by the United States than by Russia. I also emphasized the fact that President Nasser had expressed a sincere desire to talk face to face with President Eisenhower, provided such a conference would not be humiliating to his country nor would in any way threaten his country's sovereignty.

President Eisenhower responded most favorably to this comment and stated that he would like to talk with Mr. Nasser provided, of course, that he could do so without embarrassing our allies—the British, the French, and Israel.

President Eisenhower was keenly interested in what we had to say. He was courteous, gracious and extended the interview fifteen minutes beyond the prescribed time. At the close of our conversation, he re-emphasized his opening observation that he was most interested in getting the opinions and impressions of an honest man who had no ulterior motives other than the welfare of the United States.

President Eisenhower asked me to submit my observations and recommendations in a brief report. He said that when he gets things in writing, he can make sure that they are adequately followed up. He also suggested that I have a talk with Secretary [John Foster] Dulles. This interview was arranged and I talked briefly with Mr. Dulles the following day, Wednesday, July 22nd.

August 9, 1958. Left Huntsville this morning with the intention of driving to Salt Lake to have my Buick car repaired. However I thought it folly for me to drive clear to Salt Lake City when I could probably have it fixed at the Buick agency in Ogden, so I drove to Browning's on Washington Blvd. As I entered the show room, I found to my surprise that I had unintentionally run into a state-wide gladiola show. It was a wonderful exposition of some of the most beautiful gladiola flowers in the world; there were sixty varieties. It was early in the morning, but many people were there, and I soon found myself surrounded by them—men, women, and their children from all parts of the State. However, I had a very pleasant time with them. Pictures were take[n] for the local newspapers, and radio interviews held.

August 13, 1958, First Presidency meeting. It was decided that the sacrament should not be administered to the inmates of the Utah State Prison because of the sacred nature of the covenants and obligations and because of their inability to keep them.[28]

August 29, 1958, 9 a.m. Presided at the regular meeting of the First Presidency. At this meeting a letter was read from Dr. Hubert Eaton of Forest Lawn, of Los Angeles, California, which reviewed arrangements he has made to secure two replicas of [Bertel] Thorwaldsen's statue of the Christus.[29] He reported that the Italian Company quoted $6,400 for two replicas, one for Forest Lawn, and one for the Church, for erection on Temple Square. The cost of transportation will be additional. Marble of suitable texture and grain for our cold climate will be used in the statue to be prepared for the Church.

President [Stephen L.] Richards requested for himself and Sister Richards the privilege of presenting the statue to the Church.[30] President [J. Reuben] Clark and I concurred in granting the request and reserved the right to have a suitable plaque prepared and erected, acknowledging the gift. Explanation was made that a suitable canopy to protect the statue in cold weather can be erected.

---

28. Sacrament meeting was still held for the inmates, but the sacrament was not provided. A Sunday school lesson was usually given after the more formal service, and then the men who provided the religious devotions met separately to partake of the sacrament.

29. The statue was created for the national cathedral of Denmark (Church of Our Lady) in 1821, along with matching statues of the twelve apostles.

30. Richards had suggested the replica and arranged for its sculpting through his contacts as owner of Wasatch Lawn Cemetery in Salt Lake City. He also anonymously paid for it. The massive replica was displayed for the first time on Temple Square in 1967 in a building designed to house it and given the descriptive moniker of North Visitors Center. Matthew O. Richardson, "Five Things You Never Knew about the Christus Statue," *LDS Living Magazine*, www.ldsliving.com.

September 5, 1958, excerpts from a discussion of apostasy among the French missionaries, London, England.[31]

President McKay: The third point is regarding the most unfortunate condition in France. Brother [Henry D.] Moyle, will you please make a statement regarding it.

Brother Moyle: I think Brother [Hugh B.] Brown, who has been in Paris, and I have not, should speak. I held some meetings last Saturday, and Sunday, in Brussels.[32]

Brother Hugh B. Brown: Well, while in Basel [Switzerland], President Milton L. Christensen of the French Mission called me on the phone and said that there was very serious trouble, and asked me if I could come over. I was just leaving for Rome, but I flew to Paris and he told me the nature of the trouble when I arrived. He said that there was a group of missionaries who were preaching polygamy and a lot of other things, denouncing the Manifesto and circulating literature sent to them by the Fundamentalists.

Question by President McKay: Why did he permit it?

---

31. The controversy among the French missionaries involved nineteenth-century teachings on polygamy and related issues. McKay and the other church officials from Utah met on this date in a London hotel, two days before the temple dedication on September 7–9. The French missionaries were expected to arrive the next day, September 6, to participate in the dedication and to attend the temple. The notes for this meeting were taken by secretary A. Hamer Reiser.

32. Less than a week earlier, Moyle had recorded: "There are 5 or 6 elders who are converted to the fundamentalist movement and cannot sustain President McKay. Two have gone home. There are 8 more who should, including President Christensen's second counselor [William P. Tucker], with whom Brother Hugh B. Brown spoke in Paris yesterday. It broke out in the Nancy, France, district. The elders started preaching their doctrine to the saints [church members]. All the missionaries have the question of the validity of the Manifesto on their minds. The condition is not good.

"In each mission we have visited there are serious problems with elders, etc. I see no escape from the re-establishment of a European Mission, or in any event, keeping someone here for six months or more every year. The mission presidents are all bewildered and have had no answers to most of the letters for months past. It is not good to have mission presidents in the frame of mind ours are in. Last night Brother and Sister Christensen were just beside themselves, at a loss to know what to do. They have learned to love their second counselor, who is the ringleader and who is encouraged by long letters and literature sent from a former missionary, now attending the B.Y.U. If reports are true, and I think they are, he should be excommunicated for the propaganda he is carrying on to disrupt the work and the thinking of the elders. Brother Brown is reporting the matter to President Joseph Fielding Smith in London." Moyle diary, Aug. 31, 1958, typed excerpt in Quinn Papers.

Brother Brown: It seemed to have been going on for some time. They had been meeting secretly. They had been holding protected meetings—a group of the leaders—Elders. They would admit only those whom they thought worthy of "higher things." A man who went home just before Brother [Harold W.] Lee[33] was released [as mission president] had apparently been doing some of this, but he left, and upon arrival home he sent a whole package of this Fundamentalist literature back to his companion, including a 100-page letter setting out the troubles the church is in, and the solution of them all. It was sent to the counselor of the Mission President, a missionary by the name of [William P.] Tucker.[34] Tucker, with this material, called in a few of his close associates and companions and began to teach it to them. That went on before the President discovered it. Tucker was the counselor in the Mission Presidency. He traveled over the Mission. He was leaving some of this literature. When I arrived in Paris, he, (President Christensen) told me the situation, and I asked where Tucker was; and he said he was down in Geneva on an assignment, and I asked him to phone at once and bring him into the office, which he did.

I sat down and talked to Tucker for three hours. I talked with him and used every method that I could think of, persuasion and prayer. I wept with him. He sat there looking me in the eye. He did not take his eye off me while I talked with him. I said, "Do you accept the [1890 Wilford Woodruff] Manifesto [banning plural marriages]?" He said, "I do not." "Do you believe that polygamy should be practiced now?" He said, "I know that there are righteous men who are practicing it with the knowledge of the General Authorities."

"Do you believe that President McKay is two-faced and is talking out of both sides of his mouth and not telling the truth?"

---

33. Harold Willey Lee (1907–78), originally from Cardston, Alberta, was a BYU French professor and department chair who received his PhD from Stanford University. As a young man, he had studied at BYU and served a mission to France.

34. William P. Tucker (ca. 1936–67) converted to the LDS Church in Pasadena. After his excommunication in France, he traveled to Mexico and joined the LeBaron family's Church of the Firstborn, soon marrying the former French missionaries Marilyn Lamborn and Nancy Fulk, although he and Fulk would separate. For a while Tucker served as a fundamentalist mission president in California, but eventually drifted away from the LeBarons and died of appendicitis in his early thirties.

"I believe just that. But I do not and I would not know until the Lord reveals it to me."

I said, "I am here representing the General Authorities looking into this matter, and I am telling you that you are wrong."

He said, "I do not accept you as an Apostle. I take my direction from the Lord and only from Him."

I won't take too much of your time. I made no impression whatever on Tucker. I was impressed that I should instruct the President to send him home at once, but with this meeting coming up, and inasmuch as there was another of the Brethren on assignment, I did not want to over-step my bounds.

I told him to stop his operation, and that we shall not allow him to meet with any missionaries again until we can have the meeting here.

Two other young men had been affected, and they had already made arrangements to go home. Apparently they were of the same opinion. Brother [Gordon B.] Hinckley had talked with the president about them and they had gone home. Still two others with whom I had talked had the same attitude.[35]

Brother Hinckley said: The first indication was about ten days ago.

Brother Brown: There were two other men who had talked the same way. One was stony-faced. I asked when they got their first impressions and they refused to answer. They said they would not implicate anybody. One young woman nearly 30, a fine woman, had also become so imbued with it. This young woman was ready to go into polygamy. She was wait-ing for an opportunity. I talked with her for some time, but I think she has completely changed her mind. Tucker—the counselor to the Pres-ident—he almost put them under covenant not to tell, but she broke down and told me the whole thing. She said she had lost confidence in the General Authorities of the Church and thought that they were two-faced, and she said, "After hearing you, I ask forgiveness. I thank God you

---

35. Hinckley was an Assistant to the Twelve. He later wrote, "I talked with them at length and gave them my assurance that no good would come of their actions, and that the day would come when they would regret what they were doing. I bore them my testi-mony of the gospel and tried every way I knew to persuade them to reverse their course, but to no avail. At that point there was little for me to do but make sure they had a way to get home. We felt we owed that to their parents" (in Dew, *Go Forward with Faith*, 203).

came and I want to tell you I will never have anything to do with this again. I will personally accept your statement."

There were two other ladies in the French Mission—American missionaries—who I think will have to go home. I think someone must see them individually and decide each individual case on its merits. They are saying there are two Priesthoods, and John the Revelator is the man who presides over you and he has given them instructions through this man Tucker that he does not need to ask for instructions from you or me or anyone else. I have never in my life run into anything quite like it. I had all those cases in Granite [Utah] Stake under Dr. Talmage. We handled cases of those polygamists, including John Burt.[36]

Tucker is a missionary from home. He is a brilliant young man, too brilliant for his own good. He is the most defiant, self-opinionated person I have ever met.

Brother Moyle: President Christensen and his wife, if they said it to me once, they said it a half a dozen times: "They hated to do anything with Tucker because they had learned to love him."

President Christensen came into the mess and he did not know what he ought to do with it. He evidently did not know it existed until ten days ago.

Brother Hinckley: About ten days ago, President Christensen phoned the Bishop of these two boys. The boys' parents had received requests for money for the boys to come home, so the boys' Bishop called, and he sent a cable to President Christensen asking for a report on the situation. President Christensen cabled, and then telephoned and said these boys had no faith and no testimony. They were determined to come home. I told him I would talk with a member of the Presidency, [and] if they were insistent on coming home, he could hold them there [for a short time]. Brother Brown would be there in Paris in a few days. The parents sent money to one of the boys, the other boy's parents sent no money. Then President Christensen called to make a plea for the London meeting, and I talked with President [J. Reuben] Clark and he said we shall approve the London meeting, and we sent a cable to that effect.

President Christensen did not say that polygamy was in it at all.

---

36. A number of polygamous fundamentalists were excommunicated in Brown's stake on September 7, 1935. Quinn, *Extensions*, 824; Quinn, *Elder Statesman*, 252–53.

These two young men had lost their faith. He said they were getting wonderful results in the French Mission, and the devil was really at work. Not only these two young men, but about ten others. I suggested that he talk with Brother Brown and give him the word of the London meeting, and you (President McKay) would be here and the matter could be resolved at that time. That was about ten days ago.

Henry D. Moyle: This last Sunday, they held a public meeting down in Brussels. They had a wonderful conference. I spent all Saturday with the Elders and President Christensen, but did not know how far this group of Elders had been affected. They had some 37 Elders from the Brussels and Liège Districts, which goes as far as Lille [130 miles west] in France. After a whole day's work interviewing them and talking to them, they held a testimony meeting.

I did not attend the testimony meeting. That was held Sunday night after three big meetings Sunday called by President Christensen. It was a regular District Conference. Testimony meeting was a continuation of the Saturday meeting. The upshot of the matter is that the Elders of these two districts are all right. At 10 o'clock President Christensen came to my room in the hotel and said he had a report from Nancy, France, District Headquarters, that they had a big meeting at which the District Supervising Elder had publicly, from the pulpit, preached these Fundamentalist doctrines. All the Elders from Nancy seemed to be affected. So far as he knew, it was the first time it had broke[n] out in public.

Another thing—I met with all the Elders in West Germany in the Meeting that we held in Dusseldorf where there were 57 Elders present. The spirit was pretty good, but I think there is something there that needs pretty careful attention.

When I got to Stuttgart, I felt the very devil himself was there. There was not anything I could pinpoint, but I think a feeling that there might be some relationship between the feeling I had at Stuttgart and in the French Mission. I am sure that is the French situation. The first thing after I talked with the Elders, instantly they started to ask me about the Manifesto and Brother [John W.] Taylor and Brother [Matthias F.] Cowley. I cut them off pretty short. I told them that they were not in their missions to discuss that question. I am afraid it has affected some others. It is pretty hard to keep it confined. They correspond with one another.

Brother [Thorpe B.] Isaacson: I was in Paris and I met Brother Brown. I was not staying at the Mission Home. The next morning, President Christensen and his wife went to Brussels and they volunteered to have the missionaries take me to the plane. We were staying at the hotel and one of the missionaries whom I had interviewed for his mission came. The other man is a son of a very fine stake president, Elder [Cecil E.] Hart from Idaho Falls. I had been to their home twice, and I knew this boy, when he was about 14 and again about 19 or 20. So I took another walk in Paris. I was astounded at how reluctant they are to tell anything. I said to Hart: "You are all right, Brother Hart; knowing your father like I do, they could not mix you up, could they?"

He is a fine chap. I do not think they have hurt him, but I did not get a positive answer. He said, "No, they could not hurt me, but there is a lot of teaching going on that you do not know what to think."

While I think that they have not touched him, I think they have him disturbed. This man Tucker was with him. This boy Hart is a fine boy, but someone will have to reinforce him. I think every missionary over there will have to be reinforced and put straight.

Brother Moyle: All those 37 missionaries need something to support and sustain them. President Christensen is absolutely lost.

President McKay: Where is Tucker from?

Answer "From California."

Hugh B. Brown: He is from President [Howard W.] Hunter's Stake—Pasadena. He was a companion of Elder Shore. Elder Shore is the one who started this, yes, beginning the last few months. He is a student going to school.

Question: Is Tucker an unmarried man so far as you know?

Answer by Brother Brown: He says he is unmarried. And Shore is an unmarried man, so far as I know.

They have all kinds of mysteries—the Adam-God idea. They are talking about many things that I have not heard of. He said, "You are not up-to-date." President Hunter will be here Sunday. Tucker is from his Stake. (Insert by Brother Reiser [keeping notes]—By the way, I think Brother Brown [was the one who] said all these things although my notes do not indicate it definitely. But I am quite sure it was Brother Brown.)

He (Tucker) pledged them to say nothing about it.

President McKay: Now, Brethren, we had better call a meeting of the Mission Presidents tomorrow, Saturday, at 10 o'clock.

Our Elders in Europe, as indicated here in France, are preaching the eternity of the marriage covenant as being plural marriage itself. They are misled. They should get clearly in mind the thought that the principle of that great revelation is the <u>eternity of the marriage covenant</u>, and what that principle is, the Prophet Joseph [Smith] explains clearly. The marriage bonds of man and wife will last through the eternity—just as plain as the English language can express it. When the Prophet Joseph received the great revelation on the eternity of the marriage covenant, he asked the Lord about Abraham, Isaac and Jacob and David and Solomon, each of whom had more than one wife; and then the Lord explained that "If I give to him a virgin by this same covenant, he has not sinned because I have given her to him." That is marriage under the covenant. "If he has ten virgins, and he is married under the covenant, it is right because I have blessed it, and if he does not have them given under the covenant, he is committing adultery." Marriage with more than one wife is just as legal as with one wife because it comes under the eternity of the marriage covenant.

But the Church did away with the practice of plural marriage because of the law. President [Wilford] Woodruff said he was going to do away with that practice, but he did not deny the principle of the eternity of the marriage covenant. It is in force today as it has always been in force, but the <u>practice</u> of plural marriage is not permitted, and anybody who indulges in it or permit[s] marriage into it, has violated the law of the Church and merits excommunication.

In the Book of Mormon times, they had the same experience. The Lord called the plurality of wives an abomination, but that did not do away with the eternity of the marriage covenant, for it is an eternal principle. The "Cultists" think with polygamy they will receive greater blessings in the Hereafter, and that the Authorities of the Church are deluded. They do not understand the difference between the eternity of the marriage covenant, and a practice of plural marriage.

Brother Brown: They are reading into it that you must be in polygamy to get to the highest degree of glory.

Brother Hinckley: A meeting of the French missionaries is scheduled for [a week from] Wednesday. President Christensen would like some of the

Brethren present Wednesday at 10 o'clock. He would like some of the Brethren to meet on that occasion. They have [the old mission headquarters at] Ravenslea Hall[37] lined up for the meeting on September 10th. All the French missionaries are coming, and he hopes this thing will be nipped at that time.

Brother Hugh B. Brown: I wonder whether we ought to see these brethren separately rather than to open up with all the missionaries.

Brother Moyle: When Brother Christensen said that he had authority to bring all his missionaries, I felt sorry that that authority had been given. I would like to see that cancelled. I do not believe it would be good to have them come. I think it is a matter which has got to be handled on an individual basis. They are coming tomorrow. I would not have them come to the Temple.

Brother Hugh B. Brown (I believe this statement was made by him, although I am not sure): I think Brother Moyle is exactly right. I think there are too many polluted. They are not worthy to go through the Temple.

President McKay said: It is 10 o'clock. We will adjourn this meeting, and if you will just wait here in the hotel, we will reassemble after we get through with this appointment. We will decide on the action pertaining to these missionaries. They should not come. You meet the Mission Presidents and present this matter to them.

If they are coming, we should interview everyone of them singly.[38]

---

37. The Ravenslea chapel, sometimes referred to in the diary as the old mission home or the building on Nightingale Lane, was the mission's headquarters during World War II. Although there were no active missionaries, the congregations organized under the mission leadership still needed administrative oversight. Baugh, "Church in Twentieth-century Great Britain," 21.

38. The next day Moyle recorded the following: "All the general authorities met at the mission home at 6 o'clock a.m. with President Christensen and 105 French missionaries for the purpose of screening out any unworthy to go to the [London] temple. President [Joseph Fielding] Smith, myself and Brother [Hugh B.] Brown met the questionable ones. By 8 o'clock we had interviewed all of them. Each of the other brothers worked alone, referring doubtful ones for us to resolve. 10 missionaries, 4 lady missionaries and 6 elders, were denied cards to the temple. They each admitted they were so far out of accord with President McKay and the general authorities that they should not go. They do not believe in the Manifesto or any of the authorities since. I have never seen people so rebellious. Too bad it was not discovered sooner, and wonderful it was not let go any longer. It demonstrated the need for more frequent visits of general authorities. I recommend one of us here all the time. We arranged to meet this [group of] ten tomorrow at the [new] mission home [at Princes Lane], while the French Mission conference is held [five miles distant at the] South London Branch, Nightengale Lane. I was assigned to meet with the ten with Bishop [Thorpe B.] Isaacson, Brother Brown to meet with the 95." Moyle diary, Sept. 9, 1958.

September 10, 1958,[39] excerpts of letter from President Milton L. Christensen of the French Mission.

On September 10, an Elder's Court was held in London at [the new Hyde Park mission home at] 50 Princes Gate,[40] under instructions by President David O. McKay and under the direction of Elder Henry D. Moyle.[41] ...

---

39. The letter is dated September 13, but is placed here based on the date of the event reported.

40. The Hyde Park mission home at 50 Princes Gate, Exhibition Road, would be dedicated six days later on September 16, and three years later President McKay would return and dedicate an adjacent chapel.

41. Moyle wrote: "I picked Bishop [Thorpe B.] Isaacson up at the Cumberland Hotel at 8:45 a.m. We met President [Milton L.] Christensen of the French Mission at the [new] British Mission headquarters [at Hyde Park], with also 10 of his missionaries whom we had not permitted to go to the temple yesterday. ... We started the meeting with prayer. I was mouth. I then pleaded with them for an hour, followed by Bishop Isaacson, President Milton Christensen, and a little later we sent for [the mission mother][,] Sister Christensen[,] and had her plead with them. We then interviewed them separately, the four of us being present, Brothers [Hugh B.] Brown, Isaacson, Christensen and myself. The nine of them [one had left with Mrs. Christensen] were more rebellious than ever and wanted to be excommunicated, so they said. They all wanted to be dishonorably released from their missions. We told them they would be released. They stayed around [for the excommunication proceedings].

"I sent for Brother Hugh B. Brown who was speaking to 95 remaining missionaries at the old headquarters in Nightengale Lane, London S.W. When he came we decided we had best try them [the nine missionaries] for their membership. We asked them if they would waive notice and consent to be tried by a court that we might convene, and all be tried together. They consented readily to all. So we four called in four elders of the French Mission who had come with Brother Brown. ... The eight of us constituted the court. I presided. President Christensen [and three] Elders ... were named to represent the accused, the other four the prosecution. We had them individually consent to the court. The trial proceeded with a minimum of difficulty. They all pleaded guilty to the charge of apostasy and indicated a desire to be excommunicated. The specific act of apostasy was the denial of President David O. McKay as a prophet, seer and revelator.

"We heard from the four members for the prosecution, then the nine defendants, then the four for the defense. Finally we gave them all a chance to say anything further they desired. They said the church's stand upon polygamy was one reason why we had lost the priesthood. None of them sustained any of us as general authorities. They were absolutely unbending. They were obsessed with their own righteousness. The court withdrew after they had all admitted they believed polygamy should be practiced in the church ... and after due deliberation, by unanimous vote, they voted to excommunicate all nine missionaries. We reconvened court and pronounced sentence upon them individually. We assured them of our willingness to help them come back in the church the moment they repented. They evidently were not guilty of any immorality or other offense against the rules of the mission.

"In the morning I called them to repentance, but all my words went unheeded. They

The following missionaries were found guilty of apostasy and were accordingly excommunicated from the Church of Jesus Christ of Latter day Saints: ...

These nine missionaries, together with another sister missionary who has since asked to return home with them, will sail from LeHavre, France on the Greek Line "NEW YORK" on September 16, 1958 and arrive in New York City on September 26.

Briefly here is an outline of what happened preceding the above action: Recently some of our missionaries have been studying and delving into teachings not in accordance with the accepted doctrine of the Church, and widespread and painstaking labor has been done to stamp this out. These teachings, however, were of a very secret nature, and because of this, it was not until towards the end of the month of August that we were able to pinpoint where the trouble was stemming from and to extract from some of the above named missionaries the confession that they believed these teachings, basically those of the widespread group known broadly as "fundamentalists."

On August 23, Elder Hugh B. Brown of the Council of the Twelve Apostles arrived in Paris, and interviewed four of our missionaries. We found them to be in an apostate condition, and two of them, after requesting permission, were allowed to return to the United States. Upon arriving the following week in London, and after reporting to President McKay and President [Joseph Fielding] Smith, Elder Brown called to say that it had been decided that all missionaries would be interviewed by one of the General Authorities Tuesday morning, September 9 before being allowed to attend the morning session of the dedication of the Temple.

This was accomplished early that morning, with interviewing being done by the following members of the General Authorities: Joseph Fielding

seemed to have a great affection for President Christensen but would not heed his counsel. It was a sad day. I saw President McKay at 9 a.m. as he was leaving for Wales. ... He gave me his final advice with reference to these missionaries and charged me with the responsibility of explaining to them the difference between the principle of Celestial marriage and the practice of polygamy. He also instructed me to be merciful for the sake of parents and friends as well as themselves. There was no opening left by them for us to do anything for them, so at 4 p.m. we left them [to decide their travel plans]. Hugh Brown and Bishop Isaacson went to the 95 [missionaries at the Ravenslea chapel] to explain." Moyle diary, Sept. 10, 1958.

Smith, Henry D. Moyle, Richard L. Evans, Hugh B. Brown, Thorpe B. Isaacson, ElRay L. Christiansen, and Gordon B. Hinckley. It was found at that time that ten of the French Missionaries were in an apostate condition, and should not be admitted to the Temple. Nine of them requested that they be excommunicated, and requested also that it be done together.

Hours were spent that day and the following morning by the above named authorities and by Sister Christensen and myself in laboring and pleading with these young men and women, asking that they repent and come back to finish the fine work that they had started in the mission field. This work, however, was in vain, and although exceeding love was shown by all those who plead and reasoned with them, they stood firm. Again they requested excommunication, and that this action be taken with them as a group.

The above named Elder's Court was then called, and these nine missionaries were excommunicated from the Church of Jesus Christ of Latter day Saints, for apostasy. This action was based on their negative answers, give[n] independently to the question of whether or not they sustained David O. McKay as a Prophet, Seer and Revelator.

Our hearts go out to these young men and women, to their parents and families, for we know that they have taken a step which will adversely affect their eternal progress. They were among our finest missionaries, until they came under the influence of these teachings. We pray that some day in the near future they may be loosened from this diabolical power, and that they might again seek baptism into the Church of Jesus Christ of Latter day Saints.

September 23, 1958, 8:30 a.m. Elder LeGrand Richards and I had a conference with Elder Harvey William Harper this morning at 8:30 o'clock. Brother Harper gave up his mission in France and came home because he had become confused over his association with a group of missionaries who had been secretly teaching polygamy and had joined with the "Fundamentalists" under the leadership of Elder William P. Tucker ... a member of the French Mission Presidency who had come from California as a fully authorized missionary of the Church.[42]

---

42. Others besides Harper had left the mission early but were not excommunicated. Marlene Wessel, who later married Douglas Wayne Owens (mission secretary

I asked Elder Harper when he was first approached with the idea that it is right to practice polygamy now and that those who oppose it have apostatized from the Church. He answered that he got that information while serving as a missionary in the French mission.

I then asked him when he changed in his thinking and when he came to the conclusion that the General Authorities of the Church are the authorized representatives of the Church. He answered: "<u>I knew it in the Mission Field, but I did not know that I knew it.</u>"

Elder Harper bore his testimony to me that he knows that he has made a grave mistake; that he does have a testimony of the truth of the Gospel, and would like to make restitution for what he has done and also to finish his mission.

<u>At 4 p.m.</u> I had a consultation with Gordon Hinckley, Assistant to the Twelve, who had been appointed by me while in London to go to France and investigate conditions at Mission Headquarters. He said that he had spent hours going through mission files and correspondence, and that he could find nothing that would lead to a suspicion of what was going on—that Elder Tucker and his followers were sworn to secrecy.

Brother Hinckley said that he had gone to the dock to see the nine missionaries who had been excommunicated while in London who were [leaving] on a Greek liner for New York. He told them he did not come to preach to them; that they had had better men than he talk to them (Elders Joseph Fielding Smith, Henry D. Moyle, Richard L. Evans, Hugh B. Brown, Bishop Thorpe B. Isaacson) but that he had come in the interest of their parents to see that they had enough money to get home safely; that he also wished to bear his testimony to them and to say to them that they would live to regret what they were doing on that day—leaving the mission field, probably for Mexico to practice their mistaken ideas.

Brother Hinckley said all the missionaries, excepting Elder Tucker and one of the girls, seemed morose and down-cast.

I told Brother Hinckley that after talking today to Elder Harper, I am inclined to let him return to the mission field—not to the French

---

and future Democratic US Congressman from Utah), was allowed to return to serve out the rest of her mission in France. Two other missionaries who left early were excommunicated at home. Some of those still in the mission said they regretted staying. Mehr, "Trial of the French Mission, 42, 44

Mission—but to receive a transfer to the Eastern States. I told him that I had talked to President Stephen L. Richards about it, and that he was in agreement with this plan. Brother Hinckley will now effect the transfer to the Eastern States Mission. I also instructed him to get in touch with President Jacobsen, President of that Mission, and let him know the whole story about Brother Harper so that he may watch the situation. (see 2:40 p.m.) …

2:40 p.m. Elder Harvey William Harper with whom I had consultation this morning returned to the office as per agreement. I told him of our decision to let him finish his mission in the Eastern States. Told him to report to Gordon Hinckley.

September 24, 1958, 7:30 a.m. <u>Visited Elder Ezra Taft Benson in the LDS Hospital</u> where he has been confined for the past few days for a check-up. He suffered a gall bladder attack last Monday evening while delivering an address in Salt Lake City.

Brother Benson seemed to be feeling very well. He said that the doctors are calling at 10 o'clock this morning to release him. He said that they had found that there was nothing wrong with his heart; that he had suffered a gall bladder attack; that the stone had passed through and that he is now all right.

I mentioned to Brother Benson that he had <u>"stirred up" the democrats in giving his talk the other evening.</u> He asked me if I had any objection, and I told him that he could do nothing else since he is US Secretary of Agriculture. Brother Benson said that he had forty appointments ahead of him, and that three fourths of them are non-political.

I told him to go ahead, and congratulated him on the success that he is having with the farmers.

October 8, 1958, 9 a.m. <u>Elder Henry D. Moyle</u> made a further report to the First Presidency on <u>pari-mutuel betting.</u>[43] He said that Utah county residents, upon checking the names of supposedly qualified voters on the horse-racing and pari-mutual betting petitions filed at the State Capitol,

---

43. The church would again take a strong stand in 1992 and help defeat an attempt to legalize betting in the election that year. Pari-mutuel implies gamblers wagering against each other instead of against an oddsmaker.

have found the names of many deceased persons, many persons who have moved away, and in addition, the names of many people who claim never to have seen the petitions and deny having signed them. Richard Bird, attorney, thinks there is good chance to defeat the petitions on the grounds of illegal signatures. The residents affected are willing to be plaintiffs in appropriate legal action to defeat the petitions.

It was agreed that appropriate legal action to defeat the petition be supported and that the aid of stake presidents be sought in checking the petitions which may be presented from other counties with a view to discovering if there may be any illegal signatures upon them, and that decision as to joining in the resolution await the outcome of this action.

October 12, 1958. ... I met at the office Elder Ezra Taft Benson where for twenty minutes he consulted with me about his work in Washington [DC]. He brought to my attention a copy of the Washington Farm Reporter (Report No. 839) of October 4, 1958 in which some statements [appear] regarding "Mr. Benson's remarkable political come-back"—that in New York there is "considerable interest in Benson as a potential Republican presidential candidate for 1960."[44]

In our conversation I said to Brother Benson "do not seek the candidacy; let them come to you and if they do, we shall consider it."

October 26, 1958. President McKay quite miserable today because stitches are irritating his eye. The doctor reports they are not yet ready to be removed. President McKay remained in bed most of the day.

October 31, 1958, 10 a.m. to 12 noon. Held a meeting with my counselors at my home. During our two-hour meeting we gave consideration to the letter signed by Presidents of the Stakes in the Idaho Falls area reviewing public interest and action being proposed by citizens of Idaho Falls for the circulation of a petition to the legislature for the establishment of a state college at Idaho Falls. The letter included President [Ernest L.]

---

44. Benson opined: "I've said over and over again that I have no political aspirations. All I want to do is to serve President Eisenhower as best I can as long as he thinks he needs me. Then I want to come home." The vice-chair of the Republican National Committee, I. Lee Potter, said, "Ezra, don't throw cold water on the idea" of running for office. Benson, *Cross Fire*, 408.

Wilkinson's occurrence in the subject being brought to the attention of the First Presidency for consideration of the advisability of making an announcement as to the plans of the Church to develop Ricks College at Idaho Falls.

Consideration was also give to the memorandum of the meeting held in Idaho Falls, attended by citizens interested in petitioning for the establishment of a Junior College in Idaho Falls as well as the memorandum of legal steps to be taken for an election upon the issue and for financing the establishment of a Junior College.

After consideration it was unanimously agreed to recommend to the Council of the Twelve and the Board of Education that steps be taken to establish Ricks College at Idaho Falls. It was decided to present this recommendation to the Council of the Twelve today in a special meeting and to have Elder Marion G. Romney and Elder Hugh B. Brown go to Rexburg to present the decision to the presidents of the Rexburg Stakes, and to ask them to sustain the action, and that thereafter announcement of the decision be released to the newspapers in Idaho Falls and Salt Lake City.[45]

Later in a meeting of the First Presidency and the Council of the Twelve held at 12:20 p.m. in the Board Room of the First Presidency President [Stephen L.] Richards presented the recommendation of the First Presidency, and reported the meeting with me this morning at my home about the matter. It was later reported to me that after a discussion, on motion of Elder Delbert L. Stapley, seconded by Elder Mark E. Petersen, the recommendation of the First Presidency that Ricks College be moved to a permanent location at Idaho Falls was approved and also approved were plans to have Elders Romney and Brown present this decision to the stake presidencies and bishops of the Rexburg stakes in a meeting to be held Sunday, and that they be asked to sustain this action. Thereafter that announcement of the action be released to the newspapers in Idaho Falls and Salt Lake City.

The balance of the day I rested.

---

45. Wilkinson was elated and subsequently mused in his diary that "there is one moral to the Ricks College transfer, namely that if one is right (as I was sure I was), one should not hesitate to question the decision of the President of the Church as long as it is done properly." On the bottom of the page, there is a penciled notation: "I apparently crowed too early on the above. It now seems President McKay will reverse this decision." Wilkinson diary, Oct. 29–Nov. 3, 1958.

November 4, 1958. The following is a report from Elder Marion G. Romney and Elder Hugh B. Brown who went to Rexburg to investigate Ricks College matters at the request of the First Presidency: (President McKay was at home convalescing from eye surgery at this time.)

<u>Rexburg Stakes Sustain Action on Ricks College</u>

President Stephen L. Richards asked that the record show that Elder Marion G. Romney called and reported that he and Brother Hugh B. Brown called President [Delbert G.] Taylor and President [Orval P.] Mortensen of the Rexburg Stakes Sunday evening to Idaho Falls and explained to them the action taken by the First Presidency and the Board of Education relating to the removal of Ricks College from Rexburg to Idaho Falls and asked for their cooperation in getting a meeting of prominent Church people in Rexburg in order that the matter could be presented and explained to them. President Taylor and President Mortensen, while greatly disappointed, nevertheless said that they would do what the brethren requested and that if the First Presidency, the Twelve and the Board of Education had reached a decision, that they would abide by it and cooperate with them.

President Taylor and President Mortensen returned to Rexburg and called a meeting, which was held Sunday evening at 9:00 p.m. and which was attended by the presidencies of both stakes, members of the high councils of both stakes, bishoprics of all wards, patriarchs, and presidents of all Melchizedek priesthood quorums, total about 135. After making a full explanation of the matter Brother Romney said that the General Authorities would be pleased if the brethren present would indicate their cooperation in this important movement and someone of the group made a motion that the action of the General Authorities be given their full support. All but four of those present voted in favor of the motion and three of the four came to the brethren after the meeting and said they would like to change their vote. Brother Romney said that he felt that the Spirit of the Lord was in this meeting and that the people manifested a spirit of humility and a spirit of devotion to the Church which motivated them sincerely to take the action which they took at the meeting.

Monday morning at 7 o'clock Brother Romney and Brother Brown met the presidents of the Idaho Falls Stakes and told them of the reaction of the people in Rexburg. The brethren asked that they be especially considerate of the people in Rexburg. Brother Romney reported that the stake presidents in and around Idaho Falls were gratified with the decision and felt that the movement to secure a State Junior College would be abandoned.

Elder Mark E. Petersen subsequently reported that he had conferred with several business men in Idaho Falls, including Mr. [E. Francis] McDermott, owner and editor of the Idaho Falls papers, who expressed himself as highly pleased. He characterized the movement for a State Junior College at Idaho Falls as abortive and said the business men had not been consulted and that he felt sure that they would be loath to have taxes raised to support a State College at Idaho Falls, and that Ricks College at Idaho Falls would be welcomed by the people. He said that the notice would be published in the papers and an editorial upon the subject would be prepared.

President Richards stated that when Brother Petersen left for the north and also after he had arrived in Idaho Falls he secured commitments from most of the newspapers and radio stations that they would observe 5:00 p.m. today release for the notice, which had been authorized, and the newspapers and radio stations in Idaho Falls had agreed to observe this release time. KSL in Salt Lake City had also agreed and had kept its agreement. Some misunderstanding developed, however, and the Deseret News came out with the information in the street edition at about 1:00 p.m. Monday, which resulted in confusion. Radio stations other than K.S.L. here picked up the announcement and used it before the release time, much to Brother Petersen's embarrassment. Brother Petersen is now trying to discover how the "break through" occurred at the Deseret News.

President Richards stated that as soon as he received the report from Brother Romney he reported to President McKay and to President [J. Reuben] Clark, both of whom expressed gratification in the way the Brethren had handled the matter in Rexburg, and Idaho Falls.

November 10, 1958, 9 to 10:35 a.m. Meeting with the First Presidency on the Ricks College matter. An editorial which appeared in the Rexburg Journal November 5, 1958 about Ricks College being moved to Idaho Falls was read. A letter and excerpts from the diary of Elder Marion G.

Romney of his visits with Elder Hugh B. Brown to Rexburg and Idaho Falls on Sunday, November 2, 1958, were also read. On this occasion Elders Romney and Brown informed President [Delbert G.] Taylor and President [Orval P.] Mortensen of the Rexburg Stakes about the decision of the First Presidency and the Board of Education to move Ricks College from Rexburg to Idaho Falls. A letter from S[tephen] [M.] Meikle, banker of Rexburg, was also read.

I explained that I had called the meeting this morning because I thought it wise for me to go to Rexburg and meet Mr. Meikle and others and tell them why the decision was made. After discussion it was decided that all three members of the First Presidency should go to Rexburg and explain to influential people that the keeping of Ricks College at Rexburg was based upon the assurance that it would supply the need, but that now it is evident that it will not and that a Junior College at Idaho Falls is the greater need, and that to continue Ricks at Rexburg with a Junior College at Idaho Falls with an institute also at Idaho Falls would cause Ricks College to dwindle.

Explanation was made that Brother [Ernest L.] Wilkinson had reported that of the $878,000 to be raised by the people of Rexburg, $7,000 had been subscribed in Rexburg Stake and $28,000 in North Rexburg Stake. The decision to return this money to the donor was reviewed.

November 19, 1958. Elder Ezra Taft Benson called from Washington [DC] regarding the [Mormon Tabernacle] Choir and the possibility of their going to the Russian Fair as a part of the prospective trade and cultural exhibition program of the United States and Russia.

I feel that there is no objection to the Choir taking such a trip. However, I made no mention of taking the Choir to the Scandinavian countries and Czechoslovakia, although that was mentioned by Brother Benson.

I feel that the Lord is opening up the way for a favorable introduction of the church into Russia.

November 15, 1958, First Presidency discussion of meeting with civic/religious leaders of Rexburg.

He [Stephen L. Richards] thought that President McKay presented the matter very well to the people there; that, however, they were not of a frame of mind to receive his presentation in the light in which it was given. ... The President went through those matters, explaining them in detail, and in general, without naming the people from whom these letters had come, all of which served to justify a change of decision [about moving the college to Idaho Falls]. However, these people in Rexburg wanted to argue, and did argue, at great length the various items which it was felt justified the change [if the presidency reversed itself]. ... They would not make any acknowledgment that the Presidency were actuated by the consideration of what was the greatest good for the greatest number of people. One or two went so far as to say, "We think you are sincere in substance, but entirely mistaken."

President Richards thought perhaps he was a little severe in asking President [Delbert G.] Taylor a question [about whether he thought he was a better church member than President Ernest L. Wilkinson] when [Taylor implied][46] that this whole thing was to be laid at the feet of Brother Wilkinson. President Richards felt that it really reflected upon the intelligence of the First Presidency and the Church Board of Education. Brother Taylor said that Brother Wilkinson had "sold us a bill of goods and was a great salesman," and that when he presented the matter to the whole group of stake presidents in that area, when they were all invited to hear it, he was actuated by a selfish desire to see his own purposes accomplished. President Richards asked if he thought he, Brother Taylor, was a better member of the Church than Dr. Wilkinson. President Richards also told him that he never heard President Wilkinson make a recommendation. He only submitted the facts. The facts were so self-evident he did not need to make a recommendation. President Richards said he felt somewhat aggrieved to think a man like President Taylor would make such inferences against President Wilkinson. ...

[J. Reuben Clark said that] after President McKay had finished speaking it seemed evident that these men had come to this meeting as objectors, among the chief of whom was President Taylor—it seemed that they had come expecting to have a debate and to try to persuade the First Presidency to change their minds. ...

President Clark said President McKay made it clear that this meeting

---

46. The diary had "he inferred."

was not to be a debate; that the Presidency were there merely to tell them what the decision was that had been reached. In the course of the discussion someone asked: "Does this mean that the decision is made and there is to be no change?" and of course the answer was that the decision had been made by the Church Board of Education and the First Presidency, and no debate was appropriate.

... The objectors tried to blame the decision on President Wilkinson, saying that he had been the one who had stirred this up, and that President McKay had yielded to his importunities, and as they would have it, more or less to his insistence and imperial attitude, making President McKay reach the decision.

President Clark replied to this, stating that they were entirely wrong, and President Richards pointed out that the Presidency never had talked with President Wilkinson about this matter between the time when the original decision was made and comparatively recently, excepting one conversation. President Clark told them that President McKay did not need anyone to make up his mind; that he had heard the arguments and made up his own mind. President Taylor particularly seemed to urge that they had never had opportunity to discuss the matter; that President Wilkinson had come after long preparation and made his statement and the matter had been pushed through without the proper opportunity to make their statement. President Clark pointed out to him that at the opposition's request, the Presidency had given them a separate meeting, that they had all the time they wanted to talk, that they brought a prepared speaker, and that they had full opportunity to present their case. Finally, rather reluctantly, he seemed to admit that.

Some of them, particularly [medical] Dr. Murland F. Rigby, said how much they had prayed about the matter, and Dr. Rigby made the statement that the prayers had all led along the opposite direction from ours—at least, that was the inference—and President Clark interposed, "You know, we prayed about it, too," and after all ours were the prayers that counted in this situation and not his individual prayers, that we had the whole Church to consider. The objectors did talk about the situation in Idaho Falls, crowded streets, dirty and narrow, etc. The radio man averred the fact that all the ills that could be found in large cities were in Idaho Falls.

President Clark remarked that President McKay never lost his temper and never betrayed any irritation, notwithstanding there were times when he, President Clark, thought President Taylor's criticism of President Wilkinson was a slap against the First Presidency. At the conclusion of the meeting President [Orval P.] Mortensen [of the North Rexburg Stake] offered the benediction, and gave a very good prayer.

November 21, 1958, 9 to 11:45 a.m. Was in a meeting of the First Presidency. At this meeting it was decided to go forward with plans to provide better office quarters for Brother Hamer Reiser and Elder Gordon Hinckley. It was also decided to make an adjustment in Brother Hinckley's salary allowance, on account of his double duties in connection with the missionary department and as one of the General Authorities. The Brethren favored paying him the same allowance as the other Assistants to the Twelve receive and in addition a modification of his present secretarial salary.

November 23, 1958. This morning I rested trying to regain my physical health. The two operations for [a] cataract this year, the dedication of two temples in foreign lands [in Great Britain and New Zealand], the presiding at and conducting two General Conferences of the Church, in addition to the myriads of Church problems which have risen during this year, have taken a toll of my health, and I am having a difficult time regaining my strength.

December 3, 1958, 8:30 to 10:30 a.m. Was in the meeting of the First Presidency. In order to take care of the many pressing problems, it has been necessary to move the meeting to an earlier hour. ...

At the meeting this morning I reviewed a proposal to have stake and ward officers in the stakes of the Ricks College area manifest their support of Ricks College at Idaho Falls. After discussion it was decided to wait for a statement being prepared by President Ernest L. Wilkinson of the B.Y.U. of the history of the proposal to move Ricks College to Idaho Falls, and if the stake and ward officers be asked to react that the occasion be upon call of the stake presidents of the stakes in the district (2 in Blackfoot, 3 in Idaho Falls, 2 in Rigby, Lost River, Salmon River), the meetings to be held at the same time, the purpose of the meeting to be announced at the meeting, and the officers attending to be asked if they sustain their stake presidents in their asking the First Presidency to reconsider the decision to leave Ricks College at Rexburg.

December 8, 1958, 9:30 a.m. Met with Dr. William F. Edwards. Minutes of that meeting as prepared by Dr. William F. Edwards follow: ...

4. Education: It was pointed out that the financial demands of the educational program have increased tremendously. In the 1951 and 1952 budget for education averaged about $3 million dollars and 13% of the total Church budget. For 1959 the Unified Church School System and the Pacific Board of Education have requested a total of $29,378,000 or 37% of the total requests. The B.Y.U. alone is requesting for 1959 approximately $10,400,000 more than 1958. And this increase accounts for 57% of the total increase in requests. It was suggested that there was probably a need for a comprehensive, coordinated study of the Church educational program including the development of a financial schedule. Confidence was expressed that such a study could be made by President [Ernest L.] Wilkinson and Bro. [Wendell B.] Mendenhall that would permit long term financial planning to meet the needs of the educational program.

5. Compensation of General Authorities: I called attention to the fact that three of the General Authorities had spoken to me about their inability to meet expenses with their allowances. I find that the annual financial needs of my family are substantially greater than the allowances of the brethren. This was for his information.

December 28, 1958. Ricks College Meeting[:] Held a long meeting with President Delbert Guy Taylor, and his counselors.[47]

December 29, 1958, 9 a.m. Attended a meeting of the First Presidency and President Ernest L. Wilkinson of the Brigham Young University. Matters pertaining to Ricks College were discussed, and also details connected with the creation of the Church Junior College in Salt Lake City, and the announcement thereof were considered.

---

47. The minutes, comprising some thirty pages, detail the Rexburg stake president's contention that Wilkinson had unfairly represented the situation to McKay.

December 30, 1958. As President McKay left the office, he stated to the secretaries in his private office: "It is a funny thing—after about two hours of work here at the office, my strength leaves me; I do not like it; I am used to working twelve hours without fatigue."

9   Rebellion, Temples, and Grief, 1959

His emotions, however, were near the breaking point when he publicly said farewell to President Richards. There was hardly a dry eye in the whole audience. General Authorities on the stand were seen wiping their eyes with their handkerchiefs as the President said: "Goodbye for the present, Stephen L., my beloved friend. We shall miss you—Oh! how we shall miss you!, but we will continue to carry on until we meet again. God bless you. ...
   —Clare Middlemiss, May 22, 1959

January 5, 1959, telephone conversation.

   J. Reuben Clark: May I speak to you here for a minute on one or two matters? I have been thinking about that special committee, whatever it was called, advisory committee. I think that if it is intended to make that a supervisory committee of all those corporations, we would get into trouble. There are certain legal matters involved there, but I don't know any reason why the Presidency should not be ex-officio of each of the Executive Committees—not connect it with any one institution, but just as the majority stockholders, have a Committee and operate as proposed.

   President McKay: That is my idea.

   President Clark: We are responsible now, and we may just as well exercise it.

   President McKay: I think so too.

   President Clark: If we try to make it one committee, there are legal aspects.

   President McKay: Well, the legal matters would have to be gone into.

President Clark: I think that is what concerns Brother [Stephen L.] Richards—as for the principle, I think we are all united. I just thought this thing over the past day or two. I am grateful to say I am a little better this morning. Still I am going to ask you to let me have some time off, but I shall talk to you about that.

President McKay: Can you come to the meeting tomorrow morning with Brother [William F.] Edwards?

President Clark: There is going to be a [financial] shearing such as hasn't been held for sometime. I anticipate that he probably will not approve it.

President McKay: That does not matter. It is right. We are not set up properly now.

President Clark: No.

President McKay: No matter what comes we must face it and start out right. I am not feeling just right about the bank business. It affects all of the others.

President Clark: I think I should bring to your attention again the Building Committee. McClure commands the brethren. He is dictating what kind of meeting houses we shall have, and the local people are complaining. It is more expensive [to construct what the wards want] and so on.

President McKay: He did not dictate in Australia. We have some good ones there. I think it needs to be reorganized some way, but we can't do it all at once.

President Clark: I am calling it to your attention. It is serious. Now, David, your voice tells me you are to go home.

President McKay: I have been here long enough. This is my holiday. Take care of yourself.

January 6, 1959, 8:30 a.m. Dr. Ernest L. Wilkinson met with the First Presidency regarding the releasing of news concerning the establishment of a Church Junior College in Salt Lake City.

Later, the Deseret News carried the Announcement of the Church's plan to establish a junior college in Salt Lake County.[1]

---

1. See also the note for December 28, 1958.

January 6, 1959; excerpts from the First Presidency's letter to William F. Edwards.

It seems to us also that this program might furnish an even more satisfactory relationship of yourself to the various corporations. We think you have performed a most valuable service in the reorganization of the companies, but as you well know, we have all been a little concerned about the effect of your inclusion on all the executive committees, with, of course, the right of vote, and in addition thereto the prestige which your relationship to the First Presidency entails. If, instead of serving as a member of the various executive committees, you could be sustained with compensation as secretary to the supervisory committee, we wonder if this position might not well be regarded as more consistent with your position as Secretary of Finance to the First Presidency.

We should be pleased if you would give prayerful consideration to the matters herein suggested, and at the first opportunity we shall arrange a conference with you with the view of making satisfactory adjustment in the matter.

Finally, we wish to remind you, as we remind ourselves, that arrangements of the kind we have spoken of have very often become effective not only for the present, but for long periods to come. We are particularly anxious that no precedents be set that will not be wise for the future.

January 20, 1959. Today, in the presence of President [Stephen L.] Richards and President [J. Reuben] Clark, my counselors, I signed the contract for the purchase of the Forest Dale Golf Course[2] [in Salt Lake City], amended as proposed by the First Presidency, and the escrow agreement between the Corporation of the President of the Church of Jesus Christ of Latter-day Saints and the Salt Lake City Corporation, as drafted and approved by Clyde Sandgren, Esq., General Counsel of the Church School System, pursuant to the instructions from the First Presidency. Following this, the documents were take[n] to the Mayor of Salt Lake City for his signature.

This land will be used for the new Salt Lake City Junior College of the Church.

---

2. As early as April 1957, McKay had looked favorably on the idea of a school in Salt Lake City that would be a junior college rather than a branch of BYU and would thereby avoid competing with the University of Utah. For his discussion with Governor George D. Clyde on the topic, see the entry for January, 4, 1958.

January 22, 1959, 4:25 p.m. Brother Wendell B. Mendenhall, Chairman of the [Church] Building Committee came in. He talked about the schools in the Pacific Islands and the matter of making the Church College of Hawaii a four-year school. I expressed the opinion that the Church is not ready to establish a four-year college at Hawaii, but that we might work toward that plan.[3] ...

Minutes of a Meeting of the First Presidency
Thursday, January 22, at 4:30 P.M. with William F. Edwards.

1. Chairman and Vice-Chairmen:

Brother Edwards made the following statement: "Because of the unusual importance of KSL to the Church, as well as the investment of the Church, there would appear to be no other company with more justification for the interest and attention of the First Presidency. Presumably members of the First Presidency would wish to serve the company as Chairman and Vice-Chairmen."

Action: It was agreed that President McKay would become Chairman and Presidents [Stephen L.] Richards and [J. Reuben] Clark Vice-Chairmen.

2. President:

Brother Edwards made the following statement: "When Jay [William] Wright[4] was employed by KSL, he had deficiencies in training and experience for the position of top leadership. Salesmanship and not engineering is the paramount challenge for success in this business. Therefore, there must be some reservation as to his ability to provide the necessary leadership to re-establish satisfactory operations. Nevertheless, he has had valuable training and experience since coming with KSL; he commands the confidence of his associates; his appointment as president would be received with general approval; and it would strengthen his position in and out of the

---

3. The Church College of Hawaii was McKay's brain child from his 1921 world tour. When he saw the property, he felt impressed to say that an educational institution for the Pacific Saints should be built there.

4. After Jay William Wright (1909–2001) received a graduate degree in physics from the University of Utah in 1936, he went to work with Columbia University's Division of War Research. He then became an engineer for CBS television in New York City, where he remained until 1954 when he returned to Utah to be vice president for seven years of KSL radio and television, and then president of KSL, before becoming head of engineering in 1961 for Seattle's KING Broadcasting, which would be later be purchased by LDS-owned Bonneville International.

organization. I am personally convinced that it would be much wiser to appoint him president and give him every assistance than to attempt to locate and employ someone with greater qualifications. It would be a serious blow to the organization to reach out a third time for a new top man."

Action: After general discussion of the qualifications of Brother Wright, it was the decision of the First Presidency to recommend to the Board of Directors that Jay Wright be made president.

3. Board of Directors:

The Board is now made up as follows: Stephen L. Richards, J. Reuben Clark, Jr., Richard L. Evans, Earl J. Glade, Spencer P. Felt, Gordon B. Hinckley, Gordon Holt, John M. Wallace, Joseph L. Wirthlin, _____, _____.[5]

Action: It was the decision of the First Presidency that President McKay and Jay Wright would be nominated to fill the two vacancies.

Brother Edwards pointed out that there was a real but minor conflict in the case of Gordon Hinckley[6] because of the new music services program of KSL. It was agreed that Brother Hinckley would be spoken to by a member of the First Presidency, and he would continue on the Board unless he felt there was a conflict. ...

8. Ivor Sharp's Retirement:[7]

It was recommended that Ivor Sharp be retired as of January 1, 1959.

Action: The First Presidency approved of the retirement of Brother Sharp as of January 1, 1959. In view of his long service to the company, it was approved that he would retire with an income from the company of $400 per month.

9. Earl J. Glade:

Brother Glade received an income from KSL of $350 per month from the time he was released as Executive Vice-President from 1944 through 1951. Subsequently, he received $200 per month. There was a

5. In the diary these names are listed vertically and numbered 1–11.

6. Hinckley had been involved with church media since the 1930s, specifically programming for KSL's Sunday evening shows.

7. Ivor Sharp (1893–1972) was a son-in-law of J. Reuben Clark and had succeeded Earl Glade as director of KSL in 1938. Quinn argues that with Sharp's forced retirement and Clark's release as president of KSL, McKay was displaying some displeasure with the station. Quinn, *Elder Statesman*, 420.

general discussion of his relationship to the company and the justification of continued compensation.

Action: It was the expressed opinion of the members of the First Presidency that this compensation from the company should cease. This opinion will be conveyed to Brother Wright who may wish to discuss it with the First Presidency before action is taken.

January 27, 1959, 2:15 p.m., Laguna Beach, California. Sister [Emma Ray] McKay and I got in the car and drove over to the Hotel for lunch. As I drove into a parking place, Sister McKay commented that there was not enough room for the car, so I turned my head, looking back, and stepped on the accelerator instead of the brake. As the car was in reverse gear, the car sped backward with great force, hitting a car that was already parked, which car struck a car back of him, and a third car backed into another car.

I called the police and there was an investigation. I admitted that it was my fault, and told them that I would notify my insurance company and pay the bills.

Sister McKay and I did not feel much like lunch, so we drove back to our home in Laguna, and later Brother [Ferren L.] Christensen[8] drove us to the station where we caught the train for Salt Lake City.

January 30, 1959, 8 a.m. ... Elder Hugh B. Brown of the Council of the Twelve came in at 8 o'clock. He conversed with me about the work he is doing with persons who are coming to him relative to cancellation of Temple sealings. In addition, many persons are being referred to him who want to discuss their marital troubles, many of whom are on the verge of divorce. Brother Brown feels that it would be a good thing to have some one appointed to work with these people to see if they can give them good advice and probably save their marriages.

I suggested this morning that Brother Brown make a list of young men in the Church to whom he could refer some of the persons—such as Lowell Bennion[9] of the University of Utah Institute, and that he also name

---

8. Ferren L. Christensen (1929–2007) was the Laguna Beach ward bishop. He would become president of the Newport Beach Stake in 1968 and Regional Representative of the Twelve for the Ventura Region in 1977. In his professional career, he was a district school superintendent.

9. McKay apparently thought that at fifty years of age, Lowell L. Bennion was

a competent psychiatrist who could work with these people. A group of these men could be called to render this service to Church members. This would greatly relieve the heavy load that Brother Brown is now carrying.

Brother Brown suggested, also, that a pamphlet could be prepared to give to some of these young couples and persons who are having difficulty, so I asked him to collect the material and prepare such a pamphlet and then submit it to the First Presidency for approval.[10]

February 1, 1959. Spent about two hours at the Salt Lake Temple, studying the Temple ordinances, and meditating on Church problems. Sister [Emma Ray] McKay was at Fast Meeting. Later, when we broke our fast, we went to the Temple Square Hotel[11] for dinner.

February 2, 1959. Preston Nibley, Assistant Church Historian, knocked on my door at the office at 7:45 o'clock. Said he had received a telephone call from Mr. [Arthur C.] Porter[12] in Rexburg, editor of the Rexburg Journal. He spoke to Brother Nibley as Assistant Church Historian, asking for Brother Nibley to find him a reference to a speech that President J. Reuben Clark had made when the Church was going to close the L.D.S. College here in Salt Lake City.

Mr. Porter said it is reported to him that President Clark saved the College from closing.[13] Brother Nibley said: "Now you tell me what I should do."

---

still a young man. From the president's perspective at eighty-five, that may have seemed to be the case.

10. Brown's 200-page "pamphlet" was published in 1961 by Bookcraft as *You and Your Marriage.*

11. This was across the street to the south from the Assembly Hall where the church-owned, 30-story condominium tower 99 West is now located.

12. In 1947 Arthur Child Porter (1916–) acquired the *Rexburg Journal* from his father, the paper's founder. "Art" had attended Ricks College, served a mission to England under Hugh B. Brown (filling the position of associate editor of the *Millennial Star*), and continued his studies at BYU. He was the pilot who in 1957 flew his plane from Rexburg to Salt Lake City to convince McKay to change his mind about moving the college to Idaho Falls. He brought three passengers, along with meat from wild game that he knew McKay loved. See entry for July 11, 1957; Hemming, "Ricks College," 75n77.

13. Clark matriculated from the Latter-day Saints' University (LDS Business College) under the presidency of future apostle James E. Talmage and credited his later success at Columbia University to his tutelage under Talmage (Quinn, *Elder Statesman,* 8–9). In 1932 the church stopped funding LDS Business College but encouraged the

I said: "You go to President Clark and ask him what you should do, and what he wants to do."

February 3, 1959, 8:30–10 a.m. Presided at the regular meeting of the First Presidency. At this meeting Dr. W[illia]m F. Edwards presented items as follows:

(1) Layton Sugar Company matters

(2) Dr. Edwards, Secretary of Finance, proposed that he withdraw from membership on Board of Directors, but continue his relationship with the Boards as the representative of the Standing Committee, in his capacity as Secretary of Finance; in that position acting under assignment of the Chairman and Vice-Chairman of the Standing Committee he could meet with the officers of the companies, attend the Board meetings. He explained that in one or two instances temporarily it may be advisable for him to delay this withdrawal until after the annual stockholders meetings (August 6).

(3) Meetings with the First Presidency: Dr. Edwards pointed out that the past year has been one of moving from one crisis into another. Often we approach almost the hour before an important meeting before he is able to meet with the First Presidency and make decisions. He recommended that he be given permission to schedule a meeting with the First Presidency approximately every other week, which would permit him to clear various matters with them, and when it may be desirable to have a president of one of the companies meet with them, he could arrange ahead for this. Now that the First Presidency have the specific responsibility of being a standing committee of the Chairman and Vice-Chairmen of the various companies there should be a regular meeting.

February 6, 1959, First Presidency's meeting; telephone conversation with Delbert G. Taylor.

[First Presidency meeting:] At this meeting I stated that the General Authorities of the Church should be informed that the First Presidency expect no book to be published unless it be first submitted. The Authority

---

school to try to raise funds privately. The next year, after Clark was named to the First Presidency, the church appropriated $18,000 to renovate the school's main building. Hilton, *History of LDS Business College*, 122–23.

will still be the author, but the First Presidency wants to know what is in the book before it is published. In the minds of the people the General Authorities in their individual capacities cannot be separated from them in their official capacities.[14] ...

President McKay very worried over many church problems, especially Ricks College matters. (c[lare] m[iddlemiss]) "There have been more troubles to look after than I have had in any other week that I can remember—some very serious." D[avid] O. M[cKay].

[Call from Rexburg stake president.] President Taylor: I apologize for calling. You know about the information we promised to obtain and present to you. The information has been assembled, this information plus a great deal more comprises a pamphlet. We are anxious that you be the first to evaluate it. ...

President McKay: The Presidency will meet you—

President Taylor: I would rather have it alone with you.

President McKay: No, we shall have it with the First Presidency and the Stake Presidency and Brother [Ernest L.] Wilkinson.

President Taylor: President McKay, I would rather give you the information and have you take it to Brother Wilkinson. I would rather do it that way. We are so tired of this controversy. We would like to get from under it. If we could meet with you alone, and then you could do what you want to do. It is driving us crazy.

President McKay: You said there are misstatements, and I said you would have to state them to Brother Wilkinson.

President Taylor: We will state them in this pamphlet.

President McKay: Why don't you want to meet the Presidency?

President Taylor: They seem to be rebuking me to the point where I don't want to take it any longer. You have been so kind and lovable, but the other brethren seem to make me feel that I have lost the track. I could stay out of it entirely if you want me to. I have never had anything bother me so much in my life.

President McKay: The same with me. Why not send the information down then? I think it would be just as well. It would save you a trip.

---

14. This was in response to Bruce R. McConkie's *Mormon Doctrine*, published in 1958 by Bookcraft of Salt Lake City. McConkie was a member of the First Council of Seventy. See entries for Mar. 5, 1959; Jan. 7, 8, 14, 27, 28, 1960.

President Taylor: We would like to talk it over with you. We will come down any time, tomorrow or Sunday, or Monday morning. ... Now, you will let us meet with you and your secretary[?]

President McKay: I would rather [you] meet [with] the Presidency.

President Taylor: We would too otherwise. I think you can hand this to them after it is over with and after you have given your personal evaluation. It will be lots better for us. ...

February 8, 1959. Came down to the office this morning. Called Joseph Anderson and asked him to get a copy of Bruce McConkie's book "Mormon Doctrine"[15] and then place it on my desk.

This he did, and later I took the book to my home where I studied the book, and made an outline of questions that I shall take up with Brother McConkie when he meets with the First Presidency next Wednesday morning. I then went to the office and dictated my notes to the dictaphone.

February 9, 1959, excerpts from conversation with D. Arthur Haycock.

---

15. Bruce R. McConkie, *Mormon Doctrine* (Salt Lake City: Bookcraft, 1958). J. Reuben Clark was among the first to see problems with the book's publication, and told McKay: "I was sure we had to do something because the book would raise more trouble than anything we had had in the Church for a long while" (in Quinn, *Elder Statesman*, 224). Problems with the book would erupt over the course of the next twelve months. Red flags must have been sufficiently waved to cause McConkie to write the following letter to the Brethren, "As you may know, I am the author of a book entitled 'Mormon Doctrine', an encyclopedic-type publication which attempts to digest and explain many of the basic doctrines of the Church. Some discussion has arisen as to whether this work carries any official stamp of church approval or whether it contains only my personal views. May I say in reply that it is not a church publication; it contains my personal views only, and I am solely responsible for all statements or opinions expressed in it. I tried to present only true doctrines and approved procedures, insofar as I understood them, and it was not my purpose to speak as the voice of the Church at any point." (See typed the excerpts in D. Michael Quinn Papers, photocopy courtesy of the Smith-Pettit Foundation.)

This pre-emptive move did not assuage fears of the book's possible negative impact. The First Presidency responded: "We feel that they [McConkie's two letters] do not cover the situation as it was discussed by us, and particularly that they do not conform to the ideas that we have that you cannot be disassociated from your official position in the publication of such a manuscript. The letters do not indicate that there will be corrections of items which you yourself indicated were over[ly] or not well stated. Furthermore, we suggest that pending the final disposition of this problem no further edition of the book be printed" (Quinn Papers). McKay assigned apostles Marion G. Romney and Mark E. Petersen to do an in-depth analysis and recommend what corrections should be insisted on. See entry for Mar. 5, 1959.

President McKay: And you are ready to go ahead with this [micro-filming of George Albert Smith and John Henry Smith diaries]?

Brother Haycock: Yes sir, whenever it is cleared. So far as we have been able to determine there is nothing in the journals of George A. Smith that would be of a controversial nature.[16]

President McKay: Did you find anything in the others?

Brother Haycock: George Albert Smith, Jr. has a copy and he is going over it very carefully and Emily has a copy and if they should find anything that would be questionable at all either from the family's or Church's standpoint, they are going to clear that.

February 10, 1959, 8:30 a.m. Attended the regular meeting of the First Presidency.

<u>Dr. Kimball Young's book—"Isn't One Wife Enough?"</u>[17]

I took into this meeting a report from Elder LaMar S. Williams of an audition of a tape recording of a radio broadcast given by Marti Malone of the Speech Department of the Northwestern University, Chicago, Illinois, of a book by Dr. Kimball Young (head of the Department of Sociology of Northwestern University) entitled "Isn't One Wife Enough?", being an attempt to ridicule and slander the Church through the polygamy issue. The review had been broadcast as one of a series in the University's Americana programs. After reading Brother Williams's report of the radio broadcast, it was decided to refer the material to President [John K.] Edmunds of the Chicago Stake, with the request that he look into the matter for the Church.

---

16. Photocopies of the Smith diaries are in the Special Collections, Marriott Library, University of Utah.

17. Kimball Young (1893–1972) was a grandson of Brigham Young who was raised in Provo and graduated from BYU but had become a lapsed Mormon. With the release in 1954 of *Isn't One Wife Enough?* issued by New York publisher Henry Holt, controversy surrounding the topic of polygamy was stirred up. However, as MIT's Thomas F. O'Dea wrote in a critical review, "One suspects that the title was chosen to spice up a scholarly study" that O'Dea found credible, if also lacking in some respects (*American Journal of Sociology* 61, no. 1 [July 1955], 98). Young did graduate work at the University of Chicago and Stanford University and taught at the University of Oregon, Queens College, and Northwestern University. In 1945 he became president of the American Sociological Association. After retiring, he returned to Provo. His research notes are at BYU's L. Tom Perry Special Collections.

George Romney—Letter re: Church educational trends

I also brought to the meeting and had read a long letter addressed to me by President George [W.] Romney,[18] President of the Detroit Stake, who expresses his concern about trends he notes in Church educational policies for the development of institutions for higher learning and post graduate study in Utah and Idaho in competition with already established institutions, and his concern lest this development may reduce the Church's seminary and institute policy. It was decided to refer the letter to President [Ernest L.] Wilkinson who has been asked to see me about the matter before I answer the letter. (Later it was decided that Pres[ident] McKay would send an acknowledgment, stating that Dr. Wilkinson was sending facts.) ...

From 11:45 a.m. to 2 p.m.—During these hours the First Presidency met at their request the Rexburg Stake presidency (Pres[ident] Delbert G. Taylor, Willis G. Nelson, 1st counselor[,] and Walter F. Ririe, second counselor),[19] on Ricks College matters.

They presented a pamphlet entitled "The Proposal to Move Ricks College," which was published in answer to a pamphlet entitled "Ricks College, A Statement," prepared by Dr. Ernest L. Wilkinson of the B.Y.U.

[President J. Reuben Clark speaking:] May I ask a question? This[,] of course[,] we will all agree with[,] is a Church matter, but this [Rexburg] Committee of 1000 has appealed to the people of the United States. Am I right about that?

Brother Taylor: That is right.

President Clark: That is wholly contrary to the discipline of the Church.

Brother Ririe said that he did not think they intended to mail it to others than Church membership.

President Taylor said the information was mailed all over, that they tried hard to stop it, but they said this was a public matter. ... Those

---

18. George W. Romney (1907–95) was president of the American Motors Corporation and the future governor of Michigan and US Secretary of Housing and Urban Development. He was born in Mexico in the Mormon colony of Colonia Dublán. His son Willard Mitt Romney would follow in his footsteps as CEO of Bain Capital and governor of Massachusetts.

19. The stake presidency represented a cross-section of the community. Taylor was the owner of the Chevrolet dealership in Rexburg. Nelson was principal of Madison High School. Ririe was manager of the J. C. Penney department store.

familiar with the proposal to relocate Ricks College have known from the beginning that the idea, however fantastic[,] was Dr. Wilkinson's. Out of respect for his status as Administrator they restrained themselves from revealing his true role in the conflict, but when it was realized Dr. Wilkinson had been able to maneuver a whole community into a position where it appeared opposed to the First Presidency, Board of Education, and lifelong friends in neighboring communities, Rexburg citizens felt the problem was bigger than Ricks College and it was high time to tell the full story.

Facing an opponent who seemed to have the resources of the Church University at his disposal they found it expedient to form an organization through which individual efforts could be coordinated. Someone suggested a Committee of 1000, representing people everywhere who have affiliated themselves with the cause. ...

For those who might question the motives of its writers, let it be understood that they are all responsible L.D.S. Church members who feel Dr. Wilkinson has deliberately distorted the facts to win his case. This booklet is an honest effort to tell the full story, without malice or prejudice, in the hope and prayer that truth will prevail, justice and fair play will have their day, and in the end Ricks College will be allowed to fulfill its greater destiny at the site of its pioneering founding.

President Clark: Don't you have any information about it?

President Taylor: Yes, we have the booklet.

President Clark: Do you know the people who wrote it?

President Taylor: Yes, we know who wrote it. It is Brother Arthur [C.] Porter.[20] ... We hadn't seen the pamphlet. We knew some things that were going into the pamphlet. We knew what was going into it, but we had not a chance to read any part of it. We told them we wouldn't [use] it,[21] but when we found it covered our own information pretty well we thought maybe you would be as interested or more interested in it than in a separate presentation. We wrote our own and Brother Nelson read this as we came down and we said, "This is the better way to put it—like this is." Here are the questions here, answers to questions by Dr. Wilkinson. ...

---

20. Porter confirmed in a 1975 interview that he had been the sole author of the pamphlet. Hemming, "Ricks College," 96n137.

21. The transcript has, "We told them we wouldn't do it."

President Clark: I am trying to find out who you are accusing of being a liar; that is what your argument comes to, are you challenging the fact that someone has lied? Who is it?

Brother Nelson: This says here there are misrepresentations of the facts.

Brother Taylor: And there is.

President Richards: A misrepresentation contemplates a willful misrepresentation. ...

President Clark: May I put one question to you? When you go on your knees to pray, do you pray that the Lord will guide and direct the Prophet, Seer, and Revelator to change his mind, is that your prayer?

Brother Taylor: Well, President Clark, did the other stake presidents go on their knees?

President Clark: I am not asking that.

Brother Taylor: I do not want to talk any more about it.

President Clark: I do not see how you can talk to the point that you go on your knees to pray to the Lord to instruct the Prophet of the Lord.

Brother Taylor: When this statement was sent out by you Brethren, "Ricks College will not be moved from Rexburg," who was it then that changed the story? I cannot believe that you Brethren would start out immediately and say, "We're going to change our mind."

President Clark: You know of the law of the Church which provides that when something has been decided and turns out that it seems to be wisdom to reach a contrary decision, you know that has been done time and time again in the Church. ... May I say this, I have wondered as I have known of your position, I have wondered what I would say if I got down on my knees to change a decision of the First Presidency.

Brother Taylor: We have never asked the Lord for that.

President Clark: But you have treated it as if no decision had been made.

Brother Taylor: No, we haven't.

President Richards: Did it ever occur to you, that that pamphlet would never have been written had it not been for your activities in Rexburg? ...

President McKay: You tell that man Porter that he has done more injury to the idea of Ricks at Rexburg than all the enemies of the school since it was founded.

Brother Taylor: We have told him that.

President McKay: He has written some of the most vitriolic things we have had in the Church.

Brother Taylor: I took that back to him and said, "This is what you have done. The Brethren will be willing to accept factual things that are right. I told you that when you started this and you have completely violated it."

President Clark: It occurs to me, Churchwise, the great transgression in the matter has been to appeal, and this is what these men have done and it is what they intend it shall mean, appeal to the people and not the members of the Church, to take it away from the members of the Church and make it a community matter. That I think is terribly destructive of all Church discipline.

Brother Nelson: I cannot speak for the other brethren, but I can say in my heart I sincerely pray to the Lord with an open heart.

Brother Taylor: You assume I have never done it, but I have done it, President Clark; that is, I have sat down with you brethren step by step and you will see this thing has been sadly distorted, and I say that with all the firmness I have. You Brethren have not known the details and he [Wilkinson] has planned on moving that school for a long time. I have the evidence.

President Clark: I do not think you have. We have evidence, too.

Brother Taylor: President, Clark, I have always loved you and I always will. I have no personal ambition in this thing.

February 13, 1959; First Presidency meeting. At this meeting the booklet "Dr. Wilkinson's Role in the Proposal to Move Ricks College" prepared by the "Committee of One Thousand Rexburg, Idaho," was considered and a statement prepared by President Stephen L Richards stating Dr. [Ernest L.] Wilkinson's position on the matter as acting under the direction of the Church Board of Education was read. It was decided that the statement be released for publication in the Deseret News and in the Idaho Papers.[22]

---

22. The statement authored by Richards for the First Presidency appeared in the *Deseret News* that afternoon under the headline, "Church Decries Ricks Pamphlet." It read, in part: "From reading the pamphlet, we interpret it to be, in substance, an attack on the professional integrity of Dr. Wilkinson [and] ... upon the sincerity and good faith of the ten stake presidents, who either signed or subsequently confirmed a letter to us reporting certain developments in Idaho Falls which suggested urgent reconsideration of a decision to leave the College at Rexburg." The decision to move the campus to Idaho Falls would be reversed again the next year. See entry for June 30, 1960.

February 19, 1959, 10:25–3:30 p.m. Was convened in the meeting of the First Presidency and Council of the Twelve in the Salt Lake Temple.

At this meeting, in preliminary remarks, I said that if every member of the Church who partook of the Sacrament last Fast Day kept the covenants that he or she made that day in partaking of the Sacrament, we would be pretty close to the Millennium even now. If every person kept his covenants to take upon himself the name of Christ and to keep his commandments without any exception, worshiping God and being true to Him, treating his brother as he would have his brother treat him, and always be guided by his Spirit, I repeat, we would be pretty close to the Millennium. And that is our obligation—the obligation of the General Authorities—to make them feel the responsibility of membership in the Church of Christ.

March 5, 1959, 2:35–2:40 p.m. <u>Elder Mark E. Petersen</u> and <u>Elder Marion G. Romney</u> called at my request. I asked them if they would together go over Elder Bruce R. McConkie's book, "Mormon Doctrine" and make a list of the corrections that should be made preparatory to his sending out an addendum to all members of the Church who have purchased his book.[23]

March 6, 1959, telephone conversation with Ezra Taft Benson.

Benson: Secondly, Mr. [Abba] Eban,[24] who has been the Israeli Ambassador here in Washington is just retiring and returning to his country—we understand to stand for election for parliament over there

---

23. McConkie had faced similar scrutiny in 1955 with his proposed "Sound Doctrine: The Journal of Discourses Series," which came to the attention of the First Presidency when they saw it advertised as a forthcoming title in the *Improvement Era*, December 1955. After reading the first 150 pages of the manuscript, J. Reuben Clark suggested that it be permanently enjoined from publication. He told McConkie "it would have been better if he had conferred with the Brethren before he began the printing of his book, instead of afterward." McConkie "admitted that that [had been] a mistake" and submitted to the decision of the First Presidency (Quinn, *Elder Statesman*, 222–23). It was nevertheless published twenty years later by his son, Joseph Fielding McConkie, as the *Journal of Discourses Digest, Volume 1* (Bookcraft, 1975). For reservations regarding *Mormon Doctrine*, see the entry for Jan. 7, 1960.

24. Abba Eban (1915–2002) was born Aubrey Solomon, son of Lithuanian immigrants to South Africa. He had graduated from Cambridge University and become Israel's ambassador to the United Nations before he was assigned to Washington, DC., in 1950. Over the next two decades he would serve in four cabinet positions representing the Israeli Labour Party.

and possibly to become a candidate to succeed the present prime minister Mr. [David] Ben–Gurion. Mr. Eban has been very friendly to me
personally here. When Brother [Harold B.] Lee came through here, I
arranged for Mr. Eban to arrange his travels. He has invited me to luncheon with him the first of next week. If there is anything I can do to be
helpful to the Church, I shall do so. He will probably raise the question
regarding the Church, and I wanted to check with you. I shall, of course,
tell him of our plans which he is familiar with, to open an office in Israel.
He has encouraged us. He may ask whether or not the Church is considering opening a mission in that country.

President McKay: No. If I were you, I should give no encouragement
for the time being. The Arabs are opposed to the State of Israel.

Brother Benson: The situation has improved considerably.

President McKay: I would not give him any encouragement on our
establishing a mission there.

Brother Benson: I shall not mention it then. I shall stick to the agricultural work. Of course, I do plan to keep in touch with him. He has
asked that I do so. If the time comes that he can be helpful to us, I think
we have a friend in him. ...

President McKay: How is Mr. [John Foster] Dulles [Secretary of
State]? ...

Brother Benson: The President [Eisenhower] is <u>pleased</u>. The treatments have given good results.[25] ... <u>Secretary Dulles was very pleased
to have your greeting and blessing</u> extended to him. I told him that you
Brethren would be praying for him in the Temple. It pleased him. He
could hardly hold his emotions. I am sure it has helped a great deal ...

March 8, 1959. Spent several hours at the office going over petitions
for cancellation of [temple marriage] sealings. This is a very depressing
experience. ...

This is the gloomiest duty I have in the Church. I appreciate the
assistance rendered by Brother Hugh B. Brown. I handled 39 cases, and
there were more women in the group who had gone wrong than usual. I
am convinced that more care should be taken on the part of our bishops

---

25. The Secretary of State had colon cancer and would die in May.

in recommending people to be married in the temple. Many men particularly violate their covenants by committing adultery and forfeiting their blessings. More thought should be given on the part of bishops in letting the people understand what it means to go to the temple and enter into eternal covenants and then go out and violate them. It is a great thing to be sealed in the House of the Lord for time and all eternity—a wonderful blessing—and some of our men do not realize it.

March 12, 1959, 9:00–10:00 a.m. The First Presidency met with Dr. William F. Edwards who presented a brochure containing a complete summary of the over-all financial position of the Corporation of the President and of the financial interests of the Church. The report included [a] report of tithing received in 1958 compared by tables with the years back in 1951. The summary also included income and expenditures of the Church according to budget reports. The operating allowances of the major divisions of the Church, missions, temples, educational institutions, welfare, buildings and grounds, genealogy and administrative departments were also reviewed in considerable detail. The Church's building commitments were reviewed by table and chart. The flow of cash into and from the accounts of the Church were next reported and accounted for. Loans of various Church organizations and interests were listed. Non-budget items were similarly reviewed. The agricultural and livestock enterprises and their financial status and the investments of the Church with relation to maturity dates were analyzed. The complete reports of audits of all divisions of the Church were presented also.

March 13, 1959, 11:30–12:30 p.m. President Cecil E. Hart of the South Idaho Falls Stake called at the office regarding Ricks College matters. He reiterated the attitude of the stake presidents on their belief that the Ricks College would serve the young people of the college area more efficiently at Idaho Falls than if it were to remain at Rexburg. He deplored the attitude of the so-called Committee of One Thousand in its attack upon President [Ernest L.] Wilkinson and the Presidency of the Church.

March 24, 1959. [Regarding] Adam-ondi-Ahman, and Pattonsburg Reservoir in Missouri. After conferring with the above brethren, the First

Presidency returned to the north Board Room and met with Brother Alvin R. Dyer,[26] formerly President of the Central States Mission, and Assistant to the Twelve, on developments in Washington, D.C. on the proposed Pattonsburg Reservoir which threatens to inundate the Adam-ondi-Ahman site, near Gallatin, Missouri. David S. King, Congressman from Utah, has conferred at length with the U.S. Army Corps of Engineers in Washington, D.C. about the project. They show an earnest desire to respect the Church's wishes in the matter. It was felt that rather than the First Presidency write a letter to the Chief of Engineers, Alvin Dyer, should go to Washington, D.C. and quietly confer with David S. King, our Senators, and the U.S. Chief of Engineers with regard to an alternate site for the location of the dam farther up the river, which would preserve the properties we now hold at Adam-ondi-Ahman, as well as surrounding areas which are sacred to us as a people.[27]

March 27, 1959. A memorandum from Elder Gordon B. Hinckley was read at the meeting of the First Presidency this morning, in which he communicated to the First Presidency a message he had been asked to bring from President Delbert G. Taylor, who said that "he was greatly oppressed by a sense of having done wrong." President Taylor asked, "If you have opportunity, tell the Brethren that we know we have made some serious mistakes. We have done wrong. We sustain the First Presidency, and we want them to know that we sustain them." In conversations repeatedly President Taylor indicated that he sustained President McKay in the Presidency and appeared to be extremely repentant about what has happened.

President Taylor is now trying to appease the people's feelings and to gain their united support of the First Presidency.

---

26. Alvin Rulon Dyer (1903–77) had been an Assistant to the Twelve for five months. In 1967 he would be ordained an apostle but not placed in the Quorum of the Twelve. In 1968 he would become a member of the First Presidency. His background in mechanical engineering earned him a spot during World War II in the Army Corps of Engineers. Until 1958 he ran a company that supplied contractors with heating and air-conditioning equipment.

27. Others opposed the dam, including a local newspaper that in 1955 editorialized that it would mean "the virtual end of Daviess County" when it drowned "65,000 acres of the most productive land in the county." *Gallatin Democrat*, Mar. 3, 1955; Wilbur Bush, "Pattonsburg Dam Proposal Cause[d] Concern," Daviess County Historical Society website.

I reviewed the inquiry I made some time ago from Brother Salisbury of Rexburg for a statement of his reasons for saying that the ten stake presidents in Idaho Falls area were prompted by other feelings than their own, by some other influence, to request the reconsideration of the decision as to the location of Ricks College, and stated that Brother [Howard E.] Salisbury had taken that inquiry as an assignment to interview each of the stake presidents on the point. As yet he has made no report.

A note from Elder Mark E. Petersen reported that a message from President [Lloyd P.] Mickelsen of North Idaho Falls Stake is to the effect that the presidents of the stakes in the Idaho Falls area desire the brethren to know that they are united in their support of the removal of Ricks College to Idaho Falls. President Mickelsen said that if the First Presidency want to talk with them as a group the stake presidents would be pleased personally to assure them of their stand.

April 1, 1959, 8:30–11:15 a.m. Was convened in the meeting of the First Presidency. At this meeting we considered the following items in addition to many other matters:

(1) Institute of Religion Building on U[niversity] of U[tah] Campus. President Ernest L. Wilkinson of the B.Y.U. reviewed details of the proposal to purchase from Salt Lake City a piece of land at the south border of the University of Utah Campus upon which an institute building can be built as the University campus moves eastward.[28] He said that the proposal to purchase has been approved by the Board of Education, and had been agreed to and confirmed by the [Salt Lake] City Commissioners in Salt Lake City, and that the City Attorney, James L. Barker, Jr., had come to him to show him that the original agreement to sell the land stands despite newspaper statements to the contrary, that after the November elections the transaction can be resumed.

(2) A letter from Sister Belle S. Spafford, President of the Relief Society, written from England, reporting her observations of the work of the [charity known as the] Women's Volunteer [Voluntary] Service

---

28. A new Institute of Religion would be constructed across the street from the football stadium to the south. To differentiate from the existing building at the lower end of campus on University Street, it would be called the East Institute, the older building the West Institute. "LDS Plans Open House at Complex," *Salt Lake Tribune*, Sept. 18, 1965.

organization of England which is being carried forward under the direction of Lady [Stella Isaacs, marchioness of] Reading and her staff, and of
the care of aged women in their homes, was read.[29] ...

(4) A letter from President T. Bowring Woodbury of the British
Mission reported on taxation valuation & officer's proposal to tax the
temple in the amount $10,000 and stated that the subject is now being
reviewed by the solicitor and the special tax council.[30]

President Stephen L. Richards will go to London to make a investigation of this matter.

April 16, 1959, 7:15 a.m. <u>Met by appointment Dr. Ernest L. Wilkinson,</u>
President of the <u>Brigham Young University</u> who took up the following
with me:

1. <u>The question of whether President Wilkinson</u> should have <u>access
to the tithing records</u> of the faculty of the Brigham Young University. The
faculty itself has already voted that compliance with Church standards is
one of the criterions for promotion. This question was <u>discussed at our
meeting of the First Presidency today.</u> ...

<u>Tax Problem Associated with Swiss Temple, Switzerland</u>

<u>1:15 p.m.</u>—Brother Henry D. Moyle came in to my private office, at
which time we talked over the matter of the request the Church submitted
to the tax authorities of the Canton of Berne for a reconsideration of the
tax exempt problem, or if possible remission of taxes on our Temple property in Zollikofen, Switzerland. In this application we explained all reasons
which, according to our opinion, justified a tax exemption in every respect.

Inasmuch as <u>President Stephen L. Richards is now in London</u> looking into tax problems associated with the <u>London Temple</u> and other
holdings in England, it was decided that he should go to Switzerland and
look into the tax matters there.[31]

---

29. For more, see the entry for April 24 below.

30. At first a question was raised about whether it was appropriate to tax the
buildings associated with the temple—the offices and housing for temple officiators and
visitors. When that was resolved, it was pointed out that the temple was not a "public
place of worship," and that became a point of contention. It was eventually decided that
it would be right to tax the temple and all other structures on the temple grounds at half
the normal rate. Cowan, "Tale of Two Temples," 30.

31. See the entry for April 29 below.

April 24, 1959, 10:15–11:45 a.m. The First Presidency listened to a report from Sister Belle S. Spafford, General President of the Relief Society, on her trip to London, England to fill an assignment with Lady Reading of London.

Sister Spafford, who became acquainted with Lady Reading when she visited Salt Lake City, May 29, 1958, and at whose invitation she went to England, made a study of the old age program in England, and also of the Women's Volunteer Services Program which was instituted by Lady Reading, and which has been in force since the beginning of the second world war.

Sister Spafford attended a number of dinners and social functions. At one dinner, attended by a number of distinguished guests at which Queen Elizabeth and Sir John Hunt who climbed Mt. Everest, were toasted, Sister Spafford was toasted as a distinguished guest from Salt Lake City.

She also received a very nice message from the Mayor of Southgate, who invited her to dinner at the Town Hall Council Chamber Room. She stood by the side of a distinguished army officer, who, upon learning she was from Salt Lake City, and asked if she would pardon him if he asked a personal question. He asked her if she had any opportunity to mingle with the Mormon women in Salt Lake City, and he was quite surprised when Sister Spafford told him that she was the head of all the Mormon women.

I have listened to many reports of officials returning from assigned duties, but few if any have given a report more impressively, more appreciatively, with a clearer comprehension of an assignment than did Sister Spafford. She fully realized the magnitude and value of the organization founded by Lady Reading.

Sister Spafford in her earnestness and eloquence really stirred our emotions as she spoke of her love and admiration for Lady Reading, and of the possible world-wide benefit and magnitude of the work that she has inaugurated.

April 29, 1959, 8:30–11 a.m. President Stephen L. Richards who has just returned from an assignment in London, England, and Bern, Switzerland gave a detailed report on—

(1) The Swiss Temple and his interview with Mr. Schmidt, the lawyer representing the Church. Said that the present problem arises from

the fact that the local taxing authorities in Switzerland are loathe to grant exemption of even half of the full allowance on the Temple free from tax under the present mortgage, and the authorities have raised the question as to income taxes from the Church. The established practice in Switzerland whenever a building is built is to place a mortgage upon it immediately. The mortgage is in the name of the mortgagor who can endorse and sell it to the bank or a lending company. This mortgage is made payable to the bank, which collects the interest. The Swiss government looks with favor upon the arrangement because it brings much capital into the country. A great deal of foreign capital is invested in these mortgages. If a mortgage had been placed upon the Temple at first, there would have been no trouble about the taxes now.

Only three churches in Switzerland are entitled to tax exemptions— the Catholic church, and two Protestant churches. There are certain cantons in which the National Church, the State Church, is entitled to exemption, and no other churches are given exemption. Other churches can gain exemption by mortgaging the property.

President Richards then gave in detail his views regarding the validity of the present mortgage on the Swiss Temple.

He said the Swiss Temple is beautifully landscaped and well kept. Advised that the land recommended to be purchased across from the Swiss Temple be purchased—it is offered at 100 francs per square meter, and will cost about $60,000. ...

(2) Tax on London Temple

President Richards explained that the London Temple tax matter was in litigation before he arrived in London. The tax valuation officer had appraised the property including the whole temple grounds, the manor houses, and the buildings. Representatives of the Church there protested the assessment, and the case now comes before something like a Board of Equalization. This Board has authority to grant exemption, and they are laymen, but have legal talent to advise them. They call it a Tax Tribunal. It will probably be within the next two months that the decision will be reached. Preparation is being made for the hearing before this Tribunal. The lawyer, Mr. Forges, is a barrister hired by Mr. Sharman. He has a pretty good conception of the position of the Church on the issue.

President Richards told Mr. Forges that he would prepare a statement for him which would indicate the place of the temple in our worship. We held a discussion as to how much of the endowment ceremony could be told. I stated that the temple ceremony could be presented to show emphasis upon cleanliness of thought and living; the value of the promises made in the presence of the Lord and the binding nature of the promise to live their religion in daily lives; the emphasis upon loyalty to a companion in marriage; and the consecration of all to God. When we so bind ourselves to live spiritually in this world, but not of the world, then we are prepared to enter into the presence of the Father in Heaven.

President Richards will prepare the statement of the relation of the temple service to public religious worship of the Church for the benefit of the lawyer as [he] agrees with the Church upon the subject.

"New Era" for the British Mission

President Richards then reported that the missionaries of the British Mission asked him to express to President McKay their thanks for his launching for them what they call "the new era" for the British Mission. President [T. Bowring] Woodbury is the epitome of enthusiasm.[32] He has called 500 local part-time missionaries who can go out once a week in missionary service. The results are good in new conversions,[33] as well as in getting children [of members] over nine years of age baptized and in giving part-time missionaries enthusiasm of missionary work.[34]

April 30, 1959, meeting of First Presidency and Twelve. President [Stephen L.] Richards gave the following report on the British Mission:

President T. Bowring Woodbury of the British Mission reported the

---

32. Henry D. Moyle later wrote: "Never in all my life have I met a man with more energy or more enthusiasm, more determination or more courage than President Woodbury. He speaks up in a very forceful, diplomatic way and is constantly letting people know that the Church is founded upon truth" (Moyle diary, Nov. 30, 1959, typed excerpt in Quinn Papers). Thomas Reinhold Bowring Woodbury (1908–72) was a Utah native whose wife, "Bubbles" (Beulah Larkin Blood), was said to have been as exuberant a speaker as he was. They both attended the University of Utah, and he became president of a company that manufactured power lawn mowers.

33. The diary has "conversations" rather than "conversions."

34. Unfortunately, the push for increased baptisms had led to what came to be known as the baseball or kiddie baptisms, missionaries recruiting boys for a church baseball league that, they told the young men, required their baptism in order to be allowed to participate. It became the task of succeeding missionaries to undo the damage this caused.

mission is in good condition. He is overjoyed at the idea of this "new Era" which he attributed to President McKay, and he is emphasizing this and has been very successful. He has already called over 500 district missionaries (local missionaries) who give at least one night, if not two nights a week, to missionary service. President Woodbury is overjoyed with the prospect of what these missionaries will be able to do and are going.

He has also discovered that hundreds of children over nine years of age have not been baptized, so President Woodbury is directing the work of these local missionaries to first of all get these children baptized. They are also meeting with part-member families and delinquent families more than they are with non-members.[35]

May 6, 1959, 8:30–9:30 am. Attended First Presidency's meeting. First we met with Dr. W[illia]m F. Edwards, financial secretary to the First Presidency, and considered matters pertaining to Layton Sugar Company matters—the announcement of the purchase offer of Utah–Idaho Sugar to farmers and the shareholders of Layton Sugar Company—future management organization of Layton Sugar Company, stockholders' meeting to be held May 20, etc. ...

We then held a meeting of the Standing Committee of the Chairman and Vice-Chairman of Z.C.M.I. [department store]. All members of the First Presidency and Dr. W[illia]m F. Edwards, Secretary to the Committee were present. Retail and wholesale operations of the Company were considered. At this meeting the Standing Committee approved the

---

35. A year and a half later, following a visit to the British Mission, Henry D. Moyle reported to the First Presidency and Twelve: "We now have an ample supply of young men in the branches to provide companions for our young women members, which has never been the case before in the history of the European Mission. Then too, these teenagers—nearly all of them—want to get into the building program and learn building trades. This thrills the mission presidents because they have been a little bit worried about having too many teenagers baptized, but they seem to be fitting in perfectly" (Moyle diary, Dec. 15, 1960). The building program included volunteer labor in the form of "building missionaries" or "church builders." This gave young people "the opportunity to learn construction skills" (Gary B. Hansen, "A Firsthand Account of the New Era in Great Britain: 1958–1961," online at garybhansen.com). At this point in time in 1959, the church had fourteen chapels under construction in Great Britain and sixty-three other building projects planned (Derek A. Cuthbert, "Breakthrough in Britain," *Ensign*, July 1987).

recommendation of the management that the company withdraw from the wholesale business.

The Standing Committee of the Chairmen and Vice-Chairmen of Zion's First National Bank (all three members of the First Presidency present[,] with Dr. W[illia]m F. Edwards, Secretary to the Committee present). ...

There was presented for review the architects' sketch of the proposed new main office building at Main and First South [in Salt Lake City] to be erected at an estimated cost of $3,857,000. There was a full discussion of the various means of financing the proposed building. The Standing Committee approved the architectural plans which will be presented to the Board of Directors when they next meet.

May 13, 1959, 11:15 a.m. Received a courtesy call from Wilber M. Brucker,[36] Secretary of the Army, Washington, D.C. and Mrs. Brucker. ...

Mr. Brucker was in Salt Lake to speak at a luncheon meeting sponsored by the Bonneville Kiwanis Club, Salt Lake City Chamber of Commerce, and Salt Lake Sertoma [Service to Mankind] Club. Among other things, I noticed from the newspaper that Secretary Brucker said that "this country must tighten its belt to overcome greater communist momentum and secure superior strength in the future; that symbols of freedom such as Berlin must be maintained; that backing down or appeasement will only increase pressures for more backing down; that this country can afford to maintain arms superiority; that the present condition of the world demands that 170,000,000 Americans contribute to the defense team."

I later remarked to the Brethren that I do not see an indication on the part of the Communists that they are modifying the original thought of [Karl] Marx—that the only way is destruction of capitalism, then they can build their hope for a millennium of Communism. In the present attempt, the same determination is shown to hold to that original thought; that for three days now the big powers have been in session, and have accomplished not a thing in their attempt at unification. Referring to present conditions and Communism, I said I thought it did not look very

---

36. Wilber Marion Brucker (1894–1968) had been Michigan's governor in the 1930s, three decades before George W. Romney. In addition to that, he had been the state attorney general and general counsel for the army during the McCarthy Hearings. At this point in time, he was Secretary of the Army. His military involvement extended back to the Pancho Villa campaign of 1916–17 and World War I in 1917–18.

hopeful for peace. The Communists are getting stronger and stronger, and when they feel they are prepared to strike, I think they will strike. I do not like to express this thought, but that is my feeling. I hope that the nations will accomplish something at their present conferences in Geneva, but thus far they seem not to have accomplished much of anything. Let us hope and pray that they will show a spirit of yielding, but so far they have held to that abominable, demoniacal ideal, (atheistic in the extreme) of Marx, who let his own wife starve and his children starve to death. It is the most atheistic, diabolical spirit of the devil that we have ever had in the world, and we are going to suffer from it.

May 19, 1959, 7:30. Just after I had concluded a conference with Bishop Pickering of the 27th ward (my home ward), Elder Gordon B. Hinckley, Assistant to the Twelve, came in and brought a message from Sister Stephen L. [Irene] Richards who had phoned to him from their summer cottage at Wasatch Lawns, to the effect that President Richards had not been well during the night—that he had been seized with irregular heart pains and was feeling chilled. They had called Dr. Harlow Richards, his nephew and physician who came out immediately and decided that President Richards should go to the hospital. They secured a private ambulance this morning and had taken him to the LDS Hospital for one or two days' tests. However, Sister Richards reported that she was not worried; that everything would be all right.

7:45 a.m. Soon thereafter I received a call from Dr. Harlow Richards from the hospital who notified me that President Richards had passed away on his way up to the operating room where they were going to give him some tests. About this same time President [J. Reuben] Clark came in and said that he had learned of the passing of President Richards.

It seems that President Richards had recognized his son, Dick [Richard Merrill Richards], who had come down from Spokane on business and happened to be in Salt Lake in the morning. He had gone up to the hospital. President Richards recognized him at the hospital door, and it was to Dick that he said: "I feel that I am going to faint." The news of his passing was a terrible shock to me.[37]

---

37. No where else in his diary does McKay mourn the loss of a colleague as he does in this instance. Biographer Francis Gibbons described the loss as "one of the chief

Brother Benson [on the telephone]: Hello, President McKay, this is Brother Benson. I just got the flash over the wire here about Brother Richards.

President McKay: Well, we are all broken up about it—it is sudden and a shock. ...

Brother Benson: It is an awful shock, and I know what a shock it is to you!

President McKay: He has been as close to me as a brother could be, a friend of the truest kind. He has been wonderful, and of great value to me. It is a great loss to the Church. He was a great intellect, a great soul. He was as loyal to me as his grandfather [Willard Richards] was to the Prophet [Joseph Smith] and just as close.[38]

May 20, 1959. The regular meeting of the First Presidency—the first without my dear friend, companion, and advisor—President Stephen L. I could not believe that he had gone, and kept looking for him to come in. ...

Note by c[lare] m[iddlemiss]: President McKay is deeply grieved and shocked over President Richards' death—it is very noticeable that the passing of his beloved counselor and friend is weighing heavily upon him.

May 21, 1959. President McKay did not return to the office—was very shocked to learn that Sister [Irene Smith Merrill] Richards has suffered a mild heart attack—the shock of losing her husband has been too much for her.[39]

May 22, 1959, note by Clare Middlemiss. It was very evident to all present

---

sorrows of [McKay's] entire administration," explaining that "when President McKay learned of the death of his friend, he broke down and wept." The "sense of desolation ... never quite left the Prophet during the rest of his life." Gibbons, *David O. McKay*, 400–01.

38. This sentiment reflects Richards's view as well. On his calling to the First Presidency, he stated, "I have felt that the only reason for my being in the presiding counsels of the Church is in the devotion of Willard Richards [his grandfather] to the prophet Joseph Smith. ... I would like to be as true a friend to President David O. McKay as my grandfather was to the prophet" (in Winder, *Counselors to the Prophets*, 369).

39. One of the apostles noticed that "President McKay was visibly affected by the death on Tuesday of his first counselor, Pres[ident] Stephen L. Richards. He looked very old and haggard and grief-stricken" (Spencer W. Kimball diary, May 21, 1959, typed excerpt in Quinn Papers). Two months later J. Reuben Clark was worried that President McKay was still "depressed" (Clark diary, July 13, 1959).

that it was extremely difficult for the grieving President to conduct the funeral services. However, he brought his emotions under control, and handled the situation masterfully—the services proceeded smoothly and efficiently. His emotions, however, were near the breaking point when he publicly said farewell to President Richards. There was hardly a dry eye in the whole audience. General Authorities on the stand were seen wiping their eyes with their handkerchiefs as the President said: "Goodbye for the present, Stephen L., my beloved friend. We shall miss you—Oh! how we shall miss you!, but we will continue to carry on until we meet again. God bless you, Irene, and your choice sons and daughters. During this inevitable separation may there ever echo in your hearts, as if they had come from the voice of your beloved husband and devoted father, the words of the Savior to his disciples when he had to leave them. ..."[40]

June 11, 1959, 1:30–2:10 p.m. Elder Henry D. Moyle came to my office following [the] Council meeting [First Presidency and Quorum of the Twelve] to take up some Welfare matters with me.

Following our conversation on Welfare problems, I told Brother Moyle that I had chosen him to be my second counselor.

June 12, 1959, 8:15 a.m. ... Yesterday afternoon following Council meeting, I had a conference with Elder Henry D. Moyle at which time he presented several welfare problems to me. After we had considered these matters, I said to him, "Elder Moyle there is another matter that will have to be considered immediately as it pertains to your trip to Europe—(Bro[ther] Moyle having received permission from me a few days ago to take his wife and grandson to Europe during the summer vacation)—you heard what Brother Marion G. Romney said about his being in Europe this Summer and visiting the German Missions at which time we told

---

40. In the Gospel of Luke, Jesus says, "I have prayed for thee, that thy faith fail not: and when thou art converted, strengthen thy brethren" (22:32). The Gospel of John adds, "And now I am no more in the world, but these are in the world, and I come to thee. Holy Father, keep through thine own name those whom thou hast given me, that they may be one, as we are" (17:11). McKay's grief lasted for weeks. In mid-July, J. Reuben Clark worried that "President McKay sounds depressed, and those who have seen him indicate that he acts that way. If anything should happen to Sister McKay, almost anything might be looked for" (Clark diary, July 13, 1959).

him that we should like him to make the same visit that you made last year during your trip and go behind the Iron Curtain. I know that you would like to go again this year, and that is all right for you to arrange that trip, but I am going to say something to you now—<u>I should like you to be my second counselor!</u>"[41]

Tears welled up in his eyes, and he said "My goodness! Then, I'll not go to Europe!" That was his first reaction, and I said to him, "Yes, you had better take Sister Moyle, as you have planned, but I thought you should know about this now, and if you feel all right about it and can support the President—"

"Support him! I should say I can!" interrupted Brother Moyle. Then Brother Moyle told about when President [Heber J.] Grant chose me [McKay] as his counselor and he [Moyle] said, "I responded to that appointment [of McKay] with all my heart, and have ever since."

I then said, "Do not say anything about this as yet; you may talk to Alberta (Sister Moyle), and no one else."

So this morning, Brother Moyle came in and said: "Sister Moyle and I didn't sleep all night—we have decided that we had better not go to Europe; we feel that I should stay here and be by your side to help you."

I was very pleased with Brother Moyle's attitude. ...

8:30 a.m.—Following Brother Moyle's departure, I called President [J. Reuben] Clark and asked him to come to my private office. I said to him: "President Clark, I think the time has come when we should reorganize the First Presidency, and I should like to have you as my First Counselor."

"Well, now," he said, "I do not want you to feel obligated to take me, but I feel honored in being asked, and I pledge you my wholehearted

---

41. Moyle's biographer states probable reasons for his new calling. He was a "leader with solid business experience ... [who] was needed to pick up many business-related assignments that President Richards had been carrying. ... The accelerating missionary program needed strong leadership, and here Elder Moyle's enthusiasm had been demonstrated. Finally, President McKay saw Henry Moyle as a friend as well as a colleague—a recipient of affection as well as respect" (Poll, *Working the Divine Miracle*, 187). Another factor was that the Moyles and McKays shared common bonds and ties. Thomas E. McKay, the prophet's brother, who was Moyle's mission president in Germany from 1909 to 1912, gave Moyle permission to leave the mission to attend the University at Freiberg. Another McKay brother, William M., was Moyle's first tracting companion (*Working*, 23, 25, 27–28, 33, 37). Later, after establishing a successful law firm, Moyle hired McKay's oldest son, David, as a member of the firm (65–69).

support, and all that I have I want to give to the Cause and to the support of the Church and the First Presidency, and I pledge my allegiance to you."

I thanked him, and then told him that I should like to have Brother Henry D. Moyle as my second counselor.

President Clark was agreeable and said that Brother Moyle would give good support.

9 a.m.—Called a special meeting of all members of the Twelve who are in the City. We met in the office of the First Presidency. I announced to the Brethren that the purpose of the meeting was to present for their approval the reorganization of the First Presidency.

I said that some of the members of the Twelve will be mentioned at the Mutual Improvement Association Convention as advisors, and that I thought this matter of appointing counselors in the First Presidency should have attention first so that the people might be informed of the true situation.

I told the Brethren that undoubtedly all had felt the loss of Brother Stephen L. Richards, that his clear vision, sound judgment, loyalty to the truth and the Church, and to the Brethren are greatly missed. However, I stated that he had been called Home and that this work is greater than any man or any set of men. I said further that the Savior is at the head of the Church, and He has been with us as we have deliberated and presented to Him the problems that we are facing, and the need of His continual guidance.

I then recommended that President J. Reuben Clark, Jr. be sustained as first counselor in The First Presidency, and that Elder Henry D. Moyle be sustained as second counselor. Elder Harold B. Lee moved for the approval of this recommendation, and the motion was seconded by Elder Spencer W. Kimball, and unanimously approved.

President Clark and President Moyle then briefly expressed their feelings and their willingness to give their all in serving the best interests of the Church.

I then said that it would be necessary to release Brother Moyle from his position with the Welfare Committee and that he would talk with Brother Harold B. Lee in regard to a reorganization of that Committee.[42]

---

42. Moyle was heavily involved in the creation of the LDS Church Welfare Program. As president of the Cottonwood Stake, he experienced first-hand the severity

I also said that I should like to have Brother Moyle sustained today as head of the Missionary Work, and would refer to him and his associates some matters which will need immediate attention. Brother Moyle expressed himself in favor of the proposed changes, and the recommendation was unanimously approved by the Council.[43]

June 18, 1959, meeting of First Presidency and Twelve. Since Elder Marion G. Romney is leaving soon to tour the European Missions, he inquired regarding the counsel he should give to the Saints in Europe regarding their emigrating to this country so I gave the following instructions to him:

There is no command regarding this matter, but we wish the people to build up the Branches where they live so that those who never can get away from those countries over there will be built up spiritually, and receive their temple endowments and all blessings they could obtain if they were to come here. We want them to be loyal and true to every principle of the gospel in their own land and to know that the Lord will be with them. I should like our good Saints in foreign lands to have favorable meeting places where they can partake of the sacrament, participate in the auxiliary activities, and build up the branches in those lands. In many cases our members would never be able to come to Utah and obtain the blessings that we enjoy in Church work and Church services. The same condition exists in South Africa where an entire generation of men and women had never even seen a member of the Council of the Twelve. I think we should have a temple there some day. It is a long way for these people to go to a temple and the distances are great in that country and under present conditions they are obliged to live and die without having the blessings of the Temple and realize the significance of them.

---

of the Depression on his stake members. At one time, three of his bishops and four of his high councilmen were unemployed. Along with Hugh B. Brown of the Granite Stake and Harold B. Lee of the Pioneer Stake, Moyle helped to implement the fledgling program. Initially it was known as the Church Security Program (1936) and was later renamed the Church Welfare Program

43. According to Spencer W. Kimball, President McKay said, "The Savior is at the head of [the church] and I think he has been with us as we have deliberated and presented to him the problems that we are facing and the need of his continual guidance. We believe that now we will present to you, with His approval, the names of the Brethren to complete the First Presidency." Kimball diary, June 12, 1959.

July 1, 1959, 7 a.m. Sat for <u>Ortho Fairbanks</u>, sculptor.[44] This is probably the last sitting Brother Fairbanks will need to continue his work on the bust that he is doing of me.

I have been very impressed with the ability and sincerity of this young man. I feel that he is talented and really gifted in his art. I think he is a noble young man, and have learned to respect and admire him.

Later I was greatly surprised to learn through my secretary, Clare Middlemiss, that Brother Nicholas G. Morgan, Sr., who employed Brother Ortho Fairbanks to do this bust of me, intends to have <u>twelve busts finished in white Italian marble and one placed in each of the Temples of the Church</u>. Of course, I feel very reluctant about this being done, but it seems that I shall have nothing to say about it as Brother Morgan, with the endorsement of President Henry D. Moyle, has already gone ahead with arrangements for this to be done.

9 to 10:30 a.m.—as convened in First Presidency's meeting. ...

I read to the Brethren at the meeting this morning a letter from John Talmage,[45] assistant to Governor [George D.] Clyde, which reviewed the Governor's interest and position with respect to the Sunday Closing Law and explained again the governor's veto of the bill to enforce Sunday closing to certain grocery stores.

After consideration, it was agreed that the Statement of the First Presidency on observance of the Sabbath, recently published in the Deseret News be republished in the newspaper and that a circular be prepared of a statement for distribution to the homes of the Saints by the Ward teachers. Assignment was made to carry out this purpose.

---

44. Ortho R. Fairbanks (1925–2015) was a grand-nephew of Avard Fairbanks, whose monumental *Tragedy at Winter Quarters* is well known and whose angels sit atop the spires of four temples. He was also a grandson of the art missionary John B. Fairbanks, whose murals adorn the rooms of the Salt Lake Temple. Ortho received a BA and MFA from the University of Utah, served a mission to New Zealand, and taught at the Church College of Hawaii (BYU–Hawaii). He sculpted the statue of Karl G. Maeser for BYU's Provo campus and the bust of Brigham Young for the LDS Conference Center.

45. John R. Talmage (1911–2001) was the youngest child of apostle James E. Talmage (1862–1933). After receiving a degree in journalism from the University of Utah, he worked for the *Deseret News*; he eventually became managing editor. He had been a navy captain during World War II. He authored the biography of his father, *The Talmage Story: Life of James E. Talmage—Educator, Scientist, Apostle.*

July 21, 1959, 4:30–5:30 p.m. I met with <u>Elder Joseph T. Bentley</u> who presented the following to me:

(1) Suggested that inasmuch as President [Ernest L.] Wilkinson is receiving no salary for being President of the Brigham Young University, he wonders if it would not be a nice gesture for the B.Y.U. Board to pay for his trip abroad. President Wilkinson has already left for Iran, and later he will go to Europe for a vacation.

Later, I took this matter up with President [Henry D.] Moyle, and we agreed that the B.Y.U. should present this gift to President Wilkinson.[46]

July 29, 1959. President J. Reuben Clark, Jr. called to report that he is better. He says that he is able to walk around a little. Stated that he is taking "pills, pills, pills," then added: "Do you remember what Sister Richards said about President Stephen L. Richards?—that he is one of the pill-ers of the Church! (laughter) Well," concluded President Clark, "I am two pill-ers!" (laughter).

"The Lord be with you—our love and blessings to you," replied President McKay.

August 20, 1959. At Council meeting today a letter was read to the Brethren from the Advisors to the Music Committee suggesting the advisability of appointing the Director of the Tabernacle Choir as a member of the General Church Music Committee.

I related briefly conditions in connection with the release of Elder J. Spencer Cornwall nearly two years ago and explained that the First Presidency had decided to consult Brother Cornwall in regard to the advisability of his being honorably released as leader of the Choir, and it was decided that I should talk with him about the matter. I called Brother Cornwall into the office and presented the matter, indicating that we were considering the advisability of a reorganization so far as the chorister of the Choir was concerned with the thought in mind of asking him when the change might wisely be made and whom he might suggest for his successor. When the question was raised as to how this should be accomplished and when, Brother Cornwall answered very abruptly, "as of

---

46. Wilkinson's trip cost approximately $5,000, the equivalent of about $50,000 today.

now!" In answer to his retort, I said, "All right; it will be right now." I told him he should take charge of the Choir the following Sunday as certain appointments had been made [by him involving the program].

Later [the assistant conductor], Brother Richard P. Condie[,] was appointed as his successor, but having in mind the incidents relating to Brother Cornwall's release, the First Presidency, in presenting the appointment to Brother Condie who manifested an excellent spirit, said that they would like him to take charge of the Choir for two years, and they would like to see what he could do in that time; that after two years his successor would be appointed. Brother Condie made the response, "Suppose I make a success of it?" In answer to this question I told him: "You will be released in two years." Brother Condie accepted this in good spirit, and there was a record made of that conversation. Now the two years will be up within a month or two. Accordingly, the question now arises as to whether Brother Condie should be continued in this position. I think that Brother Condie has done a very good job in directing the Choir; and in considering the matter, this morning the First Presidency in their meeting felt that Brother Condie had given complete satisfaction, and had really done a wonderful job.

Brother Richard L. Evans said that he felt personally, not as a musician, but as one who has been closely tied to this situation for 30 years, that we have the best Choir singing today that we have had in that 30 years of time, and that recordings of the Philadelphia Orchestra and the Choir are now on the best-seller list across the nation, and are having a tremendous reception. The Choir is happy and there is a sweet spirit among the members. Said he felt that Brother Condie has done a remarkable job.

I presented to the Council the recommendation that we appoint Brother Condie a member of the General Church Music Committee, which implies that his two years will not end his service as Choir leader.

This was approved by the Council, after which I said that I believed that the sentiment of the Brethren represented the feelings of the Church generally—those who understand music especially. The Choir members who were opposed to Brother Condie two years ago are now reporting that they have received more definite instruction and training than they have ever had before, and that there seems to be a general feeling that we are proud of our Choir and proud of Brother Condie and his achievements.

August 25, 1959, 9–10 a.m. Attended the First Presidency's meeting— President [J. Reuben] Clark was present for the first time after a several weeks' absence due to illness. We were happy to have him back.

September 1, 1959. While Elder Richard P. Condie was with us in [the First Presidency's] meeting this morning, I asked, "When are your two years up?" Brother Condie replied, "The fifteenth of September." I said: "Well, you go right on." Whereupon, Brother Condie said, "As one Scotsman to another, I love that."

September 8, 1959. The first to call to extend congratulations on my birthday [today] was Elder Hugh B. Brown of the Council of the Twelve. The warmth of his friendship, his devotion to the Church and to me in helping to discharge some of the duties associated with this office are deeply appreciated by me. I was very grateful for his visit this morning. ...

On September 10, 1959 I said to the Brethren assembled in Council meeting in the Salt Lake Temple that I had received many cards, letters, telegrams, cablegrams, and messages of greetings on the occasion of my 86th birthday ...

I stated that when I look back over my association with men and women I am convinced that there are a lot of good, honest, true, loyal men and women in the world—many who want to do right. We hear about the gangsters and those who cheat and lie, particularly among the Communists, but the majority of men and women want to do right, and it is our duty to show them what is right—that is our responsibility. We must, as a Church, declare to the entire world that Jesus Christ is the one and only one who has given the Plan of Salvation leading to peace.

I said that I find that most of our young people want to know what is right, and if they know it, I feel sure they will do it. I further said "You might call me an optimist, but I have faith in mankind; they are God's children, and His glory is to bring about their salvation and redemption. We may be discouraged, but the way is opening up. The Presiding Brethren of the Church are carrying the responsibility most magnificently. The people love them. They are listening to their message, and through our non-member friends, the Gospel is going to be taken to people whom the missionaries cannot reach. I feel happy and not discouraged."

September 13, 1959. During this time I studied 28 requests for cancellation of their temple [marriage] sealings, Elder Hugh B. Brown of the Council of the Twelve having made preliminary investigation of each case for me. This meant the signing of my signature 168 times on the various letters to the parties concern[ed], and to the Temple Presidents notifying them of the cancellations. This in addition to writing "Approved" and date on each report given by Elder Brown.

October 9, 1959, 12:30 p.m. Interviewed Brother Howard W. Hunter,[47] President of the Pasadena Stake, Arcadia, California, in my private office regarding his being chosen as the new apostle to fill the vacancy in the Council of the Twelve caused by the appointment of President [Henry D.] Moyle to the First Presidency.

Brother Hunter, of course, was shocked at this news—many tears were shed as he pledged his allegiance and accepted this high and holy calling. I told him that his name would be presented for the sustaining vote of the members of the Church at the[48] Tabernacle tomorrow morning.

October 15, 1959, 10–1:30 p.m. Was convened in the meeting of the First Presidency and Council of the Twelve held in the Salt Lake Temple.

At this meeting I gave the charge to the new Apostle—Elder Howard W. Hunter, ordained him an Apostle of the Lord Jesus Christ, and set him apart as a member of the Council of the Twelve.

October 22, 1959, 2:15 p.m. ... I met in my private office Elders Mark E. Petersen and Richard L. Evans. They presented the matter of publishing an abridged edition of the Book of Mormon, which will contain all the

---

47. Howard William Hunter (1907–95) was a successful attorney in southern California and prominent church member who was notably involved with bringing the LDS temple to Los Angeles. He was originally from Boise and had worked in banking. He also played saxophone in a band. In 1994 he would become president of the church.

48. The diary has "at the in the".

parts of the Book of Mormon as contained in the Sunday School lesson on the Book of Mormon for the year 1940.

The committee feels that this will prove to be a very <u>convenient book for investigators</u>. They stated that no word or comment within the book will be other than the words of the Book of Mormon itself.

I told them to go ahead with the matter, and submit a prospectus to the First Presidency.

November 7, 1959, 9 a.m. At this hour had a meeting—a very important and unpleasant one—with Lester F. Hewlett,[49] president of the [Mormon] Tabernacle Choir, and Jack Thomas, Tour Manager.[50]

President Henry D. Moyle and Brother Stanford Darger were present during part of the discussion. Further facts are to be obtained regarding the matter discussed.

November 13, 1959, 11:30 a.m. <u>Met by appointment J. Bracken Lee</u> who was recently elected as Mayor of Salt Lake City. He was accompanied by Bishop Thorpe B. Isaacson. This was merely a courtesy call, and Mr. Lee expressed a desire to conduct the affairs of the city so that it will be pleasing to those who have elected him.

November 19, 1959. Today at Council Meeting I reported that during the past few days the First Presidency had been considering the problems in the European Missions, and that I now presented to the Council, for the First Presidency, the advisability of reopening the European Mission, and instead of sending the Brethren of the General Authorities to visit the various missions over there, that we appoint one of the General

---

49. Lester Franklin Hewlett (1896–1962) was born in Salt Lake City and served a mission to England. As he grew older, he became involved in his father's food manufacturing company, which specialized in "coffee, teas, extracts, and spices." In the 1930s he advised the church as it established the food manufacturing arm of the Church Welfare Program, Deseret Industries. He had been president of the choir since 1938.

50. In ten days the choir would receive a Grammy Award for its 1958 collaboration with the Philadelphia Orchestra. The new conductor, Richard P. Condie, had improved the choir's sound by dismissing those who lacked adequate training or skill, and had proven to be "hot-tempered," prone to "yelling and screaming," and dictatorial. Nor did he himself have adequate training in directing a choir; he had to be convinced by Eugene Ormandy of the Philadelphia Orchestra to take lessons in conducting. Hicks, *Mormon Tabernacle Choir*, chap. 6.

Authorities to preside as President of the European Mission, to work with the various missions just as the European Mission President formerly did. I continued that it is now felt that the headquarters of the European Mission should be on the continent rather than in London as formerly.

I then proposed that Elder Alvin R. Dyer, Assistant to the Twelve, be called to become the President of the European Mission with headquarters in Frankfurt am Main in Germany.[51] I stated here that I felt that we should first establish European Mission Headquarters and the other matters pertaining to getting publications and lesson helps to the German-speaking missions, etc., could be developed later in connection therewith.

The Brethren unanimously approved of the reopening of the European Mission and also of the appointment of Alvin R. Dyer as the President.

December 25, 1959. As is traditional with the McKay family, all of our children and grandchildren returned to our home [for Christmas]. It was 11 o'clock when they arrived.

Presents were distributed to each of them by Sister [Emma Ray] McKay and me. The children had all joined in giving to Sister McKay and me a colored television set—an RCA.

Another joyous and happy occasion! Later in the day Sister McKay and I were guests of our son Lawrence and his wife Mildred at a delicious dinner.

During the day a beautiful snow fell, which added to the joyous spirit of Christmas. All in all, Christmas Day, 1959, was perfect!

December 26, 1959, 9:30 a.m. This morning took my car over to the Hotel Utah Garage, and left it there so that the mechanic could put the snow tires on.

I then walked over to the Church Offices, taking the path at the rear of the building. The snow storm yesterday had left quite a bit of snow and ice on the pathway. Workmen had also been digging the road up, and in order to avoid the holes, I climbed up on the foundation of the

---

51. As president of the European Mission, Dyer was to oversee areas of the continent where missionaries were not stationed and to coordinate the activities of the other mission presidents. As the European regional headquarters, Frankfurt am Main would house editors and translators to produce magazines and manuals in eight languages, along with attorneys, accountants, and specialists in real estate, government relations, and church records.

building. In doing so, I slipped on some ice and went tumbling down to the ground, hitting my head on the ice. I managed to get up and make my way to my private office. I was so shaken up that I had to lay on the couch for awhile.

10 Doctrinal Difficulties, 1960

The First Presidency held a meeting. We decided that Bruce R. McConkie's book, "Mormon Doctrine," recently published by Bookcraft Company, must not be re-published, as it is full of errors and misstatements, and it is most unfortunate that it has received such wide circulation. —January 8, 1960

January 4, 1960, 8 a.m. Bank Merger Considered—the First Presidency met by appointment (previously arranged through President Moyle), the following bankers: David M. Kennedy, Chairman of the Board, Continental Illinois National Bank & Trust Company of Chicago; Howard J. Stoddard, President of the Michigan National Bank, Lansing, Michigan; Taylor H. Peery,[1] businessman from Palo Alto, and formerly an officer of the Bank of America; W. LaMar Webb,[2] President, Zion's First National Bank, and William F. Edwards, Finance Secretary to the First Presidency.

This was one of the most important meetings ever held on financial affairs of the Church. Three leading bankers of the country (named above) willingly responded to a telephone invitation to come to the office

1. Horace Taylor Peery (1902–64) was a prominent California financier whose grandfather, David Harold Peery, had been a Utah banker. He was reared in California and graduated from Stanford University, served an LDS mission to Germany, worked in New York, and returned to Stanford for an MBA. During World War II he became a lieutenant colonel on General Eisenhower's civil affairs staff. Afterward he became a vice president of the Bank of America and co-founder with John Arrillaga of a prosperous real-estate company. McKay performed Peery's 1931 marriage.
2. Walter LaMar Webb (1908–91) had degrees from the University of Utah and Harvard School of Business Administration. For a time he was senior vice president of Wachovia Bank and Trust in Winston–Salem, North Carolina, and he had just been named president of Zions Bank in 1959. He was originally from Ogden and Salt Lake City.

of the First Presidency to confer with us on banking affairs. They left their businesses at short notice, coming by plane at their own expense. It was necessary for them to leave at noon by plane in order to meet other commitments of their own.

We discussed with these bankers the advisability of the Zion's First National Bank joining with the Walker Bank of this city and the First American Bank,[3] and the impact that this merger would be upon the Church, and upon banking interests generally here in the West.

These men thanked us for the privilege of discussing this matter with them, and refused to have the Church reimburse them for their expenses in coming to Salt Lake City.

What a reservoir of strength this Church has in men who are seemingly indifferent—outstanding men—men of judgment—who wish to cooperate with us and render service!

We concluded that the Zion's First National Bank will not consider further the proposal of merging with Walker Bank & Trust Company and the American First Bank. ...

[Excerpt from the minutes]

Is the concept of a state bank to operate more as an adjunct of the Church Financial Department to serve the direct banking needs of the Church sound and practical?

President Moyle, in particular, emphasized the importance of the Church having a bank which it controls to handle Church funds. An important consideration is the confidential nature of the church business. Another important consideration is the question of safety.

No final conclusion was reached, but Brothers Kennedy, Perry, and Stoddard questioned seriously the advisability of organizing a state bank to operate more as an adjunct of the Church Financial Department. Brother Stoddard, in particular, questioned if a charter would be granted for such a limited operation.

The question was asked, if Zions First National merged with Walker,

---

3. Walker Bank, which had been acquired by Transamerica Corporation in 1956, had become Firstamerica Bank in 1958 due to antitrust regulations (see footnote at Nov. 9, 1956). Meanwhile, Zions Bank had merged with First National Bank of Salt Lake City in 1959 to become Zions First National Bank, contrary to the advice of David Kennedy recorded in this diary on January 14, 1959. See "Zion's Bank Elects Webb President," *Salt Lake Tribune*, Jan. 14, 1959.

might the charter of Zions First National be continued but the business restricted to serve the needs of the Church? Brother Stoddard was firm in his opinion that the Comptroller of the Currency would not permit a national charter to be used in this limited manner. Brother Kennedy concurred in this opinion.

Brother Kennedy led out in suggesting that the banking needs of the Church might be better served through use of established banking facilities.

a. Deposits: Brother Kennedy suggested that banks might be selected in regional areas and that all funds raised by wards and stakes within the regions could be sent directly to the selected regional banks. Arrangements could then be made by these regional banks to send automatically at the end of each month deposited funds to a limited number of "key" banks. This arrangement would eliminate the possibility of anyone outside of the Church organization identifying the amount of Church contributions. He also expressed the opinion that if these banks were carefully selected, the funds of the church on deposit would be even safer than when concentrated in one bank.

b. Disbursements: Brother Kennedy expressed the opinion that the disbursements of the Church could be handled with accounts at the limited number of "key" banks. Again, this would eliminate any possibility of information regarding total disbursements of the Church becoming known. He stressed the confidential way in which such information is maintained by leading banks. He was of the opinion that this program would provide even less possibility of information becoming known than exists at the present time.

c. International Services: Brother Kennedy expressed the opinion that some of the large banks would be able to give the Church even better service in their international transactions than now available through Zions First National Bank. He said that all of the large banks without international departments would open up the possibility of competition and result in even better service. Asked if the Church withdrawing from Zions First National Bank would weaken the relationship with banks such as First National City, Brother Kennedy responded that this should have no adverse effect.

Brothers Perry and Stoddard agreed in general with the position taken

by Brother Kennedy. It was observed that this greater use of banks throughout the Church could have a favorable influence.

6. Advisability of Church Withdrawing from the General Banking Business.

Brothers Kennedy, Perry, and Stoddard were of the opinion that
if the Church continued to control Zions First National Bank and the
bank continued to solicit deposits, then the bank should provide banking
services to its customers. They felt this was necessary from the points of
view of (a) proper relations with the public; (b) the management of the
bank; and (c) the minority stockholders.

There was general agreement that if the services of the bank were to
be restricted, the Church should offer to acquire the stock of the minority
stockholders.

Concern was expressed by Brothers Kennedy, Perry, and Stoddard
that if the bank were to confine its operations to one office in the downtown area, that business would gradually move away from the bank and
dissatisfaction would develop and that time would work against the operation. It was pointed out during the discussion that many good Church
people, including bishops, are transferring their business to other banks
because of convenience.

Nevertheless, there remained the basic question that if it is considered desirable that the Church control a bank to meet its own banking
needs, it may be better to continue Zions First National Bank on a confined basis than to attempt to organize a new state bank.

7. Church Selling Zions First National Stock.

Considerable attention was given to the possibility of the Church
selling its stock of Zions First National Bank, but with the bank remaining an independent institution. In case of such a sale, it was suggested that
the First Presidency should withdraw entirely from the management. It
was agreed that if this were done, the word "Zions" should be deleted
from the management. If a satisfactory sale were made, this would permit
First National Bank to go forward providing desirable banking services
for the benefit of the community. This would be consistent with the interest of the minority stockholders.

However, this discussion was not carried to a conclusion. Many
problems would be involved. The interest of the Church in Zions First

National Bank has influenced many of the customers of the bank and employees, and the withdrawal of the Church could have a considerable impact upon the organization. It was brought out that if such a sale were to be made, it would probably be desirable to withdraw in advance of the sale or concurrently with the sale the surplus capital funds.

President Clark, in particular, stressed the importance of the First Presidency being relieved of the responsibilities that go with the management of a large competitive bank. President Moyle expressed the feeling that the First Presidency should be tied in more closely to the management of the bank if it is to continue to operate as at present. ...

9. Business Connections of General Authorities.

Each member of the First Presidency expressed the opinion that it is desirable for the Church to maintain certain important business interests and for the General Authorities to maintain reasonable business connections. It was observed that the Church involves the lives of its members every day of the week, and it is desirable for the General Authorities to remain in contact with the everyday business world.

10. Other Business Interests of the Church.

It was pointed out that the responsibilities of the First Presidency are different with respect to the bank than the other business interests of the Church. It was recognized that if the Church withdraws from the general banking business, this need have no bearing upon the policy toward other business interests of the Church. ...

The First Presidency concluded that in view of the possible legal involvements, Zions First National Bank will not consider further the proposal of merging with the Walker Bank and Trust Company. President Moyle was authorized to notify John Wallace, Chairman of Walker Bank and Trust Company, of this decision.

January 6, 1960. Received telephone call from [Salt Lake City] Mayor J. Bracken Lee regarding statement that he has made to the papers that the Church will not build a Junior College on the Forest Dale property,[4] and

---

4. BYU had purchased the 169-acre Forest Dale golf course from the city on June 19, 1958 (Wilkinson, *Brigham Young University*, 3:151), and had given the city two years to vacate the property. See note under Jan. 20, 1959.

that the city will try to re-purchase the property. The [Salt Lake] Tribune reporter also called to verify this story. The reporter was told that when Mayor Lee made a courtesy call to my office in company with Bishop [Thorpe B.] Isaacson, I made the statement that the Church had not decided when they would build a Junior College on that property, and Mayor Lee interpreted what I said as meaning that the Church was not going to build one.

This matter was later turned over to President Ernest L. Wilkinson of the Brigham Young University who was instrumental in getting the Forest Dale property for the Church, and the matter was finally settled and announced in the local newspapers that the Church would not sell the property back to the city.[5]

January 7, 1960. By telephone, Henry Smith of the Deseret News, asked for instructions in the matter of a newspaper report of the interest of the Salt Lake City Commission in the re-purchase of the Forest Dale Golf Course. After consideration, it was agreed that it will be better if nothing is said about the matter in the newspapers. It was explained that the Mayor had been informed that nothing has been done about building a Junior College on the property. No decision about the building will be made until the Church gains possession of the property in 1961.

I stated that the whole question of Junior Colleges, institutes, and seminaries is before the First Presidency. The rapid expansion of the Brigham Young University and the matter of providing additional Junior Colleges in several places and giving training in basic courses in education rather than in the "fringe" subjects were mentioned as warranting a full review of the general subject with President [Ernest L.] Wilkinson.

January 7, 1960, 10:15–12:45 p.m. ... The First Presidency met with Elders Mark E. Petersen and Marion G. Romney. They submitted their report upon their examination of the book "Mormon Doctrine" by Elder Bruce McConkie.[6]

---

5. For Wilkinson's response, see Wilkinson diary, Jan. 6, 1960.

6. Their findings are summarized in the next paragraph. J. Reuben Clark was extremely agitated over the possible impact of the book: "I was sure we had to do something because this book would raise more trouble than anything we had had in the Church for a long while." Clark memorandum, July 9, 1958, qtd. in Quinn, *Extensions of Power*, 224.

These brethren reported that the manuscript of the book "Mormon Doctrine" had not been read by the reading committee; that President Joseph Fielding Smith did not know anything about it until it was published.[7] Elder Petersen stated that the extent of the corrections which he had marked in his copy of the book (1067) affected most of the 776 pages of the book. He also said that he thought the brethren should be under the rule that no book should be published without a specific approval of the First Presidency.

I stated that the decision of the First Presidency and the Committee should be announced to the Twelve.

It was agreed that the necessary corrections are so numerous that to republish a corrected edition of the book would be such an extensive repudiation of the original as to destroy the credit of the author; that the republication of the book should be forbidden and that the book should be repudiated in such a way as to save the career of the author as one of the General Authorities of the Church. It was also agreed that this decision should be announced to the Council of the Twelve before I talk to the author.

Elder Petersen will prepare an editorial for publication in the Improvement Era, stating the principle of approval of books on Church doctrine. A rough draft will be submitted to us for approval.

[Cover letter from Romney to McKay, Jan. 28, 1959:]

The author [McConkie] is an able and thorough student of the gospel.

See also McKay diary entry, Mar. 6, 1959, herein; Prince and Wright, *David O. McKay*, 49–53; Quinn, *Elder Statesman*, 222, 501–02; Quinn, *Extensions of Power*, 844–45.

7. This statement, taken at face value, seems strange. Having married Smith's daughter, McConkie was in frequent communication with his father-in-law on matters social, religious, and especially doctrinal (McConkie, *Bruce R. McConkie Story*, 106–107, 118–19). McConkie edited for publication his father-in-law's letters and other writings under the title *Doctrines of Salvation*, and according to his biographer he elicited responses on subjects not adequately covered and "put them into writing" for his father-in-law to literally sign off on. "President Smith never found it necessary to change so much as a word of what Elder McConkie had written," we are told (ibid., 3). It seems unlikely that they would not have discussed McConkie's encyclopedic work— especially since a substantial amount of it quoted and rephrased Smith's books and addresses (David John Buerger, "Speaking with Authority," *Sunstone*, Mar. 1985). Smith was thanked in the preface: "Joseph Fielding Smith, ... made many valuable suggestions as to content and construction" (6). That McConkie would have kept this a secret seems uncharacteristic of their relationship and writings.

In many respects he has produced a remarkable book. Properly used, it quickly introduces the student to the authorities on most any gospel subject.

As to the book itself, notwithstanding its many commendable and valuable features and the author's assumption of "sole and full responsibility" for it, its nature and scope and the authoritative tone of the style in which it is written pose the question as to the propriety of the author's attempting such a project without assignment and supervision from him whose right and responsibility it is to speak for the Church on "Mormon Doctrine." Had the work been authoritatively supervised, some of the following matters might have been omitted and the treatment of others modified.

A. [Discourteous] references to churches and other groups who do not accept "Mormon Doctrine."
1. "Reorganized Church of Jesus Christ of Latter-day Saints" who sometimes refer to themselves as "Josephites." (Exhibit II–1, pages 50, 141, 362)
2. "Christian Churches" generally. (Exhibit I–2, pages 139, 455)
3. "Catholic Church". (Exhibit II–3, pages 13, [6]6, 129, 130, 216, 241, 242, 314–315, 342, 346, 350, 422, 499, 511, 697)
4. Communists and Catholics. (Exhibit II–4, pages 260, 131)
5. Evolution and Evolutionists. (Exhibit II–5, pages 37, 77, 136, [229–38],[8] 659)

B. Declaration as to "Mormon Doctrine" on controversial issues.
1. "Pre-Adamites". (Exhibit III–1, pages 17, 262)
2. Status of Animals and Plants in the Garden of Eden. (Exhibit III–2, pages 36, 234–35)
3. Meaning of the various accounts of Creation. (Exhibit III–3, pages 157–8, 167–8)
4. Dispensation of Abraham. (Exhibit III–4, page 204)
5. Moses as a translated being. (Exhibit III–5, pages 206, 445, 466, 727–8)
6. Origin of Individuality. (Exhibit III–6, page 404)
7. Defiling the priesthood. (Exhibit III–7, page 437)
8. Manner in which Jesus was Begotten. (Exhibit III–8, page 494)

---

8. Romney had "0, 228, 238" but probably intended to reference the entry on evolution on pages 229–38.

9. Written sermons. (Exhibit III–9, pages 634–5, 716)

10. Resurrection of stillborn children. (Exhibit III–10, page 694)

C. Miscellaneous [speculative] Interpretations. (Exhibit IV)

Frequency of Administrations, page 22

Baptism in the "molten sea," page 98

II Peter 1:19, page 102

Paul married, page 112

Status of those "with Christ in His Resurrection," page 128

Consecration of oil, page 147

Councils and schools among the Gods, page 151

Limitations on Deity, page 154

Sunday not a proper day for family reunions, page 254

Geological changes at the time of the deluge, page 268

The Holy Ghost a spirit man, page 329

Facing east in temples when giving the Hosanna Shout, page 337

Details on family prayer and asking the blessing on food, page 526

Women to be gods, page 551

Interpretation of Doctrine and Covenants 93:1, page 581

Interpretation of "Every spirit of man was innocent in the beginning,"
page 606

Resumption of schools of the prophets, page 613

Time of beginning of seasons, page 616

Interpretation of III Nephi 21:20, page 618

D. Repeated use of the word "apostate" and related terms in a way which to many seems discourteous and to others gives offense. (Exhibit V, pages 123, 125, 160, 169, 212, 223, 383, 528, 538, 548, 596).

January 8, 1960, 11:55–12:15 p.m. The First Presidency held a meeting. We decided that Bruce R. McConkie's book, "Mormon Doctrine" recently published by Bookcraft Company must not be re-published, as it is full of errors and misstatements, and it is most unfortunate that it has received such wide circulation. It is reported to us that Brother McConkie has made corrections in his book, and is now preparing another edition. We decided this morning that we do not want him to publish another edition.[9]

---

9. McConkie's authorized biography, written by his son Joseph Fielding McConkie

We decided, also, to have no more books published by General Authorities without their first having the consent of the First Presidency.[10] ...

We also discussed the matter of <u>choosing new [members of the board of] Directors</u> for the <u>Zions First National Bank</u>. Elders Harold B. Lee and Delbert L. Stapley were suggested as new directors and approved. Brother Louis T. Ellsworth, president of the Surety Life Insurance, was suggested. He has a small deposit now with the bank. I suggested that they hold this suggestion up for further investigation.

January 13, 1960, 12 noon. <u>Brother Henry Smith</u> of the Deseret News came in and reported that there is a rumor that President Ernest L. Wilkinson of the B.Y.U., is seeking someone to take his place at the B.Y.U. I told Henry Smith that there is nothing to the rumor.

<u>Received a telephone call from Dr. Ernest L. Wilkinson</u>, President of the Brigham Young University, Re:—<u>Forest Dale Property and [Salt Lake City] Mayor J. Bracken Lee's attitude that the city should buy the property back from the Church.</u>

President Wilkinson reported that he is getting inquiries from "City Hall" in Salt Lake City as to whether the Church is going to sell the Forest Dale property it purchased last year from the City.

I told President Wilkinson that we did not know anything about Mayor Lee's proposals, and that we are not going to sell the property or do anything about it until we consult with him. I said further that he (President Wilkinson) could call Mayor Lee and tell him the

---

(*Bruce R. McConkie Story*), interpreted these events differently by referring to the controversy as a bit of "flap and fuss" (182), without mentioning the most serious issues raised with the Brethren. The biography claimed the real reasons were McConkie's "identifying Roman Catholicism as the 'great and abominable church' spoken of by Nephi in the Book of Mormon" (182) and the "authoritative tone of the book" (183). If the book were controversial or without substantial merit, the son argued, his father would not have been "called to the Quorum of the Twelve in 1972" (183). "No one who knew him could question his integrity or discipline," the biography read, "particularly where matters of priesthood direction were concerned" (184), which is at odds with the documentation.

10. For another perspective, see Horne's *Bruce R. McConkie*, in which Horne found that wording from McConkie's *Mormon Doctrine* later appeared in the Bible Dictionary, which is published as part of the church's Standard Works. Both Horne and Joseph Fielding McConkie understated the displeasure of the First Presidency with McConkie, beginning with his previous book, *Sound Doctrine*, and with Joseph Fielding Smith over his book, *Man: His Origin and Destiny*.

matter has been referred to him (President Wilkinson). I said that I would tell Mayor Lee that I had referred the matter to him (President Wilkinson).

I then told President Wilkinson that I had other matters about which I should like to talk to him, and he asked me to designate the time, which I shall do upon my return from [an upcoming trip to] California.

Later I called President Wilkinson and told him that the First Presidency had not discussed with the City Commission nor Mayor Lee the matter pertaining to the Forest Dale Property; that in the first place I understand that we do not get possession of the property until 1961. President Wilkinson turned to Clyde Sandgren who was by his side and asked him, and he said that was right—1961.

I then repeated to President Wilkinson that we had said nothing about plans for a Junior College; that no commitment whatsoever has been made, that we should say nothing until we are sure; until at least we have possession of the land.

I said: "Now if the Mayor calls again, the matter is in your hands. You may have this—(a commitment made by one of the brethren in our consultation this morning)—that pending our decision regarding our Junior College, if the city wants to continue to rent it from us for a golf course, that might be a consideration."

President Wilkinson said: "I think that is wise. I'll suggest that; I'll tell Mayor Lee that I will sit down with him, and if the City wants to rent it, we might work out something."

January 14, 1960, 8:30–9:50 a.m. Was engaged in the meeting of the First Presidency. Among matters discussed at this meeting were the following:

(1) Elder Mark E. Petersen's Proposed Editorial on Books by General Authorities. A draft of a proposed editorial for the Improvement Era, prepared by Elder Mark E. Petersen, on the subject of selecting good books, and upon the approval of the publication of books by the First Presidency, was read. After consideration it was decided that the general statement, without the reference to [Bruce R. McConkie's] "Mormon Doctrine," and [Milton R. Hunter's and Thomas S. Ferguson's] "Ancient America and the Book of Mormon," which should be handled separately, would be a suitable editorial on the subject of

selecting good books.[11] Further action on the matter of publishing a statement relating to the approval of [specific] books by the First Presidency was deferred awaiting consideration of the subject by me with President Joseph Fielding Smith. ...

(2) I signed letters to three banks in the East transmitting deposits to each of $100,000, and I approved also of making deposits of $50,000 in selected banks in Ogden, Provo, an Logan. (see copy of letter of appreciation from Mr. Frank M. Browning of Ogden following).[12]

January 27, 1960, 8:30–9:30 a.m. Brother Thomas Stuart Ferguson of the New World Archaeological Society who lives in Oakland, California[13] ... called by appointment at his request on the First Presidency. He is very enthusiastic regarding the accomplishments of his organization. It would seem from what he says that they have done a good work. The Church has contributed a considerable amount in support of work that his organization has been doing in Central America. We referred him

---

11. A draft of the proposed editorial, "Seek Ye Out of the Best Books," is found in the J. Reuben Clark Papers (drawn to my attention by Stirling Adams). After a lengthy review of the need for books and proper education of church members, Petersen wrote: "Wise reading material is necessary also in the field of religion. There again the unreliable is ever present. Speculation becomes rife at times. Private interpretations of doctrine and extremes of dogma are thrust upon an unsuspecting public, some of whom seem to accept any unusual idea that is promulgated if they see it in print. ... Books of this nature are occasionally published among the Latter-day Saints. ... At times members of the General Authorities of the Church have published such material, some of which has been misunderstood, some being actually inaccurate or speculative. When the Brethren have done this they have acted upon their own responsibility, doing so without the knowledge or consent of the presiding authorities of the Church. Those publications should not be accepted by a discriminating public as the official views or doctrines of the Church, nor even as being representative of the Church. One such book was the recently published 'Mormon Doctrine' by Elder Bruce R. McConkie of the First Council of the Seventy. This volume presumes to give the final word on many doctrines of the Church, some of which have never been completely explained even in revelations. Another on the speculative side, is 'Ancient America and the Book of Mormon' by Hunter and Ferguson, which advances unacceptable views on the geography of the Book of Mormon and other topics, and which, together with works of a similar nature by other authors, tend to confuse the thinking of Latter-day Saints."

12. On January 19, Browning acknowledged "this grand gesture" that was implemented with the deposit of "$50,000 of the funds of our beloved Church."

13. See the entries and footnotes under Apr. 7, 9, 14, 1953; Mar. 10, 1955.

to President Ernest L. Wilkinson of the Brigham Young University, to whom this matter of archaeological work has been assigned.[14]

January 27, 1960, 3:00 P.M. ... At the request of the First Presidency, I called <u>President Joseph Fielding Smith</u>, and told ... him[15] that we are a unit in disapproving of Brother Bruce R. McConkie's book, "Mormon Doctrine", as an authoritative exposition of the principles of the gospel.

I then said: "Now, Brother Smith, he is a General Authority, and we do not want to give him a public rebuke that would be embarrassing to him and lessen his influence with the members of the Church, so we shall speak to the Twelve at our meeting in the Temple tomorrow, and tell them that Brother McConkie's book is not approved as an authoritative book, and that it should not be republished, even if the errors (some 1,067 of them) are corrected."

Brother Smith agreed with this suggestion to report to the Twelve, and said, "That is the best thing to do."[16]

I then said that Brother McConkie is advocating by letter some of the principles as printed in his book in answer to letters he receives. Brother Smith said, "I will speak to him about that." I then mentioned that he is also speaking on these subjects, and Brother Smith said, "I will speak to him about that also."

I also said that the First Presidency had decided that General Authorities of the Church should not publish books without submitting them to some member of the General Authorities, and President Smith agreed to this as being wise.

January 28, 1960, 8:30–9 a.m. ... Was engaged in the meeting of the First Presidency. I reported to my counselors that I had talked with President Joseph Fielding Smith about the decision that the book "Mormon Doctrine" should not be republished and about handling the matter to

---

14. In 1959 the New World Archaeological Foundation had been attached to BYU's Department of Archeology at Wilkinson's request.

15. The transcript has "told me that him".

16. Contrariwise, McConkie's biographer claimed that Joseph Fielding Smith was pleased with the book: "He (Joseph Fielding Smith) thought so highly of it that he kept his copy at home. He was afraid that if he took it to the office, someone might walk off with it or borrow it and forget to return it." McConkie, *Bruce R. McConkie Story*, 191.

avoid undermining Brother [Bruce R.] McConkie's influence. President Smith agreed that the book should not be republished, and said that he would talk with Brother McConkie. It was decided that the First Presidency should inform Brother McConkie before he learns of our decision from some other source, so Brother McConkie was asked to come into our meeting this morning.

When he arrived I informed him of the desire of the First Presidency with reference to his book not being republished, to which he agreed. The recommendation was also made that he answer inquiries on the subject with care. Brother McConkie said, "I am amenable to whatever you Brethren want. I will do exactly what you want. I will be as discreet and as wise as I can." In answering letters he said that he would express no views contrary to views which the First Presidency has expressed. He said that he would conform in every respect.[17]

Many other matters of importance were considered at our meeting this morning, and then we dismissed to attend the Council meeting in the temple.

10 a.m. to 2:45 p.m.—Was engaged in the meeting of the First Presidency and Council of the Twelve in the Salt Lake Temple.

At Council meeting I reported to the Brethren our decision regarding Elder Bruce R. McConkie's book "Mormon Doctrine," stating that it had caused considerable comment throughout the Church, and that it has been a source of concern to the Brethren ever since it was published. I said that this book had not been presented to anyone for consideration or approval until after its publication. I further said that the First Presidency have given it very careful consideration, as undoubtedly have some of the Brethren of the Twelve also, and that the First Presidency now recommend that the book be not republished; that it be not republished even in corrected form, even though Brother McConkie mentions in the book

---

17. McConkie's son said his father was "invited to be seated but chose to remain standing. I also know that it was his practice (because he told me to do the same) when you are getting scolded, you offer no excuses—you just take it. After the experience President Moyle observed, 'I've never seen a man in the Church in my experience that took our criticism—and it was more than criticism—but he took it better than anyone I ever saw. When we were through and Bruce left us, I had a great feeling of love and appreciation for a man who could take it without any alibis, without any excuses and said he appreciated what we had said to him'" (in McConkie, *Bruce R. McConkie Story*, 185).

that he takes all responsibility for it; and that it be not recognized as an authoritative book.

I said further that the question has arisen as to whether a public correction should be made and an addendum given emphasizing the parts which are unwisely presented or misquoted or incorrect; but it is felt that that would not be wise because Brother McConkie is one of the General Authorities and it might lessen his influence. The First Presidency recommend that the situation be left as it is, and whenever a question about it arises, we can answer that it is unauthoritative; that it was issued by Brother McConkie on his own responsibility, and he must answer for it.

I reported that the First Presidency had talked with Brother McConkie this morning, and he said he will do whatever the Brethren want him to do. He will not attempt to republish the book, nor to say anything by letter, and if he answers letters or inquiries that he will answer them in accordance with the suggestions made by the Brethren, and not advocate those things concerning which question has been raised as contained in the book.

The Brethren unanimously approved of this.

I then said that the First Presidency further recommend that when any member of the General Authorities desires to write a book, that the Brethren of the Twelve or the First Presidency be consulted regarding it. While the author need not get the approval of these Brethren, they should know before it is published that a member of the General Authorities wants to publish a book. I said it may seem all right for the writer of the book to say, "I only am responsible for it," but I said "you cannot separate your position from your individuality, and we should like the authors to present their books to the Twelve or a Committee appointed." I asked the Brethren of the Twelve to convey this information to the other General Authorities. On motion, this became the consensus of the Council.

February 1, 1960. One letter I dictated was to a woman in answer to her question about the <u>wearing of the garments</u> while sun bathing. I said to her: "The wearing of the garment is a personal responsibility, and conditions that justify temporary removal should be determined by each person."[18]

---

18. McKay was signatory to a First Presidency statement in 1942 about "the wearing of the garment [being] an individual responsibility. ... The conscience of the wearer must guide when circumstances seem to justify a modification of these obligations. The

February 4, 1960, 8:00-8:30 a.m. The First Presidency had an <u>interview with [Utah] Governor George D. Clyde</u> at his request. The Governor reported this visit [was in accordance] with other governors [and] with [the recommendations of] President [Dwight D.] Eisenhower and others on <u>Civil Defense projects</u>, having particular <u>reference to air-raid shelters</u> from atomic and hydrogen bombs and fall-out from such bombs.[19]

Governor Clyde's report was not a very encouraging one as to the improbability of an attack. The entire hour was occupied entirely with discussing the necessity of securing bomb shelters, not only in government, but in our own Church buildings and in private dwellings. Steps will be taken not only by the government, but by other organizations and by the Church to have bomb shelters in new buildings that are being erected.

February 16, 1960, First Presidency meeting. The billboard advertising soliciting attendance at "Mormon Church" meetings was considered, and it was agreed that since it does not comport with the dignity of the Church that this billboard advertising should be discontinued.

February 18, 1960, 10 a.m.–1:45 p.m. Was engaged in the meeting of the First Presidency and Council of the Twelve in the Salt Lake Temple.

One matter considered at this meeting was Brother Mark E. Petersen's report on an assignment given him to [conduct an] investigation [of] a game called "Exaltation," which has been prepared by the Bookcraft Company, and which is being sold in various stores, Z.C.M.I., Deseret Book Company, etc., and said that he had made an investigation of the game and explained to the Brethren just what the nature of it is.

I commented that the Church is a sacred institution; that it is the only "Light" that the world has today; the only means by which peace can be established and the world saved, and anything that will cast reflection upon it should be avoided. I said I certainly did not think such games are

---

sacredness of the garment should ever be present and uppermost in the wearer's mind."
Bergera, *Statements*, 444–49.

19. The Cold War offered new fears to the world and to the United States in particular. A primal fear was aroused by the documented effects of atomic bombs dropped on Hiroshima and Nagasaki, and it caused cities to seek protection by sponsoring bomb shelters, some intended for the community as a whole and others for specific neighborhoods, and to encourage organizations and individuals to do the same.

uplifting when played in a group of people who are assembled for pleasure and recreation. I said that devotion and reverence are elements that need to be developed. Humor, amusement, recreation, are elements intended to build character also, but the name of deity should not be associated with amusement and pleasure. I feel that the association used in this game is not reverential, and I think it would be well to let the Bookcraft Company know that we look upon the selling of this game in that way.

February 19, 1960, 8:30–12:45 p.m. The First Presidency met in their regular meeting with the Presiding Bishopric, and then continued with their own meeting.

We first had a long conference with Dr. Louis Moench[20] relating to psychiatric problems of our missionaries. Dr. Moench has given excellent service to the missionaries in this respect and we expressed our appreciation to him.

Dr. Moench said some problems are arising in the mission field which can possibly be avoided if some changes can be made. In response to a question as to whether or not the physician who examines the missionaries should discover mental illness that may exist, Mr. Moench said that it is sometimes difficult to detect this kind of illness from a physical examination, and that such an examination would not disclose it. Unless the person was extremely disturbed it would not show up in the usual physical examination. However, there are tests that will show most of these things if the tests can be given before the missionary is called. It is extremely embarrassing to have a boy come into the mission home, and then to discover that he is not mentally well enough to go on a mission. Dr. Moench then said: "I think we should do some testing before young men are considered for a call. There should be a physical examination and some kind of psychiatric test. We have a test which the Bishop could use and send the results in here and then some screening could be done here before the missionary call is issued."

Dr. Moench explained that the test materials could be delivered to

---

20. Louis Moench (1914–98) had been a cardiologist associated with the University of Utah College of Medicine. As he became interested in psychiatry, he went back to school and completed a residency at Harvard University's McLean Hospital and then became a member of the LDS Hospital staff. His son followed his father's lead in psychiatry and also became an advisor to the Church Missionary Department.

the Bishop who would have the prospective missionary fill out the test. It could then be returned to the office of the First Presidency to be studied by a psychiatrist or a psychologist. He said that the test is very simple to administer, but the bishop could not screen or score it; it requires a mechanical scoring device and someone familiar with the test. The bishop could give the test and send the examination in. The data could be transferred to an IBM punch card system and then become available in a form which the specialist could study. And if the prospective candidate passed, it would be easier to issue the call after that.

A long discussion was held regarding ways and means to handle this problem.

March 3, 1960, meeting of First Presidency and Twelve. President McKay said he had but little to report. When he left the meeting last Thursday, he went home and found Sister [Emma Ray] McKay sitting on a chair and unable to say a word, nor could she move her arm. He said they called in the doctors and decided to take her to the hospital. At nine o'clock that night the President said he received a telephone message at home from his son, Dr. Edward McKay, saying that there was a lady there who wanted to speak to him, and when he took the telephone, it was Sister McKay's voice. He said that was the sweetest thing he had ever heard in his life. She said, "Hello, I can talk." It was thought that everything was fine, but the next morning she was speechless again. She has had a slight stroke. The President said his wife is making remarkable recovery; that when their daughter Lou Jean came here from the East, she said to her mother, "You are looking fine today. Are you comfortable, mother?" Sister McKay answered, "I am comfortable." This morning at 6 o'clock the President learned she had had a good night's rest, and the nurse said she moves her right arm, and that is the first time she has done so for a week. She is making remarkable recovery, and wished President McKay to express to the Brethren her appreciation of their faith and prayers. The President said that since the occasion of her illness he had spent as much time as he could at her bedside.[21]

---

21. Emma Ray McKay had suffered a series of lesser incidents since the previous summer, and after the stroke the McKays felt compelled to move out of their home on South Temple street to an apartment in the Hotel Utah. Gibbons, *David O. McKay*, 417–18.

March 5, 1960, 2:30 p.m. Elder Ezra Taft Benson and his son Reed called at the office by appointment previously arranged by telephone call from Brother Benson at Washington, D.C.

They entered into a two-and-a-half-hour discussion with me on national political affairs, especially on questions pertaining to candidates for the presidency of the United States.[22]

I made no commitments, but advised that they watch the political trend between now and April Conference. Reed then asked the question (having in mind the suggestion that has been made that his father run as a candidate for presidency) if there is anything that he could do or say that there might be other candidates considered besides the Vice President on the Republican ticket. I answered, "You must never mention this—let the political leaders get together and make the suggestion, but do not let it come from you; you may acquiesce, but let them do the suggesting."

March 17, 1960. Attended the regular meeting of the First Presidency and Council of the Twelve in the Salt Lake Temple. We had some of the most distressing problems that we have had for a long time.

April 6, 1960. Met in my private office by appointment at his request Elder Ezra Taft Benson who discussed with me again the matter of his running for the presidency of the United States. I told him that there is no change in my advice as given to him on March 5, 1960, when he called; viz., that the pressure for this candidacy must come from outside groups, and not from him nor from his son Reed.

April 8, 1960, 12:15–1:10 p.m. Chief of Police Cleon Skousen (just recently dismissed by [Salt Lake City] Mayor J. Bracken Lee)[23] called at

---

22. See the entry and note for Oct. 12, 1958.

23. The controversy over Skousen's firing is one of the more colorful chapters in Salt Lake City history, the best account of which is in Lythgoe's *Let 'Em Holler*, 265–95. Skousen was fired on March 21 by a vote of 3–2. He was appointed in 1956 by Lee's predecessor, Adiel Stewart, after consulting with FBI head J. Edgar Hoover, who endorsed his former employee and member of the BYU faculty. The firing sent shock waves across the political landscape. See Wilkinson diary, Mar. 21, 22, 1960.

the office, and gave me some pertinent facts pertaining to the controversy between him and Mayor Lee.[24]

My confidence in Chief Skousen is absolute![25]

April 13, 1960, 8:30–10:30 a.m. Meeting of the First Presidency was held. We again considered at length the proposal to establish a Polynesian Village at Laie [Hawaii]. The suggestion was made to [stake] President Edward L. Clissold and Wendell B. Mendenhall that the Bureau of Information building [visitors center] be moved to a place which would be an advantageous location with relation to the unloading of the bus passengers who arrive at Laie. The area suggested for the Bureau of Information would be the first place the tourists would be met before they start on a tour of the grounds of the Temple, the [Church] College [of Hawaii], and the village. The proposal was made that a suitable building be planned for the Bureau to permit two groups to be given a film and other presentation on the work of the Latter-day Saints in the Islands, and an account of the temple before the tour starts. The proposal included provision for the commercial items such as films and curios to be completely removed from the Bureau of Information and to be sold elsewhere in the area.

I stated that the present purpose of visitors to Laie is to see the Temple, and if arrangement is made for them to be taken first to the Bureau of Information to hear the message of the Gospel and of the Church in the lecture and exhibit rooms and subsequently to visit the temple and other attractions, that my earlier concern about the proposal would be cleared up.

---

24. The genesis over the firing was a disagreement over the city budget, Lee wanting a substantial fiscal reduction in the police department and Skousen saying it would cripple law enforcement. Lee said he offered Skousen an opportunity to resign with a good recommendation, but Skousen countered, "Well, let's be very clear on this. The Mayor didn't ever extend me the courtesy of resigning. He just up and fired me" (*Deseret News*, Mar. 23, 1960, in Lythgoe, 273). In the end most observers conceded that they were both too stubborn, too opinionated, and at polar opposites on far too many issues to amiably work together.

25. According to Skousen, McKay was a factor in his accepting the chief of police post, when McKay offered him a leave of absence from BYU (Lythgoe, 266, 290). Skousen returned to BYU, and McKay remained a staunch ally. For insight into the First Presidency's view of this, see Wilkinson diary, Mar. 25, 1960.

April 14, 1960, meeting with Edward L. Clissold and Wendell B. Mendenhall. After consideration in detail it was agreed the planning of the [LDS Bureau of Information] building to be oriented primarily to the purposes of missionary work and the visit to the [Laie] temple grounds first and thereafter to the Polynesian Village, meets the desires of the First Presidency.

The importance of having the native culture and dances presented in the village on a high plane and to avoid indecent and pagan aspects featured in the night clubs of Honolulu was emphasized.

April 15, 1960, 8:50–10:40 a.m. Was engaged in the meeting of the First Presidency. ...

At our meeting this morning we read a letter proposed to be sent to Mr. Leland B. Flint[26] communicating a conditional offer to sell stock owned by the Church in the Zion's First National Bank. One of the conditions stated was the acquiring by the Church of the name, Zion's Savings Bank & Trust Company, for the name of a private bank to be operated by the Church to carry on its Financial Department affairs.[27]

My interest in retaining some banking functions for the accommodations of members of the Church whose long loyalty to the Church and to the Zion's Savings Bank is one of the important reasons for the Church continuing to have a bank, was considered at length and it was suggested that ways be sought to continue this relationship without competing in the commercial banking or trust fields.

The letter contains a proposal for the transfer of the stock to the purchasers, for the election of officers by the new board of directors, and for continuing the operation of the bank for the benefit of the community and for the state of Utah.

---

26. Three individuals, Leland B. Flint of Kennecott Copper, Judson S. Sayre of Norge Appliance Company, and Roy W. Simmons of the Lockhart industrial bank, formed a company called Keystone Insurance & Investment that acquired Zions First National Bank. Keystone was later renamed Zions Bancorp when a public stock offer was made.

27. The idea of retaining the name was abandoned. The church continued to purchase and manage real estate through an entity called Zion's Securities Corporation. It would also offer banking services to employees through Deseret First Credit Union. Otherwise McKay gravitated toward the advice of the four bankers he consulted on January 4, 1960.

I <u>took the letter for study</u> and later returned it to President [Henry D.] Moyle.

April 22, 1960. My son Lawrence[28] called at the house with a statement regarding the sale of the Zion's First National Bank for my approval. I had him insert a paragraph as follows: "To continue many of its financial relations, it is probable that the Church will organize its own bank. It is not planned, however, that this bank will in any way be competitive with your bank or any other banking institution."

Later the full statement by the First Presidency regarding the decision to take the church out of the commercial banking business, together with the account of the sale, was published in the local newspapers. ...

As a consequence of the above sale, <u>I resigned this day as Chairman of the Board of Directors of Zion's First National Bank.</u>

April 25, 1960, 11–11:10 a.m. Mr. Alfred I. Biorge, President of the Controls Engineering & Distributing Company, ... and Mr. Donn E. Cassity, Attorney at Law, ... called at the office and wanted to know if the Church would have any objection to former [Salt Lake City] Chief of Police Cleon Skousen running for Governor of the State.[29]

I said that that is a political matter; that every citizen has a right to seek nomination for any office that is available.

They mentioned an aspirant who says that he has $75,000 to spend for the nomination, and I said that that would be folly to let Governor Clyde and Brother Skousen run for the same office and split the Mormon vote, and let this man come in. They said that he (this aspirant) is a Democrat, and I said "Well, that is a different matter." Clyde, one of the county commissioners, and Skousen will be aspirants for the Republican nomination.

I said that the Church has no objection to Skousen's running for nomination—that he has a right to come out if he chooses to do so.

---

28. D. Lawrence McKay was an attorney at McKay Burton & Thurman in Salt Lake City. One of the original partners, Henry D. Moyle, resigned in 1947 when called to the Quorum of the Twelve Apostles.

29. In the 1960 gubernatorial election, George D. Clyde was re-elected over Democratic challenger William A. Barlocker by a count of 196,00 to 176,000.

April 28, 1960, 8 a.m. At the request of <u>President Ernest L. Wilkinson ... I gave a blessing to him at this hour.</u> This blessing was given to President Wilkinson as President of the Brigham Young University and Chancellor of the Unified Church School System.[30]

May 2, 1960, 5:45 a.m. With Brother Allan Acomb at the wheel, drove up to Rexburg, Idaho. As I wanted this to be a surprise visit to the Ricks College, I did not tell anyone where I was going except members of the family and my secretary, Clare Middlemiss.[31]

The trip up to Rexburg was pleasant and uneventful. I studied a little on the way, talked, and admired the scenery.

We arrived at Rexburg at 10:20 a.m., unannounced, and the students were just coming out of their devotional exercises. I had understood that their assembly would be about 10:45 a.m. The students were very surprised to see me when I stopped in front of the building, and suggested that they reassemble and hold another service, which they did. Dr. Hugh C. Bennion, dean of the faculty, conducted the meeting. Following prayer and singing, I spoke to the students for about thirty minutes, admonishing them to know where they are going and to live up to the principles of the Church.

I was disappointed and surprised that President John L. Clarke of the college was not in attendance. I learned from his secretary that he had gone to Idaho Falls. He came into the meeting when it was half through.

Following the exercises, <u>I shook hands with about five hundred students.</u> Then I went to President Clarke's office where I had a conference with him. I asked him to furnish me with some data regarding the College which I wish to study.

We left Rexburg at 11:45 a.m., and started back to Salt Lake City. Along the way, having had nothing to eat, we stopped and had a sandwich and some hot chocolate which Brother [Allan] Acomb[32] had in the car, furnished by Bishop Gordan Affleck of the Church Offices.

---

30. For Wilkinson's narrative, see his diary, Apr. 28, 1960.

31. This was not entirely true; see Wilkinson diary, May 6, 1960.

32. Whenever McKay ventured very far out of town, his driver was Allan MacKay Acomb (1910–2004), who had been an Air Force colonel during World War II and afterward attended George Washington Law School. He was employed by the church as a purchasing agent and was otherwise chief clerk of the Utah House of Representatives, a member of the Utah State Board of Pardons, and a member of the church building committee.

We ran into a heavy rain storm in Rigby, and had rain all the way to Malad, Idaho.

We arrived back in Salt Lake City at 5 p.m., and went directly to the Hotel Utah where we had dinner, and then Brother Acomb drove me home.

It was a very successful visit, and I wanted to partake of the spirit of the School and see just what they are accomplishing under the adverse circumstances of this year, which was one of the most difficult years for Ricks College. I was very glad I made the trip–it was about 500 miles. It was one of the best trips I have made in many a year!

May 4, 1960, First Presidency meeting. Among many other important Church matters considered was the prospects of <u>opening a Mission in Greece</u>. Elder Harold B. Lee's letter brought the opinion of [former] U.S. Ambassador [to Greece][,] [James W.] Riddleberger[,] that the people of Greece pride themselves on having religious freedom by which they seem to mean the freedom of churches to worship, but that if vigorous prose-lyting missions be undertaken by any denominations, which convert many from among the Greek Orthodox people, such denomination might have their visiting permits cancelled. It was agreed that the matter be held in abeyance, and that when and if the opening of a mission be undertaken, it be by direct approach for permission from the proper authorities.[33]

May 10, 1960, First Presidency meeting. I commented upon the departure of the spirit from the body [at death] as an occasion for looking up to God rather than down to the mortal remains, and recounted an experience of being present with David Eccles and Bertha Eccles when [David's brother] Stewart Eccles passed away in an Ogden Hospital. As David Eccles, Bertha Eccles, and I were in the room at the bedside of Stewart, we heard Stewart quietly, but clearly and plainly speak, saying, "Yes Father, I recognize you, Father. May I come back?" (His father [William Eccles] had passed away years before). Bertha was crying. She said, "Oh, Brother

---

33. After several decades of attempting to obtain entrance to Greece, a mission was finally created there in July 1990. However, as of 2019 there were still only three LDS congregations in the country. Church members in Greece were previously included in the Austrian or Swiss missions for administrative purposes.

McKay, administer to him." I answered, "It is too late; he is gone." In just a few moments Stewart's heart stopped, and he was dead.

President [J. Reuben] Clark related his standing at the coffin of Mr. Knox, his friend in Washington, for whom he had deep affection. "As I went up to look at him, something said to me—I would not say it was an audible voice—'What you love is not here; it is gone.'" I said to Pres[i-dent] Clark, "I know that feeling, and it is real!"

1:25 p.m.—Left for home for lunch. I ate hurriedly and was back at the office at 2 p.m. at which time a special meeting of the Church Board of Education was held.

This was a history-making meeting dealing with the future ed-ucational policies of the Church for the next 15 to 20 years, relating particularly to Junior Colleges and higher education.[34]

May 11, 1960, board of trustees, Zion's First National Bank. Pres[ident] J. Reuben Clark, Jr.: I know nothing about banking and never did. I do not even know enough to be able to maintain a modest banking deposit of my own. There are some things that are elemental that have always been in my mind. I have been able to think about banking and bank problems only as I have been able to think about my own, and as I say, I am not successful and never have tried to be business-wise. I have had some experience, it is true, in rather large operations. I was in this respect, most importantly, the President of the Foreign Bond Holders Protec-tion Council organized under Franklin Delano Roosevelt to handle in a semi-official way the credits of the world owing to citizens of the United States. Money meant so little to me, it never scared me. I cannot think about it more calmly than I can think about my own; and I might say to you men here, indicating what some have recognized in me, the most flattering thing that was ever said to me in my life, that tickled my vanity

---

34. There are discrepancies here regarding dates. The meeting said to have oc-curred on May 10 actually occurred, according to the minutes of the meeting, on May 12—and not for the Church Board of Education (minutes of that entity, during this time period, are for May 4 and June 1), but rather for the BYU board of trustees, who heard Wilkinson outline a program to accommodate projected growth for the next forty years. Wilkinson mentioned five possible strategies and recommended one that would cap BYU's enrollment and build ten junior colleges around the country to accommodate between 4,000 and 5,000 students over the space of twenty years.

most, was an observation made by Mr. [Dwight W.] Morrow with whom I worked in Mexico for some time.[35]

He said, "Clark, you are the least influenced by mere wealth of any man I ever knew." Wealth means nothing to me except a responsibility to use wealth in the right kind of way. ...

Pres[ident] David O. McKay: Now, I am sure the quicker we get out, the quicker you will get through with your business. In departing I would just like to say this: The strength of any organization, financial as well as religious or social, depends upon two things—first, the character of the directors and leaders, the character from the foundation of this bank and from the present has been the source of its strength. The second is the devotion of those men to the growth of the organization. "Losing oneself", to use a scriptural phrase, "for the good of the organization" is the secret of success. A poet-philosopher put it in these words: "For great and low there is but one test. Tis that each man will do his best. Who works with all the strength he can, shall never die in debt to man."[36]

May 19, 1960, 8:30–10 a.m. Was in the meeting of the First Presidency. I took two letters into the meeting to read to my counselors—an anonymous letter from "a member who will see more of the Lord than most of you," complaining that the sale of the Church's interest in the Bank will make available considerable money to be laid away for the retirement of the higher officials of the Church, "who have never worked hard in their lives; who travel all over the world at Church expense while poor missionaries pay their own way."

The other, a letter from Mrs. Donna Livermore of Pontiac, Michigan, a non-member, commenting upon my statement that "the Mormon Church would not withdraw from its business enterprises," and saying that the Church's being involved in business is the business of no one but

---

35. Clark worked under US Ambassador to Mexico Dwight W. Morrow (1873–1931) as a legal advisor and succeeded him as ambassador. Morrow, an attorney, was a partner in J. P. Morgan; in 1926 US President Calvin Coolidge asked him to advise the government on aviation, and his recommendation led to the creation of the US Army Air Corps, which later became the US Air Force.

36. This poem is Edgar A. Guest's "True Nobility." The minutes, attached to the diary, quote McKay saying that "there is a tinge of sorrow in leaving this group. It is a pleasure to meet once a month or more frequently and greet as fellow laborers; there is a feeling of friendship, of brotherhood."

the Church. "I am not of your faith, but lived in Idaho where I saw kindness and charity and help given to people in your religion not equaled by any other Church having business of its own. I say 'more power to you.' I like your Christlike attitude toward each other."

We then discussed the ZCMI option to buy Redwood Road Property, and rumors of the Church's interest in the sale of ZCMI.

Murdock Travel, Inc.

Details for setting up the corporation of "Murdock Travel Inc." were presented by President [Henry D.] Moyle. These have been gone over carefully with Brother [Franklin J.] Murdock who now says that he would be satisfied with a salary of $12,000 (his base pay now) and 15% of the stock. The suggestion that the Brigham Young University travel arrangements be handled also by this corporation was considered and it was agreed that a director or two to represent the Brigham Young University could be added to the Board and that the Board then be Elders Delbert L. Stapley, Gordon B. Hinckley, John Vandenburg, Lawrence McKay, Franklin J. Murdock, and two from the Brigham Young University.

The articles of incorporation will be filed in Nevada and Brother Murdock and his staff in the office will be the original incorporators. Subsequently the changes of directors can be made without giving publicity to the proceedings. Brother Murdock has written for the transfer of the licenses from the various transportation agencies to the Murdock Travel Inc. After consideration of the assets which Brother Murdock is turning to the corporation it was decided to split the difference and give him $12,000 and 12% of the stock.

June 6, 1960, 11 a.m. Received a courtesy call from United States <u>Senator Barry Goldwater</u>[37] of Arizona. He was accompanied by Bishop Thorpe B. Isaacson. He impressed me as a good man and one who is favorable to

---

37. Barry Morris Goldwater (1909–98) of Arizona attended a private school in Virginia and married the daughter of a successful industrialist. During World War II he became a pilot in the Army Air Force and advanced to the rank of colonel, afterward helping to establish the US Air Force Academy in Colorado and Arizona Air National Guard. From 1952 to 1964 he was in the US Senate, and ran for the US presidency in 1964, losing badly to Democrat Lyndon B. Johnson. In 1969 he re-entered the Senate and stayed to 1987. He is most famous for his book, *The Conscience of a Conservative*, published in 1960.

the Mormons. Senator Goldwater thought it would be a wise thing to have Brother Benson come home as he fears he is going to be embarrassed by both the Republicans and the Democrats.[38] I told the Senator that some time ago the Church had a good place for Brother [Ezra Taft] Benson if he felt to come home at that time. This information was conveyed to President [Dwight D.] Eisenhower so that he might have an excuse to release Brother Benson if he desired to do so, but President Eisenhower felt that he needed Brother Benson's services, and did not feel to release him at the time.

June 10, 1960, 8:30 a.m. The First Presidency's meeting was held. One matter of importance was the reading of a letter of instructions prepared by the First Presidency for the General Authorities of the Church, setting forth the action of the First Presidency and the Council of the Twelve on the <u>subject of interviewing prospective missionaries</u>. The letter was approved as prepared. A letter was also read and approved (a copy of which is being sent to Stake Presidents and Bishoprics) <u>setting forth new qualifications and standards for young men and women being selected to serve as missionaries for the Church.</u>

I reviewed instructions relating to the interviewing of prospective missionaries, and explained that <u>young men who are found morally unclean will not be called on missions</u>. I stated that Bishops have the responsibility of interviewing boys before they are ordained deacons, teachers, and priests, and that these interviews give opportunity to create an atmosphere in which the boys will live and grow up to manhood. It is hoped that they can be influenced to keep their lives clean and to accept the responsibility of protecting the moral cleanliness of themselves and of the girls of the Church.[39]

June 17, 1960, 8:15 a.m. President J. Reuben Clark, Jr. called at the office. He inquired regarding Sister [Emma Ray] McKay's health. I told him of

---

38. Goldwater is referring to the increasingly unpopular agricultural policies under Secretary Benson.

39. The letter of July 21, 1960, advised "local Church officers" that they "must exercise more care and discrimination in recommending young men for missions. These young men must have a desire to serve as missionaries, and must be willing to put in the time and effort required of those who are now serving in the mission field. They likewise should have been well trained in the program of the church and know enough of the doctrine to go into the world and teach it" (Bergera, *Statements*, 271).

the set-back she has had the last few days, and he said: "there is nothing you can do, Brother, but sit back and watch—it is terrible; I know; you will just have to take it."[40]

June 25, 1960, 8 a.m. Met by appointment President Ernest L. Wilkinson, and for the next two and one half hours went over the steps that have been taken concerning Ricks College which seemingly proved that the people in the Ricks College area [had been convinced and] were unanimously in favor of moving Ricks College to Idaho Falls. President Wilkinson went over the whole business and finally said that it will cost nearly as much to build Ricks at Rexburg as it will to build a new college in Idaho Falls—$7,014,000 at Idaho Falls, and $5,600,000 for new buildings at Rexburg.

President Wilkinson made a claim that if we change our decision to move Ricks College, his influence would be nullified on the Church school system. I told him that I should have to take the blame for vacillating, but that when the matter of moving Ricks College to Idaho Falls was presented, and I was given the signed petition from the Stakes in the Ricks College area, asking that the change be made, I went along with the Brethren that it should be moved, but that I had never really felt right about the decision.[41]

June 30, 1960, 10:00–2:25 p.m. Meeting of the First Presidency and Council of the Twelve convened in the Salt Lake Temple. At this meeting I gave a report on Ricks College. This was in very deed an Apostolic meeting.

<u>Confidential Report of Ricks College Location</u>
<u>Made by President McKay at Council meeting Held June 30, 1960.</u>
President McKay said he had a matter he wanted to present to the Brethren as members of the Twelve and as members of the Board of Education, a matter, he said, which had given him a lot of worry, and on

---

40. Clark had endured the unpleasant death of his wife, "Lute," and of his parents and siblings. Quinn, *Elder Statesman*, 101–02, 185.

41. Two weeks prior to this meeting, on June 11, Wilkinson himself had experienced misgivings on the Ricks issue. Finally on June 25, "it was quite apparent to me," he wrote, "that he [McKay] had made up his mind to leave Ricks College at Rexburg, and therefore he seemed to brush aside practically every argument I made in favor of sustaining the two decisions of the board of education to transfer it to Idaho Falls."

which he needed the help of the Brethren, which matter pertains to the Ricks College. The President reviewed items relating to the proposition to move Ricks College to Idaho Falls. He presented the following facts:

In compliance with a letter sent by the General Board of Education of the Church of Jesus Christ of Latter-day Saints to all stake presidents of the Church which instructed each stake to organize a board of education and to establish an academy, the Bannock Stake, at a Priesthood meeting held on August 17, 1888, chose a Bannock Stake Board of Education.

The first Board consisted of: Thomas E. Ricks, Rexburg, President; William F. Rigby, Rexburg, Secretary. Members: James E. Fogg, Rexburg; Jacob Spori, Rexburg; John Donaldson, Teton; William M. Parker, Parker; Richard Jardine, Lewisville; James E. Steele, Iona.

President Ricks, in consultation with Superintendent of L.D.S. schools, Karl G. Maeser, chose Jacob Spori to be principal. It was called Bannock Stake Academy and they used the Rexburg First Ward chapel.

Opened first term of ten weeks on November 12, 1888. Jacob Spori served as principal from November 1888 until spring of 1891, assisted by Alex F. Nelson and Sarah Ann Barnes.

History of Actions and Decisions Regarding Ricks College

1. April 8, 1957. Very important meeting from 10 a.m. to 2:10 p.m. held in the Board Room on the Main Floor of the Church offices. Stake presidents of the following stakes were present: Blackfoot, East Rigby, Idaho Falls, Lost River, North Idaho Falls, North Rexburg, Rexburg, Rigby, Salmon River, Shelley, South Blackfoot, South Idaho Falls, Star Valley, Teton, Yellowstone.

Meeting was held in the interest of the future of Ricks College with emphasis on the advisability of moving the College from Rexburg to Idaho Falls.

President [Ernest L.] Wilkinson presented facts relating to this very important problem, and each of the stake presidents present expressed their opinions and viewpoints about the matter. No decision was reached on this problem.

2. June 1, 1957. In company with Elder Marion G. Romney, President Ernest L. Wilkinson, with Allan Acomb at the wheel, left for Rexburg, Idaho where at 1:30 p.m. we held a meeting with all 15 stake presidents

and six specially invited civic leaders: Dr. Blaine H. Passey[42]; Mr. J. Fred Smith, Mayor of Rexburg; Mr. John J. Walz, president Rexburg Chamber of Commerce; Mr. Lane L. Wilcken, St. Anthony, Idaho Manager of First Security Bank of Idaho; Mr. S. M. Meikle, Rexburg, Idaho, President Idaho Bank of Commerce; Mr. Louis Felt, Blackfoot, Idaho, Vice President, First Security Bank.

President McKay asked each person present at the meeting to personally write him a letter giving his views of what should be done about Ricks. The following stake presidents sent letters <u>favorable to the moving of Ricks College</u>: William J. Lewis, Yellowstone Stake presidency; William A. Strong, Teton Stake President; George Christensen, Rigby Stake President; Parley A. Arave, Blackfoot Stake President; Cecil E. Hart, South Idaho Falls Stake President; J. Cleve Hansen, Lost River Stake Presidency; Charles P. Brizzee, Idaho Falls Stake Presidency; Lawrence T. Lambert, South Blackfoot Stake President; Leonard E. Graham, East Rigby Stake Presidency; George E. Grover, Shelley Stake Presidency; Lloyd P. Mickelsen, North Idaho Falls Stake Presidency. The following also sent favorable letters: Lane L. Wilcken, Manager First Security Bank of Idaho at St. Anthony; Howard E. Salisbury of Ricks College.

<u>Against removal were</u>: Marvin C. Meyers, 2nd Counselor, North Rexburg Stake; Delbert G. Taylor, Rexburg Stake Presidency; E. Francis Winters, Star Valley Stake President; Willis G. Nelson, 1st Counselor, Rexburg Stake; Edwin C. Flamm, 1st counselor, North Rexburg Stake; H. Earl Stokes, Salmon River Stake Presidency; John J. Walz of Rexburg Chamber of Commerce; J. Fred Smith, Mayor of Rexburg; S. M. Meikle, President of Idaho Bank of Commerce, Rexburg, Idaho; John L. Clarke, President of Ricks College; Eldon C. Hart, Business Manager of Ricks College; Blaine H. Passey, M.D., Rexburg, Idaho.

<u>Neutral</u>: Orval P. Mortenson, North Rexburg Stake President.

3. <u>July 11, 1957</u>. Ricks College Not to be Moved to Idaho Falls. During the meeting of the First Presidency I presented to President Stephen L.

---

42. Blaine H. Passey (1919–2011) was a local physician who had pushed for the recently completed Madison Memorial Hospital in Rexburg and would soon become president of the Upper Snake River Valley Medical Society. He was born in Idaho, studied at Ricks College, and is credited as one of the original members of the local historical society. In World War II he was a medic who was present at the invasion on Omaha Beach and the Battle of the Bulge.

Richards by long distance telephone call to Bellingham, Washington, (as I also presented to President [J. Reuben] Clark who was in attendance at the meeting) my conclusion that it is not worth the cost to move Ricks College to Idaho Falls; that the plan proposed by President Wilkinson at the latest meeting of the Board to make Ricks College a part of the Brigham Young University has merit; that the school will grow where it is and that the support of the people of the area will be given, and the honor of the General Authorities of the Church in their minds will be preserved.

President Richards agreed to the announcement being made that it is decided by the Executive Committee of the Brigham Young University and the First Presidency that Ricks College will not be moved to Idaho Falls. President Richards thought it would be well to call Mr. D. F. Richards of Idaho Falls and give the announcement to him.[43] First news of the decision was given by me to Mr. Richards by telephone call to Idaho Falls.

That same day I presented to the Executive Committee of the Brigham Young University Board of Trustees, and of the Church Board of Education a summary of my reasons why Ricks College should not be moved to Idaho Falls as follows:

I. Granting that every reason advanced for its removal to Idaho Falls is sound, it is not worth the price because:

(1) Justified or not, thousands of people, young and old, will be imbued with the thought that the assurance given by the First Presidency, by the President, and by the Church School administration, that Ricks College will remain at Rexburg was not kept.

(2) Housing in Idaho Falls less advantageous than at Rexburg.

(3) Dormitories needed at Idaho Falls as well as at Rexburg.

II. Accommodations for Students. Pledges for 1,570 students from $12 to $20 a month.

The Church is built upon Faith and Trust. Once confidence is lost, the foundation of society begins to crumble. Our integrity will be measured by our conduct.

4. <u>October 31, 1958</u>. From 10 a.m. to 12 noon held a two-hour meeting with my counselors at my home as I had just returned from the hospital after undergoing eye surgery. They presented to me a letter

---

43. Richards was the executive with American National Bank of Idaho Falls who was going to help finance the college.

signed by presidents of the stakes in the Idaho Falls area reviewing public interest and action being proposed by citizens of Idaho Falls for the circulation of a petition to the legislature for the establishment of a state college at Idaho Falls. The letter included President Wilkinson's concurrence in the subject being brought to the attention of the First Presidency for consideration of the advisability of making an announcement as to the plans of the Church to develop Ricks College at Idaho Falls.

(President McKay said that President Stephen L. Richards and President Clark brought a letter to him at his home at a time when he was convalescing from eye surgery, this letter being dated October 29, 1958, addressed to the First Presidency, reading as follows:)

My dear Brethren:

During the semi-annual conference of the church we [five stake presidents in the Idaho Falls area] advised Administrator Ernest L. Wilkinson of a movement in Idaho Falls for the establishment of a State junior college and asked him if he would be kind enough to advise you that while we were entirely willing to abide your final decision in the matter, we felt that with this movement underway the choice would now be between having a small Ricks College at Rexburg or an outstanding [larger] Ricks College at Idaho Falls. This was not so apparent when your decision to leave Ricks at Rexburg was made.

A few days after Conference Brother Wilkinson advised us that he had presented the matter to the First Presidency and that you had taken the whole question under advisement. While he gave us no indication of your feeling, he did suggest that if, without making any commitment as to whether we would or would not favor a State junior college at Idaho Falls, we could discreetly cause the postponement of the [state] Junior College election, we should do so in order that you would have time to fully consider the matter. At that time we informed him that we thought we would be able to probably postpone the circulating of a petition, which is the first step in the calling of an election to determine whether there shall be a junior college. We have been able to postpone the circulating of this petition until after the general election on November 4, but it is now apparent that the petition will now be circulated immediately after that date. Once the petition is signed and sent to the state capitol it will be necessary for the election to proceed.

In our opinion, if you now feel inclined to again consider the permanent location of Ricks College, we should like to suggest that you do so at once before the circulating petition is signed as the preliminary step in the election process. We feel quite certain, for instance, that if you decide on Idaho Falls as a permanent location for Ricks College it would be much better for an announcement to be made before the junior college election gets underway. If the announcement is made after petitions are filed and the election is in progress, there might be criticism of the motives of the Church.

We recognize that we have been instructed that things of this nature should be taken up through Administrator Wilkinson. We have therefore phoned him as to the urgency of this matter, telling him that we could hold up the circulation of petitions for only about a week. In that situation he has informed us that he had no objection to our writing direct to the First Presidency. We are sending a copy of it to him so that you may obtain his advice also.

Our two purposes in writing are first, to inform you as to the facts as to what is happening; and second, to obtain your counsel as to what we should do with respect to the proposed election to determine upon the creation of a State junior college, the first step of which will get underway probably in about nine days. The election law requires that the petition for the junior college be signed by only 300 people, and it is apparent to us from sentiment that is being generated in Idaho Falls, that it will be possible for the proponents to obtain signatures of many times this number.

We should finally add that in our opinion the transfer of Ricks to Idaho Falls would mean four times as many students as at Rexburg. We think we have an even greater obligation to the larger number who will not go to Rexburg than to the smaller number who will go there; further, a large [church-sponsored] junior college at Idaho Falls would give us much more influence in educational matters throughout the State. The Governor has already commented adversely on the Church not availing itself of the opportunity to build a junior college in Idaho Falls. In view of this new development, we frankly believe that the matter of the proper location of Ricks will be properly settled as you face it squarely on the merits involved. We repeat, however, we are willing to abide by your decision after you deliberate with a full knowledge of the facts.

The letter was signed by the following stake presidents: Cecil E. Hart, South Idaho Falls; George Christensen, Rigby; Lloyd P. Mickelsen, North Idaho Falls; Lawrence T. Lambert, South Blackfoot; J. Burns Beal, Lost River. The President said that is the letter and conversation that resulted in the reconsideration of the decision that Ricks should remain at Rexburg.

5. November 2, 1958. Elders Marion G. Romney and Hugh B. Brown went to Rexburg and told them of that decision [to relocate Ricks to Idaho Falls].

6. November 4, 1958. A meeting was held Sunday evening at 9 o'clock, attended by the presidencies of both Rexburg stakes, members of high councils of both stakes, bishoprics of all wards, patriarchs, and presidents of all Melchizedek priesthood quorums—a total of about 135. After making a full explanation of the matter, Brother Romney said that the General Authorities would be pleased if the Brethren present would indicate their cooperation in this important movement and someone of the group made a motion that the action of the General Authorities be given their full support. All but four of those present voted in favor of the motion, and three of the four came to the Brethren after the meeting and said they would like to change their vote. Brother Romney said that he felt that the Spirit of the Lord was in this meeting and that the people manifested a spirit of humility and a spirit of devotion to the church which motivated them sincerely to take the action which they took at the meeting.

At 7 o'clock in the morning on Monday, November 3, 1958, Brother Romney and Brother Brown met the presidents of the Idaho Falls Stakes and told them of the reaction of the people in Rexburg. Asked them to be considerate of the people of Rexburg.

Elder Mark E. Petersen subsequently reported that he had conferred with several business men in Idaho Falls, including Mr. McDermott, owner and editor of the Idaho Falls papers, who expressed himself as highly pleased. He characterized the movement for a State junior college at Idaho Falls as abortive and said the business men had not been consulted and that he felt sure that they would be loath to have taxes raised to support a State college at Idaho Falls, and that Ricks College at Idaho Falls would be welcomed by the people.

7. December 12, 1958. The First Presidency sends letter to the following

stakes: East Rigby, Shelley, Idaho Falls, Salmon River, South Idaho Falls, Blackfoot, South Blackfoot, North Idaho Falls, Lost River, Rigby.

In the letter the stake presidencies were asked to call a special meeting of the stake and ward officials named in the letter on Sunday, December 21, 1958 and have them express themselves freely upon the subject. The brethren were asked to report to the First Presidency as soon as possible, on the meeting [in each stake].

It was also suggested that the enclosed statement prepared by Administrator Ernest L. Wilkinson of December 12, 1958, be read at the meeting. After the reading a proposal to sustain the stake presidencies' position should be submitted to those present for their sustaining vote. (Each stake president received 150 copies of the statement.)

8. <u>December 21, 1958</u>. Special Meetings held in various stakes in Idaho. All stake presidencies replied by letter and informed the brethren that the stake and ward officers invited to the meeting "unanimously" sustain the First Presidency in their decision.

The President said he believed this to be a fair review of the actions that were taken. Recently he made a special private trip to Ricks College and found the school in excellent condition. President John L. Clarke of Ricks College was not present when President McKay arrived. The devotional exercises were being dismissed due to a misunderstanding on his part as to the time when these services were held. However, all the students went back, as well as the teachers, and another devotional exercise was held, at which there was a very good spirit.

President McKay said that now the problem is before us just as it was before. All indications favor going to Idaho Falls. The President had had a two and a half hour conference with President Ernest L. Wilkinson some time ago, and President Wilkinson had asked for time for him to come back from Mexico and prepare his reports and his argument, and for two and a half hours he presented in his masterful way reasons why we should continue with our plan to move Ricks to Idaho Falls. President Wilkinson explained that it would cost as much to remodel and restore the Ricks College at Rexburg as it would to build a new college at Idaho Falls; that it would, however, cost nearly two million dollars more to move to Idaho Falls than to remain at Rexburg. It will certainly be necessary to have a new library building, and we must have a gymnasium, and also dormitories at Ricks College.

The President said he could not feel right about moving the school from Rexburg to Idaho Falls, and spending seven million dollars in building a new school, leaving standing at Rexburg at least three new buildings on the campus, even though we should have to spend five million dollars in Rexburg. An expenditure of two million dollars for dormitories and a library and gymnasium will give us a pretty good school at Rexburg. He said there is no question in his mind that if we do not go to Idaho Falls, sooner or later there will be erected a junior college there, and if we left Ricks at Rexburg it would be a small school if it had to compete with the State College at Idaho Falls, and under necessity we would have an Institute at Idaho Falls competing with our Church school at Rexburg.

But even with those facts in mind, the President said he could not bring himself to the thought of spending seven million dollars and moving the school to Idaho Falls. He felt that we ought to keep the school in Rexburg and spend a million or two [million] dollars making it a good school, utilizing the 500 acres we have there, and the water that is already developed, and give an opportunity to our people to attend a Church school or to attend the State college at Idaho Falls if they want to, with our Institute located there.

The President said that when he visited Ricks College on May 2, 1960 he found there were only four less students from Idaho Falls attending Ricks College than Rexburg students. There were in attendance 922 students in the college in this most adverse year; <u>164 were from Rexburg; 160 were from Idaho Falls</u>; and others were from various places. The President said that the following quotation came to his mind in connection with this difficult problem:

> Dim as the borrow'd beams of moon and stars
> To lonely, weary, wand'ring travellers,
> Is Reason to the soul; and as on high
> Those rolling fires discover but the sky,
> Not light us here; so Reason's glimmering ray
> Was lent, not to assure our doubtful way,
> But lead us upward to a better day.[44]

---

44. John Dryden, "Religio Laici" ("A Layman's Religion"), 1682.

The President said that when he faced this problem <u>he felt cloudy about the sale of the buildings</u>, tearing them down, and the building of a new college at Idaho Falls. He therefore wanted to take the Brethren into Council, for he said that when they go out of this room today as a Board of Education they will have to deal with the problem; that at present he was speaking to them as the First Presidency and members of the Twelve. President McKay said he had said nothing about rumors and statements and letters he had received, nor had he said anything about the fact that when we decided that Ricks should remain in Rexburg nothing was done to improve Ricks. He had tried to present the other side. He said his feeling is that whether they have a State junior college at Idaho Falls or not we should keep Ricks at Rexburg, build the dormitories for a million dollars, and the library and whatever is needed, and start at once to improve Ricks where it is and let Idaho Falls take its course.

President Joseph Fielding Smith moved that we sustain the President.

Elder Delbert L. Stapley asked the President if we felt that in the commitment that was made in July, 1957 it was rather a permanent commitment, and that the people of Rexburg thought Ricks College would not be moved.

The President answered that they did accept it as such. That was before we met with them afterwards and told them why it was decided to change, and they were willing to abide by our decision.

President Moyle said: "I agree with President Smith that there is only one course that we can pursue, and that is to sustain you, President McKay, in whatever your inspiration directs you to do, and as far as I am concerned I hope and pray that whatever course is taken that it will bring peace and satisfaction to your soul, and eliminate from you the feelings of uncertainty that you have had about it up to date."

Elder Marion G. Romney said that he had been very close to the situation and had had very strong feelings about it, but that the overriding feeling in his soul was to sustain the President. He said he felt that the President's impression is more persuasive on what should be done than anything else, and he therefore seconded the motion by President Smith. He further said that he had felt until what the President had said today that all the argument was in favor of going to Idaho Falls, but that he could go out of this meeting wholly committed in his feelings that the right thing is to leave it at Rexburg if that is the way the President feels, because he thought the President's inspiration was much more persuasive than any argument the other way.

Elder LeGrand Richards said that there were many of our people in that part of the country who would be very happy if this body decided to keep the college at Rexburg. He felt to sustain the President in his feelings.

Elder Hugh B. Brown said he was wondering if the President wished this Council to take action on this question as the Twelve, or whether the final decision would be reached by the Church Board of Education.

President McKay said it was not the intention to take action today; that he was asking the Brethren for counsel. He wanted to know how the Brethren felt, and he had given them his feelings.

Elder Hugh B. Brown said he was one hundred percent in harmony with supporting the President's feelings in the matter.

Elder Stapley said he felt the same way.

President Moyle said he thought it would be wholly in keeping with the spirit of the Brethren here today, and very appropriate for the Council to go on record here as sustaining President McKay in whatever decision he felt to recommend to the Board of Education when this comes up officially before the Board, and that we ought to be controlled by the President's inspiration and decision.

Elder Mark E. Petersen said he felt very much the same way as the other Brethren; that he had felt from the very beginning it would have been better to leave the college at Rexburg. He suggested, however, that when the final decision is made we avoid giving publicity to it. He thought it would be far better to move quietly and do what we are going to do without making any public announcement.

President McKay agreed with this. He said that in the budget we should provide for the necessary expenditure to build the necessary buildings at the college; that this is our business, and we should go ahead with it without making any announcement. President McKay said he would take the blame that would come to him because of the seeming vacillation.

President Smith said, "We will all share it with you."

Elder Spencer W. Kimball said he was one hundred percent behind President McKay in what he felt to be the revelation of the Lord to him.

Elder Stapley said he felt the same way; that he did also share the thought expressed by Brother Petersen; that he had always felt that we had a commitment as far as the Rexburg area people are concerned.

President Moyle said there was one bit of history the President did not refer to this morning; that in 1955 or 1956 the Executive Committee, with President Wilkinson, met with the First Presidency and presented this for the first time, and that he, President Moyle, was one of those who urged the move from Rexburg to Idaho Falls; and that he sat there and listened to all three of the members of the First Presidency say: "Brethren, we can never do that. The roots have been planted too deep." He said that from that moment he had accepted what the Presidency then decided, and felt that was the thing to do.

Elder George Q. Morris said he was wholly in accord with what the Brethren had decided to do. He wondered, however, what was going to happen in Rexburg because of the bitterness that had been engendered; what these people will say. He thought that they would perhaps claim the credit for the Victory, and that they had brought about what they intended to do. He thought they would be crowing about it and saying they had succeeded.

President McKay said he wished to add another item which he thought was very important in connection with this matter, namely, that after his two and a half hour conference with President Wilkinson, during which he referred to the personal attacks upon him—and they had been vicious—he said: "Well, if any such movement as this is made my influence will be at an end." The President said he did not like that personal element; that he felt the decision was for the good of the whole thing.

Elder Petersen again cautioned the Brethren regarding publicity in regard to the matter, and thought that perhaps we should not appropriate any money for expansion in Rexburg for two or three years.

President McKay answered that we will have to do something for Ricks next year; that, however, we can start in a modest way by providing housing facilities, a library and a gymnasium.

President McKay said that since his conversation with President Wilkinson last Saturday, at which time he told him he was going to consult the Brethren of the Council, President Wilkinson telephoned last night and expressed the hope that he would have an opportunity to present the matter to the Council. The President said he, of course, had no right to present any argument to this Council on the matter; that the decision must be made by the Board. The President said that today as never before our charge as Apostles should be considered sacred, and one of those charges is that we keep this to ourselves.

President McKay then presented to the council the motion that had been made and seconded, and the Brethren present voted unanimously in favor of it.

Elder Petersen then mentioned to the Brethren that President John L. Clarke of Ricks College had expressed to him several times the thought that it would be very inspiring to the students if the Brethren of the General Authorities could stay over a day when attending conferences in that area and speak at the devotional exercises, the same as is done at the Brigham Young University.

President McKay mentioned that these devotional exercises are held on Mondays.[45]

August 5, 1960, 3:30 a.m. Awoke at this early hour this morning in new and strange environments—could not go back to sleep so got up and dressed. Our first night in the Hotel Utah—I am not sure that I shall like being away from our home at 1037 East South Temple, but shall give it a try.

August 10, 1960. A memorandum from Elder Spencer W. Kimball recited his having been authorized, and his having restored blessings to a woman, who, in the interim during her excommunication and restoration, gave birth to a child. The question asked of me today is whether or not the restoration had effect of placing the child as though it had been born in the covenant. After consideration, I stated that the child should be sealed to the parents, and the child was not born in the covenant since it was born before the restoration of the mother's blessings.

Child born During Father's Excommunication

I also ruled that in the case of a child born to a faithful mother in the

---

45. This decision to reverse course was kept confidential, even from Ernest L. Wilkinson, who nevertheless recognized that the wind had shifted (Wilkinson diary, June 30, July 31, 1960). It was not until mid-October that he conceded to himself that it was over: "I think probably the thing to do now is to accept it without further protestation" (Wilkinson diary, Oct. 19, 1960; also Apr. 22, 1961).

interim during the <u>excommunication of the father</u> and the restoration of his blessings, <u>it would be born in the covenant since the children go with the mother.</u>

August 17, 1960, 8:45–11:25. President [Henry D.] Moyle and I (President [J. Reuben] Clark excused) met with the Chairman of the Building Committee (Wendell B. Mendenhall) and architect Harold Burton who presented to us plans and sketches showing proposed developments ...

Of especial interest were the plot plan and sketch of the proposed Office Building to be built on the Church Office Block, showing contemplated underground garage with relation to the existing buildings which are to remain on the block.[46] It was explained that the two wings of the building to accommodate the Missionary Department administrative offices and library and the missionary lecture classrooms and dormitories, all comprising four floors will balance the general location of these buildings with relation to the central core of the office building. It was also pointed out that the central core for the building will be <u>thirty-five stories</u> on a module plan which will permit private offices, large or small as desired, to accommodate the offices of the auxiliary organizations of the Church, the Building Committee, and other general offices.

I stated that the Church Office Building [Church Administration Building] now standing will be mainly for the offices of the General Authorities and the offices of the Melchizedek Priesthood; the other office building for the Presiding Bishopric and the Aaronic Priesthood. Provision for the financial department with the Presiding Bishopric was also mentioned.

Brother Burton, the architect, explained that the underground garage will provide parking for 2,220 cars on four floors, access to the floors being by ramps.

Seven rooms indicated in the Missionary Building for classrooms and for setting apart missionaries were considered. It was agreed that the missionaries can be set apart in the Church Office Building. Further inquiry in the intended use of these buildings was requested.

The dormitory floors planned for the Missionary Building were next

---

46. Construction of the twenty-eight-story Church Office Building would begin in 1962 and take ten years to complete and would finally not house missionaries.

considered. The dormitory floors provide 140 beds per floor, or 420 beds for all floors. It was agreed that the plan be altered to provide for the girls' dormitory to be on a floor independent of the dormitory for the Elders.

The general plan for the 35 floors of the main building was next considered. The architect said that with space for elevators, stairways, storage, and for office rooms, there will be 29,410 square feet on each floor, and for offices a net of 2600 feet. This space can be divided by partitions in any desired way, or can be left open for general offices. the total space available in the building is to be 943,220 square feet [and] with the underground garage the total [would be] 1,323,910 square feet. The general estimate of cost of this building—$40,000,000—the underground garage, 14,000,000.

With the understanding that independent dormitories for Elders and Lady Missionaries would be provided in the missionary section of the building, the general concept for the office building was approved.

September 8, 1960, First Presidency and Twelve. Remarks by President J. Reuben Clark, Jr.[:] I think that the minutes of this meeting ought to carry our message of love, trust, and confidence in the President of the Church on this, his natal day, that we love, we trust him, we believe the Spirit of the Lord is with him, and that the warmest prayers we have in our hearts are that his life may be preserved in years as long as they are happy to him. When I wished him well this morning, I wished him many returns of happy years. He has been a great inspiration to us and the people. He has been a great leader. He enjoys the confidence of the people. We rejoice in that confidence. There is nothing that is good that we do not wish and pray will be bestowed upon him by our Heavenly Father, that He will continue in the future as in the past to give him His inspiration, His wisdom, and the revelations of His messages of love and appreciation and confidence to you, and made these prayers in the name of the Lord Jesus Christ. Even so, Amen.

Following President Clark's spiritual message, I said that I wanted to take this opportunity to express to them, my beloved brethren, the deep love that I have in my heart, and gratitude for their loyalty and for the unity of spirit that pervades the Council. I told them that I wished to express appreciation to my two counselors—loyal, faithful, true servants of the Lord; that I appreciate their support; I appreciate their wisdom and what they do for this Church and the Presidency as members of the First Presidency of the Church—President Clark for his wisdom, his willingness to do things which sometimes cause him physical inconvenience; President Moyle for his willingness to work night and day and their united support as expressed at this meeting so beautifully by President Clark and the Brethren, by President Joseph Fielding Smith and all the members of the Twelve, for the feeling of brotherhood mentioned in the opening prayer and the prayer at the [temple] altar.

I told the Brethren that my heart goes out to them as I ask God to bless them—I asked them to accept of my love this morning and appreciation and gratitude for their faith and prayers. I thanked President Clark for his message and all the Brethren for their confidence as expressed this morning. I said that I prayed that God would magnify each as he stands before the people in the various conferences, and that they (the people) will see in them [individuals] specially chosen of Christ to bear witness of His reality, of His Sonship, His Fatherhood, and that through them the people of the world may be aroused to the fact that He is our Father and the Son of the living God, our Savior and Redeemer, and no greater truth is needed in the world today than that very fact that Jesus Christ is the Son of our Father in Heaven, the Savior of the World, the Redeemer of Mankind.

I said that I had read only yesterday an article in the magazine "Special Speeches" in which a supposed philosopher <u>ridicules the principle of losing one's self for the good of others; living for others, making others happy</u>. This writer comes right out and condemns that principle, and yet he claims to be a philosopher. <u>There is no other source of happiness in the world</u>, and here in one of our latest magazines this man comes right out, almost as determined to deny that principle as the communists are to deny the existence of God himself. It seems that Satan, as President Moyle said today, has never been so active and determined to oppose the Truth as he is at the present time. He realizes that his Time is probably growing short.

I then asked the Brethren to please accept of my love and confidence and blessings, and as far as it lies within my power to bless them as President, I pray for God's blessings to attend each and every one of them, that His spirit will rest upon the whole Quorum and that they may be united as Christ was on that night at Gethsemane with His Twelve, and his prayer—"Holy Father, keep through thine own name those whom thou has[t] given me, that they may be one, as we are." (John 17:11, 15)

President Henry D. Moyle then commented that he was sure the Brethren all wished to thank me for the blessing I had given them, and he suggested that before I leave, that there be read to the Council a tribute that came this morning from the British Mission. He said that this tribute had been embossed very beautifully on a sheepskin scroll. The tribute which was read at the meeting of the First Presidency this morning was then read to the Brethren.

Following the reading of the scroll, I expressed appreciation for this wonderful tribute, and mentioned the fact that I was a missionary in Scotland sixty-three years ago, and that it did not seem possible that the missionaries are now counting the converts by the hundreds, when at that time they were counted by the dozens.

I said that I should like to carry the spirit that has prevailed in the Council this morning directly to my family and asked to be excused at this point to go to them. I again asked the Lord to bless the Brethren and departed from the meeting.

Never have I attended a meeting which was filled with a more beautiful spirit of Brotherly love! The brethren started out my [eighty-seventh] birthday anniversary as one of the most satisfying experiences of my life.

September 12, 1960. Was shocked and grieved to learn of the sudden passing of my dear friend, Joseph [John] F. Fitzpatrick, publisher of the Salt Lake Tribune. ...

I have always appreciated John Fitzpatrick—he was a true friend to the Church, and proved it in many ways. One of his latest kind acts was his refusal to print in the Tribune a complaint signed by a number of citizens in Salina regarding the erection of a hospital in Richfield which came to Mr. Fitzpatrick's hands, and was never printed in the Tribune. The Catholics were involved, but Mr. Fitzpatrick did not permit the attack to be printed.[47]

---

47. In early 1960 ownership of the hospital in Richfield was transferred to the Catholic Church. The little town of Salina had a previously established medical facility and considered itself a rival of Richfield. Bishop, *History of Sevier County*, 184–87, 235–36.

September 13, 1960, First Presidency meeting. I said that protests are coming [and] to [consider] permitting the use of the [Salt Lake] Tabernacle for political meetings. We considered the part to be taken by the brethren of the General Authorities in the political meetings.

It was decided that individual members of the General Authorities may attend these meetings as they please, but that they be advised to take no part.

I stated that I had advised Elder Hugh B. Brown not to participate by offering prayer or by introducing the speaker. It was suggested that Elder Ezra Taft Benson refrain from participating in the campaign.

September 16, 1960, 8:30–9 a.m. Held regular meetings with my counselors. We met with Elder Glen Fisher who has recently returned from the South African Mission.[48]

September 21, 1960, 9–11:30 a.m. The regular meeting of the First Presidency was held. ... I stated that the committee should bring back to the [Church] Board of Education a plan, and then the Board is to decide whether or not the plan be adopted. We agreed that until the income of the Church will justify the junior college program, it should not be undertaken; and the answer warns the committee not to project a program which will cut into the reserves of the Church. ...

While at my apartment at the Hotel, talked to Ezra Taft Benson in Washington, D.C. Told him that we do not want him to enter the political campaigns this Fall.

October 4, 1960, 8:30–10 a.m. Attended First Presidency's meeting. President [J. Reuben] Clark indisposed at home.

Preaching the Gospel to Those with Negro Blood

Among other matters, President [Henry D.] Moyle and I considered

---

48. The report by the president of the South African mission, Glen Gibb Fisher (1905–93), would have far-reaching implications for LDS involvement on the continent. Fisher had visited with Nigerian converts who had never experienced personal contact with the church (see June 22, 1961). Fisher was born in Magrath, Alberta, and became a merchant in Hill Spring, fifty miles to the west. He and his wife, Holly, served church missions from 1946 to 1960 in Western Canada, the Midwestern U.S., and South Africa, successively.

two letters written by President William Grant Bangerter[49] of the Brazilian Mission, which gave details of opportunities for proselyting in new areas in the Brazilian Mission, and with special relationship to the racial mixture and the high percentage of persons of Negro blood. The problem of providing leadership for the branches where, because of racial mixture, there will not be men holding the priesthood, was also presented and considered.

I said to tell President <u>Bangerter to preach the gospel, but for the present, until the Lord gives another revelation, those who have Negro blood are not to receive the priesthood.</u> I said that I spoke to them about that when I was in Buenos Aires. A man asked about it. He said he was going to marry a girl, and I told him he was at perfect liberty to marry her, and that she was entitled to be baptized and become a member of the Church and to be confirmed a member of the Church, and that their children may be so blessed, but that they will not be entitled to the priesthood. That is definite, and he will have to conform to it until the Lord tells us otherwise. If they who have negro blood in their veins do not want to accept the gospel, that is their privilege. Even at that, the Church offers them more than any other church in existence, and they are entitled to it. We should tell President Bangerter to go on preaching to these people and baptizing them, but they must be told before baptizing them what the limitations are.[50]

October 7, 1960, 8:30 a.m. Held a meeting with President J. Reuben Clark, Jr., and President Henry D. Moyle. <u>We three decided upon the calling of the following men to be Assistants to the Twelve</u>: [Nathan Eldon Tanner, Franklin D. Richards, Theodore M. Burton].[51]

---

49. William Grant Bangerter (1918–2010) would become an Assistant to the Quorum of the Twelve in 1975 and would be advanced to the First Quorum of the Seventy within two years of that calling. From a suburb of Salt Lake City, he graduated from the University of Utah and worked as a building contractor. He became a mission president in Brazil and then in Portugal. His brother Norman would become the governor of Utah in 1985.

50. See Grover, "Mormon Priesthood Revelation," 39–53; "Religious Accommodation," 23–35.

51. Nathan Eldon Tanner (1898–1982), a nephew of apostle Hugh B. Brown, would be called to the Quorum of Twelve two years later. The year after that he would become McKay's second counselor. He had been a school teacher, businessman, and member of the Legislative Assembly in Alberta, Canada. Franklin Dewey Richards (1900–87), a grandson of apostle Franklin D. Richards (1821–99) and cousin of apostle

After we had taken up the matter before us, <u>President Clark broke down and said that he would not be able to attend Conference</u>—said he is not well enough; that his legs are weak, and that he cannot get up the steps. <u>I wept with him, and reluctantly said that he probably should not attend the meetings.</u>[52]

October 8, 1960. I missed President [J. Reuben] Clark today, especially at the morning session when he was not present to present the names of the General Authorities and general auxiliary officers of the Church for the sustaining vote of the people—a duty he has performed for many years!

October 13, 1960, with Henry D. Moyle and Alvin R. Dyer. [The European Mission] President [Alvin R.] Dyer described conditions prevailing in the Communist-controlled part of Germany where careful and very close watch is kept upon the activities of the members of the Church by police of the Communist country. The local, full-time missionaries are found to be unable to do regular proselyting because of the suspicion and distrust which [means] they are kept under surveillance by the police. We agreed that the full-time missionary work behind the Iron Curtain by local members be discontinued, and that the full-time missionaries be released, and that proselyting be done on a part-time missionary basis. The work of the Church meetings are conducted under serious restraints because of the feelings on the part of the people that they may be spied upon by the Communist authorities through fellow members of the Church.[53]

LeGrand Richards, would later serve in the First Quorum of Seventy. He was an attorney and former commissioner of the Federal Housing Administration in Washington, DC. Theodore Moyle Burton (1907–89) was also related to past and present church leaders, as a grandson of the former counselor in the Presiding Bishopric Robert T. Burton and a cousin of Henry D. Moyle of the First Presidency. Like Richards, Burton would also later be placed in the First Quorum of Seventy. He had received a masters degree from the University of Utah and PhD from Purdue, and had been an attaché to the US ambassadors to Germany and Austria, as well as later president of the LDS European Mission.

52. Clark had an elevator installed in his home in 1957, but by 1959 he could no longer walk without assistance. He did attend one session of the church's weekend-long general conference. Quinn, *Elder Statesman*, 174–75.

53. For more on this, see Gilbert W. Scharffs's *Mormonism in Germany*, published by Deseret Book in 1970.

October 14, 1960, 11 a.m. President [Henry D.] Moyle came in and consulted with me about President [J. Reuben] Clark's being carried by chair up the steps to the Church offices when he is able to come, and also up the steps of the Temple when he is able to attend the Thursday meetings. I said I felt that it would be better for President Clark not to exert himself in this way. President Moyle said that he agreed with me. I said if we have to hold a meeting with President Clark we can go up to his home.

October 20, 1960, 8:30–9:50 a.m., meeting of First Presidency. President [J. Reuben] Clark excused. We considered and made decisions regarding sixteen matters of Church importance. One item concerned the <u>new Archives Building</u>. We decided that it would be economical to arrange to provide five or six floors for the Archives, and <u>to build a multi-purpose type of office accommodation above for occupancy of the Auxiliary organizations of the Church during the time the new large office building is being erected</u>. I said that this is the thing to do; it is economical, and it will serve the purpose of the Church for years to come, so the architect can continue to plan <u>for fifteen stories for the Archives Building</u>.[54]

October 25, 1960, 10–11:30 a.m. Was engaged in the meeting of the Committee on Expenditures. Following the meeting, President Moyle and I had a serious consultation with Brother Wendell B. Mendenhall of the Building Committee. At this time I cautioned Brother Mendenhall to move slowly on some of these important Church buildings which are causing a vast expenditure of money; that these things had caused much concern in my mind.[55]

October 26, 1960, 2:30–3:15 p.m. Received a courtesy call from the following: <u>Senator Lyndon Johnson of Texas, the vice presidential candidate for the Democratic Party</u>. ...

Senator Johnson and I, for 40 minutes, discussed matters pertaining to the younger generation, both of us agreeing that the young people are

---

54. The anticipated archives would not be built until almost half a century later and would be ten stories shorter than initially anticipated. Lynn Arave, "New Church History Library: 48 Years in the Making," *Deseret News*, Oct. 23, 2008.

55. See note at Dec. 27, 1960.

as sound and patriotic as older generations, and far better prepared to face the problems of life. ...

In our conversation Senator Johnson inquired about the missionary system, and then talked about his ranch in Texas, inviting me to visit him sometime at his place.

I thoroughly enjoyed my conference with Senator Johnson and the others, and felt that Senator Johnson is a very fine person.

October 28, 1960, 3:15 p.m. Took Sister [Emma Ray] McKay to see a special showing of the movie "Inherit the Wind," as guests of the manager of the Lyric Theatre.[56] This movie portrayed the story of the great "Monkey Trial" when William Jennings Bryan was the prosecuting attorney at the time the legality of teaching [Charles] Darwin's theory of evolution in the schools was taken to the courts. I was especially interested because I had personally met William Jennings Bryan on three occasions, and had followed the real court trial. When I was Principal of Weber College, William Jennings Bryan, at my invitation, came to Ogden and addressed the students of the College.

November 8, 1960. Elder Richard L. Evans was asked to remain for a discussion of the case of a missionary from Colorado,[57] a convert of two or three years, who had been guilty of transgression two years ago. Elder Evans' careful interview with the missionary brought out the impression that the missionary had repented and that he is a young man of good character and should normally be recommended to be called as a missionary, though the views of others would seem to be that he should not be recommended for [a] call.

---

56. The Lyric Theater had been at 132 South State Street since 1905. As the Orpheum Theater, it had staged live drama until 1918, when it switched to motion pictures and then to a widescreen format in 1953. Two decades later it was acquired by the LDS Church for dramatic presentations to tourists. It was torn down (the façade was retained) in 2003 and replaced with a parking garage. "Promised Valley Playhouse, *Cinema Treasures*, cinematreasures.org/theaters.

57. Missionaries were interviewed and set apart by members of the Quorum of Twelve Apostles at what was called the Salt Lake Mission Home, northeast of Temple Square (now the location of the Church History Library). Missionaries were given instructions for two weeks, taken through the Salt Lake Temple, and sent off to learn languages on their own in their assigned countries, without formal lessons.

President [Henry D.] Moyle explained that he and Brother Evans meet the newly-arrived missionaries at the Missionary Home Monday mornings and instructions are given in the importance of a clear conscience before they go to the Temple and into the Mission Field. Missionaries needing to make confessions do so. Missionaries who disclose transgressions are not now sent into the Mission Field, but are returned to their homes from the Mission Home.

I emphasized the importance of REPENTANCE and the possibility of saving a soul. I said that I think we are not justified in sending a boy home who makes a confession, and who has kept himself clean since his transgression. If he has truly repented, we are not justified in prohibiting him from going on a mission.

I then said that if you brethren feel that this boy in question is telling the truth, and if we then refuse to let him go on his mission, I feel that we are doing him an injustice, and the Lord will not be pleased with us. When we say we shall not send any [such] boy on a mission, we are taking judgment into our hands, and that decision really belongs to the Lord. If a boy lies, that is his responsibility, and he will not amount to anything here or anywhere else.

President Moyle then said that he felt that way yesterday morning, but that he did not tell them (the missionaries) that he who confesses and repents will be forgiven.

I said that I feel that that attitude is Christlike, and that I feel that He would do it.

Brother Evans said that the boy confessed and was repentant.

I said "Go thy way and sin no more."

Brother Evans said "That is my feeling, President; I feel that any time we close the door forever, we discourage repentance and confession and confidence."

I said that if we do not forgive, then we do not acknowledge that there is power in repentance; that I think repentance is a most Godlike principle. Of all principles, repentance is the most Godlike. I then said that I think we had better have an understanding about this with the Twelve.

President Moyle said that it becomes a matter of discretion for the Twelve to determine whether the repentance is sincere, and if it is, then the missionary should be allowed to go on his mission.

I said that I could see no other way; otherwise, we become somewhat pharisaical in our judgment and condemn a soul irrespective of his desire to do right. I said that I would let this boy who has confessed go on his mission.

November 14, 1960. Following lunch, Sister [Emma Ray] McKay and I called on President J. Reuben Clark, Jr. at his home on 80 "D" Street. We found him looking well, his voice was strong, and he said he is thinking of coming back to the office. We were happy to see him, and he seemed very appreciative of our call.

November 18, 1960, meeting with Henry D. Moyle and four others.[58] Inquired as to the height of the General Office Building. Brother Mendenhall said that it had been approved for 39 stories. I said "That is going to overshadow the Temple—that[,] with the Kennecott Building, and the new Archives Building." Brother Dunn said, "All three [are narrow] spires[59]—they are not competing with it as massive buildings would." Brother Mendenhall said that it has been recommended that the Archives Building be 15 stories—the floor space has not been changed, and that ground space for the future has been saved. I said that we cannot now change the Kennecott building, but that we can modify the buildings on the Church Office Block.

Genealogical Building

Brother Dunn then exhibited a map of the area where the Genealogical Building is to be located on the triangular space bounded by Hempstead Road, Wasatch Boulevard, and Foothill Boulevard.[60] He explained that this will provide a single wing on the east and two stories and a semi basement on the west. It will provide parking for 700 cars. The building is planned to accommodate about 2,000 people including

58. Also in attendance from the Church Building Committee were chairman Wendell B. Mendenhall, consulting engineer Howard Barker, project director J. Howard Dunn, and committee vice chair John H. Vandenberg.

59. The diary states that "all three have spires," which is not the case. If the Church Office Building had retained the plan for a more substantial base, perhaps the tower would have looked like a spire of sorts, but not the vertical rectangle that is the Kennecott Building.

60. Apparently what became the Family History Library to the west of Temple Square was initially planned to be part of the Institute of Religion complex adjacent to the University of Utah.

officers and staff and the people who will come to do research work. The plans provide for a small auditorium for lectures. ... I said that we would have to go over these plans again.

December 21, 1960. Announcement of the <u>erection of a home for the elderly people of the Church was made in the newspaper this evening.</u>[61] <u>This has been a dream of mine for many years, and I am happy that we have now launched out on this project.</u> It is my desire that the old folks of the church can retire in a dignified manner in their own environment where Church affiliation may be carried out under the direction of their Loved Ones.

December 22, 1960, 8 o'clock a.m. Upon my call, President [Henry D.] Moyle and I (President [J. Reuben] Clark being indisposed at home) met with the members of the Council of the Twelve in the First Presidency's Room of the Church Administration Building.

I expressed pleasure that the First Presidency had received a letter from the Council of the Twelve dated December 19, 1960, signed by the Brethren of the Twelve who are in the city, and endorsed by those who are absent. I said that inasmuch as the items presented in the letter, which refer to the Regionalization of the Church for facilitating Stake and Mission work, would affect the future policy of the Church, I deemed it advisable that the First Presidency and the Twelve consult together relative thereto before further steps be taken in the matter.

The letter was read, and then followed a long discussion by the Brethren on this matter. After listening to their comments, I made the following statement to the Brethren:

"I shall preface my remarks with a statement with reference to a condition in our country. About 20 years ago we shifted in this country from the established program of the Forefathers [in] founding the Constitution and [providing for leadership by] the Senate and House of Representatives and the President of the United States to a Rule by Committees. You who have had anything to do with farm matters or

---

61. This was a private venture supported by McKay, located a block northwest of Temple Square, called the Salt Lake Home.

stock raising know that we have been ruled by Committees, and we are largely shifting that way now in the Government.

"In this Church we are so organized that the Priesthood will control. It does not matter how large we grow, how many hundreds of thousands or millions, we have certain established rules. There is a little ward here presided over by three high priests, and the bishopric have representatives holding the Priesthood. There are quorums in that Priesthood and there are auxiliaries, each one assuming certain responsibilities. We have so many wards in a stake, and that stake is presided over by three high priests, assisted by twelve councilors. Those stakes constitute the Church. It does not matter how far you go or how wide.

"Now a bishop may not be very effective in his administration, but that is his responsibility, and the Lord has said that man must be chosen by the First Presidency and the Twelve, and we are responsible. No matter how large the church grows the 15 men sitting here are responsible for the appointment of those men, and that must never be taken away from you. That is the stakes.

"Now the same with the missions. We have to choose men to preside over those missions. Some are effective, and some are ineffective, but you are responsible for those mission presidents. You can divide those missions as you wish, but be careful that you do not take away from the constituted authority of the Church the divine right by ordination and by setting apart, and leave that to some Committee. You always have to have your hand on that. And as I see this this morning, the recommendation that we change our policy is merely a means of educating these men who are appointed by you men. It is an education more than an assignment of dictation.

"I have looked with a little question upon assigning a man to preside over a certain district and giving him responsibility. He must never get out from under your influence and your guidance. If we do that we will be running this Church by Committees, just as the Government has been running the country by Committees, and as it is being run now by Committees. You are the constituted Authority.[62] Some men who may

---

62. As the church began establishing regional headquarters and establishing the Church Correlation Committee to oversee curricula and activities, McKay was worried that the apostles might capitulate some of their responsibilities to committees and office workers. Seven years later sixty-nine regional heads would be called, later replaced by members of the Seventy to oversee twenty-one geographical regions.

be chosen to preside over missions may not be so effective as others. That is inevitable, and when you have such men you are going to have trouble with missionaries. Give a man so many missionaries that he cannot do his work, the work is going to lag and it is going to be injured probably by inefficient missionaries.

"Now, in our changing of our policy here, let us keep as near as we can to the revelations of the Lord, and we will never be wrong if we do that. In this regionalizing, or in this move to regionalize, you cannot shirk the responsibility of presidency and guiding. The suggestion that you all together constitute the Missionary Committee, I think is a good one. It is your assigned duty to watch over this Church and set things in order in all parts of the world, just as much in Europe and China as here in the United States, and you must never get away from it. You cannot get away from it.

"I think it would be a good thing if you brethren would sit with the Missionary Committee each week, in addition to your weekly meeting, and assign these missionaries, get the reports, and know exactly what is going on. I am not sure about these three men. You would have a Committee. Perhaps there would be more efficiency by assigning them that way. That is the tendency that is prompting this division now—to make more effective and more efficient this missionary work. You will have to do the same thing to make more efficient stake work.

"And now the stakes are growing. You Brethren of the Twelve will be sent to Europe to visit the London, the Manchester, the Birmingham Stakes. You will also have to visit the missions over there. We are multiplying missions for efficiency. You men will have to do that. Your Assistants—the Assistants to the Twelve—will have to do it. Some will come home having made a superficial investigation, a superficial visit, and some will come home having made an efficient supervision and visit. That is the personality and efficiency of each one, but you will never get away from the organization of the Church. You members of the Twelve with the Assistants now given to you have to set in order the Church throughout the world. Now it is just a question of how best to do that."

The Brethren then discussed the matter further, after which I said that nothing would be done until we are all united one hundred percent, and then we shall know we are right. I said that there should be an understanding that the Quorum of the Twelve will constitute the Missionary Committee. However, this matter will be postponed along with the other until the Twelve have studied the matter further and bring in their report. I said the whole subject should be further considered, and that the Brethren who are now absent should have the privilege of being as thoroughly advised as the Brethren who are here in regard to what is contemplated, as it involves a change in the policy of the Church; that no principles are involved, but we do want to know where we are going when we adopt such a policy as proposed.

December 27, 1960, 8 o'clock a.m. Met with the Budget Committee, consisting of Elders Delbert L. Stapley, Joseph L. Wirthlin, with Elder George Jarvis and Brother Olson of the Finance Department attending.

Elder Stapley stated that instructions to the Budget Committee were to keep the 1961 budget within the anticipated income of the Church, and that the assignment presents difficulties because the Committee does not know what commitments the First Presidency has made, and asked for our directions before putting the budget into final form for the council on Disposition of Tithes.

He reviewed the report submitted, including schedules showing requests have been made totaling $107,144,000, whereas anticipated revenue is estimated at $82,500,000. His statement of the reductions which the departments have agreed are acceptable was presented, showing the budget reduced to $99,830,000, which is still $17,000,000 over the anticipated income.

We then made further reductions in the budget bringing the amount over the estimated income down to $9,000,000.

The educational budget was carefully reviewed. The Budget Committee's analysis was first considered with relation to the Pacific Board of Education, whose projects were reviewed. I said "We shall hold the Church Board of Education responsible for these schools and when they go to the Islands on Church appointments, they must include visits to the schools as members of the Board of Education."

The request for $5,000,000 for Ricks College was considered, and it was decided that this be reduced to $3,000,000.

Other ways and means of reducing the budget were considered and it was decided that we shall have the meeting of the Committee on the Disposal of tithing after the first meeting of the Council.[63]

63. The church was in a precarious financial position at this juncture. See Prince and Wright, *David O. McKay*, 199–226; Quinn, *Extensions*, 219–20.

11   Seventies, Vacancies, and the Negro, 1961

The fact is that we do not welcome negroes into our social affairs because if we did it would lead to inter-marriage, and we
do not favor inter-marriage. We recommend that negroes marry
negroes, and that whites marry whites, and we cannot modify that statement. We object to negroes marrying whites for
their own happiness. I said that we cannot change our attitude
until we receive a revelation from the Lord directing otherwise.
—September 26, 1961

January 20, 1961, 8 a.m. Mr. John Gallivan, General Manager of the
Salt Lake Tribune, and Gus Backman of the Salt Lake City Chamber of
Commerce, called upon me in the office of the First Presidency. ...

We then discussed the legislative bills which are to be presented to
the [Utah] State Legislature, and the attitude which the papers should
take toward them. Some of the bills are favorable and some are not.

January 31, 1961, 9–10 a.m. Was engaged in the regular meeting of the
First Presidency. Among matters discussed this morning was the plan for
the supervision of missions by the Council of the Twelve as worked out by
the Missionary Committee and Brother Harold B. Lee of the Twelve. The
plan provides for assignments of the Twelve to visit mission regions, to be
made by the First Presidency. President [Henry D.] Moyle said that the
Committee agreed that the program they presented the other day would
not work. Application of the plan now proposed was considered in relation to persons to be given the direction of regions. I said that the Church
has grown to such a size that we have got to do something; that we cannot

go along without doing something, and that everybody is committed to the necessity for greater supervision than we have had in the past.

February 2, 1961, 10 a.m.–2 p.m. Was engaged in the meeting of the First Presidency and Council of the Twelve in the Salt Lake Temple. At this meeting we unanimously approved the recommendation that members of the Twelve become members of the Missionary Committee, with President Henry D. Moyle as Chairman. ...

I then told the Brethren that I should like to have them take under advisement the matter of making members of the First Council of Seventy High Priests. The Prophet [Joseph Smith] changed that and made them all Seventies. Some of them were High Priests at one time, and a discussion arose as to which would be higher in authority, and the Council of Seventy have not been High Priests since. Now they are sent out under the direction of the Twelve, and cannot set apart Stake Presidents. They have to stand aside while the Brethren of the Twelve do the ordaining of High Priests. It would make them more effective as visitors under the direction of the Twelve if they had the authority to ordain High Priests. This question will be discussed at a later date.

February 5, 1961. No special appointment. Was at the office most of the day studying church matters. My eye is sore from the slight operation performed by Dr. [Richard W.] Sonntag yesterday, but I have not been hampered in using it today.

February 7, 1961. President J. Reuben Clark, Jr. attended Expenditures Committee meeting after an absence of three months ... I told President Clark that it was in very truth good to see him back at his desk.

February 15, 1961, 3 p.m. President Ernest L. Wilkinson reported an incident that happened the other day when the Brigham Young University basketball team played with the Utah State University in Logan. Trouble was started by a negro who is on the State University team. Much criticism has come because the State University has brought in negroes from the outside to play on their basketball team. President Wilkinson reported [USU] President Daryl Chase'[s] favorable attitude toward the negroes. Fathers and mothers up there are concerned because the negroes have been dating the white girls at the College.

February 16, 1961. My secretary, Clare [Middlemiss], reported having received two overseas telephone calls from a <u>Mr. Mack Williams of the Scottish Daily Express, Glasgow, Scotland</u>, and also from a Mr. Dixon of the same newspaper. They were very insistent that they speak to me directly, so my secretary came into the meeting of the First Presidency to report the matter. She said that Mr. Williams had said to her that there is a "<u>lot of criticism in Scotland regarding the methods used by our Elders in getting new converts</u>; that they are persuading teen-age boys and girls to join the Church and taking them out of the control of their parents." They were given the answer by my secretary that there was a misunderstanding, because one of the teachings of the church is that parents are to be held responsible for the training and teaching of their children. I instructed Clare to tell Mr. Williams who was waiting on the phone that he should get in touch with President Bernard Brockbank, the Mission President in Scotland, who would be pleased to give him the true facts in the matter. Mr. Williams later called back and said that he could not reach President Brockbank, so he was told to get in touch with President Woodbury in London.

March 16, 1961. Today at Council meeting I mentioned that the suggestion has already been approved that the Ricks College remain at Rexburg for the present: that President Ernest L. Wilkinson was of the opinion that it would be well to call the Presidents of stakes in that area together, or that I should go up and meet them again. I have received letters from the presidents of stakes in Idaho Falls and have visited by appointment with four of the leading men in Idaho Falls. They manifested a good spirit, but of course they expressed the hope that the school would be moved to Idaho Falls. I am of the opinion that nothing would be gained by calling these stake presidents together again, or by my going up and meeting with them; the matter has been fully studied and considered, and I therefore recommend that the Church make the appropriation that was authorized several years ago for the improvement of the school at Rexburg, and go right ahead and take care of the matter.

Elder [Harold B.] Lee expressed the thought that there was much wisdom in this suggestion, and that he was recently in Idaho Falls, and Brother William J. O'Bryant, who is the mayor, is coming up for re-election either in April or July, and his enemies are trying to make the delay in the decision regarding Ricks College a political matter.

I said that if the election is in April, it would be best not to make the announcement at this time, but if it is not until July, we perhaps should not wait. The Brethren unanimously approved of the suggestion made regarding this matter.

March 17, 1961. Received an anonymous letter containing a check for $16,034.00 made out to the Corporation of the President. The donor, who wishes to remain unidentified, in his letter postmarked "Salt Lake City," said: "Please accept the same as a contribution for such purposes as you see fit—however, if a better use for the money is not known, it would be pleasing to us if the same was used in helping to bring the Gospel to the Jews."

March 29, 1961, 9:30–10:15 a.m. Held the regular meeting of the First Presidency. At this meeting I discussed with my counselors the matter of sending out members of the First Council of Seventy to set the Church in order without giving them authority to set apart Stake Presidents or to ordain Bishops, and commented on the fact that they are going out and doing the work of high priests and should be given that authority.

I explained that in the early days of the Church, the First Council of Seventy were high priests and when the question arose about this the Prophet took the high priests out and seventies took their places. In response to President [J. Reuben] Clark's inquiry as to whether or not when a president of seventy is chosen I would propose that there be conferred upon him a special authority and to make him a high priest or only confer a special authority, I said that when a vacancy in the Council of Seventy is filled, special authority would be given to set in order the affairs of the Church and the individual should be ordained a High Priest.

The revelation (Doctrine & Covenants, Section 107, Verse 94). "And the seventh president of these presidents is to preside over the six;" was also considered and the relation of this to the present need of the Church was discussed. President Clark's question, "Will you make it a general rule or apply it to specific persons?" was answered by me by saying, "Under present conditions, I should apply it to specific cases. Every man who is appointed to go out to a stake, every one of the First Council of Seventy appointed to visit a stake, should have authority of High Priests to set in order the needs in that stake. I should not make it general; I should make it individual. I should confer upon each one who goes out to set the Church in order."

President [Henry D.] Moyle said, "You have a precedent established by President [Heber J.] Grant. He conferred upon the Assistant the authority of the Apostleship."

I said: "They are Apostles with every right and power of the Apostles except only the choosing of patriarchs, and they are given the same charge. They do not have the right to choose a patriarch, and they are not members of the Quorum, but they have the authority of the Apostle." I then said that only the members of the First Council who are sent out to do the duty of High Priests would be given authority.

President Clark said, "If it is a special ordination, my query is answered."

I then said that we shall present the matter to the Twelve at our meeting in the Temple tomorrow.

March 30, 1961, 7:25 a.m. Consultation with <u>President Joseph Fielding Smith</u>. I explained that under the arrangements being made <u>to divide mission fields into areas and placing them under the direction of one of the General Authorities of the Church</u>, that the stakes within the areas can be taken care of by the General Authority assigned to the area. I also informed President Smith that the Presidency will probably have a <u>recommendation to make that the Seventies be given authority to set in order everything pertaining to the stakes</u>. I felt impressed to say to him: "We shall give them that authority."

I said the President[s] of the Seventy will be ordained High Priests and sent out to set the stake in order and everything pertaining thereto. [They have] the same authority as [an apostle],[1] and by virtue of the

---

1. The diary states that "he has the same authority as a Seventy," in reference to the seven presidents of the seventy, although in the previous day's entry a president of the seventy was said to have the same authority as an apostle when representing the Twelve. It is probably a transcription error, not that a seventy "has the same authority as a Seventy."

appointment of the First Presidency, [they have] authority to attend to every duty in the stake. I am sure that is right! I said nothing to President Smith about the seventh president of seventy presiding over the other six. We shall take this matter up a little later. ...

10:10 to 12:00 p.m.—Was engaged in the regular meeting of the First Presidency and Council of the Twelve, held in the Salt Lake Temple.

Seventies—Ordination to High Priests. Presented to the Brethren in Council Meeting today the matter of ordination of Brethren of the First Council of Seventy to High Priests in order that they may attend to ordinations when they are assigned to go out into the Stakes. ...

ORDINATION OF BRETHREN OF FIRST COUNCIL OF SEVENTY TO HIGH PRIESTS. President McKay, speaking to the Brethren, said that the Church is growing, stakes are increasing in number, and work of the General Authorities is becoming heavier and heavier all the time, and their presence is needed in the stake conferences. He mentioned that the Twelve now have eleven associates called Assistants; also the First Council of Seventy who go out regularly, and the Presiding Bishopric. He said that the Seventy, who labor under the direction of the Twelve in accordance with the revelations, are not authorized to complete all the work for which they are sent out; that at one time in the Church high priests and seventies both were called into the First Council of Seventy. The question arose regarding the authority, etc., of these brethren, and the high priests were released, and since that time only those who were ordained to the office of seventy have occupied a position in the First Council.

President McKay said that the First Presidency now recommend that those members of the First Council of Seventy who are appointed to represent the Twelve at the quarterly conferences be ordained high priests so that they can attend to all the regular duties to which they are assigned. They will not join the high priests' quorum, he said, because they will hold to their present appointment, but as they go out they will be given authority, which they already have as holders of the Melchizedek Priesthood, to set in order everything necessary.

The President said that this authority would not be given to all of them, and it will not change the order and calling of the seventies into the First Council of Seventy. They shall be chosen as heretofore, but when the First Council of Seventy are used to go out to represent the

Twelve and to do that work just as the Assistants do, they should have the power and authority to do everything that will help in the work.

President McKay asked if the Brethren had any questions.

Elder Ezra Taft Benson said he assumed that this would not include the ordaining of patriarchs.

President McKay answered no; that even the Assistants cannot do that. In answer to a further question by Brother Benson, President McKay said that, however, they will be able to ordain bishops and set apart presidents of stakes and high councilmen. They cannot, however, choose patriarchs. That responsibility rests with the Twelve. Nor can they attend to the restoration of blessings. They can merely attend to the local work.

President Joseph Fielding Smith moved approval of the decision of the First Presidency. Motion seconded by Elder Ezra Taft Benson and unanimously approved.[2]

April 4, 1961, 10:30 a.m. Received a courtesy call from <u>Ralph Harding, Congressman from Idaho</u> (Democrat).[3] He is a returned missionary from Malad, Idaho. He expressed his desire to be of service to the Church in Washington as the Brethren may call upon him.

April 18, 1961, First Presidency. I reviewed briefly the proposal to erect the new office building which includes a plan to put in a foundation sufficient for a multi-story building, that construction will not at first go

---

2. Since the church's founding, the seventies, as a quorum, have experienced the greatest change. Their mission and responsibilities were argued back and forth over the decades. This decision by McKay set the stage for additional reforms. In 1964 he bestowed upon the First Council of Seventy the marriage sealing authority (January 12, 1964). Later, under Spencer W. Kimball, stake presidents were permitted to ordain seventies upon approval of the First Council (March 29, 1974), and Kimball eventually formed three quorums of seventy and dissolved the office of Assistant to the Quorum of Twelve, absorbing the assistants into the new structure of quorums of seventy (October 1, 1976).

3. Ralph Ray Harding (1929–2006) was, as stated, a Democratic US congressman. He had defeated the long-time Republican incumbent, Hamer H. Budge, by a narrow margin (51–49%). In 1963 the Blackfoot, Idaho, Democrat would play a major role in a church controversy (see entry for Dec. 23, 1963). He served in the 87th and 88th Congresses under Presidents Kennedy and Johnson as the youngest serving congressman in the nation at the time and sponsored legislation to establish the Peace Corps, support Civil Rights, and back equal pay for women. He had served an LDS mission to Kansas and Oklahoma, graduated from BYU and Idaho State University, and was a veteran of the Korean Conflict.

to full maximum height as proposed, and that the building which the missionaries will occupy would be one wing of the structure, extending from State Street west on North Temple. I said that I favored an adequate foundation being put in, but that a skyscraper should not be built. President [J. Reuben] Clark concurred in this view.

April 19, 1961, First Presidency meeting. I said that heretofore the First Presidency has made appointments of members of the Twelve to visit foreign countries, and that now I feel that the responsibility of making these Stake appointments at home and abroad should be with the Twelve. I further said that we need to appoint a Committee of the Twelve to assist President Joseph Fielding Smith in assignment of Brethren to Stake conferences. I shall talk with him, suggesting the need of such a Committee to study the conditions and needs of the Stakes, and to make assignments of General Authorities in accordance therewith. I said that I would present the matter to the Council of the First Presidency and Quorum of the Twelve at their meeting in the Temple tomorrow.

(3) I expressed my feeling that special appointments to visit missions [rather than established stakes] should be made by the First Presidency and approved by the Twelve.

(4) First Council of Seventy. We agreed that members of the First Council of Seventy who are sent to Stakes and Missions to set in order the affairs of the Church be ordained high priests, and have authority to serve as such. They will not, however, be members of the high priests' quorums, but are given special authority to set in order the Stakes and Missions to which they are assigned. ...

[After the meeting] Elder Delbert L. Stapley brought in some old Mormon gold coins, issued in 1849 and 1850, and again in 1860. ... One of the directors of the Mountain States Telephone Company who is interested in this field and visits collectors' stores, discovered some of these coins in St. Louis.

Elder Stapley exhibited the coins that this friend of his had sent to him, asking if the Church would be interested in their purchase. The ones so exhibited were as follows: one two and a half dollar; five five dollar coins. The two and a half dollar coin was made in 1849. Four of the five dollar coins were made in 1850, and one with the Beehive and Lion House in print was made in 1860. Elder Stapley also showed me samples of the original bank notes issued by the Kirtland [Ohio] Safety Society Bank.

The Church has several of the Kirtland Society Bank notes, but have only one of the gold coins, which is a five-dollar piece.

I was astonished to learn that we do not have some of these coins on hand, and decided that we should attempt to locate some of the coins, perhaps by advertising for them. Later, in presenting this matter to the Council of the Twelve, it was decided that Elder Richard L. Evans be asked to try to locate some of them, perhaps by advertising.

The coins now in the possession of Elder Stapley will, together with the three Kirtland Bank Notes, be purchased for the Church for $4,220. Later, the Brethren in the meeting of the Council of the Twelve, when this subject was brought up, moved that the Church purchase them.

April 25, 1961, 8:30–9:10 a.m. Was engaged in the meeting of the First Presidency. I reported to my counselors that I had talked with [BYU] President [Ernest L.] Wilkinson about buildings for Ricks College at Rexburg, and that I had informed him that the First Presidency has decided to proceed with the construction of the following buildings at Rexburg:

1. A library and classroom building
2. A science building
3. Residence halls for approximately 200 students

I said that I informed President Wilkinson that this decision has been made and has the approval of the Council of the Twelve.

May 4, 1961, 8:30–10 a.m. Was engaged in the meeting of the First Presidency. Before we began our regular business, we met with Dr. LeRoy Kimball[4] and David L. McKay, the appointment being made by me at the request of Dr. LeRoy Kimball.

---

4. James Leroy Kimball (1901–92) practiced medicine for over forty years in Salt Lake City, where he pioneered the electrocardiograph machine. He was from Alberta but received his undergraduate degree from the University of Utah and a medical degree from Northwestern University. He purchased his great-grandfather Heber C. Kimball's home in Nauvoo in 1954 and renovated it. Six years later, in 1960, it was dedicated by apostle Spencer W. Kimball as a church historic site—the first step toward preserving the old Mormon neighborhood of Nauvoo.

We had a long and very interesting conversation with Dr. Kimball regarding the acquiring by the Church of Historic property in Nauvoo, Illinois. ...

[From the First Presidency minutes:] President [Henry D.] Moyle said that the ultimate justification for such a development would be to build a temple for the members of the Church in the Middle West on the Nauvoo Temple site and this despite the fact that the Catholic Church has cut off the view to the river.[5] Dr. Kimball asked if the Church has the [architectural] plans of the [original] Nauvoo Temple and was informed that it is believed the Church does have them.

President McKay said, "Why not call Dr. Kimball on a mission to pick up some of these homes for the Church?"

President Moyle said, "I am agreeable."

President McKay said, "He can do it rather than have the people become aroused, thinking the Church is doing it."[6]

May 9, 1961, 8:30 a.m. Went into my meeting of the First Presidency. Among other matters we considered, (1) A letter ... which suggested the Church make more contributions to reputable, charitable organizations and spend less on new office buildings and "plush chairs" for our Relief Society rooms. This letter was ordered filed. I remarked that this man does not know that we are doing more for charity than any other Church in existence.

May 26, 1961. Telephone Conversation with Elder Ezra Taft Benson Re: Serving on a Committee to look into the question of exchange of humans for tractors in Cuba.

Elder Ezra Taft Benson telephoned to me at 3 o'clock this afternoon and said that Dr. Milton Eisenhower[7] had been appointed by

---

5. Forty-one years later (June 2002), a new temple would be dedicated in Nauvoo.

6. Soon Kimball would create a company called Nauvoo Restoration Inc. to acquire the old Mormon homes and buildings in Nauvoo, persisting at it for twenty-five years and for two years, 1971–73, as president of the newly formed Nauvoo Mission.

7. Milton Stover Eisenhower (1899–1985) was the younger brother of Dwight D. Eisenhower and president of Johns Hopkins University. He had earlier been the information director at the US Department of Agriculture and had recommended Ezra Taft Benson for the cabinet-level position of Secretary of Agriculture. People assumed that Eisenhower had a PhD, but it was an honorary doctorate from the University of Nebraska; otherwise he had a bachelor's degree in journalism from Kansas State University.

President John F. Kennedy one of a three-person committee to look into the question of exchange of humans for tractors in Cuba. One thousand two hundred and fifteen freedom fighters that are imprisoned in Cuba may face death[8]—we do not know. [Fidel] Castro has made the proposition that he would exchange them for 500 American tractors. It may be blackmail. President Kennedy has appointed Mrs. Franklin D. Roosevelt, Walter Reuther, and now he has asked Dr. Milton Eisenhower, and has authorized him to add two or three members to his committee to deal with the agriculture aspects of the deal. Brother Benson said Dr. Eisenhower called him to see if he would lend his name to the committee.

I answered: "You cannot lend your name on that Committee." Brother Benson said: "I do not feel that I should; Dr. Eisenhower apparently feels that I cannot refuse the President. He said that our duty will be largely to raise the funds for the tractors. They propose to get the names of the prisoners, and send one [of] fifty of the tractors[,] as Castro cannot be trusted." I said Castro cannot be trusted any more than [Nikita] Khrushchev[9]—"their word does not mean a thing!" Brother Benson said the sentiment in South America is very strong against Castro, and some of the people are raising funds to help purchase the tractors so that the prisoners can be freed. I said, "Well, it is a terrible thing, but you must not associate yourself or your name with this committee—with Mrs. Roosevelt, and Walter Reuther."[10]

June 5, 1961, 9 a.m. Took time to listen to a recording sent to me by [a husband and wife] of Calgary, Canada, in which they make a confession of their sins and ask for forgiveness. The tape recording was returned

---

8. The U.S.-backed Bay of Pigs invasion had occurred the previous month, on April 17, 1961, and had left six volunteer battalions of Cuban expatriates stranded.

9. Nikita Khrushchev (1894–1971) was the Soviet premier who led the USSR during the height of the Cold War. His background included growing up in a poor village midway between Moscow and Kiev. His father had been a union organizer prior to the Bolshevik Revolution, and Nikita followed his lead as a political functionary after World War I.

10. Anna Eleanor Roosevelt, widow of the late President Franklin D. Roosevelt, was a socially liberal activist. Walter Philip Reuther, president of the United Auto Workers union, was equally prominent as a political agitator. Neither of them occupied the portion of the political spectrum McKay would have favored, even overlooking the danger of the church seeming to take sides in such a controversy.

to them together with a letter telling them that if they have entirely repented a just Heavenly Father will forgive. They were instructed to confide in their local Church authorities.

June 9, 1961, 11:30 a.m. Went up to the office of the First Council of Seventy where, by appointment, I met with the members of that Council. Brother Levi Edgar Young was present.

I explained to these brethren the proposition that they are sent out under the direction of the Twelve to set in order matters in the stakes and wards, and that under the arrangement that has heretofore prevailed they were unable to ordain High Priests to any position in the stake, or even assist in such ordinations; that, however, the Brethren of the First Presidency and the Twelve were now united in recommending that when members of the First Council of the Seventy go out to fill such appointments under the direction of the Twelve, they should be empowered with all authority necessary to set in order the stakes and wards.[11]

The brethren of the First Council voted unanimously for this change and seemed to be pleased regarding it. ...

While these Brethren will be ordained High Priests they will not belong to the High Priests Quorum, but will belong to the First Council of Seventy.

June 10, 1961, 8 o'clock. I met by appointment at his request, Brother Willard Marriott of Washington, D.C. who asked what his attitude should be with his hotel business in states that permit the sale of liquor in hotels.

I told him that my attitude is that this is a matter of a business company, and he is to conduct it on as high a plane as he possibly can and wherever it conflicts with the duties of his Church, we shall have to release him. These hotels are run by Hotel Boards made up of non-members of the Church in Texas, Chicago, Illinois, Washington, D.C., and other places in the United States. Some of these members of the Board

---

11. On one occasion in 1942, Oscar A. Kirkham (1880–1958), who had been set apart as a seventy the year before by President Heber J. Grant, unknowingly set apart a bishop during a stake conference visit. He apologized and commented, "I wish the President and Apostles would give us the authority to attend to ordinations of that kind," adding that it was "humiliating" for the First Council of Seventy to be denied the opportunity to perform these necessities during visits to stakes. See Quinn, *Extensions*, 149.

say, reported by Brother Marriott, "Why should we permit Marriott to let his religion affect his business interests?"

I said, "So far as I am concerned, there is no more difference in your hotels conducting the hotel regarding the sale of liquor in accordance with the laws of the State, than for Z.C.M.I. to sell tobacco, tea, and coffee."[12] I further said, "If a Chairman or a member of the Board of these hotels permit the business to interfere with his Church duties, it is up to the Church to deal with him. Otherwise, I cannot see any objection to it."

June 13, 1961, 8:30–10 a.m. Went in to the meeting of the First Presidency. ... I reported to the Brethren at our meeting that I had received a letter from Donald F. Jensen[13] of South Carolina reporting that he is expecting to lead a movement of conservative Republicans to the extent of making a speech supporting state rights; also that he had been asked to extend his remarks to include strong statements in opposition to the <u>integration of negroes and whites</u>, in which he would quote statements by Abraham Lincoln. Brother Jensen asks for counsel in the matter. In discussing the question, the Brethren felt that there would be <u>no objection to Brother Jensen's making a speech</u> in support of state rights. However, they questioned the wisdom of his discussing the integration question. I said that I would convey this word to Brother Jensen, <u>perhaps through his brother, Keith Jensen, who is a member of the Presidency of the South Carolina Stake</u>.

Note: President McKay called Keith Jensen the next day, June 14—see following notes of conversation, and also letter from Donald Jensen. ...

Telephone conversation between President McKay and Keith A. Jensen, 1st Counselor in the South Carolina Stake, speaking from Columbia, South Carolina, regarding a letter written to President McKay by Donald F. Jensen (brother to Keith A. Jensen) June 14, 1961. ...

---

12. The church-owned ZCMI department stores not only sold these items but advertised them. See such display ads as, for instance, "Legget & Myers ... tobacco on sale by Z.C.M.I. and branch stores," *Deseret Evening News*, Feb. 17, 1881; "There are enough fancy teas at ZCMI [Darjeeling, Earl Grey, Twinings] to stage another Boston Tea Party," *Salt Lake Tribune*, Aug. 5, 1959; "New ZCMI Instant Coffee," *Salt Lake Tribune*, Nov. 11, 1960; as well as mention of beer "by the case" and "liquors" cited by Quinn in *Wealth and Corporate Power*, 442.

13. Donald Fogg Jensen (1933–86) had majored in political science at BYU. He was president of the state-wide Young Republicans during his time in Utah. See "Jensen Attends Confab," *BYU Daily Universe*, Nov. 13, 1959.

President McKay: He [Donald] is chairman of the delegation of the Young Republican National Federation—a national organization in which he leads a movement of what he calls "conservatives" to the extent of making a speech supporting states-rights. Now that is good, and he should be commended for his interest in that National Federation.

President Jensen: Yes sir.

President McKay: But he says this: "Beyond this, I have been asked to extend my remarks to include strong statements opposing integration of Negroes and Whites and to quote President Abraham Lincoln's statements regarding the same. President Lincoln very sharply attacked such an idea as even allowing Negroes the right to sit on juries, etc." Now your brother asked me confidentially what he should do on that matter of integration.

President Jensen: Yes sir.

President McKay: His first part, on states-rights, he should be absolutely free to go right ahead.

President Jensen: Go right ahead on states-rights?

President McKay: As a Republican, yes! Do his duty there … be absolutely free. But [as for] … the other matter, I think we should not get into it at all.

President Jensen: Yes Sir.

President McKay: We cannot get into this matter because they are allowed to join the Church. We should like to leave the solution for the Southern States people to handle. If the Government judiciary had kept out of this the Southern States would have handled it properly. Now I do not like to write anything, so will you have a talk with your brother?

President Jensen: Yes sir, I certainly will.

President McKay: Give him the spirit of it—tell him he is free to do what he wishes, but on the matter of integration of the Negroes the less he says about it the better it will be.

June 14, 1961, 9 a.m. The regular meeting of the First Presidency was held. The following are some of the items we took up: …

7. First Council of the Seventy—Reference was made to the announcement that I made Sunday morning in the MIA June Conference that four of the members of the First Council of the Seventy had been

ordained high priests, which ordination took place Sunday morning at 8 o'clock. Elder Levi Edgar Young had inquired both from my secretary and Brother Anderson, secretary in the office of the First Presidency, as to the reason why he had not been given this ordination.

I explained that the action did not include making all of the first Seven Presidents High Priests, but only those who are going out to set in order the affairs of the Church. Those ordained were Antoine R. Ivins, S. Dilworth Young, Milton R. Hunter, and Bruce R. McConkie.

President [Henry D.] Moyle mentioned that Elder Ivins seemed to have the understanding that in the future when selecting brethren for positions in the First Council of the Seventy, Presidents of Stakes and others who are High Priests could be chosen, and that perhaps the Assistants to the Twelve might now be made a part of the First Quorum of Seventies.[14]

I explained that it was not the intention to call High Priests into positions in the First Council of Seventies, nor was there any thought of filling up the First Quorum of Seventies in the manner mentioned. For the record, I said that some time ago (June 9) I met with the First Council of Seventy, Levi Edgar Young being present, and explained to them the proposition that they are sent out under the direction of the Twelve to set in order matters in the stakes and wards, and that under the arrangements that has heretofore prevailed, they were unable to ordain High Priests to any position in the stake or even assist in such ordinations; that, however, the Brethren of the First Presidency and the Twelve are now united in recommending that when members of the First Council of the Seventy go out to fill such appointments under the direction of the Twelve, they should be empowered with all authority necessary to set in order the Stakes and Wards.

The brethren of the First Council voted unanimously for this change, and seemed to be pleased regarding it. I stated further that while these brethren will be ordained High Priests, they will not belong to the High Priests Quorum, but will belong to the First Council of Seventy.

President Moyle suggested that, if I felt inclined to do so, it would be

---

14. This occurred fifteen years later under President Spencer W. Kimball when the Assistants to the Twelve Apostles were absorbed into the quorums of the seventy at the October 1976 conference.

perhaps wise to explain again the situation to Elder Ivins in order that he may have a correct understanding.

Referring to the First Quorum of the Seventy, <u>I said that it has been generally understood that the First Quorum is made up of the first seven presidents of the first ten quorums, but that this is not authoritative and that the first quorum has never been organized. I mentioned that it has also been stated that the First Quorum should include the senior president of the first 63 quorums. I said that I did not feel right about ordaining Levi Edgar Young a High Priest inasmuch as he is not able to visit the Stakes and Wards at the present time due to his condition.</u> ...

8. <u>President J. Reuben Clark, Jr.</u>—At our meeting today President Clark said to me: "Whenever you feel it would be well to relieve me of my position because I cannot get around, it will be satisfactory to me." I said: "Let me tell you, you are not going to be relieved of your position. We are going to call in another man to do work that we need done, but we are not going to release you of any position. You are the first counselor in the First Presidency, and you will remain that, so you need not be worried. We shall call in the necessary help. The Lord bless you! The work will go on, and you come whenever you can. There is no embarrassment to us."

President Clark answered: "You do whatever you think best, and if that means relieving me, it will be all right."

June 15, 1961. Elders Spencer W. Kimball and Mark E. Petersen called and discussed at length their recommendation, which was concurred in by the Twelve, regarding confining the activities of the mission presidents to a supervision of proselyting, and setting up in the districts of the missions "embryo" stake organizations. President [Henry D.] Moyle joined these brethren in urging that such a program be instituted for the reason that the membership in the mission, it is felt, are not receiving proper opportunities for development in the priesthood and other organizations, and as a result many are losing their interest in the Church.

<u>I stated that I am opposed to the setting up of an administration of this kind. I said that I feel that such a program would mean a dual leadership in the same area, which I think would be inadvisable.</u> I feel that the President of the Mission could carry the responsibility if he had the right kind of counselors, and suggested that consideration might appropriately

be given to the advisability of calling from headquarters counselors to assist the Mission Presidents. The Brethren were agreed that some conclusion should be reached in regard to this matter before the holding of the Mission Presidents' Seminar in order that such program as may be decided upon could be explained to the Mission Presidents when they are in the city. The question is to be given further consideration. ...

Seventies—Ordaining of to High Priests

Today at Council Meeting, I reported to the Brethren that I had held a meeting with the members of the First Council of Seventy, and that on Sunday morning, June 1, 1961, I had invited four of them to come to my office and that President Henry D. Moyle and I had ordained the following High Priests—Brothers Antoine R. Ivins, S. Dilworth Young, Milton R. Hunter, and Bruce R. McConkie.

I said that in regard to the ordination of these Brethren, I know it is right, and that the Lord approved of it, but that I do not know that we are compelled to give it to all of the Brethren of the First Council of Seventy just because we give it to those whom we send out to represent us. When they are appointed, they will go representing the Twelve, and they should be empowered with authority to do the work—that is clear to me.

In answer to a question as to whether these Brethren can ordain Bishops, I answered yes, that they could do virtually everything that the Assistants can do; that, however, they do not join the High Priests' Quorum, but that the First Council of Seventy is their quorum. Nor does it follow that we shall call High Priests into the First Council of Seventy. We are not going to do that, as the Prophet has ruled on that matter.[15]

To the question if the members of the First Council of Seventy who have been or may be ordained High Priests can perform marriages in the Temple, I answered No, nor can they select and ordain Patriarchs.

June 21, 1961, 9:00–11 a.m. The meeting of the First Presidency continued. Help for the First Presidency. I announced to my counselors this

---

15. In 1986 the seventies quorums throughout the stakes were disbanded, and the men were distributed variously to the quorums of elders or high priests. Quinn observed that "when President McKay allowed members of the Council of Seventy to perform similar functions as the assistants, he first ordained them to the office of a high priest, ... ironically, this was the status for which founding prophet Joseph Smith dropped five members of the Council of Seventy in 1837" (Quinn, *Extensions*, 150).

morning that if it meets with their approval, I should like to call some-body to help the First Presidency, but that the present members of the Presidency would continue as they are.

President [J. Reuben] Clark said: "May I say right here—do with me as seems to you best." I answered: "That is what we are going to do, and keep you right where you are."

President Clark said that he was more grateful than he could say, but that he would not feel right to go to his grave with a charge that in any way his own selfishness had interfered with the operation of the Church. I said: "It is not going to interfere with it, but I am sure this is going to aid us all. The Church is growing, and we shall present this matter to-morrow at Council meeting." President Clark reiterated, "Please do not consider me for a moment; I appreciate it, and love you for it, and all that, but this is the work of the Lord."

June 22, 1961, 8:15 a.m. Called Elder Hugh B. Brown of the Council of the Twelve and asked him to come down to my private office.

I then explained to him that the heavy volume of work accumulating in the office of the President requires some additional help. I then said: "Elder Brown, I feel, and in this I have the support of President [J. Reuben] Clark and President [Henry D.] Moyle, that the Quorum of the First Presidency should be enlarged to four members—Brother Brown, we wish you to become a member of the First Presidency of the Church."

Brother Brown, after swallowing a lump in his throat and wiping his eyes, said, "President McKay, I could nominate eleven other men in our Quorum, any one of them would be a better man than I."

Whereupon I said: "I remind you, Brother Brown, that the right of nomination does not rest in you, but in me, and you are the nominee."

It was a touching scene for a few moments when the eyes of both of us were filled with tears, and then Brother Brown said, "President McKay, I pledge to you the very best I have. I should like to get under one corner of your load and lift a bit, and I hope you will be perfectly free to assign me any duties that you think I am capable of handling. I have loved you through the years and am happy, though humble, at this opportunity to become even more closely associated with you."[16] ...

---

16. Brown's journal records, "I was, of course, overwhelmed, but inasmuch as the

[First Presidency meeting:] I reported that it was my intention to present to the Twelve in our meeting today the matter of calling one of the Brethren of the Twelve to assist the First Presidency. I mentioned that I had spoken to Elder Hugh B. Brown this morning in regard to his being chosen for this service. President Moyle indicated his approval.

Negroes in Government Installations in Tooele

President Moyle reported that Brother Eugene Merrill reports having a plan, which President Moyle encouraged him to follow up, by which it is hoped that the War Department will be encouraged to make use of two of their plants in California and retain their colored contingents there instead of sending them to Tooele. There will be two to three hundred Negro families in this contingent.

Missionary Work in Nigeria

I referred to the situation in Nigeria where many of the native people it is reported desire to join the Church. We have been corresponding for years with them through LaMar Williams[17] and others, and have sent them Church books and materials. They have organized themselves in a church, which Church they have given the name of the Church of Jesus Christ of Latter-day Saints. I said that we cannot escape the obligation of permitting these people to be baptised and confirmed members of the Church if they are converted and worthy, but they should be given to understand that they cannot perform these ordinances nor can they hold the priesthood. In discussing the matter, it was the sentiment of

---

call came from the President of the Church, I had but one course to take and that was to humbly accept the responsibility" (in Campbell and Poll, *Hugh B. Brown*, 239). Brown found it significant that he was to be a counselor "to" and not "in" the First Presidency.

17. LaMar Stevenson Williams (1911–96) was a long-time employee of the church's Missionary Department. He realized something important was afoot in Nigeria when a "Joseph Smith Story" brochure arrived in 1959 from Nigeria with a request for information written on the back. The sender was Honesty John Ikong. Williams proceeded cautiously by bringing the head of the Missionary Department, Gordon B. Hinckley, into the loop. Soon South African Mission President Glen G. Fisher would be consulted, as recounted in E. Dale LeBaron's 1992 biography, *Glen G. Fisher: A Man to Match the Mountains*, and James B. Allen's "Would-be Saints: West Africa before the 1978 Priesthood Revelation" in the 1991 issue of the *Journal of Mormon History*. See also Fisher's report to the First Presidency, September 16, 1960, recorded herein, and entries for August 16, October 13, 1961, for Williams's appointment to investigate the matter further.

the Brethren that it would be well to have President [All]dredge[18] of the South African Mission call on these people and that LaMar Williams might join him there, the two of them going together. It was felt that President [Al]ldredge might properly assign one or two missionaries to serve among these people. The thought was also expressed that perhaps Brother Williams might be left there for a time as one of the missionaries to work with these people.[19] ...

[During meeting of First Presidency and Twelve:] I referred to the fact that President J. Reuben Clark, Jr. has been incapacitated for some time now, which has worried President Clark more than it has his associates. He has been coming to the First Presidency's meetings of late and also attending the meetings of the Council, but the work has increased a great deal and it is felt that we should have more help in the First Presidency. I mentioned that there is historical evidence of other times when the Presidency had to have added help, and that I felt it was in keeping with the mind of the Lord that we should do so at the present time.

I told the Brethren that I had spoken to President Clark yesterday, and that President Clark had suggested that it would be all right to release him, but that I had told him that he would not be released; that he would continue in his present position in the First Presidency. President Clark broke down and wept, and said he appreciated it. I told President Clark that we were going to call in another counselor and let him share the burdens of the First Presidency.

I then told the Brethren that the First Presidency are united in recommending that another counselor in the First Presidency be chosen, and that he share in the responsibility of the First Presidency. I asked if there was any objection to this or any remarks to be made. There being no objections voiced, or comments made, I asked all who were in favor of the proposition to so indicate by vote, and the vote was unanimous.

---

18. The diary misspells Alldredge as Eldredge. The mission president in Johannesburg in the early 1960s, Otha Layton Alldredge (1907–1988), had been to South Africa as a young missionary and returned to marry Hilda Frieda Hubert of Bloemfontein and together to establish a chain of American-style drive-through ice cream shops with pitched roofs with dormers, called Doll Houses. Alldredge was born in Tooele County, Utah. The family later returned to the United States, and he and his wife both died in Salt Lake City.

19. For the story of unproselytized Nigerians, see Prince and Wright, *David O. McKay*, 81–94.

I then announced that the First Presidency had chosen Elder Hugh B. Brown for this position: that President Brown has been laboring closely with the First Presidency in the cancellation of temple sealings, and that I felt that he should be chosen and sustained here this morning as a counselor in the First Presidency.

I further announced that Brother Brown would be taken from the Quorum of the Twelve and join the First Presidency, and that in due time his successor in the Twelve will be chosen, perhaps at October Conference time. I thereupon asked Brother Brown if he would accept that call and responsibility, to which Brother Brown answered, "In humility, I will, President McKay."

I then asked all who could sustain Brother Brown as a counselor in the First Presidency of the Church to manifest it, and the voting was unanimous.

Thereupon President Moyle and I of the First Presidency and the Brethren of the Council of the Twelve, all being present, with the exception of Elder Ezra Taft Benson, unitedly laid our hands upon the head of Elder Hugh B. Brown, and I was voice in ordaining and setting him apart as "a counselor to the First Presidency of the Church of Jesus Christ of Latter-day Saints."

This appointment was given to the newspapers as soon as possible following the setting apart.[20]

June 23, 1961, 8 a.m. First meeting of the First Presidency where a Quorum of four were present—Elder Hugh B. Brown, newly appointed counselor, attended his first meeting with the First Presidency. In behalf of the First Presidency, I extended a hearty welcome to him as a member of the First Presidency's Council. ...

Sketches of the proposed administration building to be erected on

---

20. Spencer W. Kimball recorded: "I then went into the temple meeting. ... Most all the brethren were present[,] except President [J. Reuben] Clark did not come. After the usual business was over, President McKay presented Elder Hugh B. Brown as another counselor in the First Presidency, explaining that since President Clark is unable to carry on the work and that the pressures are tremendously heavy, he had felt to have another counselor. We then set apart Elder Brown to be the counselor in the First Presidency, all of us laying our hands upon his head, and President McKay being mouth" (Kimball diary, June 22, 1961).

the northeast corner of the Church Office block, also sketches of the proposed underground parking arrangement, together with tunnels proposed to be constructed from the Church administration building to the Bureau of Information and the Tabernacle were exhibited. ...

One of the sketches of the proposed new administration building as previously submitted provided for a tower of 35 stories. Another sketch that was exhibited was for 18 stories, it being the thought that perhaps it would be well to build 18 stories first, with the building. Brother [Wendell B.] Mendenhall suggested that perhaps there should be a compromise as to the height of the building and complete it now instead of erecting only a portion of it with the understanding that additional stories might be built later.

In discussing this matter, we agreed that the building should be completed at this time, and that it should not exceed 30 stories, and as a matter of fact it might not go higher than 28 stories.

June 27, 1961, 8:45 a.m. ... President Ernest L. Wilkinson of the Brigham Young University came into the meeting of the First Presidency and brought with him to visit us Musa Bey Alami[21] and his party from Jericho, Jordan. There were in the party, in addition to Mr. Alami, Lily Haykal, daughter of the Jordanian Ambassador to the United States, George Jahariya, Agricultural Expert, Reem Hamama, Inspector for 23 of the Frontier villages; Amer Salti, one of the [orphan] boys from Jordan attending the B.Y.U. There were also present Dale Clark [originally] from Farmington, and Dean Walker of the B.Y.U.

Musa Bey Alami extended an invitation to me to visit Jordan. I told him that I should very much like to visit Jordan, but that I was unable at the present time to make any promise because of the illness of Sister [Emma Ray] McKay.

---

21. The Arab Development Society founded by Musa al-Alami (1897–1984) helped refugees in the wake of the 1948 Arab–Israeli war in the desert near Jericho, in drilling for water and planting crops. With the help of Utah farmer Burt Bigler (they were introduced through the director of the United States Agency for International Development, Dale D. Clark, who was from Farmington, Utah), al-Alami added a dairy to the settlement. Musa's father had been mayor of Jerusalem, and he himself had graduated with honors from Trinity College in Cambridge. Bigler, "Personal History"; "Musa Alami, Founder of an Arab Aid Group," *New York Times*, June 16, 1984.

Mr. Alami said they have sixteen wells in operation now. I said that I was very pleased to see Mr. Alami again and commented on his wonderful achievement in providing wells for his people. Mr. Alami had been sick with a heart attack, but he said that as soon as he was able to travel he decided to do one thing before anything else, and that was to come and pay his respects to me and President Wilkinson for what had been done.

Mr. Alami made the following statement: "I feel, and I am saying it in all humility and sincerity, that the association with the Brigham Young University and their effort to help has given us more courage and more hope than any gifts or grants which have been made to us by either Point 4 or the Ford Foundation or any other institution in England, and I will tell you why—all these other institutions give these grants; they may be big grants. We have a million dollars from the Ford Foundation; we get $100,000.00 from Point 4; we get several hundred thousand dollars from several other institutions in England—they were all given as part of their routine grants, but this gift of cattle with all that followed it was a gift from the heart, and we feel that no gift and no cooperation can be effective unless it is coupled with love."

Mr. Alami said that they now have milk, which they have not had before, that he had not tasted milk for five years, and that the people there had never heretofore tasted milk, whereas now they can drink any amount they want. He said that people from all parts of Jordan are coming to Jericho to see the cattle and to inquire about the Brigham Young University and the Latter-day Saints Church. He said there has not been anything done in Jordan, in spite of the millions of dollars spent there, that has met the success of this gift. These are the only pedigreed cattle in the country and this is the only up-to-date farm with first-class equipment.[22] It will help serve 111 villages which lie on the frontier between Jordan and Israel.

Mr. Jahariya related how when the cattle arrived, reporters and photographers came and took pictures and when they arrived in Jericho a little after midnight everyone in the settlement—men, women and

---

22. The cattle were purchased in Holland and shipped by way of the Suez Canal and Gulf of Aqaba under Bigler's guidance. A milking barn was constructed, equipment assembled, alfalfa planted, and Palestinians tutored by Utah dairyman Ned Smoot and others. Bigler, "Personal History."

children—was up waiting to see the cows. The following day the people were there from all over Jordan to see them.

I asked Mr. Alami how many boys are being helped by the project and he said there are permanently 160 boys in residence there, and that 400 have already graduated and have fine jobs. Mr. Amer Salti who is at the B.Y.U. is one of these boys. President Wilkinson said that there is another boy from Jerusalem at the B.Y.U. who came on his own.

Musa Bey Alami left with me a copy of the bible (the cover of which is in mother-of-pearl) which he had autographed.

June 29, 1961, 8:15 a.m. Elder Ezra Taft Benson came in and asked about the disposition he should make of his many government records and also his personal records. I told him that we would leave to him and President Joseph Fielding Smith, Church Historian, the matter of going over the papers and recommending what papers, if any, should go into our records here in the Historian's Library, and which, if any, should be placed in the Congressional Library. They are to report back.

I stated that Brother Benson gave a grim report of conditions in Washington from which place Brother Benson has just returned. Brother Benson has received an invitation from the senators and congressmen to go back to Washington as an adviser. I feel that if this matter comes up again that Brother Benson should remain here, that we need him at home.

Laraine Day[23]

A letter addressed to me from Laraine Day (moving picture and television actress) was read. She mentions a rumor that the garments are to be re-designed. She appeals for elimination of the sleeve.[24] She also

---

23. Laraine Day (1917-2007) was arguably Mormonism's most successful starlet, portraying nurse Mary Lamont in seven *Dr. Kildare* movies and hosting a television series, *The Laraine Day Show*. She was born Laraine Johnson in Roosevelt, Utah, and grew up in southern California. She was married to singer Ray Henderson for five years (1942–47) and had three children. When they divorced in 1947 and she married the legendary baseball manager Leo Durocher the next year, it caused a stir. The couple divorced twelve years later, after which she married screen writer and Mormon convert Michael M. Grilikhes (1923–2007), with whom she had two additional children.

24. The movement to redesign the garment came from Klis Hale Volkering, a church member in Southern California associated with the Max Factor cosmetic company, according to BYU archivist James V. D'Arc.

mentions the book "The Twenty-Seventh Wife," by Irving Wallace,[25] and said that she was incensed by it, and that there is talk in the motion picture industry of making it into a moving picture. It was decided to send the letter to Elder Richard L. Evans for his report and suggestions.

June 30, 1961, 9–10 a.m. Was engaged in the meeting of the First Presidency ... President [Hugh B.] Brown referred to letters being received from people in Nigeria, who bear their testimony and ask if someone cannot come and help them. I said that we are going to send to Nigeria to look into the situation President O. Layton Alldredge of the South African Mission and probably Brother LaMar Williams who has been corresponding with these people.

I said that in this matter we are facing a problem greater than the Twelve of old faced when the church was shaken by the question of whether or not the Gentiles should have the gospel. I said that the Lord would have to let us know, and when he is ready to open the door he will tell us. But until he does, we shall have to tell these people in Nigeria that they can go so far and no farther.[26]

In this connection President Brown referred to a conversation he had with Elder N. Eldon Tanner, Assistant to the Twelve. He reported that Sir [Alfred] Savage,[27] former [finance minister] of Nigeria, is in London, and that he is a friend of Elder Tanner. Also, that a man by the name of

---

25. The book by Irving Wallace (1916–91), his sixth (he would author two dozen more), had just been released. Two of his books would become feature films. He began his career by writing screen plays for four movies and authoring episodes of the television series *Have Gun—Will Travel*. The book in question was about the acrimonious divorce of Brigham and Ann Eliza Young. It would not became a movie.

26. See previous discussion of this issue under June 22, 1961. The initial contact in 1946 came from O. J. Umordak's request for more information. Little transpired in the intervening fifteen years. When Honesty John Ikong sent a similar request, it presaged the Civil Rights movement in the United States and presented the church with theological, logistic, cultural, and political challenges.

27. The diary incorrectly gives the name as *Arthur Savage* for Alfred William Savage (1903–80), who had been finance minister in Nigeria from 1946 to 1948. He had not been the governor general, as the diary repeatedly asserts, although he had been governor of Barbados and governor general of British Guiana. Tanner met him in Barbados in the early 1950s on business. In British Guiana in 1953, Savage declared himself the sole governing authority in the country and dismissed the legislature. It was because the left-leaning People's Progressive Party (PPP) had won the national election. The next time elections were held was 1957, and the PPP won again, as it did in 1961.

[George A.] Drew is the [Canadian] High Commissioner [to the United Kingdom] [and] is a friend of Elder Tanner. Brother Tanner reported that diplomatically speaking, it would be very well for us to make further inquiry through Messrs. Drew and Savage before we go to Nigeria, and Brother Tanner also thinks they would be willing to give us letters of introduction and letters of recommendation. President Brown suggested the advisability of having Brother Tanner fly down to Nigeria and join Brothers Alldredge and Williams in Nigeria. I said that I think this is an excellent suggestion, and that I shall talk with Elder Tanner before he returns to England.[28]

July 1, 1961, 7:15 a.m. By appointment at my call, met with members of the First Presidency and members of the council of the Twelve in the office of the First Presidency. (President [J. Reuben] Clark still being indisposed was absent) ...

Missionaries to the Negroes in Nigeria

Then I spoke to the Brethren about the importance of a problem that is almost as serious as the one that was faced by Peter, James, and John, and the Twelve in their day. Paul left the synagogue, members of which had rejected him, and said he would go to the Gentiles, and historians give him credit for being the author of the decision to take the gospel from the Jews to the Gentiles, but that was done in the Lord's own way and in the proper way.

Peter, as Head of the Twelve, received a revelation when he had the vision on the housetop, in which a sheet was let down and various kinds of meats were shown him, and he dreamed that the Lord said, "Arise Peter, stay and eat." Peter answered that he had never eaten anything that was unclean. The Lord then said, "Callest thou not unclean that which I have cleansed."

It seems that at the very same moment three men stood at the door and invited him to come and give the gospel to one Cornelius. Peter accepted the call, and sat with other Gentiles.

That was a difficult thing for Peter to do, and there occurred the only exception that we have in sacred history where the Holy Ghost was

---

28. For more background, Prince and Wright, *David O. McKay*, 82.

poured out before baptism, and Peter said, "Can anyone refuse baptism since he (Cornelius) has received the Holy Ghost as well as we?" Peter baptized Cornelius and his household.

Then a meeting of the Twelve was called at which James presided, as he was in charge of the branch in Jerusalem, and Peter testified on that occasion as to the case of Cornelius, that he had received the Holy Ghost, and that he was entitled to the gospel. Paul also witnessed that the Gentiles had received it, and so the great decision was made that the gospel is for all the world, and James and the others of the Twelve ruled that the Gentiles could accept the Gospel and need not be circumcised as the Jews were.

I reported to the Brethren that there has been considerable correspondence with the Negroes in Nigeria on the part of Brother LaMar Williams, and even previous to the present correspondence, and that some of the negroes in Nigeria have taken upon themselves the name of the Church of Jesus Christ of Latter-day Saints. They are asking for some one to come and give the gospel to them.

I stated that these people do not know as yet that they cannot have the Priesthood, although they have received literature from us—the Book of Mormon, and other books and tracts—and are teaching the gospel as they understand it. The Lord has not revealed any thing other than that they are entitled to baptism and the laying on of hands for the Gift of the Holy Ghost, and can participate in all the auxiliary work and in Sacrament meetings, but they cannot have the Priesthood.

I told the Brethren that in the past two attempts have been made to have the President of the South African Mission visit these people in Nigeria, but because of political conditions they have not had a good visit with them. It is now learned that two of the British Government officials who have had much to do with affairs in Nigeria are in Great Britain, and that President N. Eldon Tanner is well acquainted with them.

The thought has occurred that probably now would be a good time to let the President of the South African Mission on his return home from the Mission Presidents Seminar now being held in Salt Lake City go with President Tanner to Nigeria, have a conference with these people, and let Brother Tanner report back conditions to us. I shall have a meeting with President Tanner this morning about this matter.

President [Hugh B.] Brown explained that Brother Tanner feels that it would be necessary to see Mr. [George A.] Drew, who is the [Canadian] High Commissioner, and is now living in London, and still has some jurisdiction in Nigeria, and also Sir [Alfred] Savage, former [finance minister] of Nigeria, who is now in London.[29] Brother Tanner has already talked with this gentleman, and it would probably be wise for him to see both of these men in London on his way to Nigeria, and perhaps obtain some credentials from them. They have previously expressed a willingness to do anything they can for us.

Elder Mark E. Petersen raised a question as to whether or not the Government of South Africa might be offended were we to attempt to do proselyting among these Nigerian people.

Elder Harold B. Lee, speaking to the subject, also mentioned that when he was in South Africa, a little over two years ago, consideration was given to the matter of increasing our missionary quota, and that when he contacted the Ambassador in Washington, and later with President Glen G. Fisher of the South African Mission, and went to Pretoria, the capital, they asked one question—"Do you proselyte among the Bantu?" When they closed down on missionaries coming into the country, they made an investigation of every Church that had been sending in foreign missionaries, and that was the question they asked, and if they had learned that we were proselyting among the negroes, there would have been a real question as to permitting us to do missionary work in South Africa.

President Brown stated that Nigeria is a long way from South Africa, and that there is no political connection between those countries, that according to Mr. Savage, Nigeria is much further advanced in civilization than is South Africa, in fact, that Nigeria is the furthest advanced of any of the countries in Africa.

I concluded the discussion by saying that we should send to Nigeria the President of the South African Mission to ascertain what the situation is, and make his recommendation; that President Tanner accompany him, representing the General Authorities, and that nothing be done

---

29. The diary again misidentifies Sir Alfred Savage as the "former governor general of Nigeria," which has been corrected here. The text is also incorrect about "Mr. Drew" being the British High Commissioner of Nigeria, which is undoubtedly a reference to George A. Drew, Canadian High Commissioner to the United Kingdom. Tanner had probably suggested that Drew might introduce him to the British diplomats in Nigeria.

until a report has been received from these Brethren. I said the question before us this morning is whether or not the Brethren would approve of sending these two brethren to Nigeria in answer to the calls that have come from the people of that country comparable to what Paul received when he received his vision to go to Macedonia.

Elder Ezra Taft Benson moved approval, and the motion was seconded by Mark E. Petersen, and unanimously approved. ...

[In a subsequent meeting] I then presented to President Tanner the question of Nigeria and missionary work among those people. He told me that he is well acquainted with the former [finance minister] of Nigeria—Sir [Alfred] Savage, and also with Mr. Drew the High Commissioner of [Canada].[30] He said they are personal friends and that they have offered to do anything they can to help him. He believes they will give him letters of recommendation and introduction to the officials in Nigeria. He said that he would be glad to go to Nigeria in company with the President of the South African Mission and look into this matter and report back to us.

July 5, 1961, 9:30 a.m. Arrived at my private office. Had consultation with my secretary Clare [Middlemiss], regarding my personal diaries and other records she has been keeping for me for twenty-six years. Read a few pages of my diary for the past several busy days, and told her I approved of them. Said that I would like to take my diaries to the Hotel [Utah] for the present; that a place is being prepared for them in the new home in Huntsville. However, this matter will be given further thought.

July 18, 1961, 8:40–10 a.m. Regular meeting of the First Presidency was held. ... I reported to my counselors that I had received letters from two different parties calling attention to the heavy assessments that had been levied against them in their wards in connection with contributions to building funds. I said that in one instance the woman writing the letter said that the bishop had advised her to borrow $1500 from the bank to contribute to the building fund, that her son has polio and that her husband has lost his regular job and she is now asking that their names

---

30. Once more the diary assigns Savage the governorship of Nigeria and Drew the post of British High Commissioner in Nigeria, both of which are incorrect.

be taken from the Church records. I said that such demands are contrary to everything that we have taught, and that I think it is a subject that I might well speak upon at October Conference.

July 19, 1961, 8:30–11:30 a.m. Was engaged in the meeting of the First Presidency. ... President [Hugh B.] Brown reported that he has a letter from President N. Eldon Tanner regarding the expressed desire of the people in Nigeria to receive the gospel in which he reports an interview he had with Sir Alfred Savage, former Governor General of [Guiana], and one of the top diplomats in London who is a close friend of President Tanner. This gentleman pointed out that these people are not of a kind that we can place confidence in them—that they would join any organization that would offer them personal benefits. He feels quite definitely that it would be ill-advised to go into this area if we expect to have any responsible organization; that they read an article in some magazine about some church, and then immediately contact the organization relative to joining it.

I said that I feel that the matter should be placed in the hands of President Tanner to make further investigation and perhaps obtain further information from the leaders of the groups in Nigeria with whom we have been corresponding. I said that any statement to these people about their not being permitted to hold the priesthood should not be placed in writing but should be conveyed orally.

July 27, 1961, 9 a.m. ... Elders Marion D. Hanks and A. Theodore Tuttle came in by appointment for the purpose of being ordained high priests.

I referred to the recent occasion when I met with the First Council of Seventy and mentioned to them the recent action of the First Presidency and Quorum of the Twelve when it was unanimously decided that the brethren of the First Council of Seventy should have full powers under the Quorum of the Twelve to set in order matters pertaining to the Church in the stakes and missions. I then asked Elders Hanks and Tuttle if they were in full accord with that action, and they answered in the affirmative. Presidents Moyle and Brown and I then laid our hands upon the head of Elder Marion D. Hanks, and I was voice in ordaining him a high priest. We then laid our hands upon the head of A. Theodore

Tuttle, and <u>President [Henry D.] Moyle, at my request, was voice in ordaining Elder Tuttle a high priest.</u>

July 28, 1961, with Richard L. Evans, Thorpe B. Isaacson, and Joseph L. Wirthlin. Brother Evans explained the need of locating and developing at least one additional [Salt Lake] Tabernacle organist, stating that both Richard B. Condie and Frank W. Asper recommend Robert Cundick. He explained that he feels it would be a better program to invite a number of persons to perform as guest organists for a three-month period during which time they would give some noon and some evening recitals, and also help with the Choir, particularly during rehearsals. The names of Melvin Dunn, presently employed as the Tabernacle organ technician; Robert Cundick, a teacher at the Brigham Young University; Harley Belnap, William Richards, a son of George J. Cannon, and a young man from Wenatchee, Washington, were suggested as some who might be invited as guest artists.

It was made clear that these brethren would not be expected to give up their present employment or ties, and there would be no commitment for their services beyond the guest period during which they would be given a modest compensation for their time. It was suggested the compensation would be worked around a figure of approximately $200 per month depending on the circumstances and the amount of time involved. We authorized Elder Evans to go forward with this project and then to report back to the Presidency.

August 3, 1961, 8:30 a.m., meeting of First Presidency. President [Henry D. Moyle] is in Florida, and President [J. Reuben] Clark still indisposed at home. President [Hugh B.] Brown and I read a number of letters containing matters of general church interest. ...

An inquiry regarding the appointment of a third counselor in the First Presidency, and asking as to which other Presidents of the Church have had three counselors, was referred to President Brown for handling. ...

A letter referring to the recent decision to ordain the members of the First Council of Seventy to High Priests and quoting from the Documentary History of the Church corrected a practice of ordaining Elders to High Priests before they were ordained Seventies, and does not preclude the giving of additional authority and duties to the First Council of Seventies.

August 14, 1961. Brother Cleon Skousen telephoned to say that he had learned that General Douglas MacArthur will be in Salt Lake City during October Conference, and that he thought it would be a very nice thing to him to speak at one of the sessions of the Conference in the Tabernacle. He said that Elder Ezra Taft Benson said that General MacArthur had once said to him, "If I can ever be of help to the Mormon people, please let me know." Elder Benson could extend the invitation to General MacArthur when he goes back East.

I said that it would be best not to ask him to come as a speaker, but to invite him to attend Conference, and then if he comes I could acknowledge his presence and ask him to say a few words; that I think this would be the proper way to handle this.

August 16, 1961, 8:30–11:00 a.m., meeting of First Presidency. ... At our meeting this morning President [Hugh B.] Brown called attention to appeals from natives in Nigeria for baptism into the Church. He stated that these natives bear testimony to their faith in the Gospel. After discussing the matter it was decided to ask LaMar Williams, who has been corresponding with these people, to go to Nigeria accompanying some missionary who may be enroute to the South African Mission for the purpose of meeting with these people on his own responsibility and not under appointment by the Church or with authority to take any action that would involve the Church, the purpose of the visit being to ascertain the situation regarding these people, whether or not they are truly converted to the Gospel and are sincere in their desire to become members. Brother Williams would be expected to tell these people that we have no paid ministry and that if they become members of the Church they could not hold the priesthood. It was felt that before making this assignment we should obtain President N. Eldon Tanner's approval in light of the contacts he has made in London. The Brethren were agreed that neither President Tanner nor President Alldredge should be requested to make such a visit and that the visit of Brother Williams should be entirely unofficial. Brother Williams in meeting with these people could tell them that he had come on his own responsibility in answer to their correspondence to look into the situation there.

August 17, 1961, 10 a.m.–3 p.m. The regular meeting of the First Presidency and Council of the Twelve convened in the Salt Lake Temple at 10 a.m. This was the first meeting since we adjourned on Thursday, June 22, 1961.

Following some regular business regarding Stakes and Wards, we discussed the following:

(1) Position of the Church with reference to Communism. Some of the Brethren called attention to the <u>extensive activity of some of our stake presidents in the Los Angeles area, largely directed by President Hugh C. Smith</u>.[31] Brother Cleon Skousen is taking an active part in this campaign, and that regularly organized meetings are held in the Los Angeles area, and <u>that this campaigning is being carried into our Sacrament meetings</u>.

Elder Ezra Taft Benson mentioned that Brother Skousen is field director of the American Security Council, which is a national organization set up [in 1958] by businessmen and business corporations primarily, and financed by voluntary contributions, that some very distinguished Americans serve on the Advisory Committee and the Board, and they have headquarters in Chicago. Their objective is to try to inform the American people on the issues involved in Communism and Socialism. He said that personally he thought the Communism threat is very real and very dangerous, and that there is need for some organized effort to meet this great threat.

Elder Benson and others of the Brethren indicated that they thought that perhaps Brother Hugh C. Smith has been a little extreme in his efforts to combat this menace. The Brethren were agreed that we should fight Communism as citizens, but they questioned the wisdom of doing so as the Church, and particularly in our Sacrament meetings.

<u>It was suggested that the First Presidency prepare a carefully worded memorandum on this subject to be handed to the Brethren of the General Authorities for their use when visiting quarterly conferences, setting</u>

---

31. Hugh Charles Smith (1910–1995), president of the San Fernando Stake, was born in Canada and married Margaret L. Wright in the LDS temple in Cardston, Alberta, in 1934, after which the couple relocated to Southern California and he became co-owner of Columbia Pest Control.

forth the precise feeling of the First Presidency about this matter. It was suggested that emphasis should be placed on the spiritual nature of our Sacrament meetings.

It became the sentiment of the Brethren that this be done, but I said that in this connection, however, we must be careful about condemning any efforts that are anti-Communistic because Communism is a real danger in our country. It is a termite movement, the purpose of which is to make the state dominant over the individual. Our Sacrament meetings should be reserved for spiritual enrichment and spiritual instruction.

August 24, 1961, meeting about purchasing historical properties. I asked Dr. [J. LeRoy] Kimball how much it would cost to pick up the balance of the 100 acres [in Nauvoo, Illinois]. Dr. Kimball said that he had expended about $85,000 now including the Brigham Young home, that if we figured $500 an acre it would be $30,000 and that we might need $60,000 to get the rest of it, perhaps more. He thought that what he had spent and what the Church had spent has cost us perhaps $110 an acre or $120,000 and if we picked up the rest of the land at $60 an acre or $70,000 the total cost would probably be $200,000. Then on top of that would be the cost of restoration.

I said the first thing to do is to get possession of these properties and the sooner the better. It was suggested that Dr. Kimball go back with the idea of purchasing as much as he can and as it becomes available, and that he do it in an orderly way rather than wholesale. ...

[With the First Presidency:] I called attention to the discussion in the Council Meeting last Thursday regarding the various discussions that are going on particularly in California in the Sacrament meetings and elsewhere regarding Communism. I read to the Brethren of the First Presidency an editorial issued by the First Presidency, consisting of Heber J. Grant, J. Reuben Clark, Jr. and David O. McKay, under date of July 3, 1936, setting forth the attitude of the Church regarding Communism.[32] It was the sentiment of the Brethren that this editorial should

---

32. "Communism is not the United Order, and bears only the most superficial resemblance thereto," the editorial asserted. "Communism is based on intolerance and force, and the United Order upon love and freedom of conscience and action. ... We call upon all Church members to eschew Communism" (in Bergera, *Statements*, 90–91).

be copied and placed in the folders of the General Authorities as they go out to visit the stakes. It was felt that there should be no hesitation in giving circulation to this article. It was decided to take it to the Council this morning to be read to the Brethren. <u>It was the sentiment of the Brethren that we should not open our meetings to national organizations and individuals to discuss the communistic trend</u>, but that any instruction on the matter should go through proper channels and there would be no objection to the Brethren of the General Authorities reading this in quarterly conferences. <u>I said we do not want the Brethren to go out with the idea that we, as a Church, are not publicly and emphatically against Communism.</u>

[With First Presidency and Twelve:] I referred to the discussion on the subject of Communism held in the Council Meeting a week ago, at which time it was recommended by the Brethren that the First Presidency prepare a statement setting forth the attitude of the First Presidency regarding the matter, which statement it was suggested be given to each of the General Authorities to take with them when visiting the stake conferences. At my request there was read to the Council an editorial over the signatures of the First Presidency, President Heber J. Grant, J. Reuben Clark, Jr. and David O. McKay, which appeared in the Improvement Era in August, 1936.

<u>I stated that a copy of this article would be given to each of the Brethren that they might take it with them in their visits to the quarterly conferences, that the people might be advised through the regular channels of the Church rather than having the matter discussed in Sacrament meetings, or by special self-appointed unofficially appointed speakers.</u>

Elder Spencer W. Kimball suggested that it might be well to enlarge this statement somewhat in order to make it applicable to our people in foreign countries as well as in the United States. It was also decided that the statement would be read at the General Priesthood meeting of the Church in connection with the October Conference, at which time the one presenting it would make such additional remarks as could be quoted for use in foreign countries when dealing with the subject of Communism.

August 25, 1961, 8:30 a.m. Attended the regular meeting of the First Presidency.

Chancellor of Church School System

I mentioned that Ernest L. Wilkinson's title as Administrator of the Church School System should perhaps be changed to Chancellor, that Administrator is a title given to educators on a lower status than the president of a university, and that where one is head of several universities he usually has the title of Chancellor, as is the case in various educational setups throughout the United States. We decided to change the title to Chancellor of the Church School System.

Florida and Georgia Farms

I said that I felt that a very good choice was made in appointing Van Moss as assistant to Leo Ellsworth, in taking charge of the farms in Florida and Georgia.[33] I said that I awoke this morning with the impression that we ought to begin to develop another phase of that great ranch. I feel that with the aid of Brother Ellsworth, Brother Moss and the capable assistants there, the future of the ranch financially is established, that, however, these men, too, would in time pass away and we must look to the future of the ranch. I consider this ranch the greatest ranch in the United States and one which we do not want to sell or let go into the hands of someone else. I asked if the Brethren[34] didn't think it time for us to begin to establish wards and stakes in that ranch, and get into the hands of individual Church members orchards, dairying projects, fruit groves and all the crops which can be grown so successfully in that rich soil. I said that our aim is not to have an income to the Church alone, but our aim is to save the people and help the Lord in bringing to pass the immortality and eternal life of man, and I said that I felt that now is the time for us to begin to have places where young men who cannot make a living down here in Sanpete County; that people who have to leave Berlin and other stricken places, will have to be helped, that we could help establish them on these

---

33. Called Deseret Farms, later the Deseret Ranch, the company began in 1950 with 450 square miles of rangeland in Florida, a feed lot in Georgia, and a few thousand head of cattle. By 1963 the number of cattle had increased to over 70,000 (see entry for Apr. 2, 1963) and there were 170 acres of alfalfa. There would eventually be 1,700 acres of orange groves. Ellsworth was hired from his ranch in Arizona. Dan Brown, "Cattle Gamble Pays Off," *Salt Lake Tribune*, Dec. 13, 1959; John Hollenhorst, "LDS Church Ranch Making Big Impact in Florida," *KSL News* online, May 18, 2011; Poll and Larson, *Working the Divine Miracle*, 137–39; Kelley, *No Place for Zion*, 22.

34. The diary repeats "if they" after "Brethren."

lands requiring them to pay back to the Church what we are investing in the ranch and the Church's investment would then be in souls.

The Brethren of the Presidency were united in this matter and felt it was a real inspiration. President [Henry D.] Moyle suggested that if I would just give the word to Utah–Idaho Sugar Company the matter would be on its way.

August 29, 1961, 7:30–8:30 a.m., dictation to Clare Middlemiss. This period was interrupted by Henry Smith of the Deseret News who came in and asked me for a statement regarding my 88th birthday. He asked me what I thought had contributed to my long life and I replied, "For one thing—do not worry! Do something about your problems and then do not worry about them. If you cannot do anything about your problems then what good does it do to worry?" I told him that I loved life as much as ever and I love people.

September 1, 1961, 4:00 p.m. Called on President J. Reuben Clark, Jr. at his home where he has been confined for several months, and wished him many happy returns on his 90th birthday. I found President Clark looking well, free from pain, and enjoying the association of his friends and family gathered around for his birthday celebration.

September 7, 1961, 3:30 a.m. Arose and took a hot bath—still feeling a little tired[,] I rested for 45 minutes before beginning the day's work. ...

3:00 p.m.—When I returned to the office from Council Meeting I was greatly surprised to be greeted by a large group comprised of heads of departments, secretaries and other Church Office associates who had gathered in the office of the First Presidency in honor of my 88th birthday. ...

I told the employees that "it is very hard for me to express my feelings on occasions of this kind but that I wanted to say that I love and appreciate everyone of you." ([secretary:] At this point the President choked up and it was very difficult for him to speak—everyone present was very touched and tears flowed freely.) I said that I wished that when they were 88 years of age they could feel as good as I do and look as young as they do now. There was a wonderful friendly spirit present and I enjoyed my moments with them.

September 8, 1961. For the past several years I have been prone to consider <u>Old Age</u> as a disagreeable unwelcome trespasser, skulking along to claim any faculty that might show the strain and usage of the passing years; this year at eighty-eight I look upon him with a degree of compassion akin to appreciation. Indeed, if it were not for "Old Age" I should not have seen seventy-five, or eighty, or eighty-five, and most assuredly not <u>Eighty-eight</u>.

Now I am content to let him walk by my side, but shall continue as long as possible to deny the demands of Old Age to take from me the good health Kind Providence still gives me!

This has been a memorable 88th Birthday, and I am thankful and grateful for the Lord's goodness to me!

September 15, 1961, First Presidency in meeting with Ernest L. Wilkinson. <u>BYU Faculty and Communism</u>—I asked President Wilkinson if there were any Communists on the faculty of the Brigham Young University, and President Wilkinson said he was very sure that there are none. <u>I mentioned a report that I had received to the effect that someone in Provo had claimed that Brother Paul [Professor Richard D. Poll], a member of the [history] faculty, is a Communist, but President Wilkinson said that he has been unable to get any items of any kind to prove this assertion and that he personally is satisfied that he does not favor Communism.</u>

September 19, 1961. <u>Communism</u> (Note by C[lare] M[iddlemiss]): Today when <u>Mr. Victor Riesel</u>[35] visited President <u>McKay, he asked if the Church was pacifistic and would be opposed to bearing arms</u> in the case of a showdown with communism. President McKay declared the Church was <u>militantly opposed to the godless atheism of communism and would not hesitate to oppose force with force if it became necessary.</u>

September 22, 1961, First Presidency meeting. We were agreed that it would be appropriate to make Bishop [Joseph L.] Wirthlin secretary

---

35. Victor Riesel (1914–95) was a noted journalist for the *New York Post*. He most famously uncovered corruption in labor unions and was accosted on the street in 1956 by members of the Lucchese crime family in Manhattan, who threw sulfuric acid in his face, permanently blinding him. He nevertheless continued writing his nationally syndicated column.

and treasurer of the Deseret Title Holding Corporation in connection with the proposed release of Bishop Wirthlin as Presiding Bishop of the Church at this coming conference. I mentioned that with the release of Bishop Wirthlin his counselors would also be released. ... I said that I would call Bishop Wirthlin into my office and tell him of this appointment and of his proposed release as Presiding Bishop.

In regard to counselors in the Presiding Bishopric, I said the new Bishop will have the right to choose his own counselors.

I recommended to my counselors that John H. Vandenberg[36] be chosen as successor to Bishop Wirthlin. ... I shall visit President [J. Reuben] Clark at his home and present to him the matter of the proposed reorganization of the Presiding Bishopric. ...

Presentation of General Authorities—Sustaining of Hugh B. Brown as Counselor

We gave some consideration to the matter as to how the First Presidency should be presented at the October Conference. I said that I felt that the Brethren should be presented as they were ordained and set apart—David O. McKay as President, J. Reuben Clark, Jr. as First Counselor, Henry D. Moyle as Second Counselor, constituting the First Presidency; then Hugh B. Brown as Counselor in the Presidency of the Church of Jesus Christ of Latter-day Saints, the four to be voted upon in that order. I said that it was not an innovation in the Church organization, and in that way we keep in mind the revelations of the Lord regarding the three presiding high priests constituting the First Presidency. In other words, we sustain the First Presidency and Hugh B. Brown as counselor in the First Presidency. It was suggested that if any explanation is made in regard to this matter, the General Priesthood Meeting would be the better place to make the explanation. I agreed to this suggestion.

---

36. John Henry Vandenberg (1904–92) was sustained as the ninth Presiding Bishop on September 30, 1961. He would become an Assistant to the Twelve and member of the First Quorum of Seventy after McKay's death. His parents were Dutch emigrants, and his wife, Ariena Stok, was also from Holland. He had met her on a church mission. He attended Weber Academy in Ogden (Weber State University), became an accountant for a livestock company at the Ogden Stockyards, and worked for the rest of his non-church career for a sheep and wool merchandiser in Denver.

September 23, 1961, 10 a.m. <u>I called on President J. Reuben Clark, Jr.</u> at his home at 80 D Street, <u>and presented to him</u>, as I have done for 27 years (having been chosen Counselor one year after he became Counselor to President [Heber J.] Grant), <u>official Church matters</u>. His devoted daughter, Louise, (Mrs. Mervyn Bennion)[37] answered the door and took me to President Clark who was in his wheelchair with a shawl around his shoulders. With tears in his eyes he listened to the matters that I presented to him, and gave his approval of the proposals made. <u>I could see that it would be impossible for him to be with us at our Conference meetings.</u> This was my last conference with him in this mortal life. He did not pay much attention to the details. He said, "What you Brethren have decided, I approve."

We went back even to our schooldays. We remembered that he and Sister [Emma Ray] McKay graduated together from the University of Utah. There were six graduates who got degrees that year, in 1898; Sister McKay (Ray Riggs), Molly Connelly (Mary Elizabeth Connelly), President Clark, Dr. Chamberlain (Ralph Vera Chamberlain), Dr. Hills (Herbert Thayer Hills), and Albert Johannsen.

President Clark was very emotional as he recalled the schooldays, and particularly the 27 years that we have stood shoulder to shoulder in the First Presidency. We caressed and bade each other goodbye. I left the house with a heavy heart and went directly to our apartment in the Hotel Utah.[38]

September 26, 1961, 8:30 a.m. Attended the meeting of the First Presidency. Among many matters we considered the following: ...

(3) <u>Church's Attitude Toward Negroes—A letter was read from Stewart L. Udall, [US] Secretary of the Interior,</u>[39] addressed to President

---

37. Clark's cherished son-in-law, Mervyn Bennion (1887–1941), was killed in the attack on Pearl Harbor twenty years earlier. Bennion was a graduate of the US Naval Academy (third in his class) and had advanced shortly after World War I to the rank of captain and the command of the *USS Bernadou* destroyer. At the time of his death, he was captain of the *USS West Virginia* battleship.

38. Being confined to a wheelchair and attended by his daughter and friends was hard for Clark. He suffered a stroke three days later, from which he would never recover. Quinn, *Elder Statesman*, 174–78.

39. Stewart Lee Udall (1920–2010) was born in St. Johns, Arizona, where his father was the stake president. He attended the University of Arizona, spent four years as a gunner on an air force bomber during World War II, practiced law, and was elected to the US

[Henry D.] Moyle and President [Hugh B.] Brown stating that he is deeply concerned over the growing criticisms of the Church with regard to the negro question and the rights of minority groups. ...

In connection with the letter from Secretary Udall, consideration was given to ... correspondence [that] has reference to a proposed transfer of 500 negroes within the next 12 months from Benicia Arsenal, Benicia, California, to Tooele, Utah, for duty at Tooele Ordnance Depot, and has particular reference to the matter of housing these negro families in the Tooele area, and raises the question as to whether these negroes will be encouraged and welcomed to attend social gatherings, Mormon churches and other churches, and the community swimming pool, as well as other community affairs, the same as members of other races in the city of Tooele.

I said that we should give the usual reply to Secretary Udall, that we always give on this question, namely, that we admit negroes into the Church by baptism, but we do not permit them to have the priesthood. So far as the matter of accepting the negroes in the Tooele area, that will be left entirely to the community of Tooele whether they accept them, loan them the money, or otherwise receive them, that is their responsibility. The fact is that we do not welcome negroes into our social affairs because if we did it would lead to inter-marriage, and we do not favor inter-marriage. We recommend that negroes marry negroes, and that whites marry whites, and we cannot modify that statement. We object to negroes marrying whites for their own happiness. I said that we cannot change our attitude until we receive a revelation from the Lord directing otherwise. I said it is a most difficult problem for us to meet when negro boys and girls attend our meetings, when a negro woman comes with her son to sacrament meeting and 11 boys out of the Primary are put on the stand to be recommended to receive ordination to the office of a deacon and the little negro boy has to sit down by his mother's side. It is a most heart-rending experience, but if we change it, we open the door for the priesthood to be given to the negroes. I said that I had to tell them just that in Brazil, and when the question was raised following a meeting

---

Congress as a Democrat. To Moyle and Brown, he wrote, "I am deeply concerned over the growing criticism of our church with regard to the issues of racial equality and the rights of minority groups. ... It is my judgment that unless something is done to clarify the official position of the church these sentiments will become the subject of widespread public comment and controversy" (Prince and Wright, *David O. McKay*, 68).

there, one man got up and said that he was in love with a negro girl and raised the question as to whether if he married her their children would be prohibited from receiving the priesthood, and I answered publicly that they would. I said that we have faced this question in the past, and we shall have to face it now, and I believe that our attitude is right.

September 28, 1961, 8:30–8:55 a.m. Held a meeting with Presidents Henry D. Moyle and Hugh B. Brown. Discussed with them important matters concerning the selection of new General Authorities.

8:55 a.m.—As I returned to my private office the telephone was ringing—it was Dr. LeRoy Kimball, to tell me that President [J. Reuben] Clark is "sinking." Dr. Kimball said he does not know just how long it will be before the end comes. My heart sank as I heard this news.

September 29, 1961, 9:15 a.m. President [J. Reuben] Clark's illness. Returned to my private office where I rested for a few moments. My secretary came in a few minutes later and told me that Dr. LeRoy Kimball was on the line. He had called to tell me that President J. Reuben Clark, Jr. is a little better than he was yesterday; however, that he thinks it is just a matter of days before he will be gone.

September 30, 1961, 7:30 a.m. Met by appointment in my private office Elder Gordon B. Hinckley, and interviewed him regarding his filling the vacancy in the Council of the Twelve. He was moved to tears, and said that he would do whatever we ask him to do.[40]

7:45 a.m.—I then met with Brother Boyd K. Packer[41] and told him that we should like him to accept a call to become an Assistant to the Twelve. Brother Packer was really overcome, and the tears flowed freely. He humbly accepted and said that he would do his best to merit the call.

40. For Hinckley's perspective, see Dew, *Go Forward with Faith*, 234.
41. Boyd Kenneth Packer (1924–) was at the time a supervisor in the church's Seminaries and Institutes of Religion. "The Twelve are waiting in the next room," McKay hurriedly informed him after their interview. "I am going to present your name as an Assistant to the Quorum of the Twelve Apostles, and I think they are going to approve you." Shortly before general conference, Moyle told the director of Seminaries and Institutes the Brethren "don't wish to call Brother Packer as an Assistant to the Twelve without your approval, but I must say," he added, "that we will call him whether you approve or not." Packer would become an apostle in April 1970. Tate, *Boyd K. Packer*, 124–25.

October 3, 1961, 8:30–10 a.m., meeting of the First Presidency. ... President [Henry D.] Moyle reported that he had been up to see President [J. Reuben] Clark; that he was taken up to his bedroom, but President Clark was sleeping, and he did not feel like disturbing him. I said that President Clark's daughter, Luacine, called me this morning. She said she felt like calling me and thanking me for the wonderful conference and for the prayers in behalf of her father. She said they were grateful for the consideration that had been extended to him. She said that he is now bedfast. I asked her how he had felt about the proceedings of the Conference, and the daughter said that President Clark had slept through most of the days of the Conference and was not aware of what was going on.

October 6, 1961, 7:30 a.m. Bishop Carl W. Buehner[42] called at the office. He apologized for some of the statements he made in his address at the general conference meeting on Sunday, October 1, 1961. "Really," he said, "if I had given way to my real feelings I would have bawled, and it would have been worse than what I did say. I feel all right about my release as counselor in the Presiding Bishopric, and will do anything you want me to do." I told him that I had always felt impressed that he would represent the church well in presiding over a mission in Germany, and that I had mentioned the fact particularly to him when I told him of his release as second counselor in the Presiding Bishopric. I said that I was very much disappointed when he told me that he did not speak German, and that Sister Buehner's health is not good. I said, "I shall tell you this morning that I still feel to let you know that I should like you to preside over one of the German Missions. I am not worried about your not speaking the German language—you know enough about it that you can fulfill a mission in that country." He said, "Oh, I can get along all right with it." Then he said, "I want to tell you that my patriarchal blessing says that I shall preside over a mission in the land of my birth." I told him that I am concerned about the health of Sister Buehner, and whatever operation she needs—and that I would see him again. ...

At 2:20 p.m., Mrs. Luacine Clark Fox, daughter to President J. Reuben Clark Jr. called for me at the office, to notify me that President Clark

---

42. This apology masked Buehner's disappointment at receiving another assignment. For more, see note at January 24, 1961.

had passed away at 2:10 p.m. My secretary, Clare Middlemiss, immediately got in touch with my [forty-seven-year-old] daughter, Emma Rae [Ashton],[43] who was at our apartment in the Hotel Utah, and left word with her. I was asleep, being pretty tired after having been busily engaged since six o'clock this morning, but my daughter awakened me to tell me of President Clark's passing.

I immediately got up and drove up to President Clark's home to express my sympathy to members of the family, and to make arrangements for funeral services. I returned to the office and called President Hugh B. Brown and all members of the Twelve for a meeting at which time they were notified of President Clark's passing. We then arranged for committees to take care of funeral services.

President Henry D. Moyle, who had just taken a plane for Europe, called me from Denver, Colorado. He said that Gordon Hinckley had called him at the Airport in Denver and notified him of President Clark's passing. I told him that we were now in meeting discussing plans for the funeral. I asked him when his first meeting in Europe was scheduled, and he said it was for Sunday, October 8, but that it was a servicemen's meeting and he was not scheduled to speak so he could easily cancel that appointment. I said that I thought it would be a great comfort to the family for him to return and to speak at the funeral; that he could then attend the council meeting on Thursday and leave Friday for Europe. ... I said, "please be back for the funeral Tuesday at 12:30 p.m." President Moyle answered, "I shall be there."

Following the meeting, we prepared a statement for the press regarding President Clark's death.[44]

October 10, 1961. Later [after the funeral] I received a telephone call from

---

43. Emma Rae McKay (1913–2006) married Conway Alan Ashton in 1939, and they had five children together. She was named after her mother, Emma Ray Riggs McKay. The daughter graduated from the University of Utah and taught high school in the Salt Lake Valley. After her husband retired from Beneficial Life Insurance Company, they filled a mission together to Scotland.

44. For many years during Clark's three decades in the First Presidency, he had been the de facto president because of the failing health of Presidents Heber J. Grant and George Albert Smith, and had trained younger men, primarily Ezra Taft Benson, Spencer W. Kimball, Harold B. Lee, Henry D. Moyle, and Marion G. Romney. Quinn, *Elder Statesman*, 138–39, 425–28.

President Clark's son Reuben [III] who expressed gratitude for the services. He said that the daughters and he were grateful for all that had been done to make this trying time easy for them.

October 11, 1961. I told Brother Henry D. Moyle, second counselor in the First Presidency, that I should like him to be my first counselor, and also told Brother Hugh B. Brown that I should like him to be my second counselor.

October 12, 1961. Was engaged in the meeting of the First Presidency and Council of the Twelve in the Salt Lake Temple.

New Counselors in the First Presidency
After the Brethren had all assembled in the Council room, I made the following remarks: President [J. Reuben] Clark has received the Call for which he has been waiting for a long while. He has finished his work, and it is our duty now as the Presidency to complete the Quorum of the First Presidency. I then said: "I recommend to you Brethren this morning that Brother Henry D. Moyle fill the vacancy caused by the passing of President Clark, and become the First Counselor to the President of the Church; and that Brother Hugh B. Brown be sustained as Second Counselor."

President Joseph Fielding Smith moved approval of the recommendation. Motion seconded by Elder Spencer W. Kimball and unanimously approved.

President Brown, the Brethren of the Council of the Twelve, and I then placed our hands upon the head of Brother Henry D. Moyle, and I was voice in ordaining him and setting him apart as First Counselor in the First Presidency of the Church.

President Moyle, the Brethren of the Council of the Twelve and I then laid our hands upon the head of Brother Hugh B. Brown and I was voice in ordaining him and setting him apart as Second Counselor in the First Presidency of the Church.

October 13, 1961, 11:45 a.m. Brother LaMar Williams came in to say goodbye before leaving for his assignment in Nigeria where he is going to investigate matters pertaining to the natives of Nigeria who have asked for baptism and for someone to come to Nigeria to help them organize the Church there. I told Brother Williams to investigate and <u>report to us</u> <u>especially how we can best get white men who are entitled to hold the</u> <u>Priesthood into Nigeria to preside over a Branch of the Church</u> if and when one is organized. I told Brother Williams that my blessings and prayers for the success of his mission are with him.

October 26, 1961, meeting of First Presidency and Twelve. I called attention to the fact that Bishop John H. Vanderberg has been serving as Assistant to the Chairman of the Building Committee, and in that capacity has had charge of the finances of the Building Committee and advances made to wards in connection with their building programs. I explained that in cases where the bishops need money to complete a project, instead of stopping the project, <u>we have been advancing money so that the build-</u> <u>ing construction could continue. I said these advances go into millions of</u> <u>dollars, and Brother Vandenberg has handled this phase of the building</u> <u>program in a masterful way for the Building Committee.</u>

I said the First Presidency <u>has not felt that there has been the proper</u> <u>relationship between the Presiding Bishopric and the Building Commit-</u> <u>tee regarding these funds,</u> because the bishops have to pay the money back to the Presiding Bishopric at a later time. Inasmuch as the <u>Presiding</u> <u>Bishopric is also handling tithing funds it would seem advisable that the</u> <u>Presiding Bishop handle that fund also,</u> instead of placing it with the Building Committee. It is therefore felt that Bishop Vandenberg should continue to handle the fund now that he is Presiding Bishop.

The Brethren approved of this recommendation.

November 1, 1961, 9:30–10:30 a.m., First Presidency meeting. … <u>Temple</u> <u>in the Washington, D.C. Area</u>—President [Hugh B.] Brown reported that while he was recently in the New England Mission, President Carr said that Brother Franklin D. Richards had called a meeting of all <u>mis-</u> <u>sion presidents in that group of missions</u> and that they <u>were going to</u> <u>select a site for the temple.</u> President Brown said that President Milan D. Smith of the Washington [DC] Stake has made certain recommendations regarding securing a temple site, and had sent some information regarding the territory there. He said that the stake and mission presidents in that area have agreed that when we do select a site it should be in Washington, D.C.,[45] rather than in Florida, New York, or elsewhere. It was the sentiment of the Brethren that the stake presidents and mission presidents have no jurisdiction in a matter of this kind.

November 9, 1961, 8 a.m. Arrived at the office late this morning. I slept for eight hours last night, the first time in a long while that I have slept this long.

November 16, 1961, 7:15 a.m. Arrived at the office—was busy with regular duties until 8:00 a.m. at which time President [Hugh B.] Brown and I met by appointment Congressman David S. King[46] who reaffirmed his allegiance to the things of the spirit and the things of the kingdom. He discussed what he thought were actions that indicated that perhaps there was an abandonment by the Church of its neutrality in politics. He mentioned cases that had come to his attention by report. One thing he mentioned was that it had come to his attention that Sunday School teachers are making broad hints and innuendoes in classes that those who follow the Democratic program are handmaidens of Communists, and cannot expect to consider themselves in full fellowship in the Church. He urged that the First Presidency say something in print as to where the Church stands on politics. He said he understood the Church had spoken officially sometime in the past, but he thinks that the average Democrat does not know where to find it. He then discussed the general direction of the Democratic administration which he thinks is in complete harmony with Gospel principles. He also set forth his political philosophy.

I remarked to him that the action of the President of the Church in choosing two Democrats for counselors should be sufficient indication

---

45. The Church officially announced the plans for the Washington, DC, temple on November 15, 1968. Groundbreaking occurred three weeks later (conducted by Brown), and the temple was dedicated November 19–22, 1974, by Spencer W. Kimball

46. David Sjodahl King (1917-2009) was elected to the U.S. House of Representatives in 1958 and 1960, defeating the Republican candidates William A. Dawson and Sherman P. Lloyd, respectively. Prior to running for office, King was an assistant to Elbert R. Curtis of the church's Young Men's Mutual Improvement Association, 1948–58. He opted to run for the US Senate in 1962 against incumbent Senator Wallace F. Bennett and lost. He would later serve as ambassador to the Malagasy Republic and Mauritius, respectively, and as an alternate director of the World Bank. His later years were devoted to church service as president of the mission in Port-au-Prince, Haiti, and from 1990 to 1993 as president of the Washington, DC, temple. He was the son of Utah Democratic Senator William H. King (1863–1949), who served from 1917 to 1941.

that the Democrats have a definite place in the Church. I said that all we need to do is to republish what we have heretofore said on the political stand of the Church.[47]

I told Congressman King that he has my confidence and very best wishes. I asked him to convey my kind regards to President [John F.] Kennedy.

December 1, 1961, First Presidency and Budget Committee. The [1962] budget, as now presented, is $20,000,000 over the estimated income of the Church. After a lengthy discussion, ... I said that we should, as nearly as possible, cut our budget down to our estimated income, and if we have to make capital investments, that is a different thing. It was decided that the capital investments, such as Archives building, new office building, garage and foundation, retirement center, Deseret Gym, auditorium, Bureau of Information, etc., should all be eliminated from the budget; also the Oakland Temple, improvements in the Salt Lake Temple, and the Los Angeles apartments, that they are not budget items.

It was also agreed that a campaign should be started to increase the tithing income; this campaign to be part of the Stake Conference programs for 1962, so that in every stake conference the payment of tithing would be considered. It was also felt that some disciplinary action should be taken regarding our expenditures in order that the wards, stakes and missions may know that we need more tithing. It was mentioned that notwithstanding there has been an increase in tithe-paying, yet the percentage of tithe-payers is still not what it should be by any means.

We shall take to the Council next Thursday the decision to carry on a tithing campaign as a part of the quarterly [stake] conference program. I said that we should hope to increase the tithing by $15,000,000 in order to keep within our budget. I said I have that confidence in the people,

---

47. The neutrality question will always be a thorny issue in Mormon political realms. Despite repeated statements by church leaders, the members, and some of the leaders, drag political-party affiliation and topics into church circles, taking at times fanatical stands where the church has spoken otherwise. Much of King's concern originated with the ascendency of the right-wing John Birch Society and partisan, inflammatory statements of recent Secretary of Agriculture and church apostle Ezra Taft Benson. See Quinn, *Extensions*, 66–115. For a concise set of statements on the church's position with regard to politics, see Bergera, *Statements*, 317–28.

<u>and I think that we can do it. I indicated that I did not in any way want to retard the progress of the Church.</u>

December 15, 1961, meeting with George W. Romney, president of Detroit Stake, regarding his possible candidacy for governor of Michigan. [48]I said that the negroes are admitted into the Church by baptism; they are welcome to become members of the Church, and members of a ward, and to partake of the Sacrament and have full fellowship in every thing but not to be ordained to the Priesthood. President Romney said he thought it would be correct to say that the negroes do not have a complete picture, but they do have a picture that has been widely distributed among the negroes in this country that we do not permit them to have the Priesthood, and they build upon that, and say we have a race bias. I said that <u>"we can offer them all that any other Church can offer, and we do advocate care in marriage; we advocate that Mexicans marry Mexicans; Japanese marry Japanese; Catholics marry Catholics, and Mormons marry Mormons; for the ... good [of] family harmony and peace.[49] We look with hesitancy, and, one might say, suspicion on our Church allowing negroes, Chinese, Japanese, Hawaiians, to mingle with each other. That, of course, would encourage marriage.["]</u>

President Romney said he thinks there is no question that most people would agree in this position, and that people of other religious faiths, who have given serious thought to the question, favor <u>intra-faith</u> rather than <u>inter-faith</u> marriages.

<u>I said that so far as the colored question is concerned, we offer the negroes, and the Indians from India, and the Mexicans, the Japanese, and the Chinese every privilege of the Gospel that any other Church can offer excepting only that the negro is not permitted to the Priesthood. I said, "Now, I think we can stand on that."</u>

---

48. George W. Romney (1907–95) was born in the Mexican Mormon colonies from which his family fled during the Mexican Revolution. His rise in the post-war business world ended with his appointment as chair of the recently merged American Motors Corporation in 1954. He remained in that position until his bid for the Michigan governorship, which he won, remaining until his appointment to the Nixon cabinet as US Secretary of Housing and Urban Development (1969–73). He later served as a church patriarch and regional representative. He was the father of future Massachusetts governor and Republican US presidential candidate Mitt Romney.

49. The diary has "for the of good family harmony and peace."

December 22, 1961. The sending of 2,000 Christmas cards, in addition to preparing gifts for many close associates, employees, friends, and Loved Ones, is quite a project. Notwithstanding all this, I love Christmas and it is a joyous time of the year.

12 Nigeria and Nigerians, Political and Polygamous Problems, 1962

Brother Tanner will go down, accompanied by Brother LaMar Williams and the two couples, and receive the Nigerian people into the Church with a full knowledge that they will have every blessing of membership excepting the Priesthood. I stated that we have made no promise, and we shall state plainly to them that they are not to have the Priesthood. —October 11, 1962

January 3, 1962, First Presidency meeting. Among other matters we considered a letter from President George Romney of the Detroit Stake. President Romney expressed his appreciation for the interest, advice and counsel given him by the First Presidency on the occasion of his visit. He reviewed recent developments in Michigan; the meeting last week of the Board of Directors of "Citizens for Michigan" at which the consensus was that he had fully discharged his obligations and should feel free to enter his candidacy for governor of Michigan; that several Democratic members and independents have urged him to run; that "Citizens for Michigan" is hopeful of receiving a grant from the Ford Foundation which will enable them to carry out some of its broader objectives; that the state's leading negro Democrats strongly advises that Brother Romney be a candidate, and that it would help rather than to hurt in the writing of the state constitution if he is a candidate; his prospective candidacy is being sought by conservative Republicans. The constitutional convention[1] is starting its

---

1. A convention was convened in 1961 to rewrite the state constitution, with Romney as vice president of the convention. It took seven months to complete the document. It was accepted by voters in 1963.

decisive period and this will be completed by January 31st. Brother Romney's maximum influence will be given in that period. He expects that by the time the committee reports the situation will be cleared. ...

He expressed the desire that his candidacy would not be hurtful to the Church by reason of the negro question. ...

After careful consideration, I said that we do not want to take the responsibility of telling him not to run, and it is not right for him to give us that responsibility. President [Henry D.] Moyle said we should say that we want him to remain as stake president, and that he should make his own decision without any feeling that if he decides to run it will be detrimental to the Church.

I said that it will not be detrimental in any way, but it will be detrimental to his candidacy if he is released before. We should let him run as president of the Detroit Stake and win as president of the stake. If he fails in nomination or election, he is still president of the stake.

January 9, 1962, First Presidency meeting. The following conversation ensued concerning the problem of taking the Gospel to those asking for baptism in Nigeria:[2]

President McKay: "A very important question we have to decide, and we will bring it up next Thursday—we have all heard the report of Brother Williams regarding Nigeria—we have several hundred people there who have taken upon themselves the name of the Church of Jesus Christ of Latter-day Saints unauthoritatively, and they are asking that we come down. What shall be our attitude toward this invitation?"[3]

President [Hugh B.] Brown: "It is probably a precedent establishing decision."

President McKay: "It is as great in the Church today as the question that nearly split the primitive Church when they preached only to the Jews."

President [Henry D.] Moyle: "Sooner or later it will have to receive the same answer."

---

2. Hugh B. Brown reflected in his autobiography that "a serious problem that has confronted us especially during the past few decades has been our denying the priesthood to the Negro. Personally, I doubt if we can maintain or sustain ourselves in the position we seem to have adopted but which has no justification in the scriptures, as far as I know. The president says it can only come through revelation." Firmage, *Abundant Life*, 129.

3. See Prince and Wright, *David O. McKay*, 60–105.

President McKay: "Before that time every Roman or Gentile had to become a Jew to become a member of the church. Paul is given credit for having carried the gospel to the Gentiles, and I suppose he did, but he had made them Jews by circumcision and of abstaining from meats and so on, but really that revelation came to Peter."

President Brown: "He opened the door."

President McKay: "It took the Lord to do it, and he and Paul were witnesses before the twelve when the Twelve had to decide whether to carry the gospel to the Gentiles. James presided at that meeting, James the brother of the Lord, because Peter was a witness and Paul was a witness, and Peter related the experience he had when he had the vision on the housetop, you remember, a sheet was lowered with several meats. In the dream, the Lord said: 'Rise, Peter, kill and eat,' and he said: 'Not so Lord; for I have never eaten anything that is common or unclean.' And the voice said: 'What God had cleansed, that call not thou common.' When he went to Cornelius, the centurion, he sat down, contrary to his teaching and training, to the table with those Gentiles. It was against the rules. But he heard Cornelius—it was Cornelius, the centurion. The Holy Ghost came upon the centurion, and Peter said: 'Can any man forbid water, that these should not be baptized which have received the Holy Ghost as well as we?' The only exception in the holy scripture that the Holy Ghost came without baptism, and it took the experience of Cornelius, and that was even after the dream. 'Can we forbid baptism to those who receive the Holy Ghost as well as we?' And he gave the testimony to the Twelve. James gave the decision that they can join the Church without circumcision. Even after that it was hard for some members of the Church to sit down to the table and eat with Gentiles. Peter sat down with them and Paul was offended with him when some members came from the Jerusalem church and Peter got up from the table and walked away. That prompted Paul's saying: 'I withstood him to his face,' because he did not conform to the ruling and he was recalcitrant. Contrast Peter's remark when he referred to Paul saying: 'Our beloved brother Paul ... hath written ... things in which are some things hard to be understood when they that are ... unstable wrest as they do other scriptures, unto their own destruction.'"

"Well, that is the beginning of the Gentiles coming into the Church.

They did not comprehend what Jesus said: 'Go ye into all the world and preach the gospel unto every creature, and he that believeth and is baptized shall be saved, and he that believeth not shall be damned.' Now we are facing just such a crisis, and we had better be united on it either one way or the other."

President Moyle: "I have never been able to reconcile myself to the thought that we won't baptize them."

President McKay: "We have baptized them."

President Moyle: "That has been my feeling."

President McKay: "We baptize them here in the Church, and they are entitled to it."

President Moyle: "After that is settled, the only question left is the procedure which we are following, not only in baptizing them, but in taking care of them after baptism."

President McKay: "There is no other conclusion so far as we are concerned, but every colored man, every negro and Indian are classed with the negroes in Africa, but they are not. An Indian can receive the priesthood, and the negro cannot receive the priesthood."

President Brown: "I am wondering, President McKay, if we are not in much the same position. Can we deny them having received the Holy Ghost unless we can say that they have [not] been converted by the holy spirit. If they have been converted and they are truly converted, if they are converted by the spirit, who are we to deny them? It seems to me that there is a comparable situation there, and I agree with Brother Moyle, we can do nothing else. It raises many problems—they are very poor people, they are pretty much illiterate. It will involve much over-seeing and guidance."

President McKay: "We will have to furnish them that from here. We will have to send your son and my son, and my grandson and your grandson."

President Brown: "To labor with them. It is a tremendous decision."

President McKay: "To have this answered properly and to take care of them properly, there will be thousands come into the Church."

President Moyle: "And they will be spared from membership in the Catholic Church."

President McKay: "I think they should remain where they are; to urge marriage among their kind. The question of intermarriage bothers me more than anything."

President Moyle: "I have been sort of obsessed with the idea all the way along that in our organization it ought to be combined as far as possible to our auxiliary organizations. I don't know whether that is sound or not, but where they are not going to hold the priesthood themselves, it seems to me that it would be consistent for them to be organized into auxiliary organizations that we are going to have, if Brother [LaMar] Williams' report[4] is right, and I am sure it is, we are going to have a concentration of them there as far as numbers are concerned to justify wards and stakes, and I have never been able to think that out in my mind. I have dealt more with the idea that they will be organized on the Sabbath Day as Sunday Schools, and we would have to have someone there occasionally for any regular administration of the Sacrament to them, and week-day auxiliary activities could be carried on in many branches without the priesthood. It is auxiliary to the priesthood unless we were to look forward and have a large corps of missionaries there rather than a small corps to travel, just a few missionaries that would travel and take care of ordinations of the priesthood, that will be necessary such as baptism, confirmation, administration of the Sacrament, administration of the sick and blessing children. They could themselves in their own auxiliary organizations take care of the balance of their activities."

President Brown: "I wonder if the time is coming when we will give the Lesser Priesthood to them, whether the prohibition or direction with respect to the priesthood upon which we rely applies to both the Melchizedek and the Aaronic priesthood. I have never thought of it before, but I wonder if we give them the Aaronic Priesthood, and then they could administer the Sacrament and baptize under the direction of the missionaries, but that is a matter I do not know about."

President McKay: "You do that and you give them the priesthood."

President Moyle: "There is no doubt about that."

President Brown: "That's the opening of the door. I don't think the time has come, but it may come when the Lord directs it, but we can go along the lines President Moyle indicates."

---

4. This was an hour-long oral report to the First Presidency by LaMar S. Williams after a month-long trip to Africa at the end of 1961. After meeting with the groups that called themselves Latter-day Saints, he became "a passionate partisan for missionary work in Nigeria," according to James B. Allen, "Would-be Saints," 227.

President McKay: "That means that there is no other line within the organization of the Church. You have the Sunday School as a part of the ward; Primary, the Mutual Improvement Association, is part of the ward, and you have the Relief society."

President Moyle: "We have Sunday Schools in the Church today out in the mission field that are only related to the mission and not to a branch or ward."

President McKay: "It is always related to a branch, always."

President Moyle: "In the mission field today we are holding Sunday Schools not related to any branch."

President McKay: "That's the beginning of a branch; it belongs to it. The authority is of the branch."

President Moyle: "Mainly they function under the mission president."

President McKay: "It functions under the mission president, yes."

President Moyle: "If we have a mission president, we have a Sunday school and other auxiliaries in each of the places where we have a concentration of membership without having anyone between them and the mission president, such as a group or branch or district president. I am just asking the question—I am not saying—is that not possible?"

President McKay: "Here is a problem that is real. Already in the Church we have colored people, members of the Church, they are faithful in attendance to their duties; they keep the Word of Wisdom, pay their tithing, attend their meetings. The children participate in the Primary from four years and on; the young girls and young men participate in the auxiliary associations. They study the lessons and associate with the white people in every way in the Church; they are just as faithful as members of the Church—those with whom we have met. In Primary the little boys and girls answer the questions and study the lessons and when they are eight years of age, they are baptized and confirmed before the Church. When a boy becomes 12 years of age, in Sacrament meeting, he goes with his fellow Primary members and the custom now is to have these young men who are about to be ordained deacons sit up on the stand and be presented by the Primary worker to the bishop as being worthy to be accepted as deacons. In that Sacrament meeting the colored boy has to sit down by the side of his mother and the other boys walk up. He has been received all the way along as a member of the Church and has participated in everything else, but now at that meeting he sits down, unworthy to be associated."

President Moyle: "It is a rude segregation."

President McKay: "Now if you give him the Lesser Priesthood, the time will come—"

President Brown: "The problem will come when he should be ordained a deacon and when he will be a priest and then an elder. The situation will not obtain in Africa for quite a long time."

President Moyle: "Suppose they migrate after baptism? We can't compel them not to."

President McKay: "You can't compel them not to."

President Moyle: "That's one of the hazards. If the spirit of gathering gets on them, they will come, and you can't stop them. It will be some time, however, before the economic condition will permit their migration." ...

"When it becomes known that we are over there, of course, and have baptized this colony, it will become known to the negroes of this country, and they will take whatever advantage they can in their fight against us."

President McKay: "No question about it. There is a disposition on the part of the southern negroes to push themselves. If I lived in the south I would not want to be associated with that."

President Moyle: "The organization's headquarters is in Chicago. That is the NAACP [National Association for the Advancement of Colored People]."

"If they would stay with themselves and marry among themselves, the question will be easy, but intermarriage would be an inevitable result, and I don't believe in it."

"There seems to be less compunction in Europe. White girls marry negroes. They have no trouble in picking up a German or French or English white girl."

President McKay: "Now brethren, we have got to decide before next Tuesday. We will present it to the Twelve and make a decision."

President Moyle: "Should you present it to the Twelve until your mind is clear as to what we should do? That will inevitably lead to an expression of many views over there. It has just been my feeling, or maybe my hope, that you would satisfy yourself as to what should be done and advise us."

President McKay: "I want to hear from them just as we have heard from you this morning."

President Moyle: "That's fine."

President McKay: "We are facing a problem just as serious as that before the original Twelve."

President Brown: "The same problem. The color doesn't matter. Shall we preach the gospel to every creature."

President McKay: "That's clear, they are entitled to the gospel, but the priesthood is another thing."

President Brown: "You don't intend to decide any change on that at this time."

President McKay: "You can't deal with this in a proper way unless you do. God bless you, brethren."

January 18, 1962, 8:40–9:50 a.m. Brother Gordon B. Hinckley ... reported on <u>reductions proposed in mission budgets</u> for 1962 in accordance with the direction to reduce the budgets by $200,000.00.

February 2, 1962, First Presidency meeting. We then discussed the matter of the proposed construction of a civic auditorium on the property that the Church owns between South Temple and First South and West Temple and First West. The Presidency have heretofore decided that we would not join with the city in the matter of having a civic auditorium. I said that in thinking the matter over, I think we should ascertain how much money we have invested in this property, and then consider whether or not we would be willing to turn the property over to the City and County that they might construct a civic auditorium thereon, they to pay us the cost of the property, but that we have nothing whatever to do with the auditorium itself; then, if at some time in the future we wanted to build our own auditorium we might build it perhaps on the site originally considered, north of the Tabernacle. I further said that any negotiations that we may have regarding this civic auditorium should be with the committee headed by Gus Backman, that the members of this committee are good citizens, and I am willing to go as far as I can to help them.[5] ...

---

5. The result was construction in 1967–69 of the Salt Palace for conventions, concerts, and professional basketball games featuring the Utah Stars. It had a 10,000-seat

[A meeting of the First Presidency and Presiding Bishopric:] Bishop [John H.] Vandenberg mentioned that at the present time the membership records do not indicate race or color of the individual, that however at times the question is raised as to how many members we have of a certain race, particularly in regard to negroes.

President [Henry D.] Moyle mentioned that President George Romney of the Detroit [Michigan] Stake called him regarding a meeting he was going to have with the negro national organization in Detroit, and he said that if the figures were available he would like very much to know how many members of the Church there are with negro blood. President Moyle said he had already sent to President Romney information he had been able to obtain from the Historians Office regarding the three negroes that came to these valleys with the pioneers in July 1847. As to the number of negroes in the Church he had referred this matter to the Presiding Bishopric. He felt it might be advantageous to know how many negroes, how many Chinese, Japanese, and other races there are. I said that to do this would result in emphasizing the number of negroes and the distinction between the Caucasian and the negro races and would perhaps raise some knotty problems and I suggested that we think further about this matter before taking any action. ...

The question was again raised in regard to permitting two young ladies who it is suspected may have a mixture of negro blood to serve as local missionaries in Brazil. Neither of these girls is dark, nor can it be readily recognized that they have negro blood, but one is a daughter of a man who, while a member of the Church, shows signs of having negro blood.[6]

I said that for the present <u>we will draw the line where it is known definitely that they have negro blood, but where they are merely suspected of having negro blood they should be given the benefit of the doubt.</u>[7]

February 15, 1962, 8:05–8:50 a.m. Attended the meeting of the First

---

capacity. When the Delta Center (now Vivint Arena) was built nearby with twice as many seats, the Salt Palace was renovated to be used strictly for conventions.

6. For more on this, see Mark Grover's "Religious Accommodation in the Land of Racial Democracy: Mormon Priesthood and Black Brazilians" in the fall 1984 issue of *Dialogue: A Journal of Mormon Thought*.

7. See the entry of January 17, 1954, for McKay's account of his personal encounter with this issue; also McKay, *Home Memories*, 226–31.

Presidency, and there I told my counselors of the meeting with Elder [Ezra Taft] Benson regarding Anti-Communistic Activities. Brother Benson is very much concerned regarding certain information that has been given out in Seattle. A member of the high council up there has written to him regarding instructions that one of the members of the First Presidency has given the president of that stake by telephone in answer to a letter of inquiry he had written to the First Presidency. He said that a member of the First Presidency had told him that they shouldn't permit any discussions of communism in their Church meetings, especially in any Sunday School or young people's firesides. He said that he could not speak for the other members of the First Presidency who were out of town. A few days later a member of the stake presidency announced in the stake preparation meeting that there should be no discussions of Communism, that the people were not well enough informed to discuss it.

President [Henry D.] Moyle recalled this conversation and explained the circumstances. He had said to the stake president in substance, that it was his judgment, and he was speaking for no one but himself [in saying] it was not proper for us in firesides and in our Church meetings to get into controversial matters, and that there was a controversy over [W. Cleon] Skousen's talks, and these things should not take place in our formal religious gatherings. He told the stake president he was not prepared to give any official statement, that when there was an official statement to be given it would be given in writing over the signature of the First Presidency, and that so far as he knew there had been no formal approval of either "The Naked Communist" by Cleon Skousen, or the "American Heritage of Freedom" [by Ezra Taft Benson].[8]

I commented that I have given public approval of Skousen's book "The Naked Communist" in General Conference, and that the "American Heritage of Freedom" is a pamphlet containing Brother Benson's October Conference address, that I knew nothing wrong with Elder Benson's talk, and thought it to be very good.

---

8. Benson's October 1961 general conference address, "The American Heritage of Freedom: A Plan of God," was being distributed as a pamphlet. In his address he warned that there was a "world-wide secret conspiracy" against the free-enterprise system. "No true Latter-day Saint and no true American can be a socialist or a communist or support programs leading in that direction," he said. *Improvement Era*, Dec. 1961, 952–57.

President [Hugh B.] Brown said that his only objection is that Elder Benson's talk puts socialism and Communism in the same category, that all the people in Scandinavia and other European countries are under Socialistic governments and certainly are not Communists. Brother Benson's talk ties them together and makes them equally abominable. If this is true, our people in Europe who are living under a Socialist government are living out of harmony with the Church.[9]

It was decided to invite Brother Benson to meet with the First Presidency Monday morning, February 19th.

February 19, 1962, First Presidency meeting. <u>Elder Ezra Taft Benson</u>, by appointment, came into the meeting. We discussed the matter of communism and <u>Elder Benson's participation on the Advisory Council of the All American Society</u>,[10] an Anti-Communist Organization. Reference was made to a letter from a high councilman in the Seattle Stake, requesting explanation as to the Church's stand on the matter of speakers referring and discussing communism in Church meetings.

After much consideration, it was decided that Elder Benson should call the president of the Seattle Stake to have this matter cleared, and to remove all questions as to Elder Benson's responsibility and participation in Anti-Communistic activities.

After the departure of Elder Benson, the First Presidency agreed that now was not the time for the Church to make a statement as to its stand against Communism, but that such a statement could be made at a later date.

February 28, 1962, First Presidency meeting. A letter from Uda Eta of Nigeria was read. The writer expressed thanks for sending the missionaries, LaMar Williams, and Elder [Marvin] Jones, to Nigeria in November 1961, and asked if other missionaries will be sent to organize the groups. Another letter from Aska Apani also expressed interest in having the missionaries.

---

9. For more on this topic, see Quinn, *Extensions*, 71, 74, 443n59.

10. The All-American Society was a recent creation of W. Cleon Skousen. It had just been called an "exemplar of the far-right ultras" in a national news magazine. "The Ultras," *Time*, Dec. 8, 1961.

I reviewed my intention to present to the Council of the Twelve tomorrow the proposal that Nigeria be made a part of the West European Mission under President Tanner; that LaMar Williams be sent down to open the mission; that he go for six months; that he take with him two couples without children; that no announcement be made, but that they be sent down with President Tanner and let them baptize the people in accordance with the action of the Twelve; have them organized into branches and direct the finishing of the meeting houses which are now partly finished.

I said: "We can do with the Nigerian Mission what we are doing with the others—furnish enough money to finish these new branch houses and give them credit for their labor on an 80–20 basis, and then we will have President Tanner and LaMar and these two couples make recommendations to us. Brother LaMar Williams has been asked to recommend couples to accompany him."

It was agreed that this suggestion be given to the Council at the meeting tomorrow.

March 1, 1962, First Presidency meeting. The following conversation ensued regarding the Nigerian question:

President McKay: "We would like to present today our recommendation regarding letters and action taken by the Twelve regarding Nigeria. I have had a talk with Brother [LaMar] Williams. He is swamped with inquiries from the so-called branches in Nigeria as to what policy will be established regarding their request to join the Church. I have this to recommend:

First, that we organize a Nigerian Mission; that the organization be placed not under South Africa, but under the West European Mission, President [N. Eldon] Tanner; that Brother Tanner with his approval and our suggestion appoint Brother Williams temporarily as president of the Nigerian Mission; that Brother Williams go down without his family; that Brother Williams accompany President Tanner down there; that they take with them two couples without children and that the four attend to the baptizing of the people in the branches."

President [Hugh B.] Brown: "Two pairs of elders?"

President [Henry D.] Moyle: "No, a man and wife."

President McKay: "A man and his wife without children. It is no place to take children down there. These men will have to choose later. We have asked for some names. They are looking for them now. President Tanner, Brother Williams, and those two couples should go down and meet these so-called branches, and that they authoritatively baptize those who have been baptizing themselves into the Church."

President Brown: "I don't think they have baptized, have they?"

President McKay: "They have been doing baptizing, but they recognize that it is without authority. They would then organize their branches under the direction of these elders. They have also in an unfinished state several chapels which they have built themselves but they have not finished them. Let Brother Tanner and Brother Williams report back to the First Presidency the unfinished chapels, and we shall present these to the Expenditures Committee on the same basis as we do in other places, 70–30, and let them build their own chapels, and we shall furnish enough cash on the same basis and let them have a place to worship, and these missionaries will continue to hold branch meetings weekly or monthly and administer the sacrament and organize the auxiliaries to be presided over by the local men and try not to make any publicity, not to give it any publicity, but it will have publicity over the Church as soon as we do it. That is as far as we can go today if that is approved."

President Brown: "We will not give it any publicity here."

President McKay: "Try not to." We then discussed the choosing of the couples to accompany President Tanner and Brother Williams, and it was decided that we would wait until recommendations had been received before considering this further. ...

10:00 a.m.–3:00 p.m.—Attended Council Meeting [of the First Presidency and Twelve] held in the Salt Lake Temple. At this meeting, I again called attention to the situation in Nigeria where a large number of natives of the black race, about 4,000 in all, claim that they are converted to the truth of the gospel and are appealing for baptism and membership in the Church. I mentioned the fact that the matter had been before the Twelve, and each one of the Brethren, as well as the Brethren of the First Presidency, had expressed himself on the question. I also mentioned that Brother LaMar Williams has received literally dozens of letters from these people.

At the meeting of the Council when this matter was given consideration, the First Presidency had promised to bring to the Council some definite recommendation based upon the attitude of the Brethren at that time, and so I presented the following suggestions for consideration by the Presidency and the Twelve:

(1) That a mission be organized in Nigeria without any public announcement or fanfare, and that it be not attached to the South African Mission, but to the West European Mission. Nigeria has been under the direction of England, and they have had a Governor–General there who was an Englishman. Now they are independent. Most of them speak English, especially the young people. One group cannot understand the native language spoken by another group 50 or 100 miles away, so when they come together the universal language is English, a sort of pidgin English.

(2) That we appoint LaMar S. Williams to return to Nigeria without his family and spend such time as is necessary with President N. Eldon Tanner of the West European Mission in organizing these groups; also that he and President Tanner take with them two married couples, with no children, to labor there. The decision as to who these couples will be will rest with the Presidency and the Twelve. These four men can then do the official baptizing of the members of these groups numbering almost 4,000 people. It is also recommended that the two couples remain there and visit these groups once a week, once in two weeks, or once every month, as may be necessary, giving them the privilege of the Sacrament after they have been baptized properly, and organizing them into auxiliaries, and appointing local authorities who are worthy and capable of guiding these groups. They will probably land at Port Harcourt, which is the largest port. The accommodations there are good, but the headquarters will probably be at Aba,[11] 40 miles northeast inland from the port. That is where the large group is located.

(3) That President Tanner and Elder Williams be authorized to inspect unfinished meeting houses which the people there are attempting to build by their own effort, and recommend to the First Presidency and

---

11. Aba, Nigeria, is a city of half a million that grew from a string of villages along the Aba and Imo Rivers that flow toward Port Harcourt and the Bight of Bonny, part of the Gulf of Guinea. Aba is where the British colonial headquarters had been and where the LDS temple would be dedicated in 2005.

the Twelve the amount of money to be appropriated to finish these meeting houses, the Church to assist them on the same basis as we help other missions—namely, 70–30, giving them credit for their local labor, and the Church furnishing the cash necessary.

President Joseph Fielding Smith moved approval of these recommendations. Motion seconded by Elder Spencer W. Kimball, and unanimously approved.

Elder Harold B. Lee asked if these brethren would set apart those who are called to preside over the various auxiliary organizations, and I answered that they would, and that they would do it authoritatively, but these local people would not serve by virtue of the Priesthood.

Elder Lee also inquired if the Brethren felt assured of the personal safety of these white missionaries, and reminded of what had happened to the whites in northern Nigeria.[12]

I called attention to Brother Williams' report wherein it was stated that no woman had been molested there for several years. I said that we would, of course, have to wait to hear from President Tanner and Brother Williams and these elders, that we should feel our way in the matter; that, however, we cannot ignore their appeals for baptism. I said they will want schools, and the government will pay the teachers. I added that I have asked for a list of people who might be considered for appointment to this mission, and would submit the list of names at the next meeting of the council.

It was thought that the first thing Brother Tanner and Brother Williams should do would be to consult the government officials. I stated that the Spirit will have to guide us, and that we are facing a very important epoch in the history of the Church.

Elder Lee expressed the thought that the Brethren of this group should have the understanding that any expressions on the subject should come from the First Presidency and not from anyone else; that we should not become publicity agents for what is happening in Nigeria.

---

12. The hostility in Nigeria between the Muslim north and the Christian and Yoruba south increased after the country was granted independence in 1960 and culminated in the civil war of 1967–70, in which 145,000 soldiers were killed and 2 million civilians died through violence and starvation. The situation became especially dire in the predominantly Christian breakaway region of Biafra.

I concluded that this is just as important in our history as when James presided over the Council that gave consideration to the matter of carrying the gospel to the Gentiles, when Peter gave testimony, as also did Paul, and James gave the decision that was carried by the Twelve.

March 12, 1962, 7:00 a.m. According to appointment, I called at the office of Dr. L[ouis] E. Viko, who gave me a physical examination. He said that my blood pressure was okay, and that I seemed normal in every respect. He took a sample of blood in order to see its condition following the recent nasal hemorrhage which I had.

I said to Dr. Viko: "I am still dragging my feet, and my voice is not so strong;" to which he answered: "A much younger man carrying the responsibility you have would be as tired—I don't believe there is another man in the world doing what you are doing."

March 16, 1962, First Presidency meeting. Among many other matters discussed at this meeting, we considered again the statement on fasting for publication in the Improvement Era. Bishop [Victor L.] Brown of the Presiding Bishopric presented for review the proposed wording of a statement about fasting, which is desired for publication in the Improvement Era. Bishop [John H.] Vandenberg said: "Fasting is refraining from two consecutive meals."

After consideration, President [Hugh B.] Brown said, "That is all we need to say," and I agreed that this is so.

Bishop Vandenberg said that it is a positive statement, and it leaves it optional.[13]

March 23, 1962, 7:30 a.m. At my request, Brother Frank G. Berg, President of the Monument Park West Stake called at the office. I reported to him the information that has come to me concerning Dr. J. D. Williams,[14] Bishop of the Monument Park Sixth Ward and Professor at the

---

13. See Bergera, *Statements*, 156–61.
14. John Daniel Williams (1926–2007) was a popular professor of political science at the University of Utah. He was founding director of the Robert H. Hinckley Institute of Politics at the university, a staunch Democrat, and an advocate for the freedom of ideas. He would become increasingly concerned during the 1960s about Ezra Taft Benson's politics and right-wing positions.

University of Utah, who gave an address at the University of Utah on February 20, 1962, on 'Ways Not to Fight Communism.' In addition to students a number of interested citizens were also in attendance.

It is reported that on this occasion "Dr. Williams made some vicious accusations against the Bensons, Mr. Cleon Skousen, Dr. Robert Morris, President of the University of Dallas, Senator Dodd, Dr. Fred Swartz, and many other individuals known to be prominent in the fight against Communism. He told the students that these men were to be feared, and that the things which they are advocating and the things which were being advocated by the Freedom Academy and the 'Americanism Up Front' Seminar recently conducted in this area, were serving only to alarm our people unnecessarily and to make them suspicious of their own next door neighbors. Dr. Williams advised his students to beware of super patriots and those known to be identified with the right wing. One statement by Dr. Williams seemed to be more shocking to those present than all else when in a state of frenzy he said: 'My apologies to those who know me as a Mormon Bishop, but by G--, I am glad I voted for a Democrat.'"

I asked President Berg to call Bishop Williams in and face him on some of these statements, and especially about his using the Lord's name in vain; that we cannot tolerate a Bishop of the Church doing that.

President Berg stated to me that he had just recently been released as President of the Monument Park West Stake, and that the President now is Brother Rex Austin Skidmore. However, I asked that Brother Berg handle this matter, inasmuch as he has been acquainted with Bishop Williams.

March 27, 1962, First Presidency meeting. ... we took up many matters of importance to the Church, among which we considered the <u>statement of Father Sweeney[15] of the Catholic Church regarding Dr. J. D. Williams'</u> remarks at a meeting of the University of Utah February 20, 1962, where

---

15. Lawrence Paul Sweeney (1929–2016) was born in Wyoming, raised in Utah, and graduated from St. Patrick's Seminary in California. In 1954 he was ordained a priest at Our Lady of Lourdes Parish in Magna, Utah. In his next assignment as chaplain at the Newman Center adjacent to the University of Utah, he took advantage of the proximity to campus by enrolling as a student and earning an MA in psychology. He became editor of the *Catholic Register* (now *Intermountain Catholic*) and wrote one book, *On the Other Side of the Street*, about homelessness. He would later become a Prelate of Honor, or monsignor.

Bishop Williams treated the subject, "ways not to fight communism." Father Sweeney wrote: "I don't understand how the Authorities of the Mormon Church can tolerate a man so radical, so vicious, so abusive as Dr. Williams in holding a high position in the Church."

Dr. Williams' reply to a question as to whether or not he considered himself to be a "middle of the roader," and the answer[s] he gave were quoted. Dr. Williams' statement "my apologies to those who know me as a Mormon bishop, but by G--, I am glad I voted for a Democrat," was quoted.

President [Henry D.] Moyle said that his son and daughter-in-law had heard Dr. Williams on this occasion and quoted him as saying, "I am a Mormon bishop and I am a Democrat, and thank God for both." He said Bishop Williams is not profane, and that he found him to be as sweet and lovable a character as any boy he knew.[16]

I said that I talked with President Frank C. Berg of the Monument Park West Stake, who was a counselor in the stake presidency when Bishop Williams was called to be a bishop, and I asked him to talk with Bishop Williams about the incident.

President Moyle said, "I would plead that before you come to any final conclusion about Williams that you give him a personal hearing."[17]

I said: "I have given him a personal hearing through the man who recommended him. He has had that personal hearing. It is through this person the matter was presented to the man himself. That is where it should be. I have given it here today. He has given answer to it. Of course, Williams would not acknowledge that he had taken the name of God in vain. He said 'perhaps I used it but not in the sense of profanity,' but others heard him, and they think he is a radical man when he gets into politics."

President [Hugh B.] Brown said: "I met Dr. Williams once and found him to be a humble, intelligent, young Latter-day Saint. That was my impression of him. I think I should say that much to you. I was favorably impressed that he was a clean young man."

I said: "I have asked his students what kind of man he is. His students like him. They say he is a fine young man."

---

16. Williams was thirty-six, Moyle seventy-two.

17. During the previous month, at a stake conference held on Temple Square, Moyle had "denounced tactics of Reed Benson [the apostle's oldest son and member of the John Birch Society] and upheld J. D. Williams as a bishop," although "without mentioning names" (Quinn, *Extensions*, 71).

March 29, 1962, 4:45 p.m. Left for home—a tiring day! It is not the long hours and hard work that makes one tired and weary, but the decisions and the things you sometimes have to do to set things right.

April 7, 1962, 7 p.m. General Priesthood meeting held in the Salt Lake Tabernacle. ...

I asked my Second Counselor, President Hugh B. Brown, to conduct this meeting. This was the first time in eleven years since becoming President that I have turned this responsibility over to someone else.

April 8, 1962, 10 a.m. Presided at and conducted the Sixth Session of the General Conference—for the first time in the history of the Church this morning's session was televised Coast to Coast and broadcast by short wave radio to Europe, South and Central America, and Mexico. ... A total of 51 television stations and twenty-four radio stations carried this session on a volunteer basis. It was estimated that sixty million persons viewed and listened to the proceedings of this session. As I said to the audience, we participated in something far greater than we knew this morning.

April 25, 1962, First Presidency meeting. We discussed a letter from [the father of a] 22-year-old daughter, whose body had been filled with cancer, had died, and because of the nature of the cancer, they had agreed to several autopsies, and had thereafter arranged for her cremation. They now plan to have the ashes brought home to Idaho, and have them scattered over the beautiful mountains there. He asked, "Please drop me a line of your feeling about what we have done." I said, "It is done. It is the[i]r responsibility. The Church favors interment and not cremation, and that's all we can do."[18]

May 3, 1962, 9:00–9:15 a.m. Brother O. Preston Robinson, General Manager of the Deseret News, and Brother Henry Smith of the Church Section, met with the First Presidency and inquired as to what they might publish regarding the proposed trip by the First Presidency to Nauvoo and the purchase of property by the Church in Nauvoo. They said that they wanted to print only that which the Brethren wanted them to print

---

18. For the church's policy over the years, see Bergera, *Statements*, 109–10.

on the subject. They called attention to an article in the Nauvoo paper stating that the Church was going to reconstruct the Nauvoo Temple. I told these brethren not to mention any such thing as a reconstruction of the temple, and said that this work was really under the direction of the [Utah] State Chairman of Parks and Historic places, Harold Fabian, who has also just been elected chairman of the United States Landmarks and Sites Commission, and that Nauvoo is a part of the over-all scheme.[19]

May 15, 1962, 8:10 a.m. Arrived at the office, at which time my counselors and I held a meeting with Dr. J. LeRoy Kimball and Mr. Harold P. Fabian, who gave a report of their recent visit to Nauvoo when Presidents [Henry D.] Moyle and [Hugh B.] Brown, and Elder A. Hamer Reiser accompanied them.

Mr. Fabian said that Mr. Conrad Wirth, Director of the National Parks Service, Washington, D.C. met with them in Nauvoo on May 4th and 5th, and said that the National Parks Service can help in the historic and archae[o]logical research about Nauvoo. He is most enthusiastic about the whole project.

Then followed a long discussion regarding how we are to go about restoring the old homes in Nauvoo, the obtaining of property, the uncovering of the foundations of the old Nauvoo temple, the manner in which the whole project is to be handled, by whom, budget, etc.

We decided to form a corporation known as the Nauvoo Restorations, Inc., with Dr. J. LeRoy Kimball as President, Willard Marriott, Vice President, and A. Hamer Reiser, secretary and treasurer, with Mr. Harold Fabian and Mr. David Kennedy as directors. The working capital to be set aside for this corporation was also discussed. ...

In making a report of this meeting at the Council Meeting in the Salt Lake Temple held on Thursday, May 17, 1962, I said that I thought the Brethren would be pleased with what will be done there (in Nauvoo) without any extravagance. I mentioned the article which came out in the local Nauvoo papers several weeks ago, stating that the temple was going to be

---

19. As discussed in the next entry, Fabian, who was not of the LDS faith, accepted an offer to join the board of Nauvoo Restoration Inc., where he became an advocate for historical accuracy over religious sentiment. The downtown area of Nauvoo had been accepted in 1961 as a National Historic Landmark. Esplin, "Place for the Weary Traveler," 17–20.

rebuilt which created quite a stir in Nauvoo circles, that, however, an effort was made by the brethren who visited Nauvoo not to give an impression that the Church was going back there to rebuild Nauvoo and restore the temple, but that whatever is done there the Nauvoo people should lead out in it, and that the Church will help. I said that thus far the Church will confine itself to the purchasing and remodeling where necessary some of the old homes; also that we plan on a renovation and remodeling of the Carthage Jail, placing a bureau of information just outside the jail; also to make an exit from the back of the jail for the accommodation of visitors so that they can go through the jail and come out at the rear.

May 18, 1962. While I was dictating letters, I had a <u>telephone call from Elder Ezra Taft Benson</u>, who was in Portland, Oregon attending a National Boy Scout meeting, and is appointed to the Seattle Stake Conference.

He asked regarding his accepting the invitation of the National Boy Scout Organization to be chairman of Region twelve, and his attendance at the Seattle Stake Conference. He said that he felt that there has been some reflection cast on him in this stake with the President and the High Council and Bishoprics, he asked that I make a telephone call to the Stake President regarding this matter. ...

I then called <u>President F. Arthur Kay of the Seattle Stake</u>, and told him that Elder Ezra Taft Benson will attend the quarterly conference of his stake, and that I wanted him to know that Elder Benson comes up there under no cloud whatsoever, and that I also approve of Brother Cleon Skousen's book "The Naked Communist."[20]

May 24, 1962. While we were in the Temple holding our regular meeting, the news was flashed around the world of the <u>successful three-orbital flight around the earth of Astronaut Malcolm Scott Carpenter</u>. Astronaut John Glenn was the first American to orbit the earth on February 20, 1962.

When I returned to the office, my secretary told me that all radio contact with the Astronaut was lost at 12:30 p.m., and that millions listening

---

20. McKay had said at the October 1959 general conference, "On the flyleaf of the book, *The Naked Communist*, by W. Cleon Skousen, we find this quotation, (and I admonish everybody to read that excellent book of Chief Skousen's): 'The conflict between communism and freedom is the problem of our time. It overshadows all other problems. This conflict mirrors our age, its toils, its tensions, its troubles, and its tasks.'"

in on radio and television were held in suspense until 1:05 p.m. when Lt. Col. John A. Powers, the mercury information officer, announced that a Navy patrol plane had reported picking up a radio beacon, an indication that the Aurora–7 was in the water, but that was no indication that Astronaut Carpenter was alive. That knowledge came at 1:25 p.m., when the patrol plane spotted the Aurora–7 and Astronaut Carpenter riding his life raft nearby. During the time that no contact could be made, it was reported that the people of America were praying for the safety of the Astronaut. I think this is a good illustration of the spirituality of the American nation. For a few minutes our man in space was lost, and there was a prayer felt in each individual's heart, a prayer that he may be safe. The spirit of pure dependence upon our Heavenly Father was manifest to a marked degree. So long as this Nation will maintain faith in a Divine Being, I think we are safe.

May 31, 1962, 6:00 a.m. I called [telephoned] Ted Cannon, Assistant Manager of the Tabernacle Choir, and told him to get in touch with Schyler Chapin, President of the Columbia Masterworks Records. I learned that Mr. Chapin is the one who desired to have the selection entitled "Meadowland"—a militant Russian song—included in the Tabernacle Choir and Philadelphia Orchestra's album recently made. I said that this is a Communistic number which we do not favor incorporating in the album.[21] It was suggested to Brother Cannon that he get in touch with Mr. Chapin, and try to convert him to leaving it out.

June 6, 1962, First Presidency meeting. The concluding three paragraphs in the book, "John Doyle Lee" by Juanita Brooks, concerning the Mountain Meadow Massacre, as follows were read: "Through all the 84 years which have elapsed since the execution of John D. Lee, the dearest hope of his many descendants has been that his name should some day be cleared. An action taken on Thursday, April 20, 1961, has made that hope a reality for them.

---

21. The song, "Polyushko–Polye," would nevertheless be recorded three years later by the Disneyland Boys Choir. The lyrics mention young men going to war, girls crying at their departure, and farmers working "with peace of mind" because the army is looking out for them.

"On that day the First Presidency and the Quorum of the Twelve of the Mormon Church met in a joint session and it was the action of the Council after considering all the facts available that authorization be given for the reinstatement to membership and former blessings to John D. Lee. On May 8 and 9 following, the necessary ordinances were performed in the Salt Lake Temple."

I said the author had no right to include that in any book. She was told not to do it, and that if she did the action might be rescinded. It was agreed that no publicity be given to rescinding the action if this is done; that it would be "fanning the flame." We decided that the matter be left without further action, and I said that we will leave it just as it is.[22]

June 15, 1962, First Presidency meeting. Among many items considered was a letter from the General Superintendency of the Sunday School relating to retaining six young women in the employ of Sunday School board since they have been married.

I said that the policy restricting the employment of married women has not been followed as it should be. I reviewed practices which involve the office of the First Presidency as well as other departments; I referred also to special employment problems arising in the Genealogical Society. I stated that the rule is honored more in the breach than in the observance, and mentioned the change of practice over the practices of many years ago.

The advisability of revising the regulation was carefully considered and it was decided that women will be hired and retained after marriage if they are capable and do their work well, but that it will be expected that they will not deliberately postpone responsibilities of parenthood.

June 20, 1962, First Presidency meeting. We read President Ernest L. Wilkinson's letter relating to the proposal to assign Dr. Lowell Bennion to the writing of five needed seminary and institute courses of study, and his release as director of the Institute at the University of Utah.[23] After consideration, it was agreed that the recommendation be approved.

---

22. Brooks's biography, *John Doyle Lee*, was published in 1961 by Arthur H. Clark Company. For more, see Levi S. Peterson's *Juanita Brooks: Mormon Woman Historian* from the University of Utah Press, 1988.

23. During this period (1961–62), Bennion was much sought after in Utah educational circles. University of Utah President A. Ray Olpin attempted to cajole him

June 28, 1962, 2:20 p.m. <u>Elder Howard W. Hunter</u> came into my private office at my request. I told Brother Hunter that I should like him to take over the responsibility of investigating requests from the people of the church for cancellation of Temple marriage sealings. Heretofore, President Hugh B. Brown has been carrying this load, but now that his duties as Second Counselor in the First Presidency are increasing, it will be impossible for him to continue with this work. Brother Hunter willingly accepted this assignment.[24]

July 7, 1962, 8:00 a.m. … <u>President Hugh B. Brown</u> came in to my private office where we held a meeting on: …

(5) The matter of <u>notation on membership record of negro ancestry</u>— We considered the question as to whether or not the race of all members should be indicated on membership records.

(6) <u>Lowell Bennion and his retirement from director of University of Utah Institute of Religion</u> discussed.

July 10, 1962, First Presidency meeting. President [Hugh B.] Brown asked whether or not, in planning the trip to Nigeria in Africa for the middle of November, Brother LaMar Williams should take his wife. <u>I said the party to Nigeria should include President Nathan E[ldon] Tanner, President of the West European Mission; Brother Williams and his wife; and two couples, man and wife without children, and that they should open up the Nigerian Mission.</u> The two couples will be left after opening the mission and baptizing the people, and organizing them into branches. Thereafter, the couples will officiate. The couples are to be chosen by the First Presidency.

July 17, 1962, First Presidency meeting. I stated in our meeting this morning that <u>I feel that the time has come for a retrenchment, and for the</u>

---

into leaving the institute and becoming an administrative and faculty member at the university. Bennion had balked because of the freedom and enjoyment he had found at the institute. There were also rumors of Bennion being called into the Quorum of the Twelve. Bradford, *Lowell L. Bennion*, 140–45; Wilkinson diary, June 6, 1962.

24. Hunter had already been given a partial assignment in November 1960: "Because of ill health [J. Reuben Clark] had to be relieved of the responsibility. President Moyle told Howard the assignment was being given him because of his knowledge and experience in handling the legal aspects of these matters." Knowles, *Howard W. Hunter*, 155–56.

rebuilding of the cash reserves of the Church; that non-producing prop-erties must be sold so that the cash reserves of the Church can be built up. I said that I should announce this policy and purpose in the Expenditures Committee meeting today.[25]

July 19, 1962, 8:00–8:30 a.m. Met by appointment Brother Graham H. Doxey of Zion's Securities Corporation. Items discussed with him were: …

(3) I suggested to him that we should like the expenditures now carried on by the Building Committee and other departments of the Church reduced to a minimum, and that the Church reserves should be increased—first, by the sale of non-producing properties, which may be sold at a great profit to the Church—these should be sold and the reserves of the Church replenished. I suggested that he consult with Brother [Wendell] Mendenhall on some of these properties in California, after which he is to bring me a list of the properties that are now at a point where they may be sold at a profit to the Church. …

A letter addressed to me … asked if the discussions in the missionary lesson program must be memorized before they may be given, or if they are thoroughly supported by an outline whether the presentation in the missionary's words would be in order. He explained that the impression is given the missionaries that if they fail to give the lessons word-for-word from memory they are in disobedience of my instructions, and "going against your words, and in a sense apostatizing." The Elder wanted to know if they must be memorized word-for-word and if an outline can be used for the discussion with the contacts. I directed that the answer be that the missionary may use the outline and should follow the spirit and his own intelligence. These excellent lessons must be used as a guide and not as a prop, and never at the expense of the spirit.

July 20, 1962, 9:05 a.m. Brother George Jarvis of the Financial Department came into the meeting and read his report of July 19, 1962, on the status of the cash and other liquid reserves of the Church, of the non-budget income, and the non-budget assets, "the Church program assets," investment stocks and loans to Church businesses. The latter item

---

25. Through the 1950s deficit spending had brought the church to a perilous financial position. Goates, *Harold B. Lee*, 381; Quinn, *Extensions*, 198–225.

he amplified as relates to the Florida and Georgia ranches. He also stated that the deposits in Canadian banks remain. Deposits in South Africa may be increased, he said, to take care of building projects approved. The buildings proposed for the South African Mission were briefly reviewed. I said that there was no urgency so far as South Africa is concerned.

I said I had already reported that the expenditures of the Building Committee should be reduced to a minimum, and every effort should be put forth to increase our reserves. I said I had told the chairman of Zions Securities Corporation to consult with Brother Mendenhall with a view to recommending disposing of all surplus properties and bringing any increase into the reserves. That is the instruction for the next month or so. That should be done before conference. I also mentioned that we have several million dollars worth of property in Florida, and I think we should dispose of any wisely because the value is there. I said that I think we should have under consideration the sale of some of that valuable property in Florida, that it is worth millions, and somebody should be looking intensely and intelligently upon the desire of Cape Canaveral to get some of our property there, that we should dispose of it if they want it. That will add millions to our reserves. I said that there is a feeling, unfounded but abroad, that the Mormon Church is holding property notwithstanding the desire of the government to obtain some of that at Cape Canaveral. I said if they want it, we shall sell it; we have reached the point in that investment where we should stop expenditures and bring in some sales and that will make a change in this.

Brother Jarvis mentioned briefly and reviewed the selling of some government securities at an opportune time. I said that was all right and that it was a good move.

July 27, 1962, Clare Middlemiss: I said to President McKay today, "President McKay, why is it that people who are too aggressive and try to get ahead of other people seem to get places and gain advantage over other persons who are more reticent to do those things?"

President McKay looked up and in all seriousness said "No, they do not gain." I said, "Well, it seems that way."

President McKay very emphatically answered, "Truth crushed to earth will rise again!"

428

July 28, 1962, 8:00 a.m. Went over to the office and met by appointment President Ernest L. Wilkinson. ... In discussing matters with President Wilkinson pertaining to the conditions in the world and the government here in our own United States, I said that I had a <u>letter suggesting that at the forthcoming October Conference of the Church,</u> or in some other way, <u>that I make a statement which would once again be an official pronouncement for the Church in favor of the continuation of the American form of government, and at the same time a condemnation of Communism and all species of socialism.</u> I shall give serious consideration to this matter.

August 3, 1962, First Presidency meeting. ... <u>President Joseph Fielding Smith and Elder Harold B. Lee</u> came into the room by appointment at my request.

We considered the <u>necessity of members of the Quorum of the Twelve discharging their duty given them by revelation to set in order the affairs of the Church in all the world.</u> I suggested that since it is physically impossible for the Twelve, their Assistants, and other General Authorities of the Church to visit stake conferences (now numbering 355) more than possibly once a year, it would be <u>more essential than ever for each one of the General Authorities to be thoroughly acquainted with all policies, plans and programs approved by the First Presidency and the Twelve.</u>

The present practice, therefore, of appointing area supervisors and expecting them to give out special instructions to presidents of stakes and mission presidents should not be encouraged, but every member of the General Authorities—the Twelve, their Assistants, the First Council of Seventy, and the Presiding Bishopric—should be given all the information regarding details and new plans now given to the so-called area supervisors.[26] In a word, each General Authority must be supplied with all information now given to the so-called area supervisors.

August 9, 1962, First Presidency meeting. President [Henry D.] Moyle said he felt that the meetings he and Brother Gordon B. Hinckley held

---

26. The church had called twenty-five men in 1961 as part-time supervisors for twenty-five global areas and asked them to advise the stake presidents and to assist the general authorities in seeing that church guidelines were adhered to. The program would soon be discontinued. Mehr, "Area Supervision," 196–97.

with the missionaries in Europe were of real value; that they had met all the missionaries in Europe with perhaps a half dozen exceptions. He said that he and Brother Hinckley have now presented this program[27] to between five and six thousand of our missionaries, and that they have made appointments to meet with the missionaries in the Northwestern States Mission and the West Central States Mission, and that they had in mind planning for Brother Hinckley to meet with all the other missions.[28]

I stated that we should not continue this program in the manner suggested, that I am very much concerned at the tendency which is growing to have the work of General Authorities of the Church done by special committees.

President Moyle said he did not think there was anyone in the Church who could do this work among the missionaries like Brother Hinckley is doing it, that he felt that Brother Hinckley should give his message to all the missionaries in the Church, and that he should be permitted to make his own timetable, that it would present tremendous results to the missionaries. He said it is a tremendous presentation, and mission presidents are very grateful for it. President Moyle mentioned that they had met only with the missionaries and not with the saints.

I indicated that the Brethren of the Twelve are subject to the President of the Twelve, and should go out under the direction of the Twelve, and not under the direction of the First Presidency. I commended President Moyle on the success of the work they have done, and said that he and Brother Hinckley had done the right thing so far as their work in Europe is concerned, that they had accomplished a great work, but we should not lose sight of the fact that the Brethren of the Twelve are under the jurisdiction of that Quorum. I mentioned the fact that we now have 360 stakes and under present conditions, there are only about 25 of the

27. Hinckley was introducing missionaries to a new strategy involving six standardized discussions they would be required to conduct with potential converts. John-Charles Duffy, "The New Missionary Discussions and the Future of Correlation," *Sunstone* magazine, Sept. 2005.

28. This was particularly strenuous for Hinckley, who with Marjorie Hinckley had just been to the Asian missions. On arriving home, Hinckley had been sent to northern and southern California and the eastern states, and he had stopped in Detroit to buy a car and drive it back. He had no sooner arrived in Utah than the phone rang and he was asked to be in London the following day. For the European tour, he and Moyle visited twenty missions in twenty days.

General Authorities of the Church who can visit these stakes, and that the Twelve have now proposed that the General Authorities should visit the stakes only twice a year. I suggested that we call the Twelve together and tell them that the responsibility rests upon them to take the message to the people, and that includes visits to missions and that each one of the General Authorities must go prepared to give the message that Brother Moyle and Brother Hinckley have been giving. If the Twelve want to send Brother Hinckley out as a representative of the Twelve to do this work, it would be up to the Twelve to send him.

President Moyle reported that the new missionary program is not going over in any of the missions that he visited, that the mission presidents are fumbling with it, and that the conditions in some instances could be described as chaotic, but that when Brother Hinckley got through with this presentation, they all said that they could now go to work. Apparently, President Moyle added, they do not know how to do it until they have been told, and it takes a teacher like Brother Hinckley to tell them.

I said that I am going to ask for a report from the Twelve as to what their program now is, that I have been preparing a plan which I should like to present to the First Presidency some time next week, relative to the responsibility and the work of the Twelve and the General Authorities, and let them know exactly what they will have to do.

August 15, 1962, First Presidency meeting. ... (2) <u>General Authorities at Stake Conferences</u>—I stated that with the release of the new Stake Conference Schedule, <u>dual Stake Conferences to be conducted by one General Authority will be discontinued</u>. I said that 360 Stakes having quarterly conferences cannot be attended by 34 General Authorities of the Church, 7 of whom are not available for appointment. <u>I stated that the duty of the General Authorities of the Church is to set in order the affairs of the Church in the world, and that this is fundamental</u>. Auxiliary organizations hold annual conferences at which the stake president and bishops of the wards are generally expected to be in attendance. <u>I suggested that Auxiliary Conventions, heretofore held independently of Stake conferences, hereafter be held under the direction of the stake presidencies at quarterly conferences not attended by the General Authorities of the Church</u>. On these occasions the stake and ward auxiliary workers can receive instructions from the General Boards. <u>I suggested that this proposal be presented to the Twelve, who will be responsible, with their associates for setting the Church in order in all the world, and that the Auxiliary programs for each conference which are not attended by one of the General Authorities of the Church will be prepared under the direction of the auxiliary advisors. I explained also that every member of the General Authorities of the Church will know the plans and instructions of the Church offered at the quarterly conferences. I stated, "We should like to suggest that the Twelve prepare and outline the activity for the holding of these annual quarterly conferences to which certain Auxiliaries will be appointed throughout the year, and that this subject be presented to the Council of the Twelve tomorrow, and that we would like them to take under advisement this new plan and make it incumbent upon every member of the General Authorities to know what the plan is and what plans and instructions are given regarding the stake work, genealogical work, and missionary work, and each member of the General Authorities will have to prepare himself and be prepared to give instructions."</u>

In response to a question by President [Hugh B.] Brown, I said the programs presented at the Stake Conferences not attended by one of the General Authorities of the Church will be under the direction of the Stake President, and that provision may be made for holding some Auxiliary instruction meetings on Saturday before the Sunday of the Stake Conference so that stake board members can receive and give detailed instructions. The Sunday morning program and the Sunday afternoon program will be meetings held under the direction of the Stake President and attended by representatives of the General Boards who will have a chance to give an auxiliary program to the entire Church. In response to President Brown's inquiry about Welfare, I said that Welfare and Missionary Work will be similarly emphasized at these conferences.

President Moyle reviewed figures on the number of stakes and the number of General Authorities and expressed the opinion that the General Authorities, who are the priesthood of the Church, <u>can conduct at least two stake conferences a year in each stake.</u>[29] He reviewed also the

---

29. In other words, 360 stakes could not be visited quarterly by 27 general authorities. However, the authorities could visit each stake twice a year, and this became a prelude to later discontinuing quarterly conferences in favor of semiannual stake meetings.

growth of the Church and the increase in the number of ordinations and interviews, and the interviewing of missionaries. He suggested that it would be well to have the Twelve work out a plan on the basis of two priesthood conferences a year when the General Authorities of the Church would be present. I said that would be all the better. ...

(4) <u>Missionary Interviews by General Authorities of the Church or by Stake Presidents</u>—President Moyle reviewed the increase in the interviewing of prospective missionaries by the General Authorities of the Church, and mentioned the delays in calling missionaries which result from waiting for a General Authority to do the interviewing. He suggested that the responsibility for the final interviews before recommending a missionary to the First Presidency be placed upon the stake presidents. I said that Brother Kimball, after interviewing many missionaries learned of a number who had had sexual experience and that the stake presidents had not made this discovery. <u>This resulted in the First Presidency and the Twelve deciding that every missionary will have to pass under the jurisdiction of the General Authorities</u>.

President Moyle said that there is enough pressure and enough urgency for us to bring this up tomorrow and ask if we can eliminate that requirement and have the Twelve place the responsibility squarely on the president of the stake and the bishops of the wards, and that the stake president's personal recommendation go to the First Presidency. I said the local brethren will have to take the responsibility.

August 16, 1962, meeting of First Presidency and Twelve. I then made mention of the action [to] the Council of the First Presidency and Quorum of the Twelve on Thursday, June 28, on the recommendation of the Twelve, that dual quarterly conferences be discontinued and a new system of quarterly conferences be developed.

I asked President Joseph Fielding Smith to speak on this question, and in response, President Smith said that these dual conferences are not successful in his judgment; that too much has to be left undone when one of the Brethren attends conferences in two stakes at the same time, and it is therefore felt that each stake should have its own conference separately. He mentioned that we have so many stakes now that the Brethren cannot visit all of them every quarter, and that when the schedule of visitors to stake conferences is made, at least one third of the stakes have to go without a visitor. It has therefore been agreed by the Twelve that beginning with the first of the year, dual Stake Conferences would be discontinued. It is proposed, he said, that one or more of the General Authorities would visit every other conference in each specific stake, and that the other two stake conferences would be auxiliary conferences under the direction of the presidency of the stake. ...

Responsibility of the Brethren of the Twelve—I called attention to the revelation that places upon this body of men the responsibility of directing the affairs of the Church in all the world. I said the Brethren should keep this in mind. I stated that the central power, the central authority, has the right to adopt whatever is found useable, applicable, productive of good, at any time. A plan may be adapted by the entire Church, provided the Brethren of the Council hold the guiding hand, but that authority, no matter how large the Church becomes, and this principle, are just the same and just as applicable.

Elder Mark E. Petersen asked if this would mean that these conferences would take the place of the regular annual conventions of the Auxiliary Organizations, and I said they would.

There was considerable discussion as to how the program would work, and I asked the Twelve to take this matter under advisement, give it prayerful consideration, and come back with a plan for 1963. I said that we have reached a point where we shall have to place more responsibility on the local people, and give them the understanding that the power and direction of all of it is in the hands of the Twelve. I said that we have had opportunity to test the various methods; that, however, we should be careful not to do as the Government is doing—that is, place too much power in the hands of the Committee.

August 21, 1962, First Presidency meeting. ... We met with [attorney and stake president] George L. Nelson who came in by appointment regarding the Sunday Closing Act. He said he came as a lawyer representing a group of business men who have asked him to prepare a bill to be presented to the coming State Legislature regarding Sunday closing. Brother Nelson said his only purpose in coming to the Presidency was to be assured of their sympathetic approval. Brother Nelson mentioned that a bill of similar import was passed by a good majority by the last Legislature and was vetoed by Governor [George] Clyde; that also, six years prior to that a bill was presented which was vetoed by Governor [J. Bracken] Lee. Brother Nelson said he hoped they had now met all the substantial objections to this bill which arose while the bill was in the Legislature and while it was on the Governor's desk. He said the Kennecott people have signified their approval, that they had gone to all the groups that could have anything to do with it, and he felt it was a step in the right direction. He said it would accomplish the closing of general business, that, however, we have exceptions in cases of hospitals, industrial plants, power plants, and things having to do with health, life and recreation. He mentioned that the Supreme Court of the United States had made a decision sustaining Sunday closing as a principle.[30]

The growth of Sunday opening is going at such a pace that it is feared all stores will be open on Sunday unless something is done about it.

I wished Brother Nelson and his associates success in this undertaking. I said I have always been in favor of the Sunday Closing Law. Brother Nelson said they were not asking for the Presidency's public approval of it, that that may not be desirable, but they did desire our approval. I said for them to go right ahead with it.

September 5, 1962, First Presidency meeting. President [Henry D.] Moyle reported that there has been a tremendous amount of talk around the building about the terrible mistake we have made by selling the bank [Zion's First National]. He said, "I hear it from all sides. I wanted you to know that the George Morris estate had 1100 shares of bank stock, and they can't sell it. It has been with Edward L. Burton, and they can't get a purchaser at $70.00 a share. I am going to be surprised if they get as much as we got for it. I want to call your attention to the fact that the bank has twenty million dollars more on deposit. It had fifty-eight million in assets when we sold. With more assets they cannot sell it for more than we sold

---

30. The case Nelson refers to is *McGowan v. Maryland* (1961), which revolved around the question of what sort of business, if any, could be conducted on Sundays. At this particular juncture, blue laws were prevalent but were not particularly onerous either. The issue in Maryland was that a department store had sold items not expressly permitted for Sunday sales, namely a notebook, a can of floor wax, a stapler and staples, and a toy.

it. We sold it for $13.00 a share above its asset value, and you remember we had letters from three banks telling us it was a pretty high price."

I said, "I wouldn't pay any attention to that."

President Moyle replied, "I wish it could be stopped. It is all tied in with the Church being bankrupt and being broke. It is so silly. We are getting 5% on money that we could not get more than 2%. This banking business is getting so competitive that they are hiring women to go from door to door to solicit accounts. Can you imagine the President of the Church sitting at the head of an institution and asking the Relief Society to bring in accounts. This competition in the commercial banking is right at the point where the Church could not engage in it." (The discussion continued as follows:)

President [Hugh B.] Brown: I have not indicated to anyone that the Church is going broke. Lee Flint asked me to dinner with him yesterday. He explained the bank set-up. He asked me to come to dinner with him. I have not had anything to say about this sort of thing. Reports come in about the loss we have sustained.

President Moyle: You can ask me and I can give you facts and figures in every detail.

President McKay: I am glad we are out of the bank. I am glad we are out of it.

President Moyle: We could not be in it. There is a law suit. The bank will have to sue the Eccles. You remember the Eccles are going to open a bank on the Cottonwood Mall contrary to the understanding. In working out this detail, Edwards did not get a contract that will hold water, but the bank must sue. How can we justify it with hundreds of members of the Church working for First Security. How can you justify bringing suit. I am mighty happy that we are out of it. We are still a very substantial stockholder, next to the largest.

President McKay: I had hoped that we would establish the Zion's Savings Bank and Trust Company, but we took the advice of the bankers back east. They said not to do it, and we have held that in abeyance.

President Moyle: The savings bank business has gone to nothing. This Prudential Building & Loan is as big as the bank.

President McKay: (To President Brown) You knew we reserved the right to establish Zion's Savings Bank?

President Brown: I think when President Moyle made his report we were told you were doing that.

President Moyle: That was the advice at the time.

President McKay: We took the advice of leading bankers of the United States, and they were united in saying that it would not be possible to establish a savings bank alone. I do not lose any sleep over that; that is all right. We shall present it to the Brethren. There is no worry about that.

September 7, 1962, 8:30 a.m. Bishop Thorpe B. Isaacson called at the office and presented me with a top coat, beautifully tailored in England, for my birthday. I registered my disapproval of his going to this expense, but he said he especially wanted to remember me this year with a gift; that he had not done so before, for fear it would be taken as "apple-polishing."[31] He expressed his deep feeling with tears in his eyes. I appreciate his love and spirit of brotherhood, which I reciprocate with all my heart. He has been a true, loyal friend through the years! ...

September 18, 1962, 8:00 a.m. Ted Cannon[32] of the Church Information Service came in. One question he brought up was the matter of a book being written by Samuel Taylor.[33] Brother Cannon said that Brother Taylor is trying to give a true picture of the Church's business holdings to offset some of the articles that have been written, giving misleading stories. The book will be written whether we give our approval or not, so I told Brother Cannon to cooperate with Brother Taylor in giving the correct information to him. ...

We had a long discussion in our [First Presidency] meeting this morning regarding the duties and authority of the First Presidency to direct the Twelve in missionary, genealogical, and auxiliary work.

---

31. In fact, Isaacson was developing a reputation in that direction. When other authorities were unable to get a hearing with the president, he was always able to get an appointment, as were Alvin R. Dyer and Sterling W. Sill.

32. Theodore Lincoln Cannon Sr. (1904–66) was the church's news director, associate editor of the *Deseret News*, and vice president of the Tabernacle Choir. His son of the same name would become the Salt Lake County Attorney. He is sometimes confused with Edwin Q. Cannon Jr., one of the first senior missionaries to Nigeria. All three were known as Ted.

33. It would take Taylor sixteen years to write *Rocky Mountain Empire: The Latter-day Saints Today*, which would be published by Macmillan in 1978. The questions he had for Cannon pertained to his chapter on "Latter-day Profits," 132–47.

At the conclusion of the discussion, President [Henry D.] Moyle said: "Do you think this correlation, which has to do with primarily the class work in the various organizations, should transfer any of the responsibilities that are now placed in the Presidency to the Twelve, for genealogical work, as an example?"

I said that the correlation work affects primarily the duplication of courses of study, and that it should not affect the organization of the Church.[34]

President [Hugh B.] Brown said that the Prophet [Joseph Smith] had a wonderful sense of propriety and of revelation when he said that it is the nature and disposition of almost all men when they get a little authority as they suppose to extend it, and to reach out for more and more.

I quoted: "Hence, many are called and few are chosen. Why are they not chosen? Because they have not learned this one lesson, etc."

President Moyle added, "That no power or influence can or ought to be maintained."

And I quoted, "Only upon the principle of righteousness."

I then said that these matters of correlation of our work are for all three of the First Presidency to decide; that when we are united, we can take the next step, and until we are united, we do not take any step. ...

NOTE: Today I autographed my photograph at the request of Elder T. Bowring Woodbury, formerly President of the British Mission, and also one for Dr. E. Sarofim, an Egyptian, who is now teaching at the London University. He is the man who cabled to me some time ago, and asked if he could be baptized. I turned the matter over to President Woodbury, who was then serving as President of the British Mission, inasmuch as Dr. Sarofim was then teaching at the University of London. This man has not yet been baptized, because he has the problem of having two wives, whom he married under the Egyptian Law. I sent word to President

---

34. The Church Correlation Program had its genesis in 1960. The First Presidency authorized a committee of general authorities to review and make recommendations to coordinate the programs of all priesthood and auxiliary organizations. At this juncture in 1962, the church had organized activities and curricula around children, youth, and adults. Harold B. Lee was the prime mover behind the new approach that required all church matters to be cleared through a Correlation Committee. Perhaps this is why McKay begins to expresses concern about "the work of General Authorities of the Church [not being] done by special committees (Apr. 9) and about not putting "too much power in the hands of the Committee" (Aug. 16).

Woodbury at the time that Dr. Sarofim would have to tell his Egyptian wife of his marriage to the woman from Switzerland. This he has done, and now President Woodbury says he is coming to Salt Lake City soon, and wishes to be baptized when he arrives here.[35]

September 19, 1962, First Presidency meeting. I said the coming of the mission presidents to October Conference hinges around the question of holding a seminar. The statement was made that we would withhold decision until after approving the recommendation of the committee on Conferences and unification of courses of study. We have that to decide. This correlation work is applicable to courses of study of priesthood and auxiliaries to avoid duplication. That is the purpose of the correlation work. That is the heart of it, and further than that as it affects the organization of the Church, we will have to decide and tell them so. That is where we stand on that.

I said that I am not thoroughly committed to the Seminar, and President [Henry D.] Moyle said, "We do not want to hold one until you are; I do not want to press it." I said, "I am in favor of bringing them into Conference and doing our work during the Conference, and let the stake conferences be carried as we are planning. I think that is an excellent plan."

President Moyle said that the Seminar is for the full-time mission presidents, and does not involve the quarterly conferences at all.

President [Hugh B.] Brown said that it is a question as to whether or not these sisters, the wives of the mission presidents, should come to the Relief Society Conference. I said that it would not do to have them travel alone; that we can decide right now that the Relief Society sisters should come when their husbands come.

President Brown said the question is whether the mission presidents and their wives are going to come to Conference, and whether we are going to hold a Seminar.

I said that it is a question of holding of the Seminar, that is all there is to it; and President Moyle said that the basic idea of the Seminar separate from the General Conference is that at General Conference time we have so many other things we cannot concentrate on the Seminar. We

---

35. The First Presidency authorized Sarofim's baptism, then questions regarding the status of his marriage and the possibility of public-relations repercussions surfaced.

hold it in the summer time just at the edge of the vacation so the Brethren would not be unduly interfered with.

I said, "It is like holding another Conference. We have our Semi-Annual Conference; we have our Annual Conference; we have our June Conference; and you have your Seminar. I would rather do away with one of the Conferences rather than add to it. I am ready to do away with the Semi-Annual Conference, and have that meeting once a year."

President Moyle exclaimed, "Amen, amen; I am too."

President Brown said, "I would support you in that. I think there would be some opposition, however."

I replied: "You will get opposition of course. For several years now, I have been convinced that the Annual Conference and the June Conference with the Mutual [Improvement Association] would be all we need; especially if we put in a Seminar for missionary work."

President Moyle said that with this short-wave, there would be few of the mission presidents who would not be able to get the proceedings of the Conference; and I said that it would make a big difference to our propagandizing. [He] said, "I am convinced of this. If we have our zone instructors covering the missions, we would have little excuse for holding a Seminar. There is a copy of a letter around the building that President [Warren E.] Pugh[36] wrote to stake presidents in California that is entirely out of line. I did not see it until it was circulating the building. It had not emanated from our office. We didn't have anything to do with it. Since Brother Burton went to California, we have not had a zone instructor over there, and President Pugh has got together with President Stone, and this is the way President Stone wanted it, and the meeting of the other stake presidents was held, and they worked this out as I found out on investigation. It was worked out with their approval, but it's wrong, basically wrong. If we had these zone instructors for all the missions and could keep in touch with the zone instructors, we would really have no need for a Seminar. But, where we have so many of them that are

---

36. Warren E. Pugh (1910–90) was president of the Northern California Mission. On his return home, after his tenure as mission president, he would resume management of the intermountain dealership for the Cummins Engine Company, along with his sons, in selling and servicing long-haul refrigerated tractor–trailers. He would be invited to join the Sunday school board and Church Finance Committee and would be elected to the Utah State Senate, eventually becoming the majority leader.

not in a zone, we ought to have some way to keep contact with them to keep them somewhere in line. Otherwise, within a period of two years, they develop diversified practices and ideas, some good and some bad."

I remarked, "It is easy to understand how the Apostasy took place in the early days."

President Brown added, "Take the heads away, and you are done."

President Moyle said, "Leave this alone, and you get something contrary to the Church. That is the way the Roman branch of the Church took precedence. As big as we are now, the amount of assistance and instruction and supervision that we can give is essential to maintain the integrity of the Church and the efficiency of our work."

I said that we are holding that whole proposition up, that it is going farther than the correlating of studies. It is going to the point of suggesting a change in the organization of the Church. That is the vital point now.

President Moyle said, "This program was suggested in 1948; it is in the files." I said that I did not remember it.[37]

President Moyle said that it was presented at great length to the Presidency and the Twelve; and I said, "Yes, but we didn't accept it." President Moyle replied, "No, we did not."

I said, "This latest suggestion is striking at the very heart of it. They wanted to see me, but I told them we shall have to take it under further consideration, and that is where it is standing." But, they are in a transition now. If the correlation committee comes in with a new plan, it will be well if this is not emphasized.

Dr. Ebeid Sarofim, Egyptian, and Two Wives—I inquired as to the status of the matter presented by President [T. Bowring] Woodbury relating to the baptism of Dr. Ebeid Sarofim, the professor at London University, who is married to two wives.

The correspondence on this case was reviewed, including the opinion of the London solicitors to the effect that no legal action in the matter would likely be taken in Great Britain since the marriages were performed in Egypt where they are legal. The correspondence indicated also

---

37. Harold B. Lee had proposed in 1948 that the church correlate different areas of activity, but President George Albert Smith had rejected the suggested change for what Lee considered "sentimental" reasons. Quinn, *Extensions*, 18–19; Goates, *Harold B. Lee*, 365–66.

that President [N. Eldon] Tanner was to receive an oral reply to his question as to whether or not Dr. Sarofim may be baptized, a memorandum stating that the oral permission would be given.

I said, "I have heard, incidentally, that this man is coming here to visit us."

President Moyle remarked, "That will give us something; it will go through every newspaper in America."

I said that President Tanner has not been notified earlier.

Review of the correspondence disclosed that Dr. Sarofim was legally married to both wives in Egypt, and one daughter came to England to attend Oxford University. President Woodbury was informed that Dr. Sarofim should inform his first wife of his marriage to a second wife. The file also indicated that Dr. Sarofim had complied with this instruction. President Moyle commented that the opinion given by the London solicitors controls was that the marriages were legal in Egypt. Both marriages are recognized as legal in the country of which he is a citizen. I presume the same rule would apply in the United States. Our courts have uniformly held that the law of the domicile of the marriage controls. I said that if he has done that, and married them legally, we will have to recognize them just as we must next November when we send missionaries to Nigeria.

Comment was made upon an earlier ruling in the matter of Indians who had married more than one wife, and it was decided that they may be baptized if they were legally married according to their tribal custom.

I said, "I do not see anything else to do. Let the chips fall where they may. A Nigerian priest, to become a member of the Church, was told that he could not be baptized lest he did away with one of his wives. He slept on it over night, and came the next morning and told Brother Williams that he had decided to let one of his wives go back to her father. That is a cruel thing to do."

President Moyle said that the Manifesto does not apply because these are not marriages under the New and Everlasting Covenant. These are marriages under the law of the land where they live.

President Brown asked, "What will you do when this man wants to take one of his wives to the Temple?"

I replied, "Let him take both of them. You will have to let both of them."

To this, President Brown asked, "If he can, why not I?" and President Moyle answered, "Because your wife won't let you."

I said that it is prohibited just as it was in the days of the Book of Mormon.

President Moyle commented, "The way I look upon the Manifesto, is that it prevents anyone from entering upon a plural marriage without the consent of the President. The President was told not to use the power he had. That is the way I look at the Manifesto. It is not to be used, or any power of the Church."

President Brown said, "The statement of President Joseph F. Smith in 1904 is pretty sweeping. I am wondering what position we are going to be in if you say to these people we will let you join the Church and let you become members and have the privileges of the Church, including the Temple. I wonder how we are going to differentiate from those who are married legally."

I said, "I think we will have to differentiate. These men practicing it now are against the law. They are law breakers against the law of the land and the law of the Church;" that this man in Egypt obeyed the law, but he cannot go through the temple in this country.

President Brown asked, "Can he go in England or Switzerland?"

I answered, "No, we will have to draw the line there. That is our only safeguard."[38]

President Moyle asked, "Would you let him take his first wife through?" to which I answered, "No."

President Moyle said, "We always have the out that the work can be done for them vicariously;" to which I replied, "Yes, That's the stand we will have to take, Brethren, and make a note of it."

President Brown said, "That is the only safety;" and President Moyle added, "Yes, we could not make it otherwise."

October 2, 1962, 8:45–10:00 a.m. Attended the regular meeting of the First Presidency. After considering a number of official matters, I asked Elder Nathan Eldon Tanner to come into the meeting. We discussed with him matters pertaining to Dr. Ebeid Sarofim, Egyptian, now teaching at

---

38. Gradually it was decided that monogamy should be a requirement, regardless of local customs—even for baptism. Quinn, "Plural Marriage," 274–75, 292n226.

the London University, who by Egyptian law, is married to two women, and who is converted to the Gospel and seeking baptism.

President Tanner said he had tried to communicate with Dr. Sarofim before he left London, but had left with President Marion D. Hanks[39] of the British Mission the matter of following it up. I said that the latest information is that Dr. Sarofim's first wife had come to England and had not met with the second wife. President Tanner said that is something he does not know, and that when he returns he will pursue the matter. He said he thinks it is a good thing to let the matter rest to see what Dr. Sarofim's attitude is. I said that for the present, we had better let it remain as it is until we learn more about the relationship. I said it is a question as to whether or not we should begin to press the matter or wait for him to do this. President Tanner said that he had applied for baptism with President T. Bowring Woodbury, formerly President of the British Mission, and that Dr. Sarofim was told that President Woodbury could not go forward until President Woodbury has authority to do so because of the plural marriage, and that is the way it stands. President Tanner said that Dr. Sarofim has applied for baptism and is left with the understanding that we would notify him. President Brown said that he understood it would be in order [acceptable] to go ahead with the baptism if there was no objection; that the attorney's opinion in writing had been received. However, I said that we shall wait until after Conference, and that we would see Brother Tanner again.

October 4, 1962, meeting of First Presidency and Twelve. ... I thanked the Brethren for their suggestions regarding someone to fill the vacancy in the Quorum of the Twelve caused by the death of Elder George Q. Morris,[40] and said that we now have before us the responsibility which the

---

39. The president of the British Mission had also been a member of the First Council of Seventy since 1953. Marion Duff Hanks (1921–2011) would become an Assistant to the Twelve in 1968 and receive emeritus status in 1992. He had a law degree from the University of Utah (he was born in Salt Lake City) and taught in the Church Educational System prior to his call to church leadership.

40. George Quayle Morris (1874–1962) died just after April conference on the 23rd. He and McKay had been friends for over fifty years, and Morris had been an apostle for eight years. After studying at Brigham Young Academy (BYU) and the University of Utah, and serving a mission to Great Britain, he had acquired his father's tile and monument company and had chaired the committee that created the This Is the Place Monument.

original Council of the Twelve had when they met together and asked the Lord to guide them in filling a vacancy in the Twelve, and that was a very important occasion in the history of the former-day Church. I said that I had always been impressed with what Peter said on that occasion, "From those who have been with us while Christ was here and who witnessed his resurrection, we are to choose a man to take his place."

I then said that the First Presidency had considered the full list of names submitted, and that one who it seems is worthy to fill the vacancy is Brother Nathan Eldon Tanner,[41] now presiding over the West European Mission. The brethren unanimously approved of Brother Tanner.

October 9, 1962, 7:30–8:15 a.m. Elder Nathan Eldon Tanner called in company with Dr. Ebeid Sarofim, an Egyptian, Professor of Law at the London University, who is visiting Salt Lake City. He has attended all sessions of the Conference. He is here at the invitation of President T. Bowring Woodbury, formerly President of the British Mission.

Our conversation was along general lines. He is a Coptic Christian, and belongs to the Coptic Christian Church. We talked about John Mark who was the founder of the Coptic Christian religion in Africa. I recounted having met a prominent man at the University who lectured on the Coptic religion.

I tried to avoid saying anything to Dr. Sarofim about his family relations, feeling that as President of the Church I should not talk about his having two wives whom he has married under Egyptian law; but when he said he wanted me to give him a blessing on his family relations, or a blessing because he is going to be baptized into the Church, I said, "I am very glad to hear of your conversion, and the Lord bless you in your association in seeking the truth."

Dr. Sarofim presented me with a very old edition of the "Koran" in Egyptian h[ie]rogl[y]phics.[42]

He then left the office, and President Tanner remained and said he would like to speak to me about this man. I said that I had tried to get him

---

41. Tanner had been called to serve as an Assistant to the Twelve two years earlier. The previous summer he had driven McKay around Scotland when they organized the Glasgow Stake. While in Utah for the October general conference, he had intended to propose increased funding for church activities in Europe.

42. The diary has "hyroglphics."

last night, and that I did not know whether or not I should talk to him about the matter. He said that he had spoken to President Moyle about it. I said, "Is there anything I should know," and President Tanner said that he is not sure whether Dr. Sarofim has spoken to his first wife, who is in Egypt, about his marriage to the second wife, and that that is the condition to be complied with before he can be baptized into the Church.

Later, when I took this matter up at the meeting of the First Presidency, President Moyle said that he had talked with President Tanner confidentially, and that he felt there should be a condition of Dr. Sarofim's baptism, and that so long as his first wife is alive he should not come to America (he having applied for a position at the Brigham Young University[43] ...

I said that he has not conformed to the first condition, and there should be no baptism here, and that President Woodbury should know that; that I had told President Tanner that the matter is now in his hands. I told him not to hurt the young man,[44] but to handle it wisely. I think he could not be in better hands than with President Tanner, and that it ought to turn out all right. Dr. Sarofim's first wife is a daughter of an aristocratic Egyptian family, and she cannot leave Egypt without risking loss of family property; the second is a woman whom he met in Switzerland, and has taken her to London with him. The two marriages—according to legal opinion—are lawful under Egyptian law.[45]

---

43. See Wilkinson diary, Oct. 8, 1962.

44. Sarofim was forty-one years old.

45. According to the minutes of this meeting, "President McKay said President Tanner had talked with him this morning about the application of Dr. Sarofim for baptism. He and Dr. Sarofim met President McKay at 7:45 a.m. Dr. [Ernest L.] Wilkinson came in later. He had in mind employing Dr. Sarofim at BYU. ...

"President McKay: Do you remember when we discussed this before we said that this man would have to report to his first wife in Egypt that he has a second wife. We received word from someone that he had done that. Now I received word yesterday ... that Dr. Sarofim had not reported to his wife that he was married to a second wife. ...

"President Brown: In that case Brother Wilkinson had better lay off this.

"President McKay: I am going to tell Brother Wilkinson to have nothing to do with it.

"President Moyle: I talked it over very confidentially with President Tanner. I felt there ought to be a condition of his baptism, and as long as his first wife is alive he should not come to America. We could not have him at the BYU.

"President McKay: He has not conformed to the first condition and there should be no baptism here. President Woodbury should know that. I spoke to President Tanner and told him it was in his hands. I told him not to hurt this young man but to handle it wisely. He could not be in better hands than with President Tanner. It ought

October 11, 1962, First Presidency meeting. I said that the important matter before us this morning is what we are going to tell Brother Nathan Eldon Tanner, particularly regarding the Nigerian situation; that we have already decided to put Nigeria under the West European Mission, and have already decided that we shall send couples down there, married couples without children, so as not to subject children to the conditions there. Brother Tanner will go down accompanied by Brother LaMar Williams, and the two couples and receive the Nigerian people into the Church with a full knowledge that they will have every blessing of membership excepting the Priesthood. I stated that we have made no promise, and we shall state plainly to them that they are not to have the Priesthood. They will receive baptism and be entitled to the sacrament, and all the opportunities offered by the Auxiliaries; that the local people can preside in the Auxiliary associations, but the Elders who will be appointed there under the direction of the President of the West European Mission will take charge of sacrament meetings, administer the sacrament, and will exercise everything pertaining to the Priesthood.

I stated that one very important question is like the one which arose yesterday, when we had an application of a Mohammedan who is really a Coptic Christian and not a Mohammedan, who under the laws of Egypt is entitled to two wives. We have already considered that he could not visit his first wife personally but she has accepted his second wife whom he married according to the Egyptian law, but we think we had better not be connected with that in any way. I told Brother Tanner to leave his conversion and his baptism to the British Mission. Then followed the following conversation:

"I have not heard from President Tanner, have you?"

President [Henry D.] Moyle said, "Not since we talked."

President McKay: "I think our decision not to have him baptized here under President Woodbury was very wise, even though he himself, a very refined educated gentleman, will feel hurt to a degree. I do not know that he will but we shall leave that in the European Mission where it began and where it should continue.

---

to turn out all right." Typed excerpt from the minutes, Quinn Papers, photocopy courtesy of Smith–Pettit Foundation.

"Now that same question of plural marriage will have to be faced within the month down in Nigeria."

President [Hugh B.] Brown: "Are they polygamous?"

President McKay: "Some of them—those who can afford it. They are recognized by the government."

President Moyle: "These leaders are polygamists. One has been told that he cannot come into the Church and he reported to Brother Williams his willingness to put away one of his wives. Both are young. After a sleepless night he came to Brother Williams and said I have decided to put away one of my wives. Which one? The younger one. He will keep her three children and send her back to her father. Well now, I think that is not right."

President Brown: "That is the very thing our fathers refused to do; President [Joseph F.] Smith and the rest of them."[46]

President McKay: "And the government approved. I think we will have to let them keep their wives and baptize them."

President Moyle: I do not see any reason for anything else.

President Brown: That is the law of the land there.

President McKay: Now of course since they are negroes, they can never go through the temple, so that question will not come up. It will come out with this man, but I think we had better refuse to acknowledge his relationship in this life anyhow.

President Moyle: It will not come up as long as his first wife is living because she cannot go to the temple. And under the rule of the Church he cannot be sealed to his second wife until he is sealed to the first wife.

President McKay: In this question in Nigeria we will not ask this leader to turn that wife out and keep these children.

---

46. This is a reference to the fact that church leaders continued to live with their plural wives after the 1890 Manifesto. The ambiguity that surrounded the Manifesto and the amnesty petition sent to US President Harrison now made the issue of cohabiting with plural wives legally and emotionally problematic. Joseph F. Smith had interpreted the amnesty agreement with US President Benjamin Harrison in 1893 to mean only that he could not take additional wives, not that he would have to leave the ones he had. An outraged US Senate committee listened to the church president admit in 1904 that he had fathered eleven children by five wives since the Manifesto. See his testimony in Paulos, *Mormon Church on Trial*, 52–53. See also B. Carmon Hardy's *Doing the Works of Abraham*, released in 2007 by the Arthur H. Clark Company, chapter 9.

President Brown: It is morally wrong, wrong to the children. He is the father of these children.

President McKay: You know what effect this will have on these "Fundamentalists."

President Brown: They will make the most of it.

President McKay: We shall not give this Nigerian matter publicity. We shall help them and build their meeting houses, and we shall give them every consideration we give in other missions. They are building their houses now one hundred per cent. They will appreciate our assisting them so every branch will have a meetinghouse. <u>Now we are all united on that attitude, are we not</u>? We shall not take it up this morning, but Brother Tanner is going back and he will want to know just what to do.

President Moyle: There is one thing not clear in my mind about Dr. Sarofim. I do not believe that the second marriage took place under the laws of Egypt. I doubt very much that it is legal if it was performed under the laws of Switzerland.

President Brown: I think our record shows that we got a report, I do not know that it is correct.

President McKay: He cannot go back to Egypt. He has never taken his second wife back to Egypt. That makes his marriage under the English law illegal. I am so glad we did not approve of his being baptized here. …

President Moyle: On this Nigerian matter, if these figures are right, if we are going to baptize 4,000 people, the question I have in my mind is how long would it take for one couple to get around and administer the sacrament to them.

President McKay: We shall have two couples and President Tanner and Brother Williams. Brother Williams will not take his wife or children.

President Brown: There will be Brother Williams and two couples besides Brother Williams.

President Moyle: Have we picked those couples?

President McKay: No, not yet. We will instruct President Tanner and they will come down in November and we want to be clear on this question.

President Moyle: I don't know anything else to do, but we have got to do it with our eyes open as to the risk we are running. Every man becomes to us a potential threat in the future. They will make a fuss that will be world-wide. I am not opposed to it. I see the potential danger that can arise in the future.

President McKay: Let us face it. Just as soon as these branches are organized the leaders will want to come here to Conference. They are entitled to a trip here just as the presidents from England are.

President Moyle: But they will have none of the local men appointed branch presidents. They will be only heads of auxiliary organizations. If you bring the Relief Society you will have to bring the Relief Society sisters here. We have not yet done that in any other than stakes. We have brought no Relief Society sisters from the missions to conference.

President McKay: I think we shall be well to guard against that possibility. Already there has been an expressed desire to have leaders come over.

President Brown: We could not pay their fare. There is no one qualified to receive the fare over and back. If there are some who can do it on their own, that is their business.

President Moyle: If you have a concentration there. I do not know how concentrated they are. You can have 4,000 members of the Church conceivably.

President McKay: We shall have double that number as soon as you baptize them. I think it will be well for Brother Tanner and Brother Williams to go to the heads of the Nigerian nation and tell them what we are doing.

President Moyle: I do too, and then you are going to be confronted sooner or later with the understanding of what you are going to do about giving them a stake.

President Brown: You cannot do that without importing all the offices. That is something we will have to meet when we get to it. It will be at least a year.

President Moyle: With 8,000 people concentrated, they will know what the organization of the Church is.

President McKay: And they have been using the name of the Church for over two years and asking for baptism to be made legal and to be properly baptized. They use the right term, but I do not see anything else to do. Make them heads of auxiliaries and throw the responsibility locally upon them and have these men who will be sent spend two and one-half years down there and administer the sacrament and conduct the sacrament meetings. Bless them and baptize their children.

President Moyle: I am wondering, I am just thinking out loud. Maybe they ought to be advised from the very beginning that it would not be possible for us to set up a regular Church organization now or in the foreseeable future, and if the question of organizing a stake were to arise, we could refer back to the initial instructions.

President Brown: If they are forewarned.

President Moyle: I don't see how we could ever organize wards and stakes down there. When you have a concentration of 400 to 500 people in branches or 4000 to 8000 people within a stake area and they are going to learn very rapidly what our Church organization is and we have stakes all around them in Europe. I think they should be forewarned about this as well as about priesthood unless we see our way clear to have such an organization within a year or so. The organization is a problem as well as the priesthood. It is almost inconceivable to carry on the work of a stake without the priesthood.

President McKay: Especially the Aaronic Priesthood. Deacons and teachers. If we could confer the Aaronic Priesthood on them, it would be no clearer. The question was asked as to what effect this will have on the missionary work in South Africa. They do not want it in Johannesburg.

President Moyle: We just could not do that in South Africa what we are doing in Nigeria.

President Brown: And that is not our fault. It is the government's fault. The government in South Africa would not permit us to do it.

President McKay: We have taken one step and it will be announced to the world next Tuesday and this will be associated with if it is right for Brother Tanner of the West European Mission and Brother Williams and anyone else of our elders and their wives to carry the Church organization to the negroes. We have got to look forward and brig the mission organization to thousands of negroes. There will be opposition when they go to the government and it depends largely upon the attitude of the government officials and what the attitude of the negroes will be. Now we will have a man who is very wise and he is in touch with the English government officials when Nigeria was in the British government. Most of these negroes speak English. We shall have no difficulty in learning

451

the language. We shall help them build their meetinghouses and these meetinghouses will soon be used as school houses in helping the children to read. When the children join the Church, the next thing will be to have them learn to read. One boy has been driven away from home and he was told that if he joined the Mormons, he will be driven away from home. The last we heard about him was he was sleeping out in the country and he was drawn to a group who called themselves Mormons. There will be hundreds of them. They will be meeting in Sunday School and the Mutual and Primary within a few months. They are going to read and we will have to have some elementary schools in the meetinghouses.

President Brown: It is a big movement. It is history making.

President McKay: If we could just give them the Aaronic Priesthood. I suppose there is no way to differentiate. The Lord will have to do it. The Lord did that after the priesthood was taken away from the ancient prophets. That law was added as a school master to bring them to Christ. And that is all they had for hundreds of years.

President Brown: It was the Aaronic Priesthood?

President McKay: The Aaronic Priesthood.

President Brown: There seems to be a differentiation somewhat. I am wondering whether this prohibition against their having the priesthood was intended to include both. We rely mostly on that paragraph in Abraham in the Pearl of Great Price. I secretly hoped that the time would come when we could give them the Aaronic Priesthood.

Here is one of the saddest things in the policy of the Church. In years past we have baptized the negro. They have been faithful and just as faithful as any human beings can be and their children have attended Sunday School and Primary and they have associated with our children in Primary. We saw one of them at our socials, a member of the Primary school, who came there before the First Presidency and the Twelve. Do you remember?

President Moyle: Yes.

President McKay: [We knew that] in a year or so that child will be associated with other members of the Primary Association, the male part, and the boys will be recommended to the bishop to receive the priesthood. And on Friday that negro boy met with others in the Primary Association and Sunday evening the other boys went with the Primary class and were put on the stand and this boy sat down with his mother and he could not be there with the other boys to be recommended. Now that is a tragedy.

President Moyle: That's where the rub comes. That is what pulls at the heart strings of fathers and mothers.

President McKay: I think the Lord is not pleased with it.

President Moyle: Being they are his children and he has opened the door for them to go into the Celestial Kingdom through baptism, that's pretty hard treatment for the children.

President McKay: Only the Lord can change it, but that is what we are facing, Brethren, and we have gone so far now that we shall have to go down to Nigeria and baptize these people.

President Brown: But they ought to go first to the government officials.

President McKay: That is what I am presenting to you this morning. That is the right thing to do.

President Moyle: I think so.

President McKay: If they want to take the stand that they will not admit us, we shall thank the Lord and say that is all right. We shall receive that, and it will be their responsibility.

President Moyle: We will go as far as the Lord will let us. ...

At Council Meeting today, we discussed the case of Dr. Ebeid Sarofim, an Egyptian who has requested baptism. It was agreed by all present that this is a matter that should be handled in the British Mission, and that he should not be admitted into the Church by baptism here inasmuch as he has two wives, even though they were both married under Egyptian law (see Council Minutes of this day for details).

October 15, 1962, 11:45 a.m. At his request, met <u>Elder A. Theodore Tuttle</u>, of the First Council of Seventy, and President of the South American Mission, in our apartment at the Hotel Utah.

He reported his work in the South American Mission—said that everything is moving along very well. I asked him particularly about the <u>attitude of the members of the Church in Chil[e][47] toward Communism</u>. Brother Tuttle said there are members of the Church who are Communists, and I said to him, "how can they be Communists and still members

---

47. The diary has "Chili."

of the Church?" He said that they joined the Communists before they became members of the church; that Communism is the political party in Chil[e]. He said that he is afraid to say anything to the members about their affiliation.

I said, "No member of the Church can be a Communist." Brother Tuttle said that they are not really Communists; that they are such in the way some of our people were twenty years ago. I said, "You mean Socialism?" He said, "Yes, Socialism."

I made it very clear to Brother Tuttle that Communism and the Restored Gospel do not harmonize, and those who accept the Church must reject Communism.[48]

October 18, 1962, meeting of First Presidency and Twelve. ... Elder Howard W. Hunter reported that recently a negro was baptized in the Great Lakes Mission, he being the husband of an Hawaiian woman who accepted the gospel when presented by the missionaries. This man was informed prior to baptism that he could not hold the priesthood, and had a full understanding of what the situation would be. Now it appears that this man's father, who is Pentecostal minister and has a congregation, has become interested in the gospel. The missionaries have not been to see him, although they have been asked to do so, and the mission president wants direction. The negro [minister]'s son, who is now a member of the Church, says his father wants to join the Church and bring in his whole congregation of colored folks.

I said that Elder N. Eldon Tanner, President of the European Mission, is arranging to go to Nigeria following the November election, and that he will be accompanied by LaMar Williams; that Brother Williams' wife will not go with them; that, however, two other good brethren will be selected to go, taking their wives to assist in opening the work there; that four thousand of those negro people in Nigeria are asking for baptism. Elder Tanner has been requested to go to the rulers of Nigeria when he arrives there, and tell them exactly what we intend to do, and if the rulers look upon the project with favor we may have a whole nation in that

---

48. For an account of Tuttle's years in South America, see Mark L. Grover's 2008 book, *A Land of Promise and Prophecy: Elder A. Theodore Tuttle in South America, 1960–1965,* published by the BYU Religious Studies Center.

country joining the Church. However, they have a right to be baptized if they are thoroughly converted, and want to come into the Church, although they do not have the right to the Priesthood and they understand that this is the case. I said the same thing applies to these negro people in the Great Lakes Mission.

We felt that it was best that nothing be done about the matter until after the November election for the reason that if we were to baptize a considerable number of negro people at this time, certain politicians might take the view that it was done to influence the negro vote in favor of George Romney in his candidacy for Governor of Michigan.

October 31, 1962, First Presidency meeting. We read a letter from President Theodore M. Burton who reported a visit made by President William S. Erekson after his release as President of the Swiss Mission to members living in Poland. President Erekson reported that he was received kindly and found the people to be very friendly. President Burton reported that he had talked with President Fetzer and President Erekson, who feel that missionary work can be done in East Germany and in Poland if missionaries are not from NATO countries, since such missionaries would be regarded as spies. Missionaries from Scandinavian countries, Finland or Switzerland, however, would not be under that disadvantage. I decided[,] with President [Henry D.] Moyle concurring[,] that missionary work in a Communist-dominated country, at present, is inadvisable. I stated that we should be dealing with governments which have no honor and who would use us as tools to further their own purposes at the very first opportunity they could get.

November 14, 1962, 5:00 a.m. ... As I left the Hotel [Utah] to take a morning's walk, I learned of the explosion which occurred on the outside of the east door of the Salt Lake Temple at 1:30 a.m. by a bomb planted by someone unknown. I immediately went over to see what damage had been done. The explosive, which was probably attached to the right-hand doorknob of the large, double oak doors, blasted a five-inch hole through the right-hand entrance door. Flying fragments of metal and debris were shot through glass panels into a set of interior doors several feet behind the large entrance doors. Nine exterior windows were shattered. Fortunately, the heavy oak doors can be repaired, and the windows replaced. I was dismayed to learn that there is no watchman on duty between the hours of 12 o'clock midnight and 6 o'clock in the morning.

I directed that all "crank letters" which have been received during the past year be turned over to the Federal Bureau of Investigation officials. I also called Bishop Victor L. Brown of the Presiding Bishopric's office and told him that I was surprised to learn that the Temple grounds were unguarded between the hours of midnight and 6 o'clock in the morning; that that must not be—that someone should be on guard every minute and especially during the night and early morning hours.

November 15, 1962, First Presidency meeting. I commented upon the several verified reports which have been received concerning baptisms of children in the mission fields without consent of parents, and said that this is contrary to all established missionary policies and practices of the Church, and always has been; that such baptisms must be controlled absolutely, and that the practice must be stopped. President [Henry D.] Moyle said that the missionary who violates this principle should be sent home, and that appropriate disciplinary measures should be taken to stop these violations. I said to him, "I am surely glad to hear you say that!"

The disposition of some Mission Presidents to tolerate the practice for the sake of a record was mentioned by President [Hugh B.] Brown, and President Moyle suggested that a letter be sent to Mission Presidents on the subject. I asked President Moyle to present the matter to the Twelve at the next meeting so that they will understand our position. ...

[With the First Presidency and Twelve:] At this meeting we discussed the matter of reports that have been received from various missions in this country and in Europe concerning the baptizing of children without the parents being fully informed of the true situation. President Moyle, in reporting this situation, said he personally felt that a missionary who performed baptisms in violation of the rules should be sent home, dishonorably released.[49] Elder Spencer W. Kimball said he would

---

49. This is perplexing because Moyle was the architect, along with his protégé, T. Bowring Woodbury, of the so-called New Era of church growth in Europe. His idea had been to work quickly and cast a wide net, and to construct chapels that would attract more converts, borrowing heavily from banks to do so. Elders Hanks, Smith,

be opposed to any such drastic measure as suggested by President Moyle; that he felt that much of the problem is with the mission presidents, and that the mission president should be asked to watch these situations. In the discussion which followed, mention was made of certain pressures that have been brought to bear in some missions, in Europe particularly, where missionaries are given a certain quota of baptisms by the mission presidents or district supervisors, and certain penalties have been attached to their failure to reach these quotas; that is, they have been deprived of certain privileges because of not being able to meet the quota. President Brown mentioned that in some cases the missionaries have been told that they should not attend Sacrament meetings, but should spend the time proselyting. I stated that the missionaries should attend Sacrament meeting; that if they are members of a stake, they should go to sacrament meeting in their stake; if they are in the mission field, they should hold their own sacrament meeting.

It was agreed that a letter should be sent to all presidents of missions giving instructions regarding the baptizing of children.

November 16, 1962, First Presidency meeting. We took up with the Presiding Bishopric the matter of guarding and careful supervision of Temple Square and Church Buildings. It was reported that one watchman is in the Tabernacle 24 hours a day, and another in the Temple 24 hours a day. The watchman is in the Temple Annex, and the contractor who is doing the repairs and building which are now going on has a watchman. These two were together when the explosion at the Temple occurred. The guard who has heretofore been at the Gate House on Temple Block has been leaving at midnight and then coming on duty again at 6:00 a.m. Hereafter, however, there will be a watchman on duty 24 hours a day. I expressed surprise that the watchman leaves the Temple grounds and comes over to the Deseret Gymnasium.

Bishop Victor L. brown presented a proposal that a man with a police dog be hired to tour the Temple grounds at night. It was suggested that the city be asked to hire this man and his dog, and that the Church

---

and Petersen, among others, were concerned about this problem. In early 1963 McKay would relieve Moyle of all responsibilities ("all but my title," Moyle said) because of the damage he had caused. Poll, *Working the Divine Miracle*, 217.

reimburse the City; that in this event the man will be responsible to the City. We approved of this suggestion. It was also suggested that the floodlights on the Temple and on Temple Square be kept on all night; that light is the best deterrent to vandalism. I inquired if the gates are kept locked, and Bishop Brown said they are, but in the area which the contractors use for an entrance, the only provision made is a low chain-link fence. We decided that the height of this fence should be increased. Additional ADT clocks[50] will be installed at a cost of $225 a year.

November 21, 1962, 8:30 a.m. ... Set apart Brother LaMar Stevenson Williams as a missionary to the Nigerian Mission to labor under the direction of President Nathan Eldon Tanner of the West European Mission. Presidents [Henry D.] Moyle and [Hugh B.] Brown assisted in this setting apart.

Received a letter from Nathan Eldon Tanner stating that he has made arrangements to fly from London to Nigeria November 29. Said he had checked with the Nigeria High Commissioner in London, and finds that everything is in order as far as his papers are concerned; that he had given him the names of both the Canadian and American representatives in Lagos, Nigeria, whom he can contact, and who should be helpful. Later, I sent a cable to Brother Tanner telling him that our blessings go with him and his companions on this eventful mission. ...

Later, President Tanner's departure was postponed due to the fact that the Nigerian Government had not approved their visas for entrance into the country.

December 11, 1962, First Presidency meeting. We read a letter from President Marion D. Hanks of the British Mission in which he reported that there is a considerable agitation in the Aliens Department of the Government because of complaints that have been made against the missionaries' baptizing children and accosting children and interfering with parental control and family solidarity. This report, President Hanks says,

---

50. When the ADT (American District Telegraph) Company was founded in 1874, it offered neighborhoods emergency call boxes that connected to a central office by way of telegraphic transmission. The clocks were a later innovation that were used by watchmen and indicated when they had visited a given location to be sure everything was secure.

came from one who works for the government in the Alien's Department. He further states that there has been so much complaint and discussion that there is some hint of an official investigation. It was decided to send this letter to President [N. Eldon] Tanner of the West European Mission and ask that he look into the matter and submit a report.

December 14, 1962, meeting of First Presidency and Presiding Bishopric. Among many items discussed with them were:

(1) Negroes and Church Membership—Bishop [John H.] Vandenberg mentioned a negro family, the mother of which is a member of the church and is the fifth generation in the Church, her great-great-grandfather having come to Salt Lake City with Brigham Young and the pioneers. Her husband is a Methodist and she has one child 9 years of age who has not been baptized. The question was asked if we are to make any effort to have her children baptized. The answer was we certainly should. The question was also asked if we should send ward teachers and Relief society sisters, etc. to these people. The answer was yes.

The bishop mentioned another problem pertaining to negroes which had been raised by a letter received, namely, that there is a senior member of the Aaronic Priesthood whose wife is reportedly the great-granddaughter of a negro. She looks white. She and her husband are Young Marrieds leaders. They do not know whether or not she really is negro, although the grandfather is reported to be a negro. It was reported that these people have boys who will soon reach the age to have the priesthood. I said, "Do not let these people suffer from just hearsay; that unless we have definite evidence that there is negro blood, we should not withhold the priesthood."

The Bishop mentioned a similar request that had come from the Vancouver Stake where a bishop observes that there are possibly negroid characteristics in a newly-baptized family. The boy of the family is of age and otherwise worthy of the Aaronic Priesthood. I said "the answer is the same in that case; that we should not let hearsay interfere."

December 27, 1962, officiating at wedding in Logan temple. During the time I was officiating at the wedding, I had a strange physical experience, one I have never felt before. As there was no chair, I had to stand during the whole ceremony, and suddenly I became dizzy and my whole body trembled, and I was unable to control the shaking. I was worried; however, I was able to continue without the audience noticing my condition.

13   Benson, Difficulties with Birchers, and Declining Health, 1963

> Lou Jean [McKay's daughter][1] reported [to Clare Middlemiss] that her father came into the dining room from his bedroom this morning and said: "Lou Jean, I cannot button my shirt; I have tried for hours, but I just cannot do it; my fingers will not operate; I think I have had a stroke! —November 10, 1963

January 10, 1963, 2:00–3:00 p.m. ... In my private office, I held a meeting with Elder Nathan Eldon Tanner who gave an excellent, detailed report of his visit to Nigeria.[2]

He told of his meeting with Government officials regarding the opening of missionary work among the Nigerian people; of the several meetings he held with groups of people who are interested in the Church; of their living conditions, etc.

Brother Tanner reported that at a meeting held at Aba, Nigeria, on Sunday, December 30, 1962, he offered a special prayer in which he blessed the land and the governments and the people. Said that he dedicated Nigeria for missionary work to be conducted as directed by the Lord through his Prophet.

---

1. Louise Jeanette McKay Blood (1906–2002) began her life in Ogden, Utah, but graduated from Queen Mary School for Girls in Liverpool and studied piano at the Paris Conservatory of Music during a time when her parents ran the European Mission. At the University of Utah, she met her future husband, Russell Henry Blood, who had himself previously studied at the Sorbonne in Paris and went on to medical school at the University of Pennsylvania and a practice in neurosurgery in Los Angeles, as well as military service in World War II and the Korean Conflict. They had one child.

2. Tanner and his wife, Sara, took a Christmas holiday trip to Nigeria and returned cautiously optimistic.

Elder Tanner stated that if a mission is to be established, it is his opinion that they should do no proselyting; but that they do a very careful job of screening before baptism. Brother Tanner submitted a copy of the form he filled out in applying to the government for a mission in Nigeria. ...

After listening to Elder Tanner's report, I was deeply impressed that it was most fortunate that I had appointed Elder Tanner to go to Nigeria to look into the opening of the work there. I do not know of another man who could have met the conditions so favorably and intelligently as Brother Tanner did. He was inspired to meet the government leaders in Nigeria and accomplished a very fine mission.

January 18, 1963, 8:30 a.m. I met with the Presiding Bishopric. President [Henry D.] Moyle was absent, being in the hospital preliminary to having some teeth extracted, and President [Hugh B.] Brown is in South America. Bishop John H. Vandenberg and Bishop Victor L. Brown were present.

Among matters brought to my attention by them were:

(1) Nauvoo Temple—Bishop Vandenberg said that they had made a preliminary study of the Nauvoo Temple excavation situation and read certain items from the study that has been made, one of which pertained to artifacts recovered. He said that no report has as yet been received from the University of Southern Illinois people who have been investigating this subject. The question was considered as to what would be done after the foundation and basement had been completely uncovered. It was thought that this project had cost and would cost a lot of money if it were continued. To complete the excavation would involve the removal of trees and houses, and the department of anthropology at the University of Southern Illinois say that work must be done very carefully to preserve what can be preserved of the font and other things. It was the recommendation of the Bishopric that the hole be filled in, that the place be landscaped with lawn and possibly a marker placed in each corner to show people the dimensions and have a monument indicating what stood there, rather than have an uncovered hole.

I said that all hopes to rebuild the temple should be discouraged as there is no intention of doing that. I also felt that people who come there would be as much interested in seeing the surface of the ground where the temple stood as they would the excavation, if not more so, and let

462

them imagine what happened there. I thought it would do the Church just as much good as for them to see the excavated hole.

January 23, 1963, 7:30 a.m. ... Met by appointment at his request <u>Elder Ezra Taft Benson</u>, and had a lengthy conference with him regarding the <u>newspaper statement</u>[3] made by the First Presidency dated January 2, 1963 pertaining to political questions in general and the John Birch Society in particular. Elder Benson said the statement seemed to be level[ed] against him and his son, Reed, and also Brother [W. Cleon] Skousen.[4]

I told Brother Benson that it was intended to apply to them. I said that the statement made by him (Elder Benson) in favor of the John Birch Society was made by him, one of the Twelve, who is an international character and received international publicity, and that that is one reason the Presidency had to make the announcement in the newspapers.

<u>Elder Benson asked if this means that they must never mention Communism, and I said that, of course, they could mention Communism by saying that it is un-Christian in America and an evil thing</u>. I said it did not hurt my feelings for the accusation to be made that the John Birch Society is a secret society (which Elder Benson says it is not) because when there is a prairie fire sweeping over the country, men who fight the fire, often start fires themselves. I told Brother Benson, however, that he must not say that the Church favors such "a fire." <u>I said further that if members of the Church want to join the John Birch Society, they may pay the $12.00 dues if they wish; that that is up to them.</u>

9:30–11:00 a.m.—Attended the meeting of the First Presidency. President [Hugh B.] Brown was absent, he being in South America. Among other matters discussed was the <u>Missionary Committee</u>. I stated that there seemed to be some sentiment among the Brethren of the Twelve that they

---

3. This short excerpt captures the pith of their statement: "We denounce Communism as being anti-Christian, anti-American, and the enemy of freedom, but we think they who pretend to fight it by casting aspersions on our elected officials or other fellow citizens do the anti-Communist cause a great disservice." *Deseret News*, Jan. 2, 1963.

4. This potential cultural and political catastrophe had been brewing for some time. With overt acknowledgment of the Benson family's involvement in the John Birch Society, many people were offended and alarmed. McKay's concern, as it is expressed in this conversation, was over the bad press this divisive issue was generating nationally. It is important to note that counselors Brown and Moyle were equally upset over the recent inflammatory events. See Quinn, *Extensions*, 71.

are not consulted regarding missionary matters; that decisions are made by President [Henry D.] Moyle and Brother [Gordon B.] Hinckley. President Moyle said that there is no truth in such an attitude; that he did not know of any decision that they had made on their own. He said the only thing they do is take care of missionary assignments; that every other item of business goes before the Committee. He said that Brother Hinckley and he make no decisions of any kind that they do not bring to me. Recommendations are sent to President Moyle for Mission Presidents and they are brought to the First Presidency. He said Brother Hinckley had been given a rather free hand, and that he was in favor of continuing it because he does his work well, and that Brother [Boyd K.] Packer is doing a fine job and that he has implicit confidence in him.

I asked what President [Joseph Fielding] Smith's position with the committee is, and President Moyle said he presides, that as far as he is concerned he would be happy if the President of the Twelve could carry on; that he would like to see it left in their hands. I said that that is a question that is being held up now. President Moyle said he had honestly felt ever since he had been told to take charge of the Missionary Committee that it would be very desirable to have that Committee under the Twelve, and let them report to the First Presidency.

We discussed at some length what would happen under such an arrangement.

January 30, 1963, First Presidency meeting. Consideration was given to the matter of the desire of the Mutual Improvement Associations to introduce a course for the Mutual Study Class on communism. The matter has been submitted to the Reading Committee, and Elder Spencer W. Kimball makes inquiry as to whether this would be a proper course of study, these books being as follows: "A Study of Communism" by J. Edgar Hoover;[5] "Witness" by Whittaker Chambers;[6] "The Naked Communist"

---

5. Hoover's book had been released the previous year by Holt, Rinehart and Winston of Manhattan.

6. Chambers became an instant celebrity while testifying during the McCarthy years to the House Committee on Un-American Activities against Alger Hiss, a State Department official. Chambers, a Russian spy, had defected into the anti-Communist camp. His book, *Witness*, was published by Random House in 1952.

by W. Cleon Skousen; "The Red Carpet" by Ezra Taft Benson;[7] "Masters of Deceit" by J. Edgar Hoover; "You Can Trust The Communists (To Do Exactly As They Say)" by Dr. Fred C. Schwarz.[8]

I said that there is no objection to a study of the books listed. In this connection, however, I said that in approving this course, it is not intended that approval be given to the activities of the John Birch Society or any other self-perpetuating group, that the Church must not in any way be associated with a self-perpetuating groups, nor should this course of study be used as a means of increasing the membership of such groups.[9]

January 31, 1963, meeting of First Presidency and Twelve. I reported to the Council that the First Presidency had given consideration to the advisability of reorganizing the Missionary Committee, and now felt to recommend that the following serve as that Committee: President Joseph Fielding Smith—Chairman, Harold B. Lee—Vice-Chairman, Marion G. Romney, Gordon B. Hinckley, and Boyd K. Packer as members of the Committee. The motion was unanimously approved.[10]

I announced that it is the responsibility of the Missionary Committee to make recommendations to the First Presidency of brethren to serve as mission presidents, as has heretofore been the case. I said further that there is one other committee to be appointed, and the members of that committee will be named later.

Later, following the meeting, I telephoned to Joseph Fielding Smith, and told him that he may feel free to use any of the Twelve whom he may choose to serve on the Missionary Committee.

---

7. Benson's book, *The Red Carpet: A Forthright Evaluation of the Rising Tide of Socialism, the Royal Road to Communism*, published by Bookcraft of Salt Lake City, was a 1962 release.

8. Frederick Charles Schwarz (1913–2009) was an Australian physician who founded the Christian Anti-Communism Crusade. He conducted a successful speaking tour through the United States and moved his organization to California, where he remained for thirty-eight years.

9. This idea was soon dropped and no study manual was prepared. See the entry for Feb. 7, 1963.

10. McKay is streamlining oversight of the department by creating an executive committee in which junior apostles Gordon B. Hinckley and Boyd K. Packer would still do most of the hands-on work but would come under the immediate supervision of more senior apostles: Harold B. Lee, Marion G. Romney, and Joseph Fielding Smith.

February 4, 1963. Spent most of the morning taking up office matters with my secretary, Clare [Middlemiss]. She showed me the hundreds of letters from all over the United States which have been received from <u>members of the John Birch Society</u>. They have come as a result of a statement made by the First Presidency concerning that Society. I told her that we should not attempt to answer these letters, but that members of the Church who have written asking whether or not their membership in the Church is in jeopardy if they belong to the John Birch Society should have an answer.[11] I dictated later a letter to be sent to the members. I also asked that a copy be sent to each of the General Authorities so that they would know what to say to members who inquire regarding the Church's stand on this matter.

February 5, 1963, 9:45 a.m. <u>Elder Gordon B. Hinckley</u> of the Council of the Twelve came in to report a telephone conversation he had had with President [Henry D.] Moyle from London last evening. President Moyle feels well. He said that <u>Dr. Ebeid Sarofim</u>, who was in Salt Lake City last October applying for baptism, has been to Egypt and consulted with his first wife, and has met all the conditions which were laid down prerequisite to his baptism. President Moyle indicated that he feels well about permitting Dr. Sarofim to be baptized, and suggested if it meets with my approval, that I cable authorization to President Mark E. Petersen to act in the matter. It was decided to send a cable to President Petersen giving him authority to take the proper action.

February 7, 1963, meeting of the First Presidency and Twelve. (3) <u>Negroes— marriage with whites—Racial Intermarriage Statute</u>. Elder [Richard L.] Evans reported that [Democratic] State Senator [Vernon L.] Holman of Panguitch had called on him last night and reported <u>regarding a bill before the [Utah] Legislature that would void or withdraw from the statutes the statute which prevents racial intermarriage, including marriage of whites with negroes</u>. This bill had gone to a second reading and he

---

11. At McKay's behest, Middlemiss wrote the following letter to those concerned over Birch Society membership: "The Church is not opposing the John Birch Society or any other organization of like nature; it is definitely opposed to anyone using the Church for the purpose of increasing membership for private organizations sponsoring these various ideologies" (in Quinn, *Extensions*, 73).

thought it might go to a third reading today. In his own feelings he said he was opposed to repealing this statute and wanted instruction.

Elder [Harold B.] Lee said that Reed Bullen had come in to see him about this same matter and said that he had talked with me about some of these problem[s]. Brother Bullen mentioned that according to the rules of Senate they could not kill a bill in committee but they could kill it in the House, and that is what they are attempt[ing] to do; to kill it so that it wouldn't come out for open discussion.

Elder Gordon Hinckley mentioned, in this connection, the Utah statute which prohibits the marriage of Caucasians and orientals, and that some of our people are being so married; that it is not uncommon for a returned missionary to marry a nisei [second-generation-immigrant] girl, and that they have to leave Utah to do so.

I said that we are facing a question of permitting the marriage of negroes with whites, and that we had better put up with a little inconvenience regarding inter-racial marriage to avoid greater troubles.[12]

(4) Communism—Course of Study for Mutual Improvement Association. After discussing an inquiry that had come from the Executives of the MIA as to whether or not a course on Communism might be an alternate course to be studied by the group that calls itself the Mutual Study Class, it was decided that in view of the fact that the whole curricula of the Church is undergoing supervision, study, and revision in harmony with the outlined plan approved by the All-Church Coordinating Council, and subsequently approved by the First Presidency and Council of the Twelve, that the introduction of the subject of Communism as proposed by the MIA Executives, at this time, would be untimely, and that the course be not introduced for the coming year. However at the same time that we are not unmindful of the need of placing before our people authentic information on the teachings of Communism, and that it would be our opinion that there be included in the Mutual Study Handbook, pages 123 to 127, in addition to the books there suggested for reading on various subjects, the following books on Communism: "A Study of

---

12. The church's position on interracial marriage had largely mirrored that of American culture at large. However, on Monday, March 18, Governor George D. Clyde would repeal Utah's miscegenation statute ("Clyde Busy Signing Bills," *Provo Daily Herald*, Mar. 19, 1963), while McKay and the other brethren would remain strongly opposed to interracial marriage.

Communism" by J. Edgar Hoover; "Witness" by Whittaker Chambers; "The Naked Communist" by Cleon Skousen; "The Red Carpet" by Ezra Taft Benson; "Masters of Deceit" by J. Edgar Hoover; and "You Can Trust the Communists To Do Exactly As They Say" by Dr. Fred C. Schwarz.

We believe that the placing of these books thus prominently before the Mutual Study Class Group will have the effect of their giving serious and prayerful study to the dangers which are faced in Communism, but at the same time will not interfere with the authentic curricula development which is now going forward.

This question of the study of Communism was suggested for the study of the Melchizedek Quorums, and when the matter was called to the attention of The First Presidency and Council of the Twelve, I advised that in my opinion, which opinion was supported by my counselors and the Twelve, that there be no such course of study, but instead there be published the statement on Communism previously published, a copy of which is attached hereto.

It was suggested that this statement on Communism be reproduced in the Mutual Study Handbook so that those who have the Handbook may have the First Presidency's statement on the subject of Communism along with the books on this subject. I gave approval for this to be done.

February 14, 1963. Immediately following the Council Meeting, President Joseph Fielding Smith, and Elders Harold B. Lee, Marion G. Romney, Richard L. Evans, Gordon B. Hinckley, and Nathan Eldon Tanner, met with President Hugh B. Brown and me (President [Henry D.] Moyle was not present he being in New York).

Elder Lee, speaking for the group, said that in setting up the matter of the area presidents—namely, the European Mission, West European Mission, South American Mission, and missions in the Eastern United States, the Midwest, etc.—they wondered what the President would think if they were to study the question of having members of the Twelve named to preside over those regions, these brethren to travel back and forth as Brother Hinckley and Brother Romney are now doing so far as their regions are concerned, rather than to be domiciled in those areas. He mentioned that in this way considerable expense could be avoided, and that we would have the services of the brethren here when they were not visiting the missions. <u>I said it was not necessary for them to be domiciled in the particular areas.</u>

Elder Lee then asked if it would be all right to bring in a recommendation from the Twelve of someone to <u>preside over each of these areas so far as the mission supervision is concerned.</u>

<u>I answered that that is just the thing to do.</u>

<u>Priesthood Board—Committees</u>—Elder Lee then said that the next question is the matter of bringing into the Priesthood Board the four committees—Welfare, Genealogical and Temple work, Missionary Work, and Home Teaching. He asked if it would be pleasing to the Presidency if they were to ask the Assistants to the Twelve and the First Council of Seventy so far as possible to serve as committees of those Boards to direct them in this phase of the Correlation work.

I gave approval.

Elder Lee then said, "Suppose we study through what we are engaged in, and present to the Priesthood Committee our thinking, and give our recommendations to you as to the personnel to fit into each committee of our General Authorities, and also the personnel of Brother Romney's committee, as well as the names of those of our area supervisors whom we would wish to name as our missionary field workers, who would also serve as members of the Priesthood Board." He said that they would also bring in suggestions of brethren of the Assistants whom Brother Tanner might use in the Genealogical work, and who also might be used in the Home Teaching Program.

President Brown asked what the brethren had in mind with respect to the present area supervisors, such as Elder Franklin D. Richards.

Elder Lee explained that it is intended that a member of the Twelve will now become a supervising president of a given area.

President Brown indicated that was much more desirable, and much more economical.

Brother Lee further indicated that in the <u>matter of mission presidents, the matter would first be taken to the Missionary Committee, and President Smith, as chairman of that committee, would bring the recommendation to the First Presidency.</u>

Elder Lee, referring to Brother Romney and his supervision of the missions in Mexico, said that it was thought that perhaps Brother

Romney should be relieved of that responsibility, inasmuch as he will have a tremendous job taking charge of the Home Teaching Program.

I told the Brethren that they were on solid ground in their thinking.

February 27, 1963. [A professor] of the Utah State University sent a letter asking for a statement of the church's position about the John Birch Society.

I directed that he be informed that the Church has nothing to do with the John Birch Society, but that joining is an individual matter. A person who joins will not lose his membership in the Church on that account. President [Henry D.] Moyle said that he had declared that since this is the Dispensation of the Fulness of Times, the Lord will reveal all things necessary for us as He pleases; that a member may join if he wants.

March 5, 1963, 8:15–8:30 a.m. Brother O. Preston Robinson of the Deseret News came in on Deseret News matters. I told him not to publish the story which appears in the Salt Lake Tribune this morning regarding President Hugh B. Brown's statement regarding Ezra Taft Benson and the Church's stand regarding the John Birch Society.[13] ...

11:45–1:00 P.M. ... The First Presidency met with the Executive Committee of the Church Board of Education and considered the matter of Junior Colleges with reference to the financial involvements which would be incurred should the Church embark on the proposed Junior College Program. ...

After a long discussion of the letter to the First Presidency signed by Elder Boyd K. Packer, and of the minutes of a meeting of the Executive Committee held, March 1, 1963, a motion was made that the Church take steps to approve of the discontinuance of the actions establishing Junior Colleges throughout the Church.[14]

---

13. Second counselor Hugh B. Brown said of the John Birch Society, "We are opposed to them and their methods," and advised church members that "we should not mix politics and religion." "LDS Oppose Birchism, Leader Says," *Ogden Standard Examiner*, Mar. 5, 1963.

14. The junior college issue had been volatile since its inception. Two opponents emerged. One of them was apostle Boyd K. Packer, who having been an Institute of Religion instructor preferred the present arrangement of the Institute program of which he had been a part. Apostle Harold B. Lee was the other opponent. He similarly believed that the proposal was excessively expensive and unnecessary. McKay vacillated back and

March 6, 1963, First Presidency meeting. John Birch Society—President Hugh B. Brown's comments concerning—I read a clipping from the Los Angeles Times under headline "Benson Not speaking For Mormons On Birch". The article quoted President Brown. President Brown explained that when he arrived in Los Angeles President [Howard B.] Anderson of the California Mission had five reporters in his office for a press interview. The reporters had a copy of the statement of the First Presidency about the Birch Society. The first question asked was if the First Presidency had issued a statement [responding to the fact] that Brother Benson is for the Birchites. President Brown said he answered that Brother Benson is entitled to his own opinion as an individual, but the First Presidency have spoken for the Church and any statement contrary to that is not the policy of the Church. When President Brown found out what he was up against he asked the secretary of the mission to get a tape recorder and to make a record of everything that was taken down. President Brown has a complete tape of everything that was said. He said he made it very clear that any statement Brother Benson made was on his own responsibility and that he was not speaking for the Church, that the statement which they had was the authoritative position of the Church with respect to the Birch Society.

I read the following statement from a copy of a letter sent from my office and signed by my secretary, Clare Middlemiss, answering inquiries about the Church and its position on the John Birch Society: "I have been directed to say that members of the Church are free to join anti-communist organizations if they desire and their membership in the Church is not jeopardized by so doing. The Church is not opposed to the John Birch Society or any other organization of like nature; however, it is definitely opposed to anyone's using the Church for the purpose of increasing membership in private organizations sponsoring these various ideologies."

President Brown said what he said was entirely in harmony with that statement. ...

I said that following the publication of the statement, I was asked to apologize for what was said against Brother Benson and his son Reed because "if we had called them 'we would have readily subscribed to your requirements.'" He [apostle Ezra Taft Benson] said "We would have done

forth on this issue, which angered Wilkinson, who in his own words had spent more time on the junior college project than on any other issue at BYU.

471

anything that you suggested." I said "yes and nobody in the Church or in the world would have known that you were doing that, but everybody knew that you are a national character and everybody knew that you favor the Birch Society and that you approve your son representing it in Utah, and when the First Presidency gave that statement it received the same publicity which your statement received, and we offer no apology." I referred to a telephone call [to my daughter], the message of which [was] … "please do not let your father have his picture taken with that man (Mr. [Robert] Welch)[15] because Sister Benson is telling people that President McKay is in favor of Mr. Welch." I said I sent a telegram to Mr. Welch stating that I was sorry that I had to go to the coast. On that day Mr. Welch telephoned to Reed Benson saying "That's too bad. I should have come a week earlier or a week later"—showing that his whole purpose was to see me.

March 7, 1963. For the first time for several months, we met in the Salt Lake Temple for our regular weekly meeting of the First Presidency and Council of the Twelve.

March 20, 1963, First Presidency meeting. By appointment, Elder Nathan Eldon Tanner came into the meeting. He read a letter which stated the following conditions for granting visas to missionaries being admitted into Nigeria: (1) The body must be one that practices cooperation with other Christian bodies; (2) It must be one that is recommended by the Christian Council of Nigeria or by overseas bodies already recognized in Nigeria; (3) It must be one whose work will be welcomed by the regional authorities; (4) It must be adequately financed.

President Tanner read briefly from an excerpt of the pamphlet "Mormonism and the Negro" by John J. Stewart,[16] which stated that negroes

---

15. Robert Winborne Welch Jr. (1895–1985) founded the John Birch Society in 1958 with University of Illinois professor Revilo P. Oliver and ten others. Welch attended the US Naval Academy and Harvard University, but had dropped out of school to start a candy company with his brother, along the way inventing Sugar Daddies, Sugar Babies, and Junior Mints. In 1950 Welch ran unsuccessfully for lieutenant governor of Massachusetts; he had previously supported McCarthy's anti-communist campaigns.

16. John J. Stewart (1925–2014), a journalism professor at Utah State University, with a master's degree from the University of Oregon, was a native of nearby Brigham City. His 54-page pamphlet, *Mormonism and the Negro*, was pro-church, its subtitle *An*

may become members of the Church, may receive patriarchal blessings, may enter the Temple for vicarious work for the dead, but may not receive other temple ordinances and may not hold the Priesthood.

President Tanner explained that elder LaMar Williams suggested that he be authorized to get a tourist's visa and go in and clear these matters up, but he was informed that this is a matter which the First Presidency must direct.

President Tanner said the action should be taken as soon as possible. He referred to an address delivered by Elder Mark E. Petersen at the BYU, which bluntly stated the Church's position on the negro question,[17] and he expressed the opinion that it would not be wise for Brother Petersen to go to Nigeria.

I said that I think Brother Tanner should follow through with this until it is settled. He should go down and take Brother Williams and other missionaries and start them out as planned. Brother Tanner explained that the Nigerian government will not let Brother Williams and the other missionaries in as missionaries, and that he does not know how long it will take to get this cleared up.

Brother Tanner reviewed the requirements of the Nigerian Government. I said Brother Tanner is the only man in the Church who can do it, but things would be left as they are until after Conference. I asked Brother Tanner to have Brother Williams continue his efforts to get a visa so he can go with Brother Tanner.

March 29, 1963, First Presidency meeting. We first met with Elder Marion G. Romney, who reported a case of a missionary's transgression and confession after he had listened to the Brethren instructing the missionaries before they go to the Temple. After a discussion of the matter, I said that the Lord has said that if you sin and repent you should be forgiven, but if the sin is repeated you should be cut off. This missionary has made

---

Explanation and Defense of the Doctrine of the Church of Jesus Christ of Latter-day Saints in Regard to Negroes and Others of Negroid Blood. He later wrote the official *Life of Joseph Fielding Smith,* published by Deseret Book.

17. Petersen had said at BYU on August 27, 1954, in "Race Problems as They Affect the Church," that the only negroes in heaven would be servants: "If that Negro is faithful all his days, he can and will enter the Celestial Kingdom. He will go there as a servant, but he will get a Celestial resurrection."

confession, and that repentance should be accepted, but he should be made to realize his responsibility to be honorable in the performance of his mission, and that he goes with our trust. I advised that the young man tell the young woman to come to Brother Romney, also, because she is a part of the responsibility.

April 2, 1963, 8:30–10:00 a.m. First Presidency meeting. … We had a long conference with Brother Leo Ellsworth and Brother Donald Ellsworth regarding Florida Ranch Development, and Utah Lake property. Leo Ellsworth reported that since the first of the year in 80 working days, 8,000 acres of land in Florida have been cleared and planted to grass.

The important question before us this morning was whether to go on with the development of the land, which would mean that we would have to increase the number of cattle, and the acquirement of additional money. Brother Ellsworth said that we now have <u>73,000 head of cattle in round figures</u> which does not include the yearling heifers. <u>One hundred thousand acres of the land are fenced</u>. If we go ahead with the development, they will <u>need another estimated $8 million</u>. The Deseret Farms has now made a $30 million loan and will pay the Church back the $25 million dollars borrowed from them, which will give the company five million dollars for the additional expense to continue developing the land and buying additional stock.

After discussing this matter at length, I asked Leo Ellsworth additional questions about the Florida property, and about going ahead along the lines discussed, and he said he believed in it and thought it should be done. I said that I agreed; that the land is increasing in value, and that <u>as soon as we can do so profitably the Company should sell some of it</u>. Brother Ellsworth said that we had an offer a few days ago for $350 an acre for all the land we hold north of Bithlow cut-off. He said he did not submit it, because he knew we would not want to sell. They were told that <u>we would accept $1,000 an acre</u>, and that we would not even look at $350.

April 3, 1963, First Presidency meeting. <u>The program for the Saturday evening Priesthood Meeting was considered. By telephone I asked Elder Harold B. Lee to come into the meeting and to give the First Presidency an outline of what is planned to be presented by the Correlation</u>

<u>Committee in the General Priesthood Meeting</u>. Brother Lee said the plan is to present with the use of charts the over-all organization and a review of the curriculum of correlation of auxiliary courses for leadership training. A chart showing the organization of the Priesthood General Board will be presented. He said this was the organization charge which he and Brother [Marion G.] Romney presented to President [Henry D.] Moyle before he went to Europe, and which later was presented in detail to the First Presidency and the Twelve. This board will be presented as divided into four groups, priesthood mission, priesthood genealogical, priesthood welfare, and priesthood home teaching. Priesthood home teaching is to include the ward teaching plan where the whole priesthood is brought into the program.

Brother Lee said this plan was presented to the Twelve and approved by them and commended.

President Moyle said he had not approved of the plan but was very upset about it.

Brother Lee explained that the home teaching plan is bishop-centered, the quorums visit their members under the direction of the bishop. He said the program has been developed step by step and has been brought to the First Presidency and the Twelve where it was approved and now is in the process of being printed.

It will be presented to the stake conferences beginning the first of June. Brother Romney is to be chairman of the home teaching committee, and Brother [Alvin R.] Dyer, managing director, is to assist him in it. President Moyle said this takes it entirely out of the hands of the Presiding Bishopric. Brother Lee said I am telling you what has been developed by the First Presidency and the Twelve.

I reviewed the provision that the quorums will be brought into ward teaching to watch over the members of the Church of their quorums. The bishop has charge of these members of the ward, and the teachers will be under the direction of the bishop of the ward, and will report to him the welfare of each individual. They will not make report to the General priesthood committee known as the priesthood home teaching committee.

President Moyle said he understood that the original commission to the Correlation Committee was to correlate the ward teaching messages to be delivered by the ward teachers and that the committee would go no farther.

Brother Lee said no step has been taken that has not been explored and approved by the Presidency and the Twelve.

President Moyle expressed the opinion that the committee has gone beyond the letter of commission given it. He said the details of the plan should not be presented to the priesthood at the Saturday night meeting until there is agreement.

I said this must not be; that we must be agreed. I directed that the presentation that Brother Romney gave be made to the council of the First Presidency and the Twelve at the meeting tomorrow. Brother Lee asked if Brother Romney should repeat it, and I said yes I think so, and that we should do it tomorrow.

President Moyle said it was his understanding when the change was made in the Priesthood Committee that it was to report to the First Presidency directly. I said that is right. President Moyle said if this is to be a sub-committee of the Correlation Committee or the General Priesthood Committee, whichever it is, maybe we ought to make a segregation of these two committees and have one man chairman of one and another man chairman of the other so that there will be no confusion. The Correlation Committee and the General Priesthood Committee—when he says this is not a sub-committee of the General Priesthood Committee I presume it is a sub-committee of the Correlation Committee. They are two committees and they are operating as one. Before anything is presented to the body of the Church Saturday night, we ought to know what it is because we cannot discuss it afterwards. I said we shall have Brother Romney present that to the Presidency and the Twelve as he did before.

President Moyle commented upon the dismissal of Brother Hinckley from the direction of missionary work without the knowledge of the First Presidency and the giving of this function to the Priesthood Missionary Committee Representative. He said he understood that when a change was made the Missionary Committee was to report to the First Presidency directly. I expressed concurrence.

President Moyle commented also upon the taking over of the Genealogical work and the selecting of a manager to take Brother [N. Eldon] Tanner's place.

Brother Lee said we shall have Brother Romney make the presentation tomorrow, and I said if you will please. Brother Lee withdrew from the meeting.

I then said we shall have that presented to the Twelve. We shall have no discussion; we shall discuss it here.

I reviewed the plan for having representatives of the Auxiliary General Boards attend quarterly conferences during the third and fourth quarter of the year alternating with representatives of the Genealogical, Welfare, Missionary, and Ward Teaching in other quarters. I said the Genealogical Department is doing good work. President Moyle said that should continue under Brother Tanner and the Missionary Work should be under Brother [Gordon B.] Hinckley. He said this conducting of the quarterly conference falls into place, we have agreed to that, but we have never agreed that the Correlation Committee could dismiss Brother Tanner from the Genealogical Department and Brother Hinckley from the Missionary Department. They have been appointed by the Presidency.

I advised that the Priesthood Meeting Saturday evening be informed as to how the quarterly conferences will be conducted with emphasis upon the various phases of Church work. President [Hugh B.] Brown and President Moyle agreed that this be done.

I then commented upon the plan of organization having one of the Twelve and one of the Assistants working with the Welfare Department and with the Ward Teaching Department of the Presiding Bishopric, and the other departments. President Moyle commented upon the anomaly of having two heads or managers, and assistant managers. I said "Not two heads, but advisors." President Moyle said they could be set up as advisors. President Brown said that would be all right. President Moyle commented when you give a man like Brother Romney the title of manager and Brother Dyer assistant manager, that leaves nothing for the Bishop to do. I said absolutely. That is not right. President Moyle said "And the same in welfare as well as ward teaching."

I said when we have someone in Welfare and Ward Teaching and Genealogy, just as we have them in the Auxiliaries, and call them advisors, that is right.

April 15, 1963, 10:00 a.m. Left for home. Later, my son Lawrence came and had me sign income papers for both the State and Federal taxes. It is unbelievable that the government can take so much money from the people! Something must be done about the power that has been given to them.

April 25, 1963, First Presidency meeting. We first met with Brother Wendell B. Mendenhall of the Building Committee who took up the matter of purchasing a building in Brussels for the headquarters of a new mission. President Mark E. Petersen came from London to see the property. The price is $82,000 including furnishings and carpeting. With a tax of $8,200, and $5,000 an estimated cost of remodeling, would bring the total cost to $95,200. President Petersen recommends that it be purchased.

I commented that the mission homes are costing us a great deal of money to maintain according to the 1962 report.

However, I said that if Brother Petersen and Brother [George R.] Biesinger[18] approve, having gone over the property, and if they are united, there is nothing else to do but to take it. I said we cannot sit here and make any other judgment, so we had better take it. Brother Mendenhall will get the message to them so they can negotiate accordingly on this.

Brother Mendenhall read a letter from President Mark E. Petersen, of the West European Mission, sent to him by the Missionary Committee, in the contents of which that Committee concurred. Enclosed with the letter was a list of furnishings ordered for the French Mission home. <u>President Petersen said he wished he could feel good about the expenditures, but that he could not</u>. He said he would not furnish his own home in such luxury, nor would the Mission Presidents furnish their own homes as such, because they could not afford it. He said some of the mission homes on the continent, and in England, have taken his breath away. He said that when the people look at these furnishings, they must think that their tithing supports such luxury. He said the people receive only $30 a week, and the women come to the Church with holes in their stockings, and the children are poorly clad. The letter included comments upon the dining room furniture and other costs.

Brother Mendenhall said that the Building Committee would like

---

18. George Ross Biesinger (1918–73) was the construction supervisor for the labor missionaries in Europe. He had overseen a similar program in New Zealand in constructing the temple, church college, and twenty-four chapels. He and his wife would retire to San Diego in 1965.

to be relieved of the responsibility for furnishing these mission homes, and that they had all the mission homes to do over in the whole European area. Said that they take a list of furnishings made out to a similar list which has been approved for furnishings of mission homes; that they use the prices which have been approved for years in the furnishing of the mission homes in the United States, and that they thought these were the average type of furnishings for the living space for the mission presidents. The mission presidents indicate what they want, and that is the only way they can satisfy them without conflict. Said that the Building Committee has stayed within the standards.

I said that what President Petersen says must be true; that they are extravagant.

President [Henry D.] Moyle then commented upon the people received by the mission presidents in the mission homes; the public officials, prominent people, governors, and mayors of cities. He also mentioned the hard wear and tear upon mission property by missionaries, and many others who come into the home, and said the quality of the furnishings must be of good grade. He said that cheap furniture was purchased for the Paris mission home, but it did not hold up and had to be replaced.

It was suggested that President and Sister Petersen be asked to take the responsibility for furnishing the Belgium–French mission home as they think it should be furnished. I said I think this is a good idea, and that if he approves of the Belgium house he would want to furnish it.

Brother Mendenhall said that he told Brother Biesinger before he left Salt Lake that he felt that we ought not to have anything to do with these mission homes, even to the picking of them, unless the European and West European Mission Presidents directed them to locate something and that they ought to do nothing with it unless directed.

I said that that is right!

May 2, 1963, First Presidency meeting. A letter received from Elder Mark E. Petersen was read. It gave details of distortion of statistics of the reports of the Stakes and Missions of the West European Mission including details of specific distortions arising from misleading statistics of the conditions in the Sunderland [UK] Stake. The letter also commented upon these as being indicative of the conditions in such other stakes as Leicester, Manchester, and to some degree, the Holland Stake.

The officers of the stake want to make a good showing and asked direction as to what to do with the large numbers of names of "unattached youth"[19] who are the only members of their families who are members of the Church, access to whose homes is refused by the parents who resent the way the children became members of the Church; many of the children have been re-baptized in the churches of their parents.

I said they cannot simply remove the names unless they act in accordance with established Church procedure. They will have to deal with them as they would with any other member, each case on its merits. President Moyle said that what you say is right. A certain percentage, as they grow older, will become more active. I said it is the duty of the missionaries; they will have to deal with each one on its merits.

May 3, 1963, First Presidency meeting. Bishop [John H.] Vandenberg reported having received a letter from Elder Gordon B. Hinckley relating to the record of members of two Samoan brothers suspected of having negro blood. He has gone into the records with President [Marion D.] Hanks in detail, and has talked with [Samoan Stake] President Percy Rivers who knows these men very well. About one brother (Malu Epu), the rumor was started years ago that this family had negro blood through a grandmother, a daughter of a man thought to have negro blood. This brother took the matter to the Samoan courts, and research brought out the facts about a man named Thomas who was supposed to have negro blood. He was in fact a white American. Fatu told the story to President Hanks in Samoan who translated for Brother Hinckley. The son and also the father have been ordained to the Priesthood. They have been and are active Latter-day Saints; their membership records show negro blood notation. Brother Hinckley thinks the notation should be deleted from the records. I said I think that notation should be deleted without question. ...

I then said that we had this same matter in South Africa. There was a ruling there that unless a man could prove his origin outside South

---

19. These "unattached youth" were the result of the "baseball baptisms" that had recently plagued the missions of England.

Africa, he should not be ordained to the Priesthood. Under such a ruling every man must prove that he is not Negroid.

May 15, 1963. President McKay reported to his secretary ... that he was so tired when he reached home ... (having had an extremely busy day at the office), he decided to take a hot bath in order that he could relax before going to bed. However, somehow, he got drowsy while bathing and fell asleep in the tub. He said that he awoke at 3:00 a.m. and found himself still in the tub in cold water. Said that he didn't say anything to Sister [Emma Ray] McKay because he thought it would worry her. Despite this experience, President McKay appeared at the office the next morning in a cheerful spirit and feeling very well.

May 24, 1963. Bishop [John H.] Vandenberg of the Presiding Bishopric explained that the information about tithing paid by members of the faculty of the Brigham Young University has been requested, and asked whether or not it should be released. Limited authorization formerly given President [Ernest L.] Wilkinson was considered. <u>I said that we do not intend to force faculty members to pay tithing, nor do we intend to release information about tithing they pay</u>. Special permission was given on one occasion, but it has not been continued regularly. Bishop Vandenberg said that it is the Bishop's prerogative to interview the person, and the responsibility rests with the person paying tithing. Bishop Victor L. Brown suggested that President Wilkinson might be informed as to whether or not faculty members are tithe payers, part tithe payers, or non tithe payers. I indicated approval. Bishop Vandenberg said that accordingly <u>they would disapprove of giving information about the amount of tithing paid</u>.

May 28, 1963, 7:30 a.m. Met with Elder Nathan Eldon Tanner and Brother LaMar Williams and discussed the Nigerian situation. The interested people in Nigeria are taking the matter into their own hands and are now about to take the matter up with the Premier. There are two groups, and two leading men with whom Brother Williams has had correspondence. One is more able than the other. He has the true spirit of a member of the Church. The head of the other and larger group is more active. He was formerly a minister of another Church. In desire he

481

has been a member of the Church for many years without the benefit of authoritative baptism. I advised Brother Tanner and Brother Williams to consider the request of these men, and to choose a leader for them; proposing using both of them, the active man to head the larger group, and the more able man who is well educated and probably will make a better presentation to the Premier, to go together and make their presentation and then come back with their recommendations. They can request that official members of the Church be admitted to the country to organize them into groups. The lawyer they have has already expended $250. I told the Brethren this morning that necessary funds will be sent to present the case to the Premier, but we shall leave it to the people in Nigeria to get permission from the Premier to request the Church to come down there. So far as we are concerned, we shall leave it absolutely to them. Instead of 4,000 people seeking baptism, there are thought to be 7,000.

June 5, 1963, First Presidency meeting. Copies of Elder Nathan Eldon Tanner's letters addressed to Mr. Charles Agu of Aba, Nigeria, and a similar letter to Mr. Dick Obot of Uyo, Nigeria, and another to both of these brethren, as well as one addressed "To Whom It May Concern," were read.

I presented a letter from Mr. J[oseph] M[odupe] Johnson of Lagos, Nigeria, Ministry of Labor, which included the statement, "It shall be the pleasure of the people of the Federation of Nigeria if you send one of your missionaries, especially Brother Tanner, to Nigeria with a view to establishing your work in Nigeria." I said that ["]we will have to have an official higher than the Minister of Labor offer, before we accept an invitation."

The letters to the individuals referred to correspondence from them of May 16, 1963, urging the Church to send representatives to assist them in their Church activity, and recited the Church's endeavor to obtain visas for representatives to go into Nigeria as requested, but that visas, for some reason, had not been forthcoming.

These brethren were informed that they are recognized as leaders of their groups, <u>one in and around Aba</u>, and the <u>other in and around Abak</u>, which they have organized under the name of The Church of Jesus Christ of Latter-day Saints. <u>They stated that if and when visas are made available, representatives will come immediately to assist in the work, which will include educational and health programs.</u>

I said that we shall make no further effort to go to Nigeria; that we shall leave them with this responsibility; that the responsibility is now upon them. I stated that five thousand people are waiting for baptism. We shall make no concession to the NAACP [National Association for the Advancement of Colored People]. They are trying to take advantage of this situation to make the church yield equality in the Church. We do not propose to make any concession.

President [Henry D.] Moyle and President [Hugh B.] Brown concurred in this position.

June 7, 1963, 8:00–8:40 a.m. Following the departure of Elder [Richard L.] Evans, Brother [Arch L.] Madsen remained for further conversation regarding his duties at KSL. Brought up the matter of giving equal rights to all persons who request free public time on KSL. Mentioned in particular requests that come from members of the John Birch Society. Later, in the meeting of the First Presidency, I spoke to President Henry D. Moyle, who had instructed Arch Madsen not to give any time on KSL to any member or guest of the John Birch Society, that we must be careful and give equal rights to all in order that both sides of any question may be presented to the people. ...

10:00 to 11:00 a.m.—Conference with President Hugh B. Brown regarding statement he had made with reference to the Church's stand on the holding of the Priesthood by the Negro, in which it was reported that President Brown said: "The top leadership of the Mormon Church is seriously considering the abandonment of its historic policy of discrimination against Negroes." ...

President Brown said that they had misquoted him. Later, however, Brother Theodore Cannon,[20] who accompanied the reporter to President Brown's office, said that he was "so shocked at what President Brown told the reporter that he himself took out his notebook

---

20. Theodore Cannon Sr. was a grandson of apostle George Q. Cannon and son of a previous director of the Church Information Service, John Q. Cannon. President Hugh B. Brown was quoted saying "the whole problem of the Negro is being considered by the leaders of the church in the light of racial relationships everywhere. We don't want to go too fast in this matter," but "want to be fair." Wallace Turner, New York Times News Service, "Mormons May Drop Anti-Negro Policy," *Arizona Daily Star*, June 7, 1963.

and started writing down what President Brown said." He further said that following the interview he called Wallace Turner the reporter, at the Hotel and asked him if he would let him read his story before he sent it to the Newspaper in New York. Because of the service Brother Cannon had rendered the reporter, he [Turner] agreed to let Brother Cannon see his story. Brother Cannon said that he was able to persuade the reporter to leave out a lot of material which was not too favorable to the Church.

June 13, 1963, First Presidency meeting. President McKay said that letters received from the Minister of Labor in Nigeria inviting the Church to send representatives to Nigeria, and one from a member of the group interested in the Church asking for a loan of $25,000, and associated matters have all been assigned to Elder Nathan Eldon Tanner to work out. I said that the woman from Uganda, Vice-President of the International Woman's Organization, whom I met the other day, said that she is acquainted with the Minister of Labor in Nigeria; that he is a leading man in the country. I said that we shall make no further efforts to have missionaries sent to Nigeria; that the matter is now in their hands.

June 19, 1963, 8:30 a.m. Went into the First Presidency's room for the regular meeting of the First Presidency. President [Henry D.] Moyle had brought in James E. Faust,[21] President of the Cottonwood Stake, and asked him to explain what he had told him earlier. President Faust said that as President of the Utah Bar Association he had received telegraphic invitation from President Kennedy to attend a conference at the White House on civil rights legislation.[22]

I told Brother Faust that he should go and find out what President

---

21. James Esdras Faust (1920–2007) would later be called in 1972 as an Assistant to the Quorum of the Twelve. Prior to this call, he was a Regional Representative of the Twelve. Four years later he was sustained to the presidency of the First Quorum of the Seventy. In 1978 he was called into the Quorum of the Twelve Apostles, and in 1995 as second counselor in the First Presidency. He had received his law degree in 1948 from the University of Utah. He served in the Utah State Legislature in 1949 as a Democrat and as chair of the Utah State Democratic Party, in which capacity he assisted the campaign of Democratic Senator Frank E. Moss.

22. President Kennedy appointed Faust to the Lawyers' Committee for Civil Rights, which would produce legal arguments against segregation.

Kennedy is trying to do. I said that I did not like to see a law passed which will make the Hotel men violators of the law if they refuse to provide accommodations for a negro when their hotels are filled with white people, or restaurant men made violators when they decline to serve colored people.

I said that business men ought to be free to run their own businesses, and not become law breakers if they choose to employ certain people; that if we have such a law as that, then it is unfair to the majority of the citizens of this country.

President Moyle expressed the opinion that it is unconstitutional because it takes away a man's right to contract, and to do business. He said there is no such power given to the Federal Government by the Constitution.

June 21, 1963, First Presidency meeting. Brother [Wendell B.] Mendenhall then commented upon problems of Georgia and Florida ranches, especially as it pertains to the management of Leo Ellsworth and the shipment of cattle from the Florida ranches to Georgia. After a long discussion regarding this matter, President [Henry D.] Moyle said "this thing can be solved, President McKay, as far as your operation is concerned. It is as simple as it can be." I answered "It is not as simple as that; you have there a personality who has given nine years of his life and his fortune." Brother Mendenhall said: "There is no question about that but there is no personality problem between Leo Ellsworth and me—he treats me fine and all that, but I tell you if you are going to keep him losing money (I think, President Moyle, you will have to verify it); that when I saw it from the beginning I constantly maintained that we are losing money all the time.["] I said to President Moyle that I did not want to be associated with it; I asked him if I could resign from the Board. ["]You cannot go on doing what is being done without losing hundreds and thousands and millions of dollars." Brother Mendenhall continued, "The value of the real estate is one thing. Leave it as it is. The more you develop the land [the harder to sell it] (enough has been developed) it should be entirely stopped, nothing but operation of cattle on a conservative business-like basis should go on. Not another dollar should be spent for land development."

485

June 26, 1963, 7:30 a.m. I met by appointment at their request Brother Gus Backman and Mr. John Gallivan[23] at which time they discussed with me the matter of a site for the new civic auditorium. I told them that I think it would be unwise to go out of the city limits; that it should be located near the heart of the city where people could walk to it.

Later in the morning, I was handed a note stating that Mr. Gallivan had called by telephone and reported that the county Commissioners in their meeting this morning "went off half cocked and passed a resolution to have the auditorium five miles out of town instead of on West Temple. They want to announce the bond issue August 6 for 15 million dollars—all of this prematurely without even having a site picked." Mr. Gallivan wanted me to meet with two or three of the Commissioners, and to tell them my feelings about where the new auditorium should be located.

I instructed my secretary to call Mr. Gallivan and tell him that <u>it would be unwise for me to meet with the Commissioners because they resent any Church influence in politics, and that I am afraid that my interference would only antagonize them rather than win their favor.</u> I said that Mr. Gallivan can better give the commissioners my views that I can personally; that I had met Commissioner Cannon this morning and had told him that I think it would be unwise to go out of the city to choose a site; that the auditorium should be built where people can walk to it. These views can be put over by Mr. Gallivan.[24]

June 27, 1963, 4:00 p.m. Left for home. I was so tired when I got home that I alarmed members of the family who were there—I could hardly talk, and they became very much concerned. I know that I have used up all my reserve energy, and that it is foolish for me to go on this way, working such long hours without rest and sometimes without food.

July 2, 1963, 8:30 a.m. ... Went into the office of the First Presidency where we met by appointment President James E. Faust of Cottonwood

---

23. John W. Gallivan (1915–2012) replaced the late John F. Fitzpatrick as editor of the *Salt Lake Tribune*, and in doing so inherited a position within the triumvirate that included McKay and Backman in deciding public policy, representing business, church, and private interests. Gallivan graduated from the Cathedral School (Judge Memorial High School) in Salt Lake City and the University of Notre Dame.

24. For more, see Alexander and Allen, *Mormons and Gentiles*, 277–78.

Stake, and past president of the Utah Bar Association, who attended at the invitation of President John F. Kennedy, the White House Conference on legislation for Civil Rights. ... The essence of the meeting was the <u>president's advice that members of the bar associations of the country</u> <u>can be helpful by taking appropriate action on a local basis to solve racial</u> <u>problems in the communities and states of the country. He thinks com-</u> <u>munication between the races can take place on a local level in the local</u> <u>communities and states and by these means each community can solve its</u> <u>own problems and it may not be necessary for the Federal Government</u> <u>to act. If solution[s] can come from the ground up it will be better than to</u> <u>come from the top down.</u> If the solution can come that way, federal legislation may be unnecessary. President Faust commented that he gained the impression that the President had some doubt that his recommendations for legislation can be enacted.

He made some specific recommendations to the colored people. He said they are creating a social problem in the United States; they drop out of school; 20% are on relief; this continues from one generation to another; they have no incentive to get themselves the necessary skills, and as a consequence they are not holding up their responsibility as citizens. President Faust said that if "I had been a colored man, I would have been upset because he was hard on them."

The President also recommended that an informal committee be organized to function within the local areas and that lawyers participate on this in the local committees. The President said he had met with labor, business and Church leaders. He recommended that lawyers be catalysts in the local communities and keep the lines of communication open between the two races so matters would not break down and get into a shooting proposition. He recommended that the lawyers with public officials and also with the local committees do something to work on the problem of school drop outs, and to provide legal aid and counsel for indigent colored people; to uphold respect for law, not only by white people but by colored people as well. It was thought he was referring to the demonstrations throughout the country. He said that breaches of the peace cannot be committed by negroes any more than they can be by whites and that he intends to enforce the law. He urged that colored men be admitted to the bar without regard for color.

The Vice-President [Lyndon B. Johnson] spoke. He is head of the Civil Rights Committee. President Kennedy asked the attorney general [Robert F. Kennedy] to speak. The attorney general was immoderate. ...

The Attorney General is more extreme than the President. The President handled the situation with considerable ability and grace.

<u>I told President Faust that I think it will be all right for him to join the committee.</u>

President Faust said he felt it [incumbent] upon him[25] to accept the request of the American Bar Association and since the other legislation was involved he thought the First Presidency should guide him. President Faust said that in the Church there is little problem. He said they have Brother Abe Howe and are grateful he is doing as well as he is.

I said that we are on the fringe of having the NAACP on us, and that I had heard recently something enlightening about Nigeria. My [nephew],[26] who is going to Nigeria to teach in the university, will be about one thousand miles from the area where the "members" are who call themselves The Church of Jesus Christ of latter-day Saints. There are about 5,000 of them and they have been active. I further said that we are going to respond to their call for missionaries to go down there, but they have been putting some obstacles in our way. We have concluded that we will let them make the advance and extend the invitation, which they are going [to do]. They wanted certain conditions with which we would not comply. I said that this young man [McKay's nephew] told me he had been studying conditions down there before he accepted the position of teaching in the university and there is united effort since Nigeria received independence from Great Britain to keep aloof from the "white man's [yoke],"[27] so they are going to resent the putting white people over the negro groups. This is the clash. We find resentment right from the

---

25. The diary has "he felt it encumbered upon him."

26. The diary has "cousin," but McKay meant his nephew, Quinn Gunn McKay (1926–), a University of Pittsburgh business professor who was in Zaria, Nigeria, helping set up a program at the newly founded Ahmadu Bello University. His background included degrees from BYU and Harvard. He had also been a marine during World War II. After Nigeria he would become dean of the Weber State College business school, and later vice president of Skaggs grocery stores (Albertsons, Safeway) and pharmacies (Longs, Osco). In 1980 he would become president of the LDS mission in Coventry, England. See also the entry for Oct. 10, 1963.

27. The transcription mistakenly has "white man's yolk."

head of the government if we send down white people to be bishops and presidents of branches. They can take care of the auxiliaries, but they will resent having a white man preside over them.

I told President Faust in the meantime to join the committee and keep us informed. President Faust asked to whom he should report, and I told him to report to the First Presidency.

July 3, 1963, 2:00 p.m. The long meetings this morning, filled with perplexing problems, had really taken its toll, because as I left the office for home I was trembling so hard that I could hardly walk. My secretary, who was greatly alarmed, called Brother Wright in the outer hall and told him to see that I got home immediately. I am more sure than ever that I should get away for a few days.

July 25, 1963, First Presidency meeting. The first item we considered was a letter from President Mark E. Petersen of the West European Mission who presented the suggestion of President William Bates of Manchester Stake for working with a thousand youth who are members of record of the Stake—one-third of whom are classified as knowing that they were being baptized when they became members and their parents are indifferent; another third are regarded as not knowing that they were being baptized and having no interest in the Church now; and a third group are children whose parents resent their having been baptized into the Church under the circumstances and in a manner in which they were. President Bates proposes that the Stake keep the first category and labor with them and try to activate them, and that the other categories be transferred back to the missions permitting the missionaries to labor with them and to remove their names from the statistics and records of the Stakes. After discussion it was agreed that the Stakes call special missionaries to work with all of these children and to make of this a special stake missionary project. President Petersen's letter of April 5 was also read. It gives additional information relating to the special aspect of these baptisms as to the records of Sunderland and Leicester Stakes and comments upon the distortion of statistics of the Stakes which they create.

I said the problem now is how to handle them. The idea of saying: "Take them off the record" is not worthy of consideration. They are members and we must keep them and deal with them as members. Where parents refuse to let them be active, the responsibility must be upon the parents. Where we have permission to deal with these children we must do it in the best ways. It is a matter of saving souls rather than statistics. We must work with these young boys and girls. We shall follow the revelation of the Lord, and place the responsibility upon the parents and let the statistics be as they are. Let us do that in the Stakes. If the parents refuse, it is their responsibility. Wherever there is a boy or girl unattached, whose parents are willing, the name should be kept in the Stake. Let us answer it that way.

July 26, 1963. Read a letter ... regarding lecture on Communism to be given by Dr. Richard Poll of the Brigham Young University who has written a critique against [W. Cleon] Skousen's book "The Naked Communist," which I have approved of publicly in General Conference (October, 1959). I said that it is unwise for Dr. Poll to be sent down there [and hired in 1948]; that he must not tear that book to pieces.[28] I said further to my secretary, "I have always been against Communism—my whole soul rebels against it."

August 9, 1963, First Presidency meeting. President [Henry D.] Moyle gave me a letter which he had written to Elder Ezra Taft Benson in response to Brother Benson's letter transmitting a copy of the book "The Politician" by Robert Welch of the John Birch Society, and explained that he [Moyle] desired me [McKay] to know what he had written before the letter is delivered.

I said that I have a letter from Mr. Welch asking that Ezra Taft Benson be permitted to join the Board of the Birch Society. I said that the letter will be answered that Brother Benson may not join that Board; that he cannot be a member of that Board and be a member of the Quorum of Twelve Apostles.

August 19, 1963, 7:30 a.m. Met Dr. L[ouis] E. Viko at his office on

---

28. Poll afterward printed his address, "This Trumpet Gives an Uncertain Sound: A Review of W. Cleon Skousen's *The Naked Communist*," as a pamphlet for students. Poll was associate director of the BYU Honors Program.

Seventh East and South Temple. He gave me a thorough examination, and said that my blood pressure, heart, etc. seem to be in good condition. However, he advised me not to plan for any more long trips such as I am planning for at the present time. He also said he feels that Sister [Emma Ray] McKay should not attempt to go.

August 21, 1963, First Presidency meeting. The letter of President Theodore M. Burton reported a successful conference of Building Missionaries in the Germanic areas and expressed interest in the attitude of the wives of the Building Missionaries who feel left out of the influence of their husbands' work and calling. He expressed the opinion that their morale would be greatly improved to the benefit of their husbands and families if the women can be appropriately set apart to render their service with the spirit of [which] their husbands are working. He said he would be pleased to set these sisters apart because he knows how much it will mean to them and their husbands. <u>I said it would be a blessing to them to let them know that they will report and be subject to the Mission President</u>; then it will be all right, <u>but only under the direction of the Mission President when they assume any position or give any instruction.</u> They will be set apart to go with their husbands who are building missionaries, and as instructions already given, <u>will be subject to the Mission Presidents</u>. Inquiry was made if the wives of building missionaries should be set apart here before they go, and <u>I said yes, but that that should be arranged by Brother [Wendell B.] Mendenhall to be done by a General Authority</u>. President [Hugh B.] Brown commented that President Theodore M. Burton is a General Authority. Comment was made that the original form for calling Building Missionaries provided a call to the man and his wife. <u>I said their missionary work will be restricted to the call of the Mission President, and they will labor as he directs. The General Authority who sets them apart should be instructed to put that in</u>, and he gave <u>direction that the call of Building Missionaries be to the man and his wife</u>.[29]

---

29. Building missionaries were of two categories: couples who had industry experience and single young men who wanted to contribute to the church and learn the trade, often as recent converts.

September 4, 1963, 1:45 a.m. Returned to the office of the First Presidency where I received a courtesy call from <u>Maestro Leonard Bernstein, Director and Conductor of the New York Philharmonic Orchestra</u>. He was accompanied by <u>Mr. Carlos Moseley</u>, Business Manager of the Orchestra; <u>Mr. John McClure</u> of New York, Production Chief for Columbia Masterworks Records; and by <u>Isaac M. Stewart</u> and <u>Ted L. Cannon</u> President and Vice-President of the Choir.

After extending my personal greetings and welcome to Mr. Bernstein, I told him that I am sorry that Sister [Emma Ray] McKay and I will be unable to go over to the Tabernacle to attend the recording sessions. I mentioned that Sister McKay is the musician in the family, and would have been delighted to watch him in conducting his famous orchestra.

I said that I hoped everything is being done to make his visit pleasant and successful, and he assured me that everyone has been very helpful. <u>He said that he is thrilled and delighted with the opportunity to work for the first time with the Choir; that he had heard such glowing reports about them, and that now he knows "none of them are exaggerated."</u> He stated that the recordings are going very well and that the Tabernacle Choir, under Brother Condie's training, is most responsive, and that he is sure the album would be successful. ...

Just before the departure of the group, I presented Mr. Bernstein and the visitors with embossed brochures on the Church, and they expressed their appreciation for them. Brother Cannon then said that the Choir staff and officers are entertaining the visitors at a luncheon later that day at the Hotel Utah.

September 12, 1963, 7:30–8:30 a.m. Dr. L[ouis] E. Viko gave me a physical examination in his office on South Temple and Seventh East. I spoke plainly to Dr. Viko, telling him that I am worried because I am having difficulty in speaking as quickly as thoughts come to me. Said that I wondered if I had had a small stroke which is causing this condition. He said there is no evidence of a stroke, but that he will arrange for Dr. Thomas of Bountiful, a neurosurgeon, to go over me. Dr. Viko said further that my heart and blood pressure are in good condition this morning. He strongly urged me, however, not to accept the appointment to go to Missouri to attend dedications of the Liberty Jail and Troost Park Monument.[30]

September 13, 1963, First Presidency meeting. President [Henry D.] Moyle stated that he will leave this noon to go to Florida for the meetings to be held next week, and that he will attend the Sacrament meeting in the Orlando Ward this Sunday evening, where he will be the speaker.

I advised that Brother Leo Ellsworth attend the meetings, and asked President Moyle that during his association with Brother Ellsworth he tell him that the First Presidency have in mind asking him to help in the project of diking the Utah Lake. President Moyle explained that in the meeting of the Board of Directors of Deseret Farms of Florida, consideration will be given to two matters: One, selling 2,500 acres of land to meet the tax situation; and two, to authorize the president of the Company to meet with the President of the Georgia Operations and the President of the Church to work out a plan whereby the problems of the two ranches can be solved. No details will be gone into.

Note: This was the last meeting of the First Presidency attended by President Henry D. Moyle. He became ill while speaking at the Sacrament meeting mentioned above, and word was received of his death early Wednesday morning, September 18, 1963.[31]

September 15, 1963. In accordance with my request, President Joseph Fielding Smith dedicated the Historic Liberty Jail [near Kansas City],

---

30. Two days later Joseph Fielding Smith filled in for the president to unveil the monument in Kansas City's Troost Park where in 1832 Latter-day Saints had constructed a log building that became the first schoolhouse in the area. The bronze monument anticipated McKay's presence, stating that he dedicated the site on September 14, 1963. In fact, he had followed his doctor's advice and stayed home.

31. Clare Middlemiss later added this entry. An account of Moyle's demise was recorded by the Florida mission president Ned Winder (1922–2005), who had been the secretary of the Church Missionary Committee for many years. Winder writes: "He [Moyle] called me one day in early September and said was coming down and looked forward to seeing us." He was invited to speak in the Winter Park ward. "As President Moyle began his talk, I was once again impressed with his bearing and power of speech. However, after about ten minutes he toned down and interrupted his speaking with long pauses. I know at least one pause was a minute long! At this time Sister Moyle, sitting next to my wife, whispered, 'I worry about Henry's health; he's had a bad case of angina.'" Moyle died the next morning. Poll, *Working the Divine Miracle*, ix–x.

and also dedicated and unveiled the monument in Troost Park of Kansas City, marking the spot where the Mormons erected a Church building which later became the first school building in the area.

I was indeed sorry and disappointed in not being able to make this trip, especially since the programs had been printed up with my name listed. Last Friday I had a conference with President Joseph Fielding Smith and told him that I had made preparations to go to Missouri to take care of matters there, but it was not considered advisable for me to make the trip.

I have never seen Liberty Jail, and was looking forward to visiting that part of the United States.

September 17, 1963, 8:30 a.m., with First Presidency. Among items discussed was the matter of <u>Church Sponsorship of an Educational Program in Europe</u>. We read President Theodore M. Burton's letter written in response to inquiry about opportunities for youth of the Church to obtain higher education in Europe, by reviewing in summary educational systems of the countries on continental Europe through elementary[,] high school[,] and university levels and the degree to which opportunities are open to members of the Church. He expressed disfavor with the suggestion that the Church undertake to sponsor elementary[,] high school[,] or university education in European countries, but suggested that the Church could render a much-needed service to the Youth of the church by establishing the institute program of the Church in favorable situations and locations, one in Great Britain and one on the continent of Europe, with dormitory facilities where the youth of the church seeking education would find a rallying point under Church sponsorship and influence while they may be enrolled in any of the many schools or universities or educational centers already open to them. He explained that grade school and high school education in most countries is paid for by the state. President [Marion D.] Hanks' letter relating to the limited opportunities for youth in Great Britain to obtain higher education was also read. President Burton stated that one of the serious handicaps at the European universities is finding suitable living quarters. He estimated from the inquiries made of the missions in Europe that 312 students at present would be interested in attending an institute as suggested. A letter signed by district presidents in the Austrian Mission supporting the proposal was also included in the correspondence.

I said this plan could work; that it is in keeping with our system at home, and that <u>we could start in England and spread it from there. I said I think we ought to do it, and that we should look favorably upon it. President [Hugh B.] Brown concurred.</u> I stated that the time has come for us to take action, and that we shall talk with Brother [Mark E.] Petersen and others. <u>I said that we should look today with favor upon the suggestion of an institute. The building of dormitories is a very important part. We shall have to come to it. We are now a world-wide Church. There is no reason why we should not do it in England where the membership justifies it, and then do it here.</u>

September 18, 1963, 5:30 am. ... My son, Dr. Edward R. McKay, called at the apartment and said that he had bad news for me, and then reported that President Moyle's daughter had called him at home and said that her father had passed away in the home of Brother Leo Ellsworth, at St. Cloud (near Orlando), Florida during the night; that Sister Moyle had found him dead in bed at 6:00 a.m., when she went to see why he was not up as he had planned to be before that hour.

I immediately got in touch with Sister Moyle. She answered very clearly and bravely over the telephone. Few women are called upon to experience such a shock.

September 19, 1963, First Presidency and Twelve. I mentioned to the Brethren this morning that I have been under the weather somewhat this past week, but that the doctors can find nothing wrong with me but age. I said that I do not mind being ninety years of age; that <u>I am looking forward to more years. I said that I supposed I would have to be here until the Lord says that I am ready to go, and that I would work as long as I can.</u> I said that my legs are lazy, but otherwise I feel fine.

September 21, 1963, 12:30 p.m. <u>Funeral Services Held—Final Tributes</u>—A large crowd consisting of members of the [Henry D.] Moyle family, associates, friends, and members of the Church were gathered in the Tabernacle, and a most fitting service was conducted.[32] ...

---

32. The *Deseret News* agreed in "Impressive Final Rites," Sept. 21, 1963.

Following the funeral services, we joined the procession to the City Cemetery where the body was interred. I got out of the car, leaving Sister McKay [wife] in the care of Emma Rae [daughter], and joined family and friends in the last rites at the grave side.

President Moyle was a very active, energetic counselor—always willing to respond to any call which was given to him. He was able, intelligent, and untiring in his duties relating to the First Presidency.

September 24, 1963, 9:15 a.m. ... By appointment Reed Benson brought Mr. Robert Welch of the John Birch Society, Belmont, Massachusetts, into the office of the First Presidency. Mr. Welch reviewed the success of the meeting of his organization in Los Angeles in which Elder Ezra Taft Benson was the featured speaker.[33] He also told of his busy personal schedule since he left Boston a week ago, and explained that his wife has been obliged to accompany his ninety-year-old mother back to her home, and, therefore, could not be present with him for this visit. He stated that about half the people attending the Los Angeles meeting were members and half non-members of the John Birch Society. Mr. Welch and Brother Benson then withdrew from the office.

September 27, 1963, 6:30 a.m. ... Preparations began in the McKay household for the entertaining of the President of the United States.[34] Chef Gerard of the Hotel Utah was in charge of the breakfast. Sister [Emma Ray] McKay was up and ready hours before the President arrived. Promptly at 8:30 a.m. President John F. Kennedy was ushered into our apartment. Following the arrival of the other guests, we went into the dining room for the breakfast. President Kennedy sat on my right; Stewart L. Udall, Secretary of Interior, sat on Sister McKay's right; Senator Frank E. Moss was placed next to the President, and Sister Moss sat next to her husband. President and Sister [Hugh B.] Brown sat beside

---

33. For more on this, see footnotes at Nov. 20, Dec. 23, 1963.

34. Kennedy had arrived the day before to deliver a major address highlighting the retreat of communism and the progress of his administration on international fronts, with political jabs at Goldwater and the conservative isolationists. He had visited McKay on three other occasions, in 1957, 1959, and 1960, and McKay's estimation of him had seemed to increase with each visit.

Secretary Udall; our daughter, Emma Rae, sat next to her mother, and I sat at the head of the table.

I asked the blessing on the food. The hotel waiter then served a most delicious breakfast. The full menu included mountain trout, scrambled eggs, lamb chops, link sausage, ham, crenshaw melon, orange juice, and milk. President Kennedy was the only one who had coffee.

The conversation at the table was very pleasant, and in the words of the President, "It was a refreshing hour."

October 3, 1963, 7:00–7:30 a.m. ... By appointment, <u>Elder Nathan Eldon Tanner</u> came into my private office. At this time I told him that I should like him to be <u>Second Counselor in the First Presidency</u> of the Church. Brother Tanner was greatly overcome. It was hard for him to understand why he, one of the youngest in point of service, should be selected.[35] I told him that it is the Lord's will. With tears in his eyes he accepted with all his heart, and said that he would do the best he could.

[Meeting with the First Presidency and Twelve Apostles][,] ... I then mentioned that the calling to the First Presidency of Elder Tanner would leave a vacancy in the Quorum of the Twelve. I presented to the Council the recommendation of the First Presidency that Thomas S. Monson[36] be approved to fill this vacancy. I said that I had not yet consulted Elder Monson, but would do so this afternoon.

On motion of President Joseph Fielding Smith, duly seconded, the Council approved Brother Monson for ordination as an Apostle and to fill the vacancy in the council of the Twelve. ...

2:30 p.m.— ... By appointment, Elder Thomas S. Monson came into my private office. I told him of his call as an Apostle of the Lord. He seemed stunned for a moment, and then broke down and wept. My heart melted with his as I remembered the Call that had come to me in

---

35. In fact, his rise was meteoric. See Prince and Wright, *David O. McKay*, 215.

36. Thomas Spencer Monson (1927–2018) had spent his life serving the church in both a spiritual and business capacity. He was called to be a bishop at twenty-two, a member of a stake presidency at twenty-seven, and a mission president to Canada at thirty-two. He worked for the *Deseret News*, the Deseret News Press, and the Newspaper Agency Corporation. He was the youngest to be called to the Quorum of the Twelve since Joseph Fielding Smith in 1910. Smith had been thirty-three at the time of his call, and Monson was thirty-six. He succeeded to the presidency of the church in 2008.

my youth. I was 32 years of age, so I could fully sympathize with Elder Monson in the great obligation that has come to him.

October 4, 1963, 8:30 a.m. President Hugh B. Brown called and reported his meeting with the members of the NAACP (National Association for the Advancement of Colored People) held last evening. He said that they have given their word that they will not march in mass demonstration against the Church, as they had planned, during this morning's meeting at the Salt Lake Tabernacle. President Brown promised them that a statement would be made during one of the Conference sessions concerning the Church's position with respect to the Negro.

October 6, 1963, 10:00–12:00 noon. Conducted the sixth session of the Conference which was broadcast to a world-wide audience listening and viewing by radio, television, and short-wave broadcasts. ... President Hugh B. Brown was the first speaker. ... Recognizing articles of recent months, both in Salt Lake City and across the nation, President Brown at the beginning of his talk made a statement on the position of the Church on Civil Rights. This was prepared and approved in advance by the First Presidency.[37]

October 8, 1963, 8:30–10:00 a.m. First Presidency meeting. ... President [N. Eldon] Tanner [was] meeting with us for the first time since his appointment as Second Counselor. In addition to the acquiring of broadcasting facilities, other matters considered were:

Civil Rights Statement in Conference—I asked if anything additional had developed from the announcement of the position of the Church on the subject of Civil Rights delivered by President [Hugh B.] Brown in the Sunday morning session of the Conference, and President Brown said that he had received from the local representatives of the NAACP expressions of thanks for the statement. A letter from Mr. Albert B. Fritz, local president of the organization, was read. It expressed appreciation for the statement and said that they look forward to further meetings with the First Presidency on the subject.

---

37. For his address, see Campbell and Poll, *Hugh B. Brown*, 256.

I stated that the statement was in fulfillment of a promise, and President Brown said it was made in response to a request for the statement. I said no more would be said about it, and President Brown and President Tanner expressed concurrence.

October 9, 1963, First Presidency meeting. Elder Mark E. Petersen came into the meeting, and asked for instructions from the First Presidency on the matter of baptizing children. He said there is some difference of opinion; that he has proceeded on the basis which he understood was the view of the First Presidency; namely, that a child 8 or 10 or 12 years old who becomes interested is to be taught the gospel if the parents are willing and understand; that if the child was coming to Primary with a member child everything was in proper order, and that the child should be baptized with the consent of the parents.

I said that that would be right; that if the parents refuse, the responsibility is upon them. President Petersen said, "This idea of indiscriminately going out and rounding up children, we do not want that do we?"

I said that I have never heard of such a thing, except in the Brighton area of England.

President Petersen said, "Our idea is bringing in families if possible. We are emphasizing family proselyting. Last month more than half of President Curtis' mission baptisms were complete families. In that way we get Priesthood and can get whole families to the Temple. We shall proceed on that basis."

President Petersen then took up other matters with regard to equipping Mission Homes, stating that he could see no reason for making "palaces" out of these Mission Homes, and I said we have never done it before, and that we do not want to do it now.

October 10, 1963, First Presidency meeting. We read a letter from Senator Wallace F. Bennett[38] which announced that information had been

---

38. Wallace Foster Bennett (1898–1993) was the Republican senator from Utah, 1950–74. He had been a high school principal in the partly Mormon San Luis Valley of southern Colorado before he inherited Bennett's Paint and Glass and became president of the National Association of Manufacturers. He defeated the LDS Democratic incumbent, Elbert D. Thomas, in 1950; in 1974 he chose not to run for a fifth term. Equally notable, his son, Robert F. ("Bob") Bennett (1933–2016) matched his father's accomplishment of being elected to the US Senate.

received that visas for missionaries to go to Lagos, Nigeria had been received. President [N. Eldon] Tanner reported that he had advised LaMar Williams to withhold publicity, and to remain calm until the visas come into his hands.

We also read a letter from Quinn McKay who reported a gathering of a group of members of the church for religious services in northern Nigeria where he is serving on the faculty of the university. A small group meets regularly every Sunday morning for classes, hymn singing and prayer. President Tanner explained that it is a group of students and teachers and government workers giving specialized service for a period of two or three years. Brother Quinn McKay explained that the Moslems are predominant in the area, and that the living standards and concepts of family life are greatly different from our own. It was decided to authorize Elder McKay to organize the small group and to conduct services of that group under the First Presidency rather than to be under any mission for the present, and that the group report to the First Presidency from time to time. ...

10:00 a.m. to 2:40 p.m.—Meeting of the First Presidency and Council of the Twelve held in the Salt Lake Temple.

Elder Thomas Spencer Monson ordained as an Apostle—also given the charge.—I said that in order that Brother Monson might participate with the Twelve, I thought it would be well to give him the charge at the beginning of the meeting. I also announced that the Quorum of the First Presidency would be completed this morning, and also the vacancy in the Quorum of the Twelve.

I then gave the charge[39] to Brother Thomas Spencer Monson, after which I asked President Joseph Fielding Smith, President of the Quorum of the Twelve to be voice in ordaining Elder Monson an apostle, and in setting him apart as a member of the Quorum of the Twelve. ...

The Brethren of the First Presidency and the Twelve united in placing

---

39. According to Hugh B. Brown, the apostolic charge was to "give all that one has, both as to time and means, to the building of the Kingdom of God; to keep himself pure and unspotted from the sins of the world; to be obedient to the authorities of the church; and to exercise the freedom to speak his mind but always be willing to subjugate his own thoughts and accept the majority opinion—not only to vote for it but to act as though it were his own original opinion after it has been approved by the majority of the Council of the Twelve and the First Presidency." Firmage, *Abundant Life*, 126–27.

their hands upon the head of President Hugh B. Brown, and I was voice in setting him apart as First Counselor in the First Presidency. ...

All the Brethren then united in laying their hands upon the head of Nathan Eldon Tanner and I was voice in setting him apart as Second Counselor in the First Presidency of the Church.

The Brethren [apostles] extended the hand of fellowship to each of these [three] Brethren in their new positions.

I remarked to them that we had participated in one of the most glorious ordinances, and that we knew to a degree what the Apostle John meant when he said, "I know I have passed from death unto life, because I love the brethren."

October 17, 1963, 7:30 a.m. ... Arrived at the office. <u>Met by appointment President Ernest L. Wilkinson of the BYU.</u>[40] We discussed the advisability of his running for the U.S. Senate. I said that I think it would be better for him to make further investigation to see what his possibilities are in this respect; that if he gets the nomination, then he should accept with the understanding that he will keep his present position at the Brigham Young University if he does not win the election.

October 25, 1963, 10:30–11:00 a.m. ... Conference with Clare [Middlemiss]. In talking about the tremendous amount of work which has gone through her hands, and in expressing appreciation to her, Clare said: "Do you wish that you had chosen a man to be your secretary when you first started your duties as a Counselor in the First Presidency," and I said to her, <u>"No, I do not—I want you to know that I have been a very fortunate man in having you as my secretary; no man would have done for me what you have done—you have given me great satisfaction, and in a thousand ways have proved yourself capable. You have good judgment, and in a refined way have taken care of your responsibilities for the good of the whole Church</u>—in meeting the people, in arranging my appointments and meetings, in handling my correspondence—you have given attention

---

40. Wilkinson had met the previous Friday with apostles Ezra Taft Benson, Gordon B. Hinckley, Marion G. Romney, and Delbert L. Stapley, and President N. Eldon Tanner. Wilkinson diary, Oct. 11, 1963.

to details as well as important matters in an efficient manner—you have never failed me in anything I have asked you to do."

October 28, 1963. In speaking of the trouble in the world, President McKay commented that the United Nations organizations does not impress him very much.[41]

And then he said: "This is a pretty good old world; I like it; I have had a wonderful life—<u>I remember that Father made a little red wagon which I could pull around</u>. I remember saying to myself: 'I must enjoy this wagon now, because later I won't have it.'" I [Clare Middlemiss] said to President McKay, "<u>This is the secret of your happiness—you have enjoyed life as you have gone along</u>," and President McKay said, "<u>Yes, I have.</u>"

November 1, 1963, First Presidency meeting. Bishop [John H.] Vandenberg explained that the Bishop of Val Verda [Bountiful] Fourth Ward, South Davis Stake, by letter presented the question relating to a boy of that ward of supposed negro lineage, who is about to be graduated from the Primary, and to be recommended to receive the Aaronic Priesthood. The basis for the supposition of negro lineage is that the father was a Puerto Rican. The suggestion has been made that the boy be given a patriarchal blessing for the declaration of lineage.

I said, "No, let that boy go on." President [Hugh B.] Brown said that that would be his feeling. Bishop Vandenberg said that they have no proof that he has negro blood. Bishop [Robert L.] Simpson said if a mistake is made the Lord will take care of it.

<u>I said that I have met this question by following the rule that we shall face the Savior and tell what our decision is with a clear conscience.</u>

November 6, 1963, First Presidency meeting. President [N. Eldon] Tanner read a memorandum addressed to him by Brother Henry Christiansen of the Genealogical Department asking for guidance as to what should be done in cases where an individual who claims membership in the Church cannot provide his baptismal date. It was reported that the Presiding

---

41. See also Quinn, *Elder Statesman*, 310–14.

Bishopric have set up a procedure for the bishops to the effect that in cases where no record of the baptism can be found, if affidavits can be obtained signed by witnesses, such procedure would suffice; that, however, where affidavits cannot be secured and no record can be found, the person should be baptized again.

I instructed that we be careful not to make an ironclad ruling on this subject; that there are many cases where the records have been destroyed by fire or otherwise. I mentioned in that connection that all the records in Huntsville, including the record of my baptism, were destroyed by fire. I think, however, that the rule should remain the way it has been set forth by the Presiding Bishopric with this precaution.

November 10, 1963. Lou Jean [McKay's daughter] reported [to Clare Middlemiss] that her father came into the dining room from his bedroom this morning and said: "Lou Jean, I cannot button my shirt; I have tried for hours, but I just cannot do it; my fingers will not operate; I think I have had a stroke!"[42]

The doctors were called immediately and tests were made. They ordered President McKay to bed for a rest.

Lawrence [McKay] stayed that night, sleeping on the couch, but no one got any sleep.

November 11, 1963. Lou Jean [McKay's daughter] reported that President McKay announced to the family this morning that it seemed to him that no one was getting any rest, so he had decided that he would go to the hospital and the folks could stay home and take care of Sister [Emma Ray] McKay.

At 4:30 p.m., Robert McKay drove president McKay to the LDS Hospital. The doctors have concluded that the stroke is mild, and that it reached its peak Saturday night.

President McKay was confined to the hospital until November 18, 1963.

---

42. McKay's suspicion was soon confirmed. Despite the periodic physical impediments that resulted from small strokes, his mind remained lucid. Gibbons, *David O. McKay*, 417; Prince and Wright, *David O. McKay*, 385.

November 12, 1963, 8:15 a.m. ... When I [Clare Middlemiss] arrived at the office, I received word that President [Hugh B.] Brown wished to see me immediately. He told me that President McKay had suffered a stroke, and was in the hospital. I was greatly shocked, but could not say very much. President Brown then said that Dr. [Louis E.] Viko would call him in an hour or so, and that he would let me know more about it.

At <u>10:00 a.m.</u>, President Brown called me into the office of the First Presidency and told me that Dr. Viko had called and said that President McKay said he was all right and for him (President Brown) to go East to attend the Bankers' luncheon already planned for him by [Zion's Bank president] Leland B. Flint. And then he said, "Dr. Viko is really worried about President McKay".

I [Middlemiss] went out of the office feeling pretty discouraged. As I reached the door of my office, the telephone was ringing. It was Lou Jean (President McKay's daughter), who said that she had called me to tell me that she had just talked to her father, and that he wanted me to call him. She said they had tried to reach me several times during President McKay's illness, but had been unable to do so. I broke down and cried, and she said: "He is all right, Clare; Dr. Viko said that it is not serious; that he has suffered a slight stroke which has paralyzed his right arm a little, but that he has a firm grip in his hand which indicates it is not too serious. The doctors want him to stay in the hospital for a few days.["] She said, "If you have any trouble getting through to him, please call me. He wants you to call him right away."

I called President McKay immediately; his voice sounded good, and he asked about office matters, and told me to keep in touch with him.

November 20, 1963, First Presidency meeting. President [N. Eldon] Tanner asked if we were prepared to announce a policy regarding Junior Colleges. Attention was called to a statement in the Salt Lake Tribune this morning in which President [Ernest L.] Wilkinson is reported to have announced that we still intend to build a college on the Forest Dale golf course property [in Salt Lake City]. I said I think we should make no statement at the present time, and expressed the feeling that Salt Lake is not a good place to build a Junior College. ...

We again gave consideration to the question of the location of the civic Auditorium and the question of whether or not the Church would be willing to lease to the county its property holdings on the two blocks between South Temple and Second South, and West Temple and First West. President [Hugh B.] Brown had discussed the matter with Graham Doxey,[43] who felt that the church should not undertake as a Church to build a new auditorium of its own, that to do so would cost approximately $25,000,000, whereas an arrangement could no doubt be made with the county for the use of the civic auditorium three times a year for the holding of our conferences and for such other use as we might wish to make of it. President Brown mentioned that Commissioner Edwin Q. Cannon telephoned him last night at his home saying that he had just received word that one member of the county Commission is ready to appoint a director with authority to select a site, and that if this were done the choice would be the site on Fifth South. Brother Cannon said, however, that he and Commissioner Marv Jenson favored the site near South Temple. I authorized President Brown to say to County Commissioners Cannon and Jensen that the Church is prepared to consider a lease of its property in the area referred to for the purpose mentioned; that they should not make it any more definite than that. ...

President Brown reported that last night after 10 o'clock, he had a call from the United Press and CBS representing broadcasting and television stations, also from the Associated Press, regarding statements made by Reed Benson in Boise, Idaho, regarding talks made by his father pertaining to the John Birch Society, indicating that his father, Brother Benson, had been assigned by the President of the Church to give the talk that was made by him at the John Welch Testimonial in Los Angeles.[44] President Brown mentioned a news article in the Salt Lake Tribune this morning giving a report of remarks by Reed Benson

---

43. Graham H. Doxey (1900–69) was vice president and manager of the church's real estate company, Zions Securities Corporation. He had previously been a partner with Howard J. Layton of a Utah real estate company. He was from Salt Lake City, studied at the University of Utah, spent three years as a young man in New Zealand on an LDS mission, and served in the army at the conclusion of World War I.

44. See note at Dec. 23, 1963. Benson had prefaced his remarks in Los Angeles by saying, "I am here tonight with the knowledge and consent of a great spiritual leader and patriot, the President of the Church of Jesus Christ of Latter-day Saints, President David O. McKay." His son interpreted this to mean that McKay had commissioned or encouraged the speech, rather than simply allowing it.

in Boise last night and said that Henry Smith of the Deseret News wanted to know whether the News should run a report of this interview at Boise. President Brown mentioned that these things are causing a lot of confusion among our people. President McKay said that we should say nothing further about the matter, and that if Reed Benson has spoken out of turn he will have to answer for it. <u>President McKay said that we should let the whole thing drop and that the News should not publish anything on the question.</u>

November 21, 1963, First Presidency meeting. President [Hugh B.] Brown reported that he was informed by Brother [Delbert L.] Stapley that President Ernest L. Wilkinson notified the Executive Committee of the Brigham Young University Board of Trustees yesterday that he intends to seek the nomination for Senator from Utah. It was reported that all of the Brethren of the Committee were unanimous, with the exception of Brother [Harold B.] Lee who was not present, that Brother Wilkinson should not seek this office. The Committee is asking whether we should interfere with his ambitions or if we should seek a new President of the BYU in case he does enter the campaign. I said that <u>I think President Wilkinson should remain as President of the Brigham Young University while he is seeking the nomination, and if he gets the nomination then we can consider finding a successor. If he is not elected, then he should continue at the school</u>.

November 22, 1963, 11:30 a.m. … Just as Dr. Hucko was massaging my injured leg and arm, news was flashed on the television that <u>President John F. Kennedy was shot as he rode with Mrs. Kennedy in an open car in downtown Dallas, Texas</u>, waving and smiling to a crowd of 250,000. He fell face downward in the back seat of his car. Mrs. Jacqueline Kennedy was not hurt; she turned and clutched his head and tried to lift it. The car sped toward the hospital with the dying President. He was shot at approximately 12:30 p.m. (C[entral] S[tandard] T[ime]) (11:30 our time), and died in the hospital at approximately 1:00 p.m. (CST) (Noon our time). Governor Connelly of Texas was also shot twice in the back, but was not mortally wounded.

All at our house are shocked and stunned at the news, as it is only a few weeks ago that it was our privilege to entertain the President in our apartment, and now to think that he has gone is unbelievable!

November 26, 1963, First Presidency meeting. President [Hugh B.] Brown reported his visit to Washington [DC] where he attended the funeral of President John F. Kennedy, which was held in the St. Matthew's Cathedral in Washington, D.C. President Brown said that the person who impressed him most was Mrs. [Jacqueline] Kennedy, that she was heroic and she was Spartan. He said he saw her on several occasions, that he saw her in the rotunda of the capitol building as she walked in holding her little boy by the hand, no one with her. She walked up to the casket and knelt by it for a little while, got up and walked out with her head erect, and then she walked from the White House to the church which was about six blocks. He said she went through the whole thing which was a grueling experience, and subsequently attended the services at the cemetery. He said that he had previously looked upon Jacqueline Kennedy as a kind of play girl, but she rose to great heights in this tragic experience. ...

President Brown said that Brothers Kimball and [Delbert L.] Stapley of the Budget Committee have asked if they are entitled to know what we have by way of liquid funds as they are making up their budget for next year. President Brown called attention to the sentiment of the First Presidency a year ago to the effect that the Budget Committee has to do only with the tithes and that other income and commitments were something for the First Presidency alone to handle. I said that the committee should prepare the budget for the disbursement of tithing funds only, that the other income of the church is something they need not worry about, and is the responsibility of the First Presidency.

November 27, 1963. Although President McKay looked well, fastidiously dressed, he seemed discouraged because he is not well enough to get out of the apartment to come to the office. He said to me (i.e., Clare Middlemiss): "I do not know what the matter is—this numbness in my arm and leg—I don't like it! I don't see why it doesn't get better!"

December 3, 1963. Clare [Middlemiss] presented to me a letter from President Ernest L. Wilkinson dated November 27, 1963, asking for approval to announce his candidacy for the Republican nomination for the United States Senate.[45]

I told her to call President Wilkinson and tell him that he may go ahead with his announcement; that he may choose his campaign manager, and that Brother Harvey L. Taylor[46] will become the acting President during his absence at the BYU.

December 10, 1963, 10:00 a.m. By appointment President Ernest L. Wilkinson called at the apartment and discussed with me the arrangements to be made at the Brigham Young University while he is away from that institution seeking nomination for the United States Senate.

I told President Wilkinson to make his suggestions regarding the men who will succeed him during the period he is away. It is understood if President Wilkinson is not elected, he will return to his present positions at the school.

December 20, 1963, First Presidency meeting. President [N. Eldon] Tanner mentioned that two of the Brethren of the Twelve had mentioned that they thought it was having a bad effect to permit couples to be married in our chapels. He also made reference to cases where couples desire to be married by civil ceremony before going to the Temple, in order that relatives may witness the civil marriage. These relatives, in most cases, are non-members, but there are cases where the relatives are members, but not worthy to receive Temple recommends.

It was mentioned that as a general rule these exceptions should be limited to cases where the parents are not members of the Church.

December 23, 1963, 10:00–11:30 a.m. … I dictated a letter to her [Clare

---

45. See also Wilkinson diary, Oct. 31, Nov. 30, Dec. 10, 27, 1963.

46. Harvey Leslie Taylor (1894–1983), Wilkinson's executive assistant, had previously been superintendent of the Mesa Public School System in Arizona. He was actually assigned to fill in as Chancellor of Church Education, a position he retained after Wilkinson's senate campaign of 1964. Taylor's education had been at the University of Utah and Columbia University. He was born near Ogden. The BYU academic vice president, Earl Clarkson Crockett (1903–75), formerly a professor of economics at the University of Colorado, would assume the presidency of BYU until Wilkinson's return. His background included degrees from the University of Utah and UC–Berkeley. He was born across the Utah state line to the north of Logan in Preston, Idaho.

Middlemiss] to <u>Mr. Robert Welch</u> of the <u>John Birch Society in Belmont,</u> <u>Massachusetts,</u> in answer to one he had sent me asking if <u>Elder Ezra Taft</u> <u>Benson</u> could serve on the National Committee of the society. I told Mr. Welch that Elder Benson's duties as European Mission President would preclude his accepting his invitation.[47]

---

47. Benson's praise of Welch on September 23 was followed by weeks of controversy, primarily because of Welch's comment at the same event that Dwight D. Eisenhower, in whose cabinet Benson had served, had been soft on Communism and even "sympathetic to ultimate Communist aims." Confronted by this, Benson replied sheepishly that Eisenhower had "supported me in matters of agriculture. In other areas we had differences." On September 25, Congressman Ralph R. Harding (D–Idaho), an active LDS Church member, criticized Benson's remark in a speech he delivered on the floor of the House of Representatives. There followed an uproar in the national press, including newspapers in the Intermountain West, denouncing people on either side of disloyalty. Benson's October general conference address about how people sometimes betray good causes was seen as a hidden reference to Brown. McKay's solution on October 18 was to call Benson to preside over the church in Europe and advise him to go immediately, which Benson did within the week. Quinn, *Extensions*, 77–78; Prince and Wright, *David O. McKay*, 299–300; *One Hundred Thirty-third Semi-annual Conference of the Church of Jesus Christ of Latter-day Saints*, Oct. 4–6, 1963, 15–19.

14　Lingering Health and Political Problems, 1964

> President Brown suggested … a word of caution to the Brethren … regarding keeping out of politics. He mentioned a letter that had come to him from a Dutch Saint which was signed by former presidents of the Netherlands Mission and by Le-Grand Richards urging the [immigrant] Dutch Saints to vote for Goldwater. President Brown said he phoned Brother Richards about it, and that Brother Richards said, "Well, it is too late to do anything now. We have sent it out, and you know and I know that we ought to have Goldwater and we ought to get him in. —August 18, 1964

January 9, 1964, 10:00–12:00 noon. Attended Council meeting [of First Presidency and Twelve] in the Salt Lake Temple for the first time in over two months! I told the Brethren that sometime ago, about the first of November, I was feeling fine and attending to duties, never missing a meeting, when something came over me, and that I have not been so well since, and unable to meet with them in Council Meetings. I said I think this condition is only temporary; that the doctors say I am getting alone fine. I remarked that I am inclined to accept their word, but do not believe all that they say. However, I said that I am getting well, but I still find myself weak on my right side. The doctor does not like the word "stroke," and I do not like to use it, and do not feel that it was a real stroke, but something is wrong, and the doctors have advised that I take things easy, but that is hard for me to do. I said that I can use my right hand now, even in signing my name—it does not look like the same old signature, but it passes on checks all right. ...

Regarding the Home Teaching Program, I presented a number of questions asking for clarification of the program. Brother [Marion G.] Romney explained the organization and functions of the Home Teaching Program. In his explanation, Elder Romney mentioned that there might be occasions that would argue the advisability of having a sister go with her husband to visit a family as a part of the Home Teaching Program. He said, however, that the instruction has repeatedly been given that the Priesthood are to be the regular home teachers, and that women would be used as home teachers only on specific occasions to go with their husbands to visit special families.

I said that I think there is danger in recognizing such a condition as this, that the home visiting is the duty of the Priesthood and that by even suggesting that a teacher might take his wife with him, instead of another member of the Priesthood, would seem to be questionable wisdom. I said that I am wondering if we were not opening the door for an aggressive wife to assume more than she has the right to assume. Elder [Harold B.] Lee said that our Stake Presidents and Bishops have been cautioned regarding this; that, however, there is that possibility, and the Priesthood committee representatives have been warned about it; that he thinks, however, that perhaps we could pull an even tighter rein on the matter.

I suggested that it would be well to tighten the rein, notwithstanding the instructions and explanations that have heretofore been sent out. Elder Lee said that my wishes in this regard would be carried out.

January 14, 1964, First Presidency meeting. President [N. Eldon] Tanner said that Brother [Lamar] Williams had reported having talked with Shirley Woodward[1] and Abner Hales, local Negroes, who are faithful Church members, and who told him that there are 50 to 75 Negroes who would like to join the Church and have the activities that the Church

---

1. Shirley Steward–Howell Woodward (1932–99) was a secretary at Hill Air Force Base who had studied at Weber State College, Westminster College, and the University of Utah. Her obituary mentioned that she was an eager participant in civil rights. She was a seventh-generation Utahn. "Shirley Steward–Howell," *Deseret News*, May 5, 1999; "Mother of Five Struggles to Success," *Salt Lake Tribune*, Dec., 17, 1967.

provides for them. Brother Williams suggested that they be formed into an LDS Branch and that we assign Stake Missionaries or others to meet with them and take care of the necessary ordinances; also that arrangements could be made for them to meet in a chapel or some other building for the holding of their services. Brother Williams said that he had talked to [local NAACP leader] Albert Fritz, who does not want us to do anything that would segregate these people.

I said that I do not favor this proposition.

January 20, 1964, 10:30–12:00 noon. My secretary, Clare [Middlemiss], came over with a number of office matters. ... I noted in the Church Section an announcement that the Church had made a <u>donation of $10,000 to the John F. Kennedy Center for the Performing Arts in Washington, D.C.</u>

As I did not remember approving of this contribution, nor had I seen a letter transmitting these funds, I called President Hugh B. Brown and asked him when we had approved of this donation. He said that it was his understanding that it had been approved; however, I called Joseph Anderson and asked him to look in the minutes and see when we had approved of this amount of money being donated for this purpose. He read to me over the telephone from the minutes of the First Presidency that this matter had been brought up by President Brown at the request of Brother Willard Marriott of Washington, D.C., who is on the National Committee sponsoring the project. The minutes stated that I had asked that before making the donation I should like a report on the amount of money being donated by other churches, and then we should decide about what we should do.

However, as the decision had been made, and the money sent directly to Willard Marriott, there was nothing more to do about the matter. Several letters have been received since from members of the Church objecting to tithing money being used for this purpose.

January 22, 1964. <u>President McKay's face was beaming and full of animation when he arrived at the office</u>. He was pleased with the heartfelt welcome given to him by all who were fortunate enough to see him. As he sat in his chair at his desk in his private office, he said: "<u>Well, this is</u>

something like it!" Just before leaving the office he said to me [Clare Middlemiss]: "Don't fret, I'll be here another five years!"[2] Of course, we all hope it will be for many years longer than that!

January 24, 1964, First Presidency meeting. There was read to me excerpts from the minutes of the Executive Committee of the Unified Church School System and Brigham Young University held January 17, 1964, concerning the situation created by the resignation of Ernest L. Wilkinson as Chancellor of the Unified Church School System and as President of the Brigham Young University, and the appointment of Harvey L. Taylor as Acting Chancellor of the Unified Church School System, and Earl C. Crockett as Acting President of the Brigham Young University. It was moved that President Wilkinson be advised that he is relieved of all responsibility in connection with his former offices, and that Acting Chancellor Taylor be given responsibility for the overall direction of Brigham Young University, Ricks College, the LDS Business College, Juarez Academy, and other Church schools in Mexico, the various seminaries and institutes, and any other facilities included in the Unified Church School System, and that the executives of these various institutions serve under his direction, he to be responsible to the Church Board of Education and its Executive Committee until such time as a Chancellor is appointed and a President of the Brigham Young University is named, or until the Board amends this action. This was approved by the Committee.

Presidents [Hugh B.] Brown and [N. Eldon] Tanner explained that the committee feel that Brother Harvey Taylor should be the Acting Chancellor of the entire Church School System, including the Brigham Young University, and that Brother Earl C. Crockett as Acting President of the Brigham Young University would be working under him. They reported that President Wilkinson, under date of December 14, 1963, had sent a memorandum to [BYU executive assistant] Harvey L. Taylor, [BYU academic vice president] Earl C. Crockett, [administrator of church seminaries and institutes] William E. Berrett, and [BYU legal counsel] Clyde Sandgren, regarding the termination of his services at the

---

2. McKay passed away in January 1970, almost six years after this statement.

BYU and stating that I had asked that individuals whom he named in the letter assume duties indicated by him in his letter. President Brown then read a letter addressed to Harvey Taylor by President Wilkinson dated January 8, in which he set forth the functions of Brother Taylor as Acting Chancellor and the functions of Brother Earl C. Crockett as Acting President of the BYU. President Brown said that the committee feel it should be clearly understood that the Chancellor of the Unified Church School System, Brother Taylor, should have jurisdiction such as the title indicates, that he is the Chancellor of the whole system, including the Brigham Young University, Ricks College, the LDS Business College, Juarez Academy, etc., except of course [the] South pacific, which is a thing apart.

President Brown also mentioned that President Wilkinson has made the statement that to the extent that his time permits he would continue to advise with the Acting Chancellor and Acting President relative to the coordinating of their activities. The committee did not feel that it was desirable that President Wilkinson pursue that course while he is engaged in his campaign work because that would seem to negate what his resignation implies. It was decided to ask the committee to notify Acting Chancellor Harvey L. Taylor and Acting President Earl C. Crockett of their responsibilities to which they have been appointed, the committee also to notify President Wilkinson of this decision. ...

Church Finances—We then considered some important financial matters of the Church. I verified President Tanner's understanding that I wanted him to take the responsibility of seeing that our Church funds, long term or whatever it may be, are deposited in such a way as to bring the best rates from the banks. After a discussion of these matters, President Tanner said that he is trying to get as clear a picture of the entire financial situation as he could, and that he would like to bring to me recommendations when he thought changes should be made. I indicated my approval of his doing this. ...

President Tanner suggested that when the First Presidency make a decision of importance, such as the recent decision authorizing the Relief society to set up a child placement agency in Nevada, that it would be helpful to the Twelve if they were informed of these decisions in order that they might know what is going on in the Church. This information could be given to the Brethren at Council Meeting. I said that I had no objection to this being done.[3]

January 25, 1964. At about 1:30 p.m. today, I received a telephone call from Lyndon B. Johnson, President of the United States. ... He said: "I need some strength from you, President McKay. Could you come to Washington for an hour's consultation with me alone sometime next week—at your convenience? I'll meet [you on] your time, President McKay." I told President Johnson that I had been ill, and that if my doctors will give me permission, and I feel stronger, I shall be honored to meet with him.[4]

January 31, 1964. It was cold and blustery as we arrived at The White House at about 1:00 p.m. We were received at the northwest gate of The White House grounds, and were admitted after showing identification. We were taken into the annex offices, and from there into the Cabinet Room.

Soon thereafter President [Lyndon B.] Johnson came into the office and said: "Hello young men," and then he came over to where I was sitting and shook hands with me, then with President [N. Eldon] Tanner, and Lawrence [McKay].

After some introductions of two secretaries (Mormon girls) and the taking of pictures of the group, we were left alone. President Johnson then explained to me that he had called me on an impulse, and that he wanted my advice. He mentioned his visits with me at Church headquarters in Salt Lake City.[5] He said that he would have come out to Salt Lake City to visit with me if he could have done so, and appreciated my coming to Washington.

---

3. Tanner's influence cannot be underestimated. His financial and managerial acumen saved the church from the serious financial problems that began in the late 1950s and early 1960s, brought about by Henry D. Moyle's domination of church finances during his tenure, 1959–63. See Prince and Wright, *David O. McKay*, 199–226; Quinn, *Extensions*, 198–225.

4. See also Gibbons, *David O. McKay*, 376–77. In paradox, McKay seemed genteel and spiritually oriented, Johnson more coarse and calculating.

5. For Tanner's account, see McKay diary, Jan. 31, 1964. At the lunch, Johnson turned to McKay and said: "I feel that the spiritual and moral fiber of this country need strengthening, and we need it badly. I would like to ask you, President McKay if you can tell me how we get it." McKay replied: "Mr. President, ... I think you are an honorable man. ... I would say to you: Let your conscience be your guide, and go forward and let the people see you are sincere, that this is the problem you have before you, and one that should be met, and lead out in it and let the people follow."

The two-hour visit with President Johnson and the tour of The White House, personally conducted by President Johnson, was a memorable occasion. ...

February 4, 1964, First Presidency meeting. I reported that I had spoken to President Ernest L. Wilkinson over the telephone suggesting that he have nothing whatever to do with the Brigham Young University while he is seeking the nomination for U.S. Senator from Utah. ...

I spoke to the Brethren [First Presidency and Twelve] telling them how happy I am to be with them this morning. I told them that my right side had been somewhat affected, and that I deplore the slowness of my recovery, but said that the doctors think I have made a remarkable recovery. I told the doctors that I did not see anything remarkable about it, although my folks think I am getting along very well.

I said that I have the use of all my limbs, but I do not get much strength in my right hand, and the right leg will not obey me as a limb should. I said that I have no pain, and that I should be satisfied at the recovery I have made.

I said that I do not like to have to hesitate in talking; however, I am very glad that I can use my right hand when eating; [but] that I cannot button my shirt, and that it takes me an hour to do so if I try to do it alone. I said that it is strange how wonderful habit is; that I try time and time again to use my left hand, and find that it is difficult to do so.

February 7, 1964, First Presidency meeting. Some consideration was given to the matter of the organization of foreign language groups in the Salt Lake Valley and the problem in connection therewith. Particular reference was made to the fact that by this means these foreign speaking people do not have the advantage of attending Sacrament and other meetings in the wards in which they reside and that as a matter of fact we are encouraging these people from foreign countries to set up separate colonies as it were. I made the statement, in which the counselors agreed, that we ought not to encourage the setting up of branches for these European Saints who speak different languages; that, however, there is a different situation where different races are involved.

February 13, 1964, meeting of First Presidency and Twelve. Elder LeGrand Richards mentioned that while visiting the Granger [Utah] North Stake Conference last Saturday and Sunday the question had been asked whether or not the calling of labor missionaries is equivalent in credit to the missionary and his family as the calling of a missionary to serve in the proselyting field. It was indicated that there is in the stake a number of young men who could well have gone on proselyting missions, but who have been called to serve as labor missionaries; that these labor missionaries are being called at the age of 18, and there are two of them now serving at the age of 17. Elder Richards inquired as to what the policy is so that the brethren would be prepared to instruct stake presidencies and others on this question.

I answered that if a young man goes on a labor mission, that means participating in the erection of a meetinghouse, and that that is not equal to a regular mission. In this connection I also mentioned that <u>labor missionaries are not to be set apart by members of the General Authorities</u>, although it is in order to set apart building supervisors.

Elder [Gordon B.] Hinckley thought that the matter needed further clarification in the minds of the Bishops; that there are cases where the young man, the family and the Bishop all feel satisfied that one who serves as a labor missionary is discharging the missionary responsibility.

Elder [Harold B.] Lee mentioned another element on the matter, namely, that in cases where these building supervisors have been called to serve as stake presidents or Bishops in foreign lands, the records indicate that they have paid no tithing, and yet their allowance is sometimes greater than the income of other officers of the stake where they serve. Elder Lee said when he had asked them what [they had to say] about their tithing record they had said that they were exempt, that they were not supposed to pay tithing, and yet they were getting more money for the same labor than a man in his own country would receive.

<u>I said that these men should pay tithing on their income or allowance.</u>

February 19, 1964. I approved a letter to mission presidents prepared by President [N. Eldon] Tanner for signatures of the First Presidency giving instructions regarding the handling of cases where children had been baptized without parents' approval or consent, or without the parents or the child understanding that he was actually becoming a member of the Church. The letter recommends that the parents and children be worked with in an endeavor to convert them to the Gospel and to activity in the Church; that, however, if they insist upon having their names removed, action should be taken after a reasonable effort by regular ecclesiastical court procedure.

February 21, 1964. I told Clare [Middlemiss] that I am greatly concerned over the letters which were sent to [Idaho] Representative [Ralph R.] Harding by President Joseph Fielding Smith and my son Robert R. McKay,[6] and that I am also disturbed over Ralph Harding's alleged claim that I had sent Elder [Ezra Taft] Benson out of the country to stop his political activity, and that I had apologized to President Lyndon B. Johnson when I visited him recently for Elder Benson's actions.

I approved the publishing of a letter … [which] had asked me if "the rumor is true that you went back to Washington, D.C. to vindicate Representative Ralph R. Harding and apologize for Apostle Benson," and "was Elder Benson sent to Europe because he had embarrassed the Church in any way?" The reply, signed by my secretary, said: "President McKay has directed me to acknowledge your letter for him, and to tell you that there is no truth whatever in the rumors you related in your letter. President McKay has also instructed me to tell you that Elder Ezra Taft Benson was not sent to Europe for any of the reasons given in your letter. Elder Benson was called by inspiration to preside over the European Mission. I am directed further to say that President McKay responded to an invitation from President Lyndon B. Johnson to talk over matters with him that had nothing whatever to do with Elder Ezra Taft Benson."

I shall have to take steps to have these accusations stopped. Wide publicity has been given to these matters over Radio, Television, and in the newspapers.[7]

---

6. For references to these letters, which were critical of Ezra Taft Benson's political activism, see footnote at December 23, 1963.

7. It is difficult to overestimate the public relations problems the church encountered due to Elder Benson's connection to the Birch Society and unsavory comments of Birch leadership about former US President Eisenhower. Harding was incensed at what he perceived to be the embarrassment to the church from this issue. See his comments in Prince and Wright, *David O. McKay*, 296–97; also Quinn, *Extensions*, 78–80.

February 26, 1964, First Presidency meeting. President [N. Eldon] Tanner read a letter which … stated that a brother had … reported hearing the teaching that God the Father and Jesus Christ are fathers, just as mortal men are fathers of their children, and also that Jesus was married, and asks if answers to these questions can be given. <u>I said that there is no evidence that Jesus was married and we do not claim or publish that He was</u>. President [Hugh B.] Brown said nothing has been revealed on the subject. I said that when I first came into the Twelve we were discussing the subject on one occasion, and the statement was made to the effect that there was no revelation on the subject. <u>I said "we use the scriptures and believe the statement in the Bible 'conceived by the Holy Ghost."'</u> President Tanner said he has heard senior members of the Twelve say that this is true. I said that we do not want to do anything about this but to give that advice to them. We do not want to make any statement that will cause controversy; use the words of the scriptures. President Brown said we accept the doctrine as given in the scripture. …

President Tanner referred to a letter from a woman who desires to join the Church, but whose husband will not consent and his parents are strongly opposed. She asks if she should break away and be baptized without his permission and whether she will do wrong by teaching her children what she knows is true. <u>I advised that the family be not broken up, but that she is responsible for teaching her children the truth</u>. President Tanner summarized saying that she could teach her children correct principles but should not be baptized without her husband's consent. I concurred.

March 5, 1964, meeting of First Presidency and Twelve. A letter was read which presented the question as to whether or not fasting includes abstaining from drinking water. … <u>I expressed approval of the statement that there is no hard and fast rule, and that drinking water is not a violation of the fast</u>.[8] …

I said that before partaking of the Sacrament this morning, I should like to refer to an <u>unfortunate incident</u> which has occurred since the

---

8. During this time the *Church Handbook* stated that "true observance of the fast consists of abstaining from food and drink for two consecutive meals, attending the fast and testimony meeting, and making a generous cash offering to the bishop." Bergera, *Statements*, 158.

Council last met in this capacity. I mentioned that a man by the name of [Ralph R.] Harding in Idaho, who is a congressman, has created quite a stir, and has been misinterpreted as far as lack of unity among the General Authorities is concerned by the Nation. I said that I had received a lot of letters relative to this matter. I said that this matter affects one of the members of the Council, and indirectly all members.

I then read to the Council one of the letters I have received regarding the situation. In this letter the writer referred to a letter written by President Joseph Fielding Smith and also one by my son, Robert having reference to and criticizing Elder Ezra Taft Benson's attitude toward the John Birch Society. The writer stated that this indicates a lack of harmony among the leaders of the Church, and that this dissension is creating confusion among members and friends of the Church. I said that I have other similar letters from faithful members of the Church.

I said that I should like to know today that there is no dissension among the members of this Council, and that we partake of the Sacrament in full fellowship and full support of one another. I mentioned that since President Smith's name is associated with Brother Benson, particularly in the matter of the John Birch Society, that I think it would be well for President Smith on this occasion to explain his association with the controversy.

President Smith said he was glad to do so, that he had received similar communications to the one read by me and that he had written to brother Benson about the matter. He said that he had had no intention of saying anything detrimental to Brother Benson; that he did say that when Brother Benson comes home, he hoped he would not get into politics and would keep his blood pure. President Smith said that was not intended as an attack on Brother Benson, but he was aware of the fact that in politics a lot of things are done that are somewhat shady. He said he was speaking of conditions that exist in the political world, and intended no reflection upon Brother Benson.

President Smith said he had communicated with Brother Benson, and Brother Benson had with him, and that he had written him telling them that he and Brother Benson are on the best of terms and fellowship with each other, and that he would not do anything in the world to hurt him, but he did say he hoped Brother Benson would keep himself out of politics.

President Smith said he wished that he had not written this private letter to Congressman Harding,[9] that it was never intended to be
circulated, and he was sorry he said [it] the way he did because it was
misunderstood, that he had no intention whatsoever to cast any reflection on Brother Benson's character, and he had done the best he could to
straighten out the matter.

I told the Brethren that I have spoken to my son, Robert, and that he
had said that he had no intention whatever of bringing me into it.

President Smith said that he had written to Brother Benson and told
him that as far as he was concerned they were in full fellowship with each
other, and that he had never intended to say a thing against his character.
I asked President Smith if Brother Benson had accepted his statement.
President Smith said yes, that he had heard from him.

I then said that Elder Benson had permission from the President of
the Church to give the lecture that he gave in the auditorium in Hollywood.[10] I mentioned that some people had said that that was one activity
wherein Brother Benson went contrary to the counsel of the Presidency
and General Authorities. I said that Elder Benson had full permission to
give that lecture and he gave a good talk, but that young Benson has associated the remarks I have made against the Communists in his talking
about the John Birch society. I said that the stand of the Church regarding Communism has nothing whatever to do with the Birch Society,
which is a private organization, and the Church in no way sustains it.

I further said that Brother Benson had said publicly that he was in
favor of the John Birch Society, and that I had told Elder Benson that he
could not, as one of the Twelve, join that society. This was before Brother
Benson was called to be President of the European Mission, and his call
as President of that mission had nothing whatever to do with the John
Birch Society. I said that I had told him back in November last that he
could not join the Society as one the Twelve.

I further said that some people have written in saying that a person

---

9. For reactions, see Quinn, *Extensions*, 79–80, 449.

10. The event was held in December 1961 at the Shrine Auditorium, an events
center built in 1926 by a Masonic auxiliary, the Shriners, with a seating capacity of
nearly 7,000. It had been an early venue for the Academy Awards, popular-music concerts, and basketball games for the University of Southern California. The university
bordered the building on two sides.

cannot be a member of the Church and join the John Birch Society. That, I commented, is the wrong interpretation. Two things I said we should know: First, that a person's standing in the Church is not affected by membership in that or any other private organization. People are free to join what they wish. Second, that Brother Benson's call to preside over the European Mission had no relationship whatever to his desire to join that Society.

I stated that so far as this Council is concerned, we have no connection whatever with the John Birch Society, no matter how good it may be and how noble its purposes; that Brother Benson received his call to go to Europe without any thought of associating his call to the European Mission Presidency with his views regarding the John Birch Society, and that so far as we are concerned this morning as the Council of the First Presidency and the Twelve, we have nothing whatever to do with it, and Brother Benson's call over there had nothing to do with it.

I then said: "We shall partake of the sacrament this morning in the spirit of the opening prayer; that we be one in all things pertaining to this Church."

March 13, 1964. The Presiding Bishopric submitted tithing reports for the year 1963, and report for the months 1964 through February. The first showed an increase of 11.5 percent; the second an increase of 9.6 percent.

March 19, 1964, meeting of First Presidency and Twelve. The question was again raised as to the action that should be taken regarding missionaries who have transgressed in the mission field, whether or not those guilty of committing fornication or adultery should be excommunicated, or if where there are extenuating circumstances they might be merely disfellowshipped.

I stated that the rule heretofore followed should be maintained, that those guilty of committing transgressions of this kind while serving as missionaries should be excommunicated.

The question was then considered as to what should be done with missionaries who have been guilty of moral transgressions while in the mission field, but have not confessed their transgressions and have received an honorable release, and after they have been home for sometime they have confessed their sins to the bishop or others. Mention was made of cases where young men had been home for months and sometimes years before they have made such confessions.

I said that such cases should be handled by the Presidents of Stakes where they reside, and that there is no justification for young missionaries set apart to serve in the missionary cause to succumb to temptations of this kind. Referring to missionaries who confess after returning home, I said that disfellowshipment was the least penalty that should be given in such cases.

March 20, 1964, 3:00–5:30 p.m. Dr. Jack Trunnell[11] called at the apartment and gave me a thorough physical examination. Said that I had been having muscle spasms in my legs; that I need a high protein diet. Dr. Parley Madsen,[12] a specialist in rehabilitation, also called at this time, and recommended that I have some special massages on my arms and legs. Said that the cane I am using is giving me no support whatsoever. Later, he sent to me a much stronger cane. There was also sent to me an "Exercycle," which I can use to strengthen the muscles in my legs.

March 26, 1964, meeting of First Presidency and Twelve. I spoke briefly to the Brethren assembled in meeting, and then told them that I should like them to give me a blessing for my health. The brethren then surrounded me and placed their hands upon my head, and President Hugh B. Brown was voice in giving me a blessing as follows:

"Our Father who art in heaven, in the name of Thy Son, Jesus Christ, and in the authority of the Holy Priesthood that we bear, we humbly place our hands upon the head of our Prophet, our President, even David O. McKay, to give him a blessing; and we pray Thee, Heavenly Father, that Thy Spirit may inspire what is said, that what we may say may be

---

11. The director of BYU's Student Health Center, Jack Byron Trunnell (1918–85), had previously been a professor of medicine and director of the Anderson Hospital and Tumor Institute at the University of Texas. From 1958 to 1962 he was dean of the BYU College of Family Living.

12. Affiliated with Weber Memorial Hospital (now Heritage Park Healthcare and Rehabilitation) in Roy, Utah, in ten years Parley William Madsen Jr. (1918–93) would be the recipient of the California governor's Physician of the Year award for his work with veterans in the Bay Area. Before graduating from BYU and the University of Utah School of Medicine, he had been a pilot in World War II and for two years a prisoner of war in Germany.

Thy word and Thy will unto him, that we may be directed by the Holy Spirit to bring to him our love, our blessing, our desire to help; and grant, Heavenly Father, that Thy Spirit may rest mightily upon him.

"Now, President McKay, we, your brethren of the Twelve and of the Presidency, lay our hands upon your head, and by virtue of the Holy Priesthood that we bear, we give you a blessing for your health, for your restoration. We bless you that there may flow into your system through the power of the Holy Spirit strength, vitality and life to strengthen your leg, your arm, your voice, and inasmuch as you are approaching and we are approaching a great Conference, that the Spirit of the Lord may rest mightily upon you.

"We bless you, dear President, that you may feel the influence of the Holy Spirit and be inspired thereby in every decision you make, and we, your brethren, assure you of our united faith and of our confidence and of our desire to assist and to bless and to help. We bless you that you may, through the inspiration of the Holy Spirit, be made equal to every occasion that may arise in the coming weeks and in the coming months.

"We bless you that your life may be spared, according to the will of our Father in Heaven, so that you may continue the great leadership that you have provided for us these many years.

"Heavenly Father, again we appeal to Thee on behalf of President McKay, who, because of age and the vicissitudes of life, feels somewhat weaker than he was. O Lord, bless and strengthen him, we humbly pray, and grant that he may know of our love and our affection and our consideration and kindness, and may the Holy Spirit rest upon him and lift him up and bless him in his mind as well as his body, that he may have the spirit of gladness, of rejoicing, for we confess before Thee, Heavenly Father, that he has given to us a great leadership these many years; and we thank Thee for the great work he has done in the mission field, having traveled more perhaps than any other man in that great cause.

"We thank Thee for his life, for his service. We do not feel that it is drawing to an end. We pray that Thy Spirit may so integrate and revitalize him as to enable him to carry on effectively so long as it is in Thy wisdom the thing to do.

"Now, dear President, we leave this blessing upon you, and with the blessing we assure you of our love and our confidence, and humbly pray that God will bless you as we appeal to Him in your behalf, that His Holy Spirit may give you strength, and that we may each of us do that which you ask us to do, and be inspired in so doing.

"To this end now we bless you and seal these blessings upon you by virtue of the Holy Melchizedek Priesthood, and in the name of the Lord Jesus Christ, Amen."

After the blessing, I excused myself from the meeting, and returned to the apartment, where I tried to get a little rest.

March 31, 1964, First Presidency meeting. I asked President [N. Eldon] Tanner to review the meeting of the Finance Committee which he attended. President Tanner reported that the committee expressed satisfaction at the progress and improvement made in the financial report and records system and the accounting of the Church. President [Wilford G.] Edling,[13] who had been concerned a year ago, said that he was quite happy with the progress made and thinks the system now gives the First Presidency the information the brethren should have. He thinks everything is being done well now. Certain information needed from the wards and branches which will prevent to a great extent a likelihood of defalcation is now being provided. The kinds of reports now being required will minimize the possibility of making up a false report. ...

President Tanner reviewed the report made by the Presiding Bishopric that the ZCMI withholds tithing of employees and remits it to the Presiding Bishopric and that I had given direction that this practice be discontinued. President Tanner reported that when he mentioned this to Harold Bennett, Brother Bennett explained that this practice began in the time of Brigham Young and has been continued; that only about [a] sixth [of the] employees are involved and that they request that the tithing be taken out of their paychecks and remitted to the Presiding Bishop's office. The practice does not extend to all employees but only to those who have requested that it be done.

Since the practice is at the request of the individual, I said that is all

---

13. Wilford Gustaf Edling (1902–91) was chair of the Church Finance Committee. Going back to his mission to Sweden when McKay was president of the European Mission, he and McKay had been long acquainted. Edling became a CPA in Los Angeles and president of the Los Angeles Stake. When he retired, he and his wife moved to Huntsville.

right and asked President Tanner to inform the Presiding Bishopric and Brother Bennett that <u>since the withholding is with the consent and at the request of the individual this may be continued</u>.

April 4, 1964, 2:00 p.m. <u>For the first time since becoming President of the Church, I asked my counselors to assist me in conducting some of the sessions of Conference.</u> This afternoon I asked President Hugh B. Brown to conduct the session.

April 6, 1964, 8:00 a.m. ... Was pleased to welcome to my office in the apartment at the Hotel Brother Paul Harold Dunn[14] of the Downey Third Ward, Huntington Park Stake, Downey, California. Brother Dunn, in company with his wife, had driven all night in order to keep this appointment with me.

I asked brother Dunn to tell me something about himself. As I listened to him, I was impressed with his sincerity and faithfulness. I then told Brother Dunn that we should like him to fill the vacancy in the First Council of Seventy caused by the death of Elder Levi Edgar Young.[15]

Brother Dunn tearfully expressed his willingness to accept this position, and I told him that he would be presented at the Conference this morning.

April 8, 1964, First Presidency meeting. President [N. Eldon] Tanner presented to me a letter from President Miller F. Shurtleff of the Potomac [Maryland] Stake, together with maps and sketches, recommending the purchase by the Church of a piece of property consisting of 300 acres for use as a Temple site and for Church schools. The site to which President Shurtleff referred is on the Potomac River. It was mentioned that

14. Paul Harold Dunn (1924–98) was thirty-nine and would serve with the seventies for the next twenty-five years, three years as president of the New England States Mission. He had degrees from Chapman College and the University of Southern California. A popular teacher in the Church Education System, he acknowledged in 1991 exaggerating his past when an investigative reporter found inconsistencies in his accounts. Lynn K. Packer, "Field of Dreams," *Sunstone*, Sept. 1991, 33–39.

15. Levi Edgar Young (1874–1963) was a son of the seventy Seymour B. Young (1837–1924). He was called into the seventies in 1909, serving fifty-five years, alongside his father in the same quorum for eleven years. He attended the University of Utah, Harvard, and Columbia University, and had a master's degree in history from the latter.

property in that area would cost about $10,000 an acre and that property values are increasing.

President Shurtleff says that membership in that area and faithfulness of the people justifies our giving consideration to the erection of a Temple there.

I said that the first step would be for President Shurtleff to discuss this matter with President Milan D. Smith [of the Washington D.C. Stake], and that then one of the Brethren of the First Presidency would have to go back and look at the property later; that we could not make a purchase of that kind near Washington [DC] without very careful thought and prayer.[16]

April 9, 1964, 9:15 a.m. ... Met with the members of the First Council of Seventy in their room in the Salt Lake Temple. A meeting was held, and then I gave the charge to Brother Paul Harold Dunn. After his acceptance, I set him apart as a member of the First Council of Seventy, and conferred upon him every authority, power, privilege, and gift pertaining to this high and holy calling. I also ordained him an High Priest.

April 23, 1964, 9:00 a.m. Called Clare [Middlemiss] and told her that I am leaving for Huntsville this morning; that Llewelyn [McKay] is driving Sister [Emma Ray] McKay and me up there.

I told her that I did not feel very well, and that I hope getting away from everything will give me renewed strength.

Note by C[lare] M[iddlemiss:] Later, the secretary learned that Dr. L[ouis] E. Viko had become quite alarmed over the rise in President McKay's blood pressure and had ordered him away from the city; he said no one should be allowed to bring any problems to him.

Ever since his illness, President McKay has been beset with problems[17] and worries associated with the general matters of the Church. Hardly a day has gone by without some urgent matter being presented to him, even when he was in the hospital. He, therefore, has been unable to completely relax and give his nerves and body time to heal.

---

16. The Washington, DC, temple would be announced in November 1968, with groundbreaking and site dedication by Hugh B. Brown in December and the dedication by Spencer W. Kimball on November 19–22, 1974.

17. The diary has "beseeched with problems."

April 27, 1964. I am feeling much better today. This Huntsville atmosphere is like a tonic. Went out alone for a walk this morning, however, I had the aid of an aluminum "walker" which Lawrence [McKay] secured for me. I was able to go one half a mile without any difficulty. It seemed good to be out in the fresh air and sunshine!

May 7, 1964, First Presidency meeting. Wendell B. Mendenhall's appeal by letter with reference to the payment of tithing upon allowances paid to building supervisors was considered, and we decided that Brother Mendenhall be authorized to handle the situation without the issuance of another letter by the First Presidency so as to avoid development of the difficulties with foreign governments and labor unions and with the United States Internal Revenue Service to which representations have been made that these supervisors serve as <u>volunteer builders</u> and not as salaried employees receiving taxable or tithable income; also that they are not subject to laws relating to minimum wages. <u>The payment of tithing upon our income received by these volunteers and upon allowances paid to them is to be left as all tithing payments are to the individual who makes a voluntary contribution.</u> ...

President [Hugh B.] Brown presented a letter which had been prepared by Elder Spencer W. Kimball and addressed to stake and mission presidents for the signature of the First Presidency relating to emigration to America of members living in foreign countries. The letter restated the policy of the Church to encourage members of the Church to remain in their native lands, but asked cooperation of stake and mission presidents in facilitating the fellowshipping of members when they arrive in the United States. It explained the setting up and the existence of foreign language groups which assist them to worship in the language of the countries from which they come until they become established in wards and stakes of the Church in the United States. Mission and other presidents in foreign lands are asked to inform American stake officers of the names and addresses of members emigrating to this country. The stake officers of the United States stakes are asked to make contact with the emigrant families and to help them feel at home and to invite them to the meetings of the wards and stakes; to accept them; to help them to get oriented in the new land and to protect them from becoming affiliated with subversive groups which may try to lead them astray.

President [N. Eldon] Tanner suggested that the opening statement of the letter be made to read that emigration from native lands is discouraged, rather than simply to say that it is not encouraged. President Brown explained that he and President Tanner deferred signing the letter until I approved.

I commented that the letter can be misapplied and may be understood to be encouragement to emigrate. I concurred in President Tanner's suggestion that the statement be that the policy of the Church is to discourage emigration. I commented that "There are thousands now where there used to be hundreds; among these thousands are those who will take encouragement from this letter."[18]

May 19, 1964, 8:00 a.m. ... Brother George L. Nelson of the Deseret News [board] called by appointment at his request and discussed matters relative to the proposal of the Deseret News Board of Directors for the retainer and retirement of O. Preston Robinson, recently released as General Manager.[19]

I told Brother Nelson that the compensation recommended by the Board for Brother Robinson is far too generous, and that they should reconsider the matter and modify it substantially and resubmit their recommendations.

May 21, 1964, meeting of First Presidency and Twelve. Followed my usual [custom of giving a] report [on my health] to the Brethren. I told them, referring to the slight stroke which I suffered last November, that I still have a defiant leg and a partially defiant right arm, just enough to make me angry, but that I am getting along pretty well with the help of a cane and an aluminum "walker" which I use at home. I said that I am better than I

---

18. The concept of a gathering had been an integral part of the church since its founding. Some 150,000 converts immigrated to America prior to the reinterpretation of the doctrine, after which it was understood that people were gathered when they were brought into the church, rather than that they needed to be assembled at a specific geographic location. Ronald D. Dennis, "Gathering," in Ludlow, *Encyclopedia of Mormonism*, 2:536–37.

19. Ernest Wilkinson was among the board members who pushed as early as January to remove Robinson as general manager. McKay decided to call him on a mission. See Wilkinson diary, Jan. 10, 16, 1964.

was one week ago when I had to leave before the meeting was out. I said that I am very happy to be able to meet with the Brethren this morning.

May 22, 1964, First Presidency meeting. I then asked for information regarding the new Church Office Building to be erected on North Temple between State and Main [in Salt Lake City], and <u>asked how high the building would be. Architect [G. Cannon] Young[20] said that it has been reduced from thirty stories to twenty-five stories</u>. Brother Cannon Young's son, Richard, came into the room at this time and presented some pictures of the grounds as they will appear after the garage has been completed, the grounds landscaped, and the new building erected.

I <u>expressed the feeling that it is not necessary to have such a large building</u>. Architect Cannon Young said that if it were considered advisable, it would not be necessary to complete the upper stories; in other words, the frame work would be completed, but the upper stories would not be finished for occupancy. He said they would run into serious problems if they endeavored now to reduce the number of floors, and the expense involved would be considerable. <u>He said that in planning the building the Temple has been the center of the entire concept and that a smaller building would not fit too well into the entire concept</u>. He thought it would be much more economical to complete the shell of the building rather than to reduce the number of floors. Under such an arrangement the other floors could be finished later.

In connection with this matter, the Presiding Bishopric's staff is making a study of the offices we are now occupying, taking into consideration the anticipated growth, and they will be prepared to give us a report as to the outcome of their project in the near future. President Tanner mentioned that people are saying that if we go ahead with this building of the size indicated, and place our offices in it, there will be a lot of vacant space in other buildings. <u>Architect Cannon Young said that from an engineering standpoint, re-designing the building would cost</u>

---

20. George Cannon Young (1898–1981) was a son of one of the principal architects of the Salt Lake Temple, Joseph Don Carlos Young. The son attended LDS University (LDS Business College) and learned the trade mainly by working in his father's office. In 1936 he passed the State Architectural Examination. Among the prominent buildings he designed are the Primary Children's Medical Center and, on the same block as the Church Office Building, the stately Relief Society Building.

considerable, our footings are already in, and we cannot build higher than the twenty-five stories because the footings would not stand a higher rise.

June 3, 1964. Report was given to me that some young men, two non-members, and one inactive member had gained admission to the Salt Lake Temple on forged recommends; that word had been received by telephone at the Temple that an attempt would be made by certain individuals who were not entitled to go to the Temple to gain admission. Accordingly, the sisters at the recommend desk became suspicious of these young men. Two of them had already been sent to the washing room, and one was held for questioning. They were interviewed by [temple] President [Howard] McDonald,[21] their names and addresses obtained, and they were sent from the Temple.

Consideration was given to the advisability of bringing some legal action against these people for forgery, but it was thought that it would be inadvisable to do this.

June 4, 1964, meeting of First Presidency and Twelve. Following the administration of the Sacrament, administered by President Joseph Fielding Smith, President Hugh B. Brown made the following remarks:

"President McKay, I have asked the privilege of saying just a word this morning. I have felt deeply impressed by the prayers and what has taken place, and especially by Brother Lee's talk on covenants, commitments and witnesses, and I feel that I should like to say (and in saying it I believe I am speaking for everyone here) that you have our love, our confidence, our blessing, and that we look upon you as the rightful holder of the office to which you have been ordained, and believe that no man who has held that office has been held in higher esteem by all of the people of the Church than you; and of course that means a great many more people than at any time before in the history of the Church. The Prophet Joseph Smith was almost worshipped by say twenty-thousand people. Brigham Young was thought a great deal of by a larger number, but now

---

21. Howard S. McDonald (1894–1986) had just been appointed president of the Salt Lake Temple. He was Wilkinson's predecessor at BYU (1945–49) and had been president of Los Angeles City College (1949–58). His EdD was from the University of California–Berkeley. As a young man, he had served a mission to the eastern states.

two million people every day and many times a day mention your name in prayer, in gratitude, in petition for your restoration, and we, your Brethren of the Twelve and the Presidency, want you to know how we feel.

"We ask God to bless you and to buoy you up. We know of your struggle. We know something of the difficulties with which you are struggling. We admire your courage, your stamina, and your faith, and I thought it would be fitting this morning, inasmuch as you expressed your love for us, that we express to you our love for you. Our prayers are for you always. We stand ready to go wherever you want us to go, to do anything you want us to do, and we want to sustain and support you in every way. We humbly pray that God will bless you and your companion. We need you. We feel lost when you are not here. Your wise counsel and advice are of inestimable value to us, and sometimes when it has been necessary, some of us have been present, when it has been necessary for you to rebuke, chastize, correct, but you have always shown afterwards an increase of love, as the Lord commended.

"As so this morning, President McKay, with one voice we say, God bless you. We love you, and we want you to stay with us as long as the Lord can permit it. I wanted to say this word of commendation and appreciation, and humbly say it in the name of Jesus Christ, Amen."

I responded by saying: "I had in mind expressing my love for you this morning before this sacred ceremony. My heart was too full to express myself adequately. Thank you, and God bless you."

June 9, 1964, First Presidency meeting. Brother [Leland] Flint [of Kennecott Copper and Zions Bank] then reviewed the work of carrying out the plan for financing the Medical Center at the University of Utah, involving the State appropriation of $4,000,000, and contributions from Corporations and individuals in the State, including the United States Steel Company, Kennecott Copper Company, the Church, Mrs. James L. White, a widow, Mrs. J[ohn] L[eonard] Firmage,[22] [manufacturer] Joseph Rosenblatt, [and] [mining heir] Clarence Bamberger. He said the

---

22. After her husband, John Leonard ("Jack") Firmage (1884–1956), died, Edna Alice Chipman Firmage (1887–1987) managed her husband's fortune while living, like the McKays, in the Hotel Utah. She inherited the Nehi soft-drink bottling plant in Salt Lake City, among other responsibilities.

project is approximately $400,000 short of completion, and explained that he had asked the major contributors to continue for one year the contribution each has given. Brother Flint said that others want to know what the Church will do, and he, therefore, asks the Church to agree to give this much more.

I asked Presidents [Hugh B.] Brown and [N. Eldon] Tanner, "What do you think we ought to do?" President Brown said, "I think we ought to do that." President Tanner said, "I think in order to get the others, we have to do it." I then said, "All right".

June 11, 1964, 9:55 a.m. Left with Presidents [Hugh B.] Brown and [N. Eldon] Tanner for the Salt Lake Temple. However, as we proceeded by car in the direction of the Temple, I felt so unwell and tired that I told the Brethren that I thought it would be better for me not to go to the meeting. I feel as though I have a cold coming on.

June 30, 1964. A [man] ... came into the office and wanted to see President McKay about genealogical records of seventy or more people who, he claims, are descendants of Elijah Able, Negro upon whom, he says, the Prophet Joseph Smith conferred the Priesthood.[23] [He] claims that Elijah Able's descendants have all had the Priesthood bestowed upon them, and he wants to know what they are to be told when they learn they have Negro blood in their veins, and should not have had the Priesthood bestowed upon them.

He said the Reorganized Church [Community of Christ] is right when they bestow the Priesthood upon negroes. I [Clare Middlemiss] answered, "Then why don't they have Temples and follow the revelations on ordinations in the House of the Lord. We actually offer the negro as much if not more than any other Church."

[He] said he did not believe that, and that he is going to publish a book upon this entire matter. He wants a statement from the Church on its stand regarding the Priesthood and the Negro.

I told him that President McKay is ill and that he would not be

---

23. Joseph Smith authorized the ordination of Elijah Abel (1810–84) to the office of an elder on March 3, 1836. Nine months later, he was ordained to the office of seventy. See Bringhurst, "Elijah Abel," 22–36.

able to see him; that he should go to President [Hugh B.] Brown. He said, "No, I will not do that; I'll leave my address and he can get in touch [with] me if he wants to."

I told him to be careful what he does; that he should leave the matter alone as he might hurt a lot of individuals, but he said he will publish the book anyway no matter what anyone says; that he has his free agency so to do. He then left the hall and went out the front door.[24]

July 2, 1964, 4:00 p.m. My secretary, Clare [Middlemiss], at my request, brought over to the apartment a telegram just received from President Lyndon B. Johnson, inviting me to serve on the National Citizens Committee for Community Relations, having to do with the "Civil Rights Bill, and a voluntary effort to preserve order and achieve the goal of equal treatment and opportunity for all Americans."

After giving deep thought to this matter, I decided there is nothing else for me to do but to accept the President of the United States' invitation. The Civil Rights Bill is now passed and it is the law of the land. Some of it is wrong—the Negro will now have to prove himself.

I, therefore, sent a telegram to President Johnson accepting his invitation to serve on this national committee.[25]

July 8, 1964, First Presidency meeting. I discussed with the Brethren the advisability of conferring the sealing power upon the members of the First Council of Seventy. I asked Presidents Brown and Tanner if they could see any objection thereto, and they both expressed themselves as favoring this proposition. I mentioned that I had already given Elder Marion D. Hanks this authority, and that Elder Paul H. Dunn, also of the First Council of Seventy, has been asked by some of his friends to perform marriages for them in the Temple.

I said that I had prayed about this matter, and have thought seriously about it, and that I can see nothing wrong about it.

---

24. There is no evidence this person ever produced a book on the topic. Several black men were ordained during the early day of the church. Abel's son and grandson were both ordained (Reeve, *Religion of a Different Color*, 210).

25. The content of the telegram and other materials were included in the diary for this date, but are omitted here.

I then said that I would confer the sealing power upon Brother Dunn as soon as convenient.

July 29, 1964, 9:30–11:00 a.m. Conference with my secretary, Clare [Middlemiss], on the responsibility she is carrying, especially since my illness. I called in Brother Darcey U. Wright,[26] manager of the [Church Administration] Building, and told him that inasmuch as Clare is spending almost night and day on her work, he should see that she should get some help in clearing up the repair and cleaning out at her house; that it is entirely too much for her to bear, and that the work that has been going on for weeks and weeks now should be cleared up, and that the man who was found lying on the floor of her basement when he was supposed to be working (a Brother McLaughlin) should be dismissed if he does not change his attitude.

Just at that moment Elder Thorpe B. Isaacson came in, and I asked him to follow through with this matter, and to call in Brother Marble's men [grounds keepers] if necessary in order to get this work cleared up; that Clare is carrying a great responsibility and that she is willing to work all hours of the day and night in helping me, and that she should be given a hand in that work out at her house so that she can continue her work at the office.

August 6, 1964, 8:30 a.m. President [Hugh B.] Brown came in to ask if I [Clare Middlemiss] had heard from President McKay. I said that I had heard nothing this morning, but that last night had seen Dr. Edward R. McKay as I was driving out of the Hotel Utah garage, and that he had just succeeded in getting his father to go to bed, and that he seemed to be feeling better.

President Brown said, "If you hear anything this morning, let me know."

Later, he called and said that he had heard through the grapevine that President McKay was in the hospital. I said, "I'll call the home immediately and ask." This I did, and [daughter] Lou Jean answered. She said that

---

26. McKay became acquainted with Darcy Urial Wright (1904–94), superintendent of the Church Administration Building, when Wright served a mission to Sweden in the 1920s and McKay was president of the European Mission (*Millennial Star*, July 31, 1924). Wright sometimes filled in as McKay's driver.

her father had had a very poor night; that Dr. Viko had decided it would be better for President McKay to go to the hospital, and that therefore arrangements are being made for him to go. She said that Dr. Madison Thomas and Dr. Viko had not found anything like a blood clot, but that he has a slight temperature, and therefore they think they should take him to the hospital. Lou Jean said that President McKay is not getting any rest at home; that he insists upon getting out of bed and getting dressed, and that this morning [his son] Dr. Edward McKay had told him to stay in bed, and a little later he found Sister McKay helping him out of bed. …

1:00 p.m.—President McKay was taken by ambulance to the LDS Hospital to Room 703.

August 12, 1964, 10:00 a.m. [President McKay's son] Lawrence came in the office and reported that his father is coming home from the Hospital this afternoon. The doctors have given permission for this with the understanding that no one see him, not even his Counselors until Monday. Lawrence said further, "We nearly lost him; he had a temperature of 103 degrees when he went into the hospital; in fact he was delirious, and he had difficulty in walking. The doctors are certain now that he had been infected with a virus."

I [Clare Middlemiss] said that President McKay probably caught the virus from one of the employees who was in his office the day before he left for Oakland [California]. He [the church employee] had a bad cold, and had a coughing spell while he was in President McKay's office, and President McKay poured a glass of water for him. The next day President McKay was in Oakland and got chilled when they wheeled him in a wheelchair around the Temple in the night air, at which time he felt a cold coming on.

Lawrence said further that the only person President McKay can see is the First Lady, Mrs. Lyndon B. Johnson, who will be here next Saturday.[27]

I said that Milton Weilenmann of the Democratic Party had been in touch with me this morning about Mrs. Johnson's appointment, and said that Mrs. Johnson is still desirous of meeting President McKay for a few

---

27. Claudia Alta ("Lady Bird") Taylor Johnson (1912–2007) was in Utah for the opening of the Flaming Gorge Dam when she paid a visit to the McKays in their Hotel Utah suite (McKay diary, August 15, 1964). She also made stops in Colorado, Montana, Nevada, and South Dakota.

moments wherever he is—in the hospital or at his apartment, Saturday at 10:15 a.m.

Lawrence said "Only Mrs. Johnson and one other may come as father is not up to a crowd—photographers, reporters, etc."

August 18, 1964, 8:30–10:30 a.m. Although not feeling very well, I met with my counselors at the regular hour this morning. ...

I reported to the Brethren the visit to our apartment on Saturday morning (August 14) and mentioned the presentations made to me by Mrs. [Lyndon B.] Johnson. ...

President [Hugh B.] Brown said that he had visited President Johnson at The White House with the Tabernacle Choir; that, as a matter of fact, he called on President Johnson a short time in advance of the Choir's visit, and that President Johnson said to him, "<u>Take my love and blessing to President McKay. He is a great American and I love him</u>." ...

Historian's Office

President [N. Eldon] Tanner said that he had an idea regarding the Historian's Office that he thought would put it in A-One shape at very little cost. He said that if I so desired he would present his suggestions to me at a convenient time, however, that he feared that it might offend the feelings of certain individuals. I said that the good for the Church should be considered first even though feelings of individuals might be hurt.[28]

I reported that I went to the hospital in August in the interest, I thought, of one of our members, and when I got to the hospital the doctors reported that I had a temperature of 103 degrees, so I had to remain and they put me to bed. This was a surprise to me.

President Tanner mentioned that the doctors had asked the counselors not to bother me at all during the past week, and that is the reason I have not heard from them.

I commented to the Brethren that I am feeling better, but that I am weak. ...

---

28. Leonard Arrington credits Tanner with the founding of the church's History Division. After his call to the First Presidency, Tanner began immediately acquainting himself with the department. He was concerned about recent research and the status of the church's narratives and laid the foundation for hiring Arrington in 1972. Arrington, *Adventures of a Church Historian*, 75–91.

President Brown reported that President Mark E. Petersen of the West European Mission had submitted to him a memorandum stating that he wished there was some way to keep Brother Benson out of politics; that Europe hates [Barry] Goldwater, and Brother Benson recently gave an interview to the Danish newspapers, and his statement in one of these papers bears this headline: "Mormon Apostle said America needs Goldwater."

Brother Petersen said that this sort of publicity hurts us in Europe, and asks if there is any way to stop it.

I said that this ought not to be done, but asked that a communication be sent to Brother Benson calling attention to the report, and asking as to the accuracy of it. ...

President Brown suggested the giving of a word of caution to the Brethren of the General Authorities regarding keeping out of politics. He mentioned a letter that had come to him from a Dutch Saint which was signed by former presidents of the Netherlands Mission and by LeGrand Richards urging the [immigrant] Dutch Saints to vote for Goldwater. President Brown said he phoned Brother Richards about it, and that Brother Richards said, "Well, it is too late to do anything now. We have sent it out, and you know and I know that we ought to have Goldwater and we ought to get him in." I said that it is not right for the Brethren to become involved in politics, and that I would like to talk to Brother Richards about it. President Brown will hand the letter to me.

August 19, 1964, 4:45 p.m. The secretary, Clare Middlemiss, received a message from Lawrence McKay who telephoned from the LDS Hospital, saying that his father had asked him to let me know that he had been taken to the hospital [again]. Lawrence said that his father had suffered a small coronary thrombosis, and a mild temperature.

August 20, 1964, 5:30 p.m. Not having heard all day regarding President McKay's condition, I [Clare Middlemiss] called the McKay residence, and Lou Jean answered, saying, "I'll let Lawrence tell you all about it." Lawrence then said that the cardiogram which the doctors took definitely shows that President McKay has a coronary occlusion—it is small and is on the side of his heart which will not do too much damage. This means several days in the hospital and a long rest following. The doctors think if he will take a rest after he gets out of the hospital he could be much better than before.

I thanked Lawrence for this information and said that I am thankful it is not any worse than it is.

August 25, 1964, 7:30 a.m. The doctor reported that President McKay had had a "fairly good night's rest," and that although he had not taken tests this morning, "he feels that President McKay is improving each day."

The doctor further said that the oxygen tent has been necessary because President McKay would show signs of lack of oxygen when it was taken from him. Now he stays under the tent for an hour or two at a time, and then is allowed to be out of it.

August 29, 1964. ... President McKay said, "Now this is very important: I feel the need of the united prayers and faith of the Brethren. I should like to ask my counselors and the Twelve to have a special meeting next Monday morning. I was going to have this blessing following one of my sacred visits to the Holy of Holies[29] in the [Salt Lake] Temple, but I cannot leave this hospital room. It is going to be a problem to arrange this so that the greatest good can come out of the blessing. Personalities are involved here. I think I shall ask President [Hugh B.] Brown to represent the First Presidency in anointing me, and the have Brother Joseph Fielding Smith seal the anointing as President of the Council of the Twelve. Members of the First Presidency and Brother Joseph can come here to my room in the hospital and the Twelve, the Assistants to the Twelve, the Seventies, and the Presiding Bishopric can hold a special prayer meeting in the First Presidency's room at the same hour that the Presidency are giving the blessing. Brother Harold B. Lee will preside at that meeting—that will be Monday at 11:30 a.m." ...

President McKay seemed worried and very anxious about this matter, and he said, "Things are not just right."

August 31, 1964, 11:30 a.m. Presidents [Hugh B.] Brown and [N. Eldon] Tanner arrived. After a few words of greeting, according to arrangements

---

29. A description of the inner sanctum of the temple is found in Ludlow, *Encyclopedia of Mormonism*, 2:651.

that had been made for the special fast and prayer meeting of all the General Authorities, Presidents Brown, Tanner, and Joseph Fielding Smith gathered around my bedside,[30] and I asked President Tanner to anoint me, and President Smith to seal the anointing.

At this same hour, the Twelve, the Assistants to the Twelve, members of the First Council of Seventy, and the Presiding Bishopric met in the office of the First Presidency, all of whom, I learned later, had come fasting, and held a special prayer meeting. Elder Harold B. Lee was voice in representing the Brethren in offering a prayer in my behalf. It was a gathering of the choicest men on earth—all of them loyal, willing and devoted.

I was very grateful to know that my beloved wife and family were also fasting and praying for me at this same hour.

September 3, 1964, 9:00 a.m. Presidents [Hugh B.] Brown and [N. Eldon] Tanner called on me at the Hospital, Room 702. I asked them to take my love and greetings to the Brethren at their meeting in the Temple this morning. I said to express my deep gratitude for the special fast and prayer meeting they held Monday in my behalf when I was administered to and anointed in the Hospital. I said to tell them that I have never felt closer to the Lord than I did when President Joseph Fielding Smith gave me that inspirational blessing, after the anointing by President Tanner, and that I have felt better ever since then, and am still improving.

I also said that I think there has never been a time when there was greater harmony and love and lack of criticism among the Brethren than at this time.

September 8, 1964, 9:00 a.m. My counselors, Presidents [Hugh B.] Brown and [N. Eldon] Tanner, came over and congratulated me [on McKay's 91st birthday]. In answer to their inquiries regarding my health, I told them that I think the worst is over so far as my illness is concerned; that I am, of course, not so robust as I should like to be, but that I am feeling fine.

President Brown asked me if there is anything I should like the counselors to do, and I replied that the doctors met yesterday, and said that I could hold meetings with them for twenty minutes, but, I added,

---

30. Middlemiss is writing in McKay's voice.

<u>after the twenty minutes is over with, we can do as we please</u>! The counselors got a good laugh out of that, and I said to them "You go right along with the work, and I shall be with you pretty soon."

September 13, 1964, 11:00 a.m. Dr. L[ouis] E. Viko called me [Clare Middlemiss] at home. He said that he had had a conference with President McKay this morning; that President McKay had wanted to dismiss all the nurses, but had compromised and said he would keep the night nurse; that Gaby, the housekeeper, would stay probably to three or five o'clock in the afternoon.

Tuesday morning President McKay will start holding forty-five-minute conferences with his counselors. Then after an hour's rest, he may hold a meeting with me, his secretary.

September 15, 1964, First Presidency meeting. President [Hugh B.] Brown reported to me that he and Brother [N. Eldon] Tanner had asked Bishop [John H.] Vandenberg to submit their suggestions for participation by members of the Aaronic Priesthood for the General Priesthood Meeting Program. Bishop Vandenberg has submitted a proposed program suggesting that the invocation be offered by a Teacher. President Brown said that he had told the Bishop that he thought the Invocation should be offered by one holding the Melchizedek Priesthood, and I agreed with President Brown's sentiment. The Presiding Bishop further suggested a ten-minute address by a Deacon on the subject, "How I Honor My Priesthood Every Day of the Week," and that the same subject is suggested for an address by a Priest. Bishop Vandenberg had also suggested that we have an address by a member of a stake presidency who has come up through the Aaronic Priesthood adult program, and then a talk by a member of the Presiding Bishopric.

I did not like the subject suggested for addresses by members of the Aaronic Priesthood, and said I think we should give further consideration to the whole matter of the proposed program. The Brethren then mentioned that the correlation Committee, with Elder [Harold B.] Lee as chairman, had prepared an outline of the Priesthood Program for 1965, which described proposed steps to be taken in promoting the 1965 Priesthood instruction program which will have as its theme, "Teaching the gospel in the Home." It was explained that this program will emphasize helping parents to teach the gospel to their families, that the lessons used by the Priesthood Quorums, Relief society and home teachers would be geared to helping the parents achieve this objective.

President Tanner explained that the intention is that the Priesthood Quorums will teach this subject in the Sunday morning meetings, the Relief society will have a lesson on the same subject in the Relief society classes, and the Home Teachers would take into the home an outline and perhaps material on the subject which the parents could use in their home evening once a month. President Tanner said that originally the committee had suggested that these meetings in the home be held once a week, but they have now changed it to once a month, and if it should be found desirable to give more lessons for the home nights, this could be arranged later. He said that they propose to prepare a course of subject material which the parents could use in their home night to teach the children, and in the Priesthood Meetings this subject will be discussed so that the father will be prepared to take it into the home, and the Relief Society will deal with the subject in their classes so that the mothers will be prepared also. The Home Teacher would take supplemental information into the home.

I said that the faithful members of the Church, the Bishop and his counselors, the Ward Teachers, and the faithful women of the Church who are the busiest, will attempt to carry out the program; that, however, the ordinary man with his business connections and his Church assignments does not feel that he has time for such a program. I said we should not undertake something that we cannot make practical, and mentioned that we have a group of young men in the Church unoccupied and unassigned, and expressed the thought that it might be considered advisable to ask the Priests in the church to use this plan, assigning to them the duty of holding these meetings, the parents and the family to invite neighbors to come into the meeting where these young men would offer the prayers, do the singing, and do the speaking. The girls of corresponding ages would assist.

President Tanner said that if the Bishop would announce that there would be no Church meeting of any kind on the night when this home evening was scheduled, and tell the people that that night is intended strictly for home night, it would influence the families to hold their home night meeting and carry out the program suggested. President Tanner also mentioned that the committee has the program pretty well outlined for 1965 and if we say nothing about it at the General Priesthood Meeting, it would leave them to go ahead with their program as best they can in Stake Conferences, which would not work out very satisfactorily; otherwise it would be necessary to hold up the program for another six months. President Tanner expressed the feeling that the family Home Teaching Program has real merit; that if these proposed subjects are discussed in Relief Society the mothers will come home feeling that they have an assignment to teach the lesson in their home during the home evening once a month, and then too, if the Home Teachers see that each home gets a copy of the outline it would result in many more homes having the home evening, and a profitable one. President Tanner mentioned the success he had had in the Calgary Stake when he was President of that Stake in carrying out a home evening program. It was his opinion that if encouraged to do so, the people could find time to hold these home evening programs, and that parents should be teaching their families. He said what the committee is attempting to do is to give the parents something to teach.

President Brown commented that the important thing to be decided is whether this program is to be introduced at the General Priesthood Meeting and Brother Lee given authorization to present it to the people of the Church at that time.

I commented that for fifty years we have tried to get a home night, and that during that period only a small percentage of the families of the Church have held a home night.

I questioned whether we were prepared at this time to present the matter to the Church; however, I said I think that the very fact of placing an outline in the hands of the head of the household who may be a backslider would emphasize to him his responsibility, whether he throws it aside or not, and that this would justify our placing emphasis upon this subject during the Priesthood Meeting. It was thought that the remarks of those who participated in the Presiding Bishop's part of the program should also be brought up for further discussion by the First Presidency tomorrow morning.[31]

---

31. See Frank O. May Jr., "Correlation of the Church"; James P. and Terri Tanner Mitchell, "Family Home Evening," in Ludlow, *Encyclopedia of Mormonism*, 1:323-25,

September 16, 1964, First Presidency meeting. The Brethren gave further consideration to the matter of the proposed Home Evening Program where the gospel would be taught to members of the family in the home under the direction of the parents on the Fast evening Sunday. President [N. Eldon] Tanner said he told Elder [Harold B.] Lee that my feeling seemed to be that a good part of the time of the Priesthood Conference Meeting should be devoted to the Home Evening theme, Elder Lee to take about twenty minutes to introduce the program to the Church, and he was very happy about it. I said that the important question is how this is to be done. President Tanner stated that he thought the way to do it is to keep striving for it, that if we can only succeed in having a few thousand families in the Church follow the program it will be worth the effort, and he felt sure that many families who are not now having their home evening would fall into line.

I indicated my approval and said that we should emphasize the necessity of the father setting the example, and if he does not do so the responsibility will be on his head.

In answer to my inquiry as to what Elder Lee will give in his proposed remarks, President Tanner said that he will present the program for 1965, which is to encourage the parents to teach religion to the family in the home. In order to give the parents assistance in this project, outlines are being prepared of religious discussions that could be used each month in the home, that the Relief society course of study will provide for a lesson on the subject each month, and the brethren in the Priesthood Quorums will study that particular subject in their Priesthood classes so that the fathers who have been to Priesthood Meeting, and the women attending Relief society, will have some background on the subject when they hold the meeting in the home on Fast Day Evening, at which time there will be no ward meeting.[32] It was also the sentiment of the Brethren that in the General Priesthood meeting the Aaronic Priesthood boys

---

2:496–97. Two years previously Harold B. Lee adumbrated the basic elements of this program. See Harold B. Lee, "The Coordination Plan Explained," *Improvement Era*, January 1962.

32. Before the consolidated meeting schedule of 1980, ward members met every sabbath morning for Sunday school and in the afternoon for sacrament meeting, the exception being fast Sundays when the testimony meeting followed immediately after Sunday school and no other church service were held that day.

and the Presiding Bishopric should direct their remarks to the theme of teaching religion in the home.

September 17, 1964, 9:45 a.m. Received a telephone call from my secretary, Clare [Middlemiss], who said that she had received a telephone call from an Assistant to the President of the United States who was on board the presidential plane enroute for Sacramento, California. He said that President [Lyndon B.] Johnson would like to make an unscheduled stop at Salt Lake City and call on me if it would not be an inconvenience to me; that their plans as of the moment were to be in Salt Lake around 5:30 p.m. Clare said that she expected another call from the plane when they reach Sacramento. ...

6:30 to 6:50 p.m.—Sister [Emma Ray] McKay and I were honored with a visit of the President of the United States.[33]

September 19, 1964. President McKay called [by telephone] and said that he had decided that the subject of Home Teaching—Teaching the Gospel by the Father and the Mother in the Home—will be the theme of the General Priesthood Meeting of the October Conference; that Elder Harold B. Lee will give a talk on this theme, and that he would then like to have two young men give short talks on maintaining the moral standards of the Church.

He asked me [Clare Middlemiss] to include this information in the program for that evening's meeting.

September 30, 1964, First Presidency meeting. President [Hugh B.] Brown referred to the coming Conference proceedings, and said that sister Clare Middlemiss had told him she would give him the list of speakers to read tomorrow in the meeting of the General Authorities in the Temple. I indicated that I might attend the General Authorities meeting, but in the event I did so, I should do very little talking and getting up and down. Therefore, my counselors would have to carry the responsibility of the meeting. I further said that I should like to attend the General Conference, but that Dr. [Louis] Viko, who is usually quite lenient in such

---

33. Johnson left McKay with a bronze presidential token. The next year Johnson would defeat US Senator Barry Goldwater (R–Arizona) for the US presidency.

matters, was rather insistent that I not do so. I said that Dr. Viko had said that they [the doctors] had granted me too much leniency already when they allowed me to come home from the hospital sooner than they would ordinarily let anyone else to do so, and that I had taken some liberties since that time. I suggested that the counselors call at the apartment tomorrow morning at 8:30 before going to the meeting in the Temple. ...

President Brown said that politicians are asking whether the Church would be willing to make a statement this year to the effect that the Church is not in politics and that it takes no side with either party. The question was raised as to whether this might be mentioned in the Priesthood Meeting Saturday night. <u>I said that we must be very careful as to what we say in order not to intensify political feelings because this is going to be a heated campaign.</u>

October 13, 1964, First Presidency meeting. I referred to the report given by President Mark E. Petersen of the West European Mission regarding the expensive building program in Europe. President [N. Eldon] Tanner said he had see the report and there was one item that he wanted to explain to me; namely, that Brother Petersen's figures gave the wrong impression in that he reports that the buildings are costing $25 to $35 a square foot, whereas in this item he has included the cost of the land and the cost of the furnishings. He stated that the buildings are costing much more than they were estimated to cost, that in some cases the cost has amounted to as much as $125,000 more than the original estimate, but he wanted to clarify the item mentioned. President Tanner said he thought there are two things that are badly needed in the Building Committee. One is to improve and tighten up our accounting. He said he had instructed Brother George Jarvis about two months ago to check three or four of these areas and place them on the same basis as the missions so that we may have a check on them all the time.

He said the other matter is that we had approved two or three months ago the transferring of the administration of the Pacific Board of Education to the Church Board of Education at the first of the year. President Tanner reminded the President also that a letter had been written to the Church Board of Education asking that they make preparations to work with Brother Mendenhall and his board so that the schools in the Pacific can be taken over without friction or misunderstanding at the first of the year.

I mentioned that I have some concern as to how the school program in the pacific will function under the church Board of Education when building operations are in charge of the Building Committee. I said that it would be necessary to watch the situation carefully because there would be two departments operating in that area.

October 13, 1964. [Clare Middlemiss:] Although President McKay says he has no aches nor pains, he is still weak, and is unsteady when he stands. With the help of his "walker," he is able to get around fairly well. He expressed the desire two or three times this morning to get over to the office, and Sister [Emma Ray] McKay, thinking of the doctors' orders, insisted that he not try to go over, saying, "The Brethren can come over here—it is just a short distance from their offices."

It has been several weeks now since President McKay has been out in the sunshine and fresh air, and one could see that he is very nervous after having been confined to the apartment for so long.

October 21, 1964, First Presidency meeting. I read to President [N. Eldon] Tanner the letter that I had received from Louis W. Latimer, President of the San Jose [California] West Stake, reporting an unsatisfactory condition in the building operations in that area which are adversely affecting the stake and ward construction activity.[34]

I said that I had had an interview with Elder Thorpe B. Isaacson, who gave me a very clear and definite report of the unpleasant conditions pertaining to the project in San Jose, and had given Brother Isaacson the assignment to make a thorough investigation of the matter and then report to me.

President Tanner mentioned that Bishop Tiffany, who is involved in the situation, had been in touch with him two months ago and made a report of conditions in San Jose. President Tanner reported the matter to

---

34. This controversy in San Jose seemed to presage and precipitate the dismissal of Mendenhall (see the May 1965 diary entry) as director of the Church Building Department. The problem of Isaacson's unwelcome intervention set the stage for conflict between McKay and his counselors (see Jan. 5, 1965). Prince and Wright, *David O. McKay*, 216–18.

[Church Building Department director] Brother [Wendell B.] Mendenhall, and subsequently Brother Biesinger and Brother Bradley, representing Brother Mendenhall, went to San Jose and looked into the situation. A month or so later, Brother Tiffany called President Tanner again and said that conditions had not improved and that he would like to talk to President Tanner. Accordingly, President Tanner asked that he come to Salt Lake immediately so that he could ascertain the facts and see where the problem really lies. This appointment did not materialize, and President Tanner said that he had heard nothing further about the matter until last night when Brother Mendenhall came in to see him, and reported that he had been over to San Jose and met with the Stake President and Brother Tiffany and perhaps others, and had gone into this whole problem. Brother Mendenhall told Brother Tanner that there is a bad feeling there.

Brother Tanner then said that Brother Mendenhall said that Brother Isaacson had called him into his office the other day, and said that he had been asked to investigate the situation. Brother Tanner then reported that Brother Mendenhall had told him that he was in a state of mind that he felt that he could not carry on any longer; that there was so much criticism and fault-finding, and that he received no support from anybody, and that something had happened that had greatly disturbed him. President Tanner then told him to come over to his office and tell him his problem. Brother Mendenhall called on him yesterday at 3:30 p.m. and had given him the information indicated above. He said Brother Mendenhall had told him that he wanted a full investigation of the matter and did not want anything covered up. President Tanner further said that in talking with Brother Mendenhall he mentioned the fact that he did not have the support of the Brethren as he should have, and Brother Mendenhall had answered that he knew this to be the case, and he felt brokenhearted about it, but he said he had done what the President of the Church had asked him to do in every instance; that when the Twelve had advised that certain things be done, he had on occasion done otherwise because he had been told to do differently. (This being Brother Mendenhall's version.) Brother Mendenhall mentioned one or two things, one of them being the Pacific Board of Education, which he said had made him most unpopular. President Tanner further reported that about nine o'clock last night Brother Mendenhall called him, and said that he had just received a telephone call from Brother Isaacson in which Brother Isaacson had said, "So you went over and reported to Brother Tanner, did you?" and Brother Mendenhall said, yes, that he had considered this matter important enough that the First Presidency should know about it, and that he did not want to bother "President McKay with it." President Tanner said that he did not understand how Brother Isaacson got the information that Brother Mendenhall had called on him at his office and discussed this matter; that he certainly did not get it from him. Brother Mendenhall had also suggested that President Tanner call him and Brother Isaacson together today, as President Tanner suggested earlier, and get to the bottom of the entire matter. President Tanner said he did not know who had asked Brother Isaacson to look into the situation, whether it was one of the Twelve or whether I had done so. President Tanner said that he wanted me to know that he would never be in the position where he was taking sides with an individual, that the situation is all that he is interested in and it does not matter to him who is involved. The problem at hand, he said, is the thing that should be handled on a straight up and up basis. President Tanner said he did not know why those concerned in San Jose had taken the matter out of his hands; that he did feel, however, that a thorough investigation should be made. He did not know whether Brother Isaacson is the one to do it or not. He said that was entirely in my hands. President Tanner said that it would seem to him that Brother Mendenhall and Brother Isaacson should be asked to meet with the First Presidency together before anything is done by Brother Isaacson or anyone else in the matter of investigating the situation, so that the Presidency could hear both sides of the matter.

I stated that I had asked Brother Isaacson to go to San Jose and look into the situation and bring back his report, and I confirmed this request by telephone interview with Brother Isaacson during the meeting.[35]

October 26, 1964, First Presidency meeting. President [N. Eldon] Tanner presented a summary of a report by A. Hamer Reiser regarding the

---

35. Mendenhall suffered the loss of his chief ally when President Moyle died in September 1963. The criticisms were over Mendenhall's perceived extravagances in the design of chapels. Prince and Wright, *David O. McKay*, 214–26; diary entry for November 25, 1964, below.

Nauvoo Restoration, Incorporated. The trustees and officers of the corporation are Leroy Kimball, President and General Manager; Harold Fabian, Vice-President; A. Hamer Reiser, Secretary and Treasurer; David M. Kennedy and Willard Marriott trustees. Brother Thorpe B. Isaacson, at my request, will be added to the Board at the next meeting, November 7.

All the accounts of this Corporation are kept by the Church Central Accounting Department. The Budget Committee appropriated $375,000 for 1964, with which money they have been buying land and other things. The National Parks Service is cooperating with them to the extent that they appropriated $15,000 for historical research and dealing with the importance of the place; also that arrangements have been made for the Great River road to pass Nauvoo precisely where the Board of Trustees have asked it to be located; the officers of Colonial Williamsburg have given without charge the consulting services of their senior Vice-President, Mr. Edwin Kendrew, and the staff has been working during 1964 on plans for the authentic restoration of the homes approved by the trustees. There were 41,000 visitors to Nauvoo during the months of May, July, and August this year. It was reported that the Brigham Young University motion picture production department is at work on a dramatic thirty-minute motion picture story on the rise and fall of Nauvoo.

A more detailed report and recommendations for Nauvoo may be found in the minutes of the First Presidency of this day.

Referring to the meeting of the Board in Nauvoo, President Tanner said that Dr. Kimball and Brother Reiser have invited him to attend this board meeting in Nauvoo, which would necessitate his leaving here November 5.

I said that I could see no reason for President Tanner's attendance at this meeting. I also expressed the feeling that we must curtail the activities and expenditures of this organization. President Tanner raised the question as to whether we are prepared to spend around $300,000 a year on this project, and I said "No".

October 27, 1964, First Presidency meeting. President [N. Eldon] Tanner referred to a report made by him to the brethren upon his return from Europe when he was given the administration of the Genealogical Society at which time he found the library in very poor condition. He said that he asked Dr. Lyman Tyler[36] of the Brigham Young University, and Leslie Thompson, librarian for the University of Utah, to serve as an advisory committee in helping to set up the right kind of library. He said that Dr. Tyler took a great interest in this matter and as a result some very worthwhile changes have been made. Dr. Tyler is continuing to take an active part in serving as an advisor in this work. President Tanner said that he had learned that Dr. Tyler is anticipating taking a leave of absence from the BYU commencing September 1965 and he had asked him if he would be willing to assist us in overhauling our Historian's library, which he indicated he would be very pleased to do. President Tanner had discussed this matter with Brother Earl Olson, Church Historian's Office Librarian, who was delighted to have this help, and he and Dr. Tyler have met a number of times relative to this work. President Tanner had also talked to President Joseph Fielding Smith, Church Historian, about the matter, explaining to him the need for coordinating our libraries, namely, the Genealogical Society Library, the Church Historian's Office Library, and the Brigham Young University Library, looking forward to the time when the Church Historian's Office and the Genealogical Society will both occupy the new administration building to be erected. President Smith had said that they would welcome such help. President Tanner said he had also talked with Elders Richard L. Evans and Gordon B. Hinckley, who are in charge of communications, and they expressed their delight at such a program. President Tanner explained that it would be the intention to set up a committee consisting of Dr. Tyler; Dr. Roach, who is the librarian for the Genealogical Society; Earl Olson, who is the librarian for the Church Historian's Office Library; and perhaps others who would form a council, so that there could be made available in a very few minutes anything that was desired from any of these libraries. President Tanner asked if it would meet with my approval to ask Dr. Tyler if he would be willing to spend his full sabbatical year at half the salary he gets at the BYU working on this project, he to start actually as

---

36. Samuel Lyman Tyler (1920–98) had an impressive career as a librarian, historian of Native American culture, and US government consultant. He grew up in Arizona and Idaho (but was born in Arkansas), served a church mission to California, and was a navy radar operator during World War II. He had a PhD in history from the University of Utah; in 1971 he became director of that school's American West Center.

a consultant right away, and that when his sabbatical year commences he could devote his full time in an advisory capacity under our direction.

I indicated my approval of this plan.

October 29, 1964. Visit of President and Mrs. Lyndon B. Johnson to President McKay's Apartment[:]

As President and Mrs. Johnson entered the living room, President Johnson walked over to where I was sitting. As I started to rise, he said, "Don't get up, Mr. President."

After we had exchanged greetings with President and Mrs. Johnson, we immediately went into the dining room where breakfast was served to us. President Johnson sat on my right, and Mrs. Johnson on my left, and Sister [Emma Ray] McKay sat on Mrs. Johnson's left, and our daughter Emma Rae at the end of the table. (Emma Rae later reported that her father gave a most beautiful prayer and blessing on the food.)

A delicious breakfast of orange juice, sausages, ham, and scrambled eggs was served. President and Mrs. Johnson drank Sanka [caffeine-free] coffee, and Mrs. Johnson remarked that she was glad that President Johnson was eating so well, because he had not eaten very much for several days. President Johnson said that it was the best meal he had had in a long time.

Before we were seated at the table, President Johnson looked out on the mountains from the East window of the dining room, and commented upon the beautiful view. As we looked out on the rose-hued sky, I told him that the sky was all aglow this morning just for his coming.

During the course of conversation, Mrs. Johnson talked about what she had heard about the Mormons who had come to settle in Texas in the pioneer days—that they were fine, hard-working, industrious people.[37] I then told them a little about how they had left Missouri and settled in the far west, and were the first to settle and build the towns and cities in the surrounding states. I then mentioned Lady Bird's gift of the letter written by President Brigham Young to President James K.

37. The First Lady's reference was to the settlement led by apostle Lyman Wight in the Hill Country along the Pedernales River, ten miles west of Lyndon Johnson's birthplace. Wight was excommunicated in 1848, and most of his followers joined the Reorganized Church (Community of Christ). See Johnson, *Polygamy on the Pedernales.*

Polk at the time the Saints were being driven out. Mrs. Johnson said that they had looked carefully through their historical documents for something that would please us. Our daughter, Emma Rae, then talked about Lady Bird's visit in August, and of how they admired her standing in the rain to talk to the students. Mention was then made of their two daughters who have been campaigning for President Johnson, and President Johnson said, "Yes, our seventeen-year-old has a boy friend, and she said the other day, 'I haven't had a weekend off since May.'" Emma Rae then talked about her five children; that one son was now in the service, and the other on a [church] mission in Europe.[38] This brought the conversation into our missionary system, and President and Mrs. Johnson asked several questions regarding it.

President Johnson then talked about the wonders of the modern-day travel, of the cities he had visited on this last trip, of the crowds, and how his hand was sore from shaking hands.

At this point, President [Hugh B.] Brown and President [N. Eldon] Tanner, and Senator Frank E. Moss arrived at the apartment. So we gathered in the living room and visited for about ten minutes. Two photographers were permitted in the room—no reporters or political representatives were allowed in. My secretary, Clare [Middlemiss], was present, and took notes in the interview.[39]

October 30, 1964. In accordance with appointment previously made, Elder Vernon Snyder[40] met with the First Presidency, and was informed that the First Presidency had decided to reorganize the Legal Department, and to extend to Brother Snyder an honorable release to take effect at once, he to be given six months' salary, plus a retirement allowance.

---

38. The oldest son of Emma Rae and Conway Alan Ashton was Alan Conway Ashton, future co-founder of the WordPerfect Corporation. Alan was in the Utah Army National Guard at the time, perhaps at Fort Ord in California doing basic training. He would soon be on a mission in Germany. His younger brother, David McKay Ashton, was also of the right age to be serving a mission.

39. In addition to McKay's account, see Prince and Wright, *David O. McKay*, 354–55. Johnson had foregone a planned $500-a-plate breakfast with politicians to eat with the McKays.

40. At seventy-eight, Don Vernon Eugene Snyder (1886–1974) was beyond retirement age. Born in the nineteenth century in Park City, the draft found him a half century later practicing law out of the Judge Building in Salt Lake City ("Draft Registration Cards," ancestry.com). In the church's employ, he oversaw an office of five attorneys.

Brother Snyder said that he felt to take his release kindly if that is what we wish, and indicated that in his opinion it would be preferable to reorganize the department rather than handle the legal work in some other way. He said that he would be pleased to cooperate in any way that he could, and expressed appreciation for having had the ability to serve the Church. I expressed appreciation to him for what he has done.

After Brother Snyder's departure, Brother Wilford W. Kirton[41] met with us, he having previously been invited to do so, and I informed Brother Kirton that it had been decided to reorganize the Legal Department, and that accordingly Brother Vernon Snyder had been extended a release, and that the Presidency would like him, Brother Kirton, to succeed Brother Snyder.

Brother Kirton expressed his appreciation of the honor extended to him, and said that President [Hugh B.] Brown had heretofore talked with him about this possibility.

Then followed a long discussion regarding the conditions on which Brother Kirton would assume the responsibility of heading the Legal Department. Brother Kirton said that he had discussed this matter quite fully with President Brown, and that President Brown had indicated to him recently that after having considered the matter further, it was thought that perhaps the Church would be served better if he, Brother Kirton, maintained his own office and treated the Church as the principal client, and in this manner he could still do some private practice as well as serve the Church in that capacity.

After discussing salary and the help he would need, we authorized Brother Kirton to make an investigation of the work load, the additional staff that would be needed, etc., and to determine what the cost would be. Brother Kirton said that he would do this, and then come back and discuss it with the First Presidency. ...

---

41. Wilford Woodruff Kirton Jr. (1922–2000) flew thirty-one missions over Germany during World War II and received a Distinguished Flying Cross. When he obtained a law degree from the University of Utah in 1948, he went into practice by himself until 1964 when he and Oscar W. McConkie Jr. (brother of apostle Bruce R. McConkie) organized the Kirton & McConkie law firm. Kirton was also president of the University Stake in Salt Lake City at the time. The firm soon had over sixty lawyers, although they devoted only about a third of their time to church cases, according to McConkie's conversation with Harvard Heath, Jan. 29, 2008. See also "Obituary: Wilford W. Kirton, Jr.," *Deseret News,* July 23, 2000.

<u>6:30 p.m.</u>—Richard M. Nixon, former Vice-President of the United States, telephoned to me from the Salt Lake Airport. He said that he had stopped in Salt Lake just long enough to speak at a dinner for Republicans held in the Terrace Room, and that he is now on his way again; that he regretted that he did not have time to call on me personally.

He said he wanted to thank me for the courtesies extended to him when he was campaigning with President Eisenhower in previous years, and said, "I shall never forget how graciously, and courteously you treated me."

I told Mr. Nixon that it was indeed a pleasure to hear from him, and that I had enjoyed very much my visits with him. I wished him well and continued success.

November 3, 1964, First Presidency meeting. I told the brethren that I had talked with my doctor this morning, and that he had inquired about my proposed attendance at the dedication services [for the Oakland temple];[42] that in answer to his inquiry as to how long I shall need to talk at the service, I reported that perhaps the prayer would take 25 or 30 minutes, and that just prior to the prayer I should wish to talk about 15 or 20 minutes. The doctor indicated that that was a long time for me to stand on my feet, and suggested that I do not stand any longer than is absolutely necessary.

The Brethren agreed with the doctor, and urged that I follow his advice in this matter.

November 10, 1964, First Presidency meeting. The Brethren brought up the matter of whether or not Dr. Ernest L. Wilkinson should be invited to return to the Brigham Young University as President of that institution. I asked the counselors what they thought about permitting him to come back, and they were agreed that inasmuch as it had been promised that he could return to the Brigham Young University, we are obligated to grant him this privilege if he desired to do so. Presidents

---

42. The Oakland, California, temple is situated in the foothills overlooking the San Francisco Bay. McKay visited the site in 1942, a year before the property was purchased. It was not until fifteen years later that construction began on an adjacent building, the tri-stake center that was given a 1,700-seat auditorium and a gymnasium where the Golden State Warriors would practice. The groundbreaking for the temple, which McKay participated in, occurred in 1962. Cowan and Larson, *Oakland Temple*, 41–65; McKay diary, May 26, 1962.

[Hugh B.] Brown and [N. Eldon] Tanner both expressed the feeling that considering his own interest it would seem that he might not wish to go back to the Brigham Young University. The Brethren were unanimous in expressing their appreciation of the fine work that he had done at the University without compensation during the past thirteen years. It was also mentioned that many of the members of the Board feel that it would be better to have a change. It was agreed that I should offer the position to him and that he has the right of refusal.[43]

November 12, 1964.
DEDICATION OF THE OAKLAND TEMPLE

9:30 a.m.—The services commenced with a choir from several Stakes assigned to attend the first session singing: "The Morning Breaks, the Shadows Flee." Elder Eldred G. Smith, Patriarch to the Church, offered the opening prayer. The Choir then sang: "Oh, How Lovely Was the Morning." I then took my place at the pulpit, and gave the Opening Remarks, expressing sincere appreciation for the Temple and for those who have been instrumental in its erection. I then told of the prophecy by President Brigham Young and Willard Richards in a letter to the Saints in California who had just come around Cape Horn with Samuel Brannan, that "in the process of time, the shores of the Pacific may yet be overlooked from the Temple of the Lord" and the later inspiration of Elder George Albert Smith who in 1924 "envisioned a Temple would one day surmount the East Bay hills—one that would be visible as a beacon to ships as they entered the Golden Gate from the far-flung nations of the earth." I expressed appreciation for the committee of three men—Elder Eugene Hilton, Chairman, Elder Delbert F. Wright, and Elder A. B. Graham who were moved upon by the Spirit to select this very site where the Temple now stands.[44] I also told of my

43. Notice the subtle opposition that existed among some of the brethren. This was matched by the ambivalence of the faculty, many of whom had opposed his political candidacy and feared his displeasure.

44. Eugene Hilton (1889–1982) was the former superintendent of the Oakland School District and president of the Oakland Stake. He and two others formed a committee in 1934 to locate a temple site. Delbert Franklin Wright (1901–88) was a former executive with the Sperry Flour Company, first in Ogden and then in San Francisco, and vice president of General Mills in Minneapolis. He returned to Oakland in 1964 as the first temple president. Ambrose B. Graham (1886–1955) was a general contractor and real estate developer.

participation in recommending to President [Heber J.] Grant that the site be purchased in 1934. ...

Note by Clare Middlemiss, Secretary—A rich outpouring of the Spirit of the Lord was present on this occasion. There was hardly a dry eye in the whole congregation as President McKay stood at the pulpit. Some of us knew that it was a miracle that he was standing there, as he had been unable to stand alone like that since his stroke almost a year ago. In his opening remarks as he welcomed all present, and also an "unseen audience," naming all the former Presidents of the Church, an emotional thrill went through all present, and I am sure was felt even by the six thousand and more who were listening and watching by closed circuit wire in the Stake House. President McKay's voice was clear and distinct all through the hour or more that he gave his inspirational address and prayer.

At the conclusion of this session, [stake] president [O. Leslie] Stone asked that those present remain standing until President and Sister McKay and party had left the room as it was necessary to put President and Sister McKay in wheelchairs to travel down to the dining room on the lower floor.

November 25, 1964, First Presidency meeting. President [N. Eldon] Tanner said that yesterday in the Expenditures Committee and also in meeting with the Budget Committee, all had come to the conclusion that we are spending money for chapels, stake centers, etc. that we need not spend; in other words, that the standards are higher than they need to be and our income is not going to be such that we can carry on with that program and increase the number of buildings. He mentioned two things that we must do. One is that we should avoid using a lot of extravagant materials and services, and also that we must reduce the size of the buildings. He mentioned that the Building Committee has attempted to stay within the standards that have been set and that frequently the stake presidents and bishops have been critical of these standards and have come to the General Authorities endeavoring to obtain permission to have something different from the standards that have been decided upon. President Tanner said that at the Expenditures Committee yesterday, all agreed that it would be well to set up a committee of three consisting of Bishop [John H.] Vandenberg, some member of the Twelve, and a member of the

Building Committee, and have them make a study as to the needs, how much space required, how many classrooms needed, whether air conditioning was necessary in the particular area involved, etc., and bring back a report as to what would give the best service under the circumstances, thereby making it possible for us to serve more wards and more stakes with satisfactory service. He explained that under the present arrangement sometimes wards that are in better financial condition than others get permission to erect buildings and purchase furnishings of a rather extravagant nature and are in a position perhaps to pay their share of the cost; that however, the Church in matching the ward or stake's proportion is using tithing funds that have been paid by all the members of the Church and it is therefore not really fair to other wards who are unable to build in such proportions.

I gave my approval for the setting up of such a committee for the purpose indicated, and the First Presidency approved for membership on the committee Elder Marion G. Romney of the Twelve, Bishop [Robert L.] Simpson of the Presiding Bishopric, and Brother Holdaway of the Building Committee.

November 30, 1964, 8:00 a.m. By appointment at his request, met with Dr. Ernest L. Wilkinson. We had a long talk regarding the Brigham Young University, and the matter of his taking over the positions of Chancellor of the Unified Church School System and President of the Brigham Young University. I told him that I should like him to resume his work, and he said that he would be very happy to take up the reigns [reins] again.[45]

December 1, 1964, 7:30 a.m. ... For the first time since my heart attack on August 19, 1964, decided to go to the office for meetings. My son, Dr. Edward R. McKay, accompanied me. It was wonderful to enter into my own office again at the Church Administration Building. As my secretary did not expect me so early, she was not present, and my desk was swept clean of papers, letters, etc. It did not look natural. ...

Note by C[lare] M[iddlemiss]: After another half hour, President McKay put on his coat, hat, and rubbers and started to leave. As

---

45. Wilkinson's reaction was measured. He was aware of the discordant faculty members who were opposed to his return. See Wilkinson diary, Nov. 30, 1964.

he slowly walked across the room with his secretary on one side, and Brother Darcey Wright on the other, he stopped in the doorway and said:

"You know, I am still thinking about the dedicatory services of the Oakland Temple. Just before rising to the pulpit there in the Temple, I wondered if I would be able to go through with standing there for over an hour to give the address and prayer, and then there came to my soul the assurance that I could go through with it; I had no doubt, and I was able to give an address at each session and to read the dedicatory prayer so that everyone could hear them!" The President seemed lost to his surroundings as he talked of this event. It was a thrill to see and hear him!

He then proceeded on his way out the back door to get into his car. He stopped on the landing just before descending the stairway, and was very interested in looking at the great expansion of run-ways leading to the new mammoth underground garage which is nearing completion. It was raining steadily, but he stood there exclaiming at the work that had been done. As the President was walking on the slippery sidewalk to get to his car, he slipped and almost had a bad fall, but the men caught him just before he went all the way down. As he got up, he was smiling, and jokingly said, "That leg would not obey me, and that is what it gets!" Tears were in our eyes as we watched him and admired his determination, courage and cheerfulness. We never cease to wonder at him!

December 2, 1964. Announcement of Return of Dr. Ernest L. Wilkinson to his Former Educational Positions of the Church. Was engaged in Church Board of Education and BYU Board of Trustees.[46]

December 8, 1964, First Presidency meeting. Brother [E. Earl] Hawkes[47] suggested the use of the [Salt Lake] Temple Grounds in a manner to portray the significance of the Christmas season. He thought the grounds

---

46. Under this date is a copy of a letter sent by ten BYU professors recommending Wilkinson's return. In the afternoon McKay authorized a press release announcing the former school president's reinstatement.

47. Elden Earl Hawkes (1908–72) was publisher of the *Deseret News*. He had previously worked for the *Record American* newspaper in Boston, where he saw the Christmas decorations that so impressed him. He had also worked for other Hearst Corporation newspapers in Detroit, Manhattan, and Washington, DC. He was originally from Idaho and had graduated in accounting from Utah State Agricultural College.

could be made a fairyland which would be virtually the most beautiful spot in the entire State and community to which thousands of people would come if appropriate decorations and program were provided, which program would consist of talks with a religious significance and music by the Tabernacle Choir, high school choruses, etc. He referred to the arrangement that is presented on the Boston Commons at Christmas time, and showed pictures of various displays that are provided, and discussed the various features of their program. He suggested that if such a project were considered advisable it would be necessary to start planning right away for the 1965 Christmas holiday season. Brother Hawkes suggested that someone might wisely go to Boston, inasmuch as he felt they do one of the best if not the very best jobs along this line that are being done, and take pictures of their various displays to assist us in our development of such a project. It was explained that people who visit the Temple Grounds during such period would be required to obey regulations just as is the case during the summer months.

We listened with interest to this suggestion, but made no definite decision at this time. ...

President [N. Eldon] Tanner mentioned that Lawrence McKay had told him that Leo Ellsworth had conferred with me regarding the Florida and Georgia farms operations and is still unhappy about conditions there and feels that he should be given the full responsibility of the complete operation. President Tanner said that Lawrence had informed him, and he knew this to be true himself, that Leo will not take direction from the Board or anyone else, and that he will not talk with Van Moss who is in charge of the operation in Georgia. President Tanner said that he feels, and the Board agrees, that the feed lot in Georgia is in better shape than it has ever been, that Paul Warnick, the accountant, audits the books regularly and from appearances the operation will be in the black in the very near future. President Tanner further said that he had tried to get a report from Leo, but that he [Ellsworth] does not send him a letter, a report, or anything else. President Tanner had told Leo that if there was anything with which he was dissatisfied he should bring his problems to him, but he has failed to do this, and the only suggestion he has ever made is that he should operate both places. President Tanner said that Lawrence McKay, who has recently visited the farms, had said that there is no comparison between the way things are now being operated and former conditions. President Tanner thought it would be a serious mistake at this point to place Leo in charge, that Van Moss had taken a reduction of $5,000 in salary when the two men were brought together here and matters discussed, that they had shaken hands and said they would work together the best they could, and yet Leo will not answer the telephone when Moss calls him, and does not otherwise cooperate. President Tanner said that if Leo were given complete charge, Brother Moss would resign and the members of the board would ask to be released, thinking that there was no need of their remaining, inasmuch as Leo does not follow their direction.

President Tanner said he would say in Leo's behalf that he did not think anybody could have gone there and done better than Leo did with the Florida set up, but that that work is now done. President Tanner mentioned further that when he, Brother Ellsworth, and I met together about a year ago, he, Brother Tanner, had said it was understood that Leo would go there for two or three years and get the clearing done, get the thing into operation the way it should be, and that he understood that he would not want to remain longer than that; that, however, Leo has not been happy and is determined not to be happy. <u>President Tanner said he recommended strongly against his being given the administration. President Tanner further said that he could not understand why Leo had not come to him and told him he was not happy rather than going to me, inasmuch as he is president of the organization. President Tanner further explained that Moss does not decide what amount should be paid for the cattle.</u> That question is decided by the Board, although Moss does make his recommendations regarding the price to be paid, and other matters pertaining to the operation. President Tanner said that if I want his suggestion, it would be <u>that we release Leo and give him the finest letter I can write, because Leo has contributed more to this operation than any other man in the outfit.</u>

I said I think that all concerned, members of the Georgia and Florida boards, should get together with Leo next Monday and talk things out. President Tanner questioned the wisdom of bringing all the Board members together with Leo and Brother Moss, fearing that things would be said that would be of no value and possibly very harmful. I said that in the event Leo were let out, Brother Moss would have to take charge. President Tanner said he would not favor having Brother Moss take charge of the whole operation; he thought there were two ways that it could be done: Dave Hawkins could carry on the administration of Florida, or Bryce Stringham, who is in charge of the Canadian Ranches,[48] could be brought down to take charge of the Florida operation. He said that if Dave Hawkins were to take over the Florida Ranch, he would ask Marvin Meyers to work very closely with him. President Tanner said that Brother Meyers has told him two or three times that he has tried to get in touch with Leo, but that he will not answer his phone and that he had left requests for him to call, but he had failed to do so.

I decided that a meeting of everybody concerned would be held Monday, December 14, in the office of the First Presidency.

December 9, 1964, First Presidency meeting. The Presidency considered at some length the question as to what the attitude of the Church should be regarding continuation of the Nauvoo Restoration program. President [N. Eldon] Tanner said that when he met with the Nauvoo Restoration Board in Nauvoo recently, he suggested that a qualified architect in that field of operation, an archaeologist, and the historian who is working with them, should make a study of the whole question, determine what the outlay will be, when it will be, and what will be accomplished. Dr. [Leroy] Kimball and his associates said that if we would give them the money and the authorization to go ahead, they could get additional help for this project from the parks, the government, and various foundations, and thus the Church would not be required to put up all the money, and that when the project is finished it would carry itself without further cost. He reported that under authorization from the Presidency a lot of good land in Nauvoo has been purchased and put into proper condition; also a number of the old houses have been purchased. It was mentioned that the First Presidency had appropriated a considerable sum of money for the development of Nauvoo, some of which money has not been used as

48. The church owned the 88,000-acre Deseret Ranches of Alberta. It also owned (or would soon own) the 201,000-acre Eleven-Bar Ranch in Wyoming, the 120,000-acre Agri-Northwest ranch in Washington, a 70,000-acre Sooner Land and Livestock Company in Oklahoma, and livestock operations in Argentina and New Zealand. "LDS Church Real-Estate Holdings Include Farms, Ranches, Buildings," *Deseret News,* July 2, 1991.

of this date. It was made available to them only as from time to time they might require it. President Tanner suggested that another way in which the matter could be handled would be to turn the project over to the federal parks organization and let them make such reconstruction as they might desire to do, in which event we would lose control of the situation and would not be able to direct the story that is to be told there. It was mentioned that Dr. Kimball is asking for another three or four hundred thousand dollars for the 1965 budget.

I said that we are not prepared to give them the money they are requesting.

December 10, 1964, First Presidency meeting. President [N. Eldon] Tanner reported that the [finance] committee is working on the budget for 1965. He said that he had asked Brother George Jarvis to answer a number of questions regarding the Church's financial condition and that he would be prepared to bring the whole picture to the President within a few days with a recommendation as to how we can curtail our expenditures. He said that our income and reserves will not justify our continuing the program we have heretofore followed, that we must avoid dipping further into our reserves. He mentioned that a tentative date for meeting the committee on the disposition of tithes had been set for Friday, December 11, that he thought, however, we should wait until after the first of the year until we have the picture clearly in mind and know just where we are going and what we are going to do. He suggested that the committee on the disposition of tithes be given as clear a picture as possible without revealing to them any information that the President does not want them to have.

I said that in making out the budget we should limit the expenditures to the estimated income. President Tanner said that in order to do this it would mean cutting our building program in half. I answered if that is necessary, we shall cut it in half. President Tanner mentioned also the expenditures at the BYU for dormitories and other purposes, and said he thought we could curtail our activities along that line.[49]

49. While Tanner was so adeptly solving the building and expenditure problems, he was undermined, according to Prince and Wright, by a behind-closed-doors decision of which Brown and Tanner were unaware. Tanner had proposed keeping the existing building committee structure and working through the problems. But McKay, at the urging of Assistant to the Quorum Thorpe B. Isaacson and others, "appointed a

December 15, 1964, First Presidency meeting. President [Hugh B.] Brown called attention to an interview recently had by the First Presidency with George L. Nelson and E. Earl Hawkes of the Deseret News recommending that a committee be formed to make arrangements for appropriate decoration of Temple Square during the Christmas holidays of 1965. In such decorations, Brother Hawkes had suggested that we might wisely have a manger scene, portrayal of the Wise Men, probably pictures of camels, etc., also that appropriate music might be furnished for the occasion.

I agreed that we should adopt such a program, and suggested that arrangements be made as far as possible for appropriate decorations and music during this present season.[50]

December 16, 1964, 8:00 a.m. ... At this hour I met with my counselors, Elder Marion G. Romney of the Council of the Twelve, Wilford W. Kirton, and F. Burton Howard, Attorneys, and discussed with them legal matters in Mexico. Elder Romney mentioned that 6,325 people have been baptized in Mexico during the first ten months of this year, and that there are now between 35,000 and 40,000 members of the Church in Mexico. he said that the problem confronting us is what we should do about our Church properties; that we have two principal problems in Mexico—one is that the Church is prohibited from holding property, and the other is that under the constitution there, clergymen must be native born. He said that if we nationalize our properties we shall be free from the denunciation program which has given us considerable difficulty. He explained that the only problem if we do nationalize our Churches is the matter of getting our missionaries into Mexico; that the constitution says that all clergy men in Mexico must be native born citizens; that, however, we have been told by government officials (Mr. Palento) who is in charge

committee consisting of Isaacson and three Apostles to reorganize The Church Building Committee and 'curtail' the building program's expenses." Prince and Wright, *David O. McKay*, 216–17.

50. It was too late to do much in 1964, but the next year saw the beginning of the annual lighting of Temple Square with 40,000 Christmas lights the first year, along with a performance of the opera *Amahl and the Night Visitors* in the Tabernacle. By 1997 there were 800,000 small Christmas lights on the square. Sarah Petersen and Abby Stevens, "Christmas Lights on Temple Square," *Deseret News*, Dec. 5, 2013.

of nationalizing in Mexico City, that this change would not affect us any more than we are currently being affected.

Brother Romney further explained that our missions are operated as cultural societies which are known as corporations, and application is made to the federal government to bring the missionaries in to work for them to teach history, sports, mutual activities, etc. He said the government officials know they are missionaries, but have told us to do it this way. Brother Romney said that we would continue to operate our missions as "Sociedad[es] Civiles," and would continue to ask for passports as heretofore. He stated that if we nationalize and indicate on our buildings that we are The Church of Jesus Christ of Latter-day Saints, we shall be absolutely in the clear and that our people will be free.

Elder Romney presented the recommendation that we proceed to nationalize our churches in Mexico, to commence with two of our Churches in Northern Mexico, and then eventually nationalize all of our Churches. Brother Howard suggested that we would gain a great deal if we would go to the Mexican Government and say that we have a plan for nationalization and that we are doing this as fast as internally feasible for us to do so. he said he thought this would satisfy the situation even if it took some years to get it all done. He mentioned that Brother [Daniel P.] Taylor had made an effort to meet the President of Mexico and tell him about the Mormon Church in Mexico, and had arranged an interview which the President was not able to meet, although he did have a short audience with him, and the President told Brother Taylor he knew a great deal about the Mormons. Brother Howard said he learned when he was in Mexico a month ago that the President had personally sent men to investigate our schools, and the man who is in charge of nationalizing Mexican properties said the Mormons are the most law-abiding Church in Mexico; that we keep the spirit of the law though we do not keep the letter of it, and the Catholic Church does not do that. He said the Mormons have a very favorable reception by the Mexican Government.

After a lengthy discussion of these problems, I said there is nothing else for us to do but follow the suggestions made by these brethren, and that now is a good time for us to comply with the Mexican law as far as we can. A letter to this effect will be given to Elder Romney to fortify him in making his presentation to the Mexican Government.

At this point Elders Romney and Howard were excused from the meeting. ...

Brother Wilford W. Kirton, Church attorney, remained and talked with us in some detail about the new Legal Department set up for the Church, the rates to be charged, the address where the department will be housed, and the reports to be submitted. Brother Kirton said that he is certain that under the program they are using, the charge for their services would be within the range of the estimated $135,000 or the total budget for the Legal Department of the church for the year. He assured us that there would be no attempt to take advantage of the church in any way; that he realized if he were to do wrong financially in the matter of serving the Church he would have to account to the Lord for his actions.

I raised the question as to the address of the Church Legal Department; namely, 336 South Third East, Salt Lake City, and the explanation was made that the Church Legal department will be kept separate from Brother Kirton's own private law work, and that the difference so far as address is concerned will be the location; that it will still carry the name of the Legal Department of the church, but the address will be the address of the lawyers, and the lawyers who have previously worked in the Church Legal Department will be working essentially for that same department on an hourly basis. Brother Kirton said that he is sure that the Legal Department under the present set up would be able to do the Church a good job, and that if at any time the church wished to discontinue this policy, they should feel free to make a change. He said that he is enjoying the work very much.

Brother Kirton was then excused from the meeting, and President [N. Eldon] Tanner made the comment that Elder Howard W. Hunter, who was in his office shortly after this new set up was completed, when told what had happened said that we could not have a better arrangement, and he could not understand how we were able to establish such a satisfactory arrangement. He said that years ago his own firm would have charged more.

December 18, 1964, First Presidency meeting. I read a letter from Brother Leo Ellsworth which had been written following a meeting of the Georgia and Florida Boards [of the Deseret Ranches] on Monday. In his letter,

Brother Ellsworth stated that he is interested to ascertain what the decision is as to his future position pertaining to operations in Florida and Georgia. I said that I had told Brother Ellsworth to remain in his present position until such time as we may decide to reorganize. I asked President [Hugh B.] Brown what his feelings are in regard to Leo's services. President Brown answered that he was not too familiar with the project; that, however, he considered Leo one of the best men in the country to handle such projects, that he is the father of the Florida project and has done a wonderful work there; that, however, the cattle operation needs careful handling if we are to avoid losing a lot of money; that the Georgia operation of which Van Moss is in charge is now in the black, and if Leo were placed in charge of the entire operation, Brother Moss, whom we consider a valuable man, would have to go.

I said that I think we should recommend to the Board that we get out of the cattle business as soon as we can, except that we should take care of the cattle increase from our own cows that we should not, however buy cattle for sale. I said that I consider Van Moss as an able man, and that he should be continued in charge at Georgia as he is now, and that we would make no changes until the entire First Presidency could discuss it and come to a unity regarding it.

December 31, 1964, First Presidency meeting. We considered a question that had been raised by President Dallas A. Tueller of the Fresno Stake as to whether a Negro in good standing may be made Assistant Ward or Branch Clerk. It was our sentiments that we are opposed to using Negro brethren in such positions.

15   A Year of Reorganization and Reiteration, 1965

Gave dictation to my secretary, Clare [Middlemiss]. She reported that Elder Mark B. Garff, newly appointed Chairman of the Church Building Committee, had called and reported that he is working on the re-organization of the Committee. He said it will be necessary for him to have a clean slate, and that he has five men in mind whom he would like to suggest, and that he would report back to me as soon as he is ready. —June 1, 1965

January 5, 1965, First Presidency meeting. The counselors then discussed with me at some length administration problems which <u>they felt needed clarification</u>. At this time, President Nathan Eldon Tanner expressed himself <u>quite freely</u> about the administrative duties of the Church. Felt disturbed and greatly concerned after their departure.[1]

January 6, 1965. Following the departure of the Brethren, I met by appointment Elder Thorpe B. Isaacson. Among other matters, as a member of the Personnel Committee, he presented to me the proposal of the Presiding Bishopric, with the endorsement of "The First Presidency," for

---

1. This referred to McKay's unilateral decision to change the complexion of the Church Building Committee. Tanner had been out of town and unaware of what was occurring. According to Prince and Wright, "When Tanner returned, the memo [informing him of the changes] hit him like a thunderbolt." On New Year's Eve he would tell McKay he wanted to "sit down and talk with [him] alone about this matter before any action is taken" (*David O. McKay*, 218). Under this same diary entry for January 5, a nine-page transcription was included under the heading, "First Presidency Administrative Problems." For excerpts and context, see Bergera, "Tensions," 198–201.

large increases in the salary of men in the Presiding Bishopric and Purchasing Department. I told Elder Isaacson that this proposal had not been submitted to me, and that I had not approved of the increases. I instructed Elder Isaacson to go to my counselors and tell them that the Personnel Committee cannot go along with this proposal, and that furthermore any requests for increases in salary should be approved by me.

January 8, 1965. Had a long conference with Elder Delbert L. Stapley on Florida and Georgia Ranches. Brother Stapley advised very strongly that Leo Ellsworth be not released from the management of the Florida and Georgia ranches, and said that he feels that Leo is the only one who can save them for us.

January 11, 1965, First Presidency meeting. I told Presidents Brown and Tanner that we should commence disposing of our Florida and Georgia Ranch properties at once, and <u>ask Leo Ellsworth to take charge of this operation.</u> I suggested that we have a conference with Brother Ellsworth, who is in the city, and place this responsibility upon him—Brother [Graham H.] Doxey to work with Brother Ellsworth on this matter.

I asked President Tanner to tell the Board of Directors that up until the present time we have been engaged in developing the property, which has been better than we had anticipated from a Church standpoint, but now the price of land has gone up and we can dispose of it at a profit, and that <u>I think that we should commence at once to make disposition of it.</u> It was agreed that the organization should be continued as at present. It was also agreed that Brother Ellsworth can give as much responsibility to Dave Hawkins as he desires in regard to the cattle situation.

January 13, 1965, First Presidency meeting. President [N. Eldon] Tanner reported that at the meeting of the Board of the Brigham Young University and the Church Board of Education held a few days ago a recommendation was passed that President Ernest L. Wilkinson be made President of the Brigham Young University and that all the other schools be placed under the direction of Dr. Harvey L. Taylor, this action being taken subject to my approval.

President Tanner said that there were two points in regard to this matter which he thought should have consideration, one of which he discussed at the meeting mentioned. President Tanner said he expressed his feeling at the meeting that the higher education of the Church could well be placed under one administration and all the other departments under another, that there is very little relationship between Ricks College and the other schools that come under the unified School System.

The other question that he had in mind was the timing; that when I met recently with the Board, it was decided to make Dr. Ernest L. Wilkinson Chancellor of the whole system and also President of the Brigham Young University. President Tanner said that it would hardly be wise to make a division so shortly after the decision to make Brother Wilkinson Chancellor, and that the division should be made with the BYU, Ricks College and the Church College of Hawaii in one division, and the Pacific schools and the institutes and seminaries and secondary education be in the other. The thought was expressed that in the event Ricks College is placed under Brother Wilkinson's supervision, it might be necessary to release the President of the School, President [John L.] Clarke.

President Tanner further mentioned that at the recent meeting of the Boards, Brother Wilkinson had said that he did not object to the proposed division, but he did think the Universities should be in one division, and the others come under another. President Tanner felt that if it were decided to make the division along these lines, this change could be made at any time.

I said that it would not do to make Brother Wilkinson President of the Brigham Young University and nothing else, and place Dr. Harvey Taylor in charge of the balance of the Church School System.[2]

January 15, 1965. I told Clare [Middlemiss] that there is no girl in the world who has rendered the service as a secretary that she has; that I respected her judgment. ... I said, "Although you may have a few enemies, because of jealousy of the position you hold, most people who count, and the Brethren of the General Authorities, hold you in high esteem." Clare expressed her appreciation, and said that she has no desire but to help ease my responsibilities and to do the best she can for the Brethren and the Church.

---

2. Wilkinson knew that some of the general authorities (primarily Lee) wanted to see his influence be lessened. See Wilkinson diary, Jan. 5, 1965.

February 10, 1965, First Presidency meeting. Reference was made to some difference of opinion between Elder Richard L. Evans and Richard P. Condie and Isaac M. Stewart with respect to the handling of the Choir, that one difficulty has to do with the kind of music that is sung by the Choir. Elder Evans would like to dominate the selection of the Choir numbers, whereas Conductor Condie and Organist [Alexander] Schreiner feel that the selection of the music should be left to them. It was the sentiment of the Brethren that Brother Condie and Brother Schreiner should select the music and present it to Brother Evans in an effort to have his cooperation. President Brown will undertake to take care of this.[3]

It was mentioned that there is also the question of a new organist, that Brother Condie reports that Frank Asper can no longer give satisfactory service, that he makes many mistakes, and letters are received from musicians all over the country from time to time complaining. Brother Condie recommends that Brother Asper be released and that Robert Cundick be appointed one of the Tabernacle organists.[4] Brother Schreiner joins in recommending Brother Cundick as the most capable man available for this position. It was suggested that in releasing Brother Asper he be allowed to do organ work in other places where he will not be so prominent as he is on the Sunday morning broadcasts. So far as Brother Cundick is concerned, the suggestion is made that he be made the second organist and that Brother Roy M. Darley[5] be made one of the Tabernacle organists rather than an assistant, these changes to be made with the concurrence of Brother Schreiner.

---

3. With the choir's increased visibility and potential for positive public relations, it was felt by some (especially at the recently created Bonneville International Corporation) that the music should appeal to a wider audience. Condie favored this as well, but "when a Broadway show-tune album was contemplated, Joseph Fielding Smith tersely observed, 'I don't think the Tabernacle Choir belongs on Broadway.' Some choir members sided with Cornwall, signing petitions against Condie's approach. Perhaps more troublesome, Condie programmed a number of the 'modernistic' works shunned by Cornwall," according to Hicks, *Mormonism and Music*, 164–65.

4. Robert Milton Cundick (1926–2016) had recently returned from a church mission to England, where he had been the organist at the church's Hyde Park chapel. He was born in Salt Lake City, had a doctorate in music from the University of Utah, and was teaching at BYU. See the diary entry for Apr. 9, 1965.

5. Roy Maughan Darley (1918–2003) had studied at Utah State University, University of Utah, and the Royal College of Music in London. Like Cundick, he had been the organist at the Hyde Park chapel, as well as at the LDS chapel in Washington, DC. During World War II he had been an army chaplain in Borneo and the Philippines.

February 13, 1965. <u>Note by C[lare] M[iddlemiss]</u>—President McKay not well. ... the housekeeper, said that the only thing he would eat was a cheese sandwich; that he sat in his chair in the office or laid on the couch most of the day. Said his breathing seemed difficult, and his color was not good.

February 23, 1965. <u>Note by C[lare] M[iddlemiss]</u>—President McKay looked much better today—his voice was good and he was keen of mind, joking and using quotations to put over his point. He is still receiving oxygen through tubes in his nostrils, which annoys him very much, but he does not complain.

February 25, 1965. At 11:30 a.m. Lawrence McKay and Dr. Edward R. McKay came over to the office. After reporting that they had just brought their father home from the hospital, they said to me [Clare Middlemiss]: "Now father's condition is such that any matters brought up to him which will worry him will have an effect upon his heart, so please do not take up any matters that will cause him any concern." I answered that I should surely follow their wishes in this respect; that, in fact, I had tried for several months now not to bring anything to President McKay which would bother him. Lawrence said that I should take everything to President [N. Eldon] Tanner, and I answered that it has always been the practice to refer anything of an official nature to the First Presidency and that it was then taken to the First Presidency's meeting for attention. Other matters directly concerning President McKay or that needed his personal attention were held until convenient for the President to give his attention to them.

March 2, 1965, First Presidency meeting. President [Hugh B.] Brown reported that he had interviewed Robert Cundick and Roy Darley with respect to their new appointments as Tabernacle organists and that a letter of release had been written to Frank W. Asper. President Brown said that Brother Cundick is very well pleased and has expressed the feeling that he should give his entire time to this assignment, as does Brother Condie. The Brethren agreed with this arrangement. The suggestion was made, however, that if Brother Cundick wished to supplement his salary by doing some teaching or other work that would not interfere with his

Tabernacle Organ assignment, he might feel at liberty to do so with the understanding that the Tabernacle Organ assignment is his first responsibility and that he should be available whenever needed.

It was agreed by the Brethren that Brother Asper should be given an allowance of $600 per month and the title of Organist Emeritus.

March 4, 1965, First Presidency meeting. Some consideration was given to the matter of the advisability of holding a regular meeting for the Twelve and the Assistants to the Twelve. The Brethren had in mind that at present all the General Authorities with the exception of the First Presidency meet together each Wednesday in a brief meeting which is confined to reports of the Brethren regarding their activities of the past week. The thought was expressed that the Twelve and the Assistants should meet together as a united body and discuss the problems that have arisen so that the Assistants would feel that they are part of the picture. Under the present arrangement the Assistants to the Twelve are left more or less dangling, awaiting any assignments that might be given them.

I said that by all means they should be given more definite supervision and assignment; that I think, however, that the matter of attaching one of the Assistants to a member of the Twelve to help him in all his various assignments was something that should have very careful consideration. It was agreed that this matter should be taken up with the Twelve with the request that they bring a refined recommendation to the First Presidency. ...

10:30 to 11:30 a.m.—Called my secretary, Clare [Middlemiss], and asked her to come over. ...

Clare stated that she had hesitated bringing any matters to me as she had been told by members of the family to take up everything with President Tanner, even personal letters such as those coming from President [Lyndon B.] Johnson and others which are entirely personal. Clare said that President Tanner would only have to take them up with me as he would not know what to do.

I told Clare that it is her duty to bring ALL matters that come to my office to me for my attention as she has done heretofore. I said that I shall instruct her when I want matters referred to the counselors. Clare explained that she has always referred anything of an official nature or matters that would involve Church policy to the First Presidency to be taken up at their regular meetings; that the files are full of such referrals. I said, "Well, you keep on as you have been doing." I said that the counselors have brought over a good number of problems to me since my illness. Clare answered that she has tried to attend to all matters that would upset me, holding others that she could not handle until my health is better.

March 5, 1965. ... I had a confidential conference with President Joseph Fielding Smith concerning a request which President [Hugh B.] Brown had made of him that he take from his safe in the Historian's Office, and hand to President [N. Eldon] Tanner, the book containing the ceremonies for second sealings.[6] President Smith said that the original copy to this is in the [Salt Lake] Temple, which President Tanner could see in the Temple, but that the copy he (President Smith) has is a copy given to him years ago ... for safe keeping; that it is locked up in the safe in his office, and has never been taken out. ...

Clare later reported to me that President Smith had taken the book of second sealings out of the Temple and had locked it up in the safe in the Historian's Office with the other copy, and that there it would stay until President McKay called for it.

March 8, 1965, First Presidency meeting. President [N. Eldon] Tanner discussed with me the desire of the NAACP Leaders that the Church support them in civil rights legislation before the Utah State Legislature. Their representatives got in touch with President Tanner on Friday, at which time President Tanner told them that we had decided not to say anything in favor or against legislation, that we as a Church feel to keep out of the political field, that we do at times express ourselves on moral questions like the liquor bill, and that the Deseret News had written an article on that subject. President McKay agreed that this was the right attitude. Brother Tanner stated that last night Earl Hawkes, General Manager of the Deseret News, had called and reported that the Negroes are going to march every day this week unless something is said. He asked if we wanted him to try to relieve the pressure. President Tanner

---

6. In addition to being president of the Quorum of the Twelve, Smith had been Church Historian since 1921. He would continue as the historian to 1970.

asked me if I think that the Deseret News should prepare an editorial repeating the statement made by President [Hugh B.] Brown in a recent conference representing the view of the First Presidency on civil rights. Arch Madsen had called President Tanner this morning and asked if he thought KSL should say anything about the Negro demonstration other than as a news item.

I said that we have said all we are going to say and all that we should; that I do not favor our repeating what had previously been said on the subject.[7]

March 19, 1965, 8:30 a.m. President Joseph Fielding Smith came over to the apartment by appointment. He said that President [Hugh B.] Brown had asked him for the book containing "second blessings," and that he (President Smith) had told President Brown that the book is to be given only to the President of the Church who is the only one who has the right to give these blessings, and that they are given at his (the President's) invitation.

President Smith explained that he has a copy of the book in the safe in the Historian's Office, and the original is in the safe in the Salt Lake Temple President's office, sealed, and a note placed on the top: "To be given to the President of the Church only."

I told President Smith that he was right in what he had done, and then I turned to Sister [Jessie Evans] Smith who had accompanied President Smith, and said, "You are a witness to this."

Later that morning, President Brown called and said he would like me to call President Smith and ask him to give the book of the second blessings to him, and I told President Brown that I would call him back about this.

Thirty minutes later I called President Brown and told him that the book was locked up and that matters had been taken care of; that the book need not be taken out again, [former Salt Lake Temple] President ElRay L. Christiansen[8] having previously taken the book out of the Temple upon instructions of President Brown.

---

7. The Salt Lake chapter of the NAACP had the day before called for a protest of the church's position. "NAACP Calls March for LDS Appeal," *Salt Lake Tribune*, Mar. 7, 1965. Despite McKay's initial decision, a change of mind occurred and Brown's previous statement of 1963 was re-issued in the *Deseret News* on March 9, 1965.

8. Christiansen had been temple president up to 1961. In 1964 he was made coordinator of temples. He was also an Assistant to the Quorum of the Twelve.

March 23, 1965, First Presidency meeting. We gave consideration to the program for the first session of the April Conference which will convene Sunday morning at 8:00. The original draft of the program provided for four speakers and six musical presentations. It was our sentiment that the session should be limited to three speakers—the first two to occupy twenty minutes each, and the third to occupy seventeen minutes. Arrangements will be made to adjust the musical program to fit into this schedule.

I said that I would be the first speaker and that I intend to take twenty minutes. I said that I had not decided as to who the other speakers for this session would be. I said that I would give the matter consideration and meet with the counselors tomorrow morning and arrange to complete the broadcast program at that time.

While we were in our meeting, I called my secretary, Clare Middlemiss, and asked her to come right over with the program for the Broadcast Session Sunday morning. Within a few moments she came over and read to the Brethren the program as now prepared. Told her to schedule just three speakers instead of four as outlined by the KSL people arranging for the Broadcast.

After we were through with our meeting, I told my counselors this morning that if I am not going to get well, I wish the Lord would take me.

April 2, 1965, First Presidency meeting. I said that I am not gaining in strength as much as I had anticipated. I said that I want to take up with the Lord the matter of my responsibility at this Conference, and the question of the speakers and the order in which they are to speak. In regard to my own Conference message, I said that I had in mind the possible wisdom of preparing my talk and having it taped because of the weakness of my voice. The Brethren suggested that it could be recorded on tape and see how it sounds. I said I was not going to say much other than the message that I propose to give in the opening session but that I would have a message. I also suggested that the Counselors should take turns in conducting the meetings after the Sunday morning session, and that they should not deliver their addresses during the sessions that they conducted.

April 4, 1965. As I had hoped and prayed for days, I was well and strong enough to go to the Tabernacle to preside at this opening session. Sister

[Emma Ray] McKay, much to my satisfaction and pleasure, was also well enough to attend. We were accompanied by our daughter, Emma Rae, and sons, Lawrence, Edward, and Robert, who assisted us in getting from the Hotel to the Tabernacle. When we arrived at the General Authorities' entrance of the Tabernacle, ushers and others were on hand to carry Sister McKay and me up the steep stairs, and then from there we walked on through the hall into the Tabernacle proper. Sister McKay took her customary chair on the north of the pulpit, and Presidents Hugh B. Brown and Nathan Eldon Tanner walked with me up to the pulpit. The vast throng arose to their feet as we entered the room. The great love and respect shown by the members brought tears to my eyes. Before I took my seat, I acknowledged the presence of the members of the Tabernacle Choir who were seated and ready for the nation-wide broadcast.

I then asked President Brown to conduct the meeting. Following the singing by the Choir and the Opening Prayer, I asked my son, Robert R. McKay, to read the message that I had prepared on "Safeguards Against the Delinquency of Youth."

Robert's reading of the address was excellent—his voice was clear and distinct, and I was grateful that he did so well.

April 5, 1965, 9:55 a.m. Again I was made happy by the fact that I was able to go over to the tabernacle to attend the third session of the Annual Conference. ...

As I reached my chair, with the assistance of Presidents [Hugh B.] Brown and [N. Eldon] Tanner, I had a strong urge to say something to the audience. When President Brown saw me starting to rise, he got up and helped me over to the pulpit. As I stood there, I said to the members "I don't know what all the fuss is about." This brought quite a ripple of laughter from the audience. I then extended my greetings and appreciation to the members and compared this meeting with an old incident in Drumtochty, Scotland,[9] where a widow's son had died while away at school, and his funeral was being held. An old friend of the family, who

---

9. This is from Ian Maclaren's short story, "The Death of a Scholar," included in his 1894 collection, *Beside the Bonnie Brier Bush*: "This is no the day for mony words, but there's juist ae heart in Drumtochty, and it's sair." The village of Drumtochty was a fictionalized invention of Maclaren's, borrowed from the name of a Scottish castle.

spoke for the assembled congregation, said, "There is only ane [one] heart here today, and it is sair (sore)." "Well," I said, "there is only one heart among those in the Tabernacle and among those members listening in at this moment—and it is one of happiness and thankfulness." ...

6:50 p.m.—As I entered the Tabernacle proper, and was assisted to the rostrum, an audience of 12,000 men arose.[10] It was a thrilling sight! After the singing and prayer, and before turning the meeting over to President Brown to conduct, I stood at the pulpit for a few moments to greet the brethren of the Priesthood. I said, "Few, if any, of you can appreciate my feelings when I say, I am happy to meet you. I had a message in my heart and I put it on paper, anticipating this moment, but I have been advised that I had better conserve what little strength I have. I say to you, I am happy to be in your presence. I feel honored to work with my counselors, and the Twelve, and the other General Authorities. My heart is filled to overflowing in appreciation for your companionship and your prayers; for your ability and willingness to carry on the Priesthood of The Church of Jesus Christ of Latter-day Saints. I have asked my son, Edward, to read a paragraph or two that I have written, and if he will do that I shall just close with a prayer in my heart for God's blessings to be with you always, in the name of Jesus Christ, Amen."

Just then, as I returned to my seat, the great congregation of Priesthood, with Dr. Richard P. Condie conducting them, spontaneously arose and began singing the words of the hymn "We Thank Thee, O God, For A Prophet."

While their song filled the air, I nodded, waved, and smiled with tear-bedimmed eyes to let them know how moved I was by this overwhelming tribute from this great body of men and boys. My heart was full. Tears were flowing freely throughout the audience as they sang.

April 9, 1965. The First Presidency met in my apartment with Elders Richard P. Condie, Tabernacle Choir conductor, and Alexander Schreiner, Chief Tabernacle Organist, and discussed the organist situation, particularly the matter of the salaries to be paid. Elders Condie and Schreiner spoke in the highest terms of the ability of Robert Cundick, and

---

10. The tabernacle held a little over half that many, even counting the 360-voice choir, church leaders seated in front, ushers, reporters, and technicians.

recommended that he be asked to devote his entire energy to his work as Tabernacle organist. Referring to Roy Darley's work, Brother Schreiner stated that both Brother Cundick and Brother Darley had been students of his, that Brother Cundick is an abler organist and has more ability than Brother Darley; in fact, there is a vast difference in their ability. Brother Schreiner said that Brother Cundick is really outstanding and that he feels that he has the capacity to succeed him when the time comes for him to be retired, that Brother Cundick is also a composer of some considerable ability.

In regard to Brother Darley, both Brother Condie and Brother Schreiner felt that he should be permitted to supplement his salary by giving lessons or outside work. It was also explained that Brother Cundick is 38 years of age, has his Ph.D and has had for some years, whereas Brother Darley is 45 years old and is expecting to get his Masters Degree this year. Brother Schreiner thought Brother Darley was at his best now. Elder Condie, referring to Brother Darley, said that he has spent fifteen years as Tabernacle organist and is in a position where it seemed to him we have to be considerate of him and give him enough compensation to keep him happy, and that he should be introduced to work that would bring out his talents more. He said that he would use Brother Darley occasionally, say at least twice a year, and give him a broadcast, and in the event Brother Schreiner or Brother Cundick or both were ill, he could fill in.

After Elders Condie and Schreiner left the meeting, the Brethren discussed further the matter of compensation for the Choir leader and organists, and it was decided that Brother Condie and Brother Schreiner should be given a salary of $1,000 each per month, that Brother Cundick should be given $900, and Brother Darley $750. As heretofore agreed upon, Brother Frank W. Asper will be paid $600 per month as organist emeritus. Brother Condie commented that he loves Brother Schreiner as a man, and as an artist he is just heaven-sent.

I told Brother Schreiner that we have been proud of his record and proud of him.

April 15, 1965, meeting of First Presidency and Twelve. One item of importance which was discussed was the <u>release of Brother Wendell B. Mendenhall as Chairman of the Building Committee</u>. After a lengthy discussion, the Brethren unanimously voted that Brother Mendenhall should be released as of May 1, 1965.

April 16, 1965, 6:30–9:00 p.m. Brother Wendell B. Mendenhall arrived at the apartment. He had received this afternoon a letter of release as Chairman of the Building Committee[11] ... He was all broken up about it and cried and sobbed as he told what he had tried to do.

The decision to release Brother Mendenhall had been discussed and unanimously voted upon by the Brethren of the First Presidency and Council of the Twelve yesterday (Thursday, April 15, 1965) in the Salt Lake Temple.

As Brother Mendenhall so overpoweringly begged for an extension of time from the May 1, 1965 date set by the Brethren, I thought it would be all right to let him remain until March, 1966, as he requested that he would need this time to culminate his work.

(This, however, did not meet with the approval of the majority of the Brethren, who discussed the matter again in the Council Meeting, Thursday, April 22, 1965. See diary of that day.)

April 21, 1965. Had an appointment with my secretary, Clare [Middlemiss]. Went over letters and other office matters with her. Reported to her the discussions I have held with Wendell B. Mendenhall regarding his plea not to be released for at least another year. I told her that he had been in to see me three times since he got his letter of release on Friday, and is calling for another appointment for tomorrow morning. He is stressing the urgent need of his remaining until 1966 to finish projects now under his direction.

---

11. Mendenhall's fate had been decided some months earlier by a committee composed of apostles Howard W. Hunter, LeGrand Richards, and Delbert L. Stapley and Assistants to the Twelve Thorpe B. Isaacson and Franklin D. Richards. In their letter to McKay, they summarized the reasons for his dismissal: "There has been great concern all over the Church regarding the extravagance, waste, high salaries, maintenance, costs of supervisors, travel, hotel, telephone, excessive building costs and other expenses, also [his] domineering [presence], in connection with the Church Building Committee, until it has reached a point where many faithful members of the Church are deeply concerned, upset, and disillusioned; and ward, stake and mission leaders are questioning our laxity handling so serious a problem" (McKay diary, Jan. 21, 1965). At the end of March, the Mendenhall matter was still being discussed (McKay diary, Mar. 31, 1965).

April 22, 1965, First Presidency meeting. The Brethren discussed at some length the Negro question, LaMar Williams' assignment to Nigeria, and related items. President [N. Eldon] Tanner reminded us that three years ago it was decided to appoint LaMar Williams to visit Nigeria and take with him some missionaries for the purpose of baptizing worthy converted people who have asked for baptism, this work to be under the direction of the West European Mission. President Tanner explained that at that time at the First Presidency's request, he went to Nigeria at Christmas time and it was understood that arrangements were completed whereby Brother Williams and these missionaries could enter Nigeria within three weeks from the time when President Tanner was there. It so happened that adverse criticism and publicity was sent from California to Nigeria from Nigerian students who were attending school in California, which criticism appeared in the press, and the Nigerian Government decided against giving visas for our people to go there.

President Tanner further stated that at that time I had decided that we should not press the matter of a mission to Nigeria, that if the people there wanted us to come in they should arrange for the government to invite us to do so. In the meantime Brother Williams has been carrying on a correspondence with the people in Nigeria who wish to join the Church, as well as with government agencies, and he has now received the information that the people there were endeavoring to have him admitted, and in the correspondence it was indicated that they have no application from Brother Williams for a visa. They have sent forms for him to fill out answering certain questions in applying for visas for himself and family. President Tanner further stated that three or four Nigerian students have come to the BYU with the help of funds that Brother Williams has collected from various people, which funds are also intended to assist them in their maintenance while here obtaining their education. Two of these Nigerian students have now applied for baptism and the Bishop of the Ward where they live, and the Stake President, have approved them for baptism next Saturday and Brother Williams is to baptize one of them. President Tanner did not know who would officiate in baptizing the other. President Tanner also mentioned that a Negro couple, converts from Panama, were attending the Brigham Young University, and it is understood that these young people came to the BYU upon the encouragement of Brother Williams. In this case it seems that the funds to maintain them were not sufficient and now the wife has left her husband and the school and gone to Brooklyn. It seems that the question has been raised as to Brother Williams' activities among the Negroes, and the concern has been expressed that we are sitting on a powder keg, as it were if anything should go wrong. President Tanner said that President Brown and he were of the opinion that we could not interfere with the baptism of these two young Nigerian students, as to do so might cause serious disturbance. They raised the question as to whether or not there should be some supervision in the matter of bringing these students to the BYU without a definite arrangement as to their scholarship or support while they are here.

We were agreed that we should not encourage more Nigerians to come to the Brigham Young University, but in the case of those who are here we should continue to take care of them until they finish their education courses, and this assistance should be given through funds that Brother Williams has collected or may collect for that purpose.

The question was raised about Brother Williams' further activities in this Nigerian situation, and mention was made of the fact that Brother Williams refers to the blessing given him by me setting him apart to preside over this particular district, in which blessing he was told that there would be obstacles, but that he should carry on and not be discouraged. The thought was expressed that Brother Williams is a little over-enthusiastic about this matter, and that perhaps if and when he goes to Nigeria he may not use the best judgment. The suggestion was made that it would seem advisable to send a solid person with him who could modify his enthusiasm. President Tanner also raised the question as to whether, inasmuch as Brother Williams has applied for his visa, we should permit him to go to Nigeria and baptize these people who are ready for baptism as was originally intended, and effect an organization there.

I said that Brother Williams should go to Nigeria and arrange for these baptisms and keep the Nigerians in Nigeria as much as possible. President Tanner will talk to Brother Williams this afternoon and tell him that we want him to discourage people from coming here from Nigeria to attend school; also that he would tell Brother Williams that it is all right for him to go forward with the matter of securing his visa in order that he might go to Nigeria and arrange for the baptism of worthy converted Nigerians and effect a proper organization among them. ...

We discussed the matter of the proposed release of Brother Mendenhall as a Chairman of the Church Building Committee. A five-page letter was read from Brother Mendenhall addressed to me giving a report of the work that has been done by the Building Committee during the ten years that Brother Mendenhall has served as Chairman of the committee. The Brethren commented upon information that had come to them indirectly to the effect that Brother Mendenhall had stated that he had been reinstated. The Brethren were agreed that time should be given to Brother Mendenhall to clear up in an orderly manner some of the unfinished work, and it was also agreed that a determination should be made as to someone to succeed him.

I said that I felt at that time that Brother Mendenhall should be given until the end of 1965 to take care of unfinished business. I accordingly dictated a memorandum to the following effect, which I said that I would read to Brother Mendenhall over the telephone: "The First Presidency in their meeting this morning, sensing the necessity of all building business being brought to a close as soon as possible, decided that all unfinished business should be taken care of by the end of 1965." It was agreed that the action of the First Presidency on this matter should be reported to the Council of the Twelve in their regular weekly meeting in the Temple today. ...

10:00 a.m.—Later, after giving further serious consideration to other matters associated with Brother Mendenhall's release, and in reading again the minutes of the meeting of the First Presidency and the Council of the Twelve held last Thursday, and noting the unanimous decision made at that time to release Brother Mendenhall, I decided right there and then to call the Brethren who were in meeting in the Temple who were also intending to discuss the matter again today, and told them that if in their judgment it would be better to release Brother Mendenhall on July 1, 1965, instead of December 31, 1965, I would abide by their decision.

I asked that I be notified immediately after they made their decision.

In about an hour I received a telephone call from the secretary stating that the Brethren again had unanimously voted that Brother Mendenhall be released as soon as possible, and therefore they chose July 1, 1965 as the date of his release.

I immediately telephoned to Brother Mendenhall and said to him, I have been in touch with the Brethren who are in session in the Salt lake Temple and it is the sentiment of that body of men in a unanimous vote that your release should come on July 1, 1965.

Brother Mendenhall immediately brought up matters in New Zealand which need his attention; that he would have to go there personally, etc. etc.; that his wife has been assigned by the Relief society Board to go there. I said in that case it would be all right for him to go if it is necessary.

April 23, 1965. My Counselors and I met by appointment [Utah] Governor Calvin L. Rampton,[12] at which time we discussed the matter of federal government youth camps to be set up in Utah. The Governor mentioned that the federal government has provided for the placing of youth camps similar to Civilian Conservation Corps camps that were set up some years ago in certain areas, to be administered under the Bureau of Land Management or Forest Service Department. He said that the government does not wish to place any of these camps where the local populace does not want them, that they would not wish to establish them in a hostile area. The Governor mentioned that they had expected to establish camps in the Milford and Clearfield areas, but that the Stake Presidents in those areas had expressed opposition to the camps; that, therefore, it was decided not to establish them in those areas. He stated that in the Panguitch area President Holman of the Panguitch Stake has advocated the placing of a camp there and that one is also being placed in the Price area where there is no opposition.[13] The Governor stated that the opposition to the establishment of these camps in the areas mentioned was on the theory that it would bring into the communities young men of rather rough character. He stated that they would be young men principally from larger cities outside the State whose home life has not

---

12. In January, Calvin L. Rampton (1913–2007) had begun what would be three terms in office, 1965–77, riding a Democratic wave with Lyndon B. Johnson's defeat of Barry M. Goldwater. Rampton was from Bountiful, Utah. With a law degree from the University of Utah, he became the state Assistant Attorney General. He served in France during World War II and ran his father's car dealership, eventually selling the dealership to pursue his own career.

13. Price, the county seat of Carbon County, had always been a culturally, politically, socially, and religiously diverse area, a rarity in other Utah counties.

always been what it should be, and that there could be a certain amount of friction, but he did not think there would be anything serious, that they would be under rather strict discipline. He said that they would be under semi-military discipline in the camps, that they would have commanding officers with various subordinate commanders, that the camps would be some distance from towns but should be located in an area where a town would not be far away.

The Governor explained in answer to my question that during the day time these boys would work on the public lands re-seeding the range, and in the forest that they would be planting trees; that they would be engaged during the day time but would be free during the evening, except that they would have the opportunity of taking educational courses which would occupy much of their time in the evenings; that in addition, entertainment would be provided in the camps.

In answer to President [Hugh B.] Brown's inquiry as to what percentage of them would be Negroes, the Governor had no information on this phase of the situation. I asked how many boys would be in a camp and the Governor said that he thought that there would be around 150 boys in each camp, perhaps more in some places. In regard to sleeping quarters he said that barrack-type sleeping quarters would be provided, large wooden buildings, and that the boys would sleep in large rooms very much as do enlisted men in the army, perhaps 30 to 40 in one large room, on steel cots.

I said that this is a government matter with which we do not wish to interfere or oppose. In answer to my question as to how many camps it was anticipated would be established in the State, the Governor said he thought that there would be six this year two that have already been established, and four others. I said that it seemed to me that in general it would be a good thing to give the young men occupation. As to the moral question that might be involved, I said that that is a matter that the Presidents of Stakes and Bishops of Ward[s] should look after. Presidents Brown and [N. Eldon] Tanner also expressed themselves in favor of the program.

Liquor Distribution—The Governor said there was another matter he wished to discuss with the First Presidency. He mentioned that the handling of liquor in Utah is a constant problem and challenge to the Governor and the enforcement agencies. He stated that one of the problems involved is that we have liquor stores which are established in order to make liquor readily available to the populace, but that it is almost impossible for the tourists who came here to know where to go to find liquor. The Governor said that he is faced with the problem now of closing the liquor store on Second South and Second East because it is becoming a community nuisance, and that since the closing of the liquor store on the west side of Second South and Third West the liquor store on Second South and Second East is drawing to that store winos and others, and that the Second south and Second East area is a residential neighborhood, that the store is across the street from a Methodist Church, and that there is also a parking problem involved.

The Governor mentioned that it was his proposal to place twelve small package agencies in hotels and large motels that cater to tourists, that this would be merely an experiment, so that the visitors to our city who desire to obtain it might be able to obtain liquor. The Governor said he was opposed to the sale of liquor by the drink and he thought there was growing pressure for the handling of liquor in that manner. He hoped that the package agency proposal would satisfy the situation. He explained that under this arrangement the liquor would not be sold by the drink, but would be sold in bottles the way it is now, that it is only a question of whether these distributing agencies should be located in residential areas or in tourist centers.

After listening to the Governor's presentation of the matter, I said this, too, is a matter of a governmental nature which I do not feel to oppose. The Governor said that he would adopt this policy on an experimental basis for a period not to exceed one year to ascertain how it would work out.

I told the Governor that no matter how it is handled, that when one touches liquor it contaminates him. The Governor said he would make a report to the Presidency regarding the progress of the program. The Governor further said that if the brethren have anything they wish to tell him he would appreciate any advice they would care to give. ...

The Governor suggested that he would appreciate it if they would designate a group of three of four of the General Authorities whom he might contact regarding matters that arise from time to time. He said he did not want to bother me with these things, but he would appreciate it if the Presidency felt disposed to designate certain members of the General Authorities with whom he could confer. The Governor said he thought it would be well to have a member of the First Presidency on the committee.

I thanked the Governor for the suggestion, and said that I would call him later and give him the names of those whom we might wish to suggest to serve in the capacity mentioned. ...

<u>John Birch Society</u>—President Brown having mentioned that the John Birch Society has charged him with certain things, I said that many accusations had come to me about President Brown's opposition to the Birch Society. <u>I asked President Brown why he was so bitter against the organization.</u> President Brown said that he did not consider it a good society, and he thought that they were doing more harm than good. He further stated that since I had told him about a year ago to be quiet on that subject, he had said and done nothing further regarding it.

I said that it is wise not to mention the society.

<u>Ezra Taft Benson's Remarks in Conference</u>—President Brown referred to the April Conference address of Elder Ezra Taft Benson and his remarks about civil rights and Communism,[14] and said that he had had many unfavorable reactions regarding Brother Benson's remarks. He mentioned an article that appeared in the Washington Post with a big headline statement as follows: "Rift in the Mormon Church, Benson Says that Civil Rights is Communistic," and that the Presidency have announced that the Church stands for complete brotherhood and fairness. President Brown said that he thought that Brother Benson should be told to take care of his missionary work and leave such matters alone.

I said that I had not noticed anything objectionable in what Brother Benson had said, and asked that President Brown bring to me a report of Brother Benson's remarks, which President Brown said he would do at once. I said that we should leave such subjects alone.

---

14. Benson said that "communists were using the civil rights movement to promote revolution," but this was edited out of the published version (see entry for May 3, 1965, which includes the portion McKay ordered removed). The expurgated part was published by Cleon Skousen in 1971 in his study manual for BYU students, *Treasures from the Book of Mormon*, 3:35–39. For a more thorough discussion of this, see Quinn, *Extensions*, 66–115.

Referring to this same matter, President Tanner said that he had received telephone calls and letters from two areas particularly, one the Phoenix area and the other Idaho, in which he was told that these things have "split the people down the center" in their thinking in Priesthood meeting classes, discussions in Sunday School classes, etc., that the complaint is made that Brother Benson is taking one position and that President Brown has taken another.

I said I had told everyone not to mention the Birch Society but let the matter die out.

April 29, 1965, First Presidency meeting. President [N. Eldon] Tanner mentioned that questions are being asked and articles written about the Church's attitude on various doctrines. He mentioned that philosophers today are attacking our beliefs and referred to statements made 50, 75, or 100 years ago by our leaders relative to God and man's relation to Him, the nature of Christ, etc. President Tanner referred to the tremendous amount of information collected by the Brigham Young University librarian, Brother [Lyman] Tyler, and that Brother Tyler had suggested that we as a Church might wish to appoint someone to keep in touch with these problems. Brother Tyler says that he has on his desk at the present time six books dealing with these subjects and that he could make available to anyone making a study necessary helpful information.

President [Hugh B.] Brown and President Tanner suggested the appointment of someone to make a study of these things in order that he might be prepared to discuss and answer questions that arise, and suggested that Truman Madsen,[15] who has his Doctor's Degree in religion and philosophy, might be given such an assignment. The Presidency agreed upon Brother Madsen for this service, with the suggestion that he submit to the First Presidency for approval any articles or letters that he might prepare in answer to these attacks.

---

15. Truman Grant Madsen (1925–2009), a grandson of Heber J. Grant, was born in Salt Lake City. He served in the New England Mission under S. Dilworth Young and returned as mission president, 1962–65. He graduated from the University of Utah and USC, received a PhD in philosophy from Harvard, and taught at BYU, later holding the Richard L. Evans Chair of Religious Understanding. He was also for a time the director of BYU's Jerusalem Center.

May 3, 1965. President [Hugh B.] Brown discussed with me the recent Conference address by Elder Ezra Taft Benson, and I authorized the elimination from this address of the following statements by Brother Benson:

> "Before I left for Europe I warned how the Communists were using the Civil Rights movement to promote revolution and eventual take-over of this Country. When are we going to wake up? What do you know about the dangerous Civil Rights agitation in Mississippi? Do you fear the destruction of all vestiges of state government?
>
> "Now, Brethren, the Lord has never promised there would not be traitors in the Church. We have the ignorant, the sleepy and the deceived who provide temptations and avenues of apostasy for the unwary and the unfaithful. But we have a Prophet at our head and he has spoken. Now what are we going to do about it?"

May 6, 1965, First Presidency meeting. We discussed the matter of the recommendation of the Twelve which was approved by the Council subject to my approval, pertaining to the assignment of mission supervisors whereby each of the Brethren of the Twelve, with the exception of President Smith, would be given supervision over a mission area, to be assisted by one of the Assistants to the Twelve or one of the First Council of Seventy, these supervisors to be domiciled in Salt Lake City. Reference was made to the recommendations and discussions of this matter in the Council as set forth in the minutes of April 8, 1965. President Tanner mentioned that when this question was first considered I was not clear as to whether or not we should continue to have the Brethren who are presiding over the South American, European and West European missions domiciled here. He also mentioned that in the early discussions of this matter Brother Mark E. Petersen was not thoroughly converted to this arrangement, but that when he was here at Conference time, he indicated that those in charge of these areas could take care of the work just as well if located here as if they were domiciled in the missions. In connection with this over-all program, it was the recommendation of the council that there be three areas in Europe, namely, the British Isles Mission, the European Missions and the West European Missions. The original proposal was that Brother Petersen supervise the European Missions consisting of the Germanic Missions, that Brother Benson supervise the British Isles, and that Howard W. Hunter give supervision to the West European Missions. However, in discussing the matter, it was subsequently decided that it would be preferable to have Brother Benson preside over the West European Missions and Brother Hunter preside over the British Isles.

I gave my approval of the mission supervision program as recommended by the Council and authorized President Tanner to so notify the Council today in the event that I could not attend.

May 12, 1965, 8:00 am. By appointment met with <u>Samuel W. Taylor</u> this morning. Presidents [Hugh B.] Brown and [N. Eldon] Tanner were also present. Brother Taylor <u>appealed for the reinstatement to membership and restoration of former blessings for his father, John W. Taylor,</u> who, as a member of the Twelve, was excommunicated from the Church March 28, 1911, and who passed away October 10, 1916.[16]

I ruled, in which my counselors agreed, that authorization be given for this reinstatement and restoration. The matter will be reported to the Council of the Twelve in the meeting of the First Presidency and quorum of the Twelve tomorrow.

May 13, 1965, First Presidency meeting. President [Hugh B.] Brown made reference to an action taken in the meeting of the Council of the First Presidency and Quorum of the Twelve last Thursday to the effect that Mark E. Petersen would have supervision over the Germanic missions, that Brother [Ezra Taft] Benson would have charge of the missions in the proposed West European Mission—consisting of the Scandinavian Countries, the Netherlands, and the French Missions, and that Howard W. Hunter would have supervision of the missions in the British Isles. President Brown said that President [N. Eldon] Tanner and he had discussed this latter proposition with Elder [Harold B.] Lee yesterday and that Brother Lee feels, in which feeling President Tanner agreed, that under all the circumstances it would be well to follow the original suggestion; namely, that Brother Benson supervise the missions in the

---

16. McKay was called into the Quorum of the Twelve on the heels of the Reed Smoot hearings, which had been the catalyst for the removal of Matthias F. Cowley and John W. Taylor from the quorum. About the same time, apostle Marriner W. Merrill had died, so three new apostles were ordained on April 9, 1906—Orson F. Whitney (1855–1931), George F. Richards (1861–1950), and McKay.

British Isles, Brother Hunter in the West European Missions in Scandinavia, the Netherlands and France, and that Brother Mark E. Petersen supervise the Germanic Missions. It was therefore felt that the minutes of last Thursday's meeting should be amended accordingly. President Tanner explained that when Brother Benson was here at Conference time, he had expressed real satisfaction in the arrangement that was then proposed that he go to England and preside over the British Isles Missions, and Brother Lee felt that if a change were made now it might be unwise and be offensive to Brother Benson.

May 14, 1965, First Presidency meeting. Elder Thorpe B. Isaacson and Dr. Edward R. McKay were present during this discussion. President [Hugh B.] Brown reported that at the meeting of the Council of the First Presidency and Quorum of the Twelve yesterday, the matter of the appointment of a supervisory committee for the Building Department was announced to the Council, this committee consisting of Marion G. Romney, Franklin D. Richards, and Bishop John H. Vandenberg, with Brother Romney as Chairman, this proposition having been approved by the First Presidency on Wednesday, May 12, 1965. President Brown said that the Brethren unanimously approved the recommendation of the committee and that Howard Dunn[17] be appointed acting manager for the time being at least. They expressed a desire to notify him as soon as possible inasmuch as matters in the Building Department are in a somewhat confused condition. Mention was made of the fact that Brother Mendenhall's tenure does not expire until July 1. It was thought that inasmuch as Brother Dunn knows the situation he could carry on until such time as he or someone else be appointed to take over this responsibility.

We then discussed the matter of Mark B. Garff[18] as a prospective

---

17. James Howard Dunn (1917–2008) had been a geotechnical engineer in San Francisco until McKay invited him in 1958 to be on the Church Building Committee. He was born in the religiously diverse farming town of Corinne in northern Utah, served a church mission to France, and graduated from USU. He and his wife married in November 1940, prior to his spending World War II in the navy.

18. Mark Brimhall Garff (1907–95) was senior partner in a Utah construction company that built the fieldhouse and student center at BYU, the library at USU, a classroom building at the University of Utah, and the downtown Kennecott Building. He had been the Danish mission president when he was only thirty years old, beginning in 1937.

manager for the Building Department. Some difference of opinion was expressed on this matter.

Elder Isaacson reminded the Brethren that about eight months ago President McKay had appointed a committee with Delbert L. Stapley as Chairman, the committee consisting of Brother Stapley, Legrand Richards, Howard Hunter, Franklin D. Richards, and himself. He said the committee had been asked to make some recommendations which they have done, and prepared some charts regarding the Building Committee set-up. Brother Isaacson further reported that Brother Stapley and he had been asked by President McKay to submit three names and that they did recommend three brethren and had discussed these three brethren with me, one of whom was Brother Mark B. Garff, and the others were Carl W. Buehner and Ted Jacobsen. Elder Isaacson further stated that in some way Elder Mark E. Petersen had learned that Brother Dunn was being considered for this appointment and he had written strongly opposing Brother Dunn for this position. The thought was expressed that any opposition to Brother Dunn was undoubtedly because he was closely associated with Brother Mendenhall in the management of the Building Committee. Presidents Brown and Tanner both indicated that they were greatly pleased with the attitude that Brother Dunn is manifesting and that they were satisfied that he would carry on the work the way we would wish it handled until a manager is appointed. After a rather lengthy discussion, I said that the matter would be held over until next Monday so that more thought could be given to it. ...

John W. Taylor—Reinstatement of—President Brown reported that the Twelve had yesterday passed favorably upon the reinstatement of John W. Taylor. He mentioned that the Brethren raised a question which they were not prepared to answer; namely, in the restoration of John W. Taylor's blessings the question was raised as to what Priesthood should be restored to him—in other words, should he be restored to the Apostleship. I said that he should simply be given the Melchizedek Priesthood and the blessings of the Temple, and that President Joseph Fielding Smith should take care of this restoration. ...

11:15 a.m.—The secretary brought over letters and office matters for my attention. While she was there Elder Thorpe B. Isaacson came. He reported to me that President Joseph Fielding Smith and Elder Delbert

L. Stapley had urged him to come over and to explain to me that they had only voted for the Committee presented, and voted that Howard Dunn be made Chairman of the Building Committee at the Council Meeting yesterday because they thought it was what I wanted.

I told Brother Isaacson that I do not want Brother Dunn in that position, not even on a temporary basis; that if we should call him to be the Acting Chairman and then release him in a short while there would only be feelings, and we do not want that. I told Brother Isaacson that I do not feel right in my heart about appointing Brother Dunn to this position.

I then reported to Brother Isaacson that Brother Mark [B.] Garff will be back in Salt Lake on Sunday and that I have asked him to come and see me then. I said that I feel that Brother Garff is a man that would do anything the Church might ask him to do; that he is a good man.

May 19, 1965, First Presidency meeting. I asked President [Hugh B.] Brown to express his opinion about Mark B. Garff for appointment to succeed Wendell B. Mendenhall as Manager of the Building Committee. President Brown recited his close association with Brother Garff arising from Brother Garff's being a member of the Granite Stake when President Brown was President, and Brother Garff's having been called on a mission at that time. He served also on the High Council in the Stake. President Brown said he is a good builder, he is inclined to be impetuous, but he is nevertheless one-hundred percent loyal. He is independent. He also said he could highly recommend him.

President Brown mentioned, however, that President [N. Eldon] Tanner thinks Brother Garff may be too impetuous. President Brown explained also that the Brethren seem to be divided on the subject as to whether or not Brother Garff should be selected. Some feel that Brother Howard Dunn is the best man because he has knowledge of the workings of the committee. Some feel that he is too much of a Mendenhall man. He is, however, quite independent. Others suggested Brother Dunn to carry on as manager until the first of July when Brother Mendenhall will be released.

I commented upon Brother Garff's knowledge of the building program of the Church, his practical experience, his power to make decisions and his having a mind of his own and being loyal. I asked President

Brown to arrange to have Brother Garff come to the apartment for a confidential talk with me this morning.

President Brown then reviewed the first committee appointed to consider the subject: Elders Stapley, LeGrand Richards, Howard W. Hunter, and Thorpe B. Isaacson; and the committee appointed last week: Elders Marion G. Romney, Franklin D. Richards and Bishop John H. Vandenberg. He mentioned Brother Garff's preference to work directly with the First Presidency rather than through a committee.

I asked President Brown to meet me in the morning at 8:30 when the decision will be made and information given for the Council of the Twelve.

9:30 a.m.—Brother Mark B. Garff came to my apartment at my request. I told him that I should like him to take over the management of the Building Department. After talking over the whole problem with him, I told Brother Garff that he is to report to no one but me and the First Presidency; that he is free to come to me before he sees anyone else at any time.

Brother Garff mentioned the committee that has already been appointed and said, "President McKay, you cannot ask me to do this job and then dam the ditch with men with whom I cannot work."

I told Brother Garff to study the matter and then to come back to me with his recommendations. I said that the committees that have been appointed will be released, and that I would present the entire matter to the Council of the Twelve for their approval and action and get the whole thing settled tomorrow at our meeting of the First Presidency and council of the Twelve.

May 20, 1965, First Presidency meeting. I asked that the following memorandum which I had dictated be read: "Matter to be taken up at Council Meeting Thursday, May 20, 1965: Yesterday morning (May 19) I met by appointment in my apartment Brother Mark B. Garff, at which time I asked him to take over the management of the Church Building Department. After talking over the whole problem with him, I told Brother Garff that he is to report to no one but me and to the First Presidency. I told him that both committees that have already been appointed will be released. I am presenting this matter to you for your approval and action."

I then asked President [Hugh B.] Brown if he approved, and President

Brown answered in the affirmative. I said that we would present this memorandum to the council at their meeting this morning.

I reviewed the committees appointed to give their recommendations on the Building Committee. President Brown asked if the committees are to be released, and I replied that this should be decided now. I said that the announcement of the appointment should be made after the Council has acted and approved.

June 1, 1965, 12:00 noon–12:40 p.m. Gave dictation to my secretary, Clare [Middlemiss]. She reported that Elder Mark B. Garff, newly-appointed Chairman of the Church Building Committee, had called and reported that he is working on the re-organization of the Building Committee. He said it will be necessary for him to have a clean slate, and that he has five men in mind whom he would like to suggest, and that he would report back to me as soon as he is ready. Brother Garff also commented that he is astounded at the expenditures over in that department.

I commented that Brother Garff should have a free hand in reorganization matter, and that I will sustain him in that.

June 3, 1965, First Presidency meeting. The Brethren reported that a representative of the Time and Life magazines had called on them this morning and asked regarding the Negro situation. The representative is a member of the Church. President [Hugh B.] Brown stated that President [N. Eldon] Tanner and he were not able to give him very much information except to tell him that we have no official organization of the Church in Nigeria, that such work as has been done in Nigeria has been done by the people on their own account and we are not authorized as yet to send official representatives there, having been unable to get visas.

President Brown said this magazine representative raised the question as to the Negro holding the Priesthood and they told him that all that they could tell him was that as of now the Negro cannot hold the Priesthood.

Nigeria—LaMar Williams to do Nothing Further about Work in Nigeria—President Tanner reported that Brother LaMar Williams had made another application for visa to Nigeria and had been turned down by the authorities. President Tanner told LaMar that he should do nothing further in this matter, that he thought perhaps he might be irritating them by his constant requests.

I said that the matter should not be pushed.

June 4, 1965, First Presidency meeting. Reference was again made to the following case which had been considered by the Presidency a few days ago. A Mexican woman had married a man who she thought was an Indian, but she later learned he had some Negro blood. There were born to this marriage boys who have been raised in the ward with their comrades who have attended Primary, Sunday School and Seminary, but now they cannot be given the Priesthood whereas their comrades are ordained. Their friends pass the Sacrament and they have to refrain from doing this. These boys say that they cannot stay in the Church under these circumstances and would rather go to some other church where there is no discrimination. The mother also states that she feels that if the boys go into another church, she will have to go with them and would have to withdraw from the Church. It was mentioned that the father has been teaching the Gospel Doctrine class, that he does not hold the Priesthood, and is not asking for it, knowing that he cannot have it.

The question raised was whether the time has come when the Negro should be given the Lesser Priesthood. President [Hugh B.] Brown said that he had talked with the stake president and bishop, both of whom are acquainted with the family and regret the situation very much. They say the boys are outstanding young men.

I stated that we stand with all former Presidents of the Church that these boys having Negro blood cannot have the Priesthood. It was agreed, however, that by all means we should encourage them to remain in the Church.

June 10, 1965. Went over a copy of the financial report of the Church as of May 28. I was pleased to know that our position is much improved over what it was a year ago.

June 15, 1965, First Presidency meeting. President [N. Eldon] Tanner said that he had received a telephone call today from a Brother James Larkin[19]

---

19. James Joseph Larkin (1925–2011) was born in Brooklyn. He graduated from

in New York who referred to a recent article in Time magazine regarding "Nigerian Mormons," and said that he had spent two years in close relationship to the government in northern Nigeria, also in Lagos, the capital of Nigeria; that he knows the government officials very well and has respect for them. Brother Larkin indicated that he felt sure if he could talk with these officials face to face and explain to them the conditions that prompt our desire to obtain visas to Nigeria, that unless there is some commitment to the contrary, he could influence them to change their attitude. Brother Larkin said that he was available to help in the situation if we desired this service. He stated that the attitude of the Church toward the Negro question had been a stumbling block to him before he joined about two years ago; that, however, he understands the problem now and thinks he can explain it to others.

I said that I am convinced, after studious thought and prayer, that we should go into Nigeria and give them what we can give them in accordance with the revelations of the Lord. As of now, the Lord has not yet revealed to us that we should give the Negro the Priesthood, but we can baptize them, give them membership in the Church, and give them the benefit of the Auxiliary organizations. They may partake of the Sacrament and hold meetings. If we accept Brother Larkin's offer to go into Nigeria for us, he should make the investigation on a more or less confidential, quiet basis, going to Nigeria without letting anyone else know about it.

Referring again to the Negro question, I said that we are now face to face with a great principle that is as vital to the Church today as was the principle of letting the [gentiles][20] be baptized in the Christian era, and mentioned the occasion when James sat with the Brethren of the Twelve and rendered the decision that the [gentiles] could have the Gospel. I said that it is up to the Lord to decide the Negro question.

Columbia University, was an air force radio operator during World War II, and became a public relations official with British Overseas Airways Corporation. When Nigeria became independent in 1960, he founded a public relations company to represent the country. He was successful in other areas, as well, including becoming vice president of a New York radio station and producing the television series, *Madhouse Brigade*, which won a 1980 Emmy Award.

20. McKay (or Middlemiss) wrote "Jews" but meant gentiles, both here and later in the same sentence. For the biblical story, see Gal. 2:9; Acts 15:13–14; 21:18–19.

June 19, 1965. Resting at home. It is still necessary for me to have oxygen most of the time.

June 22, 1965, First Presidency meeting. In discussing new quarters for the Deseret News, President [N. Eldon] Tanner stated that he thinks we should start at once to get things ready for the new Church Office Building; that we should order the steel, prepare final specifications, and commence the building right away. He also mentioned the need for releasing Brother Wendell B. Mendenhall as a member of the committee having in charge preparations for the construction of the new building and the appointment of Brother Garff as Brother Mendenhall's successor.

I stated that Brother Mendenhall should be taken off the committee for the construction of the new building at once, and asked Brother Tanner to make the change this morning. President Tanner mentioned that Brother Garff does not want to do anything in connection with the Building Department until the first of July, and I said that I think this is a mistaken idea on his part.

I said also that the newspaper announcement of Brother Garff's appointment should be made right away. In this connection President Tanner said that there is gossip going around to the effect that Brother Mendenhall has been excommunicated, that he had misappropriated funds, etc. President Tanner thought that perhaps we should make some statement to correct these rumors. I said the announcement of Brother Garff's appointment should be made at once, and that nothing should be said regarding the rumors referred to.

June 23, 1965, First Presidency meeting. Mention was made of the interview by the First Presidency yesterday of James Larkin regarding the Nigerian situation. Reference was made to the fact that Brother Larkin reports his close acquaintance with government officials in Nigeria, that during the past six years he had spent the majority of his time working with Nigerian problems and has spent about two years in Nigeria. Brother Larkin has offered his services in going to Nigeria to meet with government officials if the Brethren desire him to do so relative to obtaining visa privileges for representatives of the Church. At my request, President [N. Eldon] Tanner and Brother Larkin had met with LaMar

Williams regarding the Nigerian problem and prepared a brief statement of the situation which was read at this meeting.

I stated that I think the time has not yet come to go into Nigeria.

June 24, 1965, First Presidency meeting. President [N. Eldon] Tanner reported that he had informed Brother James Larkin that the Church did not favor sending him to Nigeria at the present time. President Tanner said that he told Brother Larkin that I have taken the position quite firmly that we are prepared to do anything we can to make it possible for the people in Nigeria to enjoy the blessings of the Gospel, but that I do not feel that we should urge the government to grant us visas; on the other hand we should leave that to the local people who are working on it.

I said that is the right thing to do.

July 1, 1965, First Presidency meeting. We gave further consideration today to the matter of what instruction should be given regarding the observance of the Fast. Reference was made to instructions heretofore given that it was not necessary to abstain from drinking water. Attention was also called to items in the minutes of the council Meetings held November 19, 1909 and June 29, 1922, in which meetings it was reported that the Brethren of the Council, in expressing themselves in regard to this matter, had agreed that there was nothing to the revelations indicating the duration of the Fast, and that the evident meaning of the Fast is to abstain from eating and drinking, and it has normally been considered that a proper Fast consists of refraining from eating two meals on Fast Day, and the Fast is usually broken after the Fast Meeting. ...

I stated that in thinking about this subject, it had come to me quite clearly this morning that in observing the Fast Day, we should refrain from eating two meals and that a proper Fast is to refrain from eating and drinking.[21] ...

I further stated that in consideration [of] the practice of Fasting, the spiritual element of Fasting and Prayer should go together with the Fast itself.

July 7, 1965, First Presidency meeting. We had some discussion regarding political matters and made particular mention of the Negro question and

21. See also Mar. 16, 1962.

the recent charges of the colored organization NAACP regarding alleged Mormon discrimination. We were agreed that the best way to handle this situation is to take no notice of their charges and to say nothing whatever relative thereto.

Right-to-Work Law—President [N. Eldon] Tanner reported that this morning he had attended a breakfast at the Alta Club[22] in connection with the United Fund drive, that Governor [Calvin L.] Rampton sat next to him and the right-to-work question came up. The Governor said that he was well acquainted with the attitude of the First Presidency on this matter. President Tanner told him that he was glad he did know what the attitude of the First Presidency is regarding any question that affected man's free agency. The Governor said that when he and all other Democratic nominees accepted their nomination they made a commitment, including President [Lyndon B.] Johnson himself, that they would work for the repeal of Section 14(b) of the Taft–Hartley Law, and that he had to carry out his commitment. He explained that this was a part of the Democratic platform.[23]

July 9, 1965. Elder Thorpe B. Isaacson of the Personnel Committee had received a letter signed by the First Presidency instructing them to give three months severance pay to the retiring members of the Building Committee, where as previously they had been instructed by me that these committee members were not to get severance pay.

I emphatically told Elder Isaacson that I do not want them to have this sever[a]nce pay; that most of the members resigned of their own free will when Brother Wendell B. Mendenhall was released.

I instructed Elder Isaacson to tell President [Hugh B.] Brown that I had decided at one of our meetings of the First Presidency that this severance pay should not be given as these men had all done very well while

---

22. The Alta Club, located across from the Church Administration Building since 1898, was a place where wealthy businessmen could relax, dine, play cards, and read the newspaper. It is three stories tall and built out of massive sandstone blocks in an Italian Renaissance style.

23. McKay had always opposed compulsory membership in labor unions and was in favor of "right-to-work" laws. Section 14b allowed states to preserve a worker's right to be employed without joining a union.

at the Building Committee, but that President [N. Eldon] Tanner had brought the matter up again and pleaded for these men to get the money.

Following the meeting, Elder LeGrand Richards, Chairman of the Personnel Committee, and Elder Isaacson called on President Brown and told him that I had instructed the Personnel Committee not to give three months severance pay to members of the Building Committee. President Brown became very upset because of these instructions, and shocked Elders Richards and Isaacson with his attitude.

July 13, 1965, First Presidency meeting. There was read to us a letter from Senator Frank E. Moss [D–Utah], and congressmen John E. Moss [D–Calif.], Ken W. Dyal [D–Calif.], Morris K. Udall [D–Ariz.] and Richard T. Hanna [D–Calif.],[24] in answer to the First Presidency's letter addressed to these brethren setting forth the Church's attitude regarding the proposed repeal of Section 14(b) of the Taft-Hartley Law. Senator Moss and the Congressmen indicate that they "act in conformity with the highest principles of our Church in declining to be swayed by the views expressed in the communication of June 22, under the signatures of the First Presidency." Congressman Udall in an addendum to the letter states that he considers himself bound by the referenda of the electorate of Arizona to vote against repeal of Section 14(b), but that he has serious personal reservations about its wisdom, although he does raise a question as to the advisability of publishing the First Presidency's communication.

Attention was also called to a letter from Senator Wallace F. Bennett indicating his position in opposition to the proposal to repeal Section 14(b), also a letter from Delwin M. Clawson,[25] a member of Congress from California, which indicates that he is committed to the preservation of the right of individual free agency.

In connection with this same matter, President [N. Eldon] Tanner referred to his earlier report of a statement made by Governor [Calvin

---

24. These were all LDS members. Their response to the First Presidency is included in Prince and Wright, *David O. McKay*, 326–27.

25. Delwin Morgan Clawson (1914–92) had been mayor of Compton, California, and a multi-term Republican US Congressman, 1964–78. He was born in Thatcher, Arizona, where about a third of the population is LDS, and graduated from Gila College (now Eastern Arizona College), which was church-owned until 1933.

L.] Rampton in a conversation with him to the effect that the proposed repeal of Section 14(b) of the Taft-Hartley Act was a part of the 1964 Democratic platform. ...

President Brown reported that yesterday he and President Tanner had a conference for an hour or more with four of the union officials of Salt Lake City, all members of the Church, who came to discuss with them the attitude taken by the First Presidency regarding the proposed repeal of Section 14(b) of the Taft-Hartley Law.

Presidents Brown and Tanner thanked these gentlemen for their visit and told them that the First Presidency had made their statement and felt that the position taken was sound. President Brown said these union officials were not militant but were positive in their opinion that Section 14(b) should be repealed.

July 14, 1965, First Presidency meeting. President [Hugh B.] Brown reported that there are three Nigerian students at the Brigham Young University who have received scholarships from the fund established by LaMar Williams, that the fund has been exhausted and the committee has suggested the financing of these students will be needed to take care of their schooling. It was reported that there are two or three ways in which this could be handled. President Raymond E. Beckham of the Brigham Young University Stake, Bishop Richard B. Wirthlin of the BYU 41st Ward, and LaMar Williams state that they would have no difficulty in getting the money if we gave them the go-ahead signal authorizing them to contact a few people to raise money for this purpose. Second, they might be requested to return to their homes, but this is not felt advisable under the conditions. Third, the church could take the responsibility of taking care of them.

In this connection it was mentioned that two of these people are good students and devoted Church members, having been baptized. It was also stated that there was a misunderstanding between their leader in Nigeria and Brother Williams, that Brother Williams had told them that they would have a scholarship here, but in Nigeria they had a misunderstanding of what this scholarship contemplated.

I said that we should give President Beckham, Bishop Wirthlin, and Brother Williams the go-ahead sign to raise the money.

July 15, 1965. <u>Building Committee—Audit of</u>. Although it was agreed yesterday when I called President Brown into a meeting with Brother Mark Garff ... there would be an independent audit, President Brown ... said that President Tanner is strongly opposed to an outside audit on the grounds that it exposed to non-members what he calls our "dirty linen," and he felt our own auditors could make the audit just as well. President Brown said that there seems to be some feeling on Brother Garff's part, and that of others, that there would be a whitewash job done if it were left to our auditors.

July 16, 1965, 11:00 a.m. ... Called Mark B. Garff and asked him to come over to the office in the apartment. At this time we discussed again the matter of whether or not a firm independent of the Church should make an audit of the Building Department. Brother Garff said that on three different occasions he has received instructions from me to go ahead with an independent audit, but that my counselors have instructed him to have the church auditors make the audit. He reminded me that just last Wednesday (July 14, 1965), President [Hugh B.] Brown was called into a meeting in my apartment, and after a discussion President Brown agreed that an independent audit should be made. However, the following morning, he [Brown] brought the matter up again in the First Presidency's meeting, and the question was again raised as to whether there should be an independent audit. I called Brother Garff while in that meeting regarding the Church's making the audit, but a definite decision was not made, and he was to report to me later. Brother Garff said that the counselors called him into a meeting yesterday at 2:00 p.,m. and emphatically told him to have the church auditors make the audit. Brother Garff said he talked to Harold Davis, one of the auditors, and asked him how the Church or any business could make an impartial audit of itself. Brother Davis answered that that is why he is here; that he is the church auditor, and that he thinks they can do a better audit than anybody else. Brother Garff asked him how he can keep his seven or eight men, and others whom he will contact all around the world, from talking, and told him very frankly that he felt that he could not make an impartial audit. Brother Garff told him that he would talk to him again after talking to the President of the Church about it. Said that he intended calling me Monday morning for an appointment, if I had not called him this morning.

Brother Garff said that there is the problem of unfavorable matters showing up in the audit, and that if it is contrary to my wishes to have an outside firm audit the books, then he will abide by my decision.

I said, "Suppose we do have a Church audit and also an independent audit? What does it matter?" Brother Garff said that confidentially my Counselors told him he is to go in another direction, but that he had not acquiesced, and that he had told Harold Davis that he would not give him an answer until Monday. He said that the counselors have the understanding that I have changed my mind and that I want a Church audit, and that President Brown has told the Church auditors to proceed with the audit.

I then said to brother Garff, "I want you to have a clear slate, and personally I do not know why anyone would hesitate for you to have that slate clean. I say to you in the presence of Clare, my secretary, that we want that independent audit."

Brother Garff said, "All right that is settled. Do you want me to advise your Counselors to that effect?" I said, "Why shouldn't you? I have an idea that some others are representing me. I want you to come to me without being influenced by anyone else. I should like to know who told you that I do not want an independent audit—they have misunderstood."

Brother Garff answered, "This came out of your meeting yesterday when you called me and said that we should have a Church audit. They have told me what the church auditors can do and that we would be better off with our own auditors."

I said, "I cannot understand why anybody should hesitate to have our Church books, or business, audited by anybody, and even looked at under a search light."

Brother Garff said, "Your counselors, and [especially] Brother [N. Eldon] Tanner, feel that we should have the church auditors, and I would not go along with them. I am not going to let them cause you any more worry about this—you should not be concerned. I think the Committee is perfectly capable of doing the job you assigned us, and you are perfectly capable of telling us what you want. The whole Committee is in favor of having an independent audit."

Later, Brother Garff called by Telephone and asked that a memorandum giving him authority to go ahead with the independent audit,

signed by me, be given to him. I authorized my secretary, Clare, to prepare such a memorandum which I will sign and hand to Brother Garff.

July 21, 1965, First Presidency meeting. President [Hugh B.] Brown presented certain questions which had been submitted by a representative of
Time magazine, who had asked him for an interview regarding the statement of the First Presidency (See June 25, 1965) in opposition to the
repeal of Section 14(b) of the Taft-Hartley Law. President Brown said
that the man who is asking for the interview is a member of the Church
who lives in Salt lake City. He said that Time is preparing an article for
publication, and has asked him to get the facts.

The questions submitted are as follows:

(1) Did any special event prompt President McKay to issue the
statement?

(2) Is this statement considered by Church members to be a religious
and moral declaration from the Prophet of God, being in effect an expression of the will of God that the law makers vote against the repeal of
that section of the Taft-Hartley Law?

(3) Is it an expression of an opinion only on the part of the First
Presidency taking it out of the category of divine message relating to
morals and church doctrine and making it the opinion of the Church on
political matters?

(4) Would a Mormon congressman be considered to have rebuffed
the President of the Church if he voted against this repeal? If so, would
that rebuff have any effort on the standing of the congressman in question?

(5) Such pronouncements on the political questions of the day are not
uncommon from the First Presidency. Perhaps one of the most difficult
things to understand is how the Church members know if this is to be virtually a commandment from God through His Prophet. How can he tell?

President Brown mentioned that the statement of the First Presidency has been referred to [Michigan governor] George Romney for his
opinion by [church member and contractor] Newell J. Olsen of Logan,
and that Brother Romney had written him, President Brown, attaching
correspondence he had had with Brother Olsen on the matter, in which
Brother Romney told Brother Olsen that he had not at any time taken a
position supporting outright repeal of Section 14(b). It would seem that

Senator [Frank E.] Moss and [former] Congressman [David S.] King of Utah had quoted Governor Romney as being in favor of the repeal of this section. After some discussion of the matter, it was decided to answer the questions by the representative of Time as follows:

(1) That there was no special event which brought forth the statement by the First Presidency.

(2) That in answer to the inquiry as to whether the statement should be considered as a religious and moral declaration from the Prophet of God, being in effect the will of the Lord, the answer is that the statement sets forth the attitude of the First Presidency of the Church; that, however, that part of the statement reading as follows is from the Lord: "It is our sincere desire and earnest prayer that no action will be taken by the President or the congress of the United States that would tend to interfere with the God-given right of men to exercise free agency in seeking and maintaining work privileges."

(3) As to whether the balance of the statement is an expression of opinion by the First Presidency, President McKay said it is only an opinion. It was suggested that that part of the statement sets forth the attitude or stand of the First Presidency.

(4) As to whether Mormon congressmen will be considered to have rebuffed the President of the Church if they vote against this repeal, and if so would that rebuff have any effect upon the standing of the congressmen in the Church, the answer is no.

It was thought unnecessary to answer the fifth question regarding pronouncements on political questions by the First Presidency.

July 30, 1965, First Presidency meeting. President [Hugh B.] Brown mentioned some rumor that is going around to the effect that he had softened the stand of the First Presidency as expressed in the statement regarding the proposed repeal of the right-to-Work amendment. President Brown wanted me to understand what he did say. He stated that he said to the representative of Time Magazine who had called on him just what I had told him to say and no more, and that this man had come back yesterday and confirmed that and stated that he had reported exactly what President Brown had told him; that, however, when it went to New York, they changed it there and had given it headline value. President Brown then read to me the statement as contained in the minutes of the First Presidency's meeting which was agreed upon by the First Presidency at that time. He reiterated that he had done nothing that he was not authorized to do. I said that I am glad to hear that.[26]

August 19, 1965; meeting of First Presidency and Twelve. Elder Harold B. Lee reported that he had received the appointment to attend the South Los Angeles Stake Conference on Saturday and Sunday last, that, however, because of the rioting that took place in South Los Angeles among the Negroes,[27] he conferred with President [Harold F.] Whittier of the Stake by telephone, who told of the terrifying experiences the people were going through, that the feeling was tense, the situation dangerous, and there was a serious question whether we should hold a Conference and bring about two thousand members, some of them through the black belt, knowing that the Negroes had been incited against the Church. He said the whole thing was much like an armed camp, virtually under military control. In a later telephone conversation with President Whittier he said that the police had given strict orders to everybody not to hold congregational meetings. Accordingly, it was decided not to hold the conference that had been scheduled.

It was reported that our Santa Monica Stake building was broken into and there was some damage; also that the Huntington Park Stake building had some windows broken which had been replaced.

Elder [Spencer W.] Kimball mentioned that he is scheduled to hold a conference this weekend at Burbank, and he assumed that he should arrange to attend. President [Hugh B.] Brown suggested that it would be well to check with the Stake President and see that everything is all right.

Other interesting general matters were reported by the Brethren, after which I made the following comments:

["]Unfortunately, the last three months I have been under the weather,

---

26. Newspapers picked up the controversy. One headline read, "Leader Explains LDS Labor Law Statement: Pres. Hugh B. Brown Eases Bind" (*Ogden Standard-Examiner*, July 26, 1965). By then, the newspapers had the First Presidency letter and the politicians' response. McKay contacted the *Deseret News* to reconfirm the original intent.

27. This has reference to the Watts riots that had erupted on August 11 and resulted in the deaths of thirty-four people, twenty-five of them African-American. Property losses were estimated to be in excess of $200 million (in 1960s dollars).

I suppose because of a slight stroke. I have been blessed in that I have not had any pain. Dr. Viko was surprised. He said, 'You have had a heart attack, but you have not had any pain in the first attack nor the second.'

["]I have been absolutely free from any pain whatever, for which I am very grateful. The most embarrassing part of it is my tendency to stutter when I am talking. ...

["]I am very thankful indeed to be able to come here this morning and be in this meeting. My wife Ray protested against my coming to this meeting, but I would not have missed the meeting and the reports for anything.

["]It is good to hear the great things ahead for the Church. The matter you reported, Brother [Gordon B.] Hinckley, is of great significance. It is a satisfaction to know that the Lord is at the helm and there are great things ahead for the Church, and there is a great responsibility resting upon the Presidency and the Twelve to take care of the things the Lord has in hand for us. We pray sincerely not only as the Presidency but as members of the Twelve that we might be equal to the added responsibility which comes to us because of the favorable attitude of men of importance who are willing to contribute their means to the building up of the Church. I hope that we as the Presidency and the Twelve will be equal to the added responsibilities which the Lord has for us in the future. I am glad to meet with you this morning."

August 20, 1965, First Presidency meeting. Reference was made to an action recently taken by the First Presidency in answer to a question as to whether a child born as a result of artificial insemination should be considered as born in the covenant. At that time the decision was made that it would not be born in the covenant. President [N. Eldon] Tanner mentioned decisions heretofore made pertaining to children born illegitimately to women who have been sealed in the Temple to the effect that such children were born in the covenant. It was decided to reverse the former ruling regarding the child born as the result of artificial insemination; namely, that the child should be considered as born in the covenant.[28] ...

Mention was made of a clip sheet of an article published in the Wall Street Journal regarding the Church and making particular reference to

---

28. This despite the church's general opposition to artificial conception. See Bergera, *Statements*, 27–29.

the Church's attitude recently expressed regarding the proposed repeal of Section 14(b) of the Taft-Hartley Law. The article expresses the view that the Church had modified its original statement on this subject. I asked President [Hugh B.] Brown regarding the statement attributed to him in the article to the effect that "Congressmen have the right to tell us we can jump in the Lake." President Brown said that he had made no such statement.[29] ...

A letter was read from Senator Wallace F. Bennett enclosing a copy of an amendment to the Taft-Hartley Act repealer, which amendment is a conscientious objection amendment. Senator Bennett suggests that the First Presidency may wish to refer this item to legal counsel to determine whether membership in the LDS Church would qualify an individual to claim the right given under the amendment. It was decided to tell Senator Bennett that we do not wish to become involved in this matter.

August 25, 1965, First Presidency meeting. ... We met with LaMar Williams in regard to his appointment to go to Nigeria and take charge of the work of the church in that country. In discussing the matter with him, we had in mind that Brother Williams has received a temporary visa to go to Nigeria, with prospects that he can later obtain a permanent visa to do missionary work there.

Arrangements have been made for Elder Bryce Roger Wright[30] of Canada to accompany Brother Williams. It is understood that Brother Wright is among other things a typist and could be of real assistance to brother Williams. It is also the intention for Brother Wright to remain in Nigeria for his mission unless it may develop that Brother Williams cannot get a permanent visa, in which event Brother Wright could go to South Africa to complete his mission. It is Brother Williams' suggestion that he and Brother Wright go to Nigeria, and in the event Brother Williams is

29. For the article under discussion, see "Utah & the Mormons: As State Bids for Business, It Comes into Conflict with Church," *Wall Street Journal*, Aug. 10, 1965.

30. Bryce Roger Wright (1944–2003) was a young man from Lethbridge, Alberta. Besides having typing skills, he had the added advantage of being from Canada and therefore not needing a visa to enter Nigeria. However, he and Williams no sooner arrived than the First Presidency changed its mind and called them back. Wright was diverted to the British Mission in London (see entry for Nov. 4, 1965). After his mission he became a structural engineer. "Obituaries: Wright," *Lethbridge Herald*, July 4, 2003; Allen, "Would-be Saints," 236.

able to get a permanent visa, he would then return home and get his family and take them to Nigeria also. Brother Williams met with the First Presidency in their discussion of this situation and the First Presidency gave instructions to him regarding the proposed operations in Nigeria.

It was agreed that we should not in any way become involved with the educational program in Nigeria, that we should be entirely independent of the school there.[31] Elder Williams, upon arriving in Nigeria, will arrange to register the church there and then apply for a residential visa. Brother Williams stated that the people who have been investigating the Gospel in Nigeria are well acquainted with the fact that they cannot be given the Priesthood. I said that it should be definitely understood by them that we are making no concessions in this regard.

We emphasized that we do not wish Brother Williams or any of the missionaries to do proselyting work in Nigeria. The purpose of the mission largely is to confer with and baptize those who are ready for baptism, with the understanding that they should be carefully screened before baptism, and after these baptisms have been performed auxiliary organizations could be set up such as the Primary, the Relief society, the Sunday School, and the Mutual Improvement Associations.

In regard to Sacrament Meetings, it was to be understood that the Sacrament must be administered and passed to the congregation by the Priesthood and that it would not be proper for local people who do not hold the Priesthood to perform the service that Deacons perform of passing the Sacrament to the congregation. In other words, it will be necessary for the elders to handle the Sacrament, although, as is done elsewhere, the Sacrament may be passed from one to another on the benches by the individual members.

Elder Williams was cautioned to be very, very careful in regard to procedure and policy among these Nigerian people.

It was decided to set Brother Williams apart as President of the Nigerian Mission, and this ordinance will be taken care of later. It was also stated that the First Presidency should be Brother Williams' contact in all matters pertaining to the mission; that in other words, Nigeria

---

31. One of the larger groups seeking recognition from the LDS Church, with about 10,000 congregants, had established an educational facility called Brigham Young School. Allen, 240.

should not be attached to one of the missions at the present time. Elder Williams said that it had been decided to leave here for this mission on October 11. He mentioned that there are in other areas of Nigeria about 40 Latter-day Saints, white people, all told.

Elder Williams mentioned that the missionaries who were originally assigned to go to Nigeria with him had completed their missions elsewhere, that since returning home, however, they have indicated their readiness to go to Nigeria if the Brethren wish them to do so.

September 10, 1965, First Presidency meeting. President [Hugh B.] Brown reported attending with Elder [Marion G.] Romney the inspirational meetings of the Mexico Stake Conference held September 4 and 5, 1965. More than 2,000 persons attended, but not all could get into the building, the class rooms and the patio. Many were turned away. A tentative appointment had been arranged for President Brown and Elder Romney to meet the president of Mexico [Gustavo Díaz Ordaz], but a series of conferences he was holding with governors of the states of Mexico made it impossible.

A report was submitted by a government inspector who had investigated the President of the Mission [Harvey H. Taylor], President Harold [Brown][32] of the Mexico Stake, and Brother Dan Taylor,[33] Superintendent of [LDS] Schools [in Mexico]. He was given complete information and taken on a tour of the schools. He praised the Church for its service to Mexico and to the people. The inspector spoke to the people in the conference and encouraged the youth to heed the counsel of their Elders.

---

32. The diary has Harold Bowen, but the stake president was Harold Brown (1917–2009), an individual who worked for the CIA, according to his obituary (www.serenicare.com/notices/Harold–Brown). He was raised in the Mormon colonies in Chihuahua, so he grew up knowing Spanish. He served a mission to Argentina, worked at the US embassy in Uruguay, and was called as mission president to Argentina before completing a degree in political science at BYU. He went on to receive a doctorate at Harvard. From 1962 to 1970 he was the stake president in Mexico City and thereafter a regional representative.

33. Daniel Pierce Taylor (1924–2015) was born in Colonia Dublán. Like many who grew up there, he graduated from BYU. He returned to Mexico in 1958 as director of the Juárez Academy, and two years later became superintendent of church schools, necessitating a move to Mexico City where his father was mission president. While in office, the son increased the number of church schools in that country from four to thirty-five. He left the church's employ in 1968, and returned in 1973 to oversee church construction there. "Benemérito de las Américas," 97–98.

Elder Romney is invaluable to the Church in Mexico,[34] President Brown said. The Church, school, and building matters are in his hands. The government cooperates in many ways. It is pleased with the work being done in the schools. Steps are being taken to gain recognition of the Church and to obtain a permit to place the name of the Church on Church buildings.

The Church has been regarded as a social organization, taking care of social welfare of the people, and engaging in activities which have been recreational. The MIA program of activities has been used. Through Brother Romney's efforts the government is considering the application to recognize the Church as a Church to teach the Gospel. President Brown said he was issued a permit to preach the Gospel in Mexico. He expressed the opinion that the future of Mexico is more encouraging than it has been for a long time.

I said that this information on Mexico should be given to the Twelve, and that Elder Romney should give this report to the First Presidency and the Council without delay when they meet on Thursday.

President Brown said that four pieces of land have been acquired at different times to use as building sites, and that buildings must be commenced on two of these pieces of land immediately in order to protect the Church's title. There is a walkway through one of these properties, which will become permanent if permitted to go too long. In one other place foundations are dug and building is in progress. Brother [Mark B.] Garff or one of the men in the Building Department should look into the building program there. Membership is growing rapidly.

President Brown said that as you look at these people you become aware that you are talking to Indians, Lamanites, intelligent and enthusiastic, and that this is one of the most promising of all missionary fields.

September 17, 1965, 8:30 a.m. ... Upon invitation, [Salt Lake City] Mayor J. Bracken Lee, assistant Chief of Police Marvin Butterfield, and Homer Holmgren, City Attorney, met with the First Presidency. President N. Eldon Tanner excused.

We discussed rumors regarding a possible demonstration by Negroes at the October Conference. These city officials reported that they

---

34. Romney was born in Colonia Juárez, one of the LDS settlements in Chihuahua.

are prepared to handle any situation that should arise. I said that Negroes and others should not be permitted entrance upon the Tabernacle Grounds, or in the Tabernacle proper if carrying placards; otherwise, if they are peaceful there would be no objection to their entrance to the grounds or admittance to the Tabernacle. Brother [Wilford] Kirton, Church attorney, will be prepared to notify the police in case of need. The First Presidency will arrange to give counsel and instruction to our people to remain quiet and avoid anything that would cause a disturbance. It was the unanimous sentiment that this Negro demonstration matter is merely rumor, although it was agreed that we should be prepared for any emergency.[35]

September 24, 1965, 8:00–9:20 a.m. ... A special meeting of all the General Authorities was held in the Assembly Room on the third floor, at which Elder Mark B. Garff and his assistant, Fred Baker, of the Building Committee, made a report and presentation pertaining to the program heretofore followed in connection with building operations and proposing a new program which the new Building Committee is adopting.

I called on Elder Gordon B. Hinckley to open the meeting with prayer, and Elder A. Theodore Tuttle offered the closing prayer.

This presentation was practically the same as they gave at the First Presidency's meeting yesterday, and at my request Brother Garff gave the report this morning as I wanted the General Authorities to know about this new program, and to hear about their findings on the old program.

At the conclusion of the meeting, and before the closing prayer was offered, I made the following statement:

"Brethren, upon your shoulders rests one of the greatest responsibilities ever facing the Church. It will be up to you to discharge it under the inspiration of the Lord, and make this building program one of the far-reaching accomplishments of the Church. If Bishops of Wards, members of High Councils, and Presidencies of Stakes will make this building program applicable to local conditions, the program will be effective in

---

35. In Harold B. Lee's biography, mention is made of the "rumors of blacks invading Salt Lake City to take vengeance upon the saints and the Church." Goates, *Harold B. Lee*, 378.

forming character for the next fifty years. 'Our echoes roll from soul to soul, and go forever and ever.'[36]

"This building program touches the lives of many men, women, and children. If it is favorably effected it can be conducive to faithful membership in the Church; if unfavorable, it will be conducive to lack of efficiency in the Wards particularly, and, incidentally, in the Stakes. I believe we are going in the right direction, and that the effect on the membership will be favorable not only for the present but for years to come. We have the best group of men in the world. Your influence will be felt by the growing population. By 'growing' I mean many young people who are just beginning in life, and particularly will it be helpful to the Bishops of the Wards who have to deal with these things and who will conduct themselves in such a manner as to leave a favorable impression in the Stakes, Wards, and Branches. The Lord bless you, I pray in the name of Jesus, Amen."

It was a wonderful meeting, and an excellent spirit existed.

September 28, 1965, First Presidency meeting. President [N. Eldon] Tanner reported that with my approval he had had a visit with Truman G. Madsen and read to him a memorandum regarding his proposed study and report to the Church, and asked Brother Madsen to write a letter to the First Presidency setting out his understanding of the assignment given him. President Tanner read the letter that Brother Madsen had submitted stating that he had discussed the matter with President [Ernest L.] Wilkinson of the Brigham Young University, and that President Wilkinson feels that this assignment can be consistently related to his work at the University, and that the interests of the school and First Presidency can be coordinated. Brother Madsen asks how much of the material on the Church he gathers should be kept strictly confidential or subject to the First Presidency's approval. He will be preparing reports for the First Presidency, and he thinks that the First Presidency should have these reports before he makes any use of them. He is desirous of knowing, however, what he can use in articles and in classes that he may teach.

I said that this material should be submitted to the First Presidency

---

36. A line from Lord Alfred Tennyson's poem, "The Princess: The Splendour Falls on Castle Walls."

before it is submitted to others. President Tanner was high in his praise of Brother Madsen and of his capabilities.

September 30, 1965. My son, Dr. Edward McKay, called at the apartment and checked on my physical condition. We discussed the matter of whether or not I should attempt to stand at the pulpit and deliver the opening address of the Conference or have my son, Robert, read it for me as he did last Conference.

I decided that I would record the talk, and then if I am unable to give the talk, it will be given by tape recording rather than have anyone read it.

Called Arch Madsen of KSL, and asked him to arrange for the recording immediately. I then called my secretary, Clare [Middlemiss], and asked her to bring the manuscript of the talk to the apartment immediately. Within a few moments Clare was over to the apartment with the manuscript, and I read it over before the people from KSL arrived.

October 1, 1965. After prayer, I made the decision this morning that I would deliver my talk, and not have it broadcast by recording. I decided that I would ask President [Hugh B.] Brown to conduct the session.

October 2, 1965, 2:00 p.m. Upon the doctors' advice, did not attend this session [of general conference], so that I should have the energy to attend the Priesthood session this evening. However, Sister [Emma Ray] McKay and I watched the proceedings by Television. I asked President [Hugh B.] Brown to conduct this session.

October 15, 1965. After Clare [Middlemiss] had presented numerous letters and other important matters, I expressed appreciation to her for her devotion and steadfastness. I told her that I cannot remember when she took a vacation or any time off for herself; that she must not break her health.

Choosing of Another Counselor—I then told Clare that I think I shall choose Elder Thorpe B. Isaacson as a Counselor in the First Presidency; that I need more help. I told her to say nothing about it; that I have been giving it serious thought for some time.

October 18, 1965, 10:00 a.m. ... Had a conference with Elder Thorpe B.

Isaacson. He presented his itinerary for assignment under Elder Ezra Taft Benson to visit the European Missions. He said he is leaving [in] a week Saturday, and if the schedule outlined is followed he will be gone until the middle of December.

I told Elder Isaacson that he had better not be gone so long; that someone else would have to take the Stake Conferences.

I then said that after much prayer and serious thought, I had decided to call him as a Counselor in the First Presidency; that I should like to make the announcement before he leaves for Europe.

Brother Isaacson bowed his head and wept. He said he wanted me to know that he had never expected anything like this; that his only desire had been to help me. He then said, "I believe that I can say to you as Dr. Willard Richards said to the Prophet Joseph Smith, 'I will die for you if necessary.'" We both shed tears of brotherhood and affection. I told Elder Isaacson to plan to go over to Europe for about two weeks, filling necessary appointments; that I should like to make this announcement right away. I turned to Clare, who was present during this interview, and asked her to remind me of this.

After some discussion, Elder Isaacson left for his office.

October 19, 1965, 9:30–10:30 a.m. President and Sister Joseph Fielding Smith visited with Sister [Emma Ray] McKay and me. President Smith and I sat together on the couch in the living room, and as we clasped hands in brotherhood and understanding, talked and reminisced about our service together for nearly sixty years. Sister McKay and I enjoyed their visit very much.

October 21, 1965, 1:15–3:45 p.m. ... Met with my secretary, Clare [Middlemiss], for a few moments, and then told her to call Elder Thorpe B. Isaacson and tell him to come in.

Told Elder Isaacson that I had decided that someone should be assigned to take his Stake and Mission assignments in Europe. I again discussed with him the matter of his becoming one of the Counselors in the First Presidency. I stated that probably I should call the First Presidency and members of the Twelve into a special meeting right now, but when I noted the time, decided that it was too late to do that this afternoon. I then called my secretary and asked her to have Brother Ezra Taft Benson, who was waiting in the outer office, to come in. I told Brother Benson that I planned to call Elder Isaacson to be a counselor in the First Presidency, and asked him if he could support me in this, and he answered "One hundred percent, President McKay—I have expected it, and have been glad that you have used him over the past few months for various phases of your work."

Brother Benson then explained that he had wanted to see me about the fact that a very prominent man, representing a large group of Americans who are strongly in favor of freedom and the preserving of a conservative government, had approached him and solicited his support in their efforts to preserve freedom and conservative government in the United States.[37] He said that even the Republicans are becoming soft toward socialism and Communism, and that they may have to start a third party. I told Elder Benson that he must not have anything to do with a "third party;" that it would be completely useless; that, however, he should look into what these men have in mind.

Elder Benson then referred to an article by J. Edgar Hoover, and asked if it could be printed in the Improvement Era. He told me of the contents of the article, and I said that it would be all right to have this printed in the Era.[38] Elder Benson then left the office, and I continued my conversation with Elder Isaacson. I asked my secretary to call President Joseph Fielding Smith and ask him to come down, and when he came in I told him that I had called Elder Isaacson as my Counselor and asked him whether he could sustain me in that action, and President Smith said that he could one hundred percent. I also asked him if he could support Elder Isaacson, and he said that he could with all his heart.

I then took President Smith by the hand, and said that I wanted him also to serve as a Counselor in the First Presidency. That took President

---

37. According to Isaacson's account, which was included with the McKay diary, Benson "did not want to divulge the name of this man because it is so confidential." The man had asked Benson "to contact Senator Strom Thurmond of South Carolina," saying that with the backing of Benson and Thurmond, "they would take this [conservative agenda] throughout the states of the nation" and to the Republican convention.

38. Nothing from the FBI chief appeared in the church publication in 1965–66, but he did author an article for the church three years later. See J. Edgar Hoover, "The Evils of Obscene Materials," *Improvement Era*, May 1968.

Smith by surprise, and he said, "You mean you want me to serve in the First Presidency?" With tears in his eyes, President Smith said, "I'll do anything you ask me to do." He then reminded me of the years we have been together in the Council. I told President Smith that I knew he had been loyal to me and that I trusted him completely.

I told the Brethren that I would decide when to call them, and that they should stay close; that I would call a meeting of the Twelve and present this matter to them. I told President Smith to assign one of the other Brethren to take the Stake and Mission assignments in Europe that had been given to Elder Isaacson; that Elder Isaacson could take the Servicemen's Conference in Germany and then return home.

October 28, 1965, meeting of First Presidency and Twelve. Following the reports of the Brethren, I announced to the Brethren that after much deliberation and prayer, that I have considered it advisable to choose another counselor in the First Presidency, which would not be a violation of any precedent, and that I should like the approval of the Brethren in this. I mentioned that there is nothing wrong with me physically except when I start to talk, and then I have difficulty, and that a large part of my work involves a lot of talking. I said that I feel well enough, but my legs are not responding as I should like them to. I stated that I feel my present counselors should be relieved of some of their work and given some help. I told the Brethren that I would report to them later if they feel to approve of my choosing another man to be a counselor. Elder [Ezra Taft] Benson moved approval, and the motion was seconded and unanimously approved.

I then said that I appreciate the opportunity of meeting with the Brethren; that I love them all, and that I am sorry I cannot give them more help; that I keep pretty close to the office, to Sister [Emma Ray] McKay and family, and have enjoyed being in Huntsville the past week where the weather has been perfect—not a cloud in the sky; however, Huntsville is beautiful whether it is raining or snowing or the sun is shining.

I thanked the Brethren for their faith and prayers, and said Sister McKay is getting along very well; that she looks well and is feeling well. ...

4:30 p.m.— ... Called Elder Thorpe B. Isaacson into the office and told him that I had presented to the Brethren at Council meeting today the matter of choosing another counselor to which they gave their approval. I then called President Joseph Fielding Smith into the office, and in Elder Isaacson's presence told him again that I should like him to serve as a member of the First Presidency; that he would not lose his status as President of the Quorum of the Twelve. President Smith answered: "President McKay, I love and respect you, and I will do anything you want me to do." I said, "I know how you feel, and you have shown your loyalty. Can you work with Elder Isaacson?" President Smith answered, "Why certainly!"

I then directed my secretary, Clare [Middlemiss], to call Henry Smith[39] of the Deseret News and ask him to come over to the office. I gave him a statement regarding the appointment of the Brethren to the effect that they will be <u>Counselors in the First Presidency, and set apart as such</u>. Brother Smith is to prepare a statement for the press tomorrow and submit it to me tomorrow morning. I said that I shall have a meeting with the First Presidency and Council of the Twelve tomorrow morning and present this matter to them before anything is done.

October 29, 1965, 7:45 a.m. President [Joseph Fielding] Smith, Elder [Thorpe B.] Isaacson, and Henry Smith of the Deseret News came to my office in the Hotel. Clare Middlemiss, secretary, accompanied them. Brother Smith then read the statement which he has prepared to go into the Deseret News today, which included the following statement from me:

"Due to the increased work of the First Presidency, I should like to announce the choosing of President Joseph Fielding Smith and Elder Thorpe B. Isaacson as Counselors in the First Presidency, to assist in all duties of the First Presidency. They will be set apart as Counselors in the First Presidency. President Joseph Fielding Smith will maintain his status as President of the Quorum of the Twelve."

We approved of the statement as it is prepared. I then gave Brother Smith permission to have this printed in the papers if approved at the meeting of the First Presidency and Council of the Twelve to be held this morning at nine o'clock.

<u>9:00 a.m.</u>— ... The following is a copy of the minutes of a special

39. Henry A. Smith, editor of the Church News section of the *Deseret News* since 1931, was said to be "a close friend of President David O. McKay" (Roberts, *History of Church News*, 49). He was later appointed press secretary to the LDS First Presidency.

meeting of the First Presidency and the Council of the Twelve which was held in the Church Administration Building at 9:00 a.m.:

"President: Presidents David O. McKay and N. Eldon Tanner of the First Presidency; also the following Brethren of the council of the Twelve: President Joseph Fielding Smith and Elders Harold B. Lee, Spencer W. Kimball, Ezra Taft Benson, Delbert L. Stapley, LeGrand Richards, Richard L. Evans, Howard W. Hunter, and Gordon B. Hinckley. (President Hugh B. Brown in the South Pacific with Elder Thomas S. Monson.)

The opening prayer was offered by Elder Ezra Taft Benson.

<u>Calling of Counselors in the First Presidency</u>

President McKay referred to his announcement in the meeting of the council yesterday to the effect that he proposed to choose an additional Counselor to serve in the First Presidency, and that on that occasion the Council had indicated their approval by unanimous vote.

President McKay said: "This morning we report to you the fulfillment of that recommendation, and present the names of two brethren to act as counselors in the First Presidency; namely, Joseph Fielding Smith, President of the Twelve, and Thorpe B. Isaacson. We present those two for your consideration."

Elder Lee responded: "I being next to President Smith, if it is in order, I move the approval of your recommendation."

Elder Spencer W. Kimball said, "I would like to second it."

President McKay then said: "This will not affect the standing of either member. President Smith is President of the Twelve. This is just an addition. Brother Thorpe B. Isaacson is an Assistant to the Twelve. Brother Isaacson was notified to be present and he is here now."

President McKay then asked these Brethren: "Are you Brethren willing to accept this additional work?"

President Smith and Brother Isaacson both answered in the affirmative, and Brother Isaacson stated that he would do the best he could.

President [N. Eldon] Tanner then asked this question of President McKay: "You said that these two brethren would be counselors to the First Presidency. <u>Do you mean Counselors to the President in the First Presidency?</u>"

<u>President McKay answered, "Yes."</u>

621

President Tanner then inquired, "Wouldn't it be right and proper then to have President Smith as your First Counselor?"

President McKay answered, "No, we have two Counselors in the First Presidency already. You remain."

President Tanner then said, "These two Brethren will be Counselors in the First Presidency, not 'to' the First Presidency. You said 'to the First Presidency.' I was just trying to get this clear. They will be Counselors 'in' the First Presidency and not to the First Presidency."

President McKay said, "That is right. There will be four Counselors in the First Presidency, and President Smith will remain the President of the Twelve just the same."

President Joseph Fielding Smith then commented that this is not something that is new, because a similar situation existed in the days of the Prophet Joseph Smith.

President McKay then asked for the vote of the Brethren as to whether they favored the proposition, and the vote was unanimous. He asked if there was any opposition vote and there was none.

President McKay commented: "I am feeling a little better. The Lord is blessing me, and I am using my right hand better than I have done, but I find that talking is one of my important duties and my speech is affected, so if you will be patient with me, with my stuttering, I will do the best I can to fulfill my duties."

The President then said that these Brethren would be set apart later. The meeting adjourned."

November 4, 1965, meeting of First Presidency and Twelve. Elder Gordon B. Hinckley mentioned the work of Brother Lamar Williams, who is in Nigeria, and said he had received a telephone call from Sister [Nyal Bowen] Williams, who had told him that she had some reason to believe that Brother [Monroe] Fleming,[40] a colored man who works in the Hotel Utah, who is a member of the Church, may have some connection with NAACP, and she expressed the thought that we should be very careful

40. Monroe H. Fleming (1896–1982) was a sixty-nine-year-old waiter and coat checker at the Hotel Utah, a Mississippi native who converted to Mormonism, along with his wife, Frances, in her hometown of Salt Lake City. He was said to have encouraged prominent black musicians to perform in Utah. "Monroe Fleming, One of Fist Black Mormon Priests, Dies," *New York Times*, Aug. 5, 1982.

regarding the information we give him. Secondly, she wanted to know about her husband LaMar's trip to Nigeria, and when he was going to move his family there. She explained that Brother Williams is making arrangements to get permanent visas for himself and family with the thought that they would move there right after Christmas if he can get the visas. She further reported that day before yesterday she learned that he was negotiating with the office of immigration, and he thought that he would have a favorable response.

Elder [Harold B.] Lee commented that most of the Twelve have had occasion to be somewhat anxious about Brother Williams' connections in Nigeria, that they had talked about this in their Council meetings many times. He mentioned that Brother Williams had accepted invitations to speak at fireside groups, special interest groups, etc., and the subject they had asked him to speak about was his proposed mission to Nigeria.

Elder Lee said that Evan Wright, the former President of the South African Mission and one who had lived in South Africa for some years, had told him (Brother Lee) that he was shocked on one occasion to hear Brother Williams say that in his (Brother Williams') judgment the Negroes should receive at least the Aaronic Priesthood. Brother Wright said that if that statement were made in South Africa, or if they learned about it down there, it might close up our missionary effort in South Africa because there is a very strict policy of segregation.

Elder Lee further stated that Brother Williams had met him a couple of months ago on the sidewalk and said that he wanted to talk with him about the kind of organization he should set up in Nigeria. Elder Lee had told him that there is no other organization for us to set up but the church organization, and that he should talk to the President of the Church about anything that was to be done there.

Elder Lee said he wondered if this long delay in getting a permanent visa may not be evidence that the Lord is not ready to have this work done, and what he was concerned about is that if we go there with the NAACP on alert as they are to try to find something on the Church to warrant a demonstration, that if they learn that we baptize some Negro people and then have to send White missionaries to perform the ordinances of the Gospel, it could result in serious consequences, as to them it would indicate that we are considering the Negro as a second-class

623

citizen. He thought that to go there and do proselyting among the Nigerians would be about as dangerous a thing as we could do.

Elder Lee also referred to the work that had been done in bringing Nigerian students to attend the BYU, some of whom have been baptized while here, and that these students are attending the BYU on scholarships which Brother Williams has arranged through the help of a number of our brethren who have put up the money. He said this had created a social situation at the BYU, bringing a half a dozen Negro students in the midst of 18,000 of our own students. He stated that the Executive Committee had had little understanding of it, that it had never come to their attention, that it presented a program which it seems is going forward without proper permission, and that with Brother Williams working among these people in Nigeria, undoubtedly others will come, as many in fact as they can find money to support.

Elder Hinckley mentioned that he had been given to understand that it was the decision of the First Presidency that Brother Williams was not to encourage any more of these scholarship students.

President [N. Eldon] Tanner said that during the past six months arrangements had been made to take care of three of these students through collections, and that another student is there, making four all told; that one of the leaders who calls himself a Latter-day Saint, has sent another student from over there, and he is providing his own expense. He also stated that he understood two of these students have been baptized, perhaps three, and that Brother Williams had been definitely told to discourage any others from coming. He thought that had been the practice during the past three months.

In regard to the matter of Brother Williams' going there, President Tanner said Brother Williams had met with the First Presidency and discussed this possibility and was given approval to get his visitor's visa, he having been carrying on correspondence with these people quite regularly, that probably a year or a year and a half ago, Brother Williams was told by the First Presidency that we should not do anything further toward getting visas, that it was up to the people over there to get them, and they have been working on them. Recently Brother Williams received a letter from some man in the government telling him he could get a visitor's visa, and if he would go there, they thought they could get him a permanent visa. Brother Williams was told that he could go on this visitor's visa and endeavor to get a permanent visa, but he was not to do any baptizing or proselyting, that he could meet with these people while there and find out whether he could get a permanent visa.

President Tanner further stated that a young man by the name of [Bryce] Wright, who is a Canadian and has been called on a mission, was appointed to go with Brother Williams—he being Canadian it is not necessary that he have a visa. Brother Wright was called to fill a mission in the South African Mission, but was permitted to go with Brother Williams as his companion to Nigeria, and in the event a permanent visa could not be obtained, he was to go on to his mission in South Africa. Brother Williams was instructed that he should do no baptizing and no proselyting, that while there he was to determine whether or not he could get a permanent visa and then was to return home.

Elder Lee mentioned a discussion held in the council some few years ago as to whether or not we should gather the Negro members here in the valley together and give them a little chapel and set up a branch for our Negro members, that at first they seemed enthusiastic about the possibility, that they had not gone far, however, in talking about the matter until word came from the NAACP that the Church having planned now to take a step forward, they were demanding that the Church bring them in as full-fledged members with the Priesthood and all. It was then that Brother [Abner] Howells[41] and another Negro Church member advised that in their judgment we had better let the whole matter drop.

Elder [Mark E.] Petersen commented that this was right, that the NAACP had sent a committee of three or four Negro men and one White woman to the Council of the Twelve office demanding that they be permitted to organize this group for us. Elder Petersen said that personally he would like to see Brother Williams called home and kept home, and that we proceed no further with this program. He thought it would do us great damage.

Elder [Ezra Taft] Benson said he shared the feeling of the Brethren

---

41. Abner Leonard Howell (1877–1966) was from Louisiana, where his parents had been slaves. In 1921 he joined the LDS Church. When asked to investigate the possibility of segregating wards, he was given a letter of recommendation from apostle LeGrand Richards and a card that called him an "honorary high priest" (Young, "Howell").

who had expressed themselves on this question, that he was confident in his own mind from a study he had made of the Negro question that we are only seeing something being carried out today that was planned by the highest councils of the Communist party twenty years ago, and that Martin Luther King is an agent, if not a power in the Communist party. He said that this whole thing is being directed and supported and promoted by agents of the communist party, that the Negroes are being used in this whole question of Civil Rights, integration, etc., and that the NAACP are largely made up of men who are affiliated with from one to a dozen communist-front organizations, and he thought they would do anything in their power to embarrass the Church. Elder Benson thought we ought to be very careful what we do in the Negro field, whether it be in Nigeria, here, or any other place in the world, and he felt that so far as brother Williams is concerned, his work in Nigeria should be terminated and he be brought home to report.

Elder Petersen, referring to the young Canadian who is accompanying Brother Williams, Brother Wright, expressed the hope that he would not be sent to South Africa after his stay in Nigeria, that his experience in Nigeria might upset the situation in South Africa, particularly if they thought we were favoring the Negroes in their problems. He [Petersen] expressed the hope that Elder Wright would be assigned in England or somewhere else.

Elder Lee referred to his visit to South Africa three or four years ago, at which time he was instructed to endeavor to increase the church's quota of missionaries, and that the Prime Minister there had said that because the Archbishop of the Episcopal Church having proselyted among the Negroes there and having criticized their national policy regarding the Bantu,[42] all foreign missionaries were stopped from coming there, including our missionaries, until there could be a complete investigation. He said their investigation has indicated that we were not proselyting among the Bantu nor violating the tripartite policy; therefore, we were permitted to have a quota and he made the statement to Brother Lee

---

42. Bantu is the term white South Africans adopted in reference to native black people, rather than a tribal affiliation. Linguists also used the term to refer to a family of languages spoken in twenty-one countries throughout the southern third of the continent by the Hutu, Swazi, Tsonga, Tutsi, Zulu, and others.

and Brother [Glen G.] Fisher that we had been fairly treated because of our attitude toward this situation. Elder Lee said he was also told by a number of Saints that government investigators had made inquiry as to what the Church was doing among the native Bantu. In other words, they moved among our people to see if the truth were being told by our Church leaders, and finding that we were not working among them nor favoring them, they permitted us to have a quota of sixty missionaries, and now, plus our local missionaries, we have, including those sent to Rhodesia, 75. Elder Lee said he came back recommending that we do nothing about it, that we leave it as it was and that it would not be wise for us to agitate it at the moment.

Elder Hinckley mentioned that Brother Layton Alldredge who recently returned from presiding over the South African Mission had expressed the fear that if we took an interest in the Negroes it would jeopardize our position in South Africa.

Elder Petersen moved that Brother LaMar Williams be brought home at once, and that we assign Wright to one of the missions in Great Britain. This motion was seconded by Elder [Delbert L.] Stapley and unanimously approved.

November 9, 1965, First Presidency meeting. Held a meeting of the First Presidency, at which meeting all four Counselors were present for the first time since Presidents [Joseph Fielding] Smith and [Thorpe B.] Isaacson were set apart as Counselors. I greeted the Brethren and made the following comments:

I welcome you as the counselors in the First Presidency, and acknowledge with hesitancy that I am not so well as I used to be, and have called you Brethren as Counselors in the First Presidency to help carry on the work. I pray the Lord's blessings to attend us in this Quorum of the Presidency. It is nothing new in the Church—The Prophet Joseph had several Counselors; President Brigham Young had seven at one time, I think; and this will constitute the Quorum of the First Presidency now. I should like to meet regularly with you and take up matters and preserve the Quorum as occasion requires.

I then asked each Counselor if he is willing to support me, and asked him to state his willingness this morning.

President Joseph Fielding Smith said: ["]President McKay, speaking, of course, for myself, I want to be absolutely loyal and bear you up; sustain you; pray for you, that the Lord will bless you and lengthen your life that you may have His Spirit with you always."

President Hugh B. Brown said: "I would like very much to continue, President McKay, with the loyal support which I have tried to give you, and help you in any way I can. I have no hesitancy and no reservation in expressions of love, admiration, and support."

President Nathan Eldon Tanner then said: "I can reiterate what I have said before several times. You are the President of the church and we certainly sustain you as a Prophet of God, and I just hope that I can be worthy of the great honor that has come to me to be a Counselor to you in the First Presidency."

President Thorpe B. Isaacson said: "I am very happy to be here this morning. I came home sooner than a lot of people expected, but I remember one of the statements in your letter, that we should make our visits effective and brief. I have had a great experience, particularly in the LDS Servicemen's Conference, something that would take me a long time to report. I am very glad to meet with you Brethren. I sincerely hope that we can have a feeling here of oneness; that there shall not be anything but what is right and proper and open and frank. I am sure we can develop a great love and affection for one another."

November 15, 1965. Had a two-hour conference with President Thorpe B. Isaacson. We discussed a number of important Church matters.

November 19, 1965, 10:00–11:00 a.m. … Elder Ezra Taft Benson gave a report on the serious inroads the Communists have made in this country. Now that the United States Supreme Court has ruled that the Communist Party does not have to register in this country, they will have greater freedom than ever.

Elder Benson is pleading that the Church have a course of study for our Priesthood members on Free Agency, Communism, and the Constitution such as was prepared sometime ago, but never used.

I agreed that we should have a course of study on these subjects as I am convinced that our country is already on the road to Socialism, and that the Communists are making gains here. Elder Benson asked if President [Thorpe B.] Isaacson could go back East and take a two-day seminar on Communism and conditions in our country to be given in December by the John Birch Society. I said that it would not hurt President Isaacson to be informed on these matters. (Later, President Isaacson decided not to go; that inasmuch as he has records containing all the information to be given at the Seminar, he will listen to the recordings and get as much enlightenment as if he were to take the time to go back to the Seminar.)

November 23, 1965, First Presidency meeting. We first considered the report of the Budget Committee for 1966. The various departments have requested $34 million more than the anticipated income. There may be about $13 million unspent from the 1965 budget. In discussing this matter, the Presidency were of one mind; namely, that 7 million dollars of this $13 million be added to the 1966 income for budget purposes. It was felt by adding this $7 million to the 1966 budget we should be that much nearer to living within our income, the balance of $6 million to be held in reserve.

November 24, 1965, First Presidency meeting. Before leaving the room, President Hugh B. Brown asked to speak to me alone. He expressed his personal feelings regarding several matters, including the choosing of two new Counselors in the First Presidency, and the signing of letters and documents by five members of the First Presidency.

I told him that we should have harmony, and that I have nothing but love for the Brethren. I was not feeling very well, and really not up to a long discussion.[43]

November 30, 1965, 8:00 a.m. Met the Brethren of the First Presidency. Arrangements previously had been made for colored pictures to be taken of the First Presidency, including all five members; however, President Brown was not present, having called President Tanner last evening and told him that he was going to the hospital for a check-up. Since the photographers, who had come from Logan, said that it would be impossible

---

43. Neither Brown's official biography nor his memoirs discuss his discontent over these administrative problems.

to insert a picture of President Brown in color, we decided to postpone the taking of the picture until a later date. We were disappointed, because cameras and lights were arranged all over the room, and it meant a lot of dismantling of equipment. ...

Statements About This Life and the Other Side—I remarked to Clare [Middlemiss] that this life is a "veil of tears," and she answered, "Yes, it is, and sometimes I wish I were out of it." As I stood up to go, I said, "I Have come to the point where I think it would be glorious to be on the Other Side."

Clare looked shocked and said, "President McKay, that is the first time I have ever heard you say anything like that—you must not say that—it is all right for me to say it, but you must not—it will be good-bye for me when you go." Then she added, "If you will stick it out, I will, because I cannot imagine it here without your being here." I said, "Well, it is a pretty wonderful old world, and I like it." She exclaimed, "Well, that's more like it—that sounds more like the real you!"

I smiled, and got into my wheelchair, and Brother [Darcy] Wright wheeled me to the elevator and down to the garage where I got into the car and was taken to the apartment.

December 2, 1965, meeting of First Presidency and Twelve. In giving my report, I told the Brethren that the matter of the proposed missionary work among the Nigerians had given me considerable worry. I asked the Brethren to think about the question and to be prepared to discuss the whole matter as a Council at a later date.

I then stated that I think now is not the time to open up missionary work in that country, even though there is a strong feeling among the people there that they would like the Church to be represented.

I then read to the Brethren a letter received from Mr. O. J. Oko of Uyo, East Nigeria,[44] dated November 8, 1965, urging that "Elder LaMar Williams be returned to Nigeria immediately." I mentioned the visit of Brother Williams, and his return home because of the cablegram which the First Presidency had sent to him. I said that several thousand people

---

44. Uyo is seventy miles east of Aba in the southeastern region that in 1967–70 became the breakaway country of Biafra, and where an LDS mission would be created in 2002. Stewart and Martinich, *Reaching the Nations*, s.v. Nigeria.

in Nigeria have taken the name of the Church, and call themselves members of The Church of Jesus Christ of Latter-day Saints, and that the government has changed its attitude toward us.

I asked the Brethren to give the matter careful and prayerful thought so that it may have consideration later.

December 7, 1965, First Presidency meeting. We went over report of assessments made by Bishops in some Wards for building funds, this matter having been brought to the attention of the council of the First Presidency and Quorum of the Twelve on November 18, 1965. Particular attention was called to requests by Bishops for checks by Ward members given in advance and payable monthly, when checks, in some cases, have been sold at a discount in order to raise money for building funds.

We were agreed that this type of fund-raising should NOT be permitted, and that a letter of instructions should go to Presidents of Stakes and Bishops of wards notifying them of our opposition to such practices.

December 9, 1965, 7:45 p.m. … Sister [Emma Ray] McKay and I drove over to the Temple Square to attend ceremonies for the lighting of Temple Square for the Christmas Season. It is the first time in the history of the Square that it has been decorated in such a manner for the Yuletide.

We were driven to the south side of the Temple just below the fence which surrounds the Temple where the Tabernacle Choir was already stationed, and where rows of benches had been placed for those attending the ceremonies. Thousands of people were crowded onto the Square. All was dark as we drove through a narrow lane, with police officers and others holding the people back as we slowly wended our way to the platform.

It was very cold, and a stiff breeze was blowing so Sister McKay and I remained in the car. We rolled the windows down so that we could hear the program, the singing of the choir, etc.

When it came time for me to say a few words and push the button to turn on the lights, I was helped from the automobile to the microphone where I stood to give a brief message to the thousands who were gathered there.

At a given signal, I leaned over and switched on the lights which transformed the grounds into a dazzling array of forty-thousand brightly colored

Christmas lights covering trees, shrubs, walks, and buildings. A great sound of "ohs" and "ahs" went out from the audience as they beheld the spectacle.

I then briefly addressed the crowd and said that these lights are a symbol of the light shining in the hearts of every man, woman, and child during the Christmas Season; that our minds tonight should be on the Babe of Bethlehem, whose coming into the world Christmas morning reminds us all that each should have in his or her heart the love of Christ.

Following the ceremony, I got back into the car, and we were driven back to the Hotel.

I was happy that I was able to participate in this delightful ceremony.

December 10, 1965, meeting of First Presidency and Presiding Bishopric. Bishop John H. Vandenberg reported that the tithing receipts for the year to date are 8.03 percent above what they were a year ago. We then discussed with the Presiding Bishopric the desirability of encouraging the people to increase their fast offering payments and also their tithing payments. Bishop Vandenberg mentioned efforts that are being made along this line and made particular reference to the showing of the film "The Windows of Heaven" and stated that they are hoping to present this picture on television over KSL so that all people, members and non-members alike, might have the privilege of seeing it.

I said that it would be a blessing to the people, not because we need the money, but that the windows of heaven would open to them if they would pay their tithing.

December 19, 1965. Note by C[lare] M[iddlemiss]—Dr. L[ouis] E. Viko called secretary, Clare Middlemiss, at her home and said that he had examined President McKay this morning and that he found that President McKay is not so well; that his leg is a little more involved, and his heart is not quite so good as usual. He said that they have persuaded President McKay to cancel all appointments, and that that is why he called. He then asked the secretary to see that President McKay does not accept any appointments for the next week or ten days.

The secretary told Dr. Viko that she knew last week President McKay was not feeling so well; that he breathed heavily and seemed more tired than usual; that she had even made a note of it in his diary.

Dr. Viko said that he had tried to get President McKay to use oxygen again, but that he had turned it aside.

Dr. Viko further said that after he had given advice to President McKay, the President looked up at him and smiled and said: "What if I break your rules?" Dr. Viko said that there was no answer to that.

The secretary inquired if it would be all right if she took letters and other matters that had no problems connected with them to the President, and he said that that would be perfectly all right, as he needed something to keep him occupied.

16 Benson and Birchism, 1966

President [N. Eldon] Tanner called attention to newspaper notices that had been received regarding a talk to be given by Elder Ezra Taft Benson [on "the inroads Communism and Socialism are making in this country"], reading as follows: "The Honorable Ezra Taft Benson will be the keynote speaker by express permission of The Church of Jesus Christ of Latter-day Saints, David O. McKay." … I said that I feel Brother Benson should not be advertising that permission had been given him, and that in the future, should he write for such permission, I shall tell him that he is accepting the appointment on his own responsibility. —February 1, 1966

January 7, 1966, First Presidency meeting. Consideration was given to a request from Mark Anderson[1] of the Utah Forum for the American Idea for the use of the Assembly Hall to present a series of speakers at 8:00 p.m. on February 10, March 4, April 22, May 5, and June 4—these speakers to emphasize the American Idea. The speakers to appear are Ezra Taft Benson, February 10, 1966; W. Cleon Skousen, March 4, 1966; Al Leppet, April 22, 1966; John Stormer, May 5, 1966; and Clarence Manion, June 4, 1966.[2]

---

1. Mark Eugene Anderson (1926–2018) was an attorney in the Church Building Department and a John Birch Society section leader. He will later bring Robert W. Welch Jr., founder of the Birch Society, to Utah to speak. "Schedules Address," *Ogden Standard Examiner*, Aug. 22, 1966; Quinn, "Ezra Taft Benson," 46; *Deseret News*, Feb. 18, 1966, www.legacy.com. See also the entry for Feb. 18, 1966.

2. These speakers were either members of the John Birch Society or sympathetic with it. John A. Stormer, a prominent anti-Communist writer and a pastor, wrote a number of right-wing books, most notably *None Dare Call It Treason* (1964), which reportedly

President [N. Eldon] Tanner suggested that this smacks very much of the John Birch Society.

President [Thorpe B.] Isaacson stated that in approving this series it should be done with the understanding that any additional speakers should come to the First Presidency for approval. He said that he could see no objection to any of these speakers who are on the list submitted.

President [Joseph Fielding] Smith said that he would be in favor of granting the permission requested with the provision that if we find anyone of the speakers saying anything harmful to the Government we should withdraw our permission for the other speakers. This became the sentiment of the meeting. It was decided to so notify Mark Anderson in answer to his letter.

January 11, 1966, First Presidency meeting. A letter was read from … Seattle, complaining about the First Presidency's attitude toward the John Birch Society, and urging that something be done to correct this situation, and that the Church indicate its opposition to Communism. In discussing the matter, the Brethren were agreed that the Church is looking to the First Presidency to take some stand on this matter.

<u>I said that I think the time has come for the First Presidency to make a statement as to the Church's attitude regarding Communism; that this, however, should have nothing whatever to do with the Birch Society, and should be a message from the First Presidency of the Church.</u>

The Brethren agreed that there is a great need for such a message, and I was persuaded that I am the one who should prepare such a statement.

January 25, 1966, First Presidency meeting. It was mentioned that the General Authorities are asking for a letter from the First Presidency indicating their attitude toward the observance of the fast. There was read to us an excerpt from a letter dated May 20, 1963, … which excerpt met with our unanimous approval. It was decided to submit to the General Authorities a copy of this statement for their information and guidance. The statement reads as follows:

---

sold millions of copies. Clarence Manion (1896–1975) was the long-time dean of the Notre Dame University School of Law, who wrote books on the dwindling influence of conservatism in American politics. Leppet was a lesser light in the movement.

"There is nothing in the revelations indicating the duration of the fast, the accepted meaning of the fast being to abstain from eating and drinking. It has normally been considered that a proper fast consists of refraining from eating two meals on fast day, and in practice the fast is usually broken after the Fast Meeting.

"President Joseph F. Smith, in discussing this subject as contained in Gospel Doctrine,[3] made this statement: 'It is more important to obtain the true spirit of love for God and man, "purity of heart and simplicity of intention," than it is to carry out the cold letter of the law. The Lord has instituted the fast on a reasonable and intelligent basis, and none of His works are vain or unwise ... but let it be remembered that the observance of the fast day by abstaining twenty-four hours from food and drink is not an absolute rule, it is no iron-clad law to us, but it is left with the people as a matter of conscience, to exercise wisdom and discretion.'"[4]

February 1, 1966, First Presidency meeting. President [N. Eldon] Tanner called attention to newspaper notices that had been received regarding a talk to be given by Elder Ezra Taft Benson, reading as follows: "The Honorable Ezra Taft Benson will be the keynote speaker by express permission of The Church of Jesus Christ of Latter-day Saints, David O. McKay." President Tanner said that this same matter had been brought to him from two or three different sources, and that those who have mentioned it to him have indicated their feeling that it is wrong for Brother Benson to be advertised as a speaker with President McKay's express permission. President Tanner said that these people had not come directly to him, but that these comments have been sent to him.

I said that I feel Brother Benson should not be advertising that permission had been given him, and that in the future should he write for such permission, I shall tell him that he is accepting the appointment on his own responsibility.[5]

---

3. *Gospel Doctrine* is a compilation of Joseph F. Smith's sermons and writings, published in 1919 as a priesthood lesson manual.

4. This principle seemed to need frequent reiteration (Mar. 16, 1962; Mar. 5, 1964; July 1, 1965).

5. The problem had been brewing for months. Senator Wallace F. Bennett (R–Utah) had come out against the Birch Society the previous October. In late December apostles Lee, Richards, Romney, Smith, and Stapley had thwarted an attempt to have

February 7, 1966. Was grieved to learn that President Thorpe B. Isaacson was stricken with a stroke this morning and taken to the hospital. He had just come home from the hospital last week and was planning to come to the office in a day or two. He is paralyzed down his right side, and is unable to speak.[6]

February 8, 1966, First Presidency meeting. President [Hugh B.] Brown reported that he is back at the office today for the first time in several weeks, and that the attack from which he is recovering is the most serious one he has ever had. He said that he coughed incessantly for four weeks, night and day; that his lungs were affected, and he is happy to be restored to health. ...

A letter was read from [the] President of the Anaheim Stake, stating that he had received a call from the assistant superintendent of the Anaheim High School District concerning 150 acres of Church property located in Anaheim, California, and asking him when the Church would commence construction of the [junior] college in Anaheim. In answer to my inquiry as to the status of this situation, President [N. Eldon] Tanner explained that [BYU dean of students] Dr. [J. Elliott] Cameron had made a report of his investigation and study pertaining to Church schools, that this report he had given to the Executive Committee and the Board of Education, at which time it was agreed that the report would be studied when I was present. President Tanner said that Brother [Harold B.] Lee has spoken about the matter on one or two occasions wondering when the report could be studied, that it would seem that the matter is now being held awaiting a meeting with the First Presidency.

I asked that a meeting be set up for the First Presidency to look over the report with the Executive Committee and Dr. Cameron. It was decided to have this meeting in my hotel office on Wednesday, February 16, at 8:30 a.m. (This meeting was later called off by me.)

February 9, 1966, 8:00 a.m. Met by appointment Elder Ezra Taft Benson who said that the editors of the "American Opinion" magazine would

Welch speak at BYU. In mid-January, Benson endorsed the Birch Society in Logan, and the next month he praised its *Blue Book*, Welch's *The Politician*, and the *American Opinion* magazine. Quinn, *Extensions*, 85–88.

6. The effects of Isaacson's stroke prevented him from rendering further service within the First Presidency. He would pass away ten months after McKay in November 1970.

like to have my portrait on the cover of their April issue. He said this magazine is published in Belmont, Massachusetts, and is a high-class publication. He showed me several past issues with pictures of Senator Barry Goldwater, the Honorable J. Edgar Hoover, Director of the FBI, and other prominent Americans. Brother Benson said that they needed a colored photograph and some biographical material, and I asked him to get these from my secretary, Clare [Middlemiss].

After discussing the matter, I could see no reason why I should not grant permission for the editors to use my picture.[7]

February 10, 1966, First Presidency meeting. There was called to our attention an action by the Council of the First Presidency and Quorum of the Twelve, January 28, 1960, to the effect that when any member of the General Authorities desires to write a book, the Brethren of the Twelve or the First Presidency should be consulted regarding it, that while the author need not obtain the approval of these Brethren, they should know of it[s] proposed publication before it is published, and that the authors should present their books to the Twelve or a committee appointed to consider the matter.

In this connection, it was mentioned that certain ones of the Brethren of the General Authorities have published and are now considering publishing books without consulting the First Presidency or Twelve.

We decided to send a copy of the action of the Council referred to [to] each of the General Authorities for their information and guidance. ...

Junior Colleges—By appointment met President Ernest L. Wilkinson of the Brigham Young University. He reported the word that had come to him in the East that Dr. Elliott Cameron was to hold everything in abeyance for a meeting with the First Presidency and Elder Harold B. Lee, at which time Dr. Cameron would give a report on Junior Colleges.

President Wilkinson said that he had not yet had time to go over the voluminous reports of Dr. Cameron, and that he would like to make a report to me on his opinion of the reports before any decision is made regarding the junior Colleges.

I said that I should like to have his opinion, and that furthermore

---

7. On this issue, see the diary entry and footnote under March 8, 1966.

I should like the meeting called off until all members of the First Presidency can be present; that we should wait and see the outcome of President [Thorpe B.] I[s]aacson's illness before we decide to hold a meeting on this matter. I asked President Wilkinson to stay close to me during this crisis with President Isaacson.

Following President Wilkinson's departure I called my secretary and told her to call President Joseph Fielding Smith and have him call off the meeting of the First Presidency on the matter of Junior Colleges until all members of the Presidency can be present.

February 14, 1966. I called Henry Smith and told him to publish in the Church Section as soon as possible the speech delivered by Elder [Ezra Taft] Benson in the Assembly Hall on Friday evening, February 11, 1966. This pertained to the inroads Communism and Socialism are making in this country. I told Brother Smith that I should like to have it published just as it is with a modification of what Elder Benson said about the John Birch Society. I asked Brother Smith to talk to Elder Benson about it—that we should not bring the John Birch Society into it [editorially]—that we do not oppose it, but as a Church we cannot support this Society more than any other Society of like nature.

February 15, 1966. Earl Hawkes, Manager of the Deseret News, called secretary, Clare Middlemiss, and wanted to know about Elder [Ezra Taft] Benson's talk being published in the Church Section. He said that a full coverage of it had been given in the daily on February 12. The secretary said that all she knew about the matter is that President McKay had personally called Henry Smith and told him to publish the talk in the Church Section as soon as possible.

3:00 p.m.—Earl Hawkes called on me at the apartment, without appointment. He seemed very disturbed about printing Elder Benson's talk in the Church Section. When he told me that a full account of Elder Benson's talk had been given in the Deseret News on February 12, the day after the talk, I agreed that there was no need to publish it again. The matter was left that way.

February 16, 1966. She [Clare Middlemiss] reported that Henry Smith of the Deseret News had called her and said that Earl Hawkes of the Deseret News had told him that I had countermanded the order to publish Elder Ezra Taft Benson's talk of February 11, 1966, in the Church Section of the News.

I answered that Brother Hawkes had called at my home yesterday and said that the talk had been published almost in full in the daily paper on February 12. Clare said that probably I should talk to Henry Smith about this matter, so I told her to get him on the phone and tell him to come right over.

Brother Smith arrived shortly thereafter, and he explained that Earl Hawkes had told him that I do not want Elder Benson's talk published in the Church Section. I said, "Well, I do, and it is going in." I said that Brother Hawkes gave me to understand that the talk had already been printed almost in full in the daily paper. Brother Smith said, "It was just a regular coverage, and was not in any way published in full."

I then told Brother Smith to go ahead with the printing of it in the Church Section, as I had heretofore instructed him.

Brother Smith later reported that Brother Hawkes was "furious" when he heard about it; and said to Brother Smith, "Shall I go to President McKay again?" and Brother Smith said to him, "I would not if I were you; just do as he has asked."

February 17, 1966. I told the Brethren that I am a little concerned about a request that has come to me from Brother Earl Hawkes, Manager of the Deseret News, asking that I sign a letter addressed to the International Committee of the Olympics recommending the bringing of the Olympics to Utah in 1972. I said that they want me to assure the committee that there will be no interference in the Olympics on the part of the Church in Salt Lake City. I asked the Brethren how they feel about the Olympics.

Several of the Brethren questioned the wisdom of the President of the Church signing any such letter, and said the question involved is what they mean by "interference"; that normally on such occasions they serve liquor, have many of their activities on the Sabbath, and do a lot of carousing. The Brethren also indicated that undoubtedly the Church will be solicited for a contribution to help finance the Olympics in the event the games are held in Utah.

It was the sentiment of the Brethren that the Church should have nothing whatever to do with the matter.

February 18, 1966. Elder [Mark B.] Garff [of the LDS Church Building Department] stated that a condition has developed in his office that has upset him terribly which must be corrected. He said that the John Birchers are moving into his office and are selling tickets. He said there is quite a propaganda going on in his office in regard to Brother [Ezra Taft] Benson's talk and the other four or five talks that are to be given in the Assembly Hall of a somewhat similar nature. Brother Garff said that he and his associates cannot be a party to supporting, buying and selling tickets for anybody or anything that is not sponsored by the Church. He stated that he has learned that there is a number of Birchers in the Building Department offices and there is one man in particular who must discontinue his propaganda or it will be necessary for him to discharge him. He said that these people are trying to infiltrate the John Birch Society into the Building Department through Brother Benson. He said he wanted me to know what he proposed to do, so that in case any complaints should come, I would be informed. He stated that so far as he was personally concerned, he was not going to permit them to use his department as a vehicle for the John Birch Society. Reference was made to the talk given in the Assembly Hall by Brother Benson in which he referred to the John Birch Society, which was responsible for some of the problem we are now confronting. Brother [N. Eldon] Tanner mentioned that we shall have a great division in the Church and that there is now much discussion and argument in some of the Priesthood meetings in the stakes on this Birch Society question.

Elder [Mark E.] Petersen mentioned Elder Benson's interview with representatives of the Associated Press while he was in Boise, stating that the John Birch Society is the greatest organization to save America. Brother Petersen said that people reading these things think the Church is giving its endorsement to the Society. Elder Petersen further said that in his speech at the Assembly Hall, Elder Benson gave strong endorsement to the Birch Society. Elder Garff said that the problem is we have so many people confused because Brother Benson is teaching and saying that the Birch Society is the thing that will save the nation, and that people even in the Building Department accept what Brother Benson says about the Birch Society, and it puts us in an awkward position.

I stated that I had heard Brother Benson's speech in the Assembly Hall by means of a wire connection with the Tabernacle; that Brother Benson gave a good talk on anti-communism until he started talking about the Birch Society, and that he went to an extreme in his remarks in this regard.

Elder Petersen stated that the Church Information Service had received a bill for $25 for a photograph of me which Brother Benson had requested, and it is proposed will be printed on the front page of the "American Opinion" magazine, which is the John Birch Society organ. According to Brother Petersen, Brother Benson had asked a photography shop in town to furnish a colored photograph of President McKay to be used on the cover of this magazine, the bill of $25 in payment therefore to be sent to the Church Information Service. Elder Petersen said that if my picture is so published it will certainly look as though the Church is endorsing the John Birch Society.

I said that my picture should not appear on this magazine; that the Church has nothing to do with the John Birch Society. I authorized Brother Petersen to tell Brother Benson that he had brought this matter to my attention, and had been told by me to stop the printing of my picture on this magazine; that I do not want it used in that way.

I said to Brother Petersen, "You are ordered in the presence of these men to stop it." I further said that I do not want to have anything to do with the John Birch Society; that the Church has had nothing to do with it in the past, and that so far as Brother Benson is concerned, I do not think we would hear anything more about it.

February 19, 1966. Elder [Ezra Taft] Benson said that Elder Mark E. Petersen had come to him and said that I had told him that I do not want my picture placed on the cover of the April [1966] issue of the American Opinion magazine.

Elder Benson asked me if I had withdrawn my permission to have this done as given to him when he called to see me on February 9. I asked Elder Benson how far they had gone into the preparation of this, and he said that he assumed that they are well into it; that the colored picture had been sent; that the artist in New York is working on it, and that all the biographical material had been sent to them.

Elder Benson said "All I want to know is what your pleasure is in this matter." I told Brother Benson that <u>they had better go ahead</u> with it since I had given my permission for this to be done. Elder Benson then said that they have carried pictures of Senator Barry Goldwater, J. Edgar Hoover, and others; that the magazine is considered a high-type magazine.

March 3, 1966, First Presidency meeting. A letter was read … referring to the activities of Elder Ezra Taft Benson and his son Reed Benson in reference to the John Birch Society. They make particular reference to Elder Benson's recent talk in the Assembly Hall and talks that are to be given by other speakers along the same lines. These young men say that they are in total disagreement with Brother Benson's ideology and that many other members of the Church feel the same way. They sustain him as a high official of the Church, but they are confused when he speaks on political matters. They inquire if in so doing he is speaking for the Church.

In discussing this matter, I said that we would tell Brother Benson not to mention the Birch Society in his remarks, and that I do not think we should mention the Birch Society or have anything to do with it. I said that I have been careful not to mention the Birch Society in remarks that I have made.

March 8, 1966. This meeting concerned the matter of my picture appearing on the cover of the April [1966] issue of the "American Opinion" magazine, and the publicity that has been given to it by the circulation manager of the magazine. Elder [Mark E.] Petersen said that if my picture is so published, "it will certainly look as though the President is endorsing The John Birch Society." Elder Ezra Taft Benson's participation in this matter was called to my attention by the three brethren present.[8]

---

8. Three days previously, McKay had left for a needed rest at his home in Huntsville. David Lawrence interrupted his father's peace with a "very urgent" visit by apostles Mark E. Petersen, Joseph Fielding Smith, and N. Eldon Tanner, accompanied by secretary Joseph Anderson, who took an eight-page verbatim transcription of the meeting. Petersen and Tanner were extremely agitated over a letter from the *American Opinion* circulation managers to Utah chapter leaders about how McKay's picture on their cover would be a "selling point for any Mormon prospects they might be trying to sign up." The

It was decided to telephone and also to send a telegram to the managing editor of the "American Opinion" magazine, telling him not to use my picture on the cover of the magazine in question. The following telegram was sent, signed by me, from the office of President [N. Eldon] Tanner: "Confirming telephone conversation with Mr. [Samuel] Blumenfeld have been informed that you plan to use my portrait on your magazine. This is unauthorized and must not be done. /s/ David O. McKay"

March 15, 1966. Received a telephone call while in Huntsville from President Nathan Eldon Tanner, who at the time was in a meeting of the First Presidency at the Church Administration Building. He reported the telegraphic request that had been received for use in the St. John Ward Cultural Hall for presentation of a film containing the talk given by Elder Ezra Taft Benson in the Assembly Hall on the Utah Forum Program, February 11, 1966. This film is being distributed by The John Birch Society.

President Tanner said that he had discussed the matter with President [Hugh B.] Brown and David Lawrence McKay, and that it was decided to telephone to me regarding it, which President Tanner did with Lawrence McKay listening in on the line.

I concurred in President Tanner's suggestion that permission should not be given for use of one of our cultural halls for this purpose. ...

Birch Society Dinner in Hotel Utah—It was reported that the Birch Society has made arrangements to hold a big dinner at the Hotel Utah, Thursday evening, April 7th, at 7:00, and that letters have been sent out to bishops of wards inviting them and their counselors to attend this dinner and listen to an address by Mr. Welch of the Birch organization, the price per plate being $15. ...

The brethren discussed at some length what should be done in regard to this matter. It was agreed that so far as the proposed broadcast on television over KSL and other stations of Elder Benson's remarks

---

apostles perceived disastrous results for the church, and Petersen said he had encountered evasiveness from Benson on getting this project interdicted. McKay had his son get Benson on the phone and tell him, in no uncertain terms, to let the magazine know the church would take all "necessary legal action" if the project were not stopped immediately.

in the Assembly Hall, President Tanner would talk to Arch Madsen about it and tell him to stop it if he has not already committed himself to carry the program.

The question was discussed as to the advisability of presenting this whole matter to the Council of the First Presidency and Quorum of the Twelve on Thursday next. The thought was also expressed that inasmuch as Elder Harold B. Lee is in the east he should be requested to return home to be present at the discussion. It was decided to postpone presentation of this matter to the Council until a week from Thursday when President McKay will no doubt be present, as will also Brother Lee and other members of the Twelve.

March 23, 1966, 7:45 a.m. Conference with Elder Ezra Taft Benson concerning the John Birch Society, the dinner to be held in Salt Lake City during Conference time for Robert Welch, and the article which appeared in the Deseret News[9] ...

I told Brother Benson that I think it would be best for him not to speak at strictly John Birch Society meetings, but approved of his filling speaking appointments already accepted which were not associated with that group.

March 25, 1966, 7:30 a.m. Brother Ezra Taft Benson called, and again discussed matters pertaining to his acceptance of various non-Church speaking appointments concerning freedom and Communism, etc.

(See following letter signed by Elder Benson, which contains subject matter discussed and counsel I gave him, which he submitted to me for my approval. This letter was read and approved by me.) ...

---

9. On March 16 the *Deseret News* published the following statement from the First Presidency: "Letters have been received by bishops and other officials of The Church of Jesus Christ of Latter-day Saints inviting them to attend a dinner in honor of Robert Welch, founder of the John Birch Society, to be held at the Hotel Utah. It is explained in the letter that since many people will be in Salt Lake City for General Conference it will be convenient for them to attend the dinner at that time. It also is explained that Elder Ezra Taft Benson will introduce Mr. Welch as the principal speaker of the evening. In order to avoid any misunderstanding we wish to notify bishops, other Church officers, and members of the Church in general, that the Church is not involved in this dinner in any way, and furthermore, that the Church has no connection with the John Birch Society whatever."

Dear President McKay:

Thank you for seeing me at an early hour this morning.

It is my understanding that you counseled me, after referring to our visit last Wednesday a.m. and the meeting in the Temple yesterday as follows:

1. Although you had advised me last Wednesday to attend the Freedom Dinner April 7 and introduce Mr. Welch else it would appear that I "was being slapped down," you advised me this morning to attend the dinner but to arrange for someone else to introduce Mr. Welch.

2. You counseled it would be best that I not speak at strictly John Birch Society meetings such as the so-called, testimonial dinners for Robert Welch. ...

4. I also reported I had learned that American Opinion Magazine would carry President J. Reuben Clark's photograph on the front cover with appropriate tribute to him as a great patriot. You said you had already been informed of this and commented, "I think that's all right." ...

I am still convinced that the John Birch Society is a great patriotic, non-political, voluntary, educational organization which is doing great good in the fight against the Godless socialist-communist conspiracy which you have warned is the greatest evil in this world. ...

If you feel at anytime I am getting off the right track please do as you promised and "tap me on the shoulder."

Faithfully your brother,

Ezra Taft Benson

March 29, 1966, First Presidency meeting. President [Hugh B.] Brown reported that Elder Mark E. Petersen had stated that while in Spokane over the weekend, he learned that the Birch people had met with the Stake Presidency and urged that all of them attend the Birch Society dinner to be given in the Hotel Utah on the evening of April 7. He mentioned that our people in Spokane had not seen the notice published by the First Presidency in the Deseret News regarding this dinner.

President [N. Eldon] Tanner reported that following the meeting on Thursday last, Elder Benson had told him that he thought he, President Tanner, was a little hard on him in his presentation of the case pertaining to his relationship to the Birch Society. President Tanner told Brother Benson he thought that he was as reasonable as he possibly could be under the circumstances. Elder Benson raised the question as to what he should do about the dinner to be given by the Birch people the evening of April 7. President Tanner told him that he did not see how the question could have been stated more clearly to him by the President and by the Twelve, that everyone wanted to let him know that he should discontinue speaking about the Birch Society and for it, and that President McKay in the discussion had said two or three times that he should not participate further with them.

Brother Benson inquired about the dinner, that in the letter that had been sent out it was announced that he would be in attendance and introduce the speaker. President Tanner said that he told Brother Benson that he could not give him any further answer than was given in the meeting on Thursday. Elder Benson asked President Tanner if he would clear this matter for him with President McKay, and President Tanner had said no, that he felt that it was just as clear as anything could be.

President Tanner told us that he was considering writing Elder Benson a letter mentioning the questions that he had asked him and giving him his understanding relative thereto, quoting from the minutes of the meeting at Huntsville and from the minutes of the Council meeting on Thursday last.

President Tanner asked me if that would be a good thing to do. I gave my approval, with the suggestion that President Tanner show the letter to me before it is sent.

I commented that I thought that it was made very clear to Brother Benson in the meeting Thursday that we do not want anything to do with the Birch Society. ...

General Authorities—Increase in Allowance to—President Tanner mentioned that Elder Delbert L. Stapley had discussed with him on Saturday last the matter of the allowance received by the General Authorities, and suggested that they be given an increase of $50 each. Elder Stapley mentioned that the cost of living has gone up 5.6 percent since the latest increase was allowed, and that it is anticipated that this cost of living wi[ll] go up another 2½ percent. Elder Stapley mentioned that his reason for suggesting that the matter be considered by the First

Presidency is that the last time an increase was given it was done after a review which was made at the President's request.

Elder Stapley had also suggested that the allowance to widows of the deceased General Authorities be increased from $150 to $175 or $200.

I agreed to the suggestion that the General Authorities be given an increase in allowance of $50 per month each, but said that the allowance to the widows should remain at $150.[10]

April 7, 1966, 4:00 p.m. My secretary, Clare [Middlemiss], came over. She had the corrected copy of the broadcast talk I shall deliver tomorrow morning at the General Conference. She said that it had been reported to her that the recording is all set up and if at the last moment I feel that I am unable to give the talk, the recording could be used to broadcast the talk; or if that is not what I want, Robert could read the talk for me. I stated "I am going to give my talk no matter what anyone says."

April 12, 1966, First Presidency meeting. We read a letter from Wilford G. Edling of the Church Finance Committee with which we enclosed a copy of the financial committee report to the First Presidency relative to the financial operations of the Church during 1965. Among other things he states that the Committee is pleased to find and report that in 1965 the funds received exceeded expenditures by more than 21 million dollars.

Much of the spending has been cut from the Building Department under the supervision of Elder Mark B. Garff, for which I am very thankful. ...

12:00 noon—April Conference—Statement on Communism to go in Church News

Clare [Middlemiss] took up some important letters and office matters. I asked her to call Henry Smith of the Deseret News Church Section, and have him come over right away. In a few moments he was at the office, and I told him that word had come that the statement I read on Communism at the General Priesthood Meeting Saturday evening, April 9, was not to go in the Church Section. Brother Smith said,

---

10. The $50 monthly raise was the equivalent of $400 in 2019. As a 5.6 percent cost-of-living adjustment, it would mean the apostles were making about $85,000 a year, the widows about $14,000.

"Yes that is right." I said, "Well it should go in. I made that statement to 85,000 Priesthood members; the press has it, and many recordings have been made of it. I think it had better go in." Brother Smith then departed to arrange to have the statement included with my other remarks.[11]

April 15, 1966. Clare [Middlemiss] presented the matter of my Priesthood message on the Church's stand on Communism and the printing of it in the Deseret News. She said that Henry Smith had called and told her that I had deleted two paragraphs from the statement. I said that I did not want those paragraphs taken out. Clare said that many recordings had been made of the statement and that many people are calling the office to find out why these paragraphs had been deleted.

I told Clare that my son Lawrence had come over at the request of the counselors and urged that I leave those particular paragraphs out, pointing out that they would tie the Church in with the John Birch Society. Clare said that many people had written and called and wanted to know if it is all right for them to study Communism, as many have been led to believe that they are entering politics when they talk about Communism. I said, "Well, they are not, and we should know about these things—the country is well on the road to Socialism."[12]

April 16, 1966, 8:00 a.m. ... Met by appointment at his request Elder Ezra Taft Benson who spent the next hour and a half telling me about

---

11. McKay (his address was read by his son, Robert) said that "Church members are at perfect liberty to act according to their own consciences in the matter of safeguarding our way of life. ... They are free to participate in nonchurch meetings that are held to warn people of the threat of Communism or any other theory or principle that will deprive us of our free agency or individual liberties vouchsafed by the Constitution of the United States." *One Hundred Thirty-sixth Annual Conference of the Church of Jesus Christ of Latter-day Saints*, Apr. 6, 9, 10, 1966, p. 109

12. This statement was picked up by the Birch Society and was later published in one of its bulletins, thus tying in the church to the society. Benson's authorized biography gives the impression that his political activities were sanctioned by McKay. Prince and Wright, on the other hand, conclude that "the combination of McKay's unwillingness to give Benson an ultimatum and Benson's willingness to assume *carte blanche* support from McKay, no matter what qualifications McKay had intended, ensured that Benson would continue to push his political agenda as long as McKay lived. It also ensured that Benson's fellow General Authorities who disagreed with his extremism would be continually frustrated in their attempts to rein him in, for he would always appeal directly to McKay" (*David O. McKay*, 312).

a visit he had received from two or three prominent Americans who explained to him that a movement is under way to set up a non-partisan committee to try and stem the drift towards socialism in this country, and to draft Senator Strom Thurmond[13] and him as candidates for the Vice-Presidency and Presidency respectively, which they propose to support through a committee to be named "the 1976 Committee," which will consist of 100 men and will include prominent men from all over the country.

He explained that the purpose of the committee is to "inspire, promote, and guide political action which will help restore, maintain, and strengthen our Republic." The committee is to hold a meeting in Chicago on April 30, at which time they propose to announce that all conservative Americans of both parties demand an immediate nomination and election of the "Honorable Ezra Taft Benson and Senator Thurmond to the Presidency and Vice-Presidency of the United States." ...

After reviewing this matter with Elder Benson, I expressed the feeling that it would not be wise to start a third party, and Elder Benson said that he also is opposed to this, but this Committee and movement might result in a realignment between the two political parties.

I said that this nation is rapidly moving down the road of soul-destroying socialism, and that I hoped and prayed that the efforts of the 1976 Committee would be successful in stemming the tide. I told Elder Benson not to withdraw his name; to let them go ahead and wait and see what develops.

April 17, 1966. This morning, Clare Middlemiss, secretary, received a call ... regarding missing paragraphs in President McKay's Priesthood statement which appeared in the Church Section of the Deseret News last evening.

---

13. James Strom Thurmond (1902–2003) enjoyed a long political career as governor of South Carolina, 1947–51, and as a US senator, 1956–2003. During the post-World War II social and racial turmoil, he ran in 1948 for the US presidency as a Dixiecrat, with a platform opposed to civil rights legislation and integration. He changed his party affiliation from Democrat to Republican in 1964. Even though he was a firm advocate of segregation, he fathered an African-American child when he was twenty-two—a fact that was not publicly acknowledged until after his death. He was also the only senator to turn one hundred while still in office.

[The caller] asked the secretary if she knew why some of the paragraphs had been left out, and she said that she did not; that she was surprised when she learned that they had been left out. He then asked if she thought it would be all right for him to write a letter to the editor of the paper, and she answered "You have your free agency; you may do as you wish in this matter."

Note by C[lare] M[iddlemiss]—At 12:30 p.m., Elder Ezra Taft Benson, upon instruction from President McKay, presented to Clare Middlemiss, secretary, confidential information regarding the Committee of 1976, which information had been given to President McKay yesterday morning. Elder Benson explained that President McKay had asked that the secretary follow through for him regarding the releasing of certain statements to the press already prepared and approved by President McKay. Elder Benson explained that he is leaving for assignments in Europe tomorrow morning, and will not be here when this matter is released, and that, therefore, President McKay has asked that the secretary keep in touch with him about the releasing of the statement, which will be sometime following the meeting to be held by the Committee in Chicago on April 30.[14]

April 18, 1966, 11:30 a.m. My secretary, who had been trying since early morning to see me, came over to the office. She had many matters that had accumulated. She showed me folders full of letters that had come to me from members of the John Birch Society commending me for the stand I have taken on the Constitution of the United States and Communism.[15] Many letters from members of the Church are protesting the recent editorial by Elder Mark E. Petersen which appeared in the Church Section, and the published statement of the First Presidency against the John Birch Society, and also protesting over the deletion of paragraphs from the statement on Communism that I made in the General Priesthood meeting, April 9.[16]

---

14. See Prince and Wright, *David O. McKay*, 315–18.

15. It is important to note that during the conference, Lee had given a talk strongly advising that if a man was in complete "harmony with the brethren" of his quorum, that was "the absolute test of the divinity of the calling" (Quinn, *Extensions*, 90).

16. The church asserted in an editorial in the *Deseret News* on March 26, 1966, that it had nothing to do with the John Birch Society: "nothing to do with racists, nothing to do with Birchers, nothing to do with any slanted group." McKay's reference to Petersen as the unattributed author was an inhouse secret.

I told Clare [Middlemiss] that I did not wish these paragraphs deleted; that I gave them and the statement should stand as given; that many people have recordings of the full statement. Clare said, "What shall I do? People are calling your office asking for copies of the statement in full." I told her to send out the statement as I gave it, and furthermore that it should be published in full on the editorial page of the Improvement Era for June.[17]

Later, Henry Smith of the Deseret news came over at my request and said that Brother [Earl] Hawkes, General Manager of the Deseret News, had reported to the counselors about the statement being run and they were the ones who asked my son Lawrence to come to me and have the paragraphs about people's studying Communism deleted as they feared these paragraphs would tie the Church in with the John Birch Society. Henry was then instructed by Hawkes to leave the paragraphs out. At the same time he was told to print Elder Harold B. Lee's talk in full after the Church Section was already set up and ready to go.

These things are very upsetting to me, and the deletion of what I said at Priesthood Meeting is causing a lot of people to question and to wonder what is going on.

April 19, 1966. ... Clare [Middlemiss] came over at my request with a large folder of letters and telegrams requesting that the Deseret News reprint in full the statement on Communism given at Priesthood in meeting, since they had deleted three paragraphs.

I smilingly said to Clare, "Well, they should reprint it."

I then called Brother [Earl] Hawks of the Deseret News and said, "Brother Hawkes, I have received so many requests for copies of my statement on Communism which I gave at Priesthood Meeting, and in full, that I have decided to have you run it again in next Saturday's Church Section."

Brother Hawkes could hardly speak for a moment, and then said, "All right." I then called my son Lawrence and told him that I was having the article reprinted in full, and he said, "Well I must see you about it."

That afternoon, Lawrence visited with me about reprinting the

17. See note 11 above. It should be acknowledged that Middlemiss was sympathetic to the church president's political posturing. Gibbons, *David O. McKay*, 380–83.

statement on Communism, and Lawrence was so upset about its being reprinted that I decided not to have it reprinted in the News. Lawrence therefore called Brother Hawkes and told him not to run it.

Clare then told me that Doyle Green of the <u>Improvement Era</u> had telephoned and has asked to run both my address and statement on Communism given at the Priesthood Meeting in the June issue of the Improvement Era.

I dictated a letter to Brother Green giving him permission to print both the address and the statement in this issue.

April 21, 1966. Henry A. Smith of the Church Section called Clare Middlemiss, secretary, and said, "Did you know that the Church Section is not going to run President McKay's statement on Communism in the Church News; that Lawrence McKay, under instructions from his father, had called Earl Hawkes, the Manager, and told him not to publish it[?]["]

Lawrence later came in and explained to the secretary his reasons for believing that the statement on Communism should not appear in full in the Church Section.[18]

April 22, 1966, 3:30 p.m. At my request, my secretary Clare [Middlemiss] came over. I discussed with her the matter of the statement on Communism which I asked my son Robert to read at the Priesthood Meeting of October Conference. I had in my hand a copy of the Church Section and noted that the statement had been left out. I said, "I made that statement, and it will be printed in its entirety in so many places that we cannot get away from it, and I made the statement, and there it stands. I have never seen people so upset, thinking that this statement will tie the Church in with the John Birch Society. We shall have more letters than ever now asking why the statement was left out. I do not believe it ties the Church in with the Society—the Church is not sponsoring it any more than any other anti-communism organization.["]

---

18. Middlemiss continued to cajole McKay in the direction of publishing his statement in full, while Lawrence continued to block her effort. "I have never seen my son Lawrence so upset—he hates the John Birch Society," McKay told her. Prince and Wright, *David O. McKay,* 314–15.

April 26, 1966. Clare [Middlemiss] mentioned that she is worried regarding her status should anything happen to me. She said she noticed that requests are coming from all General Authorities for an increase in their allowance because of the rise in the cost of living. She said that employees are now allowed to accumulate so many days of sick leave; that outside of hospitalization, she has never taken a day of sick leave; that she rarely takes even a holiday because every available moment she works at home on office work; also that now three weeks vacation are allowed for employees who have been with the Church fifteen years or more. She said that she has not had even one week of vacation in ten years, and has worked overtime nearly as many hours as regular time without compensation.

I told Clare that she is entitled to be retired at full salary for her years of overtime work and lack of vacations which I know go back many more than ten years, and that I would see to it that she is retired at full salary.

I asked Clare to have Brother LeGrand Richards, Chairman of the Personnel Committee, give me a list of salaries of all Church employees; that I should like to see what has been going on in the matter of salaries to employees.

May 14, 1966, 8:00 a.m. Elder Ezra Taft Benson came to the apartment and spent forty minutes talking to me about what had happened relative to the press release regarding the formation of the 1976 Committee of One-Hundred, and their desire to have him (Brother Benson) run for President of the United States.

He said more publicity was given to the matter in Europe than here in this country where Brother Benson was at the time attending to Church assignments. He said that no inquiry had come for the statement he had asked me to make to the press regarding this matter, but that he had released his own statement. He also said that none of the Brethren had made inquiry regarding it, except for Elder Delbert L. Stapley.

I said that is all right; we shall wait and see what develops. Brother Benson left me a brochure covering plans of the Committee. He said they have printed 100,000 of them. He also said that Dan Smoot[19] had devoted some columns to it in weekly papers, and that several other

---

19. Howard Drummond ("Dan") Smoot (1913–2003) was a former FBI agent turned ardent anti-Communist. He was best known for his *Dan Smoot Report*, used by

sources have carried good coverage regarding it, but that it is just getting started. I commented that I had always liked Dan Smoot who was formerly assistant to J. Edgar Hoover, National Director of the FBI, and had listened to his talks many times.

Brother Benson then said that he will be in the East next week, and that the "For God and Country Rally" is being held in Boston at that time.[20] Although I had told them by letter that Brother Benson was too busy with Church matters to speak at their rally this year, I told him that inasmuch as he will be in Boston that he may as well accept their invitation to speak at this Rally.

May 24, 1966. Alvin R. Dyer came in by appointment and presented two options to purchase real estate … at Adam Ondi-Ahman [Missouri].[21]

Brother Dyer said that this property is important to the Church as it contains areas of vital Church history, and that it is needed for the establishing of a bureau with facilities to engage the millions of tourists who will be visiting this area annually now that the Pattonsburg and other dams are to be erected creating a lake of considerable size.[22] He said that wealthy men are already purchasing property for the establishing of Hotels and resorts in this area. He said that it is his recommendation that the Church exercise these options at once; that they concern approximately 140 acres, more or less, at a cost of $234 per acre, or $60,000. These options expire June 1st and 2nd, 1966.

Brother Dyer then said that it would be a good thing if I could go to this area and inspect the property and see for myself the necessity of acquiring the property in question in order to protect the property we already own at Adam Ondi-Ahman. He said that these wealthy men are willing to pay much more to obtain the land than it has been offered to us.

Birch Society members and similar groups to decry the creep of Communism and Socialism and the precarious political nature of the US government.

20. The New England Rally for God, Family, and Country was a July event, thought to be a front for the John Birch Society. See Stephen Zorn, "Birchers Set Tone for Rally," "Try Victory, Benson Says," *Boston Globe*, July 4, 5, 1966.

21. Dyer had been involved in Adam-ondi-Ahman matters as early as 1959, in buying real estate and preserving the surrounding area. See diary entry for March 24, 1959.

22. After local people opposed the Pattonsburg dam, the concept was abandoned. No other dams would be built anywhere in the area either. Ron Wilder, "Efforts Made Fifty Years Ago to Alleviate Problems with Grand River," *Chillicothe News*, July 25, 2011.

I told Brother Dyer that since I had never visited Missouri and these historic sites, I should like to go and see these places. I said that I think I shall take President Joseph Fielding Smith with me; that we could leave Wednesday, June 1, and return the next morning in time for Council Meeting.

I then called President Smith and asked him to come right over to the apartment. When he arrived, I told him that I should like him to accompany Brother Alvin R. Dyer and me to make a plane trip to Missouri and look over the land at Adam Ondi-Ahman, and at the same time visit the other Church historic places there. President Smith said that he would be delighted and pleased to accompany me.

I then told Brother Dyer to make the plane reservations for June 1, at 10:00 a.m.[23]

May 26, 1966, First Presidency meeting. Discussed the matter of suitable housing for the Deseret News, and also the matter of the new Church Office Building. I said that there is much opposition to the erection of the new building, and President [N. Eldon] Tanner said that since we had decided not to go ahead with the building, the University Club Building[24] has been built, and that if we wait until there is no surplus space, we shall never build a building because smart businessmen will go forward in erecting buildings.

I said it would complicate the problem if it were announced to the businessmen that we are going ahead with this building notwithstanding the fact that there is a lot of empty office space; that there would be much opposition. It was thought that the Deseret News could go ahead with the building behind the Montgomery Ward Building.[25] President Tanner said that he feels that the longer we wait to commence the new high-rise [Church Office] building, the more it will cost; that the price of materials

---

23. From 1966 until his death, McKay was an enthusiastic supporter of Dyer's passion for historical sites, especially for the campaign to develop the old "Center Stakes of Zion."

24. Construction was completed at the end of 1965. The University Club office tower (236 E South Temple) was twenty-four stories tall.

25. The newspaper would move into a two-story building at 100 S Regent Street, between Main and State Streets, near where the old Montgomery Ward department store was located until 1960. Now there is an eight-story building in the same location as the previous two-story newspaper office building. The newspaper staff has moved across town to the Triad Center.

has gone up this year very materially, and if we had ordered the steel last year as he had argued, we would have saved hundreds of thousands of dollars. We are going ahead with the plans for the new building anyway, which I have agreed to. President Tanner suggested that sometime when I am talking with Mark Garff that I discuss the matter of the proposed erection of the new high rise office building with him. President Tanner said the study I had asked to be made will be completed by the first of July which will furnish us with information as to the office space that is available and what the requirements are.

I asked how high it is intended to make the new building, and President Tanner said twenty-five stories; that it will not all be used the first few years, but that he thinks it would be wrong to build it with less than twenty-five stories; that more space is not necessary.

May 27, 1966, First Presidency meeting. A letter was read from ... Berkeley, California, enclosing a circular which [the writer] states is being passed among Church members in the Bay area regarding Elder Benson and the John Birch Society. In his letter [the writer] says that reports regarding Elder Benson's expressed attitude regarding the Birch Society and the talks that he has given at Birch Society functions, etc., have caused confusion and misunderstanding among the members of the Church. President [Hugh B.] Brown mentioned that information had come to him that Brother Benson is still talking about the Birch Society and that the Birch people have been showing at the BYU and in seminaries a film showing the riots on the University of California campus at Berkeley, California. In connection with it they say that the riots were instigated by the Communists and that the Birch Society are fighting these things.

President Brown further stated that the Birch people are claiming that the Communists will take over the Constitution and are asking their people to arm themselves and a great many of them have guns in their homes.

President Brown also mentioned that Brother Benson had converted some of our people in Europe to the Birch Society philosophy, and mentioned particularly Mark Anderson, who was formerly President of the Finnish Mission.

I asked President Brown to furnish me with evidence that Brother

Benson has been active within the past month in promoting Birch Society philosophy.

May 28, 1966, 8:30 a.m. In response to a telephone call from Elder Ezra Taft Benson at 7:45 this morning, I met him at 8:30. Had a very interesting interview with him.[26]

June 3, 1966, First Presidency meeting. President [N. Eldon] Tanner called attention to a letter that he has received from Aziz Atiya, who is a Coptic and is teaching at the University of Utah. Mr. Atiya claims to have located the original papyrus of the Book of Abraham, which the Prophet Joseph [Smith] translated, and which now appears in the Pearl of Great Price. With his letter, Mr. Atiya enclosed pictures of some of the papyrus and a copy of a letter which had been found dated May 26, 1846, signed by L[ewis] C. Bidamon and Emma [Smith] Bidamon, and a son of Joseph [Smith]. The letter certifies to the sale of four Egyptian mummies with records, which mummies it is stated were found to be the family of Pharaoh, King of Egypt. Mr. Atiya says that this is the greatest find that he has ever had, that it thrills him more than anything else. He states that if we are satisfied that this papyrus is bona fide, and if we wish to obtain it, he feels that he could arrange to secure it for us through some exchange arrangement. He also suggests that if we should like Dr. Hugh Nibley to check these things he would be glad to have him do so.

It was our sentiment that these things be referred to Dr. Nibley for his study and report.[27]

June 6, 1966. Brother Alvin R. Dyer came in by appointment and

---

26. In the "Minutes of a meeting with President McKay by Elder Ezra Taft Benson," the apostle gave a sanguine report on the progress of the 1976 Committee. He said that the church president "was very pleased to [hear] it and hoped I would do nothing to interfere with the movement following a natural course. He indicated the country needs strong, conservative, spiritual leadership, as it has never needed it before in our day."

27. It was previously assumed that these documents and artifacts had been destroyed in the Chicago fire of 1871. Because of Atiya's familiarity with the items pictured in the LDS Pearl of Great Price, he recognized them when he encountered them in the museum archives in New York. He was the founder of the Middle East Center at the University of Utah and a recognized expert. Nibley was a religion professor at BYU.

presented the two options to purchase real estate ... at Adam–Ondi–Ahman [Missouri].

Brother Dyer recommends, in which recommendation I concur, having visited and inspected the property in question, that the Church should exercise these options at once. I therefore, prepared a directive to the Expenditures Committee asking that they appropriate $60,000 for the purchase of these 140 acres.

I asked Brother Dyer to have Mark B. Garff of the Building Committee submit the directive and request for the appropriation at the meeting of the Expenditures Committee tomorrow morning.

June 7, 1966, First Presidency meeting. President [Hugh B.] Brown mentioned that Brother Mark B. Garff, Chairman of the Building Committee, had said that there would come before the Expenditures Committee a proposition that we purchase some land in Adam–Ondi–Ahman. President Brown inquired if that would come before the committee as a settled matter or for consideration, or what I should like. President Brown said he knew nothing about the matter. He understood that it involved a $60,000 investment and that Brother Garff had wanted to know whether he is to present it as a request from me for the approval of the Expenditures Committee, or whether I want them to look into the details. I said it is my desire that they look into the details of the situation. I mentioned that I had visited Adam–Ondi–Ahman a week ago with President [Joseph Fielding] Smith and others.

June 8, 1966. Elder Alvin R. Dyer came in by appointment regarding the purchase of the 140 acres of land at Adam–Ondi–Ahman, which I had inspected, and had later sent a letter to the Expenditures Committee asking them to appropriate the money for the purchase of this property. Brother Dyer said that the Expenditures Committee had refused to endorse the purchase when the matter was presented by Elder Mark B. Garff under my instructions. I told Brother Dyer that the Counselors had reported to me and that I shall now ask them to go forward with the purchase of this land. Brother Dyer said that from an investment standpoint alone it would be good, because the Church could turn around tomorrow, and sell it for twice as much as we are paying for it.

<u>Adam–Ondi–Ahman—Purchase of Property</u>—Elder Alvin R. Dyer, Assistant to the Twelve, met with us and a discussion was held regarding the proposed purchase of additional lands at Adam–Ondi–Ahman near the site where the Pattonsburg Reservoir is to be built. This matter had been taken to the Expenditures Committee yesterday with a recommendation that the committee authorize the expenditure of $60,000 for land in the Spring Hill and Tower Hill areas. Elder Dyer reported that aerial photographs have been made and some money expended to make proper identification of these places.

It was reported that when this matter was discussed in the Expenditures Committee meeting yesterday, some question was raised as to the need for the amount of land suggested, namely, 140 acres, and also as to the cost of the land. It was Brother Dyer's understanding that the price we would have to pay for the land is $234 per acre, whereas if there are only 140 acres and we pay $60,000 for the land, it would mean that we are paying over $400 per acre. It was understood by the brethren that the question involved is whether we want to build a Bureau of Information there and a place to receive and instruct tourists, and in connection therewith the amount of land that would be required to take care of the project. Elder Dyer explained somewhat the history of the area and the Church's need as he understood it for owning this property. In answer to an inquiry as to how many people would visit the area after the dam is completed he stated that estimates indicate that there will probably be four or five million people visit it each year.

President [N. Eldon] Tanner reported that in discussing the matter in the Expenditures Committee yesterday, the brethren indicated that if it was my desire that this land be purchased, they would of course have no objection. The land which it is proposed to buy consists of two properties on which we have options, one of which would cost us $35,000 and the other $25,000.

Elder Dyer thought this would be a wonderful opportunity for us to tell the story of the Church to the people who will come to that area for recreation purposes. Elder Dyer said that if we want the property, we should go ahead and exercise our options on it. He stated that he would check the acreage as he was not sure on that point.

Following the discussion, <u>I authorized Brother Dyer to prepare the papers for the acquisition of the property, and then go forward with the project</u>.

June 10, 1966, First Presidency meeting. President [N. Eldon] Tanner called attention to the authorization heretofore given for a committee acting under [librarian] Lyman Tyler's supervision to do historic research work and writing on Church institutions during the Twentieth Century. President Tanner explained that Brother Tyler, who is on sabbatical leave from the BYU and to whom we are paying his half salary allowance, has left the BYU and has taken over a project with the University of Utah. It is proposed to use the services of Leonard Arrington in this project to write the history of our Church institutions. President Tanner reported that Elders Mark E. Petersen, Richard L. Evans, and Gordon B. Hinckley are enthusiastic about the proposal, that they have met with Brother Arrington, who has expressed a willingness to be the general editor of this project. Those who will be associated with him in carrying out the program at present will be John Sorenson, Dean Mann, and Davis Bitton. These brethren are asking if this assignment could be accepted by them as their major Church assignment; in other words, that they would not be asked to perform other major Church responsibilities while on this assignment inasmuch as this would be unpaid service.[28]

I authorized President Tanner to write letters of commendation to these people granting the permission suggested, President Tanner to sign the letter for the First Presidency.

June 27, 1966, First Presidency meeting. President [N. Eldon] Tanner mentioned that Brother [E. Earl] Hawkes had asked if we would favor the setting up of a small committee in the interest of maintaining the Church's position in the City. He feared that we are losing our heritage by letting people come in from the outside and take over things and run

---

28. The project lasted only a few months. Davis Bitton passed away in 2007. Dean Mann, in a conversation with Harvard Heath, said he could not recall specifics, and John Sorenson could not remember much beyond preliminary interviews conducted with a few church leaders before the project was discontinued. Arrington and Bitton would nevertheless become two of the three principals in the Historical Division when it was formed in 1972.

them. He felt that there were several places where we would be justified in taking measures to maintain our interest and our position. It was Brother Hawkes' suggestion that <u>a committee of men in whom the Presidency have confidence might work together and keep in touch with what is going on and report to the First Presidency</u>. He mentioned as brethren who might be used on the committee: Roy Simmons of Zions Bank; Wendell Adams, Assistant Manager of ZCMI; Arch Madsen of KSL; and he himself as manager of Deseret News. President Tanner said that his feeling was that we should encourage these men to meet together unofficially to talk this situation over and report to us what they have in mind more specifically and how they propose to proceed. President Tanner said it would be his purpose to tell them to meet unofficially without any appointment and give us the benefit of any ideas they have. I gave my approval for this.

July 5, 1966, 8:00 a.m. ... According to appointment, I met with Brother Bruce R. McConkie, of the First Council of Seventy. Brother McConkie discussed the matter of re-publishing his book "Mormon Doctrine." I asked him a number of questions about the original publication, about the need for the book, and asked him to give me the facts about what has been done since we stopped the publishing of the book.

He said that the book has been read with care by one of the brethren, but no one has gone over the corrections he has made since the reading.

I told Brother McConkie that should the book be re-published at this time, he will be responsible for what is in it, and that it will not be a Church publication. I said that Elder Spencer W. Kimball who has in the past been chairman of the Reading Committee should check the changes that he has made as a result of the prior reading.

I asked Brother McConkie to meet with Brother Kimball and give him this message.[29]

---

29. There is a discrepancy between McKay's account of this meeting and Mc-Conkie's letter summarizing it three days later. McConkie wrote: "President McKay discussed the entire matter with me, asked numerous questions about the original publication, about the need for the book, and about what happened since its publication. We discussed the fact that the book had been read with care by one of the Brethren, but that no one had gone over the corrections I had made as a result of this reading. President McKay indicated that *the book should be republished at this time* [italics added], said that I should be responsible for what was in it, that it would not be a church publication, and that Elder Spencer W. Kimball, who has been in the past chairman of the Reading

July 6, 1966. As I [Clare Middlemiss] was leaving the apartment, President McKay's daughter, Lou Jean, called me into her room, and we had a long talk about her father. She is very worried about the long meetings and the number of people who are coming in to see him. I told Lou Jean that I had made none of the meetings this morning; that they had been scheduled by the Counselors. She said, "Well, something has to be done as Father cannot take all this much longer." She indicated that she is planning to take her mother and father to Laguna Beach. I said I thought it would be a good thing to get him away as he has hardly left the apartment in weeks and needs a change of scenery. She said that she will not let anyone call him or get to him while he is in Laguna as she is very worried about him.

I told Lou Jean that I had not been away one day; that I had been nearby excepting when I have been hiding out at home ... and that even then I have been available by telephone. I stated that her father keeps telling me not to go away; that he feels satisfied when he knows I am around to look after things for him.

July 11, 1966. Went over the report that Brother [George] Jarvis of the Financial Committee gave me on the Nauvoo Restoration. Dr. LeRoy Kimball, the Chairman of the Committee, is asking for the appropriation of $500,000 in addition to the money set aside for the 1966 budget. I told my secretary that something must be done to put a stop to this spending at Nauvoo; that it will never be a "second Williamsburg" as they claim, and that I had put President [Thorpe B.] Isaacson on the Board to hold them down in their spending. Now that he is ill, someone else must be appointed to watch the situation for me.

July 12, 1966, First Presidency meeting. A letter was read ... dated July 3, 1966, asking regarding Sunday employment. He states that he is a student

---

Committee, should check the changes I have made in it as a result of the prior reading." This letter appears in McKay's diary under the date. As Prince suggests, "At that point, President McKay, age ninety-two and in failing health, did not take the matter up with his counselors or the Quorum of the Twelve ... McConkie, who practiced law prior to becoming a General Authority, was well versed in the legal meaning of words; and so one is hard pressed to conclude that he misunderstood McKay's cautionary statement, 'should the book be republished,' as a mandate to republish" (*David O. McKay*, 52).

at the BYU and that during the summer months he hopes to earn enough money to take him through the year at the school. [He] mentions that he has been forced to resign his job because he refused to work on Sundays, that prominent members of the Church—Bishops and Stake President, have told him that it would be all right to work on Sundays during the summer. [He] inquires if this is the attitude of the Church.

We decided to answer this young man that he should not work on Sunday; that the means is not justified by the end.

August 13, 1966. Note by C[lare] M[iddlemiss]: At 11:00 a.m., President McKay called Clare Middlemiss, secretary, at her home. He seemed to be greatly disturbed. He said to her: "Where is everybody—where is President [Hugh B.] Brown and President [N. Eldon] Tanner? I have been calling the office and cannot reach anyone!"

Clare answered, "It is Saturday. President Brown is in Alaska, and President Tanner is no doubt at home today."

President McKay seemed agitated and distraught, as though he had been worried about Church matters. He said, "Can you come right over?" Clare said, "I am at home, President McKay, but if you will give me a few moments to get ready, I shall be done in a short time." Then President McKay said, "What is going on? Aren't there a lot of letters for me to sign—how are things going?"

Clare answered, "Well, all right, but of course not so good as when you are there, but things are moving along."

President McKay never seemed so upset and worried; he seemed very worried about the office and his work. Clare then said, "I shall come down this afternoon or in the morning, President McKay—any time you wish me to come." He answered, "I shall call you later."

In a few moments Lou Jean, President McKay's daughter, telephoned to me and said, "Clare, did Daddy call you and ask you to come down?—you know the doctors do not want him to see anyone this week." I said, "Yes, he telephoned and wanted me to come right down, but when he learned that I was at home and busy, he did not insist that I come; and said that he would call me later. I am well aware that he should not get into his work yet, so I did not act too anxious to come." Lou Jean said, "He has been so sick." Clare said, "I know, Lou Jean, but he is very worried about his work. Dr. [Louis E.] Viko, knowing how worried he becomes, used to have me come over to see him for a few moments just to set his mind at rest. President McKay never seemed so upset and worried as he was this morning. He is so concerned about his work, and wants to know what is going on. But don't you worry, I shall not come until the doctors and the family feel it is all right for me to come."

About forty-five minutes later, Sherry, the nurse, telephoned to me and said, "Did I get the dickens from Lou Jean because President McKay called you; but Clare, I went into his office, and he was trying to get you on the telephone. He had called the office and couldn't get anyone to answer there, and when I came in, he took hold of my wrist, and said, 'Call my secretary; I want to talk to her!'"

The nurse said that Lou Jean had said to her, "You know he is not supposed to call Clare."

The nurse answered, "I cannot help it if he is dialing her, and instructs me to get her." The nurse then said to Clare, "I think they are doing a lot of harm to him, keeping you away from him; you are everything to his work, and it would make him feel better if you could be with him a few moments; you handle him better than anyone, and you make him feel good about his work. I know what you mean to him, and what you have done for him—the family does not understand. I am going to talk to Dr. [Alan P.] MacFarlane[30] because I think it is doing him more harm to let him sit here and fret and worry about what is going on—he wants to know."

Clare said, "He has stated over and over again that he wants to be kept informed of what is going on. Of course, I can understand the concern of the children—they are so worried about him."

That afternoon, Lou Jean and Lawrence took President and Sister McKay for a drive up to Huntsville, and there was no further call from President McKay to the secretary.

Later, Dr. MacFarlane gave orders that it would be better for Clare

---

30. Alan Palmer Macfarlane (1917–2002) was president of the LDS Hospital medical staff and professor of clinical medicine at the University of Utah, previously chair of internal medicine at LDS Hospital. He had attended Utah State University, and his medical degree was from Cornell University. During World War II, he was in the US Air Force. He and his wife would help open a church mission to Hungary in 1987–89.

to see President McKay and bring him up to date on his work, but that nothing of an upsetting nature is to be brought to him.

September 12, 1966, 10:30 a.m. ... In the office of the First Presidency, with a bevy of newspaper reporters and photographers, Sister [Emma Ray] McKay and I received Vice-President Hubert H. Humphrey[31] and Mrs. [Muriel] Humphrey. Congressman David King of Utah and national and local representatives of the Democratic Party were present. President Hugh B. Brown and Nathan Eldon Tanner were also present.

I told Mr. and Mrs. Humphrey how happy Mrs. McKay and I are to greet them; that it had been a long time, because of my health that I had come to the Administration Building, but that I was very happy to be able to be there this morning with Mrs. McKay to pay my respects. I said, "This is the first time our paths have crossed," and Mr. Humphrey said, "Yes, this is my first meeting with you." He then stated that President Johnson had asked him to convey his greetings and best wishes, and I said, "You take my greetings back to President Johnson; I value his friendship, and esteem him highly." Mr. Humphrey said "the President appreciates your thoughts and your prayers in these difficult days."

Vice-President Humphrey then said that "President [Lyndon B.] Johnson is a God-fearing and hard working man; that he works too hard all the time." I said, "It is not so easy to be the President of the United States."

I mentioned that I was pleased to see Mr. Humphrey looking so well, and he said that he is in good health.

September 16, 1966, 11:45 a.m. ... Former [US] Vice-President Richard M. Nixon, who is in Salt Lake for a speaking appointment at the Republican Rally to be held in the Terrace Room of the Prudential Building at 12:30 p.m., called on Sister [Emma Ray] McKay and me at the apartment in the Hotel. He was accompanied by Congressional candidate Sherman P. Lloyd, State Chairman Richard Richards, National Committeeman

31. Hubert Horatio Humphrey Jr. (1911–78) taught political science in St. Paul, Minnesota, before becoming mayor of Minneapolis and a US senator (D–Minn.), 1949–64, 1971–78, and US vice president, 1965–69. He ran for US president in 1968 and lost to Richard M. Nixon. He was a major force behind the Civil Rights Act of 1964 and creation of the Peace Corps.

Ken Garff, and Mrs. Janice Romney, State Vice-Chairwoman. My son, Lawrence McKay, and my secretary, Clare Middlemiss, and a number of newspaper reporters and photographers were also present.

Mr. Nixon greeted me by saying, "I called on you six years ago, and you are still looking strong and vigorous." I said, "Why shouldn't I? I was glad to see you then, and I am even happier to meet you now."

Mr. Nixon said that [it] reminded him of an incident of Winston Churchill when one of the photographers taking his picture on his Eightieth Birthday said, "You know, Mr. Churchill, I hope I shall have the opportunity of taking your picture on your Ninetieth Birthday." Churchill answered, "Well, young man, you look healthy enough to live that long!" "So, President McKay," continued Mr. Nixon, "I think we can all say that to you."

Then Mr. Nixon said, "You have a very outstanding Church all over the world, and your young missionaries and other members are a great group. Your missionaries in a sense are the non-governmental Peace Corps to the world." ...

He did not talk politics, and said that that was not his purpose for visiting me.

I was very pleasantly surprised to meet him, and was pleased to note that he had matured in looks and in his thinking. Sister McKay and I both enjoyed meeting with him.

September 23, 1966. Letter was sent to all General Authorities stating that when they wish to write a book, they are to submit a request to do so to the First Presidency or a member of the Twelve. Manuscript of book, if written, is to be submitted before publication.

October 20, 1966. <u>Note by C[lare] M[iddlemiss]</u>: ... Though President McKay had suffered a severe fall in the bathroom during the night, having tried to get there without bothering the night nurse, or disturbing anyone, he had insisted upon attending Council Meeting. He said nothing about this fall only to the chauffeur on the way down to Salt Lake. He had a large bump on his head and was quite stiff from the fall.

October 24, 1966. ... President Hugh B. Brown came to the cottage [in

Huntsville]. He had with him Elders Mark B. Garff and Fred Baker of the Church building Committee.

Report was made of Mark Garff's personal financial difficulties in his business ... During Brother Garff's absence from his business, his [replacement] has been running the business, and has invested large sums of money in the stock market and has lost the money, and has also gone into construction business in California which has been a losing proposition. Now their business is facing bankruptcy unless some financial assistance is forthcoming.

I told President Brown that he, Fred Baker, and Mark Garff are to work this thing out, and that no one else is to be brought into the matter.

October 30, 1966, 8:00 a.m. Mark Garff came in by appointment with President and Sister Joseph Fielding Smith. He reported that President [Hugh B.] Brown had called him last Friday, October 28, and told him to resign. He said that he asked President Brown "Does President McKay want me to resign?" and that President Brown replied, "I am sorry, we want a letter of resignation from you."

Last Monday, October 24, when President Brown and Brothers Garff and Fred Baker came up to Huntsville to see me, I told President Brown to go ahead and give Brother Garff the help he needs to get him out of his financial difficulty, and that he was to keep President [N. Eldon] Tanner out of it. Brother Garff needs two and one-half million dollars, which will be paid back to the Church. Fred Baker was to work out the details.

Then it was reported to me that President Brown went to President Tanner and the Church legal counsel, Wilford Kirton, about the matter, and then Lawrence McKay was brought into it. Hence the decision above.

Brother Garff has saved the Church millions of dollars at the sacrifice of his own personal business, and his [replacement] ... has done some investing in the stock market which has proved to be disastrous to the company. Now they need help or hundreds of people will go down with them.

Brother Garff was willing to give his all to the Church, and now the Church should help him, and he is of such calibre that he will pay every cent back.

October 31, 1966, 8:35 a.m. Elder Ezra Taft Benson called at the apartment and spent about fifteen minutes with me regarding my appointment with Mr. William J. Grede,[32] Chairman of the 1976 Committee, and Executive Vice-Chairman and Treasurer Charles R. Sligh, Jr.[33] He reviewed with me the objectives of the Committee which was organized on April 30, 1966, in Chicago, Illinois, and called to my attention the 1976 Committee brochure which I have already seen.

Elder Benson reviewed with me the draft effort which is under way to have him stand for the Presidency of the United States and Mr. Strom Thurmond for the Vice-Presidency. Elder Benson read to me the letter which I had written to Elder Benson which is as follows: ...

"Dear Brother Benson:
Herewith is a statement concerning the movement to draft you for the Presidency, which I intend to use at the appropriate time.

Statement by President David O. McKay
'I have been informed of the interest of many prominent Americans in a movement to draft Ezra Taft Benson for the Presidency. It appears that this is gaining momentum and is definitely crystalizing into a formal draft movement. Elder Benson has discussed this with me and to whatever extent he may wish to become receptive to this movement, his doing so has my full approval.'

May the Lord bless you in all of your patriotic endeavors to help preserve our inspired Constitution and our liberties.
Sincerely yours,
/s/ David O. McKay."

32. William J. Grede (1897–1989) was chairman and past president of Grede Foundries, comprising six industrial plants (Milwaukee Steel Foundry, etc.), and of J. I. Case Company, a manufacturer of heavy equipment. He was also a founder of the John Birch Society. He attended the University of Wisconsin until his service in the army during World War I. From 1951 to 1953 he was president of the National Association of Manufacturers.

33. Charles Robert Sligh Jr. (1906–97) manufactured furniture in Grand Rapids, Michigan. Like Grede, he was involved with the National Association of Manufacturers (NAM), and "when interrogated by reporters [in 1961], NAM executive vice president Charles Sligh insisted unconvincingly, and with some embarrassment, that NAM 'has no connection with the John Birch Society, and never has, and never will.'" Soffer, "National Association of Manufacturers," 786.

This letter has not as yet been released to the press. I reaffirmed my earlier statement to Elder Benson that I would support him in any effort which he might make in his efforts to help preserve the Constitution. I then asked Elder Benson to remain during the visit of Messrs. Grede and Sligh.

November 5, 1966, 8:00 a.m. … President Joseph Fielding Smith, Mark B. Garff, and his attorney Harold Boyer came to the office in the apartment at the Hotel Utah and discussed matters pertaining to the Garff–Ryberg and Garff Construction Company …

The business is now in a precarious condition financially. The Church attorney, Wilford Kirton, was called in, and the decision was reached that the Church cannot legally help the Garff Construction Company with Church funds, notwithstanding the fact that Mark B. Garff has saved the Church many millions of dollars since he took over the management of the Building Department.

Practically the whole morning was devoted to this matter. It has given me a great deal of concern and worry as I realize that Brother Garff has neglected his own private business in the interest of the Church.

November 10, 1966, 8:00 a.m. … Elder Delbert L. Stapley came in regarding the Church's appropriating money for the Nauvoo Restoration, Inc. He urged that the project there at Nauvoo must go forward; that we cannot stop now. He said that they had many visitors last year, and that they are making many converts.

November 15, 1966, First Presidency meeting. A letter was read from … an obstetrician residing in Ogden, referring to an address by President Joseph Fielding Smith entitled "The Blessing of Eternal Glory" as recorded in the Improvement Era. [The doctor] states that it is his understanding of President Smith's talk that no Latter-day Saint should ever use a contraceptive, space the children, or plan for them.[34] He states that he is a practicing physician, is giving contraceptive advice from time to time to young couples and counseling them in their marital problems, that in his advice he is

---

34. The church's position on birth control has evolved. See articles by LDS physician Lester E. Bush, "Birth Control among the Mormons" and "Ethical Issues in Reproductive Medicine," in *Dialogue: A Journal of Mormon Thought*, autumn 1976, summer 1985.

suggesting that they avoid pregnancy until they have been married at least a year. [The doctor] states that he would be pleased to come to Salt Lake City and meet with us about this matter if we desire him to do so.

We indicated our approval of the attitude of President Smith as expressed in his address. We decided, however, to invite [the doctor] to meet us regarding the subject.

November 16, 1966, First Presidency meeting. President [Hugh B.] Brown said that each of the Counselors (President [Thorpe B.] Isaacson excluded)[35] had read Elder [Ezra Taft] Benson's October Conference sermon, which Elder Benson desires to have printed in mimeograph form[36] for wider circulation. It was reported that President [N. Eldon] Tanner had called attention to certain parts of the talk which he indicates would give one the impression that Brother Benson and I stand alone among the General Authorities on the question of freedom. Brother Brown said that so far as he is concerned [it] is felt that the talk is wholly objectionable because it does impugn the other Brethren of the Authorities as to their motives when they have advised the people to live their religion and stay away from extremist ideas and philosophies.

We decided that the talk should not be mimeographed and distributed in pamphlet form.[37]

November 30, 1966. In discussing the affairs of my office [with Clare Middlemiss], I stated that one of the biggest disappointments of my life was the sudden illness of President Thorpe B. Isaacson; that I was

---

35. The diary has "exclused."

36. Mimeograph machines provided an in-office way of producing a limited number of copies from a stencil, powered by a hand-operated crank. When reference is made later in the entry to a possible "pamphlet," it suggests something entirely different.

37. Benson's conference address was entitled "Protecting Our Freedom—An Immediate Responsibility." Brown's and Tanner's objections dealt with passages such as these: "There are some who apparently feel that the fight for freedom is separate from the gospel ... [or that if we] just live the gospel, there's no need to get involved in trying to save freedom and the Constitution and stop Communism ... We will be given a chance to choose between conflicting counsel by some ... All men are entitled to inspiration, but only one man is the Lord's mouthpiece. Some lesser men have in the past, and will in the future, use their offices unrighteously. Some will, ignorantly or otherwise, use it to promote false counsel; some will use it to lead the unwary astray, some will use it to persuade us that all is well in Zion." *Improvement Era*, Dec. 1966.

so thankful for his support and loyalty that I felt relaxed and secure. I said that I had had great hopes that he would get well, but that now it looks as though it is not to be. I expressed regret over the opposition that had been shown toward him, and said that "no man either out or in the Church has ever talked to a President of this Church as I had been talked to by a certain counselor a little while before I appointed President Isaacson as a counselor.["] This has been a source of real concern to me.[38]

December 2, 1966. Elder [Ezra Taft] Benson said that the statement I had made on Communism at the April Conference of this year is being distributed by the hundreds of thousands. Brother Benson feels that it should be reprinted in the Instructor[39] and other Church magazines. I told him that so far as the Instructor is concerned, he could speak to Lawrence McKay about that.

Brother Benson also mentioned that he had written to the First Presidency asking for permission to mimeograph his talk given at the October Conference. As yet he has received no answer to the letter. However, in our meeting of the First Presidency on November 16, 1966, President [N. Eldon] Tanner called attention to certain parts of the talks which he (President Tanner) indicates would give one the impression that Brother Benson and I stand alone among the General Authorities on the question of freedom. President [Hugh B.] Brown said that so far as he is concerned, he felt that the talk is wholly objectionable because it does impugn the other brethren of the Authorities as to their motives when they have advised the people to live their religion and stay away from the extremist ideas and philosophies. At this meeting, we agreed that the talk should not be mimeographed and distributed in pamphlet form. However, later as I re-read Elder Benson's talk, I could see no objection to its being mimeographed and sent out. In his talk he had quoted almost in its entirety (and this with my permission) the statement that I had made on Communism at the October 1966 Conference. There is nothing wrong with the talk, so I told my secretary to tell Elder Benson he could have it mimeographed if he wished. Elder Benson informed

---

38. This refers to Tanner's objection to Isaacson. See Jan. 5, 1965.

39. The *Instructor* was a magazine for LDS Sunday school teachers, was discontinued after forty years in 1970.

the secretary that he had given practically the same talk at the Brigham Young University,[40] and that they had published it in pamphlet form and that it is receiving wide distribution. So the matter stands where it is now.

December 13, 1966, First Presidency meeting. President [Hugh B.] Brown called attention to a publication entitled "Tri-State News Advertiser" of December 8, 1966, which is published weekly at Hurricane, Utah, and of which Myrlon G. Brown is editor and publisher. The front page of the paper bears a headline, "America Offered Leadership," and reproduces a picture of Elder Benson. The lead article states, "1976 committee heads patriot's name Ezra Taft Benson for President. Church President David O. McKay gives approval." The editorial on the front page contains the following statement, which is attributed to the President of The Church of Jesus Christ of Latter-day Saints: "... [There are] many prominent Americans in a movement to draft Ezra Taft Benson for the presidency. It appears that this is gaining momentum and is definitely crystalizing into a formal draft movement. Elder Benson has discussed this with me, and to whatever extent he may wish to become receptive to this move, his doing so has my full approval."

President Brown was disturbed about this, and asked as to whether or not Elder Benson's proposed candidacy has my approval, and not remembering at the moment that I had given full permission for Elder Benson to stand ready to enter into this movement should circumstances permit, and said that I had not approved; but later recalled the whole matter and that Elder Benson had talked to me about the whole matter, and that I had given him permission to participate in this movement should it come to a point where he was drafted into it. ...

I therefore instructed Clare [Middlemiss] to tell Brother [Joseph] Anderson to strike out of the above minutes the statement that I did not approve, and state that I did not recall at the time that I had give[n] Elder Benson permission and had indeed dictated and signed the letter giving my approval to the matter.

---

40. Actually, in his BYU devotional, Benson used his general conference address as the basic theme of his talk, but lashed out in greater detail and specificity. "Do we preach what governments should or should not do as part of the Gospel plan, as President McKay has urged? Or do we follow the Prophet by preaching a limited gospel plan of salvation. ... We cannot compromise good from evil in an attempt to have peace and unity in the Church, any more than the Lord could have compromised with Satan in order to avoid the War in Heaven." Benson, "Our Immediate Responsibility."

December 20, 1966, First Presidency meeting. President [N. Eldon] Tanner called attention to a letter to the First Presidency from A. J. Oko of Nigeria, reporting that the Church has been registered with the federal government in Nigeria, and stating that a photostat copy of the registration certificate will be forwarded to us later. Mr. Oko states that the Church is gaining strength in Nigeria. He mentions the need of school teachers for their secondary schools, and suggests that some of our people be sent there to help them in their secondary schools, and also other missionaries.

We were agreed that we cannot do anything about this at the present time. President Tanner will prepare an answer to the letter.

December 21, 1966, 10:30 a.m. President and Mrs. Thorpe B. Isaacson came in. Sister Isaacson said that President Isaacson was very anxious to visit me personally to extend his Christmas greetings. I stood up as President Isaacson slowly approached the desk, walking with the aid of a cane, and his left arm in a sling. All he could say, with the tears streaming down his face was "hello" as he shook my hand. We kissed each other as loving brothers, and there were many tears shed as I told him how happy this visit had made me. I said to President Isaacson, "Nothing has hurt me more than your illness which has deprived me of your loyalty and strength!" As President Isaacson could not tell me, Sister Isaacson told me what they had been doing. She said that she drives her husband down to Provo to the BYU three times a week where President Isaacson has speech therapy, and then two or three times a week he goes up to the University of Utah Hospital where he has physical therapy. She said that he is trying very hard to get well so that he can come back and help me.

December 28, 1966, 9:30 a.m. ... Mr. Joseph Rosenblatt[41] met with us at our invitation. It was explained that we had learned the other day that there was some question of dissatisfaction on the part of Mr. Rosenblatt

---

41. Joseph Rosenblatt (1903–1999), a mining-equipment innovator and manufacturer, Utah philanthropist, and civic leader, was an ecumenical activist who was often working behind the scenes to improve relations and assuage tensions between Mormons and non-Mormons. He served as president of EIMCO (Eastern Iron and Metal Corporation) for over thirty years. Born in Salt Lake City, he earned a bachelor's degree from the University of Utah, followed by a law degree, and served on the board of the Federal Reserve Bank of San Francisco, 1965–74.

and the possibility of a suit pending against the N[ewspaper] A[gency] C[orporation] and probably the Deseret News, and that when I heard of this, I thought I would like to chat with Mr. Rosenblatt about it. Accordingly, at my request, President [N. Eldon] Tanner had arranged for Mr. Rosenblatt to come in this morning. President Tanner explained that the situation as we see it and as we go back over the history of the thing is that the Deseret News and the [Salt Lake] Tribune were losing a tremendous amount of money, each of them, and in order for both to stay in business, they arranged to organize the NAC, with a definite understanding that they would have two separate editorial and news gathering facilities, the NAC to do the printing. It was the feeling that it was very important that we have two editorial positions so that the people would have that advantage. Accordingly there was no joining of the papers other than in the two fields, one the printing of the paper, including the advertisements which appear in both papers, some advertising the Deseret News does not carry, and the other the editorial department.

Mr. Rosenblatt said that he would like to say first that there is no intention of any suit, that there never has been, and as long as anything that might be done would involve him or any of the interests he controlled in entering into a controversy, no matter how the equities might lie, with an organization representing the Church or that the Church had large holdings in, there would be no suit. Mr. Rosenblatt said that the [Rosenblatt] boys decided that the continuance of the paper they were operating was no longer economically sound. He said that his position as a father is that he is deeply concerned in seeing that his boys are gainfully employed, that he did not want to find himself closing his eyes to their living off an income and not doing anything that should be done. In other words, he was anxious to help them get into something. He said that his boys were trained a little in writing and he thought that if they wanted to try to get out a paper, to go ahead; that after it had operated for about three years it was apparent that it was not economically sound. He therefore told them to discontinue it.[42] It was their contention, he said, that one of the reasons

42. His sons Norman and Stephen Rosenblatt purchased the *Holladay Neighbor*, a weekly newspaper, in 1964. Norman had been on the staff of the *Yale Daily News* while attending the university. He and his wife moved to San Francisco, where he became a hotel developer and jazz musician. Stephen followed his father as an executive at EIMCO.

that made the paper so difficult was that there was a combination which made the advertising problem quite serious. Accordingly Mr. Rosenblatt talked to Mr. Jack Gallivan of the Tribune and told him that he was interested in making the community the kind of place that it should be and that it must be, that we must have the best government in the country, not just the best law obedience; that we ought not to have a poor government in the city, the county, or the state; that the people who are here in the majority have been taught things that are contrary to the way these political institutions are run, that we do not have here now the kind of code of ethics we should have in public office. He said he had talked to Mr. Gallivan about this many times.

Mr. Rosenblatt referred to the proposed Salt Palace and told Mr. Gallivan about how he was trying to bring to the city of Salt Lake, as an attraction, sports events that are going to bring to Salt Lake all the things that are contrary to what we in this community expect. He said the thing that brings the tourists are the Temple, the Church, and all that the Church has done in erecting beautiful buildings, that it is the understanding throughout the land that the Church stands for cultural things, for a tradition which leads men to do always better things, and he told Mr. Gallivan that, because he wants to bring in a sports arena just for business reasons. Mr. Rosenblatt said people are not going to come to Utah because they can get whisky; that they can buy it all over the United States; they are going to come to Utah because of the things that we know are here and have attracted them in the past, and that we should have here, particularly next to the Temple grounds, as fine a cultural center as exists in the United States. It should be of the best architecture and it should have gardens and it should match what is going to be across the street, that we have to make sure that what comes here will encourage people to believe that this is the way men and women conduct themselves in this area, and we will not find ourselves attracting an undesirable element of population of which we have too much in the United States. Mr. Rosenblatt said that he thinks Mr. Gallivan feels that business should be ahead of every other thing; that he, Mr. Rosenblatt, does not feel that way. He said he feels the chief obligation we should have in this city is to make it as beautiful a place, as peaceful a place, as fine a community where men and women live as we can bring together and maintain a cultural level that is not equaled anywhere else. He said that we have a background and tradition here that men and women have sacrificed themselves for in this community for over one-hundred years, and we must not change it. <u>Mr. Rosenblatt said that he told Mr. Gallivan that if he was not going to do anything about such things, he was going to sue him, and he said it has moved from that to one rumor after another</u>, but he said he wanted to say to me, and to those present, that there has never at any time been any thought in his mind that they would institute a suit for violation of anti-trust laws or whatever it is against the Deseret News and the Church or the NAC. He said if the News were not a member of the NAC and it was Mr. Gallivan alone, then it would become a cold business matter and would change the situation altogether, but as it is now, he said, no suit was even thought of. …

I expressed myself as being very happy to hear what Mr. Rosenblatt had said. Mr. Rosenblatt said he had a very serious feeling about this whole situation in the city and he wanted me and each of the Brethren to let him know if there was anything more he could do. President Tanner stated to Mr. Rosenblatt that if he had any suggestions as to how we could improve the Deseret News, we should be glad to receive them; that we are trying to do two things: to keep people advised of the news and to encourage higher moral standards, and this is mostly done through our Church Section weekly, but all the time we try to have a standard upheld through our editorials.

Mr. Rosenblatt said that the thing that he had tried to say to Earl Hawkes is that while we have to be informed as to the news on the local and national scene, the great opportunity we have is here in the city and the state and there is so much that can be done here; that men must understand when they accept public office that there is an obligation here which is beyond what it is elsewhere; they must be absolutely above criticism and they must so conduct themselves as to serve the public in a way that is beyond corruption, and that it is not so much corruption as it is the slovenly way in which men do things; that we must have the disposition and willingness to sacrifice. He said he did not think that we had quite understood that there comes a time when we have to be more concerned about our obligations and our responsibilities than about our troubles, and we need to have those who serve the city, county, and state understand that when they accept a job it has to be a full-time job, it has to be a full-time devotion, and if they are not willing to do it at the price the job pays, they ought not to take it. ...

I feel that Mr. Rosenblatt is a true friend, and really a great man![43]

---

43. For information on the Newspaper Agency Corporation, see O. N. Malmquist's 1971 *The First 100 Years: A History of the Salt Lake Tribune, 1871–1971*, 373–85.

17 Grappling with Growth and Changing Contours, 1967

After making preliminary remarks and giving quotations from the First Presidency of the Church in April, 1941, and from President Lorenzo Snow in 1900 regarding the duty and work of the Apostles, [I showed] that when the Assistants were called in 1941 we had 138 stakes whereas we now have 435, which means that we have had an increase of practically 300 stakes, and that the increase will continue. —May 30, 1967

January 4, 1967, 10:30 a.m. My secretary, Clare [Middlemiss], came over—the first time in several days. She took up letters and other office matters with me.

I told her that with President [Hugh B.] Brown's frequent illnesses, and President [Thorpe B.] Isaacson's physical impairments caused by his stroke, I may have to take steps to call some additional counselors.

Clare mentioned that I looked tired, and suggested that I take a rest. She said she would come back tomorrow and take up the balance of the work she had brought with her.

I admitted that I was tired, and did not feel up to take up more work today. Clare then left, and I took a rest on the couch in the office [on the eighth floor of the Hotel Utah].

January 6, 1967, 9:30 a.m. Elder Ezra Taft Benson came in and reported the progress of the "1976 Committee." He said that they are having a meeting in Chicago on the tenth of this month; that they are in real earnest trying to get the people of the country to return to the fundamentals of the Constitution and to draft him to become a candidate for the Presidency of the United States, and Strom Thurmond as Vice-President. He said they now have automobile bumper stickers with "Benson for President" and "Thurmond for Vice-President—1968."

I said to Elder Benson, as I said before, these matters will have to take their own course, and we shall see what comes of it; that Elder Benson is not to take an active part in this campaign until and unless he is drafted.

January 10, 1967, 10:30 a.m. ... Elder Mark B. Garff, Chairman of the Building Committee, came in and reported on financial conditions. In discussing his experiences in the Building Department since I called him to take Wendell B. Mendenhall's place, Brother Garff said that he has saved the Church millions of dollars. He has cut down the number of employees in the Department proper from 800 to 200; has altered the plans for our Church buildings which will save the Church $50,000 on each building. Telephone bills, travel expenses, etc. have been cut. He mentioned many other ways in which the expenses have been curtailed.

I told Brother Garff that I am very appreciative of the service he has rendered, and feel satisfied that he is doing an excellent job for us.

January 13, 1967, First Presidency meeting. In a letter dated October 7, 1966[,] [a physician] of Ogden, Utah, had made inquiry regarding the Church's attitude toward birth control, and expressed a willingness to meet with the [First] Presidency on the matter if that were thought advisable. Accordingly, in response to invitation issued by the First Presidency, [the doctor] met with them this morning. The doctor explained that he is an obstetrician and that he had told his patients that he personally felt that they should have as many children as they can raise and guarantee that each child brought into the world would be a better member of the Church than the parents, but that if they discovered after they had had 3, 4 or 5 children that they could not wisely handle any more than that number, they should discontinue having children. He said that he had felt well about this attitude until the October 1965 conference when he read President [Joseph Fielding] Smith's talk[1] on the subject

---

1. In his October 1965 conference address, Smith stated: "When young people

which disturbed him and he feared that in giving advice to these young people he was doing something wrong, that perhaps he was out of tune with the Church in what he was telling the people. He knew that he was giving good medical advice but if it was not in harmony with the Church's thinking he wanted to be informed. He said that patients come in to see him who have had for instance five children and they feel guilty if they use contraceptives. The doctor said that he could find no place in the standard works of the Church where it is indicated that parents shouldn't space their children.

President Smith asked what he said in his remarks. The doctor said his comments were primarily the question as to how can we face God if we did not bring into the world all the children that we could. The doctor said that he had four lovely children of his own, that he and his wife have been using contraceptives. He is 39 years old and this is what bothers him. He said that from a medical standpoint he has a clear conscience but from a Church standpoint he does not know and this is what has disturbed him.

The brethren then read to [the doctor] a copy of a formal letter that is sent out in answer to inquiries regarding birth control, which letter reads as follows:

> "I am directed to call your attention to the words of President Joseph F. Smith which represented the attitude of the Church during his administration and which attitude has not changed: 'I regret, I think it is a crying evil, that there should exist a sentiment or a feeling among any members of the Church to curtail the birth of their children. I think that is a crime wherever it occurs, where husband and wife are in possession of health and vigor and are free from impurities that would be entailed upon their posterity. I believe that where people undertake to curtail or prevent the birth of their children that they are going to reap disappointment by and by. I have no hesitancy in saying that I believe this is one of the greatest crimes of the world today, this evil practice.' (Gospel Doctrine, page 278)[2]

---

marry and refuse to fulfill this commandment given in the beginning of the world [to multiply and replenish the earth] ... they rob themselves of the greatest eternal blessing. ... Those who willfully and maliciously design to break this important commandment shall be damned." *One Hundred Thirty-fifth Semi-annual Conference*, Oct. 1–3, 1965, p. 29.

2. McKay had essentially delivered the same message in a letter three years earlier,

"However, the brethren feel that men must be considerate of their wives who bear the greater responsibility not only of bearing children, but of rearing them through childhood. To this end the mother's strength should be conserved and the husband's consideration for his wife is his first duty, and self-control a dominant factor in all their relationships.

"The brethren trust that you and your husband will exercise wisdom and discretion in solving your marital problems, and that the Lord will bless you with health and strength so that you may be permitted to rear your children in accordance with the teachings of the Gospel, and that you may receive great joy and happiness in your family life. Sincerely yours,

/s/ Joseph Anderson

Secretary to the First Presidency"

[The doctor] said that he was pleased with the letter and that this answered his question satisfactorily. The brethren then asked him what his future attitude on the question would be and he answered that from now on as long as the mother is in good health she should have as many children as she may be blessed with if it does not impair the mother's health; that, however, if it is causing a breakup in the home so that the home is in jeopardy, then he would advise that they use a contraceptive. The brethren suggested that instead of advising the use of contraceptives, he advise the use of self-control. The doctor further said that now he thinks he knows where he stands as a member of the Church and that as a member of the Church he will tell them it is their obligation to have children as long as their health is not impaired. The doctor said that if there is an impairment of health he felt a contraceptive should be used, that people will not abstain from intimate relationship. [The doctor] said that he would like to have a copy of the letter which had been read to him which he would present to the obstetrics staff in their meeting at the hospital in Ogden and tell them that this is the attitude of the Church, and he felt sure that it would help to answer these questions for the doctors as far as the Church is concerned. He also suggested that he thought it would be a good thing if President McKay would say these same things

in which he wrote that "it is the policy of the Church to discourage the prevention of conception by any means unless the health of the mother demands it." Bergera, *Statements*, 42.

in the April conference. The doctor further commented that it had been his experience that when women do not want a baby that after the baby is born their attitude changes and they do want the child. It was agreed that a copy of the aforementioned letter would be sent to the doctor as per his request, that he might show it to other practitioners if he wished to do so.

[The doctor] was then excused from the meeting. After he had left President [N. Eldon] Tanner suggested that inasmuch as this question comes to the First Presidency so often and from so many sources, that perhaps it would be advisable to prepare a statement of this same kind to be placed in the Church Section of the Deseret News, the [Improvement] Era, or perhaps the priesthood bulletin so that there would be no misunderstanding regarding the position of the Church on this subject. President McKay said that the matter would have to be handled very wisely. President Tanner explained that when individuals make written inquiries of the First Presidency we write and give them this information; that, however, bishops and stake presidents have not had a letter on the subject and that some people take one position on the matter of birth control and contraceptives and some another, and it would seem that some official statement should be made for the benefit of the presidents of stakes, bishops of wards, etc. President McKay stated that he thought the policy of the Church should be stated clearly so that everyone will know about it. He also suggested that the statement appear in the Improvement Era.[3]

January 17, 1967, First Presidency meeting. President [N. Eldon] Tanner called attention to a letter he had received from Leonard Arrington of Logan reporting that he has been asked by a publishing company to write a history of Utah and the Mormons. He states that this is the first time of which he knows where a publishing company has asked a Mormon, especially an active Mormon, to write a history of this kind. He

---

3. Ironically, the next issue of the *Improvement Era* carried an editorial by G. Homer Durham, president of Arizona State University and future LDS Church Historian, arguing that the greatest challenge to humanity was overpopulation. "Litter, pollution, ill-use or abuse of land and resources must soon take their places as central concerns of thinking men and women everywhere," he wrote. "Population Growth," *Improvement Era*, Feb. 1967, p. 77. The topic was otherwise not broached in 1967 in the official magazine.

states that he would be glad to do it, but would not wish to attempt it unless he is permitted to get information from primary sources such as the Historian's Office, and that he would need copies of correspondence, diaries, minutes of certain meetings, etc. President [Hugh B.] Brown and President Tanner both felt that it was an opportunity for us to have a professional writer who is a devoted Church member prepare such a history.

We agreed that authorization might be given to use the materials in the Historian's Office, with the understanding that he could not take any of these materials out of the office, and that if he wanted anything from the First Presidency's Office, it would have to be cleared first by the First Presidency.[4]

January 18, 1967, 11:00–12:30 p.m. Conference with my secretary Clare [Middlemiss]. Told her of my great worry that all is not right; that I need more help, and that I shall have to appoint another counselor to help carry on the work, as President [Hugh B.] Brown is ill a good deal of the time, and President [Thorpe B.] Isaacson has not improved as I have hoped and prayed he would—his speech has gone almost completely; he is crippled so that it is most difficult for him to get around. I have been thinking of someone who can take President Isaacson's place.

Note by C[lare] M[iddlemiss]: At this point president McKay leaned his head back on the chair, closed his eyes, and in deep thought said to his secretary, "Name to me the Brethren." She called off the names of the Brethren of the Twelve, and President McKay said, "No, not among them—like President Isaacson." She then named the Brethren of the Assistants to the Twelve, among whom was Elder Alvin R. Dyer.[5] As

---

4. Leonard J. Arrington (1917–99) had a PhD in economics from the University of North Carolina–Chapel Hill and was a professor at Utah State University. His groundbreaking 1958 book, *Great Basin Kingdom: An Economic History of the Latter-day Saints, 1830–1900*, from Harvard University Press, so impressed the academic world that it attracted the attention of an editor at Alfred A. Knopf, who is mentioned here. The stimulus from his communication with Arrington resulted in *The Mormon Experience*, written by Arrington and R. Davis Bitton and published in 1979. When Arrington became Church Historian in 1972, he shepherded the book by staff members James B. Allen and Glen M. Leonard, *Story of the Latter-day Saints*, published by Deseret Book. For Arrington's account of this, see his autobiographical *Adventures of a Church Historian*.

5. Dyer and Middlemiss were cousins once removed. Her grandparents were Dyer's great uncle and aunt. Clarabel Middlemiss (1901–1983) never married, which is one of the reasons why she was able to devote herself full-time to her secretarial duties. She was

the secretary gave Elder Dyer's name, President McKay raised his head, opened his eyes, and said, "That's the one. I like him. He is the one I have been thinking of; he is a man of good judgment and dependability."

January 27, 1967, First Presidency meeting. In discussing the legislation that has been introduced in the [Utah] State House of Representatives regarding Sunday Closing, we felt that the First Presidency should not make a public statement; however, permission was given for President [N. Eldon] Tanner, since he said that he had had several phone calls about the matter, to talk to two or three of the senators and indicate to them how the Church feels about the matter; that we feel that they should endeavor to pass legislation that would require the closing of all business houses, markets, etc. on Sunday.

February 1, 1967, 11:30–12:30 p.m. My secretary, Clare [Middlemiss], came in by appointment to take up matters pertaining to correspondence and other office matters.

I reported to her for the diary that I had had a very satisfactory interview with Elder [Alvin R.] Dyer, and said that I am going to call Brother Dyer to be one of my Counselors, to take up the duties performed by President Thorpe B. Isaacson before he was stricken with a stroke a year ago. I said that the more I consult with Brother Dyer and talk to him about various Church matters, the more convinced I am and the more my impressions are confirmed that I should call him as one of my Counselors. I stated that I have every confidence in him.

February 15, 1967, First Presidency meeting. President [N. Eldon] Tanner stated that [he spoke with] the Professor at the University of Utah [Aziz S. Atiya] who had said that he had access to the parchment from which the Book of Abraham was translated. President Tanner said that in talking to him about two weeks ago, this gentleman said that he felt quite satisfied that we are going to be able to get this parchment but the

---

born in Salt Lake City, attended business school, and served a mission to Colorado—all before working in the Church Administration Building beginning in 1930. She was assigned to McKay in 1935. One of her responsibilities was to compile his sermons and writings for publication. Her name appeared alongside his for three anthologies: *Cherished Experiences*, 1955; *Treasures of Life*, 1962; and *Man May Know for Himself*, 1967.

matter has to be kept as quiet as possible. In answer to President [Joseph Fielding] Smith's question as to where the parchment is, President Tanner said that we do not know exactly where it is, but that it is in a museum and that this gentleman is working with the museum people in an effort to make an exchange of artifacts for this parchment, that we will pay for the artifacts instead of for the parchment. ...

Ezra Taft Benson—Nomination for Presidency of United States—A letter was read from Ernest Cook of Ogden, referring to a reference in a letter to the Deseret News to a statement by President McKay that he had give[n] his approval to the movement to sponsor Elder Ezra Taft Benson for nomination and election as President of the United States. Brother Cook asks if this is true, and if so, if he may obtain a statement of such endorsement. In discussing this matter, President Tanner mentioned that the policy has been as he understood it that no one of the General Authorities should seek a political nomination without the approval of the President of the Church. He stated that the President's approval is always obtained before the Brethren accept various Church assignments such as visiting missions, etc. President Tanner stated that for instance he is leaving today for Great Britain under assignment to attend the Manchester Stake Conference and reorganize the Presidency, that he would not, of course, do this without consulting me and receiving my approval. I said that this was the proper thing to do.

In discussing the matter of Brother Benson, the sentiment was expressed that while I had given Brother Benson permission to become receptive to the nomination, it had not yet come to the point where any draft movement had been made and that we would meet that when it came. ...

11:15–1:00 p.m.—My secretary, Clare [Middlemiss], came over and presented a number of letters and Church matters that had come to my office. After talking over a few matters, I remarked that President [Thorpe B.] Isaacson is not going to get better, that I am going to call Alvin R. Dyer as my counselor.

March 15, 1967, 11:30 a.m. President Ernest L. Wilkinson of the Brigham Young University came in and informed me regarding the charges made by students at the BYU as to surveillance of teachers. Evidently, a student had tried to organize some very Left-Wing organizations on the campus, and that because of the times President Wilkinson said that he had to be alert as to what some of the faculty members were teaching. He said that they need a man with Federal Bureau of Investigation detective experience to exercise surveillance on the campus.

I authorized President Wilkinson to employ such a person; that we need to keep on hand on such activities on the campus there at BYU.[6]

March 22, 1967, 8:30 a.m. ... Elder Ezra Taft Benson came in and visited with me regarding the efforts of the 1976 Committee to draft him for high office in the United States. He said that he is receiving many hundreds of letters from people from various parts of the country, and that the Committee is receiving about one hundred per day.

He also showed me a tape recording of the lecture given by Miss Lola Belle Holmes, a Negress, who spoke in Salt Lake City last Friday under the title, "Why I Became a Communist for the FBI." I told Brother Benson that I should like to listen to it at some convenient time.

Brother Benson then referred to the letter which Robert Welch of the John Birch Society had sent to me asking for the second time for permission to have him (Elder Benson) on the Council of the Society. In discussing this with Elder Benson, I told him that I do not feel that he should accept a position of this kind with the Society, but that I enjoyed reading Mr. Welch's letter and felt that he is sincerely dedicated, and that he displayed a very good spirit in his letter. It was agreed that Elder Benson would answer Mr. Welch and tell him that it would be impossible for him to serve on the Council at this time.

April 12, 1967, First Presidency meeting. Consideration was given to a letter ... asking if it would be fitting and proper to display the American flag in our places of worship. In discussing this matter, it was our sentiment that we answer this question to the effect that the flag is displayed only on occasions of national, patriotic observances, and that the Church has not felt that true patriotism requires that the flag be regularly displayed in our chapels.

---

6. Wilkinson's portrayal of this was less than forthcoming. He employed a student to do the spying, and the student recruited other students to assist him. See Gary James Bergera's "The 1966 BYU Student Spy Ring" in the *Utah Historical Quarterly*, spring 2011.

However, as we have decided before, there is no objection to display-ing the flag on the grounds of our Church buildings.

April 18, 1967, 8:00 a.m. Elder Ezra Taft Benson came in and first brought up the subject of the General Conference and how pleased and satisfied he was with it.

He then asked if he could bring Mr. Robert Welch of the John Birch Society in to meet me later this morning. I said that 11:00 a.m. would be a good time for him to come in. Brother Benson said that Mr. Welch is in Salt Lake City to deliver a talk at the Highland High School. I said, "All right, I'll see you following the meeting of the First Presidency." ...

11:00 a.m.— ... By appointment Elder Ezra Taft Benson came over to the apartment with Mr. Robert Welch of the John Birch Society, Bel-mont, Massachusetts.

Following greetings and introductions, Elder Benson explained that in order to save my time, Mr. Welch had written a letter to me which con-tains the subject matter he would like to discuss with me this morning.

I said, "All right, Mr. Welch, you read the letter to me." So he read very slowly and clearly the letter which he had prepared. The letter out-lined, as he sees it, the present situation of our country, the very fate of which he thinks hangs in the balance.

At the conclusion of his reading, he said that it would help the cause exceedingly if I would give my permission for Elder Ezra Taft Benson to become a member of the National Council of the John Birch Society.

I explained to him, as I have on two other occasions by letter, that it would not be wise for Elder Benson to serve in this capacity.[7]

April 20, 1967, 12:00 noon–12:20 p.m. Knowing that I was tired, Clare [Middlemiss] ... said that she would take up with me just a few import-ant letters that needed to go out. She read two or three letters that had come addressed to me from members of the Church inquiring regarding their status in the Church if they should join the John Birch Society. One member of the Society said that he had applied for a teaching po-sition in one of our Seminaries and had been told by his Bishop that

---

7. This was the third attempt in recent months by Benson to get McKay's ap-proval. Welch's letter is reproduced in the diary under this date.

his membership in the Society would prohibit his being accepted as a teacher. I instructed Clare that so long as this man did not advocate the John Birch Society during his teaching at the Seminary, membership therein should not prohibit his becoming a Seminary teacher.

April 21, 1967, 10:15 a.m. ... Met with Elder Mark E. Petersen of the Council of the Twelve. I discussed the following with him: ... the letter [by] Mr. Robert Welch of the John Birch Society [that Welch] had given to me personally when he visited me on Tuesday, April 18. After I had finished reading the letter, Elder Petersen remarked, "President McKay, Elder Harold B. Lee has some hair-raising stories to tell about the Birch Society which I am sure he will tell you, which I think would scare you to death. We have the Church, and if we live up to its teachings, we do not need to worry about what will happen to this country!"

April 26, 1967, First Presidency meeting. Attention was called to a letter ... stating that an Elder and his wife are considering legally adopting two Negro children. They have two children of their own. The Bishop asks for counsel on the matter. He inquires if the couple will be able to have these children sealed to them in the Temple.

We decided to answer the Bishop stating that they should discourage such an adoption.

May 16, 1967, First Presidency meeting. Our attention was called to instructions heretofore given to the effect that opening and closing prayers in Sacrament Meetings should be offered by brethren holding the Melchizedek Priesthood. The Presiding Bishopric have raised the question as to whether or not young men holding the Aaronic Priesthood might also be used in offering prayers in the Sacrament Meeting.

We agreed that this permission might well be extended to holders of the Aaronic Priesthood as well as those holding the Melchizedek Priesthood, and that members of the Aaronic Priesthood may also offer prayers in priesthood meetings.[8]

---

8. In September 1978, President Spencer W. Kimball determined that excluding women from praying in church "had no scriptural basis and should be abandoned." Kimball, *Lengthen Your Stride*, 166.

May 24, 1967, First Presidency meeting. Mention was made of [US] Secretary [of the Interior] St[ew]art Udall's article which appeared in the Dialogue Magazine,[9] and has been published in the press regarding the Negro question. President [Hugh B.] Brown mentioned that Rex Campbell and Lowell Bennion had called on him in his office yesterday. They felt that the Church should make an official declaration as to its present position with regard to the Negro inasmuch as there is so much comment throughout the Church and elsewhere regarding the Negro question, particularly in view of Secretary Udall's recent statement. It was also mentioned that the question will no doubt be a live one during the next year or longer, particularly if Governor [George] Romney runs for nomination as President of the United States.

In discussing the matter, we did not feel that anything was to be gained by making an official declaration on the subject. We discussed the status of the Negro and the attitude of the Church from the beginning. I said that "as the Presidency of the Church we have the right and the authority to give the blessing of the Priesthood, and that means all the rights and authority that go with the Priesthood. More than that, we have nothing to say." I said that this word should be given to all people whether they are in the Church or out of the Church, that it is our position and that as a Presidency we must stand on it. It was our sentiment that no official statement on the matter should be published at this time.

May 30, 1967, 8:30 a.m. ... Attended a special meeting of the First Presidency and Council of the Twelve held in the First Presidency's room of the Church Administration Building.

Elder Harold B. Lee, as Chairman of the Correlation Committee, referred to the memorandum relative to three vital problems which had been put into the hands of each of the Brethren for discussion at this meeting. ...

After making preliminary remarks and giving quotations from the First Presidency of the Church in April, 1941, and from President Lorenzo Snow in 1900 regarding the duty and work of the Apostles, that

---

9. Udall wrote a two-page letter, not an article, to *Dialogue: A Journal of Mormon Thought*, published in the summer 1967 issue, saying that "every Mormon knows ... the day will come when the Negro will be given full fellowship. Surely that day has come." The response was mixed, as documented by F. Ross Peterson in "'Do Not Lecture the Brethren': Stewart L. Udall's Pro-Civil Rights Stance," *Journal of Mormon History*, spring 1999.

when the Assistants were called in 1941 we had 138 stakes whereas we now have 435, which means that we have had an increase of practically 300 stakes, and that the increase will continue. Elder Lee mentioned that for the past two years we have been sending the auxiliary representatives to stake conferences, and we have observed their work, and while in the main there has been much good accomplished, the auxiliaries themselves have not been too satisfied. They have felt the need and are now moving out into regionalizing. He said that for instance the Relief Society people have taken themselves out of attending conferences this whole year, and they are now accepting invitations to go to regional meetings instead. The MIA, he said, are setting up regional meetings here and there to take care of certain phases of their work, which they feel is a more efficient way than going to stake conferences. The Sunday School is pressing for the privilege of holding regional meetings for their stake superintendencies.

Elder Lee said the other problem that has concerned them has been to place the Priesthood in its place, to give it the place where the Lord put it; that is, it is to be the center and core of the Kingdom of God, and the auxiliaries to be auxiliary to the priesthood. He said the men who have been representing us as Priesthood committeemen, as their work has been observed, it has been less than effective, and it has not be[en] recognized as authoritative. They have been committee members, which to the general officers does not connote an authority such as they might have had if they had been give a designation within the framework of the Church organization.

He said the Correlation Committee has worked for months and months on a question of making our work at Stake Conferences more effective. They feel the crying need is to get closer to our leaders, and to give the energy needed to training them in leadership. He said the Presiding Bishopric, for example, has given thought to training sessions for bishoprics. The committee thinks this ought not to get too far away from all of us, that we all ought to be in the business of training leaders; that, therefore, in their suggestions concerning stake conferences they have now come up with some suggestions as to how they think the work of the General Authorities can be made more effective and perhaps reach a greater number of our people than are now being reached by attendance at two general sessions of the conference for the general public.

Elder Lee thought that with this preliminary statement the brethren might be able to understand something of the background of the committee's approach to this problem. He felt that the matter is of serious import, and is presented with a prayerful desire to do what the President of the Church under the Lord's direction would wish. He said the committee yields fully to this, with the realization that we are not reaching the people in this vast growing Church as we should.

He said that in order to have a plan that will reach them effectively, we must understand what we have been doing and do it more effectively, that ours is the job to train people and to stay close to the weaker stakes and sort of live with them if necessary to get them into the channel of proper procedures.

The Brethren then had some discussion of the various items in the proposed program, after which Elder [Gordon B.] Hinckley raised a question. He said he was favorable to this program, that the only thing that troubled him is the title, "Priesthood Associates of the Twelve." He said that "associate" does have a connotation of being higher than an "assistant," and this troubled him just a little. He wondered if there would be any virtue in using "Regional Associates of the Twelve," which would have a limitation, and tie them to the regions to which they are attached.

President [N. Eldon] Tanner suggested "Regional Representatives of the Twelve." He said the title had bothered him more than anything about this, and that if we are going to make the appointment temporary, it would seem that we should make the designation such as to make it easy to move them, that is to release them if it became necessary. He wondered about calling them "Regional Priesthood Representatives." He expressed the wish that we had time to give the whole program more thought. He said he saw some things that made him unhappy. He said the thing that bothered him mostly is making seventy more General Authorities, roughly. When they are associates of the Twelve, he thought they were Assistants to the Twelve.

Elder Lee said we do not want any regional meetings if we do not have Priesthood authority to direct them. In answer to President Tanner's question as to whether this regional authority would be in charge of these regional auxiliaries, Elder Lee said he would be the Priesthood authority in that meeting, and would be over the Stake Presidents.

Elder Lee said this was something that we ought to be united on, and that he would say that if the Presidency and Twelve could be united on "Regional Priesthood Representatives of the Church," he thought that would be desirable.[10]

I said that that would be all right.

Elder Lee said that every time we organize a new Stake, it puts the Twelve a little farther away from the people; that we are now spreading ourselves about as thin as we can, and we are not doing the work efficiently. He felt that we must intensify the work. He felt that we are not teaching them properly, and that we must make those who go out to teach them more effective.

Elder Hinckley moved that these Priesthood associates of whom we had been speaking be designated by the title "Regional Priesthood Representatives of the Twelve." Elder [Ezra Taft] Benson seconded the motion, which was unanimously approved.

Elder [Marion G.] Romney moved the adoption of the recommendations on the three issues outlined, with the amendment as approved. Elder [Thomas S.] Monson seconded Elder Romney's motion. Recommendation unanimously approved.

Elder Lee said that the committee had approached this with faith and prayer, and some of them with sleepless nights, hoping to get something not only that they could approve of, but that they felt in their hearts the Presidency and the Twelve would want them to do, in order to keep in touch with the growing Church, which is growing by leaps and bounds. He said that something must be done that will keep us in closer touch than we are now.

President [Hugh B.] Brown said that the committee has done an excellent work.

Elder Lee then stated that there is one pertinent question that ought to be answered so that the Correlation Committee will know our wishes. He said that having made this decision, the next move would seem to be to acquaint the whole correlation group and the auxiliaries with the general outline of the plan. He said they ought to know as soon as thy can;

---

10. Later in the year, the church announced sixty-nine Regional Representatives of the Twelve, who assumed their positions January 1, 1968. In 1977 their title would be shortened to Regional Representatives.

that the next thing would be immediately to begin to make a study as to regional representatives that might be nominated. He thought that they should be set apart in a manner that the Presidency would direct, perhaps by members of the Twelve, because of the number, and they could be set apart according to the designation that has been agreed upon. He wondered if this would not be the better way to do it before making a Church-wide announcement, that the announcement could be made to the Church at the coming October Conference.

I said that that would be the better way to handle it.

Elder Lee then said that the announcement to the Church could be made at the General Priesthood Meeting in October, and by then we would have more clearly in mind the details. He said that there had been some rumblings to the effect that there is going to be a change, and the auxiliaries are pressing to know what they are going to do. He said that now having made the decision that we have, we could acquaint the auxiliary people and our own correlation workers so that they would all know what the general plan is.

President Tanner raised the question as to what we should do in regard to releasing these Priesthood committee representatives who are now in the service. It was agreed that all these representatives should be released, and then we can call back into service as these regional Priesthood representatives those whom we would like to use in this capacity.

President Tanner raised the question as to whether there would be any conflict between these representatives and the Assistants to the Twelve when they go into these various areas. It was explained that there should not be any more conflict than if a member of the Twelve were to go into the area.

Elder Lee then commented that the present Priesthood representatives will need to function until the end of the current year, and that the program should go forward as it is now until that time; and then at the October Conference we could notify the entire Church and could release the Priesthood representatives, at which time a letter of release could be sent to them by the First Presidency, and these regional Priesthood representatives could be nominated immediately thereafter. After this was done, they could go into training to make sure that all moved in unison.

10:30 a.m.—Following the departure of the Brethren, the First Presidency met for a short time. President Brown stated that it seemed evident that the First Presidency is losing its grip on the activities that are going forward, and that more and more we are being regulated and ruled by committees. He said that now that we have adopted the recommendations of the Correlation Executive Committee, which came with the endorsement of the Twelve, we need to make some changes and assignments among members of the Twelve as advisors to the various auxiliary groups. He felt that those who have been acting in the capacity are becoming somewhat stale in their various assignments. He suggested that if the President so desired, his counselors could bring to the President a list of those who are now acting in these capacities with some suggestions as to changes that should be made. He thought this would be an opportune time to do it. He felt that the First Presidency is taking rather a second place to the committees in these matters. He explained that for example the handling of the Missionary Department, which heretofore has always been under one of the Presidency of the Church, is being carried on quite exclusively by the Missionary executive Committee. He thought that there is a number of such things that ought to be given more consideration so that when this new program comes up in October, the First Presidency will be ready to designate who of the Twelve is to represent the Sunday School, the Mutual, the Primary, etc., and who will represent the missionary work. He thought we might consider dividing this representation among the Presidency of the Church and let one of them be on each of these committees in charge of certain parts of the work. He said that he would like to pull back into the hands of the First Presidency some of the things that seem to be slipping from them. He suggested that if agreeable to the President he would like to present to me when he has had the time to look it over with President Tanner and President [Joseph Fielding] Smith, a list of those who are representing the auxiliaries now, and some suggestions as to changes that should be made. He thought that this should be ready for consideration by a week from tomorrow if possible.

I said that this should be taken under consideration immediately.

June 1, 1967, First Presidency meeting. President Hugh B. Brown referred to the action taken by the First Presidency and the Twelve in their special meeting held last Tuesday, May 30. He said he considered the [regional] program rather revolutionary and wondered if it should not have been given more consideration. He mentioned that there is a number of things about it that he felt we might not want if more thought were given; that it is something of a new system. President [N. Eldon] Tanner said he just wondered if I were happy about the whole thing.

July 19, 1967, 10:30 a.m. My secretary came over to the apartment and presented a number of letters that had accumulated during my illness.

I then asked her to read to me the corrections made in the manuscript of the new general Handbook of the Church by Elder Alvin R. Dyer. The section given to Elder Dyer by Elder Harold B. Lee for corrections and suggestions pertains to the duties of the First Presidency and the Twelve, without mention of the place and duties of the President of the Church.

The [uncorrected] manuscript [as it] now [stands] reads as follows:

General Authorities of the Church
The First Presidency represents the Lord Jesus Christ and have received power and authority from Him to preside over and direct all of the affairs of His earthly Kingdom which is The Church of Jesus Christ of Latter-day Saints. They are assisted by the Council of the Twelve Apostles whose members hold with them the keys of the kingdom. The First Presidency and the Council of the Twelve are the General Priesthood Board of the Church and have the control, supervision, and direction of all Priesthood and auxiliary affairs.

Brother Dyer did not agree with the above statement and submitted what he thought should go in the Handbook. His suggestions and corrections are as follows:

President of the High Priesthood
One is appointed of the High Priesthood and is called the President of the High Priesthood of the Church. He it is whom we call the President of the Church. From him comes the administering of ordinances and blessings upon the Church, by the laying on of the hands. (See D&C 107:65–67; 132:7–8; 107:91.)

The First Presidency

By the President's choosing and the sustaining of other High Priests as Counselors, even as many as twelve, but not fewer than two (D&C 107:22; 107:79–80), the Quorum of the First Presidency is formed. Thus in this manner, with the "one appointed" presiding, the First Presidency represents the Lord, Jesus Christ, and have received power and authority from Him to preside over and direct all of the affairs of the Kingdom of God, which is The Church of Jesus Christ of Latter-day Saints. ...

Inasmuch as Elder Dyer's corrections and additions are in accordance with the revealed word in the Doctrine and Covenants, I stated, as I have already stated to Elder Dyer, that the additions and corrections as submitted by him should go in the Handbook.[11]

July 21, 1967. Mrs. June Noyes, the nurse, informed the secretary that Dr. [Alan P.] MacFarlane had said that President McKay could not ride in the Days of '47 Parade [commemorating the pioneers of 1847], although he had given his promise that he would do so. The secretary called Dr. MacFarlane and asked him if he knew how President McKay is going to ride in the parade, and he said, "no, tell me." The secretary then said, "He will ride in an air-conditioned car along the line of the parade without stopping at the reviewing stand at Liberty Park as heretofore, and then come directly up State Street to the Hotel." Dr. MacFarlane answered, "Under those conditions, he may certainly ride in the parade."

August 4, 1967, 10:30 a.m. By appointment at his request, met with Richard Isaacson, son of President Thorpe B. Isaacson, who reported that his father is still about the same and that he is discouraged because he cannot continue with his duties. He said that he is able to say a few more words, but cannot carry on a conversation. I asked Richard to convey my love and greetings to his father.

August 9, 1967, First Presidency meeting. President [N. Eldon] Tanner

---

11. This did not happen.

referred to the action we took yesterday in our meeting approving the proposed erection of Temples in Ogden and Provo, and suggested that it would be well for the First Presidency to call together the Stake Presidents in those particular districts, tell them what we have in mind, obtain their support of the project financially and otherwise, and also approve a site to be selected. He thought this should be done before the information leaks out that we are contemplating erecting these Temple so that they will feel that they are a part of the proposition.

I said that this should be done as it had been done in other Temple districts before building Temples, such as Los Angeles and Oakland. President [Hugh B.] Brown suggested that I would no doubt wish this matter presented to the Twelve before any further action is taken, and the suggestion was made that this could be done at the Council meeting to be held Thursday, August 17. President Brown mentioned in this connection that there is a site in Provo on the hillside which belongs to the BYU, which is located at 820 North about 13th East in Provo, which is an ideal site for a Temple. He thought that perhaps we should ask Brother Garff and his associates to look at this site as a possible location for the Temple. President Brown said that he had made inquiry and learned that there are two acres available to us adjoining the [LDS] Tabernacle in Provo, but that is not sufficiently large to do the kind of job we want. President Tanner asked if I would wish to look at this property before a decision is made, and I said that I do not feel physically able to do this. I approved of the proposal that Presidents Brown and Tanner proceed with these meetings with the Stake Presidencies <u>after the Council of the Twelve had indicated their approval</u>. President Brown will prepare a program and bring it to me for my consideration and approval. President Brown said that all he would wish to do is make preliminary arrangements and bring the proposed procedure to me, and then action can be taken under my direction and with my authority.

August 14, 1967, 8:00 a.m. ... President Hugh B. Brown called by telephone and said that he and President [N. Eldon] Tanner are planning to leave for Provo this morning to meet with the Stake Presidents in the Provo area to discuss with them the plans for the building of the new Temple there, and also to appoint a Committee of the Stake Presidents to choose a site for the Temple.[12] Following their meeting in Provo, they will return to Salt Lake, and at 4:00 p.m. will proceed to Ogden to announce to the Stake Presidents in that area the building of a Temple in Ogden, and will also set up a committee of the Stake Presidents to choose a site for the Ogden Temple.[13]

President Joseph Fielding Smith was not invited by the counselors to go to Provo with them, but was invited to go to Ogden at four o'clock this afternoon

August 15, 1967, First Presidency meeting. President [Hugh B.] Brown reported for my information that yesterday morning at ten o'clock President [N. Eldon] Tanner and he, together with Mark B. Garff and Fred Baker of the Building Committee, met in Provo with the Presidencies of Stakes that would be included in the Provo Temple District—that 27 of the 28 Stakes were represented by their Stake Presidencies, and they all enthusiastically endorsed one hundred percent the proposal that a Temple be built in Provo, and indicated that their people would pay such proportion of the cost as might be assigned them. President Brown said that an effort was made to make these brethren feel that they are being considered in the matter; that we were not merely telling them that this is what is going to be done, but we were asking for their recommendations.

A committee was appointed to make investigation with the Building Committee regarding a proposed site, and to bring back to the First Presidency their findings and recommendation.

Ogden Temple—In the afternoon at four o'clock, Presidents Brown, [N. Eldon] Tanner, and [Joseph Fielding] Smith, together with Brother Garff and Brother Baker of the Building Committee, met with the Presidencies of the 25 Stakes in the proposed Ogden Temple District, all of whom were very enthusiastic about building a Temple in Ogden as soon as possible. He stated that several proposed sites were mentioned

---

12. The selected site of seventeen acres was at the mouth of Rock Canyon, northeast of BYU. Brown officiated at the groundbreaking in the fall of 1969. Joseph Fielding Smith dedicated the edifice in early 1972, with Harold B. Lee reading the dedicatory prayer.

13. The Ogden temple was not announced until August 24. The site selected sat on ten acres in downtown Ogden. Its design mirrored the Provo temple. The groundbreaking was conducted by Tanner in September 1969; the temple was dedicated by Joseph Fielding Smith on January 18–20, 1972.

on which the Temple might be erected. Here, too, a committee was appointed to investigate with the Building Committee and report back to the First Presidency. President Brown said that the Counselors in the Presidency carried to each of these groups my love and blessing, and told them that because of a slight indisposition I was unable to be present. President Brown said he thought the meetings were very successful.

August 17, 1967, 11:30 a.m. ... Brother Alvin R. Dyer came in at my request, and once again said good-bye before leaving for Stake Conferences in Buenos Aires, Argentina, Sao Paulo, Brazil, and Mexico. ...

Then I said, "Brother Dyer, I am giving you notice now that I am calling you to be one of my assistants."

Brother Dyer was so taken back by my statement that he turned to my secretary [Clare Middlemiss] who was present during the interview and said, "What did he say?" She was so overcome with the spirit that she was weeping, and said, "He meant just what he said—he is calling you to be one of his assistants, or counselors."

At that Brother Dyer bowed his head for some little time and then looked up at me and said, "I'll do all in my power, in the background, or anywhere, to serve and help you, President McKay."

I said, "Did you know I have been watching you for a year now?" With tears in his eyes, Brother Dyer said, "No, I should have been scared to death if I had known." I said, "Well, I want you to go now on your trip to South America, and when you get back, you report to me. I'll make the announcement after you get back."

Brother Dyer then stood and said, "It is a great honor to serve you!" He leaned down and affectionately put his cheek against mine, and his arms around my shoulders, and our eyes were moist as he slowly walked out of the office and out the door of the apartment.

My secretary, who had been present during the interview, not knowing what was coming, was in tears, and after Brother Dyer had left she said, "I have never been so affected before—if I ever felt the spirit or felt that I was hearing revelation, it was this morning when you called Brother Dyer."

August 22, 1967. Elder Mark Garff, chairman of the Building Committee, met with the First Presidency and reported that the committee that had been appointed in Ogden to give consideration to the selection of a site for the proposed new temple, together with Elders Garff and [Fred] Baker of the Building Committee, had visited a number of sites that had been suggested. (The committee in Ogden consists of President Scott B. Price [East Ogden Stake], chairman; Floyd D. Fowers [Lakeview Stake], vice chairman; Keith W. Wilcox [Weber Heights Stake]; Albert L. Bott [Mount Ogden Stake]; and Lawrence D. Olpin [Lorin Farr Stake]). The committee and Elders Garff and Baker now present the unanimous recommendation that the new temple be placed on the tabernacle square on Washington Avenue in Ogden. As a second choice they recommend that it be located between 5th and 7th Street and east of Madison Avenue, which is a property consisting of eight acres. This latter property had been offered to the committee by President Lawrence D. Olpin of the Lorin Farr Stake.[14] Elder Garff said that the problem in connection with the second site is the matter of transportation, getting the people there from both the south and north sides of the district. He said that if we took this latter site it would also require considerable development so far as sewer and water are concerned. He stated that the committee had considered 13 sites altogether. Elder Garff said that there is ample room on the tabernacle square for the temple to be placed between the old tabernacle and the new one, and that there would also be sufficient parking on the block. He mentioned the old Third Ward chapel located on the southwest corner of the block, which he felt should be removed and a new chapel built for this ward, but said that this would not be necessary in order to provide sufficient space for the new temple. President McKay indicated his approval and his counselors were in agreement with this decision.

Provo Temple Site—Elder Garff reported that the committee that had been appointed to make a study of sites for the proposed new Provo Temple had visited 13 sites in an effort to find a suitable place, that the committee, together with Brother Garff and Brother Baker, now

---

14. The stake was named after the first mayor of Ogden, Lorin Farr (1820–1909), who was born in Vermont, converted to Mormonism, and was thirty-one years old when he assumed office. He was already serving as stake president and running a flour mill and lumber mill when he became mayor in 1851. He received the honor of seeing another settlement farther north, Farr West, named after him and Chauncey W. West. Farr was the father-in-law of apostle John Henry Smith and became the grandfather of church president George Albert Smith.

recommend as the most desirable site a property at 23rd North and 12th East. He explained that this site is free and clear from incumbrance, that we have 23 acres there and that the temple can be located on such part of the property as may be desired. He said it is a beautiful site and is protected from the outpouring of water from the rock canyon by dams, and we have no danger of flash floods reaching this property. President McKay and the brethren indicated their approval of this site. Elder Garff said that he was sure that the city will be willing to extend its bus service so that elderly people and others who do not have automobile accommodations may have transportation to that area. Elder Garff suggested that if we would withhold for a day or two the announcement of the proposed site, he thought we could get the city to put in curb and guttering there. Brother Garff was requested to confer with the city officials and see what can be done along the lines indicated, and that the announcement of both sites would be postponed until definite word had been received from the city officials in Provo.

September 1, 1967, First Presidency meeting. President [Hugh B.] Brown mentioned that in the meeting of the Council reference was made to the recent scare we had regarding a possible Negro disturbance. He said that these riots are going on all over the country and that we are very vulnerable in the general headquarters of the Church, the Hotel Utah, the Temple Square, and the approaches to the temple from the parking terrace. As conditions are now, people can enter the garage from Main Street or State Street and can enter the Administration Building without any question, and once they get into the garage there would be no great problem in getting into the temple through the tunnels. It was thought that we should have some trained police or FBI men on guard at strategic points at all times, even though there may be some expense involved, to see that undesirable persons do not get into the parking garage or upper rooms of the Administration Building or into the temple. President Brown said that the brethren of the Twelve wanted this matter presented to President McKay this morning to ascertain his feelings regarding employing men to be stationed at strategic points to be on guard all the time. This would apply also to the gates to Temple Square and the tabernacle.

President [N. Eldon] Tanner stated that the final recommendation of the Council was that we have the right kind of person or persons, who are trained in such matters, make a survey and bring us a recommendation as to what we should do, and that the Presiding Bishopric, who are in charge of the grounds, should be directed as to what they should do in the matter of security measures.

President McKay said he thought that this should be done. It was agreed that the Presiding Bishopric should be asked to make this study and come back with a report.

In this connection it was mentioned that the further question had been raised as to the wisdom of asking the brethren of the General Authorities to have unlisted telephone numbers, in other words, that their phone numbers should not be in the telephone directory; also that we should discontinue announcing in the newspapers the names of visitors to stake conferences and the dates when conferences would be held for the reason that people with improper motives could take advantage of this information by burglarizing the homes or otherwise making trouble for the families of the brethren. It was agreed to ask the Presiding Bishopric to follow through on these matters and make their report. ...

Security Measures for Church Properties—Elder Richard L. Evans referred to the alert we had sometime ago regarding possible rioting or trouble on Temple Square. He mentioned that notwithstanding the situation at that time, we do not appear to have taken measures for security in case of trouble, that there are no guards to protect our Tabernacle grounds, the Temple, the entrance to the Church Office Building, particularly the entrance into the building from the garage, that those inclined to do so could perhaps go through the tunnel from the garage into the Temple.

The Twelve in discussing the matter this morning suggested that we confer with the FBI, Police Department, or other agencies to see what kind of security measures should be taken. Mention was made of a metal door that can be let down from the ceiling just outside the tunnel entrance to the Temple, but no one knows just how to lower the door, nor who is responsible for it.

Elder Evans also raised a question as to the wisdom of publishing in the press the mission tours of the Brethren, the Stake Conference assignments, etc., that people reading in the paper information to the effect that the General Authorities and others are to be out of town could take advantage of this opportunity to burglarize the homes or otherwise create trouble. It was also suggested that consideration might be given to taking the names of the General Authorities out of the telephone book, that they might have unlisted telephone numbers. It was thought if this were to be done, it should be uniform. Elder Benson mentioned that his number is unlisted.

Elder Evans said that even if it costs tens of thousands or hundreds of thousands of dollars to do it, we should not be neglectful in taking proper measures to protect our buildings and properties and our people. Mention was made of the fact that this matter comes under the jurisdiction of the Presiding Bishopric, and that it should be called to their attention. President Brown said that the Counselors were meeting with President McKay tomorrow morning, Friday, and while there the matter would be brought to his attention for discussion and action. Elder [Harold B.] Lee asked that the Brethren be notified of such measures as may be decided upon.

September 21, 1967, 9:00 a.m.–1:45 p.m. Presided at the pre-Conference meeting of all the General Authorities in the Salt Lake Temple. It was a very inspirational meeting.

At the preliminary meeting, before the Twelve held their meeting alone, I was impressed to make the statement to all the Brethren (much to the upset of my Counselors, Presidents [Hugh B.] Brown and [N. Eldon] Tanner, who felt that I was getting a little mixed up, and that I should read the names of the Brethren who are to speak at Conference), that "there is a man in this room worthy to be named an Apostle, and I am presenting his name for your approval and sustaining vote this morning." I then said, "I should like to present the name of Alvin R. Dyer as one worthy to be ordained an Apostle, but not to become a member of the Quorum of the Twelve, but to be called upon to meet in the sacred meetings of the First Presidency and Twelve at all times."

I called for a sustaining vote, and all the Brethren voted in the affirmative to sustain Elder Dyer as a Apostle.[15] ...

---

15. Dyer's appointment bothered some of the brethren, who viewed him as having undue access to McKay. Because of his family relationship with Middlemiss, she would on occasion include Dyer's diary entries into McKay's, juxtaposed with McKay's. Dyer was sustained as a counselor in the First Presidency during the April 1968 general conference.

Later, when the Twelve met alone with the First Presidency, I presented the matter again to them, and received their sustaining vote for Elder Dyer.

After this matter was settled, I blessed the Brethren, especially for their duties that lie ahead in a General Conference of the Church. I then called on representatives from each group to speak to us and to bear their testimonies.

September 22, 1967, 11:45 a.m. Elder Ezra Taft Benson came over to the office and interrupted the meeting long enough to discuss with me the subject of the address he would like to give at the General Conference. He briefly talked about the plight of the Negroes in this Civil Rights Issue, and how the Communists are using the Negroes to further their own schemes to foment trouble in the United States. He said that he would talk on this subject from the viewpoint of bringing peace in our country instead of uprisings of the Negroes in riots, etc.

I told Brother Benson that under these circumstances, he may go ahead with his subject.[16]

Council Meeting—Remarks Concerning—Brother Benson said, "That was a wonderful meeting yesterday, President McKay (referring to the special meeting of all the General Authorities held in the Temple), and you certainly showed at this meeting that you are the President and Prophet of this Church. You were truly inspired when you called Elder Dyer and in the way you conducted the meeting under a difficult situation."

I answered, "While I am the President, I should like to follow my impressions in directing this Church, and when the Lord no longer needs me, then He knows what to do."

Within a week of McKay's death, he resumed his previous position as an Assistant to the Twelve and in 1976 was sustained a member of the First Quorum of the Seventy.

16. In his conference address, Benson quoted a First Presidency statement from the World War II era denouncing a "technique [by demagogues] that is as old as the human race—a fervid but false solicitude for the unfortunate over whom they thus gain mastery, and then enslave." Benson added that similar "masters of deceit are showing the same false solicitude for the unfortunate in the name of civil rights. ... There is no doubt that the so-called civil rights movement as it exists today is used as a Communist program for revolution in America just as agrarian reform was used by the Communists to take over China and Cuba." *Official Report of the One Hundred Thirty-seventh Semi-Annual General Conference*, Sept. 29, 30, Oct. 1, 1967, p. 35.

September 25, 1967, 3:20–5:20 p.m. Meeting with Elder Alvin R. Dyer regarding my decision to have him ordained to the Apostleship to assist me in my official duties. I told Brother Dyer that I should like him to stay close to me and keep me advised of all matters that the President of the Church should know about.

Elder Dyer stated that word had come to him through the secretary of the First Presidency that the Counselors were concerned about how he is to be sustained, and I answered that they need not be worried as I know how it is to be done.

Brother Dyer then reported to me that several of the Brethren had expressed to him their approval of his appointment, and I was pleased to learn of their reaction.

September 26, 1967, First Presidency meeting. President [N. Eldon] Tanner asked if there were any matters pertaining to the Conference that I wanted to discuss with my Counselors between now and Conference time. I said that I thought everything was in order.

President [Hugh B.] Brown then stated that the question had arisen as to the presentation of the name of Alvin R. Dyer as an Apostle. I said that Brother Dyer's name should be presented as an Apostle separate from the Quorum of the Twelve; and, after a discussion by the Counselors, that he should not be included in those who are sustained as Prophets, Seers, and Revelators. Later, I decided that Elder Dyer, as an Apostle, will be ordained by me as a Prophet, Seer, and Revelator, and should be sustained as such at Conference.

September 28, 1967, 10:45 a.m. ... At my request, Clare [Middlemiss] came over to the apartment, and I gave her the list of the Brethren to be sustained at the Friday afternoon session of Conference, and said that I had decided that Elder Alvin R. Dyer's name is to be included immediately following the list of the members of the Quorum of the Twelve Apostles, and is to be sustained as an "Apostle, Prophet, Seer, and Revelator," just as regular members of the Quorum of the Twelve are sustained. On the list Joseph Anderson prepared, Elder Dyer had been placed with the Assistants to the Twelve, and the Seventies and Presiding Bishopric, to be presented and sustained with them, and it was not intended that he should be sustained as a "Prophet, Seer, and Revelator." However, inasmuch as I shall ordain him as all Apostles are ordained—as "a Prophet, Seer, and Revelator"—he should be sustained by the Conference as such.

I called Brother Anderson, Secretary to the First Presidency, who had prepared the list, and instructed him that I wanted Elder Dyer's name placed immediately under the Quorum of the Twelve, and that he should be sustained as "a Prophet, Seer, and Revelator".

Brother Anderson said: "But when the Counselors discussed it with you the other day, it was decided he would not be sustained as a Prophet, Seer, and Revelator, but just as an Apostle, and would be named with the Assistants, Seventies, etc." I said, "Well, he is to be sustained as I shall ordain him." Brother Anderson said, "If that is the way you want it, that is the way it will be."

October 2, 1967. President Nathan Eldon Tanner met Elder [Alvin R.] Dyer in the auditorium on the third floor of the Church Office Building, the occasion being the final meeting with the Regional Priesthood Representatives of the Twelve prior to their setting apart, which took place on this day. President Tanner asked Elder Dyer if he had been ordained as yet, and he told him no, but that President McKay had told him that he wanted to ordain him. President Tanner then said he thought it would be done in the Temple the following Thursday, October 5, and that he would speak to President McKay about it.

Upon learning of this, President McKay assured Elder Dyer that [although] he [McKay] may not be at the Thursday meeting on October 5, that, however, he would ordain him at his office in the apartment just prior to the meeting if he was unable to attend the Temple meeting.

October 5, 1967, First Presidency meeting. President [N. Eldon] Tanner reported that Dr. [Aziz S.] Atiya of the University of Utah has made arrangements with the Metropolitan Museum of Arts in New York City for the Church to obtain possession of the Book of Abraham parchment which they now have in their possession, from which the Book of Abraham was translated. President Tanner explained that Dr. Atiya had been trying for some time to acquire this papyrus for the Church and had expected to exchange some other artifacts for it; that he has now received word that the museum will contribute the parchment to the Church without cost.

He stated that Dr. Hugh Nibley of the Brigham Young University has carefully checked pictures of the manuscript, that he is able to read some of the writings, and says that they are bona fide. It is suggested that Mr. Fisher [Henry G. Fischer],[17] the curator of that part of the museum where the manuscripts are located, would like to present them to the Church the latter part of October or the first of November.

President Tanner asked if it would meet with my approval if he made arrangements with the museum people to meet with me or someone else whom I might designate to receive the parchment. I agreed with this suggestion and authorized President Tanner to make the necessary arrangements for this presentation. ...

Ogden Temple—President Tanner asked if it was still my wish that the counselors call a meeting of Stake Presidents in the proposed Ogden Temple district for a further consideration of the site on which the Ogden Temple should be erected. He stated that there is considerable opposition to the proposition to erect this building on the Tabernacle Square in Ogden, and that when the matter was previously discussed by the First Presidency, it was the sentiment that the Stake Presidents in that area be called together, that we might obtain their views on the matter of the Temple site. I indicated my desire that this be done, and accordingly the Brethren will set a date for such a meeting.

Alvin R. Dyer—Ordained an Apostle—At 8:40 a.m. I received a call from Elder Dyer stating that I had said I wanted to ordain him to the Apostleship, and wondered if I would be at the Temple meeting this morning to do it; otherwise, one of the Counselors might ask if they should do it.

I told Elder Dyer that I wanted to do it, and then asked where he was, and he said that he was at his office in the Church Offices. I told him to stay there, and that I should call shortly.

---

17. Henry George Fischer (1924–2006) had been head of the museum's Department of Egyptology since 1964. He was born in Philadelphia and received his PhD from the University of Pennsylvania. He taught at the American University in Beirut for a while and authored several books on hieroglyphics. He most notably transported and installed the massive sandstone blocks of the Dendur temple ruins at the museum when the temple was threatened with inundation by the Aswan Dam construction.

After a few moments' discussion with the Counselors, I asked the secretary to call Elder Dyer and tell him to come right over.

Elder Dyer arrived at 9:15 a.m. I took his hand and welcomed him. He mentioned the funeral services of my sister, Annie,[18] and said he felt they were very appropriate. I told him how much I appreciated his attendance.

I invited Elder Dyer to sit by my side, and I asked him if he is willing to accept the calling of the Apostleship, and such other assignments that would go with it. Elder Dyer said he would do his utmost to faithfully fulfill the trust. I then asked him: "Is there any reason why you should not be ordained?" and Elder Dyer answered, "No, so far as I know." He stated that he is willing to accept the responsibility of this new call, whatever it might be.

I then asked Brother Dyer to sit on the leather ottoman placed in front of me, so that I could place my hands upon his head without standing, and asked Presidents [Hugh B.] Brown and Tanner to join me in laying hands upon Elder Dyer's head, and I was voice in ordaining him an Apostle of the Church in the following words:

"Brother Alvin R. Dyer, we lay our hands upon your head and ordain you an Apostle of The Church of Jesus Christ of Latter-day Saints (Elder Dyer's report of this blessing at this point: 'to serve in ways to which you will be assigned').

"We pray that the blessings of the Lord that accompany those who have authority to participate in these responsibilities may be yours. Be true to the calling and true to the Lord, and if you are faithful, the Lord will bless you in the performance of these duties. We bless you with all the authority pertaining to the duties of this office, and we bless you and ordain you in the name of the Lord Jesus Christ, Amen."

---

18. Annie Powell McKay Farr (1881–1967) died five days earlier on September 30. Like her older brother, she was born in Huntsville, attended the University of Utah, and became a school teacher. She married the young banker Thomas B. Farr in 1905 and moved with him to the small town of Smithfield, north of Logan. But in 1912 the couple left Smithfield to serve a mission together to the Hawaiian Islands, their children, Bramley and Genevieve, being born later in 1914 and 1920. Back in Smithfield, Annie became involved in founding a library and other civic projects. She traveled with her brother in 1963, after her husband's death, to Merthyr–Tydfil, Wales, to see where their mother was born.

The Counselors then departed for the Council Meeting in the Temple, and I asked Elder Dyer to remain for a conference with me.

I asked Elder Dyer to sit down, as I wanted to talk to him, and I expressed my feelings to him and told him, as I have a number of times, that I want him to attend every meeting that I hold with my Counselors, including those held in the Temple. He asked me how he would be notified as to when these meetings will be held, and I told him that I would have my secretary notify him.

I then said good-by to him, asking that the Lord continue to bless him in his responsibilities.

October 6, 1967, First Presidency meeting. We next discussed the Nauvoo Restoration, and the large expenditures of the Church's money on the projects that are going on. President [Joseph Fielding] Smith expressed himself, saying, "I want to make myself clear concerning the Nauvoo Restoration; I am not in favor of it. We were driven out of there [in 1846] by the forces of evil—so let the devil have it."

I assigned President Smith and Elder [Alvin R.] Dyer to look into the matter of Nauvoo Restoration—what the Church is doing; the cost, etc., and then to make a report to me.

October 12, 1967, First Presidency meeting. Elder [Alvin R.] Dyer asked me to clarify for the Brethren of the First Presidency his status in the matter of attendance at meetings, and as to what I had in mind for him to do so that there would be an understanding on the part of all; that he wanted to be where he was supposed to be and nowhere else. In response to my request that Elder Dyer explain the matter to the Brethren, he said that I had asked him to meet with the Brethren in the meetings of the First Presidency when the Counselors met with me. He said the question arose yesterday as to whether he was expected to meet in the meetings of the First Presidency when I was not present, and that I had wanted to make a statement on this matter this morning so that the Brethren would know that if he (Elder Dyer) came into a meeting of the First Presidency, he would be there by my appointment, and that Brother [Joseph] Anderson, Secretary to the First Presidency, is to advise him when such meetings are being held so that he can be present.

<u>To Attend all Meetings of the First Presidency</u>—Elder Dyer said that I had informed him that he is to attend the meetings of the First Presidency when I am present, as well as all other meetings of the First Presidency. Elder Dyer then turned to me and asked me if this understanding was in accordance with what I had said, and I said that that is right.

President [Hugh B.] Brown then inquired if it is my intention that Elder Dyer should attend all meetings of the First Presidency in whatever capacity. He said that Brother Dyer is not a member of the Twelve; that he is an Apostle, and asked me again what his status would be in the First Presidency's meetings.

<u>Called by President to be Assistant in the First Presidency</u>—Elder Dyer then made the following comment: "I might say that before I went to South America, the President asked to speak to me about going there, and asked how long I was going to be gone, and I told him that I had four Stake Conferences; and the President said, 'I want you to take these Conferences, and I am also advising (informing) you now that you are to be sustained as an Assistant in the Presidency.' He then said, 'This will be announced when you come home.' He never said anything at the time about the apostleship, and this was presented by him in his own feeling, and the way he wanted to do it in the Temple, and I knew nothing about that (the apostleship), but he did make this other statement to me before I went to South America."

President [N. Eldon] Tanner then spoke up and said, "As I follow you, Elder Dyer, what the President wants is to have you as his personal advisor and assistant."

Elder Dyer: "He has never said anything about an advisor. I think what the President was referring to—you know the revelation about this—I have read it a hundred times trying to get my own mind straightened on this, where it refers to those who may be called to assist in the Presidency up to the number of twelve if need be, that they are to assist the Presidency as Counselors in the presidency."

President Brown: "Is that your understanding; that you are a Counselor in the Presidency?" …

Brother Dyer: "I have tried to think in my own mind the reasons President McKay presented me for the apostleship. Was it to give me the status of a position in the Counselorship to the First Presidency that all the other members hold? This was his feeling, and this is what he did on his own. That is the only reason I can see for it. He said, 'Now you have the status and the blessing of holding the office of an apostle.' I am stating this correctly, President?"

I answered in the affirmative.

President Tanner: "Then Brother Dyer will attend our meetings whenever the First Presidency meets, and we can carry on that way."

I said, "That is right."

Brother Dyer: "In answer to President Brown's question, will I be there as a Counselor in the Presidency, or will I attend just as an Apostle, or both?"

Will Attend Meetings as a Counselor. I said, "You will attend as a counselor."

President [Joseph Fielding] Smith: "He would do it just the same as I do it."

President Tanner: "Brother Dyer would be here as an assistant and that is it, isn't it?"

I said, "That is right."

President Tanner: "If you are called by the President as an assistant, then that is it."

President Brown: "You are his representative in our meetings."

Brother Dyer [to McKay]: "You did not want to sustain me as a Counselor in the Presidency? Is this what you had in mind, or did you have in mind that I would be just an assistant to you as the President?"

I said, "You will be an assistant to the President."

To Attend Meetings Whether or Not President McKay is Present. Brother Dyer: "Now I understand I am to attend the meetings as your representative when you cannot be there and also when the President is present."

I said, "As you stand now, you are not an interloper."

President Smith: "I am the President of the Council of the Twelve, set apart to that position; but when President McKay set me apart it was to be a counselor in the First Presidency, and Brother Dyer is called as an assistant to the President. Brother Isaacson and I were called to be Counselors in the First Presidency.["]

President Tanner: "Brother Dyer is called an assistant to the President."

(Later, when meeting with Elder Dyer alone, President McKay said it was apparent that Elder Dyer's status should be that of a Counselor.)

November 7, 1967, First Presidency meeting. President [N. Eldon] Tanner reported that arrangements have been made to receive the Book of Abraham papyri from the Metropolitan Museum of Arts in New York on Monday, November 27. President Tanner said that they are attempting to keep the matter quiet until that time when they will arrange for the press to have representatives present. President Tanner will go to New York with Dr. [Aziz S.] Atiya of the University of Utah on Monday, November 27, to receive the papyri.

The question was raised as to where these papyri should be placed, and President Tanner suggested that for the time being at least, they be placed at the Brigham Young University in Provo, where they could be in safekeeping[,] or in the vault in Little Cottonwood Canyon, although he thought it would be preferable to have them at the BYU.

It was agreed that the Book of Abraham manuscript should be placed with the Brigham Young University. ...

Later, at the meeting of the First Presidency held Tuesday, November 28, 1967, it was decided to place these papyri in the vault in the Church Historian's Office.

November 8, 1967, First Presidency meeting. Attention was called to correspondence which originated with a letter from ... Westport, Washington, and concerning which we have had a letter from ... the Olympia Stake regarding the removal of a picture of the head of Christ from the wall of the Grays Harbor Ward chapel. [The writer] explains the reason for this removal; namely, that the Handbook of Instructions states that "murals or pictures should not be placed in chapels but should be used in the foyer or office or one of the other rooms." President [Joseph Fielding] Smith mentioned that he had seen the picture in question and he did not like the picture too well.

We felt that it might raise some serious questions in the minds of the people if we objected to hanging on our chapel walls a picture of the Savior, provided it is something that represents our ideas of the Lord. ...

Council Minutes—Deletion of Paragraph—I then picked up the

Council minutes from my desk which had been given to me, and went over them again, and I instructed Clare [Middlemiss] to tell Brother Joseph Anderson that I wanted the following statement by President [Hugh B.] Brown stricken out:

"President McKay is in a weakened condition. His bodily strength is waning. He is not as alert as he was."

I said, "I am alert; and I know what I am doing."

Later, Clare reported that Brother Anderson said he could not take the statement out unless he obtained President Brown's approval, and she answered that after all, the President of the Church had asked him to take it out; that probably he had better telephone him and get the instructions directly from him.

A little later, President Brown called Clare into his office and asked her if she had called my attention to his remarks at the Council Meeting, and she said, "No, the President reads all of the minutes of the Council meeting—he read that statement himself, and when he read it, he looked up and said, 'I am alert; I know what I am doing, and I want that paragraph stricken out.'"

Clare said that she had written up an account of her conversation with President Brown for her own records, but would not include them in this diary. At any rate, the phrase "he is not as alert as he used to be," was finally take[n] out by Joseph Anderson after he had received permi[ss]ion from President Brown to do so.

November 9, 1967, 9:00 a.m. … Received a call from President Hugh B. Brown. He asked me [Clare Middlemiss] to come into his office. He apologized for the way he talked to me yesterday. He said, "How do you feel?" I answered, "Well, I didn't sleep very much last night." I told him how I felt about some of the things he said to me, and then he said, "Well, I was upset and nervous; I want you to know that I have no ill feelings toward you—you have done a wonderful job for the President." I told President Brown that the President does what he wants to do; that "no one tells him what to do." At this we parted with good spirits and feelings.

November 16, 1967, 10:30–11:45 a.m. Consultation with Clare [Middlemiss]. She said she is having a difficult time getting to see me; that the nurse tells her almost every time she calls that I am too tired to see her. I instructed Clare to pay no attention whatever to what any of them say; that she is to see me under any conditions, at any time, unless I am confined to my bed and too sick to see her. I told her that I worry if she does not come over to see me and report the matters that are coming to my office.

Clare said that the nurses make her very nervous, because she does not want to intrude nor do any harm to me. She said she told the nurse that she could tell the minute that I was tired, and stopped even though I had protested and asked her why she was leaving. I said, "Well, you keep coming; it does me good to see you, rather than sit here and worry about what is going on."

November 21, 1967, First Presidency meeting. We decided that due to the fact that Church departments are now scattered over the city in twelve different buildings and the further fact that conditions are looking up in the business area of the city (the erection of the Office Building was previously delayed at the request of the business men in town), that we should go forward at once to erect the new Church Office Building. ...

President [Hugh B.] Brown mentioned that Richard P. Condie, Tabernacle Choir Director, has received an application from a Negro woman, member of the Church to become a member of the Choir. Brother Condie feels that if she is admitted to the Choir, they should have at least one more Negro woman to be with her when they go on trips.

In discussing the matter, we felt that if we admitted one or two Negroes into the Choir, we would be opening the doors to other applications that might be received. President [N. Eldon] Tanner suggested that we take the attitude that every member of the Choir must be a member of the Church worthy of a Temple Recommend, in which event Negro women would be unable to come because colored people are not given recommends to the Temple. In this event, they could not say that we are discriminating.[19]

Elder Dyer suggested that we say to this woman that we are not receiving applications at the present time, and we could then make certain that

---

19. It would be two years before the first black woman, Marilyn Yuille, would be allowed to join the choir, followed almost immediately by Wynetta Martin. Both were recent converts to the LDS Church. Martin was hired by BYU to teach a class on black culture to nursing students. Hicks, *Mormon Tabernacle Choir*, chap. 6. See also Martin's 1972 autobiography, *Black Mormon Tells Her Story: "The Truth Sang Louder Than My Position."*

all members of the Choir are members of the Church in good standing and worthy of Temple recommends. President Brown was asked to ascertain from Brother Condie how many non-members are in the Choir as well as those who could not receive Temple Recommends, and also what the repercussions would be if we were to release these people from the Choir. ...

President Brown called attention to a letter from [the] President of the Tampa Stake, in which [he] reports that he and his wife had joined the John Birch Society, and he is asking if it would be fitting and proper to show to various Priesthood groups in the Stake a film entitled, "The United Nations—the Peace Dove Unmasked," which had been shown to the John Birch Society members.

It was decided to advise [the stake president] against showing the film he mentions to Priesthood groups in the Stake.

November 26, 1967, 11:15 a.m. ... By appointment Elder Alvin R. Dyer called at the Hotel [Utah], and we discussed the letter that I had asked Joseph Anderson to prepare on Tuesday, November 21, 1967, in answer to one of the Stake Presidents in Florida, who is a member of the John Birch Society, and had asked for permission to show an anti-Communist film to the Priesthood of the Wards of his Stake. (See diary of November 21.)

We discussed the policy statement regarding members of the Church joining the John Birch Society which we have been sending out to all members who have inquired whether or not they could join the Society. ...

Brother Dyer said, in light of the above statement, to impose upon any member who holds a position of leadership in a Ward or Stake anything beyond that which is intended in the statement referred to— [one] that involves a "must" clause in order to holding position in the Church—would not only deprecate, but would deny personal freedom to the individual which would be contrary to the principles of the Gospel.

Brother Dyer quoted the Prophet Joseph Smith wherein he said, "I want the liberty of thinking and believing as I please. It feels so good not to be trammeled. It does not prove that a man is not a good man because he errs in doctrine." (DHC [*Documentary History of the Church*], Vol. V, page 340.)

After further discussion, I said that I feel that the policy statement is adequate in answering the particular letter in question. I asked Brother

Dyer to see Brother Joseph Anderson, who is preparing the letter concerning this, and that I wanted to see the letter so that we could go over it.

November 27, 1967, First Presidency meeting. President [Hugh B.] Brown reported that through some of our friends we have been able to acquire some valuable documents which were presented to the First Presidency last Tuesday by President [N. Eldon] Tanner, and the President asked that they be brought here so that the brethren of the Twelve might see them and become acquainted with the procedure that resulted in their acquisition; and also know something of the authenticity of the documents we now have. President Brown asked President Tanner to present to the brethren a report of what happened, and also to show to them the documents themselves. He said that as they are very fragile it wouldn't be wise to pass them around for each one to handle, that they would be placed on the table for each one to see.

President Tanner then made the following report. He said that just over a year ago Dr. Aziz S. Atiya, who is a Coptic and a great student of literature and ancient history, came to him and told him that while he was in the Metropolitan Museum of Art in New York in the department where they have their papyri and materials of that kind, as he was going through these materials in his study, be accidentally came on to a little parcel which he opened, and recognized it immediately as the original papyrus, a facsimile of which appears at the beginning of the Book of Abraham in the Pearl of Great Price, and is numbered one, which facsimile was made by the Prophet Joseph Smith. When he saw this, he immediately recognized the great discovery he had made, and he told President Tanner about it.

President Tanner then reported the matter to the First Presidency and subsequently told Dr. Atiya that we were extremely interested, that we thought this was a tremendous thing, and he said that he thought possibly he would be able to make this available to the Church, if we were prepared to cooperate with him. He said he had no idea what it would cost but he knew they would not sell it for money. He thought possibly he could get some Egyptian artifacts that would appeal to them, that he might give them in exchange for these papyri. Accordingly Dr. Atiya was authorized to do that.

After negotiating with them for some time, he called President Tanner and asked to see him immediately, and told him that he had just received a phone call from Dr. Henry G. Fischer, curator of the Egyptian section, saying that Dr. Thomas P. F. Hoving,[20] who is the Director of the Metropolitan Museum of Art, had given authorization to present these to the Church at no cost. President Tanner said that when he received this information he wrote to Dr. Hoving, and that Dr. Atiya also wrote him, arranging for the transfer of these items to the Church on November 27 at mid-day. President Tanner said that Dr. Hoving is an outstanding individual, and that he had been most gracious in all their dealings.

President Tanner stated that he had here for the brethren to see the original of Facsimile No. 1 that appears in the Book of Abraham. He said it is not entirely in the condition it was at the time the Prophet had it; and that he also had some other papyri and pictures of these various items, but it would seem advisable not to unwrap the papyri and handle them because of the fragility, and they were carefully packed when they were given to us. He said there are eleven of them.

President Tanner said that Dr. Hugh Nibley says there is no question about their authenticity, that Dr. Hoving, who is the [museum] director; Dr. Fischer, the Egyptologist; and Dr. Joseph V. Noble, who has been with the museum for years, all say that this is actually the original from which the facsimile in the Pearl of Great Price was made.

President Tanner said that in addition we have a letter, a typed copy of which he had brought with him to show to the brethren (he did not bring the original with him to the meeting). He said that in the typed copy there are two mistakes, that in the copy they have 1846 instead of 1856; and in the typed copy the word "his" is used instead of "her." Elder Howard W. Hunter was requested to read the letter. ...

President Tanner said that the museum people say that the parchment was turned over to Mr. A[bel] Combs,[21] and that when he died he

---

20. Thomas Pearsall Field Hoving (1931–2009) had become director of the Metropolitan Museum of Art earlier that year. He would stay for ten years. Born in New York City, he studied at nearby Princeton University for his BA, MFA, and PhD degrees. Fortuitously, his approach at the museum was to emphasize quality over quantity. The Joseph Smith papyri held little intrinsic interest for the museum.

21. Abel Combs (1823–92) purchased the papyri from Emma Smith in 1856, apparently as an investment. He was a metal worker who made and sold lamps.

left some of the material, a part of which is included in this collection, to his housekeeper; and then his housekeeper's son or daughter took them to the museum in 1918 to see if the museum would be interested in them, and the museum was not interested; and then his or her daughter's husband brought them to the museum in 1947, and the museum bought them at that time and has had them in its possession since that time.

President Tanner said that they went to the museum at noon on Monday, November 27, 1967, under assignment from the First Presidency and in accordance with previous arrangement. Provision had been made to have television cameras set up, and representatives of the U[nited] P[ress] I[nternational] and the A[ssociated] P[ress] were present; Arch Madsen [of KSL TV] and Earl Hawkes [of the *Deseret News*] were there with three of their men to take pictures and make reports. He said that at this meeting Dr. Hoving handed these items to President Tanner in the presence of Dr. Atiya [of the University of Utah], [and from the museum] Dr. Fischer and Dr. Noble. President Tanner said he had invited the five stake presidents in that area, and three regional representatives, and the mission president to attend this transfer, but some of them could not be present.

Following the presentation a luncheon was held to which all these men were invited; also Frank Wangemann, who is manager of the Waldorf-Astoria. He said that if anything ever touched Mr. Wangemann he thought this did, and that after lunch Mr. Wangemann talked to Dr. Atiya for some time.

President Tanner said that no one could have been more gracious than was Dr. Hoving. President Tanner said to him, "You cannot understand what this means to us and how much we appreciate it." Dr. Hoving said, "I think we can. We have things like this in our museum, thousands of them, but this is significant and important to your Church, and we think it should go home." ...

President Tanner said that at the luncheon he asked Dr. Atiya and Dr. Noble to speak, that Dr. Hoving was unable to attend the luncheon. Dr. Noble is the vice president of the museum. He said that Dr. Atiya was most complimentary to the people of the Church and the Church itself. He said how pleased he was to be a party to the turning of these manuscripts over to the Church. He said that he had made three very important discoveries in his life, and many important ones, but this was the crowning discovery of them all, knowing what it meant to the Church.

Dr. Noble made a statement to the effect that in their research they find artifacts here and there and put them all together and say that is the story, but he said that we have the actual thing here, and there is no question about it.

President Tanner said that when this was presented to the First Presidency, President McKay was deeply moved and suggested that the brethren of the Twelve should see it. The President said this is the most significant thing that has happened to the Church in a long time. ...

President Tanner showed to the brethren pictures of the other ten pieces, of which we have the originals, and said that it is the intention to send these papyri to the Brigham Young University for safe keeping, and to make it possible for Dr. Nibley to carry on his careful research. He said that we know that the Book of Abraham was not written from these papyri of which we have the pictures. President Tanner stated that he would have a copy of these pictures made, a full set of them, for each one of the brethren. President Tanner further stated that these papyri are pasted on heavy paper, and on the back of the paper on each of the pieces is some drawing or sketching.

Elder [Gordon B.] Hinckley commented that there might be some reasonable assumption that there are some of these papyri somewhere else.

The brethren urged that the utmost care be taken to preserve these items, particularly the original papyrus from which Facsimile No. 1 [in the Book of Abraham] was taken. President Brown moved that this particular piece of papyrus be left in the hands of President Tanner and Brother [Howard W.] Hunter, with instructions to carefully preserve it, and prepare it for deposit either in the vault in the canyon or the church files in the Historian's Office, President Tanner and Brother Hunter to determine this point, that it be not sent to the Brigham Young University. Motion was seconded by Elder [Delbert L.] Stapley and unanimously approved.

December 1, 1967. By appointment, met with Elder Alvin R. Dyer, at which time we discussed the matter of answering [the stake president's] letter [discussed previously on November 21] regarding his membership in the John Birch Society. After considering very carefully the answer prepared by the counselors, I decided that the Church should be consistent in its instructions to all members regarding their joining the John Bird Society; namely, that they are free to do so as long as they do not use the Church in any way in furthering membership in the Society, and also that Church buildings not be used for holding meetings of that Society, etc.

I therefore instructed Elder Dyer that he should return the letter to the Secretary to the First Presidency [Joseph Anderson] with the instructions that he re-write the letter omitting the last paragraph stating that "it would be inadvisable for Presidents of Stakes, Bishops of wards, and others in Church leadership positions to become affiliated with the John Birch Society, etc."

I stated that that paragraph amounted to telling [the stake president and his wife] that they should get out of the Society; and that I felt the Church should not dictate to them what they could do in matters of this kind; that they had their free agency to do as they wished, so long as they adhere to the policy of not using the Church to further the interests of this society.

December 6, 1967, First Presidency meeting. President [N. Eldon] Tanner mentioned a matter that had been discussed by us a short time ago pertaining to [the stake president] who reports that he and his wife had joined the John Birch Society and he asks whether it would be proper for them to show a picture to the Priesthood that had been prepared by these John Birch people. When the matter was discussed previously by us, it was decided to write [the stake president], telling him that he should not show this picture to the Priesthood, and that while everyone has his free agency relative to joining organizations of this kind, we think it inadvisable for Stake presidents, Bishops, and other Church leaders to become affiliated with the Society because of the influence it would have upon members of the Church under their jurisdiction.

President Tanner presented a letter that had been prepared to [send] to this effect, which letter was signed by President Joseph Fielding Smith and President Nathan Eldon Tanner, and which had not as yet been presented to President [Hugh B.] Brown for his signature, but President Brown said that he would wish to sign it. However, the letter was returned with the notation that the concluding paragraph should be eliminated. This was the paragraph in which reference was made to the inadvisability of Presidents of Stakes and other Church leaders becoming affiliated with this organization and similar organizations. When the letter was returned, asking that this paragraph be deleted, it was stated that I wanted the last paragraph deleted.

President Brown said that the letter as written represented what the First Presidency had decided, and he did not understand why the last paragraph should be deleted, although both Presidents Brown and Tanner said that if that was my desire, of course, they wanted to do what I felt should be done.

President Tanner said that it was his feeling that our position should be made clear because we are accused from time to time that the Church is backing the John Birch Society. If our Stake Presidents and Bishops were to join the organization and begin to hold meetings and show pictures and lectures, it certainly would look as though the Church was in favor of it. (It is understood that no member can use the Church for John Birch Society meetings.)

I said that I think the least we have to do with the Birch Society the better.

Presidents Brown, Tanner, and Smith felt that the letter should go as it was originally written, without the proposed deletion.

The letter as originally written was read and I also read it personally. In answer to an inquiry as to whether I am willing that my signature be attached to the letter without the concluding paragraph being deleted, I said that I was [willing to do so]. ...

President Tanner reported that following the First Presidency's meeting on Wednesday last, when the box was opened containing certain papyri that had been turned over to the Church through President Tanner by the director of the National Museum of Art in New York, these items were taken to the Council of the Twelve the following day and shown to the brethren for their information. Of particular interest was the original of facsimile #1 that appears in the Book of Abraham. It was agreed that these papyri should be sent to the Brigham Young University for safekeeping. President Tanner said that he got in touch with President [Ernest L.] Wilkinson, ascertained that they had a place of safekeeping and he said the place they have would be as safe as any place he knew of. President Tanner explained to him that we want to make the papyri available to Dr. Hugh Nibley to continue his studies, with which President Wilkinson agreed.[22] President Tanner explained that at the meeting with the Council of the First Presidency and Quorum of the Twelve, it was decided that we would keep the original of facsimile #1 in safekeeping here. It is not in proper shape for preservation in its present condition and is very fragile, so yesterday Hugh Nibley and the assistant to the curator at the BYU came up and President Tanner and Howard Hunter, who were assigned by the Council to take care of these things, turned over these documents in the wooden box to Dr. Nibley and this other brother, with the understanding that they would properly preserve them in glass and that they would take the necessary measures to provide proper preservation for the original facsimile #1, and return it to us so that we can place it in safekeeping here until such time as it should be decided where it might be placed permanently.

President Tanner explained that the way they take care of these items is to build up the humidity to what it should be, place the papyri under glass and seal it so that no air or moisture can get into it. In that way it can be preserved indefinitely. President Tanner said that Dr. Nibley suggested that one of these papyri, which is perhaps of least importance, might be placed with pictures of the collection in a window here where people could see them. He did not feel that we should display the originals. President Brown suggested that every precaution be taken to make certain that nothing shall happen to these papyri and that we will know where they are.

I asked President Tanner if he is sure that everything is all right, and President Tanner said that he felt quite satisfied with it, and I said that we would hold President Tanner responsible for it.

December 7, 1967. Elder Mark E. Petersen said that the Church Information Service would appreciate some help on a matter that may give some concern. He said that with George Romney entering the political

---

22. When it was all over, Nibley confessed that since he was "not yet confident in Egyptian, I frankly skirmished and sparred for time, making the most of those sources which support the Book of Abraham from another side, the recent and growing writing, ancient and modern, about the forgotten legends and traditions of Abraham." His involvement was nevertheless crucial for the church's early interpretation of the artifacts, even if it created an apologetic wall around the topic. Nibley, *Nibley on the Timely and Timeless*, xxxvi; Petersen, *Hugh Nibley*, 317

campaign for President, many anti-Church articles will be published in magazines and newspapers. He said that already efforts have been made to discredit him by trying to discredit the Church, and using it as a means of embarrassing him. He said we cannot stop all these articles, that everything is being done that possibly can be done to put the proper information out before the people. He said he was wondering if in a case where an article is published that is particularly slanderous and libelous, a libel suit would be a good thing. He felt that the editors and some of the writers in these magazines and columns think they can get away with almost anything in slandering the Church, and doing it on the basis of politics. He wondered what the Brethren would think if there were a case where there was clear evidence of falsehood and slander if a suit against some such publication were filed, whether it would slow down some of the other publications. President [Hugh B.] Brown expressed the sentiment that it would be better if Elder Petersen were to present a specific case that he thought would stand up in court. He thought we should hold the matter over until such a case might be presented, and then consideration could be given to the matter. ...

It was agreed that nothing should be done until a specific case might present itself which it is thought would stand up in court, at which time the Brethren would give it consideration.

December 13, 1967, 8:30 a.m. ... Presidents [Hugh B.] Brown, [N. Eldon] Tanner and [Joseph Fielding] Smith, and Elder [Alvin R.] Dyer and I met with Dr. Aziz S. Atiya, Professor of the University of Utah in the apartment at the Hotel Utah.

Professor Atiya called on me to give his personal report of his discovery of the papyri in the Metropolitan Museum in New York City, and of the series of events leading up to the presentation of the papyri to the Church.

He expressed himself as attributing this experience as the crowning achievement of his life. He spoke of his Coptic studies and of a book he would soon have published, a copy of which he would present to me later. These Coptic studies refer to the teachings and beliefs of an ancient Egyptian Christian by the name of Copt, who lived in the pre-Nicean period.[23]

---

23. The word Copt is generally thought to be a corruption of the Greek word for Egyptian. What is expressed here may have been Professor Aziz's own hypothesis about

Dr. Atiya, a non-member of the Church, but a good friend, said that he was browsing through the papyri collection of the New York Metropolitan Museum of Art, seeking for coptic or Islamic papyri when he saw the facsimile #1 (which he recognized immediately as being from the Pearl of Great Price) and other papyri. He said he knew it was the one Joseph Smith had had.

Upon his return to Salt Lake, he reported his find to the First Presidency through President Tanner, who reported it in a First Presidency's meeting where it was suggested that Dr. Atiya be given authority to negotiate for the Church to see if they could come into possession of the collection. He subsequently, because of his friendship with Dr. Henry G. Fischer, curator of the Egyptian section in the Museum, made arrangements for the Church to receive this collection as a gift from the Museum.

Professor Atiya referred very feelingly to previous meetings he had had with me, and I expressed deep appreciation to him for what he had done for the Church in being instrumental in the return of the papyri to the Church—bringing them "back home" as the professor put it.

I asked him if there were any expenses he had incurred that the Church could reimburse him for, and Dr. Atiya said: "What I have done in time and money is my gift to the Church, which Church I regard very highly."

All the Brethren present joined me in expressing commendation and appreciation to Dr. Atiya. ...

Dr. Atiya left shortly after 9:00 a.m., and the Brethren of the First Presidency and Elder Dyer remained to discuss the Pearl of Great Price papyri further, and to have a most interesting and important discussion concerning manuscripts and records of early Church history.

Reorganized Church—Appreciation for copies of Papyri letter—Brother Dyer read a portion of a letter received just yesterday from Wallace Smith, President of the Reorganized Church [of Jesus Christ of Latter Day Saints], expressing appreciation for [photographic] copies of the papyri and the letter of Emma Smith and his father, Joseph Smith III, regarding the authenticity of the papyri. He also gave a report of the Historian's Office of the Reorganized Church, and mentioned that he is endeavoring to secure copies [for us] of records of early history that we do not have.

a possible Greek epithet for an early settler. In any case, the traditional belief among Copts is that Mark the evangelist was the original Egyptian Christian.

President Smith said that the records which the Prophet Joseph Smith had—his journal, etc.—came down to our Church, and that except for the records which Emma Smith had in her own possession and those withheld by John Whitmer, we possess the major part of the historical records.

I told Elder Dyer to keep up what he is trying to do in being friendly with the Reorganized Church, and then asked President Joseph Fielding Smith to prepare a listing of all the historical documents that we have in our archives.

We also talked about the "Inspired Version" of the Holy Bible,[24] representing the translation and revision made by Joseph Smith, and that we should determine to what extent our current editions differ from the 1867 and prior editions. Elder Dyer reported that while he was President of the Central States Mission, he had secured a copy of the 1867 edition for Elder Delbert L. Stapley, and I asked him to get this copy from Elder Stapley and have the comparison study made.

This was a very significant meeting, both in view of the report of Dr. Atiya, and for the discussion we had concerning historical records and the "Inspired Version" of the Holy Bible and our decision thereto. I stated to the Brethren that this was a most sacred meeting and that the subjects discussed should be kept most confidential and that we should go ahead without fail with the matters as directed.

December 15, 1967. Elder [Alvin R.] Dyer, responding to the assignment given him by me, reported further on the publication of the Holy Scriptures—Inspired Version. He stated that as is known, the first edition, published by the Reorganized Church, came out in 1867. It was followed by subsequent printings. In 1944, a new "corrected version" was published, in which a number of textual changes were made from earlier editions.

He mentioned that the Inspired Version or revision is being used quite extensively by our people. Of latest report, 2,500 copies have been sold this year. And also from reports the sales are increasing. It is doubtful that our members know of the changes that have been made.

---

24. For what is more commonly referred to as the Joseph Smith Translation, see Robert J. Matthews's *"A Plainer Translation": Joseph Smith's Translation of the Bible*, published in 1975 by BYU Press.

He stated that it appears that we have three possibilities:

(1) To say nothing about the matter—to leave it as it is.

(2) Investigate the copyrights of the Reorganized Church's publishings—with the thought of publishing an Inspired Version of our own after researching to determine authenticity. (This would be difficult since we do not have the Prophet's original writings.)

(3) To stop all handling by any Church bookstores of the mutated editions of the so-called Inspired Verison as published by the Reorganized Church.

I asked Elder Dyer to make the investigation and report back to us.

December 19, 1967, First Presidency meeting. Elder [Alvin R.] Dyer mentioned that he had received a letter from the historian of the Reorganized Church regarding items that they had in their historian's office archives that might be of value to us. He felt that we are approaching a time when the Reorganized Church people will let us have access to read these documents and ascertain what they have. Their historian, in his letter, expresses the hope that the feeling to let us have access to their documents will be reciprocated by us. President [Joseph Fielding] Smith said that we have shown them many documents that we have in the Historian's office. Elder Dyer said that the thing that seemed to influence this attitude on the part of these Reorganized Church people was the presentation to them of pictures of the papyri that had been turned over to the Church by the Museum of Art in New York. They feel that this was a very generous gesture on the part of our Church, and they appreciate it very much. Brother Dyer thought that this thing is opening the way for us in the manner referred to.

December 21, 1967, First Presidency meeting. Elder [Alvin R.] Dyer referred to a letter that had been written for the First Presidency to sign addressed to [a stake president] in answer to [a] letter that had been received from him stating that he and his wife had joined the John Birch Society, and asking if they might show in their Priesthood Meeting a Birch Society film. The First Presidency had written stating that they should not show the film to the Priesthood or other Church gathering, and had stated in the concluding paragraph that because of the influence it would have upon the members of the Church under the Stake President's jurisdiction, it was felt inadvisable for Stake Presidents and other Church leaders to join the Birch Society or other similar organizations. Elder Dyer mentioned that in a meeting he had with President McKay, he had discussed this concluding paragraph and the President had expressed the thought that this paragraph should be eliminated and that he had asked Elder Dyer to convey this word to Brother [Joseph] Anderson, which he did. He had also asked Brother Dyer, so he said, to call [the stake president] in Florida and talk to him and explain to him that nothing should be done to use the Birch Society to encroach upon the Church. Brother Dyer said he did this, telling [the stake president] that under no circumstances should he use the Society to exploit the Church to build up what he felt personally. [The stake president] told him at that time that he had received the letter of the First Presidency advising him that it was inadvisable for Stake Presidents and Bishops to be identified with this organization. Brother Dyer said he asked [the stake president] how he felt about it, and he said he had mixed feelings, but he wanted to follow the counsel of the President of the Church. Secretary Anderson explained that inasmuch as the letter was a First Presidency letter it had been taken back to the First Presidency for their further consideration before making the deletion Brother Dyer had mentioned; that all four of the Brethren of the First Presidency were present, that President McKay asked that the paragraph in question be read two or three times, that he then took the letter and read the paragraph carefully and indicated his approval, that Brother Anderson then asked him if he was authorized to attach his, the President's signature, to the letter and the President said yes. Elder Dyer said that this brings up a question about answering letters one way to one person and answering them another way to another. He contended that letters have been sent to Stake Presidents and Bishops and Seminary teachers and other responsible men all over the United States where there has been no discrimination as to their position in the Church. The Presidency had merely stated the policy in these letters that they make their own choice in the matter, but they must not involve the Church.

President [N. Eldon] Tanner commented that the problem is that we find reports coming from different areas of the Church that some of the Brethren belonging to this Society get up in Church and advertise that one of these pictures is going to be shown to the Priesthood, etc.

Elder Dyer said he did not think we should create class distinction in the Church, that when a letter like this goes to a Stake President or a Bishop and he violates the advice given, it becomes a matter of action, that to tell him that he should not join such a Society is depriving the individual of his rights.

President Tanner said that he thought we could properly say that we advise against it because of the problems involved; he thought that was what cause[d] the President to decide it this way.

President McKay confirmed the action that had been taken.

Birth Control—Bill to be Introduced to Legislature—President Tanner mentioned a letter that had been received from [a doctor] of Ogden. He says that because of the increasing number of women who go out of this state for abortions and the increasing number of men who go away to be sterilized, the Utah Obstetrical and Gynecological Society, to which he belongs, is preparing to have introduced in the legislature a bill which would provide a new abortion and sterilization law that would allow good medical practice and a reasonable approach to this problem. He states that the Society would like to present to the Council of the Twelve, or as many members as might be deemed necessary, the reasons for the proposed legislation. It was our sentiment that this is a matter with which we should not become involved.

December 28, 1967, 10:45 a.m. My secretary, Clare [Middlemiss], came over. She handed me letters and memoranda that had come to my office for my attention. We discussed the letter signed by the First Presidency that was sent to [a stake president] regarding his being a member of the John Birch Society, which indicates that Stake Presidents, Bishops, etc. should not become members of that Society. Clare called attention to the fact that I have been sending letters all along stating that so long as these local authorities do not use the Church nor their influence in any way to further the cause of this Society, they have their free agency to join this or any other organization they wished to protect and maintain our freedoms and way of life.

I stated that I did not want that letter to the Tampa Stake to be sent without the deletion of the paragraph stating that it would be best if Stake Presidents, Bishops, etc. did not join the John Birch Society; that I had instructed Elder Alvin R. Dyer when he and Elder Mark E. Petersen met with me, to tell Joseph Anderson to write the letter over and delete that paragraph, but that later he had gone to the Counselors about it. They had brought it up at a First Presidency's meeting and stressed the point that Stake presidents and Bishops are showing John Birch Society films in Stake and Ward buildings, and are using their influence in favor of that Society. The Counselors felt it was very necessary to include that paragraph in the letter, and at their insistence I had given my consent.

However, the more I think about it, the more I think we should have left the whole matter where it stood, and that they should have followed the previous instructions I have [given] to Joseph Anderson when I discussed this matter with Elders Petersen and Dyer.

18 Predicaments: Policies, Politics, and Succession, 1968

Reed Benson came to my office with the personal letter from Governor Wallace to President McKay, and also a copy of Elder Benson's paper on the policies of Governor Wallace. It was at this time that Reed injected the thought that if the ticket of Wallace and Benson were elected and anything happened to Wallace, Elder Benson would be President. He also stressed how important he thought a decision made by President McKay, a prophet of God, was, and that it should be his own decision. I heartily agreed with this, but told Reed how necessary it was to such a decision for the President to have the facts and understand the problem. —February 13, 1968

January 5, 1968. One matter I decided upon, after discussing the matter at the meeting of the Brethren this morning, and later with Elder Alvin R. Dyer, is to have Elder Dyer occupy President [Thorpe B.] Isaacson's office in the northwest corner of the first floor of the Administration Building, which has been unused since Brother Isaacson's illness two years ago. President [N. Eldon] Tanner had suggested at the meeting that Patriarch Eldred G. Smith take this office, but after thinking the matter over, I decided that it would be unwise to bring him in to that office where members of the Church, mothers with children, and others would be coming right into the offices of the First Presidency where confidential work is being done, and where meetings are often held.

In talking the matter over later with Elder Dyer, <u>I told him that it</u>

was my desire that he occupy that office; that, however, I do not want President Isaacson to be offended or hurt in any way. I said that I should like to call on him myself and talk to him about it, but that I do not feel up to going in a wheelchair to his apartment. I, therefore, asked Elder Dyer to call on President Isaacson, talk the matter over with him, and see how he feels about it. Brother Dyer said that he would go this Sunday and take Sister Dyer with him.

January 11, 1968, 10:30 a.m. ... Went over to the apartment. When I [Clare Middlemiss] walked into President McKay's office, he was sitting in his chair dozing. The lights were off, the curtains were drawn, and it was dark, warm, and close in his office. As I quietly took my coat off, he woke up and smiled brightly. I opened the curtains and showed him the blue skies and bright sunshine, what little of it he can see from his office window. I said that it was a beautiful day—a day really for a trip to Huntsville. He said, "It is always a day for a trip to Huntsville—rain, snow, or sunshine!" ...

President McKay took joy in reading letters from members and friends who had written to express their love and appreciation to him for his remembrance of them during the holidays.

January 15, 1968. I discussed with Clare [Middlemiss] the matter of President [Thorpe B.] Isaacson's office which has been unoccupied since his illness two years ago. I said that President [N. Eldon] Tanner had suggested in a recent meeting of the First Presidency that Patriarch Eldred G. Smith occupy the office, but that after giving the matter much thought, I feel that this would be unwise because it would mean the bringing into the office of the First Presidency mothers with their babies, and many members of the Church seeking Patriarchal blessings and they would have to wait around and pass right through the private offices of the First Presidency.

I stated that I had had a conference with Elder Alvin R. Dyer regarding the office, and inasmuch as Elder Dyer needs another office because of the undesirability of the one he now occupies, and the further fact that I should like him nearer to the First Presidency, I have decided that he (Elder Dyer) should take that office. I asked Clare to tell Elder

Dyer to move into the office immediately. She said, "Do you want me to get him on the phone now so that you can tell him?" and I said, "No, that is not necessary; I have already talked the matter over with him and he is the one who should go in there; you call him and tell him that I want him to move in that office immediately."

Clare said that she would get the word to Elder Dyer as soon as possible. ...

Later, I was amused and somewhat surprised to learn of the reactions of several persons regarding Elder Dyer's occupying President Isaacson's office. Richard Isaacson, son of President Isaacson, attempted to clear up the misunderstandings that some persons have about the occupancy of his father's office, stating that his father had been very pleased about Elder Dyer's coming into his office. He said his father had asked for a piece of paper, upon which he had written as best he could the following: "The work must go on. President McKay needs help. I want Elder Dyer in there." Dick said, "I have that note and I shall always keep it."

January 16, 1968, First Presidency. Reference was made to a discussion in a recent meeting of the First Presidency at which time President Joseph Fielding Smith was asked to furnish a list of early Church documents held by the Historian's Office.

This matter was discussed in connection with a report by Brother [Alvin R.] Dyer that the Reorganized Church [of Jesus Christ of Latter-day Saints] historian had indicated a willingness to reciprocate in the matter of allowing us to view some of the early historical records that they have if we would be willing to do the same for them. President Joseph Fielding Smith had raised the question as to the nature of the records or documents the Brethren would wish to have listed. It was suggested that Elder Dyer furnish President Smith a list of items that he has in mind and when the First Presidency have considered the list they will then be prepared to answer the question raised by the Reorganized Church. This became the sentiment of the meeting.

January 23, 1968, First Presidency. It was mentioned that sometime ago the First Presidency decided that pictures of the papyri turned over to the Church by the Metropolitan Museum of Art in New York should not be made available for use by various publications until Dr. Hugh Nibley had had an opportunity to make a study of the papyri and felt that the pictures of it could be released to those who want them.

President [N. Eldon] Tanner said that a representative of the Brigham Young University periodical[1] called and stated that they are using copies of the pictures of the papyri in this publication; that he was informed that this could not be done until Dr. Nibley feels that these pictures can be made available.

This brother then got in touch with Dr. Nibley, who later called on President Tanner and told him that pictures of the papyri are available through other sources; that the press in the East obtained copies of them at the time the transfer was made to us. Dr. Nibley feels that it is just as well to make the papyri public now. He said he had made a study of it and translated a portion of it. Dr. Nibley will send us a letter indicating that he feels it is now proper to release these pictures to the public. Brother Howard Hunter, to whom President Tanner talked, also agrees to this.

The proposal is to let the Deseret News know that the pictures may be made available to anyone who wants them, and they may inform the public that they can obtain copies of the pictures from the Deseret News.

A letter will be written to the Deseret News to this effect, signed by President Tanner for the First Presidency.

January 26, 1968, First Presidency meeting. President [Hugh B.] Brown reported that in the meeting of the First Presidency and Presiding Bishopric a week ago, the question was raised as to whether or not the General Authorities should travel first class as they go to the Stakes and Missions. The Presiding Bishopric recommended that they do travel first class. President Brown mentioned a ruling made at one time that the General Authorities should travel economy class. President [N. Eldon] Tanner reported that the Presiding Bishopric had mentioned that some have received special permission to travel first class because of physical

---

1. The periodical was *Brigham Young University Studies*, a quarterly that would publish fifteen photos of segments of the papyri in the Joseph Smith collection for the winter 1968 issue. These would be accompanied by Hugh W. Nibley's eight-page "Prolegomena to Any Study of the Book of Abraham" and James R. Clark's longer "Joseph Smith and the Lebolo Egyptian Papyri." Clark was, like Nibley, a member of the religion faculty.

impairments; namely, Elders [Alvin R.] Dyer, [Alma] Sonne, and Bishop [Victor L.] Brown. It was the suggestion of the Bishopric that now, inasmuch as the board members and Priesthood representatives will not be traveling to the extent that they formerly did, and the cost of travel is being reduced, when one of the General Authorities travels, he should travel first class. It was mentioned that some of the Brethren like to work when they are on the plane traveling from one place to another and that there is not really sufficient space to do so when they travel economy class; also that they have considerable more cigarette smoke to contend with when they travel second class.

I said that I think the Brethren should travel first class.

February 13, 1968, from apostle Dyer's journal.[2] At 6:30 A.M. I [Dyer] received a phone call from Elder Ezra Taft Benson at my home. He asked if I would come to his office as soon as I reached the Church Office Building. This I did arriving at his office at 7:30 A.M. (On the telephone he spoke of an important matter that he should see President McKay about.)

When I arrived at the office, Reed Benson was with his father. I soon learned the purpose of Elder Benson's anxiety. A Press Conference was held in Washington D.C. a short while ago for former Governor [George C.] Wallace[3] of Alabama, at which time he announced his candidacy for the Presidency of the United States. This he had vowed to do if either of the parties failed to evidence a trend toward getting the country back on the principles that the founding fathers had established it upon.

As I learned, this Press Conference was attended by Reed Benson,

---

2. Beginning here, McKay's diary is occasionally interlarded with excerpts from the Journal Record of Alvin R. Dyer.

3. As governor of Alabama from 1963 to 1967, George Corley Wallace (1919–98) gained notoriety by standing at the door of the Foster Auditorium during registration at the University of Alabama to prevent black students from entering. This catapulted him into the national spotlight and the American Independent Party's endorsement. In the US presidential election, he garnered 10 million votes. While he campaigned, his wife, Lurleen Burns Wallace, was elected governor in his absence. She served a year in office beginning in 1967 and then tragically died of cancer in 1968, after which he would be elected governor three more times. Running for president again in 1972, Wallace was shot and paralyzed, forcing him to drop out of the race. Later he renounced racism and reached out to African Americans.

who afterward spent some time with Governor Wallace. It was evidently during this conversation that the possibility of Ezra Taft Benson running with Governor Wallace as Vice President was given some concern.

Brother Benson related to me that Governor Wallace subsequently called him concerning the possibility of occupying the ticket, which would be a <u>third</u> party, with him. Brother Benson said he had never really met the man and consequently would want to meet with him for a conference before pursuing it further.

Elder Benson[,] advised of his Stake Conference assignment on February 10–11, 1968, in Milwaukee, had arranged a meeting with Governor Wallace in Chicago on Sunday afternoon. This seemed agreeable. However the meeting there did not materialize due to the illness of Mrs. Wallace, who has been operated on three times for cancer and is now undergoing cobalt treatments; instead, by telephone arrangement from Chicago, Elder Benson, having picked up his son Reed in Washington, flew to Montgomery, Alabama.

(<u>Conference Held in Governor's Mansion</u>)—The Conference between Elder Benson and Governor Wallace took place in the Governor's Mansion on Monday, February 12, 1968. Reed Benson was also present. The Conference lasted approximately 3½ hours, during which time Elder Benson reports he became satisfied with Governor Wallace's concepts and determinations concerning the operation of the Federal Government. ...

(<u>His Willingness To Run Dependent Upon President McKay's decision</u>.)—It appears that Elder Benson informed Governor Wallace that he would respond to his request only if President McKay would give permission so to do. It was determined that the Governor would make a request for that permission by direct and personal letter to President McKay.

I was informed that Reed had the letter in his possession, and they were now soliciting my help to get the matter before President McKay. The request was also made of me by Elder Benson that I be present when the matter was presented.

(<u>The President's Illness</u>)—Before proceeding with the Journal which will relate how the meeting with the President was held, it is important to refer to the fact that since the meeting which President McKay attended with the Quorum of the Twelve in the Temple on the past Thursday, he has been ailing somewhat physically. The doctor, seeking to arrest this setback, had ordered no further meetings with the President until he felt better. No meetings had been held by The First Presidency.

This complicated the whole affair, but through discussion with Dr. [Alan P.] Macfarlane Elder Benson was able to get approval for this one appointment after the doctor checked the President's condition about noon-time. The appointment was set for 3 P.M. for Elder Benson and me to meet with the President.

(Reason For Urgency)—The urgency for Elder Benson to see the President on this particular day stemmed from the need of Governor Wallace to name his running mate in seeking the names quota in the State of Pennsylvania in order to be placed upon the ballot. This being required in that State.

It was known by me that Governor Wallace had obtained petition quotas in a number of states including California.

(Circulation of Non-Authenticated Statement of the Prophet Joseph [Smith] in California)—In the discussion which I had with Elder Benson and Reed on this morning I was told that Wallace would seek the Presidency on The American Independent Party, a name very similar to that which the Prophet Joseph Smith is alleged to have said would rise up in America at a time when the Republican and Democratic parties would be at war with each other. The name of the party which the Prophet is supposed to have used is the Independent American Party.

It developed that a group in California, calling themselves "Mormons for Wallace," used the supposed prophecy to get members of the Church to sign the petition in that State.

(Comment: With regard to the alleged prophecy, … sufficeth it to say, there is a very real doubt as to whether the Prophet ever made this statement.)[4]

(My Own Anxiety Over The Whole Matter)—My own concern in

---

4. In a reminiscence, Mosiah Hancock (1834–1907) said that when he was ten years old, he heard Joseph Smith say that in the future there would be three political parties and one of them would be called the Independent American Party. The three parties would unite against a common outside foe, according to Hancock's recollection of Smith's statement, at which time "the boys from the mountains will rush forth in time to save the American Army from defeat and ruin." The army would welcome these reinforcements, saying, "Give us men, henceforth, who can talk with God." "The Life Story of Mosiah Lyman Hancock," typescript, p. 29, MS 8175, LDS Church History Library.

this matter at this point was to make sure in my own thinking that my mind remained open. I did not want to become set against Elder Benson's acceptance of the Wallace offer, neither did I want to indicate to them that I favored it. The important thing was to go to President McKay with the facts both positive and negative, and in no way attempt to influence him in the decision which Elder Benson sought. I determined also that Elder Benson should present his case and not I.

Elder Benson had prepared a paper listing the things that Governor Wallace stood for and which he too supported. ... To satisfy myself on several points I asked Elder Benson a number of questions:

What had happened to the "76" group who had announced his candidacy for the Presidency on a party emanating from this group, and upon which he had obtained a letter of permission to run, which letter had been publicized.

He stated that this group had more or less faded.

I asked what part the John Birch Society would take in a Wallace–Benson ticket, and if Welch, the leader of the John Birch Society, was in support of Wallace.

Reed Benson answered this, but not too conclusively. He said he did not know of any open support indicated by [Robert] Welch. I was not completely satisfied with this phase of the situation, but felt to let it pass.

I asked Brother Benson—in light of the "76" situation and now this, if it were simply his desire to get back into public life. He answered that it was not—only if he could serve his country in helping to turn the trend away from Socialism. To me it seemed that Elder Benson is completely sincere in his desire to serve his country.

At this point I expressed the thought that perhaps Reed and I should see the President first, and then have Elder Benson come in, but prompted by the feelings of Clare Middlemiss, the President's personal secretary, whose counsel I sought and who has had much experience in these matters, it was determined that I [alone] would see the President first at 3 P.M. and Elder Benson would follow about 10 minutes later.

I am not completely sure that Elder Benson was in full accord with this procedure, but I explained to him that from my own experience in seeking counsel from the President it had proved beneficial to have one person outline the problem and the issues to be decided upon without any slants or recommendation; that the President could then reach his decision in the matter. Whether or not this registered with Elder Benson I do not truly know. At any rate this is the way the President was approached.

COMMENT: During the time before the appointment, Reed Benson came to my office with the personal letter from Governor Wallace to President McKay, and also a copy of Elder Benson's paper on the policies of Governor Wallace. It was at this time that Reed injected the thought that if the ticket of Wallace and Benson were elected and anything happened to Wallace, Elder Benson would be President. He also stressed how important he thought a decision made by President McKay, a prophet of God, was, and that it should be his own decision. I heartily agreed with this, but told Reed how necessary it was to such a decision for the President to have the facts and understand the problem.

The nurse called me by telephone and asked that the appointment with the President be changed to 3:30 P.M. I informed Elder Benson of the change.

At 3:30 P.M. I was at the President's apartment and by the side of the President. He said how glad he was to see me, and while he did not look too good, he said he felt he was getting better. He held onto my hand for quite some time.

I told the President of the reason for my visit with him before Elder Benson joined us; for I felt that he should have the facts and issues involved stated beforehand. He completely agreed with this.

With his permission I took Governor Wallace's letter from the envelope. He asked me to read it, which I did very slowly. ... I then mentioned that Governor Wallace was seeking the office of President of the United States on a 3rd party ticket, and that if Elder Benson ran with him it would be on a 3rd party effort. The President almost immediately said he opposed a 3rd party setup.

I also mentioned to the President several of the issues involved. Such as the Negro situation, the use of a non-authenticated prophecy of Joseph Smith concerning a 3rd party by the California contingency of "Mormons for Wallace," and the possibility of that erroneous usage on a widespread basis.

I also mentioned the fact of George Romney seeking the Republican nomination for President, and what effect having a member of the

Quorum of the Twelve with apparent Church approval, who would be in national opposition, might have upon the Church.

At no time in my preliminary visit with President McKay did I make any recommendation one way or another, nor did I slant what I said about the issues involved.

(Elder Benson Arrives)—Elder Benson arrived about 10 or 12 minutes after I did. He sat next to President McKay, having exchanged mutual greetings and well wishes. I stated to Elder Benson that Governor Wallace's letter to President McKay requesting his permission and blessing for Elder Benson to become a candidate for the Vice President of the United States on a ticket with Governor Wallace as candidate for President had been read.

Elder Benson then related to the President the story of his involvement in the situation. (Note: This part I have already covered.) Elder Benson spoke of his great desire to serve his country, and that he felt after meeting with George C. Wallace and questioning him and receiving his views concerning the needs of the Country, he would be willing to accept the invitation of Governor Wallace to run with him—but only if it met with President McKay's approval and blessing.

Elder Benson read from the paper he had prepared, already referred to, and with many of the points the President seemed in agreement—especially reference to the Socialistic trends in the Country. However the alleged prophecy of Joseph Smith concerning a 3rd party—as used in California—was spoken against by the President [McKay] most positively. He also stated that his name should not be used in the Wallace campaign.

Elder Benson told the President that had it not been for the illness of his wife, George C. Wallace would have come to see the President personally. The President manifested a concern for her health.

(The President Gives His Answer)—At this point President McKay picked up the letter which was on the desk in front of him and for the next 10 or so minutes perused its two pages, while Elder Benson and I sat in complete silence. Finally he let the letter and his hand fall to his lap. Elder Benson said, "President, what is your decision?" The President very clearly uttered, "You should turn the offer down." There was no question in his mind. His answer was precise.

Elder Benson indicating his willingness to follow the counsel of the

President said, "If that is your answer I will abide by it." The President then said for the second time that he should not accept the invitation.

Elder Benson then asked if it would be all right for him to call Governor Wallace personally to give him the answer. The President said it would, and to advise him that a letter would follow. He asked me to prepare the letter which I did, and it was sent to Governor Wallace on February 14, 1968. ...

After the decision had been made, we sat there together. I told the President of my high regard for Elder Benson, and that I felt he had an important destiny to fulfill for our Country, but that this no doubt was not the time for it. President McKay responded quite alertly to this thought saying that he felt it was right.

Elder Benson then said how pleased he was that I was there with him, and to this the President said, "Yes, and you could have no one any better."

We both had a lingering handshake with the President as we said goodby, hoping and praying for his complete recovery from his current physical setback.

Elder Benson and I walked back to the Church Office Building together. We both were aware of and appreciated the experience of the past 30 or 40 minutes wherein we had listened to the counseling direction of a prophet of God.

I said to Elder Benson, "Well, you have your answer." "Yes," he replied, "And without any [influence or] recommendation to him." He then said thoughtfully, "You did not make any recommendation did you?" I assured him completely that I did not. The decision was solely the President's.

February 28, 1968, First Presidency meeting. Attention was called to a letter from [a doctor] of Ogden, referring to a former letter that he had written in behalf of the Utah Obstetrical and Gynecological Society with regard to abortions and sterilization. In his former letter, [the doctor had] asked for an appointment with the First Presidency and the Twelve to ascertain the position of the Church regarding proposed legislation on this subject, which letter we answered stating that we did not wish to become involved in the matter. [The doctor's] letter now under consideration states that after polling the committee, he has again been directed to ask for an audience with the First Presidency and the Twelve so that the Brethren may be fully informed as to the provisions of a proposed law on this subject. He states that whether the Council of the Twelve wish to become involved or not, it will be asked to testify in the Senate hearings, and for that reason they are anxious to have us fully informed.

In the first letter [the doctor] referred to the growing population explosion, the growing numbers of our young men going to Idaho to have voluntary sterilization, and the growing number of women requesting therapeutic abortion, and then when refused are having it done at the hands of non-medical people.

President [N. Eldon] Tanner said that he did not think that the brethren of the First Presidency and the Twelve would have to appear before the Senate, and if they did, he questioned the need of their being informed in advance. He also said that he did not think that the Presidency and the Twelve should give this committee an audience, that whatever we might say or think would not free us from responsibility for what they might do, that they would involve us in whatever legislation might be introduced.

Elder [Alvin R.] Dyer mentioned that President [Ernest L.] Wilkinson of the BYU had told him of problems they are having on the BYU campus with our young people regarding premarital sexual relations and contraceptive measures. He mentioned an article that he had read in one of the current magazines stating that one out of six single girls becomes pregnant before she is married. Elder Dyer agreed with President Tanner that we should not become involved in this situation so far as this committee is concerned. He suggested, however, that the Twelve be asked to appoint a committee to look into all phases of the problem and prepare a report and recommendation to present to the First Presidency for their consideration.

Mention was made of the fact that there is a difference of attitude on the part of some of the Brethren, and that this would perhaps give us the benefit of the united consensus of opinion of the brethren.

President Tanner mentioned that some of the universities have been considering this problem for months, and perhaps years, and that now two universities have approved giving advice to coeds in the university as to how they can prevent pregnancy.

Elder Dyer mentioned that one of our Stake Presidents in Wyoming had reported to him that eight of the girls in his Stake had become pregnant and he did not know how many others would become pregnant were it not for the fact that they were using contraceptive methods. He felt that a modern statement from the First Presidency without the involvement of outside committees, setting forth the Church's viewpoint, could be timely.

President Tanner questioned the wisdom of making public any statement that we might wish to prepare on this subject, but he did feel that all the Brethren of the General Authorities should be united on their understanding of this question.

I asked that there be brought to the next meeting of the First Presidency a copy of the letter which we have been sending on this subject in answer to questions that have been received.

After discussing several other matters of general nature, the Brethren departed at 10:00 a.m.

March 1, 1968, First Presidency meeting. We gave consideration to answering inquiries which come to the Church regarding the Negroes holding the Priesthood. We considered a letter that had been prepared to a Stake President; in which letter quotations were made from President Brigham Young and President Wilford Woodruff which refer to the pre-existent unworthiness of the spirits of Negroes in receiving the curse of Cain. President [Hugh B.] Brown said that since people do not believe in a pre-existence, such statements only lead to confusion, and he recommended that they be stricken from the letter. President [Joseph Fielding] Smith concurred, saying the less we say in these letters about this subject the better it would be, and that if we said anything by way of reference as to the reason for the Church's stand, we should quote the passage from the Book of Abraham (P[earl] of G[reat] P[rice], Abraham 1:26–27.)[5]

I approved the deletion of the statements by Presidents Young and

5. These two verses are part of Joseph Smith's translation of the papyri purchased in 1835 from a traveling exhibitor. They refer to the founder of Egypt as "a righteous man [who] established his kingdom and judged his people wisely and justly all his days," but whose father, Ham, was "cursed … as pertaining to the Priesthood"; therefore the lineage of the pharaohs would "not have the right of Priesthood, notwithstanding the Pharaohs would fain claim it from Noah, through Ham." Exactly who these descendants of the pharaohs might be is not explained.

Woodruff, stating that the more we said about the subject, the more we shall have to explain, and that the statement should be clear, positive, and brief.

Communism—Discussion of Classes on the Constitution and Communism—President Brown called attention to a letter that had been received from the President of the Tempe Stake in Arizona regarding a series of adult classes that are projected to be held in Mesa and Scottsdale for a discussion of the constitution, Government, Communism, and related matters. President Brown stated that he had talked to President [George I.] Dana [of Tempe] this morning on the telephone and he is convinced that those conducting the classes are affiliated with the John Birch Society etc.

Later Elder Dyer called to report to me that Bishop [Marion] Vance of the Tempe Stake had called on me personally and that he had a letter addressed to me as President of the Church appealing for permission to continue the classes which are merely for the study of the Constitution, Communism, etc. He says he is not a member of the John Birch Society; that the President of the Stake is not opposed to the classes, rather that he is in favor of them, as are his two counselors, and that they are not "Birchite" meetings. Bishop Vance was advised to follow the Stake President's instructions.

I asked Elder Dyer to follow through on this matter; to get in touch with President Dana and find out the facts in the matter. Elder Dyer later telephoned to President Dana and reported that he had stated that the new series of classes proposed by Bishop Vance will be held during the M.I.A. in the Third Ward, Bishop Vance's Ward, as a Special Interest Class.

1. The teacher of the class is a Brother Spradling who is a full-fledged member of the John Birch Society, and who has worked with Bishop Vance in organizing the classes.

2. Bishop Vance feels that he has placed the idea in proper reference by shifting the classes to the M.I.A. time (rather than in the early morning hours as heretofore) to fit the instruction of the M.I.A. organization for Special Interest study on the Constitution.

3. President Dana said that he would like to see classes held where the principles of the Constitution could be discussed; that he and his Counselors had attended some of the early morning classes, and in fairness to the group sponsoring the classes, all of whom are sincere men,

especially Bishop Vance, the subject matter discussed had no direct reference to "Birchite" principles.

4. He felt that the class is being conducted in a subterfuged manner (with the teacher being a member of the John Birch Society) to further the John Birch Society. But here, President Dana said the problem is this: "Those attending the classes are sincere, honest men and faithful members of the Church, but there are some who are against it which is tending to split the people." For this reason he feels that a directive or counsel from the First Presidency is needed. He stated that the main opposition to the holding of the classes comes from members of the Stake High Council, in which G. Homer Durham,[6] a liberal Democrat, takes a leading part.

5. President Dana stated that Bishop Vance, while not a full-fledged member of the John Birch Society, is a "Home Member." This is one who receives all printed material of the organization and is committed unequivoca[l]ly[7] to its action, but who does not openly agree to identification.

6. Classes, or "Constitutional Seminars" as they are called, are also being held in the Mesa Stake, and are even perhaps more widespread.

7. President Dana stated that when counsel is sought of members of the Quorum of the Twelve, one says one thing and another says something else. One says to hold the classes, and the other says they should be stopped, thus only the First Presidency can clear the air on the subject.

Following this report, Elder Dyer urged President Dana to send him tapes containing the subject material that is being taught in these classes.

I told Elder Dyer that the whole matter of these classes being held in Arizona should be looked into and further facts obtained, and I instructed him to follow the matter up and report back to me.

March 6, 1968, 11:30 a.m. Clare [Middlemiss] came over with office matters. She presented several letters for my signature. She also presented

---

6. George Homer Durham (1911–85) was president of Arizona State University in Tempe. He had a doctorate in political science from UCLA and had been a professor and vice president at the University of Utah. In 1969 he would be named Utah Commissioner of Education. Eight years later the church would call him to the First Quorum of Seventy, and later as Church Historian. He was the son-in-law of apostle John A. Widtsoe.

7. The diary has "unequivocably."

matters pertaining to the forthcoming Annual Conference of the Church. She reminded me of the three new appointments I shall have to make at this conference—a new Seventy to replace Elder Antoine R. Ivins;[8] a new Assistant to the Twelve; and the appointment of Elder [Alvin R.] Dyer as my Counselor.

I stated that I have given the matter a great deal of thought and prayer; that I need someone like President [Thorpe B.] Isaacson to be close to me. Clare said that she understood, and that she realizes that I have a great decision to make; that her desire is to see me satisfied and that some of the burdens I am now carrying be lifted from me. She said it made absolutely no difference to her what is done, that she cared only about seeing me relieved and that Church matters are carried on as I should like them to be. I said, "I know that comes from your heart." I could not help the tears that rolled down my cheeks as I expressed appreciation to Clare and asked her to stay close to me. She said that she had talked to Dr. [Alan P.] MacFarlane and he agreed that she should come over to the office every day for a short time to relieve me of any worries I might have on my mind and to take care of any office matters that I might have to turn over to her.

March 8, 1968, from Dyer's First Presidency minutes. President [N. Eldon] Tanner brought up a matter which excited my [Dyer's] interest. It concerned a request by Leonard Arrington, whom it was reported was writing a history of the Church for the past 100 years, that the financial statement read for many years at General Conferences of the Church by a representative of the Auditing Committee, regarding disbursement of Church funds received, (but never amount received), which report has been discontinued, be included in the history for each year.

The question I asked was why we are writing another history prior to 1930, since this has been written in comprehensive form by B. H.

---

8. Antoine Ridgeway Ivins (1881–1967) had passed away just weeks after the October general conference. His father was apostle Anthony W. Ivins and his grandfather on his mother's side was apostle Erastus Snow. He spent most of his life employed by the church in managing the LDS sugar cane plantation in Hawaii and, beginning in 1931, as a member of the First Council of Seventy, presiding over the Mexican mission. As a young man, he had attended the University of Michigan, graduated from the University of Utah, and studied law in Mexico City.

Roberts. President [Joseph Fielding] Smith commented that we had a good written history to that year and no need for another.[9]

I commented that contemporary histories could only prove confusing to members and non-members alike. President [Hugh B.] Brown said it would not be detrimental if only a summary was given up to 1930, and then it could be comprehensive after that year. My answer to this was that any summary would have to be stated in the virtual words of the Comprehensive [History] compiler of the 1930 and prior history. Otherwise, we would have variant historical records and that I opposed the matter of it being attempted.

COMMENT: (Visit with Joseph Fielding Smith)—After the meeting I [Dyer] went to President Smith's office, [meeting with Smith in his role] as Church Historian, to discuss the matter with him further. He said he knew nothing about it; and when I restated what President Tanner has said about Arrington working with Earl Olson, Assistant Church Historian, on the research, he stated that he knew nothing about that either, and that Arrington, anyway, should not be writing it.

I suggested that the whole matter be looked into. President Smith said yes and that I was the one to do it. I told him I would check on a few things and report back to him; then we could take the matter to President McKay if need be. He said that this would be fine and said, "You go ahead."

(Minutes of Meeting Pertaining to Approval to Go Ahead with This Project)—As a matter of proper relationship of the assignment given in June of 1966 to proceed with this project, that segment of the minutes is included herewith.[10]

March 20, 1968, First Presidency meeting. Elder [Alvin R.] Dyer called attention to a matter that had been discussed previously by the First

---

9. Smith may have been referring to his own *Essentials in Church History*, published in 1922. In any case, the reference to B. H. Roberts's work, spelled out more explicitly in the next paragraph, was to Roberts's massive, six-volume *Comprehensive History of the Church of Jesus Christ of Latter-day Saints*, published in 1930.

10. Dyer reproduced the same excerpt from the minutes of a First Presidency meeting McKay had included in his diary on June 10, 1966. In that meeting the First Presidency had authorized Arrington, Bitton, Mann, and Sorenson to write a history of the church through the twentieth century, which had not been done before.

Presidency relative to an arrangement treating the subject of the [US] Constitution and government authority in Ward Priesthood Meetings one Sunday each month. He mentioned a seminar[11] on this subject that is being held in Arizona, concerning which we had written one of the Stake Presidents, and said that at least five separate letters had come to him [Dyer] from representatives of groups, one in Oregon, which group carries the name of TOLD. This latter group, he said, has stationery on which there is a reproduction of the painting by Arnold Friberg of General Moroni speaking in behalf of freedom. These people are asking for permission to continue to use this picture which is copyrighted by the Church on their stationery. He said they are holding classes on matters pertaining to the government and the constitution. He mentioned a similar letter that had been received from another group in Montana and one from Salt Lake City. Elder Dyer said that these classes are spreading all over the Church and he thought the way to let our people know where the Church stands is to place into our Priesthood teaching courses a lesson for one Sunday a month on this subject. When this matter was previously discussed by the Presidency, President [Hugh B.] Brown was requested to confer with Elder [Harold B.] Lee, who is chairman of the Correlation Committee, regarding it. Elder Dyer said that he understood that President Brown had talked with Brother Lee who had said that their lessons are all arranged now for the Priesthood course and it would be difficult to change them.

Elder Dyer said he had been in the discussions regarding replacing the home teaching lessons in the Priesthood monthly meetings with other material, and he felt the change had not gone so far that lessons along the lines indicated could not be substituted. He also mentioned that some people are asking to hold these discussions during the Sunday School hour and others during the Mutual hour, and he thought that unless the Church takes the initiative in the matter and gives them the proper material and opportunity, these groups will continue.

President Brown said that he would not oppose the proposition if the committee felt it a desirable thing to do. He suggested that Brother Dyer follow the matter up with the committee. Elder Dyer said that he

---

11. The diary has "seminary."

would be glad to do this if he could do it as an assignment from the First Presidency. President [N. Eldon] Tanner suggested that if we were inclined to make that change we could direct the committee to give the matter consideration and bring back their recommendation. Brother Dyer said that it was his understanding that he would present it to them as a recommendation from the First Presidency that they consider it. President Tanner said there was one thing that gave him some concern in his thinking about this matter and that was that we have said that they cannot use the Church buildings or Church organizations for these discussions, and have taken a firm position on the matter, and yet we have told our people that they are free to join any of these study groups and learn all they can and do what they should in the interest of freedom, etc. He said he sometimes thought that if our people attend these meetings and not promote them they can do much good, but promoting such discussions has some hazards.

Referring to reproducing the General Moroni painting on their stationery and otherwise, it was agreed that we ought not to authorize its use.

March 26, 1968, First Presidency meeting. Elder [Alvin R.] Dyer reported that at the request of the First Presidency he discussed with the Correlation Committee the matter of devoting one Priesthood Meeting a month in each Ward to a study of governmental matters and particularly the [US] Constitution, he had talked with Elder [Thomas S.] Monson who is chairman of the adult group of the Correlation Committee and lent him his file so that he could have the complete picture regarding the units that are springing up all over the Church outside of Church jurisdiction. He had asked Elder Monson to consider the possibility of holding such meetings this year. Elder Monson had answered that the Priesthood lessons this year are all on the press so they could not make a change. He said that he and his committee would take it under consideration to see what might be done at a later time, probably next year.

March 27, 1968. Senator Robert F. Kennedy,[12] with whom I had set up

12. Robert Francis Kennedy (1925–68) was the brother of assassinated US President John F. Kennedy. He had been the US Attorney General, 1961–64, in his brother's administration. Shortly after the president's death, Robert successfully ran for the US Senate as a Democrat from New York. In 1968 he announced his candidacy in the US

an appointment for 2:30 o'clock this afternoon, arrived at the apartment. A telephone message had been received that the Senator's schedule had been delayed, and arrangements had been made for 5:30 p.m. However, it was 6:25 o'clock before the Senator finally arrived. He was accompanied by Elder Alvin R. Dyer, Brother Wayne Owens,[13] his campaign manager, and the following representatives of the press, radio, and television ...

We had a very interesting and pleasant time together. All present were especially interested in seeing the large volume containing many pictures and items concerning the visits President John F. Kennedy had made to my office and later at the apartment when he was President of the United States. His brother, Robert, showed much interest in the book, and when he saw the record of the last speech President Kennedy had made at the [Salt Lake] Tabernacle in September 1963, and items concerning the breakfast Sister [Emma Ray] McKay and I had given him on Friday, September 26, 1963, Senator Kennedy remarked: "My brother enjoyed the breakfast with you and Mrs. McKay, and admired all of the fine things you and your Church stand for, and it is a great honor for me to meet you." He then said that he thought the speech President Kennedy delivered in the Tabernacle that September of 1963 was "one of the best speeches he had ever given." He said that President Kennedy had played a tape of his speech for his mother and father. ...

Following a very delightful visit, I told the Senator that I was glad to see him "person-to-person," and that I am glad that we had this close contact.

The Senator then arose and thanked me for taking the time to receive him, and I told him that it was an honor for me to meet him.

---

presidential primary to challenge the incumbent, Lyndon B. Johnson. After a stunning victory in California, he was fatally shot on June 5, 1968, and died a day later. During his campaign he delivered a memorable speech at BYU in which he promised President Wilkinson that "all Democrats would be off the campus by sundown" and recalled spending part of his honeymoon in southern Utah.

13. Douglas Wayne Owens (1937–2002) was Kennedy's campaign coordinator for the Western states. He was born in the small southern-Utah town of Panguitch, served his church in France, graduated twice from the University of Utah (including a law degree), and worked in Washington, DC, in the offices of US Senators Frank Moss (D–Utah) and Edward Kennedy (D–Mass.). In 1973 Owens was elected to the US House of Representatives. Two years later he was named president of the LDS Montreal Mission, after which he was reelected to Congress for two more terms. His wife, Marlene Wessel, was among the missionaries who left their French mission early in 1958, but in her case returned to finish her mission and was not excommunicated (see Sept. 23, 1958).

The Senator, after shaking hands with everyone present, left the apartment. His manager, and representatives of the press etc., after expressing their farewells, followed him out the door.

7 to 7:30 p.m. Names of General Authorities to Fill Vacancies Considered—Inasmuch as the General Authorities pre-Conference meeting is to be held tomorrow morning, I asked Elder Dyer and my secretary Clare to remain for a few moments so that I could go over the list of names that had been submitted by all the General Authorities at my request for the new General Authorities to be sustained at the coming Annual Conference of the Church.

At my request Clare had tabulated the names so that I could study the ones who had been suggested by the Brethren. I stated that I would give thought and prayer to the names to be considered, but said that I had made up my mind to call Elder Marion D. Hanks as one of the Assistants to the Twelve, and Hartman Rector[14] of the Potomac Stake, who lives in Virginia, as one of the Seventies. ... I also told Brother Dyer that I had decided to present his name to be a member of the First Presidency.

March 28, 1968, 8:00 a.m. At my request Elder Alvin R. Dyer came over to the office at the Hotel [Utah] Apartment. I also had asked my secretary, Clare Middlemiss, to be present to take notes. ... I also informed Elder Dyer that I had decided to present his name at the meeting of the General Authorities this morning as a counselor in the First Presidency. I instructed Clare to return to her office to make a list of these brethren for me so that I could present their names to the General Authorities. I asked her to hand this list and the list of the General Authorities to speak at the various sessions of the General Conference to Elder Dyer so that he could hand them to me in the Temple.

March 29, 1968, First Presidency meeting. President [N. Eldon] Tanner brought up the matter of the Independence [Missouri] Visitors Center project, which did not clear the Budget Committee on March 26, 1968.

---

14. Hartman Rector Jr. (1924–) converted to Mormonism in 1952 as a career navy officer who had been a pilot during the Korean War. H was born in Missouri and graduated from Murray State Teachers College (now university) in Kentucky. As part of his assignment as a seventy, he would preside over the Italian mission. Before his call to the seventy, he had already twice served as a mission president.

He stated that his feeling is that I should know of the opposition to it, but that if it is my desire that it should go forward that would settle the matter.

Elder [Alvin R.] Dyer spoke up and said that the desires of the President of the Church approving the project had been given twice in writing, and that members of the Expenditures Committee had also now received a letter from the President of the Church again stating his wishes for immediate approval of the project.

We held quite a discussion about this matter. Presidents [Hugh B.] Brown and Tanner claimed that approval had been obtained from me without a full discussion to inform me of the facts, although I had been fully informed of all the facts, and had even gone over the plans for the new Center with [architect] Emil Fetzer and [Building Department chair] Mark Garff, and had approved of them, and had sent letters to the Counselors that the project should go forward. It seems that the Counselors are now objecting to the project, and stating that Elder Dyer is the only one in favor of it.

President Tanner said that Elder Mark E. Petersen was against the project, as was Mark Garff of the Building Committee. Elder Dyer said that he is certain that Elder Petersen is not opposed to it, as he [Petersen] knew of my letter to the Counselors—having a copy himself—and if they (the Counselors) had spoken just one word in the Expenditures Committee meeting to signify that I had approved of the project, there would not be all this situation; but they (Presidents Brown and Tanner) had said nothing, and this was difficult for him (Elder Dyer) to understand.

Elder Dyer then turned to me and asked me <u>if it is still my desire to have the Visitor's Center at Independence built, and I answered, "Yes, it is."</u>

President Brown then said to me, "Wouldn't you like to have the matter brought before the Quorum of the Twelve?" I said that this would be all right.

Elder Dyer said that inasmuch as the President of the Church had already given approval in writing for the project, and that it had gone too far to be interfered with, he objected. He said, "All that you brethren are attempting to do is to change the mind of the President."

President [Joseph Fielding] Smith said: "Why do we want to put up a building there?" Elder Dyer said that this had all been discussed before in a First Presidency's meeting when the letter came from the

Manager of the City of Independence stating that they would like to use our vacant Temple property for a Boy's Club if we did not use the property ourselves. Fearing condemnation of our Temple land there, it was decided that we should build a Visitors Center on the land. Elder Dyer then said that he would not question the matter being brought before the Twelve if they were told all the facts pertaining to the condemnation procedures of our Temple land. President Brown answered, "Oh, so you claim to know more than the Quorum?" and Elder Dyer said, "President Brown, you know I do not mean that. I am saying that they will have to know all the facts before they can decide.["]

However, after all the discussion, the fact still remains that I feel that we should do something with our property in Independence, and if I remember correctly the matter was brought before the Twelve sometime ago by Elder Mark E. Petersen when he received a copy of my letter approving of the project.[15]

April 3, 1968, First Presidency meeting. It seemed that the matter of choosing additional counselors in the First Presidency most concerned the counselors this morning. Secretary [Joseph] Anderson was asked to read the following excerpt from the minutes of the Council meeting of the First Presidency and Quorum of the Twelve held Thursday, March 28, 1968, at which meeting I was not in attendance:

> Elder [Harold B.] Lee mentioned that there is something that is confusing the Church which he wished to mention, namely, the appointment of counselors in the First Presidency. He said that if these brethren were given the designation of counselors "to the First Presidency," there would be no discussion or confusion. He referred to the 22nd verse of the 107th Section of the Doctrine and Covenants reading as follows: "Of the Melchizedek Priesthood, three Presiding High Priests, chosen by the body, appointed and ordained to that office, and

---

15. This exchange hearkens back to the problems that existed when Thorpe B. Isaacson worked in concert with McKay without involving the other counselors. McKay would likewise increasingly rely on Dyer, and this special trust, resulting in unilateral decisions, became a matter of concern to the other brethren. This may have been manifested when, after McKay's death in January 1970, Dyer was returned to his position as an Assistant to the Twelve and was not chosen to become a member of the quorum when the vacancy was filled the next April.

upheld by the confidence, faith, and prayer of the Church, form a quorum of the presidency of the Church."

Elder Lee thought the Twelve should make an expression on the matter here for what it is worth. He said we have precedents; that, for instance, when Brigham Young became the head of the Church as the President of the Twelve after the Prophet's death for three years he presided over the Church as President of the Twelve, and at that time two brethren were sustained as counselors to the Twelve. That was done again in President [John] Taylor's time when President Young's counselors were made counselors to the Twelve.

President [N. Eldon] Tanner said that as he understood it Brother Lee was suggesting that he would like an expression from the Twelve as to a resolution recommending that additional counselors should be designated as counselors "to the First Presidency" instead of counselors "in the First Presidency."

Elder [Marion G.] Romney moved that this be the sentiment of the Council.

Elder [Mark E.] Petersen suggested that this change should be made also in the list of General Authorities that is used when they are sustained in the stakes. He said there is a lot of talk about it.

Elder Lee said that this does not take anything away from these brethren, but it does define accurately what the Lord has said. President Joseph Fielding Smith said he thought that this was absolutely right.

Elder Romney suggested that it would set forth the matter more accurately if the First Presidency were sustained, and then the counselors "to the First Presidency" were sustained in a separate vote. President Smith agreed with this upon being asked his opinion about it.

Elder Romney's motion that it be the sentiment of the Council that these three additional counselors be designated as counselors "to the First Presidency" was seconded by Elder Howard W. Hunter and unanimously approved.

Elder Lee said that he felt the President should be informed of the discussion that is going on all over the Church by gospel scholars and others, and of the action taken this morning by the Council of the Twelve. He said he felt that the revelation is explicit on the matter.

It was agreed that this should be called to the President's attention at once so that if it meets with his approval, these brethren would be sustained in the manner indicated at the coming conference.

After hearing the foregoing President McKay indicated his approval and said he felt that that is the way it should be. ...

Counselors—Sustaining of as "Prophets, Seers and Revelators"—The question was raised as to whether, in presenting the General Authorities of the Church at General Conference, the counselors to the First Presidency should be sustained as Prophets, Seers and Revelators. Elder Dyer maintained that when one is called to the apostleship he is automatically a Prophet, Seer and Revelator by virtue of that calling. He also mentioned that when he was chosen to be an apostle last October this matter had come up and that I had ruled at that time that he was to be sustained as a Prophet, Seer and Revelator because of his calling to be an apostle. He mentioned that it was in Kirtland, Ohio when the apostles were first designated as Prophets, Seers and Revelators, that before that time they had not been sustained as Prophets, Seers and Revelators, but that the Prophet Joseph Smith at that time said that they who hold the apostleship were Prophets, Seers and Revelators and they were so sustained at that conference in Kirtland. President Smith agreed with President Tanner that this had reference to the Twelve. It was mentioned that President Smith is sustained as a Prophet, Seer and Revelator as President of the Twelve, that President [Thorpe B.] Isaacson is not an apostle, and that Elder Dyer is the only one involved.

I gave my consent for Elder Dyer to be included in the group to be sustained as Prophets, Seers and Revelators.

The First Presidency—Signatures on Letters, Documents etc.—The question was raised as to whether the letters to be signed by the First Presidency in the future should carry the names of the three brethren of the First Presidency, namely, President David O. McKay and his counselors Hugh B. Brown and N. Eldon Tanner, or if the signatures of the counselors to the First Presidency should be included. The suggestion was made that inasmuch as it has been decided that the First Presidency consists of the President and his two regular counselors that it would seem that the First Presidency letters should carry their signatures only. President Smith indicated that it was his feeling that that is the way it should be done. President Tanner questioned the desirability of attaching four or five signatures to a letter sent out by the First Presidency except in very special cases. President Smith and Elder Dyer concurred in this feeling.

I said: "All right."

Elder Dyer said that he thought that as counselors to the First Presidency they should be kept advised, and it was decided that President Smith and Elder Dyer be given copies of letters setting forth decisions made by the First Presidency in their meetings.

April 4, 1968. In accordance with appointment, I met Elder Alvin R. Dyer in my office in the Hotel [Utah]. I asked him to explain to me again what the counselors are so concerned about in the sustaining of the counselors at the coming Conference. He said that the issue in question is whether or not the counselors, other than the first and second counselors, should be sustained as counselors "in" the First Presidency or counselors "to" the First Presidency. Elder Dyer said that he felt that sufficient time had not been given to the matter yesterday morning at the First Presidency's meeting to give me a chance to go into the matter and understand the real significance of the issue, or what it would mean in operation.

Brother Dyer said that he had not said much in the meeting yesterday because President [Joseph Fielding] Smith seemed to concur, but that later, when he learned of President Smith's true feelings in the matter, he felt, as did President Smith, that the matter should be considered again. He said that President Smith had commented that he would like to talk to me about it if I wanted him to.

I told Elder Dyer to get President Smith on the telephone and have him come right over. He was attending the Seminar of Regional Assistants to the Twelve, but excused himself from the meeting and came right over.

President Smith soon arrived and expressed to me his real feelings in the matter, stating, "I do not know what the Counselors (Presidents [Hugh B.] Brown and [N. Eldon] Tanner) mean by the word 'To,' or any other word. I feel that any man that the President calls to be a counselor is IN the First Presidency, and nothing can change that."

Counselors to be sustained as "In" the First Presidency[:] I said that the sustaining should be done as it had been done previously when I called President Brown, President Smith, and President [Thorpe B.] Isaacson— Counselors "in" the First Presidency. That they will be sustained as such.

At this point I called <u>Joseph Anderson</u> and told him to come right over, since he is preparing the list of the General Authorities to be presented for the sustaining vote of the Church, so that he could make minutes of this meeting and have the list properly prepared.

Just before he arrived, Sister Clare Middlemiss had brought over the list of General Authorities which previously had been prepared by Joseph Anderson. On this list Brother Anderson had changed the word "In" to "To."

<u>I told Brother Anderson to change the word "To" to "In," and to notify Presidents Brown and Tanner that the change had been made by me</u> this morning. <u>Brother Anderson</u> was quite upset, and I was displeased with the manner in which he accepted my instructions. He argued with President Smith and Elder Dyer, taking it upon himself to say: "I do not agree with your interpretation of Section 107:79; it is erroneous."

Elder Anderson at this point asked that Presidents Brown and Tanner be called over to defend the other side, and I said, "It is not necessary; I have given him instructions as to what he was to do."

April 6, 1968. <u>I noted with concern that President [Hugh B.] Brown</u> in presenting the names of President Joseph Fielding Smith and Elder Alvin R. Dyer had them sustained by the members as counselors "<u>to</u>" the First Presidency instead of as counselors "<u>in</u>" the First Presidency as he had been notified to do. This matter will have to be settled later.

April 9, 1968. Brother [Alvin R.] Dyer reported that my desires had not been adhered to with regard to the sustaining of President [Joseph Fielding] Smith and him as Counselors IN the First Presidency; that President [Hugh B.] Brown had presented them as Counselors TO the First Presidency. Furthermore, that he, Elder Dyer, has not been sustained as a Prophet, Seer, and Revelator.

I told Brother Dyer that I am vitally concerned about this, and asked him to bring the matter up in a meeting of the First Presidency.

As Elder Dyer got up to leave the office, I said to him: "I want you to stay close by my side." I had a good feeling of the spirit of brotherhood as he came over to shake my hand and to say goodbye to me.

April 11, 1968. Later I read the minutes of the meeting held in the [Salt

Lake] Temple today, and have asked my secretary to include them with my diary of today so that a record will be made of the discussions the Brethren held regarding my appointments of additional counselors. ...

My decision, after I had time to give more thought and prayer to the matter, as in the case of President Hugh B. Brown, President Joseph Fielding Smith, and President Thorpe B. Isaacson when I called them to be counselors, was that President Smith and Elder [Alvin R.] Dyer be sustained at the April Conference as counselors "IN" the First Presidency instead of "TO" the First Presidency. President Hugh B. Brown was so instructed through secretary Joseph Anderson on April 4, 1968 following a meeting with President Smith and Elder Dyer.

April 16, 1968, First Presidency meeting. President [N. Eldon] Tanner mentioned that Jack Gallivan, Max Rich,[16] and Gus Backman had called on him about the proposed liquor by the drink referendum. They explained that they had prepared a proposed bill which they have titled: "An Act For the Enforcement of Liquor Control."[17]

President Tanner said that he is meeting with Elders Marion G. Romney, Gordon B. Hinckley, and Howard W. Hunter today for the purpose of discussing this matter.

I expressed concern with the measure, and stated that we should pursue the matter of seeing to it that our people are informed on the policy of the Church concerning this important matter.

Elder [Alvin R.] Dyer suggested that, to the extent that we were

---

16. Maxwell Evans Rich (1913–79) had replaced Gus Backman as director of the Salt Lake City Chamber of Commerce. A career military officer, he had been awarded three medals for heroism in World War II, and from 1953 through 1964 he was adjutant general of the Utah National Guard. In 1970 he would be named director of the National Rifle Association.

17. There were three possible ways one could consume alcohol in public in Utah at the time. There were licensed "taverns" that sold only beer. It was otherwise illegal for restaurants and private clubs to sell alcohol, but one could purchase a bottle of wine at a state liquor store and bring it to a restaurant, where the waiter would uncork it and pour it, or a bottle of whiskey and take it to a private club where the bar tender would place it in a locker with the patron's name on it. Opponents argued that this encouraged people to consume an entire bottle of alcohol rather than a glass or two, but voters were unconvinced. The 1968 ballot measure to liberalize the restrictions went down in defeat. For the role of the media in the controversy, see Raymond E. Beckham's 1969 BYU master's thesis, *The Utah Newspaper War of 1968: Liquor-by-the-Drink*; also Quinn, *Extensions*, 365.

able to do so, we should <u>enlist influential non-members to work on an overall committee to defeat the measure</u>: that we should capitalize on the experience that the Church had of single-handedly attempting to persuade the members to oppose the repeal of the Prohibition Law some years back, and despite the appeal of President Heber J. Grant, Utah, predominantly Mormon, voted for repeal—ironically being the State which helped to reach the majority vote for repeal. Brother Dyer said that as he recalled this experience, it was the apparent issue of making a challenge by the Church which caused so many inactive members to go along with non-members in voting for the repeal.

Brother Dyer suggested that Weston E. Hamilton[18] would be a good man to help with non-members of influence to work for the defeat of the referendum to be placed before the voting public later this year.

I agreed with this, as did President Tanner, and said that we should seek all the outside help we can get to help in defeating the measure. ...

<u>3:00 p.m.—Elder Alvin R. Dyer Set Apart as Counselor In the First Presidency</u>—According to appointment, Elder Alvin R. Dyer called at the office in the Hotel Utah apartment. He was accompanied by Brother Joseph Anderson, secretary to the First Presidency. Just after their arrival my secretary Clare Middlemiss arrived and gave to me a sheet of paper which contained the wording of the setting apart and blessing I had asked her to prepare from a previous setting apart of the Counselors in the First Presidency. Sister Middlemiss said to me as she handed me the sheet, "This is the corrected statement you went over yesterday." With that explanation she left the office.

I took some time going over the wording of the blessing, and suggested further changes. I then asked Brother Dyer to read the wording of the setting apart and after he had finished reading it, I asked Joseph Anderson to read it aloud to me. I then said it was all right, and that the more I read it, the better I liked it.

---

18. Even though Weston Eugene Hamilton (1911–94) was a devout LDS member who was on the Church Finance Committee, he was nevertheless a bridge to the business community through his position as executive vice president of the Utah Retail Merchants Association and as a member of the State Liquor Commission. He was also the senior vice president of Zions First National Bank. He graduated from Utah State Agricultural College and was the personnel manager at Remington Arms Company during World War II.

April 18, 1968, First Presidency meeting. A discussion was held concerning the results of a certain group of men to have placed upon the Fall ballot a referendum for a change of the presently State-controlled liquor law to that of a legalized State-controlled bill for liquor by the drink.

President [N. Eldon] Tanner told of a visit to his office by Jack Gallivan, Max Rich, and Gus Backman in the interest of a good law to properly control liquor by the drink, since it appeared to these men that the people would no doubt support the referendum for liquor by the drink. President Tanner stated that he felt that their efforts represented a clever and insidious method to gain support for the referendum.[19] He said the only way we can defeat it is to organize throughout the Church and throw this weight against it.

Brother Gordon Hinckley said that we have three alternatives, and that we must decide on one of them, and the work accordingly. He said one is to do nothing, and as surely as we do nothing there will be liquor by the drink after the first of the year. He said we have a copy of their bill which clearly provides that. Two, we can try to defeat their referendum by trying to encourage enough people in the state not to sign it and thereby disqualify them from getting the number of signatures they want. That, he said, he thought was impossible. Three, go forward with our proposal, which will not be a Church proposal. He said [Public Safety] Commissioner [James L.] Barker[20] has already presented this to the city commission, and it is possible that the Salt Lake City Commission would become the official sponsor, at least three of the commissioners, and possibly one of the other two, would go along with it.

He said he is reliably informed that these other people now have a

---

19. The interest on the part of the Salt Lake City Chamber of Commerce and others had to do with the fact that the Salt Palace arena would be completed in July 1969, plans were underway to bid on the 1972 Winter Olympics, and there was a push to make Utah more attractive as a vacation destination.

20. The Public Safety Commissioner was in charge of the police and fire departments. In this instance, James Louis Barker (1920–2015), who had been on an LDS mission to Argentina, balanced his professional work with his assignment from the church to oversee the missionary outreach to Spanish-speaking people in Utah. He was a graduate of the University of Utah and Ohio State University law school. His suggestion was that private clubs be allowed to mix drinks using mini-bottles (therefore consuming the entire bottle), but that the state remain vigilant in controlling what he and other opponents called "liquor by the drunk" ("Barker's Right: There Is a Liquor Problem," *Salt Lake Tribune*, Apr. 6, 1968).

purse of $85,000.00 at least; that they have some of the ablest men in the state working on this, and have their referendum forms all printed; that they are ready to go out into the fifteen counties of this state which they think are the most vulnerable to get the necessary signature[s] to have their referendum placed on the ballot; that our effort will have to be a two-stage fight: One, to get the necessary signatures in fifteen counties that we can count on to get this [other referendum] on the November ballot; and two, to campaign in behalf of the project so that the electorate of the state would sustain this proposal. He thought it would take at least $100,000.00, a very good organization, and an immense amount of effort.

I said that we must be prepared to prevent liquor by the drink; that if we were to get liquor by the drink, we would have trouble.

President Tanner emphasized again that he was sure these men (Gus Backman, Max Rich and Jack Gallivan) would attempt to use anything that I [McKay] might say to promote their own cause; that we must be sure to avoid this—that our slogan is no liquor by the drink and state control. They need not fear that I shall go along on any proposal they might have.

Elder [Delbert L.] Stapley moved that we fully support the committee and vigorously go forward in overcoming the proposed liquor law proposed by this opposite group, namely, liquor by the drink, and that we authorize our committee to take such measures as are necessary, which means spending some money in order to defeat what the liquor interests want, namely, liquor by the drink. The motion was seconded.

I then asked if the brethren were all united on the matter, which they indicated they were. The matter was then put to vote and unanimously approved. I firmly stated: "Let them know we mean something."

May 8, 1968, First Presidency meeting. President [N. Eldon] Tanner referred to the discussions that had been held in the Council meeting regarding the petition that is being circulated by certain interests for a referendum to be placed on the ballot in favor of liquor by the drink. He said this matter is being given consideration by a committee of the Twelve, that the committee has conferred with James Faust, President of the Cottonwood Stake; George L. Nelson, President of the Monument

Park Stake; Wendell Ashton [of East Millcreek Stake][21] and others, and there is some question whether we should oppose the referendum entirely or put in an alternative for the people to vote on. He said this matter will be brought up for discussion tomorrow morning in the meeting of the First Presidency and Quorum of the Twelve. He explained that the people who are circulating this petition must get the signatures of 10% of the voters on the petition in 15 of the counties of the State, that they will have no trouble in getting signatures in Salt Lake and perhaps in some other counties, but the question is whether we should enter into a campaign to prevent them from getting the signatures they need.

I said this matter must be decided definitely.

May 9, 1968. In Council Meeting Elder Marion G. Romney opened the report by the Committee from the Quorum of the Twelve who had been assigned to the program of opposing the liquor by the drink referendum. Elder Romney raised the question as to whether a strong effort should not be made now to defeat the referendum in its initial form rather than to initiate an alternative bill. It was agreed by all present that our first effort should be made to defeat the referendum and that all Stake Presidents in Utah should be called and advised of this determination; they in turn to advise their Bishops, and that a strong article would be placed as an editorial in the Friday evening Deseret News.

May 24, 1968, First Presidency meeting. President [Hugh B.] Brown referred to a request that had been received from Truman Madsen of the BYU for an appropriation to assist in doing some research in New York and other eastern states on early Mormon history and activities. He mentioned that when this request first came to the First Presidency it was denied. He asked for $7,000 at that time to assist in making this research. Brother Madsen is now renewing his request stating that it is thought that they can get along with $5,000. He says that those who would do

---

21. Wendell J. Ashton (1912–1995) was an executive with Gilham Advertising in Salt Lake City. He had been the managing editor of the *Deseret News*, and in 1972 he would become director of LDS Public Affairs. He had graduated in business from the University of Utah. On his mission in Great Britain, he had served under Hugh B. Brown, the mission president at the time. His younger brother, Marvin J. Ashton, would become an apostle in 1971.

this research work are Larry Porter,[22] a Ph.D. instructor in Church History; Kenneth Godfrey,[23] an Institute Director at Palo Alto, California; and several professors at the BYU.

President [Alvin R.] Dyer inquired if this pertains to the Prophet's first vision. He said if so he thought we have in the Historian's Office considerable information on the subject that these brethren might properly review. President Brown said that the research pertained to other topics. He felt we would be justified in encouraging Brother Madsen and his associates to go forward in this research, which he now states can be done if the Church will give him a grant of $5,000. President Dyer stated that any records or information these people might find should become the property of the Church Historian's Office, and that the BYU could have a copy of it if they desired.

With this understanding, we agreed to grant Brother Madsen's request.

June 5, 1968. Sister [Emma Ray] McKay and I were shocked to learn of the tragic shooting of Senator Robert F. Kennedy while campaigning in Los Angeles as a candidate for the presidential nominee of the Democratic Party. …

The fact that I had had a personal visit with Senator Kennedy at the apartment just a few weeks ago (March 27, 1968) made this news especially shocking to me. It recalled vividly the assassination of President John F. Kennedy who was also shot just a few weeks after Sister McKay and I had entertained him at breakfast in our suite at the apartment in 1963.

June 19, 1968, First Presidency meeting. President [N. Eldon] Tanner reported on the finances of the Church, indicating the solid condition in

---

22. Larry C. Porter (1933–) would become the author of a series titled *Sacred Places: A Comprehensive Guide to Early LDS Historical Sites*, as well as co-author with Susan Easton Black of two collections of essays on Joseph Smith and Brigham Young. He received his PhD in religious history from BYU and was on the faculty of the Department of Church History and Doctrine. He would become one of Madsen's successors as the Evans Professor of Religious Understanding.

23. Kenneth Wendell Godfrey (1933–) was from northern Utah, graduated from Utah State University, and received a PhD from BYU. He became the Institute director for LDS students attending Stanford University and president of the Mormon History Association. Among other achievements, he co-authored, with his wife, Audrey, and Jill Mulvay Derr, *Women's Voices: An Untold History of the Latter-day Saints.*

which the Church now rests in its financial position as of May 31, 1968. During the past several years the Church has placed in certificates of deposit and in other investments its surplus funds. Interest received on money invested in 1963 was $3,800,000, but for the first nine months of September 1967 up to and including May 31, interest on investments amounted to $7,500,000. The increase is due to the increase in interest rates, and also due to the fact that much more surplus funds the Church has at present than heretofore. The Church is trying to accumulate in its surplus account sufficient money to carry us a few months no matter what might happen. In addition to funds in this country, we have money in various countries which totals 3.8 million dollars of which 2.6 million could be taken out of the various countries. This is in addition to Canada, which has some 28 million dollars of Church assets which includes 20 million which could be taken out of that country also. The tithing income for the first five months of 1968 shows an increase of 11.3% over the same period a year ago.

I was pleased to learn of the substantial condition of our finances.

June 26, 1968. President [Alvin R.] Dyer read to me a statement which was published in the Salt Lake Tribune on Saturday, June 22, 1968, giving an account of remarks made by Dr. Sterling M. McMurrin, Professor of Philosophy and Dean of the Graduate School of the University of Utah, in a speech given before the Salt Lake Branch of the National Association for the Advancement of Colored People and the Utah Citizens Organization for Civil Rights.

Dr. McMurrin called attention to "the illogical, impractical, and foolish stand of the Church concerning the Negro and stated that the Church had reversed its policy in not allowing its members to have freedom of thought," etc.[24]

Some of the Brethren are very upset over Dr. McMurrin's attitude toward the Church, and feel that he should be tried for his membership. He

---

24. An Associate Press story quoted McMurrin saying that resistance to the Civil Rights Movement was "one of the foremost moral problems of our times," that the LDS policy against blacks was the result of "crude superstitions" that had "no official status in Church doctrine." Jo Ann Hacker, "Ex-Commissioner of Education Raps LDS Negro Policy," *Salt Lake Tribune*, June 22, 1968. See also the entry and footnote under September 10, 1953.

was under question several years ago when he openly made the statement to President Joseph Fielding Smith that he did not believe in the vision of the Prophet Joseph Smith, and made other remarks indicating his disbelief in the Church. However, President Dyer said that Dr. McMurrin has already "cut himself off from the Church," and now that the Church is under such criticism regarding its stand on the Negroes holding the Priesthood, it would be unwise at this time for the Church to take steps to excommunicate Dr. McMurrin. Although I was disturbed over Dr. McMurrin's statements and attitude, I made no commitment concerning this matter.

June 27, 1968. There was called to the attention of the brethren a matter that was considered in the meeting of the Council of the First Presidency and Quorum of the Twelve May 23, 1968 pertaining to the giving of Patriarchal Blessings by fathers holding the priesthood. It was reported that Elder Bruce McConkie had stated while at the Brigham Young University where he gave a talk that the father, if he should receive the inspiration, can pronounce the lineage of his child. Some of the brethren of the Council did not agree with this statement. They felt that there should be no dispute over the right of the father to give his son a father's blessing and let it be recorded in the family records if that were desired, but they would question the statement that the father, in giving his son a father's blessing, could declare his lineage and call it a patriarchal blessing as compared with an ordained patriarch's right to declare the lineage. President [Alvin R.] Dyer said that President John Taylor had stated that if the father has had a patriarchal blessing wherein his lineage was given to him, he can, under certain circumstances, also pronounce the lineage of his son in giving him a blessing.[25] President [N. Eldon] Tanner commented that the father and son sometimes do not have the same lineage.

The brethren were all agreed, however, that even in the event the father may have the power to designate the lineage we should discourage fathers throughout the Church from pronouncing the lineage of their children. I stated that this is definitely right.

July 5, 1968. President [Alvin R.] Dyer called my attention to the fact that we are receiving a number of letters and inquiries concerning the

---

25. Durham, *Gospel Kingdom*, 146.

Church's stand relative to a Third Party and the candidacy of George Wallace of Alabama, in particular, who is now running on the American Independent ticket. He referred to a letter addressed to me personally from Clyde B. Freeman, Chairman of the American Independent Party in Utah, and also letters from Mark A. Benson[26] of the Dallas Stake and Mr. I. D. Workman, all of whom had referred to [a] statement made by President [Hugh B.] Brown in his Commencement address at the Brigham Young University, wherein he implied that the Church did not favor, nor was it the policy of the church, to sustain a Third Party.

Politics—Church's Position on Third Party—I emphasized the fact that the Church takes no official stand with regard to political parties; that it has no policy in the support of, or in opposition to any political party which would choose to place its ideas before the American people.

Later, on August 7, 1968 I went over a draft of a letter prepared at my request by President Dyer on this subject, and instructed that it be sent to Mr. Clyde B. Freeman in answer to two letters he sent to me; and also to others writing on the Church's stand on political matters.

I stated in this letter that the Church does not take a stand in political matters such as he presented in his letter; that members of the Church, exercising their own free agency, are at liberty to support whom they will for this (Independent Party) or any other political position; also that any statement made by a member of the Church in support of a political party or a particular candidate must therefore be regarded as their own statement, and does not reflect in [any way] whatever remarks they may make [about] the policy of the Church.

July 16, 1968, First Presidency meeting. We read a letter from President W[illia]m. L. Nicholls of the Atlanta Stake who points out that Atlanta is a sort of headquarters for the Negro situation; that the march of the poor to Washington [DC] began there, and that Martin Luther King lived in Georgia. President Nicholls mentions that the ministers

---

26. Mark Amussen Benson (1929–2012) was Ezra Taft Benson's second son—an executive with the Castlewick Corporation, manufacturer of cookware and cooking utensils, in Dallas. He graduated from BYU and Stanford and was a disciple of Cleon Skousen—a board member with Skousen's National Center for Constitutional Studies. In three years Benson will become president of the Indiana–Michigan mission. He will later become president of the Ensign Stake in Salt Lake City and a regional representative.

of various churches have expressed themselves from time to time on the civil rights question, and he asks for advice as to whether he should take an interest in the civil rights problem.

It was agreed in our discussion that the Stake President should be encouraged not to participate in these activities, nor to openly oppose them, but merely to take a completely neutral stand in the matter.

Sterling McMurrin Case—The discussion concerning the Negro led to the statements of Sterling McMurrin, Professor at the University of Utah, a member of the Church, which were recently published in the Salt Lake Tribune reporting a speech that Brother McMurrin had given to the N[ational] A[ssociation] [for the] A[dvancement] [of] C[olored] P[eople] wherein McMurrin had belittled and berated the Church for its stand in refusing to give to the Negro members of their Church their full rights in receiving the Priesthood. McMurrin also referred to the acquiescent following of the Priesthood and leadership of the Church; of the hierarchy of the Church not giving sufficient freedom of thought and action in speaking out upon such matters as were mentioned in his talk to the colored people.

President [Alvin R.] Dyer expressed his feelings regarding the Negro situation as it applies to the Church. He referred to a letter he had received from a man in Idaho concerning the giving of the Priesthood to the "Black Man." In answering the letter, President Dyer took the liberty of pointing out four things pertaining to the Lord's way of disciplining the various races of people and stated that it was not only the "Black Man" who was in the process of discipline, but in fact all of mankind, referring specifically to the Jew, the Lamanite, and also some 300,000 white men who hold membership in the Church who have not yet received the Priesthood simply because it is not time for them to receive it due to their own unwillingness to abide by the commandments of the Lord. He mentioned that according to those who attempt to stir up feelings against the Church for not giving the Priesthood to the Negro, they would have us ordain everyman in the Church who becomes a member to the Melchizedek Priesthood regardless of his worthiness or understanding of its principles. It is the same principle that must be applied to the "Black Man" in the receiving of the Priesthood. President Dyer said he received a very satisfactory answer from this man who, no doubt, was a "Black Man" stating that the answers were completely satisfactory to him.

President [Joseph Fielding] Smith spoke up and reported his experience with McMurrin years ago wherein he [McMurrin] had openly admitted to him that he did not believe in the divinity of the First Vision of the Prophet Joseph Smith. President Smith indicated that this man should be excommunicated from the Church.

President Dyer ventured the thought that if this were done it could do the Church more harm than good, and perhaps in the eyes of the Lord Sterling McMurrin has already been excommunicated from the Church on the records which are without question of greater potency than those which we keep among men where our methods are less complete and effective. He said he felt that we should state the truth as the Church believes it, and this would under-rate and place at naught the statements that McMurrin has made; because he has made mistakes in his remarks to this people, both scripturally, morally, and factually.

I stated that I think we should be careful as to how we handle this McMurrin case and the Negro question.

July 19, 1968] 9:30 a.m. Held a meeting of the First Presidency with President Hugh B. Brown, President Joseph Fielding Smith, and President Alvin R. Dyer. President [N. Eldon] Tanner was absent, still being on his vacation in Canada.

The discussion for the entire time of the meeting concerned the letters that have been received relative to President Hugh B. Brown's statements in his commencement address at the Brigham Young University on May 31, 1968. The letters made mention of portions of President Brown's talk in which he made statements which are contrary to remarks made by Elder Ezra Taft Benson.[27] Special reference has been made to the following comments by President Brown:

---

27. This has reference to Benson's May 21 devotional address at BYU, in which he warned of the threat posed by Communism, said the US Supreme Court was guilty of treason, implied that the Civil Rights movement was inspired by foreign operatives, and called for renewed efforts to save America. Ten days later in speaking at BYU's commencement exercises, Brown took the opportunity, illustrated in the excerpt in this diary entry, to denounce political extremism and incivility and to support elected officers, congruent with the church's twelfth article of faith.

"First, I would like you to be reassured that the leaders of both major political parties in this land are men of integrity and unquestioned patriotism. Beware of those who feel obliged to prove their own patriotism by calling into question the loyalty of others. Be skeptical of those who attempt to demonstrate their love of country by demeaning its institutions. Know that men of both major political parties who guide the nation's executive, legislative, and judicial branches are men of unquestioned loyalty, and we should stand by and support them.

"Beware of those who are so lacking in humility that they cannot come within the framework of one of our two great parties. Our nation has avoided chaos like that which is gripping France today because men have been able to temper their own desires sufficiently to seek broad agreement within one of the major parties, rather than forming splinter groups around one radical idea. Our two party system has served us well, and should not be lightly discarded." ...

Conclusion—We came to the conclusion that the Church does not oppose the candidacy of any individual; that it is the right of Church members to support whom they will; that we believe in honoring, sustaining, upholding the law; and also that we should sustain and support men in governmental positions after they have been elected to office by the vote of the people, even though they may not belong to the same party that we do.

The Brethren decided that this matter should be taken to the Council of the First Presidency and Quorum of the Twelve for their consideration and action at the next meeting of the Council in the Temple which will be held on August 22, 1968. However, President Dyer then said that it appeared to be President Brown's wish that the matter be presented [independently] to the Quorum of the Twelve for discussion, and I quickly answered that if it were presented to the Quorum of the Twelve, then it would be the Quorum of the Twelve's policy, and that such policy could not be sent out from the Church; that the same would have to come from the President of the Church. (President Dyer stated that it was plain to see that the President recognized that only from the president of the Church could come a basic policy statement for the Church. While he may listen to the counsel and discussion of the Quorum of the Twelve, and his Counselors, yet he is the one to determine the policy.)

It was agreed before the meeting ended that this problem is two-fold, and that the <u>first phase</u> of it produced a foregone conclusion that every member of the Church has the right to vote for whichever candidate he desires to do so without any fear of reprisal in membership standing in the Church. The <u>second question</u> as to whether a leader of the Church should support a third party and impugn others who run on other party tickets, and also whether he should <u>criticize and berate the head of the existing government of the United States, the Supreme Court, and the cabinet of the President—undoubtedly this will be the last area where the discussion will develop</u>.

August 7, 1968, First Presidency meeting. A letter was read … reporting that there are three individuals in [a] stake who have been advised by their doctor that they should use coffee regularly as a stimulant and as a diuretic. One of these individuals is a paralytic and the other two are elderly. The stake president asks for counsel on the matter. It was decided to answer … suggesting that if these individuals need caffeine such as is in coffee they could perhaps obtain from their doctor capsules that could be used instead of drinking the coffee, inasmuch as if they were allowed to go to the temple even though they drink coffee it might have a harmful influence on others. <u>In the event a capsule will not answer the purpose it was agreed that these persons should obtain written statements from their physicians to the effect that because of their health they should be permitted to use coffee regularly as a stimulant and/or a diuretic.</u>

August 20, 1968, meeting of First Presidency and Twelve. Because of the surplus over the budget, <u>the Budget Committee approved the proposal to go forward with the new office building</u>, the plans and specifications for which will be completed by September, at which time they will be put out for bids and the steel will be ordered. … it is felt that we may be able to build this building in three years, whereas it was formerly thought it would take four; in which event the building will be completed by 1971. A question was raised by Brother [Harold B.] Lee in regard to the height of the building. He did not think that our building should be higher than any other building here. The proposed building would be 29 stories high, including three stories on the top for storage, maintenance, etc., which would be five stories higher than the University Club Building. He said the foundations are built to carry the building even higher than that. This would make it possible to bring all our offices except the Relief Society, which is in its own building, and the Distribution Center which is using the old Deseret News Building on Richards Street into this one building. The computer work would be in the basement of the Utah Hotel Motor Lodge.[28]

President [N. Eldon] Tanner said that it was his feeling in regard to the height of the building that if we did not have the Kennecott Building or the University Club Building it might be wise to reduce the height of our building, but that the increase in height will not be offensive aesthetically. He said he believed that it was the general sentiment of the brethren that we should go forward with the building as planned.

President Tanner mentioned that the building will have two wings, four stories high each, which will make the high rise building appear lower than otherwise. The building he said will certainly be serviceable and functional. Two years have been spent working with the architects and members of the committee, and it is thought that we should go forward with the building as planned.

President [Alvin R.] Dyer mentioned that there has been a feeling among some people in the city that it would be better to have a number of smaller buildings to house the Church offices at different locations. He commented that when we build a high rise building like this, the higher the stories the less the cost per square foot would be. President Dyer said that he had seen the picture of this proposed building and the plaza section, which will be called the mall, between the new building and the Church Office Building, and that there will be a clear view of the Temple from First Avenue, and in between the buildings will be a beautiful garden plaza. He felt to sustain the proposal that we go forward with the building along the lines specified. He mentioned that this would take care of our office requirements for the next ten years. President Tanner commented that the building will be 70–75% occupied as soon as built,

---

28. This motel was a satellite facility to the Hotel Utah. A half block northwest of Temple Square, it had 150 rooms, a swimming pool, restaurant, auditorium, and an exhibit area for trade shows. Today the Global Service Center, which contains the church's IT department, is located in about the same spot.

and the floors not needed at this time will not be completed but will be shells until they are needed.

President Tanner asked me if we <u>should go forward with the building and I indicated my approval of this project.</u>

August 26, 1968. Knowing that I am interested in the plight of the Czechoslovakian people, since the Communists went into their country with their armed might to stop all attempts of the people to get out from under the Communist yoke, Clare [Middlemiss] reported that Americans who were in the country and witnessed the Russians with their tanks and guns shooting down the people in the streets—even children—were horrified.[29] ...

<u>I stated that the Communists will never surrender their main aim— that of world conquest—no matter what they say or do.</u>

September 9, 1968. President [Alvin R.] Dyer referred to the pressure that has been placed upon Elder [Ezra Taft] Benson by the Third Party ticket representatives, and especially George Wallace, the Presidential candidate.

This matter was brought to me by Elder Benson early in the year,[30] and at that time I told Elder Benson not to accept George Wallace's offer because of Church responsibilities. At that time George Romney was also seeking nomination on the Republican ticket as a presidential candidate. I informed George Wallace by letter that it would be impossible for Elder Benson to accept his invitation, and Elder Benson, who said that he was not seeking this position, also wrote to Mr. Wallace and told him that he would not be able to accept his invitation. Now this matter has come up again, and they are pressing Elder Benson to accept and to run with Mr. Wallace as they feel he has a good chance to win.

I said that my decision is still the same, and that I feel that Elder Benson should not launch out on this political campaign; that it could

---

29. This had to do with the Soviet (with other satellite countries') invasion of Czechoslovakia on August 20–21 to crush the "Prague Spring." In the previous months, Czech attempts to liberalize their society worried the Soviets and gave them justification to enter with armored divisions to "quell" what was considered to be an incipient revolution. Some 650,000 troops remained until September and left only after assurances by Czech leaders to abandon their reforms.

30. See the entry and footnote under February 13, 1968.

lead to confusion and misunderstanding in the Church. I also expressed the opinion that Mr. Wallace cannot win, and then what position would that put Elder Benson in. President Dyer said that Elder Benson only wants to serve his country, but most important, to be directed by what the Prophet of the Lord says in this matter. I expressed my feelings that Elder Benson is truly a great man.

Later, Elder Dyer reported that he had contacted Elder Benson relating to him the details of his meeting with me, and of my decision concerning the Vice-Presidency. Elder Benson said: "I feel relieved and will abide by the counsel of the president."

September 10, 1968, First Presidency meeting. President [N. Eldon] Tanner called attention to a letter from Elders Mark E. Petersen, Victor L. Brown, Joseph Anderson and D. Arthur Haycock,[31] who had met as a committee in response to the suggestion of the First Presidency and [to] give consideration to the question of the proper handling of letters received by members of the General Authorities from time to time in which questions are asked regarding doctrine, Church policy, history, etc. It is the recommendation of this committee that all such letters received at the office of individual brethren of the Authorities should be referred to [Joseph Anderson][,] the Secretary to the First Presidency[,] for answer. In regard to the answering of such questions by secretaries [to individual members of the presidency] it was the recommendation of the committee that the secretaries not attempt to assume the responsibility of answering these questions. The brethren of the presidency felt to approve this recommendation and it was also suggested that when questions are presented by individuals over the telephone the information should not be given out by secretaries in answer thereto but they should be referred to the Secretary to the First Presidency.

---

31. David Arthur Haycock (1916–94) was employed by the *Deseret News* but had been church president George Albert Smith's personal secretary and Ezra Taft Benson assistant when Benson was US Secretary of Agriculture. He had also been president of the Hawaiian mission. In 1970 he would return to the Church Administration Building as secretary to Joseph Fielding Smith, Harold B. Lee, Spencer W. Kimball, and Ezra Taft Benson in succession. He was born in Farmington, Utah, and studied at the LDS Business College and University of Utah.

September 27, 1968. Dr. [Alan P.] MacFarlane called me [Clare Middlemiss] this afternoon. He asked how I felt and I said, "Tired," as I had been working night and day on [General] Conference. The doctor said that President McKay should have no meetings longer than an hour; that he stayed too long at Council Meeting yesterday—3½ hours. President McKay said he was exhausted when he came home, although he had enjoyed meeting with the Brethren. Dr. MacFarlane said he has an ulcerated sore on the end of his spine from sitting too much. The Doctor feels he should remain off it as much as possible, hold only hour meetings from now on, and then perhaps he would feel well enough to go to Conference. I said that I could see no reason this week for a meeting with President McKay; that I had seen him in Huntsville last week—the first time in a month—had arranged with him for all conference matters, and that the Brethren were busy preparing their speeches. He said, "Good, I hope he does not have to see anyone." I said that Vice-President [Hubert H.] Humphrey will be here Monday, but that President [Hugh B.] Brown is handling all of his appointments and meetings. Dr. MacFarlane said, "Vice-President Humphrey shouldn't see President McKay as the President hasn't seen any of the others [this year] including Richard Nixon."

October 4, 1968, First Presidency meeting. Read a letter addressed to me from Robert E. Dansie, legal counsel, American Independent Party of Utah, requesting the use of the [Salt Lake] Tabernacle for Governor George C. Wallace, U.S. Presidential Candidate, to give a major address at 10:00 a.m. Saturday, October 12. The letter also states that 6,000 students and faculty at the Brigham Young University have signed petitions requesting that he be invited to speak there. Mr. Dansie also states that he hopes that my schedule will permit Governor Wallace to visit with me when he comes.

President [N. Eldon] Tanner and President [Alvin R.] Dyer said that inasmuch as Governor Wallace is a candidate for the presidency of the United States, that state conventions of 50 states have placed his name on the ballot, it would seem that he should be entitled to have the consideration he requests inasmuch as the candidates for the two national parties have spoken in the Tabernacle.

I gave approval for Governor Wallace to speak in the Tabernacle and asked President Dyer to telephone Mr. Dansie telling him that his request has been approved, including his request for Governor Wallace to speak at the Brigham Young University.

October 17, 1968, First Presidency meeting. Reference was made to a letter from Elder Spencer W. Kimball, who has just returned from visiting the missions in Great Britain, making suggestions regarding action that should be taken relative to the large number of children in Great Britain who were baptized in 1961–1963 without the proper consent of their parents, and sufficient understanding on the children's part.

Attention was called to a letter that the First Presidency had written to stake and mission presidents in Great Britain in February 1964 on this same subject, stating that where the parents of the child request that the name be removed from the records, in such cases the bishop, branch president or mission president should see that every reasonable endeavor is made first to convert the parents; second, to fellowship the child; third, to satisfy the child that his membership in the Church will be a blessing to him if he will participate in the activities; that every reasonable effort should be made to try to fellowship these young people and convert their parents. Elder Kimball has prepared a draft letter for the signature of the First Presidency addressed to the stake and mission presidents in the British Isles suggesting a course to be followed; namely, that each district president personally contact 25 or more of these young people, and that each member of the high council and district council do the same, thus distributing the burden on many leaders.

President [Alvin R.] Dyer questioned the advisability of adopting this course, stating that it would be a very difficult assignment, if not almost impossible, for a high councilman or a district councilman to make investigation regarding 25 persons and give each case the attention that it should have. He thought the assignment should be made on an individual basis. President [Hugh B.] Brown suggested that we assign this project to Elder Kimball to follow through on it and not involve the First Presidency in another directive letter. It was thought that in his letter Brother Kimball could say that the First Presidency has authorized him to follow the matter through. President Dyer suggested that a note be given to Brother Kimball advising against the wholesale processing of these young people.[32]

October 24, 1968, First Presidency meeting. Reference was made to questions that have been raised by presidents of stakes and mission presidents in Germany, the British Isles, etc., and also by the [Improvement] Era, regarding talks that have been given in conference by the brethren of the Authorities such as the one given by Brother [Ezra Taft] Benson at the recent General Conference regarding the responsibilities we have to oppose socialism, etc. A letter had been received from the President of the Manchester Stake stating that certain talks at the conference could create a problem, and he asks for some clarification before the conference pamphlet is published. He mentioned an address by one of the brethren reminding the people that we are under obligation to heed the counsel of the General Authorities as being from the Lord, and that on Friday morning an address was given denouncing all forms of socialism in governments, and specifically mentioning England. He explains that over half of the members of his stake in England vote socialist and that members of the stake presidency, high council and bishoprics support that cause, that there is therefore some confusion in regard to how they should accept these statements. <u>The brethren were agreed that in General Conference the Authorities should talk about principles and leave politics or pointed attacks on politics out of their talks.</u>

October 30, 1968. President [Alvin R.] Dyer referred to a decision made some months ago that the First Presidency letters should be signed by me and the first and second counselors. He said it was his recollection that it was the decision then also that copies of correspondence which the First Presidency meetings develop would be brought to the attention of President [Joseph Fielding] Smith and himself so that they could keep in touch with things. <u>It was agreed that in the matter of letters that result from decisions made by the First Presidency in these meetings, copies of these letters will be shown to President Smith and President Dyer for their information and that they might indicate thereon that they had seen them.</u>

---

32. See also Kimball and Kimball, *Spencer W. Kimball,* 272.

778

November 7, 1968. At the Council meeting held today in the Salt Lake Temple, according to the minutes, an open discussion was held with regard to procedures to be followed now that we have won the mandate of the people on the Liquor-by-the-drink issue in working with the Legislature and so forth.

Elder Harold B. Lee pointed out that care must be taken in endeavoring to dictate to members of the [Utah] State Legislature as to what they should do in the Legislature with regard to this. He said that this is a matter that needed to be carefully handled, and Brother [Alvin R.] Dyer agreed with Brother Lee that it could be dangerous to us and put us in a bad light, but that, nevertheless, something must be done to offset the efforts now by the opposition to obtain some compromise, for example, to permit Liquor-by-the-drink in the clubs, etc. But it seems to be the determination of this body to exercise the mandate that has been won, and to see to it that the present law is strengthened, and that there be no compromise with the principle of [opposition to] Liquor-by-the-drink.

November 14, 1968. President McKay looked very well this morning; he seemed so much like his old self, without that worried, tired look in his face which he has had of late. His eyes were bright, smiles came often, and he seemed happy.

I [Clare Middlemiss] took up several matters, and then said I had better leave and not tire him too much. He said, "What are you going in such a hurry for?" I answered, "I shall be back soon!" And he said, "I will be here for a long time yet." ...

Items Read in Minutes of the First Presidency and Council of the Twelve Meeting held Today—Elder Harold B. Lee expressed the thought that the legislative committee, composed of Nathan Eldon Tanner, Marion G. Romney, and Howard W. Hunter, should have a lobby representative to the [Utah State] legislators to avoid any direct connection that could be construed by outsiders as undue influence upon the legislators coming from the Church.

A discussion ensued including such thoughts as when the Committee is sought out by legislators that this tended to give the Church a status with regard to the position of the Church on legislation and that the legislators were anxious to know what the Church's stand was on various matters. So long as they would come to the Committee there could be no violation of proper propriety in such matters. (From Minutes of President Alvin R. Dyer)

Washington D.C. Temple—President [Hugh B.] Brown was not at the Temple meeting on this day so President Tanner therefore brought up the matter of approval given to the erection of a Temple in the Washington D.C. area. This approval met some reaction among some members of the Quorum of the Twelve. Elder Lee stated that there wasn't much that could be done about it, since it had been approved by the Presidency and this was like the Ogden and Provo Temples—the Quorum of the Twelve were merely informed that such were to be built. He stated that a Temple in Washington D.C. was perhaps the poorest location in the East because of the tremendous amount of criminal disturbance in that area and the many Negroes that live in Washington and suggested that perhaps the Valley Forge area out of Philadelphia would be a more suitable place for the erection of a Temple. Elder Mark E. Petersen seemed to sustain the feelings of Elder Lee. Elder LeGrand Richards stated that he felt that a Temple at Washington was a proper location to serve the concentration of members in that area and other areas as well that would funnel into that point.

The other members of the Quorum of the Twelve seemed noncommital and completely resolved to the fact that the President of the Church had made the decision for the erection of the Temple in Washington and therefore did not make any comments.

President Tanner stated that he was not present at the meeting when the decision was reached and could not therefore report on what took place. Since I [Dyer] had been in attendance, he asked me [Dyer] to make a report. I then stated simply that President Brown had brought the matter up after President Tanner had left and President McKay had permitted discussion on the matter and comments from members of the First Presidency and, after receiving them, had simply said that we should go forward with the project. (From Minutes of President Alvin R. Dyer)

Because of the feelings of Brother Lee and Brother Petersen, President Dyer suggested to President Tanner that the matter should be taken back to President McKay and that a re-confirmation be asked for on the

project in light of their opposition to it. President Tanner thought that
this should be done.

November 22, 1968, First Presidency meeting. There was read to the brethren a memorandum to the First Presidency by Joseph Fielding Smith
relative to a proposed exchange of documents by the Church of Jesus
Christ of Latter-day Saints and the Reorganized Church. The memorandum states that Earl E. Olson, Assistant Church Historian, had been
sent to Denver to meet with Richard Howard, historian of the Reorganized Church, relative to an exchange of manuscripts between the two
churches, and that as a result of this meeting the Reorganized Church is
desirous of obtaining copies of the following manuscripts which we have
in the Historian's Office:

1. Photographic prints of each page or parts thereof of the [surviv-
   ing] Book of Mormon [dictation] manuscript.
2. 35 mm positive microfilm of the following items:
   a. The Book of Kirtland Revelations
   b. Other revelations of the early church through the Nauvoo
      period, including those not published in the Doctrine and
      Covenants
   c. The Far West Record
   d. The Book of Elders Licenses, Kirtland and Far West
   e. Egyptian Grammar and Alphabet and related pages
   f. Documentary History of the Church through 1844
   g. Nauvoo List of Church Members, 1842–1845

In exchange for these papers the Reorganized Church offers the following.

1. 35 mm positive microfilm of the following items:
   a. The Book of Mormon [printer's] manuscript
   b. The original manuscript to the Inspired Version of the Bible
   c. The 1867 R.L.D.S. Committee manuscript of the Inspired
      Version
   d. The Joseph Smith Bible (1828 H & E Phinney Ed[ition]) in
      which marginal notations were made to correct the verses in
      the Bible
   e. The Book of John Whitmer

2. Photographic prints of each page of the following:
   a. Sheets from the Book of Commandments manuscript (4 sheets)
   b. Letters of Joseph Smith, written and/or signed by him
   c. The Scott letters of the Nauvoo period (approximately 3)

The memorandum sets forth suggestions and agreements as to the use to be made of these materials. President Smith, who is the Church Historian, felt that we could agree to this exchange without any question.

President [Alvin R.] Dyer said that this is really a sort of breakthrough in our relationship with the Reorganized Church and he felt to favor the proposal.

The First Presidency were unanimous in indicating their approval. I personally was very happy over this exchange.

December 11, 1968, First Presidency meeting. At the beginning of the meeting, we met with Elders Spencer W. Kimball and Mark E. Petersen of the Quorum of the Twelve and discussed the report which they had presented at a recent meeting of the Council of the First Presidency and Quorum of the Twelve regarding an assignment that had been given them by me about eight years ago to develop a program to help those of our people who are involved in homosexual and perversion practices.[33]

I was greatly shocked and dismayed to learn of the extent of the penetration of this dreaded practice, which has spread even to the membership of the Church. Elder Kimball mentioned that this problem has grown all over the world, and that it has now come out in the open, whereas formerly it was undercover. Now, an effort is being made to make this perversion respectable, and the newspapers and magazines deal with the question almost constantly.

Elder Kimball said that if their assignment is to be continued, they need much more help; that he and Brother Petersen cannot carry the program without additional help with all the other responsibilities they have.

After a discussion of this matter, Elder Kimball said their recommendation would be that a Church Committee be appointed, and if it

---

33. See Kimball and Kimball, 382–83. Over a period of seven years to 1968, the two apostles "counseled almost a thousand individuals, nearly all in Salt Lake City, Ogden, and Provo." Kimball, *Lengthen Your Stride*, 86n4.

were preferred to rotate the assignment and choose some of the other Brethren to take care of this matter, they would welcome such a change.

There ensued a discussion wherein President [Alvin R.] Dyer felt that any continuation of investigation into this matter, and the consultations to be had with those so afflicted, could perhaps be set up in a correlated manner through the Church organization with a certain few being given the responsibility and called to direct the work; that it be handled through the Stake Presidents and Bishops. However, <u>President [N. Eldon] Tanner and Elders Kimball and Petersen felt that it is best to let the Committee continue on by adding some ten or twelve others to it to carry on the work, exclusive of any direct connection whatsoever with Stakes and Wards, only as the Committee may want to consult with the Bishops</u>.

President Dyer feels that this is a Church-wide problem and something should be done to get it into the proper channels of organization to reach more people who are so afflicted; however Elders Petersen and Kimball and President Tanner were not in agreement with this and said that this is a special work and could not be committed just to the Bishops and Stake Presidents throughout the Church.

It was agreed, therefore, that Elders Kimball and Petersen should continue to go forward with this work and they were authorized to submit a list of names for approval of the brethren, (perhaps one or two sisters), whom they would recommend be asked to assist them in this work. It was also suggested that Elder Kimball and Elder Petersen report to me at least once every six months. It was indicated that they would need at least ten other people to assist them to commence with, and that as the work developed and the program increased, they could give consideration to the recommendation that it be brought under the Correlation Committee.

December 20, 1968. At 9 a.m. in accordance with previous arrangements made with President McKay, the Counselors in the First Presidency and all members of the Quorum of the Twelve (with the exception of LeGrand Richards who was in California) held a meeting with President McKay in his apartment at the Hotel Utah. Joseph Anderson, secretary to the brethren, was present to take minutes.

President McKay greeted the brethren and invited them to be seated in the living room where chairs had been provided. Following prayer and opening preliminaries, each of the Brethren stood and bore testimony of the Gospel, expressing their love and appreciation for President McKay and for his life of service, the great work that he had accomplished, and the example which he had set before them and the world.

This was a most memorable occasion for all of the Brethren, and one that shall never be forgotten.

President McKay was visibly affected, and deeply appreciative of the expressions of each one of the brethren. He stated that never before in the history of the Church was there a greater need for unity and common understanding among the brethren. He was speaking very legibly, so that Elder Harold B. Lee who sat next to President McKay leaned over to President [Alvin R.] Dyer and said, "The President is speaking very well this morning." President Dyer said, "Yes, this was the case also on the previous day when I met with him on some Church matters. Henry Smith [of the *Church News*] was present also and had read the Christmas Greeting of the First Presidency to him, and the President listened carefully, made some corrections, and then approved the message."

President McKay told of his great love for the Brethren, and stated that those who were there that day upon that occasion were participating in an event that perhaps had not been held before. He encouraged all of the Brethren to go forth and carry on the great responsibilities that devolve upon them.

The President shed many tears as did all who were present on that occasion. As the brethren prepared to leave, after each had spoken and the President had spoken to them, and had given his blessings and best wishes to them, each one of the Brethren filed by President McKay, shook his hand, and wished him the Season's Greetings and the blessings of good health.

December 27, 1968, First Presidency meeting. President [Alvin R.] Dyer called attention to an earlier discussion by the First Presidency regarding a proposed exchange of historical documents between our Church and the Reorganized Church [of Jesus Christ of Latter Day Saints]. President Dyer mentioned that he had been asked to check into this matter before granting the proposed exchange, and he now reported on the question. He said he felt that we were being asked to furnish the Reorganized Church much more than we were getting from them. He mentioned items which he thought we could well afford to exchange, namely, (1) Photographic print of [dictation] manuscript pages that we have in our possession of the first copy of the Book of Mormon in exchange for which they would give us a photographic print of their complete copy of the Book of Mormon [printer's] manuscript, which he understood to be the second copy made which was done by Oliver Cowdery; (2) They would like a copy of a Book of Elders Licenses at Kirtland and Far West. This is just a record of ordinations. He felt there would be no problem here; (3) Nauvoo list of Church members. He felt there would be no harm in giving them this. They would give us in exchange for these items as indicated a copy of the complete second Book of Mormon manuscript, the original manuscript of the Inspired Version of the Bible, and the 1867 manuscript of the Inspired Version of the Bible. We would also want to obtain a copy of the book of John Whitmer which they have in their possession. President Dyer felt if we could get copies of these items from them it would be very beneficial and he could see no objection to our granting permission for them to have copies of the three items he mentioned. They have, however, he explained, asked for a number of other items which he thought should be carefully screened before our permission is given.

I asked the counselors to give the matter further consideration and to bring back their recommendation.

December 31, 1968. Another year has come and gone, and each year seems to fly by faster than the preceding one. What a busy and eventful year it has been! I am thankful that I have been well enough to carry on with my duties and responsibilities most of the time—holding meetings with my counselors as often as possible, and meeting with the Brethren in the Temple when my health would permit; in addition to holding frequent meetings with my secretary [Clare Middlemiss] on office duties.

All our children are well, happy and busy with their children and now some of them with their grandchildren. Sister [Emma Ray] McKay has had two accidents from falls during the year, but has miraculously recovered from both of them—one a broken hip, and the other an injury to her back. Although I have been confined to my wheelchair most of the time, and have had several minor illnesses during the year, I feel pretty well, and have no aches or pains.

19   Continued Difficulties, Despondency, and Death, 1969–70

> After Dr. MacFarlane left the apartment, Clare visited with President McKay for 15 or 20 minutes. He had his eyes closed. Clare took his hand and said, "Good Morning, President McKay, do you know who this is?" He opened his eyes and said, "Of course I do, it is Clare—Good Morning." Clare asked him how he felt and he said, "I feel very weak inside." —April 2, 1969

January 8, 1969. President [Alvin R.] Dyer reported on the letter he had received from ... the San Diego Stake with regard to the Society that had originated there, purportedly to fight Communism, which had taken the name of the <u>Society of Moroni</u>.

President Dyer reported that in accordance with my instructions he had counseled them concerning this matter not to use the name Moroni or any other name that would infer that the group is Church affiliated[,] and that they had ceased to use this name.

January 10, 1969. President [Alvin R.] Dyer said of the attendance of President [N. Eldon] Tanner at the Inaugural [of US President Richard M. Nixon]: "I [Dyer] feel that it is a mistake for one member in the Presidency to go to such events as this. Normally, this would be the responsibility and prerogative of the President of the Church. This is also true when Temple Presidencies are released and new ones are called. It would appear to me that at least two of the Counselors should go so that the two could more fully represent the President and also that this prominence would not be given to a single member of the Presidency. But apparently this is not the wish and desire of President Tanner, who pursues these matters and desires to go alone."

January 13, 1969, minutes of a First Presidency meeting. The brethren reported to President McKay a discussion that was had in the Council meeting on Thursday last regarding the application of a black man to be baptized. When Elder [Marion G.] Romney was in South Africa some time ago President Badger[1] of the mission made him acquainted with this man and at that time Elder Romney suggested to President Badger that he confer with the South African government authorities to ascertain what their views on the matter were, whether it would affect our missionary relationship in that land if we were to baptize this man. President Badger conferred with the government people and received word that it would be all right to baptize the black man but that there must be a complete separation between the blacks and the whites; in other words, that they could not come together in the same meetings. A question now presented by President Badger as to whether this man, if baptized, could have his black friends investigate the gospel looking forward to having them baptized also. The question was raised as to whether we would be justified in denying a man baptism who is converted and asks for baptism. It was also reported that Elder [Ezra Taft] Benson had mentioned that according to reports that are being received, negroes belonging to the Black Power organization are attempting to become members of the Church in order to gain information about the Church and to be better prepared to emphasize their claim that the Church discriminates against the negroes by not giving them the priesthood. President [N. Eldon] Tanner said that the feeling of the brethren in the Council meeting was that we should make it clear to these negro people in South Africa that they are welcome in the Church but as long as the government takes the position that there

---

1. Howard Carl Badger (1914–89), president of the Johannesburg Mission from 1967 to 1970, had been a missionary in South Africa in the 1930s, and his father, Ralph A. Badger, had been president of the mission from 1906 to 1908. During World War II he was a chaplain in Europe, and after the war he became a real estate developer in Utah. His uncle, Carl A. Badger, had been an assistant to US Senator Reed Smoot (R–Utah) during the first decade of the twentieth century.

must be a complete separation between the whites and the blacks, we think it unwise to bring them into the Church. In discussing the matter the brethren mentioned that baptized negroes couldn't hold a sacrament meeting without white men holding the priesthood being there to bless and administer the sacrament, that as a matter of fact they couldn't have baptismal services without a white man doing the baptizing, and other meetings likewise. President Tanner asked President McKay if he felt that the attitude of the brethren of the Council was in agreement with his thinking, and he said yes for the present.

January 14, 1969, minutes of a First Presidency meeting. Elder Howard W. Hunter met with the First Presidency this morning and presented to them a problem pertaining to genealogical work which he said the committee had been discussing for several months. He explained that over the years the rule has been that if a woman has had more than one marriage in her lifetime we would seal her to her first husband, everything else being equal. This would pertain only to people who are dead. If a woman had been married two or more times and had children by each marriage, heretofore she has been sealed to the first husband. If she had no children by her first husband but had children by her second marriage, many times she was sealed to the second husband so that the children could be sealed to their own father. He said there have been cases where the family has said that the mother or grandmother, whoever it might be, did not want to be sealed to her first husband, that she did not respect him and had more affection for her second or third husband, as the case might be, and sometimes under such circumstances she was sealed to the second or third husband. He said that where we have trouble is in cases that go beyond the point of memory, that, for instance, when we go to the parish records in England, and the other registries, and we find the woman has been married to several men, we do not know what her wishes or desires were and so ordinarily she would be sealed to her first husband, except in cases when we had enough information to indicate that the second or third one would be the appropriate husband to seal her to. He said all of this is a little arbitrary and is based upon lack of facts. He mentioned the recent decision of the First Presidency going into the computer program to the effect that we would go through the parish register of marriages and seal all women to their husbands wherever we found their record of marriage in the parish records. He said this results sometimes in a woman being sealed to more than one husband, that sometimes where a woman has been married more than once she is sealed to two persons. This was approved by the First Presidency. In these cases the woman would have the right of choice in the hereafter.

Elder Hunter said that our brethren in the Genealogical Society who have been serving for many years have suggested the desirability of [taking this approach generally][,] sealing women to more than one man where they have been married several times. This pertains to people who are dead. He explained that when a woman is sealed to her first husband and there have been several marriages, the matter is left in the hands of the Lord and her choice in the hereafter, but this does not give the posterity a positive line to follow. He said the brethren of the Genealogical Society have had the feeling that it would be better to seal such a woman who has had more than one husband to each of her husbands and let the children of each marriage be sealed to their parents. This would still give the woman the right to make her selection in the hereafter. He said that frequently they have people come into the Genealogical Society office and say that their great grandmother, for instance, said before she died that she loved her second husband more than the first and that they would like to have her sealing to the first man broken so that she could be sealed to the second. Elder Hunter said that they were commencing to wonder if they followed the right course through all these years. He thought it was perfectly proper that in life a woman be sealed to only one husband, but after death and many years have passed and there are posterity from the lines of several husbands, it becomes a difficult situation.

There was some discussion and explanation made regarding this proposed change. In this connection mention was made of the fact that in cases where a sealing was cancelled between a couple who have children born in the covenant that these children are not permitted to be sealed to anyone else than their natural parents and that the matter is left to the hereafter for decision as to whether they should go with the mother or the father. The brethren emphasized in the discussion that the fact that the work is done for these people does not necessarily mean that it will be accepted, that, however, the work must be done for everyone and it is like putting it in a bank as it were to be held subject to the worthiness and acceptance of the individual.

After a rather lengthy discussion of the matter President McKay indicated his approval.

February 5, 1969, First Presidency meeting. President [Alvin R.] Dyer reported that yesterday in accordance with approval given by me he had met in his office with Vernon Romney,[2] the new Attorney General of the State [of Utah]. President Dyer explained that the committee that has been set up to study sex education and pornography materials would soon be ready to report their investigation, which committee is composed of Alma Burton, Robert Matthews, and another brother who are in the Institute program of the Church.[3] President Dyer said before making any recommendation as to what might be done to counteract the type of sex education they are getting in the schools he wanted to get the Attorney General's attitude on the matter. ... He [Romney] expressed a willingness and desire to work with us on this sex program, even to give any help needed with the legislators, if it should go that far, in preparing legislation that would be legal and sound. President Dyer said that it looks like it will take legislation to keep out of our schools the kind of materials that are infiltrating our school systems.[4] Attorney

2. Vernon Bradford Romney (1924–2013) served two terms as Utah's attorney general, 1969–76. After participating in the invasion of the Philippines and Okinawa in 1944–45, serving a church mission to upstate New York, and graduating from the University of Utah in 1950, he joined the staff of US Senator Arthur V. Watkins (R–Utah). He took night classes at George Washington University and received his law degree there. In 1976 he was the Republican nominee for governor of Utah but lost to Democrat Scott Matheson. Michigan Governor George W. Romney was a cousin.

3. The Assistant Church Administrator of Seminaries and Institutes, Alma Pexton Burton (1913–98), had received an EdD from the University of Utah. Robert James Matthews (1926–2009) was a recent PhD graduate in ancient scripture at BYU and taught seminary in Provo. He would soon become a member of the BYU religion faculty.

4. School districts around the country had begun adopting a curriculum developed by the Sexuality Information and Education Council of the U.S. (SIECUS), founded by the medical director of Planned Parenthood and condemned by Robert Welch of the John Birch Society as a "typical Communist tactic." In the upcoming general conference, Ezra Taft Benson will state that "the church is opposed to sex education in the schools." That sentiment will be echoed by Alvin R. Dyer saying that "we must not be insensible to evil influences that are being thrust upon us by the perverted principles of sex education." Mark

Romney had said that he is the Attorney General but he is also a member of the Church and has six children and wants to keep this stuff out of the schools the same as we do.

Church Department of Finance Reorganization—President [N. Eldon] Tanner reported in connection with the recent embezzlement of a large sum of money from the Church Financial Department that a careful investigation of the Financial Department had been made by Peat, Marwick and Mitchell, who will make a report in the near future. President Tanner said the conditions were such that it will be necessary to appoint a new comptroller for that department succeeding Brother [George Y.] Jarvis,[5] that it will therefore be necessary to ask Brother Jarvis for his resignation. President Tanner said that this does not mean that Brother Jarvis was in any way involved in the embezzlement but that there is a weakness in the administration of that department making this embezzlement possible, and there are things that need changing and the need for a stronger administration. President Tanner said that he proposed as Brother Jarvis' successor, vice chairman Alan Blodgett,[6] and to give him as an assistant a very fine man who is now with the Advance Planning Department. President Tanner said it was his feeling that we should then have a complete study made of the department beyond what the auditors have done, that it might be considered advisable to make separate departments of the three divisions or to consolidate them into one department with managers of the various divisions. It was agreed that President Tanner should handle this situation in the wisest and kindest way possible so as not to cause any reflection upon Brother Jarvis, that, however, he should be asked for his resignation.

E. Petersen will add that "sex education belongs in the home." *One Hundred Thirty-ninth Annual Conference ... Report of Discourses*, Apr. 4, 5, 6, 1969, 13, 57, 64; Jerry Buck (AP), "Foes of Sex Education Aim Wrath at SIECUS," *Ogden Standard-Examiner*, May 28, 1969.

5. George Young Jarvis (1904–2000) was born in Provo, a great-grandson of Brigham Young. He served a mission to France, received a master's degree from American University in Washington, DC, and worked for the Department of Agriculture and Department of Commerce, and for the American Bankers Association in New York, before he was hired by the church in 1946 to oversee finances in Europe, then to be the church comptroller. In 1969 he will be reassigned to Europe to represent the Church Financial Department in Frankfurt.

6. J. Alan Blodgett (1933–) did, in fact, succeed Jarvis as managing director of the Church Financial Department in 1969 and remained until 1985. He was from Vale, Oregon, and graduated in finance from BYU.

February 12, 1969, First Presidency meeting. A letter was read from Dennis R. Judd, John W. Rider and Brent W. Brown referring to Brother Ezra Taft Benson's remarks at the recent quarterly conference of the Illinois Stake.[7] They claim that his talk dwelt largely on political matters, that he discussed "Godless communism" and "Socialism" and linked these "insidious influences" to the decisions of the [US] Supreme Court, the Civil Rights movement, and other political matters. President [Alvin R.] Dyer mentioned that he could see no objection personally to making references to the principles of free agency and unrighteous dominion, that these are gospel principles, but it was another matter when we begin to localize these things and tie them to officials in government, that this creates confused feelings among the people. President Dyer mentioned a letter that he had received from someone else in regard to this same conference and Elder Benson's remarks on that occasion. President [Hugh B.] Brown had received a letter from another man on the same question with which he enclosed copy of a letter he had written to Brother Benson about the matter, together with a copy of Brother Benson's reply saying that if he would keep his eye on the prophet he would be all right, that if his, Brother Benson's, teachings are published in the [Improvement] Era he might know that they have the sanction of the Church.

I asked what conclusion the brethren had reached regarding the matter. President [N. Eldon] Tanner said the same conclusion that was arrived at about two years ago, that Elder Benson should discontinue this kind of thing, and particularly in stake conferences, and should limit himself to talking about the gospel and its applications. President Tanner said that he thought I made as clear a statement on the subject as he had heard made in the meeting of the Council of the First Presidency and the Twelve at that time.

I said that there is no reason why we should not continue that understanding.

---

7. Dennis R. Judd (1943–) and Brent Whiting Brown (1941–2008) were PhD candidates in political science at the University of Illinois. Judd would become a faculty member in Chicago, editor of *Urban Affairs Quarterly*, and in 2003 would have an annual book award named after him by the American Political Science Association. Brown was born in Arizona, served a mission to Brazil, and became a professor and vice president at Arizona State University. John Rider's identity is unknown.

February 28, 1969, First Presidency meeting. President [Hugh B.] Brown commented that he thought a reorganization of the presidency of the Brigham Young University was needed before long, that we should get a new president, that President [Ernest L.] Wilkinson is reaching the age where in any other institution he would be retired.

President [Alvin R.] Dyer suggested that simultaneously with any change he thought the whole school system and department of education should be brought under Correlation, that so long as they are permitted academic freedom to write whatever they desire they are bound to run counter to the policies of the Church.[8] President [N. Eldon] Tanner said that he thought that a change would be desirable but he did not think we would get anybody who would control the situation better than is now being done.

March 5, 1969, First Presidency meeting. President [N. Eldon] Tanner also presented for the consideration of the brethren a draft letter that he had prepared ... relative to a 14 year old girl who had become pregnant out of wedlock. The specific question pertained to whether she should attend MIA and associate with the girls of her age group or if she should be asked to stay away from MIA during her pregnancy. The draft letter to be signed by the First Presidency suggested that it would be unwise for the girl during pregnancy, whether living in her own home or a foster home, to attend or associate with her age group in Church gatherings. The letter also suggests that if she has friends or relatives who live away from the area where she has her membership and her problem is known, it would be desirable to have her placed in such a home; that, however, wherever she lives people should be encouraged to show love, kindness and consideration to her during this trying time in her life. The letter was approved as drafted, with minor amendments.

---

8. The Correlation Department either edits or censors, depending on one's point of view. "It is not censorship," the church maintains. It is rather the way to ensure that "programs, materials, and activities ... comply with policies and meet standards approved by the council of the First Presidency and Quorum of the Twelve Apostles." To whatever degree that is appropriate for a church, it would be odds with the mission of a university. Frank O. May, Jr., "Correlation of the Church—Administration," *Encyclopedia of Mormonism*, 1:323.

April 2, 1969, 11:10 a.m. President McKay had an appointment with Dr. [Alan P.] MacFarlane. He talked to the President and advised him not to attempt to attend any sessions of [General] Conference. "Your condition is such that you might not hold up for an entire meeting, and you would dislike to have to be taken out of the meeting before a large Conference audience." President McKay reluctantly agreed with him, but said if he felt better he would change his mind.

Dr. MacFarlane then left the office and visited with secretary Clare [Middlemiss] a few moments. Talked about President McKay and the inadvisability of his attending Conference sessions. Clare agreed saying she had never seen the President so tired and weak.

Dr. MacFarlane then asked Clare to tell President [Hugh B.] Brown that President McKay will not attend any of the meetings.

After Dr. MacFarlane left the apartment, Clare visited with President McKay for 15 or 20 minutes. He had his eyes closed. Clare took his hand and said, "Good Morning, President McKay, do you know who this is?" He opened his eyes and said, "Of course I do, it is Clare—Good Morning." Clare asked him how he felt and he said, "I feel very weak inside." ... He smiled and[,] [Clare said][,] it was good to see him smile.

May 8, 1969. It was mentioned that in the Council meeting last Thursday consideration was given to the question of whether or not the sealing power might be given to the Presiding Bishopric. It was explained that these brethren are the only ones of the General Authorities who do not have the sealing power and President [N. Eldon] Tanner thought it would be well if this permission might be granted them. President Tanner mentioned that many brethren are given the sealing power who are faithful, devoted brethren and have served as bishops and in other Church positions in various Church areas.

When the matter was discussed in the Council meeting Elder [Harold B.] Lee indicated that the reason for not giving this authority to the Bishopric is a matter of policy, that is, that they are in charge of the temporal matters of the Church and that the sealing work in the temple is not their particular field of service. President [Alvin R.] Dyer mentioned that when this was discussed in the temple he had mixed feelings about it. He realized that there are men who are not General Authorities who have the sealing power but the Lord had given a special calling to the Presiding Bishopric to administer temporal affairs. He wondered if it might not confuse their position if they were given powers and authorities dealing with spiritual matters.

President Tanner recommended that this authorization be given unless I could see some reason for not giving it. He asked me if I had any objections and I said I did not favor it.

May 12, 1969, 9:30 a.m. Meeting of the First Presidency in the President's Hotel [Utah] Apartment. Present were Presidents Hugh B. Brown, Joseph Fielding Smith.

President Brown and President Smith called at the hotel apartment this morning and discussed with me the matter of a message to be given by President Brown from the First Presidency in his devotional talk tomorrow at the BYU. President Brown stated that Elder Ezra Taft Benson had made a talk at the Y last week which was a very inflammatory speech against the government and the United Nations.[9] He said it left the students with the feeling that what Brother Benson said was the Church's position. President Brown felt that the First Presidency should make a statement of their position regarding sustaining law. He had prepared a statement which was read to me emphasizing that we believe in being subject to kings, presidents, rulers, and magistrates, in obeying, honoring and sustaining the law. The statement that he proposed for the First Presidency to sign consisted mainly of a quotation from President Joseph F. Smith on that subject. President Brown stated that he thought we should get such a statement before the students before the school closes and the devotional at which President Brown will speak tomorrow will be the last devotional of the school year. He further stated that he thought [US] President [Richard M.] Nixon was doing a good job and that he thought he should have our support.

President Smith agreed with the statement as presented and said that we must sustain the government, that while the government makes mistakes sometimes he believed that President Nixon, who is now president, is doing the best that he can.

---

9. Neither Brown's nor Benson's biography discusses this confrontation. See Wilkinson diary, May 13, 1969. Wilkinson was himself an opponent of the United Nations and shared many of Benson's views on political and governmental matters.

I, in commenting on the matter, said that I did not think that any government officials should be accused of these things.

I authorized President Brown to have my signature attached to the statement.

May 20, 1969, minutes of meeting with Alvin R. Dyer.[10] President Dyer reported that he had received a telephone call from Ezra Taft Benson in Washington, D.C., that Brother Benson is quite concerned about a statement by the First Presidency regarding upholding and sustaining the government that was read by President [Hugh B.] Brown in his recent devotional talk at the Brigham Young University. President Dyer said that Elder Benson made specific reference to two paragraphs in President Brown's talk and had asked him, President Dyer, to read these two items to President McKay, which he promised to do. President Dyer mentioned that the talk had been read to President McKay and received his approval before it was delivered. The items mentioned were as follows:

"We make no statement on how this country can or should try to disengage itself from the present regrettable war in Vietnam; that is a problem, a very difficult problem, which must be solved by our government officials in whom we have complete confidence."

President McKay said, "That is good."

President Dyer then read to him the other item which he said is part of President Joseph F. Smith's statement on patriotism as contained in President Smith's book "Gospel Doctrine." The statement reads: "Loyal citizens will probably be the last to complain of the faults and failures of our national administrators. They would rather conceal those evils which exist, and try to persuade themselves that they are not only temporary and may and will in time be corrected. It is none the less a patriotic duty to guard our nation whenever and wherever we can against those changeable and revolutionary tendencies which are destructive of a nation's wealth and permanence."

President McKay said, "That is a good statement."

---

10. A prefatory note indicates that the minutes were taken by Joseph Anderson, also that the meeting had to do with "President Brown's talk at the BYU including the statement from the First Presidency." This was repeated in a typed header introducing the entry for May 21.

President Dyer said that he had told Brother Benson that he thought it was a good statement but Brother Benson is quite concerned about it. President Dyer said he could see nothing wrong with it himself.

May 21, 1969, minutes of a meeting with Alvin R. Dyer. President Dyer read to President McKay a telegram that had come addressed to President McKay from Reed Benson, son of Ezra Taft Benson, pertaining to the recent talk by President Hugh B. Brown at the Brigham Young University devotional, in which President Brown read a statement from the First Presidency setting forth the Church's attitude toward sustaining government officials. Brother Benson states that he was grieved to hear of the statements of the First Presidency which President Brown had quoted. President Dyer said that President Brown in his address referred to the war in Vietnam and stated that we have confidence in our government officials that they will do everything they can to settle that most regrettable incident. He said this is the particular part of the statement they disagree with, that they do not think the government is doing everything that can be done, and he feels that the First Presidency ought not to make a statement saying we support the government in their efforts to try to settle the war in Vietnam. Brother Benson sets forth in his telegram a number of reasons why he feels that we should not have complete confidence in our government officials. He concludes the telegram by saying: "You are a great soul, President McKay, as well as the mouthpiece, and if you want me to have complete confidence in our government officials I want to know it and then if the spirit confirms it I will adjust my life accordingly." President Dyer said it seemed to him that this is a disrespectful wire. President Dyer reminded the President of the interview [he] had with him yesterday when certain statements from the First Presidency's announcement by President Brown were read, at which time the President indicated his approval of the statements. President Dyer mentioned that Henry Smith [of the Church News] was present for the reason that he wished to be sure whether or not the First Presidency wished the talk by President Brown and the statement therein by the First Presidency published. He asked President McKay if authorization should be given to Brother Smith to go ahead and publish it in the Church News and the President said yes. President

Dyer commented that we must have confidence in men placed in government positions, that [US] President [Richard M.] Nixon was elected by the vote of the people and that one of our articles of faith says that we believe in honoring, obeying and sustaining the law, and being subject to kings, presidents, rulers, magistrates, etc. He said that it seems evident that President Nixon is making a real effort to end the conflict in Vietnam, and President McKay stated it as his belief that this is so.

May 29, 1969, First Presidency meeting. President [Hugh B.] Brown mentioned that occasionally cases come to the attention of the Twelve where men for one cause or another are out of harmony, and certain members of the Twelve have issued instructions on the basis of hearsay evidence regarding the handling of such cases. He stated that it was his understanding that the Twelve should not instruct any [church] court to excommunicate a man, that all that they should do is to tell them to try the case, hear the evidence and form a judgment.

I said that is right.

Communists—Handling of Church Membership—President Brown mentioned a specific case that had come to his attention where a man had been charged with being a communist and the man in question had written a letter saying that he was not a communist, never had been, that his allegiance is to the Church. He states that he does have some leanings to a certain type of socialism. President Brown said he would like to discuss the matter with the Twelve this morning and I said that would be all right.

President [N. Eldon] Tanner inquired if a man were an avowed communist, would our position be to excommunicate him or disqualify him for any position in the Church. He said that if he admits that he is a communist and carries a communist card, should our position be to excommunicate him or just say that he cannot hold office and must cease all activities as an office holder. I said I did not see why our Church should have anything to do with the communists.[11] It was my decision that communists should hold no positions and that if action were to be

---

11. Sixteen days later, on June 14, 1969, the church will call native East German Johannes Henry Burkhardt (1930–) to oversee some 5,000 Latter-day Saints in the German Democratic Republic and advise him to cooperate with the Communists. Kuehne, "Freiberg Temple," 100–01, 108.

taken against them it would be done in the usual manner of their being cited to appear before a Church tribunal.

June 17, 1969, First Presidency meeting. President [Hugh B.] Brown reported that a number of people are of the opinion that the time has come when we should change the president of the BYU, that President [Ernest L.] Wilkinson is nearly 70 years old and has done a great work; that, however, there is considerable unrest[12] and a need for new leadership. President Brown also called attention to a matter that had been previously discussed pertaining to the appointment of a commissioner of education for the Church. He wondered what my feelings on the matter were. He said that if it was agreeable to my thinking a search would be commenced for applicants for these positions and bring the applications to the Presidency. President Brown said that he thought it would be desirable to make any change before the beginning of the next school year and asked me if they should go ahead with this.

As I indicated previously I am in favor of finding and appointing a commissioner of education for the Church. I am not in favor of the release of Ernest L. Wilkinson as president of the Brigham Young University.

June 19, 1969, First Presidency meeting. President [Hugh B.] Brown mentioned the mission presidents seminar that is to be held next week at which instructions will be given to the new mission presidents. He referred to the fact that the missionary training program is uniform throughout the Church and consists of a number of lessons. He said that in some cases these may be applicable but in others not so effective. He thought it would be desirable to meet with the Missionary Committee and go over this series of lessons with them and try to get them to bring them up to date and make them current. He said that each missionary is supposed to memorize these lessons. He wondered what I would think if President [N. Eldon] Tanner, President [Joseph Fielding] Smith, President [Alvin R.] Dyer and he were to sit down with the Missionary executive Committee and discuss this matter frankly with them before the seminar, and decide what is the best method of presenting the gospel.

---

12. This unrest was a result, in part, of the "spy ring" scandal that offended the faculty, students, and some general authorities.

President Brown mentioned that while on his recent trip to Canada and elsewhere he met with a number of missionaries and learned that they are somewhat confused in regard to this question-and-answer method that we are now using. President Brown said that his own feeling is that the missionary should be guided by the spirit and not keep his eyes fixed upon some document. He mentioned that when Henry Moyle was in the [First] Presidency he had charge of the missionary work, and that previous to that time one of the First Presidency had directed this work.

President Dyer said he thought it was right that the Presidency should be closer to the missionary work. He said that when he was set apart the President had said that he was to continue his interest in missionary work, but that he had had nothing to do with it.

I agreed with the suggestion that the counselors confer with the Missionary Committee about these matters.

June 26, 1969, First Presidency meeting. President [N. Eldon] Tanner summarized the financial report of the Church for the month of May and for the first nine months of the fiscal year showing a surplus for the month of [$]5½ million, and for the year [$]29½ million—an unexpected increase.

July 3, 1969. President [N. Eldon] Tanner, accompanied by Secretary Joseph Anderson, met with President McKay at 12:30 p.m. and presented the following matters[,] and actions were taken as indicated: ...

President Tanner reported to President McKay a matter he considers of serious importance. He mentioned that KSL had applied to the Federal Communications Commission in Washington [DC] some months ago for renewal of their license, which approval was granted by a small majority but there was a lot of opposition. The charge is made that KSL serves the Church and not the public and that because we own the Deseret News and KSL radio and television station we are controlling the media of communication. Later some people in Utah supported by others whom we do not know appealed the decision of the Commission. There are seven members on the Commission, two of whom belong to our Church. When the appeal was considered by the Commission three members voted for renewal and three against, and one member, who is a member of the Church, abstained from voting. The matter is now being referred to the federal court of appeals. President Tanner said that when this matter was discussed at the meeting a few days ago of the board of the Bonneville International there was fear that our station would not get its license renewed, which would mean that KSL could not operate.

Robert L. Barker, who is a lawyer in Washington, who is looking after this and is one of our Regional Representatives, says that it looks bleak. President Tanner said the KSL station is worth ten to twelve million dollars today while it is operating, that if we do not get our license renewed it will not be worth more than two million dollars because all that we would have left for sale would be our equipment. President Tanner said that he had talked to President [Hugh B.] Brown about the matter this morning and had talked with Lawrence McKay yesterday. He said President Brown felt that he, President Tanner, should report the matter to President McKay, and also the proposed solution to the question, which he thought we should seriously consider. President Tanner said that if we were to dispose of the station to friendly buyers who would operate it the way we want it operated, they could get the license renewed and we could get our money out of the station. He mentioned as the people he had in mind to whom the station might be sold: Bill Gay,[13] one of the top men in the Howard Hughes operations; Howard Anderson,[14] the President's grandson-in-law; [Michigan banker] Howard Stoddard; [oil and gas company founder] Glenn Nielson;[15] and people like that. He said that he understood these men are trying to buy a station in California and want to form an organization to do it. President Tanner asked President McKay if it would meet with his approval for him to discuss

---

13. Frank William ("Bill") Gay (1920–2007) was president of the Summa Corporation, which oversaw Hughes's Las Vegas hotels. He was also vice president of Hughes Tool Company and chairman of the board of Hughes Air Corporation. Born in Salt Lake City, he had attended college at UCLA.

14. Howard Ballantyne Anderson (1928–2014), whose wife Midene McKay (1929–) was a granddaughter of David and Emma Ray McKay, was, like Bill Gay, an executive with the Summa Corporation. In the LDS Church, he had been president of the Los Angeles Stake and president of the California Mission. He was born in Denver and graduated from the University of Utah.

15. The director of the BYU Development Office at the time, Glenn E. Nielson, had founded the Husky Refining Company in 1938 in Cody, Wyoming, where he was stake president for fifteen years. As the company grew, the headquarters moved to Calgary. Nielson was himself from Canada. He was born in Cardston and studied economics at the University of Alberta. He had also served an LDS mission to England.

this with some members of the KSL board, namely, Gordon B. Hinckley and Thomas S. Monson, who are on the executive committee; Robert L. Barker, Arch Madsen and Lawrence McKay, and perhaps Richard L. Evans. He said he would like to discuss the matter in some detail with these brethren with the feeling that if we think that is the thing to do we begin to plan accordingly. He mentioned that if we could sell it to men of this kind who are good Church members they would serve the Church to the best of their ability and they would carry out our programs as nearly as they could the way we want them carried out. President Tanner mentioned also that there is a court case now pending to determine whether or not the [Salt Lake] Tribune and Deseret News are contravening the Anti-Trust Law.[16] An effort is being made to change the arrangement that the newspaper union has. They claim that we control the media of communications. President Tanner suggested that he be given permission to talk with these men and report to the President what their thinking is. President McKay indicated his approval.

July 10, 1969. President [Alvin R.] Dyer mentioned discussions heretofore had with the Twelve in regard to the preparation of a resource-key manual for parents[,] to assist the parents in the matter of teaching their children regarding maturation and reproduction [sex education] in a way that would be in harmony with the gospel. He said people are saying that this should be taught in the schools and not in the home but the parents need a guide of some kind prepared by our own people. He mentioned that this matter has been submitted to the Correlation Committee, that Brother [Harold B.] Lee in turn referred it back to the Correlation secretaries and that these secretaries, over the signature of Antone Romney,[17] are recommending that a task committee be appointed to prepare this material. President Dyer said he has a meeting this morning with Brother

---

16. This was because the two newspapers had joint interest in the Newspaper Agency Corporation, which handled their advertising, printing, subscriptions, and delivery but had nothing to do with editorial content.

17. Antone Kimball Romney (1902–82) was dean of the School of Social Sciences at University of California–Irvine. He was born in Rexburg and had completed his undergraduate studies and master's degree in sociology at BYU and went on to Harvard for a PhD in social anthropology. He taught at the University of Chicago and Stanford University before UC–Irvine.

Lee on this question, and he inquired if they are following the direction the brethren wish them to go. The material he said would be prepared by Church writers and submitted back to the Correlation Committee for approval and probably be incorporated in the family home evening manual.

I felt that this was a good idea and asked that it be submitted to the First Presidency when prepared.[18]

July 31, 1969, First Presidency meeting. A letter was read from ... a group of missionaries at the Language Training School in Laie, Hawaii, asking if the Word of Wisdom is now a commandment. They report that their discussion manual says it is a commandment and that a letter they received from Elder LeGrand Richards states that to his knowledge it has never been made a commandment. In discussing the matter President Joseph Fielding Smith mentioned that he recalled many years ago hearing the President of the Church announce in conference that from then on the Word of Wisdom was a commandment. It was also mentioned that in the days of President Brigham Young he had presented to the conference the proposition that the Word of Wisdom be considered as a commandment in the future, which proposition was approved by the vote of the conference. It was also mentioned that letters from the First Presidency during recent years at least have indicated that the Word of Wisdom has not been given to the Church as a commandment and a copy of the letter that is usually written was read to the brethren to this effect, indicating that while it was not given as mandatory it should be observed by all saints in the light of a commandment as the same blessings follow its observance if given to the Church as a law.

After hearing the discussion and the facts in the matter, I said that it should be left as it is.[19]

August 7, 1969, First Presidency meeting. President [Hugh B.] Brown reported that President [Alvin R.] Dyer had been asked to prepare a

---

18. For background, see Kenneth L. Cannon's autumn 1976 article in *Dialogue: A Journal of Mormon Thought*, "Needed: An LDS Philosophy of Sex."

19. The ebb and flow of this can be ascertained from Lester E. Bush's autumn 1981 article in *Dialogue*, "The Word of Wisdom in Early Nineteenth-century Perspective." See also Paul H. Peterson's 1972 BYU master's thesis, *An Historical Analysis of the Word of Wisdom*, and Thomas G. Alexander's 1986 *Mormonism in Transition*.

statement on the proposition of making Ricks College [Rexburg, Idaho] a four year college, which he has done and has [the report] ready for presentation. President Brown expressed the thought that this matter should go first before the Board of Education. He said he had talked to Elders Harold B. Lee, Marion G. Romney and Howard W. Hunter about the matter of appointing a Church Commissioner of Education, which matter was brought before the First Presidency previously. He stated that some of the brethren had in mind recommending Neal Maxwell[20] for this position. President Brown said he thought that in the event Brother Maxwell is the one the President wished to appoint as commissioner, Brother Maxwell should take the lead in promoting this four year college and coordinating the work of the educational interests of the Church. He asked me if it would meet with my approval to take this matter of the appointment of a Commissioner of Education before the Church Board of Education and then take up the matter of the four year college in Rexburg, and also the tenure of office of President [John L.] Clarke of the Ricks College. I said that this would be all right. It was explained that it is the intention now only to present the proposition of a commissioner to the board but not clear any name for that position.

August 20, 1969. Elder Mark B. Garff reported that the building costs of the Washington [DC] Temple, as presently proposed, could not be built for the ceiling estimate of ten million dollars set by the First Presidency. He spoke of fourteen million plus two million for furnishings and landscaping for a total of sixteen million dollars.

This projected amount was unsatisfactory to the First Presidency. All expressed the feeling that it was too high, although it was the consensus of feeling that the Temple should reflect the image of the Church in the Nation's capital.

---

20. Neal Ash Maxwell (1926–2004) received a degree in political science and a law degree from the University of Utah. He interrupted his schooling to participate in the War in the Pacific and to serve a mission to Canada. In Washington, DC, he became an assistant to Senator Wallace F. Bennett (R–Utah) and a CIA operative (Peggy Fletcher Stack, "LDS Apostle Neal A. Maxwell Dies at 78," *Salt Lake Tribune*, July 22, 2004). On returning home, he became an administrator at the University of Utah (eventually executive vice president), and in 1970 the tenth LDS Commissioner of Education. Eleven years after that, he was ordained an apostle and gained a reputation as one of the most articulate speakers and writers in the church.

It was suggested by President [N. Eldon] Tanner that the increase of 16% in building costs in the Washington area, since the early estimates of cost, be added to the ten million, and that a ceiling cost of twelve million dollars be established for building costs with landscaping, driveways, and furnishings as extra. I approved of this and was sustained by my counselors.

Mark Garff was instructed to meet with the architects and advise them of this decision. This will require the lowering of the spires and other building height modifications.

President [Alvin R.] Dyer made the comment that we needed to take a new look at the cost of our temples, that the simplicity and purpose of that for which temples are erected seemed almost lost in the surge to make our temples great outward showplaces. Reference was made to the extremely high costs of the Los Angeles, Oakland, and now the proposed Washington Temple, that even the Provo and Ogden Temples were too high.

President Dyer made mention of the fact that the Mohammedan Temple of Mecca, which received the religious fervor of three hundred million people, was nothing but a square black stone building with no windows and but one small door and that the interior was practically bare.[21]

President Tanner stated that he felt that henceforth our temples should not exceed one or two and one half million dollars.

September 5, 1969, minutes of the First Presidency meeting. President [N. Eldon] Tanner reported that a letter had been received from Oliver Holmes, Executive Director, National Historical Publications Commission, addressed to the First Presidency. The letter explains that for several years this commission in Washington [DC] has approved projects involving the publication of papers of outstanding Americans. The pattern has been for the commission to make grants of funds to universities and noted scholars and match these funds in the various projects. Under this arrangement they have published the papers of George Washington, Alexander Hamilton, Thomas Jefferson and others. It is now the feeling of the director

---

21. Although the 43-foot-tall cube known as the Kaaba looks plain, it consists of granite walls, a marble floor, and gold waterspouts, and is part of the world's largest sanctuary, the Great Mosque of Mecca, which cost an estimated $100 billion to construct. A renovation scheduled to be completed in 2020 is costing $11 billion. See "The World's Twenty Most Expensive Buildings," *London Telegraph*, July 27, 2016.

of the commission that they should give first priority to the publication of the papers of President Brigham Young. Under this arrangement the Utah State University and other Utah universities might cooperate and the National Archives would make available without charge any Brigham Young papers that are now in the National Archives. The work would possibly not be completed for another four years. They are asking that the Church make available to them materials from the Church Historian's Office. It is proposed that Brother Leonard Arrington and Dr. George Ellsworth [of USU] be the editors in chief. It is stated that the project would be undertaken in the most scholarly manner so that it would be well received by the scholars of the nation and would be published at no cost to the Church. They state that the papers should not include any unfavorable sermons of Brigham Young and that we could edit the materials that would be used. In discussing the matter the brethren felt that there could be some things written that would be in the files that ought not to be published and would be misconstrued. It was decided to give the matter further thought.

September 10, 1969. Lawrence and Llewelyn McKay came over and discussed with their father the Negro question. President Alvin R. Dyer was also present.

September 11, 1969, First Presidency meeting. President [Hugh B.] Brown referred to the matter that was passed one a week ago regarding the appointment of a church commissioner of education, and now named for the consideration of the brethren for this position Brother Neal Maxwell. He stated that this matter had been presented to President McKay and the First Presidency who indicated their approval, but felt that it should come to the Twelve. Brother Maxwell is executive vice president of the University of Utah, and has been given an honorary doctorate, but has not received his Ph.D but does have a master's degree.

Elder Richard L. Evans moved approval, and he and others of the brethren spoke highly of his qualifications and his faith in the gospel. Some question was raised by certain of the brethren. In this connection it was mentioned that the suggestion has been made that whoever is appointed to this position should be considered for the appointment of Assistant to the Twelve.

Elder [Gordon B.] Hinckley mentioned the wonderful influence he felt that Brother Maxwell wields at the University of Utah and the need for such an influence. He said that while he had the highest respect for Brother Maxwell, he did not know who would take his place at the University and have the same strength as a church member. He thought he represented the Church's point of view there courageously. He mentioned also his academic standing with reference to his degrees. He thought that the Church ought to have men who can be questioned anywhere as to their academic standing.

Elder Evans commented that 70 per cent plus of the students at the University are members of the Church, and that perhaps 85 per cent of the students come from this metropolitan area, that some of the areas at the University are as alien to the Church and the State and the people as can be, that a faithful Latter-day Saint cannot be successfully appointed to a position in the medical school, and some other areas.

After a rather lengthy discussion of the matter, it was decided to hold up the matter until such time as a larger representative group of the Council is assembled.

September 24, 1969, First Presidency meeting. President [N. Eldon] Tanner mentioned having received a letter ... express[ing] concern because of the Church attitude toward the negro, and mention[ing] that in conversing with President George Albert Smith's son[22] recently he stated that President Smith had said that categorically the Church's position on the negro question was one of custom and not of revelation. President Joseph Fielding Smith said: "He is wrong on that." President Smith further stated that the Pearl of Great Price is clear on the matter and that it has been accepted as scripture. The brethren asked me if I wanted to make any ruling on the matter and I answered that I did not want to make any statement on the question this morning.

October 8, 1969, excerpt from Alvin R. Dyer's minutes of a meeting with Hugh B. Brown.[23] President Brown then asked how I [Dyer] felt with

22. The late church president's only son was George Albert Smith Jr., a Harvard University professor and lapsed Mormon. Clayton Christensen, "On Teaching," *Perspective* (BYU–I), spring 2017, 44–45.

23. The entry is prefaced by: "Note: The following minutes by President Alvin R.

regard to President Joseph Fielding Smith becoming the President of the Church in the event of President McKay's death. My answer to him involved a number of things which I shall hereafter make a part of the account of the discussion. First, however, here are President Brown's statements as I recall them.

"President Smith could not possibly assume this position. He sleeps now through most of the meeting and is too old."

"The matter of the President of the Quorum of the Twelve becoming the President is after all simply a tradition and need not be followed."

"I think that Brother [Harold B.] Lee should come on in and take the position as President when President McKay passes away."

My response to these statements, intermittently given, was as follows:

When the mantle of President falls upon a man, a change takes place in him to enable him to fulfill the calling and this would be true with Joseph Fielding Smith. The order of succession of the President of the Church is not merely a tradition, but a tradition based upon basic laws of God pertaining to this order. I referred to the summarization of these laws in my writings and that they are inviolate unless a direct revelation is received to make it otherwise and that such revelations would come to the Senior Apostle or the Presiding High Priest which, by the death of President McKay, would be the President of the Quorum of the Twelve and this is Joseph Fielding Smith.

I stated that the only way that this procedure and the placing of President Smith as head of the Church could be altered would be if he, himself, refused to accept the calling. Then it would fall to the next in line of the Quorum of the Twelve. ...

I stated further that Brother Lee's time will no doubt come, but that it is the right of President Smith to hold an office. If the Lord does not want President Smith to be the President, he would make it known to him or would remove him. I told President Brown that I could not in any way sustain his thinking regarding this fundamental matter.

October 14, 1969, First Presidency meeting. President [N. Eldon] Tanner

---

Dyer I wanted included in my Diary of this day. They concern the matter of succession to the presidency which President [Hugh B.] Brown discussed with Brother Dyer." The excerpt I included begins with this: "<u>Regarding President Joseph Fielding Smith</u>:"

reported that while he was in Europe he saw a man who is in a bishopric, a man in the Sunday School Superintendency, two brethren who administered the sacrament, and one who spoke in the sacrament meeting, all with long hair. He said they seemed to be sincere, devoted people, and while their hair was long they were clean and well groomed. The brethren expressed the sentiment that where a person is clean and to all intents and purposes is trying to do the right thing, they would not see why we should discriminate against him because his hair is long. In other words, they did not think we should make an issue of it. President [Hugh B.] Brown felt that those who are in presiding positions such as stake presidents and bishops should talk to these people and see why they are wearing their hair long, whether it is simply a habit or if there is some other reason. President Tanner said that one reason why he mentioned it is that there is a lot of criticism about the position that has been taken at the BYU.

October 24, 1969. I [Clare Middlemiss] called the nurse, Mrs. Noall, at 9:00 a.m. and asked if I might see President McKay for a few moments this morning. She said, "President McKay is sitting right here; let me ask him." She turned to President McKay, "Your secretary Clare wants to come over."

He answered, "Have her come right over."

I arrived twenty minutes later at the office in his apartment. President McKay seemed to be in an extremely tired condition, and it was hard for him to keep his eyes open. I took hold of his hand and said, "Good morning, President McKay, this is your secretary Clare." His handshake was quite weak, and I said, "President McKay, that isn't like your handshake. Your handshake is usually firm and strong." He turned his face and smiled and tried to grasp my hand a little harder. I said, "That is more like it, President McKay." He gave me a wan smile, and his eyes were soon closed. I was unable to take up any letters with him.

Theresia Mayr,[24] who accompanied me over there, was taking some notes on some scrapbooks that were on the shelves in his office. During

---

24. Theresia Mayr (1914–2000) was a secretary in President McKay's office and would continue assisting the church presidents through three more administrations. An emigrant from Austria, she had worked as a secretary in the Swiss mission office for five years before moving to Utah.

the time that we were there, which was about 45 minutes, President McKay seemed to be aware of our presence. He kept opening his eyes and looking over toward me and seemed to want to tell me something, but was unable to get enough energy to express himself.

He looked very wonderful, and there was a spiritual feeling in the whole room, so much so that I was in tears most of the time that I was there (although President McKay was unaware of this).

The nurse who had been tending to Sister McKay had asked us to wait until she had returned. Later I asked her what the doctor's report was on President McKay after he had examined the President yesterday. The doctor said that the President's blood pressure was normal for him and that his lungs were clear, but his blood test showed that the poison in his body is not being thrown off thus causing these extreme tired spells which he is having more frequently. ...

I left the apartment feeling very dejected.

November 13, 1969. I [Clare Middlemiss] received a call from President Alvin R. Dyer stating that a letter had been read to the Temple Council Meeting, written and signed by Dr. Alan MacFarlane allegedly at the request of the McKay family, more specifically Dr. Edward McKay after a McKay Family meeting at which time Lawrence McKay had declared that he would not read a conference talk of his father's again, and that Robert McKay had seconded a motion put to the family. Furthermore, the letter from the Dr. was read to the entire Council in which the Dr. stated that President McKay is now mentally deficient and could not sign letters or documents of policy. Furthermore, personal letters were to be taken from President McKay's secretary of 35 years (Clare Middlemiss) and given to Joseph Anderson to go over and answer—the last thing President McKay would have ever wanted.

Elder Harold B. Lee stated at the Temple Meeting, "Where the President is not[,] there is no First Presidency; that President McKay cannot be written off; that the President recognized him a week ago and seemed all right although he is getting weaker.["]

Henceforth, no letters were given to secretary Clare Middlemiss and no word was said to her about it—just taken away and no explanation as to why.

* * *

[Minutes of a meeting of the First Presidency and Twelve:] President [Hugh B.] Brown mentioned that we find ourselves in rather a delicate position in matters pertaining to the President of the Church, that President McKay's son Lawrence had come to President [N. Eldon] Tanner some time ago with a recommendation which President Tanner had been following up. He said it has now come to the point where we need to take action. President Brown said that so far as he and Brother Tanner were concerned, they approach the matter with trepidation and humility, that it could easily result in someone being charged with attempting to usurp authority to which he is not entitled. President Brown asked President Tanner to make a statement on the matter.

President Tanner referred to statements he had made two weeks ago on the subject to the effect that Lawrence McKay had gotten in touch with him on October 31 and referred to two matters, namely, editorials appearing in the Improvement Era and in the Instructor, and also the question of conference talks by the President. Lawrence had said that his father until this conference has been able to review and go over the talks that were prepared for him and approve them, but he said that he is not able to do it now, and he did not think that they should be preparing talks for him or giving them in conference. Then he said regarding the editorials he thought they should be discontinued; that, however, we could use materials from his previous talks or editorials or written material, and editorials be prepared on that basis, and let the public know what it is.

President Tanner said that when Lawrence talked to him that that raises another question in his mind about which we have been concerned for some time; that he did not want to say anything because he did not want in any sense to do anything that would offend the family or the President of the Church. He said the President's signature is appearing on letters, correspondence and documents as approved, and all this has been done while he could not sign his name;[25] that now he is not able to approve these things. President Tanner said he asked Lawrence what he thought about that, and he said he thought it came under the same category. President Tanner then asked Lawrence how the family felt about these things, that this was a sensitive and delicate matter. He thought

---

25. Letters were being signed by an autopen. Prince and Wright, *David O. McKay*, 397–98.

that Lawrence should confer with the family and see how they felt. Lawrence called President Tanner on Monday and said that he had spoken to all the family except one who was out of the country, and that they were all of one mind that these things should not be.

President Tanner said that he then discussed this matter with Presidents Joseph Fielding Smith and Alvin R. Dyer in a meeting when President Brown was away, and it was decided that it would be well to confer with Brother [Richard L.] Evans who is in charge of the Era editorial department and Lawrence McKay together relative to this matter. He stated that Brother Evans was out of the city and the meeting was not held. President Tanner did report to Brother Evans what Lawrence had said, that Brother Evans had raised a question and said that his concern was whether we would be telling the people that the President cannot speak to them any more.

President Tanner then called President Brown who was in Germany on the telephone and went through this situation with him and asked his feelings, and he said he felt the same as Lawrence did and the way the others had expressed themselves.

President Tanner said that before calling President Brown he spoke to Brother [Harold B.] Lee about the matter and told him he thought it was serious enough that it should be brought to the Twelve, and he felt that that was what should be done. Accordingly he did not [hesitate to] take it to the Council two weeks ago, and in that meeting after some discussion it was agreed to continue the three or four editorials in the Era that were approved by President McKay prior to October Conference, and that we would refer to Lawrence the question of the editorials in the Instructor and tell him of our discussion. President Tanner said he did that and Lawrence said that the editorial for the Instructor for December had been prepared by Sister Clare Middlemiss who has been preparing these editorials, and that this one for December had some current matters in it. He thought it should be run but after that they would take care of the matter.

President Tanner stated that at the previous meeting when this matter was discussed the question of legality came up, and Elders [Marion G.] Romney and [Howard W.] Hunter were assigned to meet with Wilford Kirton, our legal adviser, to discuss these matters, that they did meet and there was a discussion of some length. President Tanner was present, also Brother [Joseph] Anderson was there to take notes. President Tanner said he asked Brother Kirton to make a study of the matter and do what research he could in order to save time, and to bring to these other brethren his findings. Brother Kirton read a statement which had been approved by Brother Romney and Brother Hunter.

President Tanner said that in the discussion it was pointed out that there is provision for the President of the Church to be removed from office on account of transgression or misconduct, but no other provision.

President Tanner stated that in the discussion Brother Romney had raised a question regarding the authorized agents when they were appointed, and that Brother Kirton had answered the question that President Brown and President Tanner were appointed authorized agents some years ago, and that appointment is registered with the [Utah] Secretary of State.

President Tanner said that because President Brown had not returned he felt it was not wise to take this up with the Council, but said he would like to have done it Wednesday at the General Authorities meeting. He stated, however, that when they attended the Wednesday meeting they were not ready to present the matter at that time because they thought that the additional information that had been received should be discussed with the Presidency and the Twelve and a full and complete understanding reached here.

President Tanner said that after President Brown returned they were talking with Brother Kirton about another matter, and that he, President Tanner, said he thought this should be dealt with, [and] that Brother Kirton then went over this and explained the position that he set forth in writing in the memorandum.

President Tanner said that in order to be more positive and assured regarding the feelings of the family he thought it might be desirable to call Dr. Edward McKay and talk to him about this. Accordingly President Brown called Dr. McKay by telephone and President Tanner and he talked to him over a conference phone, that President Brown was on one phone and he [Tanner] was on the other, and President Brown told Edward what Lawrence's position was, and he said that he had supported Lawrence in this, and he felt that the situation was as explained by him.

President Tanner said, "Edward, is this the thing you would like us to do?" And he said, "No, but I think it is the thing that has to be done."

President Tanner said that in order to do more than depend on the family, and put the family in that awkward position it was decided to phone Dr. Alan P. MacFarlane, President McKay's physician. This was done and Dr. MacFarlane said that he would give us a letter stating his position.

President Tanner then said he would like Brother Romney and Brother Hunter to say anything they wished to about the matter. President Tanner said that to sum it up the position is this, that the majority of the First Presidency has to carry on as far as the Presidency of the Church is concerned as the administration, and as far as the corporation of the President is concerned President Brown or himself, President Tanner, may act as authorized agents.

Elder Romney said that he understood it the same way, that as far as the Corporation of the President is concerned, President Brown and President Tanner can serve as agents. He had read the appointment that was issued by President McKay appointing these two brethren agents of the Corporation. He said that he was in harmony with Brother Kirton's and President Tanner's statement as well as Brother Hunter's, as he understood it, that that is legally sound.

Elder Hunter said that their discussion on this was from the standpoint of the Corporation, not the religious aspects of it. He said that the general rule of agency is if the principal becomes mentally competent, then the power of attorney for the agent to act terminates, but the rule seems to be different with respect to a corporation sole under the law of Utah. He said they read the statute on it, and all of them concluded from reading the statute and examining it that the authority given to the agent to act for the corporation of the President does not terminate upon incompetency; only upon revocation, and therefore he thought they were all in harmony as to legal consequences.

Elder Romney stated that an amendment went into the law in 1947 that the agency persists until it is terminated, and that was at the time when President [J. Reuben] Clark was first counselor to President [Heber J.] Grant and President [George Albert] Smith, during which time President Clark had to act.

Elder Lee mentioned the fact that the President is sustained as

Trustee-in-Trust. Elder Hunter stated that as Trustee-in-Trust there are many things that might be in his name as trustee for the Church and that constitutes a trust, but the Corporation of the President is a separate entity, and it is an entity within itself.

Elder Lee asked if as Trustee-in-Trust he holds legal title to the properties of the Church.

Elder Hunter said there may be some things that he would hold as trustee. Elder Lee then asked how much of that has been dissipated by this other entity which delegates to someone else.

Elder Hunter said that everything in the Corporation is not in the trust. The President is the Corporation and upon his death his successor has become the Corporation.

Elder Lee then referred to the instrument where President Brown and President Tanner are agents. Elder Romney said that President McKay issued it and appointed these brethren to represent him; that anything you put into that Corporation is in it, and what you have not put in is not in it.

Elder Lee said that apparently they were talking of three different matters, two of them are legal points; that we have the Trustee-in-Trust and the Corporation of the President, and this new holding corporation in which the President has delegated agents to act in his stead.

He said these are legal matters, but now there is another matter that pertains to the ecclesiastical relationship of counselors, and he thought the [health of the] President is a very important issue. He called attention to the 107th Section of the Doctrine and Covenants ...

Elder Lee said that when this question came up back in the days when Brother McKay apparently had some concern, he requested that David Yarn[26] research this very question, which he did, and prepared this article which appeared in the Improvement Era in January, 1964. ...

26. David H. Yarn Jr. (1920–2012) was dean of Religious Instruction at BYU. The reason he was tapped for the article, "The Function of Counselors," may have been because of his involvement with the J. Reuben Clark Papers project, of which he was general editor for the series published in five volumes by BYU Press. His conclusion was that the counselors are appendages to the president and lack any authority on their own. He began teaching at BYU in 1950 in the Department of Theology and Religious Philosophy with a master's degree from Columbia University. He would receive a PhD from Columbia in 1957. He was born in Atlanta and had studied as an undergraduate at Georgia Institute of Technology and BYU.

Elder Lee said the situation is not different from what it was in the last months of President Grant's life, or different from the experience of President George Albert Smith, that we had exactly the same condition with them that we have with President McKay. He said that when this situation developed President Clark held to this very fine delicate principle, that he would never sit in the place where the President had sat. ...

President Tanner then reported that at the latest meeting of the Presidency the conclusion was reached that the President is the only one who has the power to delegate the sealing power; therefore, during this time it was felt that nothing can be done about giving or taking away the sealing power.

Elder Lee further stated that in routine matters before the determination of a new policy, until the President acts, he thought that none of us, not the first counselor or the second or both counselors, or any of us can determine a new policy or new changes without the President of the Church until the Lord releases him. He said we have a very sacred responsibility to preserve the place of the President of the Church, that the Lord appointed him, and the Lord has to release him, as he understood. He said that we must have these things in mind, but as far as the legality of doing business under this corporate set-up, this is a separate matter from the ecclesiastical situation. ...

Concerning President McKay's signature on correspondence, Elder [Gordon B.] Hinckley asked if it was the intention to continue to place his signature on correspondence. President Tanner said definitely not, that from now on all correspondence will be signed by President Brown and President Tanner, or by one of them; that all legal documents will be signed by one of them as an agent. He thought that correspondence should not have his name placed upon it nor should his name be placed on documents when he does not know what is being done.

Elder Hinckley then raised the question about missionary calls. It was mentioned that all these calls go out with President McKay's signature on them. President Tanner said that in discussing this matter it was felt that nobody could be hurt by that being done; the same with the payroll, etc. It was the feeling that those should be permitted; that when it comes to the other question of signing for missionaries, he did not know that had been discussed.

817

Elder Hinckley said that all missionary calls carry only one signature and that is the signature of the President of the Church. It is supposed that the President authorized that when he had his full competence, and we have acted under that authorization and instruction, but more and more people are beginning to ask questions.

Elder Lee said that from what Elder Hinckley had said, he did not suppose that there was any question on that matter; that also the President had authorized President Smith to confer the sealing power upon these brethren mentioned, and the President is still alive. Elder Hunter said there is no legal consequence to this.

Referring to the keys of the Melchizedek Priesthood, Elder Lee mentioned the fact that when the Brethren of the Twelve were blessed and ordained and set apart as members of the Twelve by this ordination they were given the authority to hold every office in the Church, and that means up as well as down, that potentially these brethren all hold in suspension as apostles the authority to preside over the Church, if they are chosen by the Presidency and the Twelve and sustained by the vote of the membership.

President Tanner then asked the question, "Are we agreed on these two signatures?" Elder Lee said that that has already been authorized and there is no question. He thought it would be proper to use the President's name on the checks and on the missionary calls.

President Brown stated that in order to get action on a number of these things the Presidency are meeting regularly as the counselors in the First Presidency in the absence of the President; that President Smith is there as a member of the First Presidency, and that it was thought well to have someone representing the Twelve to be with the counselors in these meetings in order that the Twelve might be represented. It has been suggested that Elder Lee be asked to do this. Elder Romney moved that Elder Lee as the senior member of the Twelve who is not in the Presidency sit with the counselors in their meetings. Motion seconded by several of the brethren and unanimously approved.

President Tanner mentioned that two weeks ago it was decided that the minutes of the discussion of this subject at that time should not be made a part of the record, but he thought that a minute of this discussion should be made and fully recorded. He stated that from now on the correspondence coming to the President or the Presidency will come to Joseph Anderson's office instead of President McKay's office, and that minutes of the meeting will not go to the President's office either.

Elder [Mark E.] Petersen said he agreed with what President Tanner was saying but that secretaries have access to the minutes, and he wondered if anyone should have access to what has been done here today. The brethren agreed that the members of this Council should have copies but no one else; that, however, the secretary who types the minutes would necessarily have access to them.

November 17, 1969. The secretary Clare Middlemiss[27] having received no letters began to wonder what had happened. Then she received a telephone call from a woman who had sent a telegram to President McKay but had received no answer. Clare inquired over at the First Presidency's office only to learn that it had been placed on Joseph Anderson's desk. Later, she saw, when returning the telegram, a pile of President McKay's personal mail already opened on Anderson's desk; also one letter with the stamp of the First Presidency, purely personal, with a gift of a leather cutting of a portrait of President McKay[,] was put on my desk to answer.

I took it to President [Alvin R.] Dyer and told him I could not stand this kind of treatment anymore; that I would not answer letters to President McKay opened by Joseph Anderson; that if he opened them he would answer them. President Dyer answered, "How can we find out if they are personal or not?" I said, "The same way we have done for 35 years—I know when they are official or personal, and official letters have always been referred to the First Presidency, and you know with your whole soul that President McKay would want me to continue with his work as I have been doing all along." There was no sympathy or offer of help from him—the person whom I had gone all the way to help to get where he is thinking he would defend and do what he knew President McKay would want. Very distressing day. ...

I returned to my office and called Lawrence. I asked him if the family had met and requested that personal mail addressed to President McKay be turned over to Joseph Anderson—and did he know about the letter

27. Middlemiss is referring to herself in third person, after prefacing her entry with this: "Note by Clare Middlemiss, secretary."

from Dr. [Alan P.] MacFarlane declaring his father "mentally incompetent." I told him that the editorials by President [Heber J.] Grant and President [George Albert] Smith were taken from their writings, and that I cannot understand why such an issue is being made on editorials now. I further said it would break his father's heart if he should learn what was done in Council Meeting, and also about the letter President [Hugh B.] Brown asked Dr. MacFarlane to send regarding President McKay's "mental deficiency." When sometime ago President Brown made up the statement that President McKay was "not as alert," President McKay had it stricken from the record, saying, "I am as alert as I used to be!"

Lawrence said he knew nothing about this latest report to the Council and that he knew nothing about the letters. He also said that the family had not met regarding these matters and especially about Joseph Anderson taking over his father's letters.

I said, "If he does take over the letters, I might as well close the office, including all the Christmas business that is now coming soon["]; that Joseph Anderson would never nor could not take care of all the letters and business coming to President McKay's office.

November 19, 1969. This morning I [Clare Middlemiss] called at the apartment to ask the nurse if I could see the President, and she said, "Yes, he is very good this morning, very lucid, and has been asking the blessing on the food for the last few days." She said she will call after the President has had his breakfast and let me know when I can come.

At 9:15 a.m.—The nurse, Mrs. Noall, called and said the President wants to see you right away. When I reached the President's office in the apartment, he was sitting at his desk, well groomed as usual and looking very well. He gave me a bright smile as I entered the room, and I told him I had a few office matters to take up with him, and he said, "Good."

The following matters were taken up with him:

FIRST: I said to him: "President McKay, have you given orders that all your mail should be delivered to Joseph Anderson for his attention and answering?"

He looked at me with surprise and answered emphatically, "No! I do not want Joseph Anderson to have my mail—you are to have it, and my office is to be carried on as usual until I am gone."

I said, "Does this include the sending to your office of minutes of the meetings held by the First Presidency; also minutes of the Council Meeting held in the Temple each Thursday?"

He said, "<u>Yes,</u>" and repeated, "<u>everything is to go on as usual</u>."

He then asked me to get <u>President Joseph Fielding Smith</u> on the telephone. The President said to President Smith, "I want all my mail addressed to me to be given to my secretary, Clare Middlemiss, as has been done all these years. I do not want Joseph Anderson to have my mail. Also all minutes of the meetings of the First Presidency and Thursday Council Meetings are to come into my office as per usual. Will you please give these instructions to the Counselors."

President Smith answered, "Yes sir, I will do that today."

After this conversation, President McKay said to me: "Before you said anything to me, <u>I knew you were going to bring this problem to me.</u>"

He then said, "I am glad you are still with me to take care of my work for me. You know just how I want it done." ...

After these matters, thinking that President McKay had had enough for the morning, I excused myself and said I would leave and come back tomorrow with other business. He thanked me and said, "All right, hurry back!" ...

That afternoon when I came back from lunch, I found a pile of mail on my desk, many letters of which had been opened by Brother Anderson.

December 4, 1969.[28] President McKay during the last few months has been perfectly alert and lucid except for the times his toxic condition has brought on temporary spells of drowsiness.

December 8, 1969, 10:00 a.m. I [Clare Middlemiss] arrived at the Hotel [Utah] and held a brief meeting with President McKay. He was quite drowsy at first. When I started talking to him about office matters he became very alert.

I asked President McKay if he wanted his office to go on as usual, and he answered, "By all means." I then said, "President McKay as you know a week ago I told you that President [N. Eldon] Tanner had

---

28. This is an excerpt from an entry again prefaced with, "<u>Note by Clare Middlemiss, Secretary.</u>"

ordered all your mail to be given to Joseph Anderson for handling, and you immediately called President Joseph Fielding Smith and requested that he tell the counselors that all your mail is to go directly to your office as per usual."

I then said, "I am receiving your mail, but President McKay the Minutes of the First Presidency Meetings and the Temple Council Meeting are not being sent to you any longer. Also all First Presidency letters are leaving the building with only the signature of Presidents [Hugh B.] Brown and Tanner." President McKay exclaimed "What are they trying to do? I have not given them authority to do that."

For several months now when President McKay has looked worried, I have asked him what he is worried about, and without explaining everything he has said, "Something is wrong; all is not right."

I then showed President McKay a report by Elders Ezra Taft Benson and Bruce R. McConkie telling of the dedication of the land of Indonesia for the preaching of the gospel.

As I felt the President had had enough for this morning, I told him I felt I should return to the office and attend to his mail and Christmas matters. He smiled brightly and said, "You can do it better than anyone else." I answered, "I would be pretty dull if I couldn't attend to your work as you wanted it done." At this point he said, "You know just what I want done. You know you get younger every day." I said, "'You are looking wonderful President McKay," and the nurse added, "And alert too."

I said goodby and told him I would see him soon, and he kept smiling warmly at me as I left.

December 26, 1969, 9:30 a.m. I met with President Alvin R. Dyer, Elder Mark E. Petersen, and Henry Smith regarding the Negro question. President [Hugh B.] Brown made a statement to the press yesterday which has caused quite a bit of controversy.[29]

---

29. This statement by Hugh B. Brown was made on December 15 to a *San Francisco Chronicle* reporter and appeared in local papers ten days later. The part that troubled the brethren was Brown's "opinion" that the priesthood ban "will change in the not too distant future ... in the ordinary evolution of things as we go along, since human rights are basic to the church." This view was not shared by many in the church hierarchy. See Prince and Wight, *David O. McKay*, 100–02.

January 5, 1970.[30] Following the short meeting with President McKay this morning, the First Presidency continued their meeting in the First Presidency's Board room of the Church Administration Building. During the meeting President [Joseph Fielding] Smith slumped over in his chair. He had an attack later identified by the doctor as an artery stoppage to the brain. President [N. Eldon] Tanner and President [Alvin R.] Dyer stood up, each taking a hold of a hand of President Smith and endeavoring to feel his pulse. There was no pulse. President Dyer then attempted to feel the artery in his neck and massaged his neck slightly and he immediately started moving. ...

January 16, 1970. <u>Last Visit of Clare [Middlemiss] to See President McKay at Apartment</u>—President McKay was sitting up in his chair dressed immaculately as usual. As I came down the hall I could hear him coughing heavily in order to remove accumulated water that had gathered in his lungs. My heart sank as I heard him and went on into his office and saw how gray his face was. When I said good morning to him, he stretched out his hand to me and clutched my hand without opening his eyes. I said, "President McKay, I just came to see how you are; I have no work to bring up." He responded by saying, "You come over here anytime. I want you to be here." I turned to the nurse and said, "Did you hear that?" To think that even in his suffering he would want me to come over with his work was very touching to me!

Then the nurse wheeled him to his bedroom, and I had a strange feeling that it was the last time that I would officially be in his office. I stood alone in his office, extremely downcast, and looked at his books that he had loved and read so much throughout his life of study.

When I returned to the office in the Administration Building, I said to my secretary: "Well, President McKay is not good; and I think he was saying farewell to me."

I called the nurse later on in the day to find out how he was. She reported the doctor had been there to see the President, and he said there was nothing to be done to relieve the condition regarding the water which was accumulating in his lungs.

---

30. Once again the line, "<u>Note by Clare Middlemiss</u>," precedes the entry.

January 17, 1970, report by Lawrence McKay. President McKay's breathing became so light around 10:30 p.m. that the nurse became worried and called Dr. Alan MacFarlane. After his examination of President McKay, Dr. MacFarlane called Dr. Edward McKay and members of the family. Dr. Edward McKay reported that "he never saw anyone fight from that time on so hard as his father did not to go into a coma." He was lying on his side struggling for his breath. Then finally his physical body took over, he turned onto his back, and he lapsed into a coma, after which there was no struggle and his breathing became slower and slower until 6 a.m. [January 18] at which time he finally stopped breathing. His countenance became relaxed and peaceful. Lawrence McKay said, "He died in peace and dignity."[31] ...

Sister [Emma Ray] McKay, who had become quite hysterical when she learned of her husband's condition, had been sedated by the doctor. She did not awaken until after his death.

January 18, 1970. Thoughts by Clare Middlemiss, Secretary[:] From the moment I received a call from Dr. Edward McKay at 6:10 a.m. regarding the passing of President McKay, I was so shocked and grieved that my voice left me. I could not believe it had happened and was in tears all day. My thoughts kept wandering over the 35 years I have been secretary to this great and noble man. It has been a rare privilege and an honor to work for him.

---

31. There is an asterisk here to indicate a footnote added to the diary that reads: "Dr. Alan P. MacFarlane said President McKay died of acute congestion of the heart. Although in failing health for several months, the Church leader had become somewhat worse the past few days from heart and kidney failure complications."

Frequently Cited Sources

Alexander, Thomas G., and James B. Allen. *Mormons and Gentiles: A History of Salt Lake City*. Boulder, CO: Pruett Publishing, 1984.

Allen, James B. "Would-be Saints: West Africa before the 1978 Priesthood Revelation." *Journal of Mormon History* 17 (1991): 207–47.

Allen, James B., Ronald W. Walker, David J. Whittaker. *Studies in Mormon History, 1830–1997: An Indexed Bibliography*. Urbana: University of Illinois Press, 2000.

Arrington, Leonard J. *Adventures of a Church Historian*. Urbana: University of Illinois Press, 1998.

———. "Banking and Finance in Utah." In Powell, *Utah History Encyclopedia*.

———. *Beet Sugar in the West: A History of Utah–Idaho Sugar Company, 1891–1966*. Seattle: University of Washington Press, 1966.

———. *Confessions of a Mormon Historian: The Diaries of Leonard J. Arrington, 1971–1997*. Edited by Gary James Bergera. Salt Lake City: Signature Books, 2018.

———. *Great Basin Kingdom: Economic History of the Latter-day Saints, 1830–1900*. Cambridge, MA: Harvard University Press, 1958.

Barlow, Philip L. *Mormons and the Bible: The Place of the Latter-day Saints in American Religion*. New York: Oxford University Press, 1991.

Barton, Peggy Petersen. *Mark E. Petersen: A Biography*. Salt Lake City: Deseret Book, 1985.

Bates, Irene, and E. Gary Smith. *Lost Legacy: The Mormon Office of Presiding Patriarch*. Urbana: University of Illinois Press, 1996.

Baugh, Alexander L. "The Church in Twentieth-century Great Britain: A Historical Overview. In Doxey, et al., *Regional Studies in Latter-day Saint Church History*, 237–59.

Benson, Ezra Taft. *Cross Fire: The Eight Years with Eisenhower*. Garden City, NY: Doubleday, 1962.

———. "Our Immediate Responsibility." *Speeches of the Year*. Provo: BYU Extension Publications, 1966.

Bergera, Gary James, ed. "Educating Zion: The Diaries of Ernest L. Wilkinson, 1951–1977," manuscript of forthcoming publication by Signature Books.

———, comp. *Statements of the LDS First Presidency: A Topical Compendium*. Salt Lake City: Signature Books, 2007.

———. "'A Sad and Expensive Experience': Ernest L. Wilkinson's 1964 Bid for the U.S. Senate." *Utah Historical Quarterly* 61, no. 4 (Fall 1993): 304–24.

———. "'A Strange Phenomena': Ernest L. Wilkinson, the LDS Church, and Utah Politics." *Dialogue: A Journal of Mormon Thought* 26, no. 2 (Summer 1993): 89–115.

———. "Tensions in David O. McKay's First Presidencies." *Journal of Mormon History* 33 (Spring 2007):179–246.

———. "Transgression in the Latter-day Saint Community: The Cases of Albert Carrington, Richard R. Lyman, and Joseph F. Smith," part 2, *Journal of Mormon History* 37, no. 4 (Fall 2011), 173–207.

Bergera, Gary James, and Ronald Priddis. *Brigham Young University: A House of Faith*. Salt Lake City: Signature Books, 1985.

Bigler, Louis Burtran, Jr. "Personal History." *Family Search*, www.familysearch.org.

Bishop, M. Guy. *A History of Sevier County*. Salt Lake City: Utah State Historical Society, 1997.

Bowen, Albert E. *Constancy amid Change*. Salt Lake City: By the author, 1944.

Bradford, Mary Lythgoe. *Lowell L. Bennion: Teacher, Counselor, Humanitarian*. Salt Lake City: Dialogue Foundation, 1995.

Bringhurst, Newell G. "Elijah Abel and the Changing Status of Blacks within Mormonism." *Dialogue: A Journal of Mormon Thought* 12, no. 2 (Summer 1979): 22–36.

Brooks, Juanita. *The Mountain Meadows Massacre*. Stanford, CA: Stanford University Press, 1950.

Buerger, David John. *The Mysteries of Godliness: A History of Mormon Temple Worship*. San Francisco: Smith Research Associates, 1994.

Campbell, Eugene E., and Richard D. Poll. *Hugh B. Brown: His Life and Thought*. Salt Lake City: Bookcraft, 1975.

Cannon, Hugh Jenne. *David O. McKay around the World: An Apostolic Mission, Prelude to Church Globalization*. Provo: Spring Creek Book, 2005.

Clark, J. Reuben Jr. Diary. L. Tom Perry Special Collections, Harold B. Lee Library, Brigham Young University, Provo.

Cowan, Richard O. "A Tale of Two Temples." In Doxey, et al., *Regional Studies in Latter-day Saint Church History*, 219–36.

Cowan, Richard O., and Robert G. Larson. *The Oakland Temple: Portal to Eternity*. Provo: BYU Religious Studies Center, 2014.

Dew, Sheri L. *Go Forward with Faith: The Biography of Gordon B. Hinckley*. Salt Lake City: Deseret Book, 1996.

Doxey, Cynthia, Robert C. Freeman, Richard Neitzel Holzapfel, Dennis A. Wright. *Regional Studies in Latter-day Saint Church History: The British Isles*. Provo: BYU Religious Studies Center, 2007.

Durham, G. Homer, ed. *The Gospel Kingdom: Selections from the Writings and Discourses of John Taylor*. Salt Lake City: Bookcraft, 1943.

Eccles, Marriner S. *Beckoning Frontiers: Public and Personal Recollections*. Edited by Sidney Hyman. New York: Alfred A. Knopf, 1951.

Esplin, Scott C. "A Place for 'the Weary Traveler': Nauvoo and a Changing Missionary Emphasis for Church Historic Sites." In *Go Ye into All the World: The Growth and Development of Mormon Missionary Work*. Edited by Reid L. Neilson and Fred E. Woods. Provo: BYU Religious Studies Center, 2012, 397–424.

Firmage, Edwin B., ed. *An Abundant Life: The Memoirs of Hugh B. Brown*. Salt Lake City: Signature Books, 1988.

Garraty, John A. *Quarrels That Have Shaped Our Constitution*. New York: Harper & Row, 1964.

Gibbons, Francis M. *David O. McKay: Apostle to the World, Prophet of God*. Salt Lake City: Deseret Book, 1986.

———. *Spencer W. Kimball: Resolute Disciple, Prophet of God*. Salt Lake City: Deseret Book, 1995.

Goates, L. Brent. *Harold B. Lee: Prophet and Seer*. Salt Lake City: Bookcraft, 1985.

Godfrey, Matthew C. *Religion, Politics, and Sugar: The Mormon Church, the Federal Government, and the Utah–Idaho Sugar Company, 1907–1921*. Logan: Utah State University Press, 2007.

Grover, Mark L. "The Mormon Priesthood Revelation and the São Paulo, Brazil, Temple." *Dialogue: A Journal of Mormon Thought* 23, no. 1 (Spring 1990): 39–53.

―――. "Religious Accommodation in the Land of Racial Democracy: Mormon Priesthood and Black Brazilians." *Dialogue: A Journal of Mormon Thought* 17, no. 3 (Autumn 1984): 23–35.

Halberstam, David. *The Fifties.* New York: Villard Books, 1993.

Haller, William. *The Rise of Puritanism.* New York: Columbia University Press, 1957.

Heath, Harvard S., ed. *In The World: The Diaries of Reed Smoot.* Salt Lake City: Signature Books and Smith Research Associates, 1997.

Hemming, Val G. "Ricks College: The Struggle for Permanency and Place, 1954–1960." *Journal of Mormon History* 26, no. 2 (Fall 2000): 51–109.

Hickman, Martin B. *David Matthew Kennedy: Banker, Statesman, Churchman.* Salt Lake City: Deseret Book and David M. Kennedy Center for International Studies, 1987.

Hicks, Michael. *Mormonism and Music: A History.* Urbana: University of Illinois Press, 1989.

―――. *The Mormon Tabernacle Choir: A Biography.* Urbana: University of Illinois Press, 2015.

Hilton, Hope A. *Descent into Madness, or the Formation of a Religious Cult: The Story of Annalee Kohlhepp Gorman Avarell Skarin.* Salt Lake City: By the author, 1993.

Hilton, Lynn M. *The History of LDS Business College and Its Parent Institutions, 1886–1993.* Salt Lake City: LDS Business College, 1995.

Hodson, Paul W. *Crisis on Campus: The Years of Campus Development at the University of Utah.* Salt Lake City: Keeban Corporation, 186–222.

Horne, Dennis B. *Bruce R. McConkie: Highlights from His Life and Teachings.* Roy, UT: Eborn Books, 2000.

Jacob, W. James, and Meli U. Lesuma. "History of the Church of Jesus Christ of Latter-day Saints in Fiji." In Underwood, *Pioneers in the Pacific*, 241–263.

Johnson, Melvin C. *Polygamy on the Pedernales: Lyman Wight's Mormon Villages in Antebellum Texas, 1845–1858.* Logan: Utah State University Press, 2006.

Jonas, Frank. *The Story of a Political Hoax.* Salt Lake City: University of Utah Press, 1966.

Kahn, David. *The Reader of Gentlemen's Mail: Herbert O. Yardley and the Birth of American Codebreaking.* New Haven: Yale University Press, 2004.

Kelley, Allison. *No Place for Zion: Deseret Ranch and the Mainstreaming of Mormonism, 1950–1985*. PhD diss. Charlottesville: University of Virginia, 2017.

Kimball, Edward L. *Lengthen Your Stride: The Presidency of Spencer W. Kimball*. Salt Lake City: Deseret Book, 2005.

Kimball, Edward L., and Andrew E. Kimball Jr. *Spencer W. Kimball: Twelfth President of the Church of Jesus Christ of Latter-day Saints*. Salt Lake City: Bookcraft, 1977.

Kimball, Spencer W. Diary, typed excerpts in Quinn Papers, photocopy courtesy of the Smith–Pettit Foundation.

Kuehne, Raymond M. "The Freiberg Temple: An Unexpected Legacy of a Communist State and a Faithful People." *Dialogue: A Journal of Mormon Thought* 37, no. 2 (Summer 2004): 95–131.

Knowles, Eleanor. *Howard W. Hunter*. Salt Lake City: Deseret Book, 1994.

Larson, Stan, ed. *A Ministry of Meetings: The Apostolic Diaries of Rudger Clawson*. Salt Lake City: Signature Books and Smith Research Associates, 1993.

———. *Quest for the Gold Plates: Thomas Stuart Ferguson's Search for the Book of Mormon*. Salt Lake City: Freethinker Press and Smith Research Associates, 1996.

Ludlow, Daniel H. *Encyclopedia of Mormonism*. 5 vols. New York: Macmillan, 1992.

Lythgoe, Dennis L. *Let 'em Holler: A Political Biography of J. Bracken Lee*. Salt Lake City: Utah State Historical Society, 1982.

———. "A Special Relationship: J. Bracken Lee and the Mormon Church." *Dialogue: A Journal of Mormon Thought* 11, no. 4 (Winter 1978), 71–87.

McConkie, Joseph Fielding. *The Bruce R. McConkie Story: Reflections of a Son*. Salt Lake City: Deseret Book, 2003.

McKay, Llewelyn R. *Home Memories of President David O. McKay*. Salt Lake City: Deseret Book, 1965.

McLintock, Alexander H., ed. *Encyclopedia of New Zealand*. 3 volumes. Wellington: Government of New Zealand, 1966.

McMurrin, Sterling M., and L. Jackson Newell. *Matters of Conscience: Conversations with Sterling M. McMurrin on Philosophy, Education, and Religion*. Salt Lake City: Signature Books, 1996.

Mehr, Kahlile. "Area Supervision: Administration of the Worldwide Church, 1960–200," *Journal of Mormon History* 27, no. 1 (Spring 2001): 192–214.

———. "The Trial of the French Mission." *Dialogue: A Journal of Mormon Thought* 21 (Fall 1988): 27–45.

Merrill, Timothy G., and Brian Q. Cannon. "Ox in the Mire? The Legal and Cultural War over Utah's Sunday Closing Laws." *Journal of Mormon History* 38, no. 4 (Fall 2012): 164–94.

Morgan, Barbara E. "Benemérito de las Américas: The Beginning of a Unique Church School in Mexico." *BYU Studies* 52, no. 4 (2013): 89–116.

Moyle, Henry D. Diary, typed excerpts in Quinn Papers, photocopy courtesy of the Smith–Pettit Foundation.

Mulder, William. "Mormons in American History." *Utah Historical Quarterly* 27 (1959): 60–77.

Nelson, Richard Alan. "From Antagonism to Acceptance: Mormons and the Silver Screen." *Dialogue: A Journal of Mormon Thought* 10 (Spring 1977): 58–69.

Nibley, Hugh W. *Nibley on the Timely and the Timeless: Classic Essays of Hugh W. Nibley.* 2d. ed. Provo: BYU Religious Studies Center, 2004.

O'Brien, Robert. *Marriott: The J. Willard Marriott Story.* Salt Lake City: Deseret Book, 1978.

Parrish, Alan K. *John A. Widtsoe: A Biography.* Salt Lake City: Deseret Book, 2003.

Parsons, Robert. "Encyclopedic History of Utah State University," online at digitalcommons.usu.edu

Paulos, Michael Harold, ed. *The Mormon Church on Trial: Transcripts of the Reed Smoot Hearings.* Salt Lake City: Signature Books, 2008.

Petersen, Boyd Jay. *Hugh Nibley: A Consecrated Life.* Salt Lake City: Greg Kofford Books, 2002.

Peterson, Anne Palmer. *Years of Promise: The University of Utah's A. Ray Olpin Era, 1946–1964.* Salt Lake City: University of Utah Press, 2010.

Peterson, F. Ross. "'Blindside': Utah on the Eve of *Brown v. Board of Education.*" *Utah Historical Quarterly* 73, no. 1 (Winter 2005): 4–20.

Peterson, Levi S. *Juanita Brooks: Mormon Woman Historian.* Salt Lake City: University of Utah Press and the Tanner Trust Fund, 1996.

Perrin, Kathleen C. "Seasons of Faith: An Overview of the History of the Church in French Polynesia." In Underwood, *Pioneers in the Pacific*, 201–18.

Poll, Richard D. *Working the Divine Miracle: The Life of Apostle Henry D. Moyle*. Edited by Stan Larson. Salt Lake City: Signature Books and University of Utah, 1999.

Powell, Allan Kent, ed. *Utah History Encyclopedia*. Salt Lake City: University of Utah Press, 1994, 27–31.

Prince, Gregory A., and William Robert Wright. *David O. McKay and the Rise of Modern Mormonism*. Salt Lake City: University of Utah Press, 2005.

Prince, Gregory, and Gary Topping. "A Turbulent Coexistence: Duane Hunt, David O. McKay, and a Quarter-Century of Catholic-Mormon Relations." *Journal of Mormon History* 32, no. 1 (Spring 2005): 142–63.

Pusey, Merlo J. *Builders of the Kingdom: George A. Smith, John Henry Smith, and George Albert Smith*. Provo: BYU Press, 1981.

Quinn, D. Michael. *Elder Statesman: A Biography of J. Reuben Clark*. Salt Lake City: Signature Books, 2002.

———. "Ezra Taft Benson and Mormon Political Conflicts." *Dialogue: A Journal of Mormon Thought* 26, no. 2 (Summer 1992):1–87.

———. "Plural Marriage and Mormon Fundamentalism." In *Fundamentalisms and Society: Reclaiming the Sciences, the Family, and Education*, 240–93. Edited by Martin E. Marty and R. Scott Appleby. Chicago: University of Chicago Press, 1993.

———. *The Mormon Hierarchy: Extensions of Power*. Salt Lake City: Signature Books and Smith Research Associates, 1997.

———. *The Mormon Hierarchy: Wealth and Corporate Power*. Salt Lake City: Signature Books, 2017.

———. Papers, Beinecke Rare Book and Manuscript Library, Yale University, New Haven, Connecticut.

Reeve, W. Paul. *Religion of a Different Color: Race and the Mormon Struggle for Whiteness*. New York: Oxford University Press, 2015.

Roberts, Paul T. *A History of the Development and Objectives of the LDS Church News Section of the Deseret News*. MA thesis. Provo: Brigham Young University, 1983.

Schapsmeier, Frederick H., and Edward L. Schapsmeier. *Ezra Taft Benson and the Politics of Agriculture: The Eisenhower Years*. Danville, IL: By the authors, 1975.

Sells, Jeffery E., ed. *God and Country: Politics in Utah*. Salt Lake City: Signature Books, 2005.

Sillitoe, Linda. *A History of Salt Lake County*. Salt Lake City: Salt Lake County Commission, 1996.

Smith, George A. Diary. Photocopy in George A. Smith Family Papers, Special Collections, J. Willard Marriott Library, University of Utah.

Soffer, Jonathan. "The National Association of Manufacturers and the Militarization of American Conservatism." *Business History Review* 75, no. 4 (Winter 2001), 775–805.

Stewart, David G. Jr., and Matthew Martinich. *Reaching the Nations: International Church Growth Almanac*. Henderson, NV: Cumorah Foundation, 2013.

Tate, Lucile C. *Boyd K. Packer: A Watchman on the Tower*. Salt Lake City: Bookcraft, 1995.

Underwood, Grant, ed. *Pioneers in the Pacific*. Provo: BYU Religious Studies Center, 2005.

Van Orden, Bruce A. *Building Zion: The Latter-day Saints in Europe*. Salt Lake City: Deseret Book, 1996.

Watkins, Arthur Vivian. *Enough Rope*. Englewood Cliffs, NJ: Prentice Hall, 1969.

Widtsoe, John A. *In a Sunlit Land: The Autobiography of John A. Widtsoe*. Salt Lake City: Deseret News Press, 1952.

Wilkinson, Ernest L., ed. *Brigham Young University: The First Hundred Years*. 4 vols. Provo: BYU Press, 1975.

———. Diary. L. Tom Perry Special Collections, Harold B. Lee Library, Brigham Young University.

Winder, Michael K., comp. *Counselors to the Prophets*. Roy, UT: Eborn Books, 2001.

Young, Margaret Blair. "Abner Leonard Howell." *African American History in the American West: Online Encyclopedia*, blackpast.org.

Photographs

As a young missionary to Scotland in 1897–99, David O. McKay was already keeping a daily diary, foreshadowing his later record of activities as church president. This image, and others in this section, are from the Utah State Historical Society's Classified, Clifford Bray, Salt Lake Tribune, and Savage Company Photograph Collections.

McKay's parents lived in this house in Ogden beginning in 1904, and David and Emma Ray lived there for a few years while he was principal of Weber Academy, now Weber State University. Even after being ordained an apostle in 1906, McKay continued to live in Ogden and commute to Salt Lake City until 1908.

The light of McKay's life, Emma Ray Riggs had studied at the University of Utah and the Cincinnati Conservatory of Music. They became engaged when she was teaching at James Madison Elementary School in Ogden, four blocks from the old Weber Academy where David was the principal.

McKay cut a dashing figure in December 1897 at twenty-four years of age, at the start of his mission to Great Britain. He had graduated that year from the University of Utah.

McKay was taking on the look of a church administrator in the 1930s when he was called to be a counselor in the First Presidency. However, there is evidence that he was preoccupied with more than the stacks of correspondence and reports one sees on his desk. Notice the three magnifying glasses that were probably used for studying historical documents.

In April 1931, McKay had already been in the Quorum of the Twelve for a quarter century. The members of the quorum at that time, standing here in front of the east door of the Salt Lake Temple, were (back row, l–r) Stephen L. Richards, Richard R. Lyman, Melvin J. Ballard, John A. Widtsoe, (middle row) Orson F. Whitney, David O. McKay, Joseph Fielding Smith, James E. Talmage, (front row) Rudger Clawson, Reed Smoot, George Albert Smith, and George F. Richards.

The McKays in formal dress in October 1935, in front of the Seagull Monument and the old Bureau of Information and Museum on Temple Square. Notice how loosely and gracefully Emma Ray's coat and skirt hang, which was typical for the 1920s–30s, along with the jabot-inspired collar, folded-crown hat, and barrel-bag purse. David O. is wearing striped slacks and a bowler hat.

McKay liked to talk about his horse, Dandy. "How like Dandy are many of you young people!" he would say. "You are not bad; you do not even intend to do wrong; but you are impulsive ... restless under restraint" (October 1968 general conference address). The horse was looked after by David's younger brother, Thomas, at the family home in Huntsville.

Heber J. Grant (center) called J. Reuben Clark (left) and David O. McKay (right) as counselors in the First Presidency in 1934.

Clarabel ("Clare")Middlemiss was McKay's devoted secretary from 1935 to 1970. She attended business school in Salt Lake City, served a church mission to Colorado, and began working as a secretary in the Church Administration Building in 1930.

Top left: J. Bracken Lee, Utah governor, 1949–57. Top right: Gustave P. Backman, director of the Salt Lake City Chamber of Commerce, 1930–65. Bottom left: Henry D. Moyle, counselor in the LDS First Presidency, 1959–63. Bottom right: Ernest L. Wilkinson, president of BYU, 1951–71, shown here with one of the pet cougars kept on campus from 1924 to about 1964.

US Secretary of Agriculture and LDS apostle Ezra Taft Benson boarding a Forest Service airplane in Missoula, Montana. Benson would become church president in 1985.

The five-story Church Administration Building was constructed in 1917 to house the First Presidency, Quorum of the Twelve, presidents of seventy, and archives and records. President McKay's office was on the northwest corner of the first floor.

US President John F. Kennedy enjoyed breakfast with the McKays in their apartment in the Hotel Utah in September 1960. They were joined by US Senator Stewart L. Udall, US Senator Frank E. Moss and wife Phyllis, McKay's counselor Hugh B. Brown and wife Zina, and the McKays' daughter Emma Rae.

McKay with his beloved but troublesome first counselor Henry D. Moyle (center) and second counselor Hugh B. Brown in about 1961. Moyle would be relieved of all duties in 1963 and die later that year.

David O. McKay with his wife, Emma Ray, and driver in the 1960s. McKay loved to drive but came to be chauffeured by Allan Acomb, who had been a colonel during World War II and probably doubled as a body guard.

The McKays at the temple dedication in Hamilton, New Zealand, in 1958. When traveling in warm climates, the president liked to wear light-colored suits, while Emma Ray stuck with her more standard wardrobe.

Index

Aaronic Priesthood, x, 44, 78, 166–67, 322, 542–46, 691; dress and grooming, 809–10; suggested for Nigerians, 407, 447–53, 459, 597
Able, Elijah, 534–35
abortion, 731, 743–45
accounting, *see* LDS finances
Acomb, Allan, 175–77, 317–18
Adams, Orval, 60, 202–03
adoption, 185–86, 691
adultery, 523–24
al-Alami, Musa, 374–76
alcohol, *see* liquor laws; Word of Wisdom
All American Society, 413
Alldredge, O. Layton, 371–72, 377–81, 384–85
American Independent Party, 737–43, 767–68, 774–75, 776–77
American Opinion magazine, 638–39, 642–45
Ancient America and the Book of Mormon, 305–06, 801–03, 708–09, 715–16
Anderson, Howard, 801–03
Anderson, Joseph, 708–09, 715–16, 718–19, 722–24, 729–31, 731–32, 755–60, 775; on death of DOM, 811, 814–19, 819–20
Anderson, Mark, 635–36, 658–59
animals, 457–58, 844f. *See also* cattle; Deseret Farms; Orlando Livestock Company; horses
apartheid, 380–81, 623, 788–89
apostasy, 237, 302–04; missionaries, 127–28, 232–44. *See also* France, mission apostasy
Arab Development Society, 374–76

Archives Building, 152, 343, 346, 400
Arrington, Leonard J., xi, xiii–xiv, 662, 685–86, 748–49, 806–07
art, 65–66, 95, 231, 492; in church buildings, 287, 715. *See also* Friberg, Arnold
Ashton, Emma Rae McKay (daughter), 395–96, 495, 496–97, 553–54, 577–78
Ashton, Wendell, 763–64
Asper, Frank, 572, 573–74, 579–80
Assembly Hall, 635–36, 642–46
Associated Press, 505, 642–43, 719–22
Atiya, Aziz S., 142–43, 687–88, 709–10, 715, 719–22, 726–27
Atkinson, Charles, 159

Backman, Gustave P., x, 32–33, 57, 162, 213–15, 353, 486, 760–61, 762–64, 844f
Badger, Howard C., 788–89
Ballard, Melvin J., 839f
Ballif, Ariel S., 121
Bangerter, William G., 340–341
baptism, 177–78, 502–03; parental consent, 456–57, 499, 518–19, 777–78; racial consideration, 788–89
Barker, James L., 762–63
Beehive House, 92–93
Belgium, mission, 478
belief, *see* theology, faith
Ben–Gurion, David, 199–200
Bennett, Wallace F., 499–500, 609–10; Stringfellow incident, 108–09, 109–10

Bennion, Adam S., 47, 139, 191–94, 209–10; on colleges, 60–61, 70–71, 73, 100

Bennion, Lowell L., 104; Institute of Religion, 260–61, 425–26; on priesthood ban, 180, 692

Bennion, Mervyn, 392

Benson, Ezra Taft, viii, 37, 106–07, 145–48, 244, 270–71, 357–59; bicentennial committee, 617–18, 650–51, 652, 655–56, 670–71, 674, 681–82; conflicts, 340, 637, 640–41, 770–72, 778, 793, 796–99; European mission, 508–09, 519, 520–23, 539, 590–91, 591–92; international trips, 194–95, 199–201, 226–27, 249; John Birch Society, x, 463, 470–72, 490, 496, 505–06, 635–36, 642–45, 645–48, 658–59, 689, 690; on civil rights, 622–27, 707; on communism, x, 362–63, 411–13, 418–20, 423, 464–65, 467–68, 588–89, 590, 628–29, 672, 673–74; presidential aspirations, 245, 313, 321–22, 688, 737–43, 774–75; Secretary of Agriculture, 44, 188–89, 211, 376

Benson, Mark A., 767–68

Benson, Reed, American Independent Party, 737–43, 798–99; John Birch Society, 463, 471–72, 496, 505–06, 644

Bible, translations, 42, 93, 121. See also Joseph Smith Bible

Biesinger, George R., 478–79

birth control, see contraception

blessings, 9; for success and well-being, 12, 44, 317, 524–26, 540–42; patriarchal, 46, 65, 206, 228–29, 767

Blodgett, J. Alan, 792

Blood, Lou Jean McKay (daughter), 503–04, 536–37, 539–40, 664, 655–67

Book of Abraham, papyrus, 659, 687–88, 709–10, 715, 718–19,

722–24, 729–31, 731–32, 735–36; racial issues, 87–90, 745–46, 808. See also Atiya, Aziz S.; Hinckley, Gordon B.; LDS historical items; Tanner, N. Eldon

Book of Mormon, 291–92, 781–82, 784–85; archaeology, 67–68, 123, 131–32, 306–07. See also New World Archaeological Foundation

Bookcraft, 93, 261, 262–63, 303, 310–11

Bowen, Albert E., 5, 67; death, 67

Boy Scouts of America, 423

Boyd, George, 104

Brazil, 90–91, 340–41; mission, 90–91, 340–41, 411. See also South and Central America

Brigham Young University, ix, 110, 203–04, 227–28, 253, 319, 321, 551–53, 715, 776–77, 809–10; athletics, 94, 159, 354–55; honor code, 809–10; leadership, 74–77, 288, 506, 507–08, 514–15, 517, 556–57, 559, 560, 570–71, 794, 800; staffing, 40, 61–63, 75–76, 112–13, 129, 211–12, 275, 390, 481, 615–16; students, 33, 582–84, 603, 624–25, 688–89, 743–45. See also Church College of Hawaii (BYU–Hawaii); Ricks College (BYU–Idaho).

Brigham Young University Studies, 735–36

British Mission, 278–79, 438–39, 441–46, 458–59, 499, 777–78; Ravenslea chapel, 239, 240–41n; change to British Isles Mission, 590–91, 591–92

Brooks, Juanita, 424–25

Brown, Brent W., 793

Brown, Hugh B., 79–80, 260–61, 370–71, 372–73, 391, 397, 520, 638, 719–22, 809–10; and church committees, 437–38, 594–95, 601–02, 668–69, 692–98; and DOM, 290,

524–26, 532–33, 540–42, 715–16, 812–19, 819–20, 846f; and Ernest L. Wilkinson, 514–15, 556–57, 800; and Ezra Taft Benson, 588–89, 590, 658–59, 673–74, 793, 794, 796–99; and stake conferences, 431–33, 612–13; First Presidency, 627–28, 629, 708, 710–12, 712–15, 758–60, 808–09; general conference, 527, 546–47; JFK, 496–97, 507; on church buildings, 504–05, 699–702, 704–06, 753–55; on church businesses, 435–37, 567–68, 579, 801–03; on communism, 411–13, 419–20, 749–51; on John Birch Society, 470–72, 505–06, 722–24; on missionary program, 185–86, 232–44, 439–41, 441–46, 468–70, 777–78, 800–01; on Nigeria, 404–10, 426, 447–53; on politics, 213–15, 225, 340, 602–03, 606–08, 609–10, 767–68, 770–72; on priesthood ban, 483–84, 498–99, 502, 596; on Ricks College, 247–49, 329–35; on temple ordinances, 291, 575, 576; on tithing, 507, 513

Brown, Victor L., 418, 455–56, 457–58, 481

Browning, Frank M., 83–86, 102–03

Budget Committee (LDS), 350–51, 507, 558–59, 772–74

budgets, *see* LDS finances

Buehner, Carl W., 26–27, 395

Building Department (LDS), 336–37, 398, 547–48, 558–59, 604–06, 614–15, 642–43, 649, 699–702, 702–04, 753–55; committee members, 569, 580–81, 584–85, 592–96, 601–02, 668–69, 671. *See also* Garff, Mark B.; Mendenhall, Wendell B.; Moyle, Henry D.

building missionaries, *see* labor missions

Burns, Robert, *see* poetry

Burton, Alma P., 791–92

Burton, Harold W., 144–45, 336–37

Burton, Theodore M., 341, 455, 491, 494–95

Cagle, William, 105–06, 107

Cameron, Elliot J., 638, 639–40

Cannon Sr, Theodore L., 424, 437, 483–84, 492

Catholic Church, 8–9, 172–73, 194–95, 196–97, 339, 565–66; criticism of, 20, 96–97, 302–04. *See also* interfaith relations

cattle, 374–76, 388n, 474, 485, 561–63, 567–68. *See also* Deseret Farms; Orlando Livestock Company

censorship, 3–4, 15, 34–35, 65–66, 137–38, 203, 310–11, 365–66, 794, 806–07; church materials, 262–63, 265, 301–03, 307–09, 424, 639; of *Temple Mormonism*, 105–06, 107–08, 109. *See also* Obscene Literature Committee

Chambers, Whittaker, 464–65, 467–68

chapels, *see* meetinghouses (LDS)

charity/aid, 57–58, 98, 141–42, 347, 362

children, views on, 163, 172–73, 212, 343–44, 794; young English converts, 478–79, 489–90, 494–95. *See also* adoption

Chile, 453–54

Christiansen, ElRay L., 105–06, 240–44, 576

Church Administration Building, (completed 1917), 186, 336–37, 704–05, 843f

church businesses, 253, 257, 258–60, 262; advertising, 56–57, 310. *See* Deseret Farms; LDS banks; Orlando Livestock Company

Church College of Hawaii (BYU–Hawaii), 94–95, 122, 258, 570–71

Church Education System, 99, 101, 104; board of education, ix, 47, 274, 319, 470, 547–48, 570–71, 629, 804–05. *See also* Institutes of Religion; junior colleges; Unified Church School System

Church Handbook of Instruction, 520n, 698–99, 715

Church Office Building, (completed 1972), 336–37, 343, 346, 359–60, 362, 373–74, 400–01, 531–32, 551–53, 599, 657–58, 772–74

civil rights, 223–24, 588–89, 590, 707, 768–69, 793; Civil Rights Act, 484–85, 486–89, 535; NAACP, 498–99, 575–76, 766–67, 769–70. *See also* King Jr., Martin Luther

Clark, J. Reuben, 5–6, 8, 9, 17, 97, 110, 174, 208–09, 213–15, 337–39, 389, 392, 842f; and church businesses, 24, 53, 93, 255–56, 258–59, 295–99, 319–20; and George Albert Smith, 1, 815, 817; calling, 2, 284–86; death, 395–96; health, 288, 341, 368, 370, 372–73, 394; on doctrine, 300n, 317–18; on policies, 44, 58–59, 76, 356–59; on Ricks College, 167, 181–82, 249–52, 261–62, 266–69, 323–30

Clarke, Harry, 8–9, 18, 24–25, 53

Clarke, John L., 570–71, 804–05; president of Ricks College, 170–71, 175–77, 317–18

Clawson, Delwin M., 602–03

Clawson, Rudger, 839f

clothing 185, 840f, 848f. *See also* temple ordinances, garments

Clyde, George D., 145–48, 154, 205–06, 287, 310

Cold War, 97, 198–99, 310. *See also* Khrushchev, Nikita

Combs, Abel, 719–22

communism, 71–72, 101–02, 223–24, 226–27, 390, 418–20, 423, 424, 490; church teachings against, 96, 280–81, 385–87, 390, 411–13, 429, 453–54, 464–65, 467–68, 636, 649–54, 746–47, 799–800; countries, 131, 198–99, 342, 455, 774; Ezra Taft Benson on, 588–89, 590, 625–26, 628–29, 640–41, 672, 673–74, 707, 793; Karl Marx, 280–81. See also *The Naked Communist*; politics, US/socialism

Community of Christ, *see* Reorganized Church of Jesus Christ of Latter Day Saints (RLDS)

Condie, Richard P., 186, 189–91, 288–90, 292, 492, 572, 573–74, 579–80, 717–18

conservation, *see* environmental practices

constitution, *see* US Constitution

contraception, 79, 671–72, 682–85, 731, 743–45. *See also* abortion

Cornwall, J. Spencer, 186, 189–91, 196, 288–90

Correlation Department (LDS), x–xi, 139, 347–50, 437–38, 439–41, 749–51, 782–83, 794, 803–04; recommendations, 474–77, 542–46, 692–98

Cowdery, Oliver, 781–82, 784–85

Cowley, Matthew, 64

crime, 162, 163n, 164, 457–58; prisons, 163, 231; Watts riot, 608

Crockett, Earl C., 514–15

Cuba, 362–363

Cundick, Robert M., 572, 573–74, 579–80

Cutler, Virginia, 61–63, 65

Darley, Roy M., 572, 573–74, 579–80

Day, Laraine, 376–77

Demille, Cecil B., 135–36

Dempsey, Jack, 221–223

Deseret Book, 3–4, 310–11

Deseret Farms, 388–89, 474, 485, 493, 561–63, 567–68, 570
Deseret News, 39, 98, 197–99, 505–06, 530, 657–58, 675–79, 735–36, 801–03; Deseret News Publishing Company, 209; editorial influence, 84, 107, 140–41, 156–57, 169–70, 287, 421–22, 463, 471, 640–41, 649–54, 764. *See also* Hawkes, E. Earl; Robinson, O. Preston; Smith, Henry
Deseret Ranches, *see* Deseret Farms
Dialogue: A Journal of Mormon Thought, 692
diaries, vii–viii, 265, 376; DOM, xii–xv, 381
Dixie College, 81–86. *See also* junior colleges; LDS schools
doctrine, 106, 520, 775–76. *See also* LDS practices; *Gospel Doctrine* (by Joseph F. Smith); *Mormon Doctrine* (by Bruce R. McConkie); theology
Doctrine and Covenants, 138, 356, 699, 755, 781–82, 784–85, 816
Doxey, Graham H., 426, 427–28, 504–05, 570
Dunn, Howard, 592–95
Dunn, Paul H., 527, 528, 535–36
Dunyon, Joy, 99, 104
Durham, G. Homer, 746–47
Dyer, Alvin R., 748–49, 753–55, 760–61, 764–65, 783–84, 805–06; and First Presidency, 698–99, 753, 755–60, 761, 778, 787–88, 819–20; calling, 686–87, 688, 702, 706–07, 708–09, 710–12, 712–15, 733–34, 734–35; on correlation, 746–47, 749–51, 782–83, 794; on historical items, 656–67, 659–62, 727–29, 735, 781–82, 784–85; on John Birch Society, 718–19, 722–24, 729–31, 731–32; on missionary program, 292–93, 342, 777–78, 800–01; on politics, 273, 737–43, 743–45, 770–72, 774–75, 779, 791n, 793,

808–09; on racial issues, 717–18, 766–67, 769–70

Eban, Abba, 270–71
Eccles, Ellen S., 162–63
Edling, Wilford G., 526
education, *see* Church Education System
Edwards, William F., 129–30, 227–28
Egypt, 226–27, 229–30, 438–39, 441–46. *See also* Nasser, Gamal A.
Eisenhower, Dwight D., 50–51, 51–52, 71–72, 150–51, 156–57, 229–30, 310; DOM guest of, 124–27
Eisenhower, Milton, 362–63
Elizabeth II, queen of England, 73
Ellsworth, Leo, 388–89, 474, 485, 493, 495, 561–63, 567–68, 570
England, 478–79, 489–90, 494–95, 494–95. *See also* British Mission, London temple
environmental practices, 208–09, 493; Wellsville Mountain Area Project, 208–09. *See also* Fabian, Harold
Europe, 20, 149–50, 455, 774. *See also* Belgium; England; European Mission; France; Germany; Greece; Netherlands; Scotland; Switzerland
European Mission, 292–93, 342, 590–91, 591–92; West European Mission, 478–79, 489–90, 539, 547–48, 590–91, 591–92
Evans, Richard L., 79, 110–11, 170, 195, 240–44, 291–92, 383, 468–70, 551–53, 572, 704–06, 807–08, 812–13
evolution, *see* science
excommunication, 127–28, 144, 335–36, 766–67, 769–70, 799; missionaries, 232–44, 523–24; reinstatement, 424–25, 591, 593
Expenditures Committee (LDS), 558–59, 656–67, 659–62
Eyring, Henry, 45, 105–06, 107

Fabian, Harold, 140, 421–23
Fairbanks, Ortho, 287
family, *see* marriage
Family History Library, *see* Genealogical Building
Family Home Evening, 21, 542–46
Family Hour, *see* Family Home Evening
Farr, Annie Powell McKay (sister), 710–11
fashion, *see* clothing
fast and testimony meeting, 261, 520n, 600, 637
fasting, 270, 418, 520, 600, 636–37
Faust, James E., 484–85, 486–89, 763–64
Federal Building (Salt Lake City), 154, 159–60, 225–26
Federal Bureau of Investigation, 24–25, 704–06. *See also* Hoover, J. Edgar
Federal Communications Commission, 801–03
Ferguson, Thomas S., 39–40, 67–68, 123, 305–06, 306–07
Fiji, 115–16
films/movies, 2–3, 123–24, 174, 213, 344; Warner Brothers film studio, 15. *See also* Day, Laraine; DeMille, Cecil B.
Finance Department (LDS), 526, 564, 649, 792
Firmage, Edna Alice Chipman, 533–34
First Presidency, xi–xii, 251, 507, 627–28, 698–99, 817; callings and ordinations of, 2, 13, 283–86, 370–71, 372–73, 391, 397, 497–98, 616–22, 686–87, 688, 710–12, 753, 761; statements of, 386–87, 411–13, 636–37, 722–24, 788–89, 463; structure, 629, 708–09, 712–15, 755–60, 778; succession, 808–09, 812–19. *See also* Brown, Hugh B.;

Clark, J. Reuben; Dyer, Alvin R.; Isaacson, Thorpe B.; Moyle, Henry D.; Richards, Stephen L.; Tanner, N. Eldon
First Quorum of Seventy, 535–36; authority to ordain high priests, 354, 357–58, 359–60, 364, 367–68, 369, 382, 429
Fischer, Henry G., 709–10, 719–22, 726–27
Fisher, Glen G., 340, 371n, 380, 626–27
Fitzpatrick, John F. x, 32n, 73–74, 158, 165, 339
Fleming, Monroe, 622–23
Forest Dale Golf Course, 257, 299–300, 304–05, 504
France, 478–79; mission apostasy, 232–44.
Friberg, Arnold, 131–32, 749–51
Fritz, Albert B., 498–99, 512–13
fundamentalist movements, 232–44. *See also* polygamy

Gallivan, Jack, 675–79, 760–61, 762–64
Gallivan, John, 353, 486
gambling, 49–50, 244–45
Garff, Mark B., 659–62, 699–702, 702–04, 753–55, 805–06; Building Department, 592–96, 599, 604–06, 614–15, 642–43, 649, 668–69, 671
Gay, Frank W., 801–03
Genealogical Building, 346–47
Genealogical Society, 551–53, 789–91
genealogy, 87–91, 346–47, 502–03
Germany, 395; former East Germany, 342, 455
Glade, Earl J., 38, 187–88, 259–60
Goldwater, Barry, 321–22, 539
Gospel Doctrine (by Joseph F. Smith), 797–98
government, *see* political freedom; politics, US

Grant, Heber J., viii, 206–08, 815, 817, 819–20, 842f
Greece, mission, 318
Guatemala, mission, 98
Guest, Edgar A., *see* poetry

Hafen, Orval, 165–66
Hamilton, Weston E., 760–61
Hanks, Marion D., 382–83 458–59, 480–81, 494–95, 535–36; calling 753
Harding, Ralph R., 359, 509n, 519, 520–23
Hart, Cecil E., 175–77, 272
Hawaii, 88–89, 154, 314; temple, 314. *See also* Church College of Hawaii (BYU–Hawaii)
Hawkes, E. Earl, 640–41, 652–54, 662–63, 719–22; on Christmas lights, 560–61, 565
Hawkins, Dave, 561–63, 570
Haycock, D. Arthur, 8, 265, 775–76
health, *see* medical issues; McKay, David O., health
Hewlett, Lester F., 292
Hinckley, Gordon B., viii, 5, 259, 551–53, 692–96, 762–63, 807–08, 817–19; calling, 394; historian's office (LDS), 538, 551–53, 685–86, 735, 764–65, 806–07; missionary program, 128n, 240–44, 429–31, 463–64, 465, 468–70, 474–77, 518; on Book of Abraham, 715, 719–22, 724–25; on home teaching, 468–70, 474–77, 512; on homosexuality, 169, 181, 201, 782–83; on racial issues, 466–67, 480–81, 622–27; Swiss temple, 159, 195
homosexuality, *see* Hinckley, Gordon B., on homosexuality
Hoover, J. Edgar, 223–24, 464–65, 467–68, 617–18
horses, 149, 841f
hospitals, 70, 210–11, 339

Hotel Utah, 622, 645–48, 704–06, 783–84; JFK visits, 496–97, 846; DOM moving into, 312n, 335, 381; Utah Hotel Motor Lodge, 773
Hoving, Thomas P. F., 719–22
Howell, Barton J., 105–06, 107, 109
Howells, Abner, 625
Huggins, Ira A., 85–86, 102–03
Humphrey, Hubert H., 667
Hunt, Duane G., 85, 96–97
Hunter, Howard W., viii, 426, 566, 590–91, 591–92, 719–22, 789–91, 813–19; calling, 291
Hunter, Milton R., 34–35; Book of Mormon archaeology, 39–40, 67–68, 305–06; calling, 366–68, 369
Huntsville, Utah, xi; Catholic Church in, 96–97, 196–97; vacations to, 7, 42, 149, 174–75, 529, 619, 734

immigration, 77, 286, 409–10, 529–30; refugees, 71–72, 374–76
Improvement Era, 305–06, 386–87, 418, 617–18, 652–54, 685n, 778, 812–13, 816
Independence, Missouri, 753–55
India, 198–99
Information Service (LDS), 642–43, 725–26
Institutes of Religion (LDS), 274, 494–95. *See also* Bennion, Lowell L., Institute of Religion
interfaith relations, 18, 142–43, 162, 172–73, 302–04; Coptic Christian Church 142–43; Episcopal Church, 10–12; Judaism, 356–57. *See also* Catholic Church
Intimate Disciple, 137–38
Isaacson, Richard, 699, 734–35
Isaacson, Thorpe B., 29, 44, 70, 144, 147–48, 321–22, 437; and church personnel, 19, 27, 35–36, 536, 569–70, 601–02; and church property,

16, 548–50, 550–51, 592–94; calling, 616–22; First Presidency, 627–28, 672–73, 686–87, 688, 733–34, 734–35, 747–48, 755–58; health, 638, 675, 699; on Islam, 229–30, 447–53, 805–06; USAC, 36–37, 49, 59–61, 68–69, 70–71, 72, 72–73. *See also* France, mission apostasy
Isn't One Wife Enough, 265
Israel (modern state), 42, 199–200, 270–71. *See also* Ben–Gurion, David; Eban, Abba
Ivins, Antoine R., 366–68, 369, 747–48

Jakeman, Wells, 67–68
Jarvis, George Y., 27, 113, 427–28, 792
Jensen, Donald F., 365–66
John Birch Society, 470–72, 483, 490, 496, 505–06, 508–09, 519, 520–23, 588, 628–29, 635–36, 636, 652–54, 658–59, 689, 690; church members affiliated with, 463, 466, 642–45, 645–48, 690–91, 718–19, 722–24, 729–31, 731–32, 746–47. *See also* Welch, Robert W.
Johnson, "Lady Bird," 537–38, 553–54
Johnson, Lyndon B., 519, 667; meeting with DOM, 343–44, 516–17, 546, 553–54; meeting with Hugh B. Brown, 538; on civil rights, 486–89, 535
Jordan, Hashemite Kingdom of, 199, 374–76
Joseph Smith Bible, 728, 781–82, 784–85
Judd, Dennis R., 793
Juliana, queen of Holland, 57–58
junior colleges, plans for new campuses, 205–06, 256, 257, 299–300, 304–05, 319, 340, 470, 504, 638, 639–40; transfer of existing schools, 81–86, 93–94, 101, 102–03, 105. *See also* Dixie College; Ricks College

(BYU–Idaho); Snow College; Unified Church School System; Weber College; and junior college listings under Lee, J. Bracken; Wilkinson, Ernest L.
journals, *see* diaries

Kennecott Building, 346, 592n, 772–74
Kennecott Copper, 101–02, 172
Kennedy, David M., 155
Kennedy, John F., 486–89, 513, 751–53, 765; Hugh B. Brown attends funeral, 506–07; meeting with DOM, 197–99, 496–97, 846f
Kennedy, Robert F., 486–89, 751–53, 765
Kidder, Alfred V., 67–68
Kimball, LeRoy, 361–62, 386, 394, 422–23, 563–64, 664
Kimball, Spencer W., viii, xiii–xiv, 2n, 184–85, 329–35, 335–36, 386–87, 507, 529–30, 608, 782–83; and church patriarch, 46, 177, 182–84; and missionary program, 368–69, 456–57, 777–78
King, David S., 399–400, 606–07
King Jr., Martin Luther, 625–26, 768–69
Kirton, Wilford W., 554–55, 566, 669
Krushchev, Nikita, 362–363
KSL TV/Radio, 53, 258–60, 483, 801–03. *See also* Madsen, Arch L.
Ku Klux Klan, 24–25

labor missions, 491, 518, 529
labor unions, 101–02, 139, 152–53; Taft–Hartley law, 601, 602–03, 606–08, 609–10
Laguna Beach, California, retreat, 12; vacations, 69–70, 260, 664
Larkin, James J., 597–98, 599–600
last days, *see* theology, millennium
Layton Sugar Company, 25–26, 279

LDS banks, 152–55, 295–99, 320–21, 435–37. *See also* Zions First National Bank, Zions Savings Bank & Trust, Zions Securities

LDS buildings, *see* Archives Building; Assembly Hall; Beehive House; Church Administration Building; Church Office Building; Genealogical Building; meetinghouses (LDS); Salt Lake Tabernacle; temples

LDS committees/departments, *see* Budget; Personnel; Priesthood; and Standing Committee(s); and Building; Correlation; Finance; Information Service; Legal; Missionary; Purchasing; and Welfare Department(s).

LDS finances, 24–25, 67–68, 306–07, 129–30, 228, 515–16, 792; accounting, 112–13, 129, 202–03, 218–21, 272, 426, 427–28, 523, 526, 597, 604–06, 649, 765–66, 801; budgets, 350–51, 400–401, 564, 629; compensation, 5, 25, 27, 35–36, 152, 153, 154, 253, 259–60, 530, 569–70, 572, 573–74, 579–80, 601–02, 648–49, 655; Corporation of the President, 219–20, 257, 272, 356, 815–19; investments, 26–27, 42, 69–70, 152, 153, 154; taxation, 19–20, 275, 275, 276–77. *See also* Personnel Committee, social security

LDS general conference, 191–94, 421, 429, 474–77, 542, 577–79, 649–50, 708–09, 753; assignments to speak, 13, 131, 212–13, 421, 527; civil rights issues addressed, 498–99, 613–14, 707; DOM health concerns, 546–47, 616, 649

LDS historical items, 8, 97, 130, 265, 343, 346, 360–61, 376, 839f; sharing with outsiders, 209, 781–82,

784–85, 806–07. *See also* Book of Abraham, papyrus

LDS historical sites, 16, 92–93, 656–67, 659–62. *See also* Liberty Jail, Missouri; Nauvoo, Illinois; *This is the Place* monument; Troost Park monument

LDS practices, *see* fasting; interfaith relations; LDS general conference; ordinances; tithing; Word of Wisdom

LDS real estate, 5–6, 6–7, 12, 92–93, 111–12, 196–97, 227–28, 257, 273, 426, 427–28, 474, 504, 565–66, 570, 612–13, 656–67, 659–62, 753–55. *See also* Building Department; church businesses; LDS buildings; LDS historic sites

LDS schools, 111–12, 116–17, 117–18; management, 23, 66, 74–77, 514–15, 547–48, 570–71. *See also* Brigham Young University; junior colleges; Unified Church School System

LDS structure and policies, *see* Church Handbook of Instructions; excommunication; First Presidency; First Quorum of Seventy; LDS committees/departments; Melchizedek Priesthood; missionary program; Presiding Bishopric; regional representatives of the Twelve; Quorum of the Twelve Apostles

LDS teachings, *see* doctrine; theology

Lee, Harold B., viii, xiii, 99, 155, 429, 518, 755–58, 783–84, 808–09, 813–19; and church businesses, 26–27, 304; and correlation, 474–77, 692–96, 749–51; on education, 47, 542–46, 803–04; on missionary program, 318, 353–54, 465, 468–70; on politics, 20, 49–50, 64, 136, 145–48, 161, 691, 779, 779–80; on racial issues, 608, 622–27, 704–06, 780–81

Lee, Harold W., 233

Lee, J. Bracken, x, 64–65, 147–48,
150–51, 292, 313–14, 613–14, 844f;
on junior colleges, 93–94, 299–300,
304–05; on University of Utah, 64,
157–58; on USAC, 52–53, 60–61, 72
Lee, John D., 424–25
Legal Department (LDS), 220, 554–
55, 566. *See also* Kirton, Wilford W.
liberty, *see* political freedom
Liberty Jail, Missouri, 17, 492–93,
493–94
liquor laws (Utah), 162, 164, 586–88,
760–61, 762–64, 779
Lodge, Henry C., 131, 200–01
London temple, 31, 275, 276–77
Los Angeles temple, 66, 131–32,
135–36, 141, 161
Lyman, Richard R., 34, 839f
Lyon, T. Edgar, 104

MacArthur, Douglas, 5, 384
MacFarlane, Alan P., 656–67, 699,
776, 811, 819–20, 824
Madsen, Arch L., 483, 719–22
Madsen, Louis L, 49, 53–54, 60,
68–69, 70–71, 75–76
Madsen, Parley W., 524
Madsen, Truman G., 589, 615–16,
764–65
Man: His Origin and Destiny, 99, 101,
104, 112
marriage, viii–ix, 69, 174, 238, 260–61,
271–72, 335–36, 508, 520, 609,
789–91; interracial, 180, 392–94,
401, 409–10, 466–67. *See also*
adoption; adultery; contraception;
temple ordinances, sealings; *You and
Your Marriage*
Marriott, J. Willard, 51, 67–68, 364–65
Maxwell, Neal A., 804–05, 807–08
Mayhew, Wayne E., 113
McCarthy, Joseph, 96

McConkie, Bruce R., 366–68, 369,
767; *Mormon Doctrine*, 262–63, 264,
270, 300–04, 305–06, 307–09, 663
McDonald, Howard, 532
McKay, David Lawrence (son), 16,
361–62, 516–17, 652–54, 669,
801–03, 807; health of DOM, 206,
503–04, 529, 537–38, 539–40, 573;
succession and death of DOM, 811,
812–815, 819–20, 824
McKay, David Oman, xv, 335, 477–78,
630, 638–39, 846–48f; and church
members, 132–33, 210–11, 290–91;
and Clare Middlemiss, xii–xv, 73,
501–02, 571, 574–75, 630, 652–54,
655, 716–17, 747–48, 810–11;
and general conference, 546–47,
559–60, 577–79; and horses, 149,
841f; and other apostles, xi, 28,
79, 202, 282–83, 290, 388–89,
532–33, 672–73, 681, 747–48,
783–84, 785–86; health, 7, 9–10,
73, 129, 132, 137, 143, 145, 224–25,
293–94, 418, 459–60, 481, 486,
489, 490–91, 492–93, 503–04, 507,
511–12, 513–14, 517, 524–26, 528,
530–31, 534, 536–38, 539–42, 573,
599, 608–09, 632–33, 655–67,
668, 715–16, 776, 795, 810–11;
longevity, 389, 502; memories, 178,
222–23, 225, 344, 835–42f; respect
for Dwight D. Eisenhower, 150–51,
156–57; succession and death, 811,
812–19, 820–21, 824
McKay, Edward R. (son), 73, 495,
536–37, 559–60, 573, 578–79, 811,
814–15, 824
McKay, Emma Rae, *see* Ashton,
Emma Rae McKay (daughter)
McKay, Emma Ray (wife), viii–ix, 2n,
36, 43, 392, 490–91, 495, 496–97,
503–04, 553–54, 824, 836–37f, 840f,
847–48f; health, 312, 322, 785–86
McKay, Llewelyn R. (son), 528, 807

McKay, Lou Jean, *see* Blood, Lou Jean McKay (daughter)

McKay, Quinn G. (nephew), 488–89

McKay, Robert R. (son), 13–14, 503–04, 519, 520–23, 577–78, 654

McKay, Thomas E. (brother), 206

McMurrin, Sterling M., 78, 766–67, 769–70

medical issues, Adam S. Bennion, 209–10; Albert E. Bowen, 67; Clare Middlemiss, 161; DOM, 7, 9–10, 73, 129, 132, 137, 143, 145, 224, 293–94, 459–60, 481, 486, 489, 492–93, 503–04, 507, 511–12, 524, 528, 530–31, 536–38, 539–42, 546–47, 559–60, 573, 577–79, 599, 608–09, 632–33, 655–67, 668, 681, 715–16, 776, 795, 810–11; Emma Ray McKay, 312, 322, 785–86; Ernest L. Wilkinson, 162; Ezra Taft Benson, 244; flu outbreak, 191–94; Hugh B. Brown, 638; Irene Richards, 282; J. Reuben Clark, 145, 288, 341, 394; Joseph Fielding Smith, 823; Spencer W. Kimball, 184–85; Stephen L. Richards, 57, 218; Thorpe B. Isaacson, 638, 675, 699. *See also* hospitals; Viko, Louis E

meetinghouses (LDS), 122, 255–56, 548–50, 558–59, 715; Nigeria, 412–13, 415–17, 449, 452

Meikle, Steven M., 171–72, 181–82, 248–9, 325

Melchizedek Priesthood, 34, 166–67, 542–46, 593, 691; high priests, 354, 356–59, 360, 364, 366–68, 369, 383–84. *See also* Aaronic Priesthood; Priesthood Committee; priesthood ban

Mendenhall, Wendell B., 111–12, 258, 478, 485, 529, 548–50; Building Department, 580–81, 584–85, 592–96; Church Office Building, 336–37, 346, 373–74, 599

Metropolitan Museum of Art, 709–10, 715, 719–22, 726–27. *See also* LDS historical items

Mexico, 565–66, 597; mission, 127–28; schools, 612–13

Middle East, crisis, 226–27, 229–30. *See also* Egypt; Israel (modern state); Jordan, Hashemite Kingdom of; Robinson, O. Preston

Middlemiss, Clare, xi–xii, 2n, 9, 536, 557–58, 686n, 715–16, 843f; health, 161; public interactions, 164, 466, 534–35; relationship with DOM, 73, 501–02, 571, 574–75, 630, 652–54, 655, 716–17, 747–48, 810–11; succession and death of DOM, 811, 813, 819–20, 820–22, 823–24, 824

military, *see* Cold War; Vietnam War

Missionary Department (LDS), 18, 353–54, 463–64, 465, 468–69, 474–77, 478–79, 800–01.

missionary program, 38, 518; discipline, 127–28, 232–44, 344–46, 473–74, 523–24; international, 14, 98, 149–50, 199–200, 318, 342, 453–54, 455; lessons, 427, 429–31, 800–01; oversight, 18, 347–50, 353–54, 368–69, 439–41, 468–69, 468–70, 590–91, 591–92; paperwork, 228, 817–18; requirements, 185–86, 311–12, 322; youth baptisms, 278–79, 456–57, 458–59, 478–79, 489–90, 499, 518–19, 777–78.

missions, *see* Belgium; Brazil; British; European; France; Greece; Guatemala; labor missions; New Zealand; Nigeria; Scotland; South Africa

Moench, Louis, 311–12

Monson, Thomas S., 497–98, 500–01, 695, 751

Mormon Doctrine (by Bruce R. McConkie), 262–63, 264, 270, 300–04, 305–06, 307–09, 663

Mormon Tabernacle Choir, 130, 249, 424, 492; leadership, 186, 189–91, 292, 572, 573–74, 579–80; racial issues, 717–18. *See also* Cundick, Robert M.; Darley, Roy M.; Evans, Richard L.; Schreiner, Alexander

Morris, George Q., 16, 191–94, 329–35

Morrow, Dwight W., 319–20

Moss, Frank E., 496–97, 602–03, 606–07

Moss, Van, 388–89, 561–63, 567–68

Mountain Meadows Massacre, 15, 424–25

Moyle, Henry D., 20, 24, 66n, 105, 124, 329–35, 337–39, 395–96, 493, 495–96, 516n, 844f, 846f; calling, 283–86, 397; church businesses, 6–7, 295–99, 321, 435–37, 483, 485; church property, 275, 361–62; correlation, 474–77; missionary program, 232–39, 240–44, 344–46, 353–54, 429–31, 439–41, 441–46, 456–57, 463–64, 466, 478–79; on Nigeria, 404–10, 447–53; on politics, 20, 49–50, 64, 244–45, 419–20, 490; on racial issues, 371, 411

Mulder, William, 203

music, 40, 100, 259, 492, 560–61, 565, 577, 837f. *See also* Mormon Tabernacle Choir

Mutual Improvement Association, 464–65, 467–68

The Naked Communist, 411–13, 423

Nasser, Gamal A., 226–27, 229–30

National Association for the Advancement of Colored People (NAACP), 409, 482–83, 488–89, 575–76, 600–01, 622–27, 766–67, 769–70; meetings with leadership, 411, 498–99. *See also* civil rights

Nauvoo, Illinois, 213, 361–62, 386, 421–23, 462–63, 550–51, 563–64, 712

Nauvoo Restoration, 422–23, 550–51, 563–64, 664, 671, 712

Nauvoo temple, 422–23, 462–63

"Negroe question," *see* National Association for the Advancement of Colored People; race and ethnicity

Nelson, George L., 434–35, 530, 565, 763–64

Netherlands, 57–58, 478–79, 539

New World Archaeological Foundation, 67–68, 306–07. See also *Ancient America and the Book of Mormon*; Book of Mormon; Hunter, Milton R.; Ferguson, Thomas S.

New Zealand, 111–12, 117–18; mission, 118–19, 121

New Zealand temple, 118–19

Newspaper Agency Corporation, 675–79, 801–03

Nibley, Hugh, 659, 709–10, 719–22, 724–25, 735–36

Nielson, Glenn, 801–03

Nigeria, x, 371–72, 377–81, 382, 384–85, 397–98, 404–10, 413–18, 499–500, 630–31, 675; BYU students, 582–84, 603; mission, 426, 447–53, 458, 461–62, 499–500, 610–12; visas, 472–73, 481–83, 499–500, 596–97, 597–98, 599–600; western perception, 488–89, 596, 622–27

Nixon, Richard M., 556, 667–68, 787–88, 796–97

Oakland temple, 556, 557–58

Obscene Literature Committee, 8–9, 18, 24–25

Ogden temple, 699–702, 710

Ogden, Utah, 25–26, 230–31; DOM's connection to, 178, 502–03, 836f; tabernacle, 137; *see also* Weber College

Olpin, A. Ray, 61–63, 157–58, 203

Olson, Earl E., 551–53, 748–49, 781–82
Olympics, *see* sports
ordinances, *see* blessings; baptism;
    sacrament; temple ordinances; First
    Presidency, callings and ordinations
Orlando Livestock Company, 6–7,
    218–19
Ottley, Sidney J., 118–19, 121
Owens, D. Wayne, 751–53

Packer, Boyd K., 394, 463–64, 465, 470
patriarch, *see* blessings, patriarchal;
    Smith, Eldred G.
patriarchal blessings, *see* blessings,
    patriarchal
Pearl of Great Price, *see* Book of
    Abraham
Perez, Taylor H., 295–99
Personnel Committee (LDS), 35–36,
    567–68, 570; Social Security, 19, 23,
    24, 35–36, 45
Petersen, Mark E., 93, 56–57, 156–57,
    191–94, 212–13, 291–92, 433–34,
    725–26, 753–55, 755–58, 782–83,
    791n, 819; on John Birch Society,
    642–45, 652–53, 691, 731–32;
    on missionary program, 368–69,
    478–79, 478–79, 489–90, 539,
    547–48, 590–91, 591–92; on *Mor-
    mon Doctrine*, 270, 300–04, 305–06;
    on racial issues, 472–73, 625–27,
    780–81; on Ricks College, 248,
    323–30
Pioneer Memorial Theatre, *see* Salt
    Lake Memorial Theatre
poetry, xi, 222, 320, 615
political freedom, 37, 40–41, 126,
    198–99, 718–19, 722–24. *See also*
    US Constitution
political neutrality, 225, 340, 399–400,
    486, 770–72; declarations of, 14–15,
    38, 41, 145–48, 546–47, 767–68

politics, international, 14, 20, 58–59,
    118, 342, 403–04, 778. *See also* Ger-
    many; Nigeria; United Nations
politics, US, ix, 18, 19–20, 37, 43,
    71–72, 74, 139, 213–14, 223–24,
    455–56, 770–72; church lobbying in
    Idaho/Wyoming, x, 49–50; "Com-
    mittee of 1976," 650–52, 655–56,
    670–71, 674, 681–82, 689, 740;
    patriotism, 127, 689–90; socialism,
    411–13, 453–54, 628–29, 640–41,
    650–51, 778, 793. *See also* American
    Independent Party; Benson, Ezra
    Taft; John Birch Society; immi-
    gration; labor unions; Romney,
    George W.; sex education; Udall,
    Stewart L.; Watkins, Arthur V.
politics, Utah, x, 20, 42–43, 136, 161,
    213–18, 292, 353, 505–06, 507–08;
    civil rights, 466–67, 575–76,
    585–86; governorship, 135, 139,
    145–48; legislature, 60, 64, 165–66,
    731, 743–45, 779–80, 791–92;
    municipal home rule, 187–88;
    reapportionment, 81, 105; Sunday
    closing law, 287, 434–35, 687. *See
    also* Backman, Gustave P.; Fitzpat-
    rick, John F.; Lee, J. Bracken; liquor
    laws (Utah); Obscene Literature
    Committee; taxes
Poll, Richard D., 390, 490
polygamy, viii–ix, 124, 136–37, 138,
    591, 593; books on, 137–38, 265;
    Ebeid Sarofim of Egypt, 438–39,
    441–46, 466; French mission, 232–
    44; Manifesto, 233, 448; Nigeria,
    447–53. *See also* Tucker, William P.
Porter, Arthur C., 181–82, 261–62,
    266–69
Presiding Bishopric, 29, 30, 92,
    358–59, 391–92, 395, 411, 502–03,
    542–46, 704–06, 736–37, 795–96.
    See also Brown, Victor L.; Bueh-
    ner, Carl W.; Simpson, Robert L.;

tithing; welfare program; Wirthlin, Joseph L.
Preston, George D., 54–56, 72
priesthood ban, criticism of, 622–27, 692, 766–67, 769–70; implementation, 87–91, 180, 201–02, 340–41, 459, 480–81, 502, 568; origins, 87–88, 534–35, 745, 808; possible changes, 116, 116n, 407, 447–53, 483–84, 596–97, 597–98. *See also* Nigeria; race and ethnicity
Priesthood Committee (LDS), 44, 78, 474–77, 692–96
Provo temple, 699–702, 702–04
Pugh, Warren E., 439–41
Purchasing Department (LDS), 129–30

Quealy Jr., Jay A., 169, 173–74, 201
Quorum of the Twelve Apostles, xi–xii, 698–99; callings and ordinations, 13, 30, 66n, 79, 291, 394, 444–45, 497–98, 500–01; consensus, 225–26. *See also* Benson, Ezra Taft; Kimball, Spencer W.; Lee, Harold B.; Petersen, Mark E.; Stapley, Delbert L.; Smith, Joseph Fielding

race and ethnicity, x, 411, 473n, 608, 622–27, 780–81; Italians, 71–72; Jews, 164; Mexicans, 612–13; politics surrounding, 454–55, 482–83, 600–01, 613–14, 707, 768–69; public appearances by blacks, 38, 40–41, 354–55; segregation, 140–41, 365–66, 371, 392–94; 466–67, 484–85; segregation within church, 512–13, 517, 691, 717–18, 788–89, 401. *See also* apartheid; marriage, interracial; priesthood ban; Thurmond, Strom; Wallace, George C.
Rainbow Randevu ballroom, 225

Rampton, Calvin L., 585–86, 586–88, 601, 602–03
Rector, Hartman, 753
refugees, *see* immigration
regional representatives of the Twelve, xi, 347–49, 692–98, 709
Reiser, A. Hamer, 138–39, 550–51
Relief Society, 21, 32–33, 274–75, 276, 542–46, 772–74
Reorganized Church of Jesus Christ of Latter Day Saints (RLDS), 534–35, 727–29, 735, 781–82, 784–85
repentance, *see* theology, forgiveness
Reuther, Walter, 362–63
Rexburg, Idaho, *see* Ricks College (BYU–Idaho)
Rich, Max, 760–61, 762–64
Richards, D. F., bank president, 181–82
Richards, Franklin D., 341, 398–99, 592–93
Richards, George F., 839f
Richards, Irene, 281–82
Richards, LeGrand, 329–35, 539, 780–81, 804; and church personnel, 23, 601–02; and missionary program, 242–44, 518; ordination, 30; on office of patriarch, 46, 177, 182–84
Richards, Stephen L., 15, 18, 137–38, 164–65, 174, 191–94, 206–08, 231, 839f; church businesses, 24, 258–59; church personnel, 45, 58–59; death, 281–82; health, 218; ordination, 2; on racial issues, 91; on Ricks College, 167, 181–82, 249–52; on temples, 17, 275, 276–77
Ricks College (BYU–Idaho), 33, 95, 361, 570–71, 804–05, 845f; Committee of One Thousand, 266–69, 272; proposed move to Idaho Falls, 167–69, 170–72, 174, 175–77, 178–80, 180–81, 181–82, 246–49,

249–53, 261–62, 263–64, 266–69, 272, 273–74, 323–30, 329–35, 355–56. *See also subentries under* Brown, Hugh B.; Clark, J. Reuben; Clarke, John L.; Petersen, Mark E.; Romney, Marion G.; Wilkinson, Ernest L.

Riesel, Victor, 390

Ririe, Walter F., 181–82, 266–69

Robinson, O. Preston, 107, 109, 140–41, 156–57, 169–70, 209, 421–22, 530; on Middle East, 226–27, 229–30

Romney, George W., 266, 403–04, 774–75; racial issues, 401, 454–55, 692

Romney, Marion G., 26–27, 57–58, 191–94, 286, 512, 755–58, 813–19; calling, 13; committees, 47, 558–59, 592–93, 695; correlation, 474–77; Mexico, 565–66, 612–13; on missionary program, 465, 468–70, 473–74; on *Mormon Doctrine*, 270, 300–04; on politics, 64, 606–07, 764; on racial issues, 180, 788–89; on Ricks College, 247–49, 323–30, 329–35

Romney, Vernon, 791–92

Roosevelt, Eleanor, 362–363

Rosenblatt, Joseph, 187–88, 675–79

sabbath, *see* politics, Utah, Sunday closing law

sacrament, 28, 231, 270

sacrament meeting, 385–86, 691. *See also* fasting; stake conference

salaries, *see* LDS finance

Salisbury, Howard E., 170–71, 178–80, 274, 325

Salt Lake City, 169–70, 191–94

Salt Lake Memorial Theatre, 144–45, 157–58, 172

Salt Lake Tabernacle, 40–41, 131, 383, 751–53, 776–77

Salt Lake temple, 575, 576, 839f, 840f; Christmas lights, 560–61, 565, 631–32; security, 197, 455–56, 457–58, 532, 704–06

Salt Lake Theatre, 206–08. *See also* Salt Lake Memorial Theatre

Salt Lake Tribune, 157–58, 339, 353, 675–79, 801–03

Salt Palace, 410, 675–79

salvation, *see* theology, death and afterlife

Samoa, 116–17, 121, 480–81

Sarofim, Ebeid, 438–39, 441–46, 449, 466

Savage, Alfred, 377–81, 382

Schreiner, Alexander, 100, 572, 573–74, 579–80

Schwartz, Fred C., 464–65, 467–68

science, 45, 120–21; evolution, 112, 302, 344. See also *Man: His Origin and Destiny*; technology

Scotland, 222–23; mission, 355, 835f, 838f

Scott, Walter, *see* poetry

scriptures, *see* Bible, translations; Book of Abraham, papyrus; Book of Mormon; Doctrine and Covenants; Joseph Smith Bible

security, for DOM, 20; Salt Lake temple, 197, 455–56, 457–58, 532, 704–06

sex education, 791–92, 803–04. *See also* contraception

Sharp, Ivor, 259–60

Sill, Sterling, 62, 65

Simpson, Robert L., 502, 558–59

Skousen, W. Cleon, 110–11, 316, 384; and John Birch Society, 463, 635–36; on communism, 385–86, 411–13, 418–20, 423, 464–65, 467–68, 490; police chief, 162, 163n, 164, 313–14

Smith, Eldred G., 3, 557, 557–58, 733–34, 734–35; censure of, 46,

177; duties as church patriarch, 65, 104, 182–84

Smith, Florence, 92–93

Smith Jr., George A., 69, 808

Smith, George Albert, viii, 1, 5–6, 8, 265, 815, 817, 819–20, 839f

Smith, Henry, 98, 300, 304–05, 421–22, 505–06, 620, 640–41, 649–50, 653–54, 798–99

Smith, John H., 265

Smith, Joseph F., 169, 173–74, 181, 201, 448

Smith, Joseph Fielding, viii, 2, 13, 47, 191–94, 519, 520–23, 540–42, 593–94, 636–37, 796–98, 839f; and First Presidency, 617–22, 627–28, 712–15, 722–24, 778, 820–21; author of *Man: His Origin and Destiny*, 99, 101, 104, 112; health, 808–09, 823; on church buildings, 668–69, 671, 701–02, 753–55; on church history/records, 492–93, 493–94, 551–53, 575, 576, 687–88, 712, 735, 748–49, 781–82, 804; on contraception, 671–72, 682–85; on missionary program, 239n, 240–44, 463–64, 465; on *Mormon Doctrine*, 300–04, 307–09; on racial issues, 201–02, 766–67, 769–70, 808; on responsibilities of general authorities, 357–59, 360, 429, 433–34, 468–70

Smith Jr., Joseph, vii–viii, xi, 137–38, 213, 437–38, 739–43, 757, 764–65

Smoot, Dan, 655–56

Smoot, Reed, 105, 131n, 839f

Snow College, 81–86. See also junior colleges

Snow, Herbert A., 24, 155

Sons of Utah Pioneers, 130, 140

South Africa, 87–90, 90–91, 447–53; mission, 380–81, 623, 788–89

South and Central America, 14, 98, 453–54. See also Brazil; Chile; Guatemala; Mexico

South Pacific, see Fiji; Samoa; New Zealand

Soviet Union, 198–99, 249, 774; see also communism; Poland

space travel, 198, 423–24

Spafford, Belle S., 33, 274–75, 276

sports, 223, 354–55; Olympics (1972), 641, 760–61, 762–64. See also Dempsey, Jack

St. George temple, 45–46

stake conferences, 164–65, 203, 358–59, 360, 400–01, 431–34, 612–13, 692–93. See also general conference

Standing Committee (LDS), 255–56, 257, 262, 279–80

Stapley, Delbert L., 139, 329–35, 360–61, 727–28, 762–63; on budget, 350–51, 507; on church businesses, 304, 570, 671; on salary/pensions, 19, 19–20, 25, 27, 35–36, 648–49

Stewart, Adiel F., 164, 187–88

Stewart, Isaac M., 492, 572

Stoddard, Howard J., 162–63, 295–99, 801–03

Stringfellow, Douglas R., 77–78, 106–07, 108, 109–10

Stringham, Bryce, 561–63

Strong, Ernest A., 123

sugar industry, see Layton Sugar Company

Switzerland, temple, 23, 31, 67, 129, 159, 275, 276–77

Taiwan, 127

Talmage, James E, , 839f

Talmage, John R., 287

Tanner, N. Eldon, x, xiii–xiv, 474–77, 520, 529–30, 538, 540–42, 545–56, 551–53, 575, 589, 704–06, 809–10; and Building Department, 504,

547–48, 548–50, 558–59, 569, 594–95, 599, 601–02, 604–06, 699–702, 753–55, 805–06; and businesses, 561–63, 563–64, 657–58, 801–03; and Ezra Taft Benson, 672, 673–74, 793; and First Presidency, 515–16, 621–22, 627–28, 672–73, 708–09, 710–12, 712–15, 755–60, 787–88, 812–19; and missionary program, 441–46, 468–70, 518–19; calling, 444–45, 341, 497–98, 500–01; on Book of Abraham, 687–88, 715, 719–22, 724–25; on colleges, 514–15, 556–57, 570–71, 794; on correlation, 692–98, 749–51, 782–83; on finances, 526, 564, 765–66; on John Birch Society, 647–48, 722–24, 729–31; on Nigeria, 377–381, 382, 384–85, 413–18, 426, 447–53, 458, 461–62, 472–73, 481–83, 484, 499–500, 582–84, 596; on politics, 516–17, 602–03, 687, 743–45, 760–61, 762–64; on racial issues, 622–27, 717–18, 788–89

taxes, 19–20, 477–78, 529, 275, 276–77

Taylor, Daniel P., 565–66, 612–13

Taylor, Delbert G., 167–69, 170–71, 175–77, 181–82, 247–48, 249–52, 263–64, 266–69, 273–74

Taylor, Harvey L., 507–08, 514–15, 570–71

Taylor, John W., 591, 593

Taylor, Samuel W., 3–4, 437, 591

technology, 69–70, 120–21, 143, 166, 629–30, 812; effects, 120–21, 143–44, 186–87, 423–24, 609; microfilm, 105–06, 107, 265; recordings, 5, 34, 223–24, 264, 642–43; television, 56–57, 64–65, 293, 421

Teichert, Minerva, 65–66

Temple Mormonism, 105–06, 107, 109

temple ordinances, 8, 31, 105–06, 107, 109, 195, 276–77, 335–36, 789–91;

endowment movies, ix–x, 67, 80, 129, 141, 161; garments, 46n, 185, 309, 376–77; racial ban, 180, 201–02; sealings, 5, 9, 139, 143–44, 211, 271–72, 291, 426, 535–36, 789–91, 795–96, 817; second anointing, 9, 575, 576. *See also* temples

Temple Square Hotel, 261

temples, ix–x, 17, 43, 45–46, 159, 275, 276–77, 287, 398–99, 527–28, 753–55, 805–06; solemn assemblies, 45–46; taxation, 19–20, 275, 276–77. *See also* specific countries (New Zealand, Switzerland), states (Hawaii), and cities (London, Los Angeles, Nauvoo, Oakland, Ogden, Provo, Salt Lake City, Washington DC)

Tennyson, Alfred Lord, *see* poetry

theology, x–xi, 143–44; death and afterlife, 318–17, 421; faith, 13–14, 100, 184–85, 423–24; forgiveness, 181, 344–46, 363–64, 473–74; free agency, 601, 793; happiness, 290–91, 338–39; Jesus Christ, 123–24, 520; Lamanites, 612–13; millennium, 164–65, 270. *See also* doctrine

This is the Place monument, 5–6, 130, 140

Thomas, Jack, 292

Thorvaldsen, Bertel, 231

Thurmond, Strom, 650–51, 670–71, 681–82

Time magazine, 596, 606–08

tithing, 100, 381–82, 400–01, 507, 513; annual reports, 219, 350–51, 523, 632, 765–66; church employees, 211–12, 275, 481, 518, 526–27, 529

Tooele, Utah, 371, 392–94

Toronto, LaMont F., 54–56, 157–58

Tracy, Stanley, 223–24

Trans–American Banking Corporation, 153–54, 155

transportation, 7, 170, 192, 736–37, 841f; airplanes, 120–21, 736–37,

845f; automobiles, 179, 317, 847f; trains, 124, 151, 155, 260
Troost Park monument, 492–93, 493–94
Truman, Harry S., 40–41, 151
Trunnel, Jack, 524
Tucker, William P., 232–39, 242–44
Tuttle, A. Theodore, 382–83, 453–54
Tyler, Lyman, 551–53, 589, 662

Udall, Stewart L., 392–94, 496–97, 692
Unified Church School System, 74–77, 388, 514–15, 559, 560, 556–57. *See also* Church Education System; junior colleges; LDS schools; Mexico, schools; Wilkinson, Ernest L.
United Nations, 14–15, 131, 200–01, 502, 718, 796–99
University Club Building, 657–58
University of Utah, viii, 40–41, 61–63, 63, 64, 142–43, 144–45, 203, 274, 425–26, 533–34, 807–08; DOM's relationship with, viii–ix, 16–17, 838f. *See also* Olpin, A. Ray
Utah Lake, 493
Utah OB–GYN Society, 731, 743–45
Utah State Agricultural College, 354–55; board of trustees, 36–37, 49, 52, 53–56, 59–61, 68–69, 70–71, 72–73, 75–76. *See also* Isaacson, Thorpe B.; Madsen, Louis L.
Utah State University, *see* Utah State Agricultural College
US Constitution, 347–48, 429, 746–47, 749–51
US Supreme Court, 205, 223–24, 434–35, 628–29, 793. *See also* Warren, Earl

Van Dam, Donovan, 57–58
Vandenberg, John H., 391, 398, 411, 481, 502, 542, 558–59, 592–93, 632

Vietnam War, 798–99
Viko, Louis E., 9–10, 129, 132, 211, 418, 490–91, 492–93, 503–04, 528, 536–37, 542, 546–47, 608–09, 632–33

Walker Bank, 153–54, 155, 295–99
Wall Street Journal, 96–97
Wallace, George C., 737–43, 767–68, 774–75, 776–77
Wallace, Irving, 376–77
Wallace, John M., 141–42, 153–54
Warren, Earl, 223–24
Washington DC temple, 527–28, 780–81, 805–06
Watkins, Arthur V., 14, 20, 44, 71–72, 74, 145–48, 150, 154
Webb, W. Lamar, 295–99
Weber College, 81–86, 100, 102–03, 836f. *See also* junior colleges
Weber State University, *see* Weber College
Weilenmann, Milton L., 106–07, 108–09, 109–10
Welch, Robert W., 470–72, 490, 496, 508–09, 645–48, 689, 690, 691, 791n
Welfare Department (LDS), 164–65, 285–86
welfare program, 26–27, 58, 70, 285n; acceptance of state aid, 58–59. *See also* Welfare Department (LDS)
West, Franklin L., 23, 47, 66
Wheelwright, Lorin, 5–6, 206
Whitney, Orson F., 591n, 839f
Whitmer, John, 781–82, 784–85
Widtsoe, John A., 31, 66, 839f
Wilcox, Claire, 137–38
Wilkinson, Ernest L., xiii, 64–65, 162, 203–04, 288, 530n, 724–25; and BYU, 40, 61–63, 94, 112–13, 211–12, 227–28, 275, 390, 481, 514–15, 517, 556–57, 615–16, 688–89, 743–45, 794, 800, 844f;

and church school system, 274,
317, 388, 559, 560, 570–71; on
junior colleges, 93–95, 205–06, 256,
299–300, 304–05, 504, 639–40;
on politics, 103, 139, 165–66, 205,
213–18, 501, 506, 507–08; on racial
issues, 354–55; on Ricks College,
33, 167–69, 174, 175–77, 178–80,
181–82, 246–47, 249–53, 266, 269,
323, 323–30, 329–35, 355–56, 361
Williams, J. D., 418–20
Williams, LaMar S., 371–72,
377–381, 384–85, 397–98, 404–10,
413–18, 426, 447–53, 458, 472–73,
481–83, 499–500, 512–13, 582–84,
596–97, 599–600, 610–12, 622–27,
630–31
Wirthlin, Joseph L., 6–7, 19, 30,
35–36, 44, 172–73, 177–78, 391
women, 512, 520; employment, 9, 69,
76, 177, 425
Women's Voluntary Service Program,
274–75, 276
Wood, Wilford C., 16, 17, 209
Woodbury, T. Bowring, 275, 278–79,
438–39
Woodruff, Wilford, vii, 238, 745
Woolley, Arthur, 72
Word of Wisdom, 804; alcohol,
162–63, 364–65, 586–88, 760–61,
762–64; coffee, 772

worship services, *see* fast and testi-
mony meeting; sacrament meeting
Wright, Bryce R., 610–12, 626–27
Wright, Darcey U., 536
Wright, Jay W., 258–59
Wright, William R. xiii–xiv

Yarn Jr., David H., 816
Ye Are Gods, 127–28
You and Your Marriage, 260–61
Young, Brigham, vii–viii, 745, 804,
806–07
Young, George C., 531–32
Young, Kimball, 265
Young, Levi E., 13, 527
Young, S. Dilworth, 366–68, 369

Zappey, Cornelius, 57–58
ZCMI, 3–4, 20, 221, 279–80, 310–11,
364–65, 526–27 Zions First National Bank, 279–80, 295–99, 304,
314–16, 319–20, 435–37
Zions Savings Bank & Trust, 24, 155
Zions Securities Corporation, 24,
159–60, 218–19

About the editor

Harvard S. Heath was curator (now retired) of the Utah and American West Archives at the Harold B. Lee Library, Brigham Young University. In 1990 he received a PhD in American History from BYU. He is the editor of *In the World: The Diaries of Reed Smoot* and a contributor to the modern edition of James E. Talmage's 1912 *House of the Lord: A Study of Holy Sanctuaries Ancient and Modern*. He was also a lead researcher for BYU President Ernest L. Wilkinson's four-volume *Brigham Young University: The First One Hundred Years*.

"These selections from McKay's diaries provide a rare and fascinating glimpse into mid-twentieth-century Mormonism. We not only see the world of one influential man, but also decades of his interactions with a set of equally famous associates. The one-sided, folksy character of McKay is complicated and deepened as the diary exposes his vigorous anti-communism and his rejection of race mixing. Given the paucity of primary sources to document the twentieth-century LDS hierarchy, *Confidence amid Change* is a matchless treasure."

 —**Colleen McDannell**, Professor of History and Sterling M. McMurrin Professor of Religious Studies, University of Utah; author of *Sister Saints: Mormon Women Since the End of Polygamy*

"Here we have a detailed account of the larger-than-life Mormon prophet David O. McKay, who presided over the LDS Church during a time of momentous change. The diaries are rich with behind-the-scenes glimpses of both the challenges and opportunities for church leaders as they grappled with an age of modernity following the Second World War. It's all there, from McKay's strong racial proclivities to an uneasiness with his apostle/politician Ezra Taft Benson's association with the John Birch Society; from the controversy about future apostle Bruce R. McConkie's seminal book, *Mormon Doctrine*, to McKay's love of poets Robert Burns, Edgar A. Guest, Walter Scott, and Alfred Lord Tennyson. Plus, we get vignettes of the church president's meetings with American presidents Dwight D. Eisenhower, John F. Kennedy, and Lyndon B. Johnson. I can't think of another primary source of modern-day Mormonism that is as detailed and insightful as this."

 —**Matthew L. Harris**, Professor of History, Colorado State University–Pueblo; coauthor of *The Mormon Church and Blacks: A Documentary History*

"Anyone who reads President McKay's diaries will come away with a much better understanding of LDS history during the critical years from 1951 to 1970. You will read of events that shaped our church internationally and locally. Marilyn Lamborn, of my Ogden ward, was one of the French missionaries mentioned in the diaries who was excommunicated in 1958. In California we lived in the same ward as Tom Ferguson, who McKay mentions sought Book of Mormon evidence among Latin-American ruins. The diaries contain an assessment of Bruce R. McConkie's *Mormon Doctrine* (over 1,000 errors) and Joseph Fielding Smith's controversial *Man: His Origin and Destiny*. They detail the roles that Ezra Taft Benson and Hugh B. Brown played in politics. We gain insights by reading the interactions among church employees during McKay's illnesses. Just read the diaries! They are instructive and suspenseful."

— **Thomas G. Alexander**, Lemuel Harrison Redd Professor of Western American History emeritus, Brigham Young University; author of *Mormonism in Transition: A History of the Latter-day Saints, 1890–1930*

"This is a superb addition to Mormon literature! Harvard Heath has carefully combed through the extensive diaries and supplementary material that comprise this remarkable collection. The diaries are exceptionally revealing, with details relative to church schools, involvement in politics, and the tragedy of the apostasy within the French mission. Most importantly, they show how a person born when Ulysses S. Grant was president of the United States adapted to the realities of the post-World War II world. They also demonstrate that attitudes on race, gender, nationalism, and use of power reflected McKay's own education and experience. As a primary document, aptly annotated, this is a must-read for any serious student of LDS history. There are insights here into the church and the times, and also into the man who looked, spoke, and behaved as a prophet."

— **F. Ross Peterson**, former vice president, Utah State University; past co-editor, *Dialogue: A Journal of Mormon Thought*

Also in the *Signature Legacy Series*

Thirteenth Apostle The Diaries
of Amasa M. Lyman, 1832–1877

Scott H. Partridge, editor

1,084 pages | $60 hardback | $9.99 ebook

Amasa Lyman was ordained an apostle in 1842 to replace Orson Pratt, who had been removed from the Quorum of the Twelve. When Pratt returned and was reinstated, Lyman became a third wheel for three years. After being reinstated, he documented his daily activities leading a group of Southern converts and slaves to Utah (and being mistaken along the way for General Winfield Scott's troops returning from Mexico), collecting tithing from LDS prospectors in California, founding the colony of San Bernardino in Southern California, and presiding over the European Mission. When he was back in Utah again, Lyman became associated with the Godbeite movement and assumed the presidency of the New Church of Zion. When the church built an auditorium in Salt Lake City, it drew up to 1,000 people per service to hear mediums channel messages from the spirit world. Lyman's transformation from apostle to spiritualist was, in his view, a constant path toward enlightenment, while others, he believed, wavered and became self-satisfied and complacent.

forthcoming volumes in this series include the journals of
the following prominent LDS figures, among others

George Albert Smith
LDS Church president
edited by Bryan R. Buchanan

Charles W. Penrose
Quorum of the Twelve
edited by Christian Larsen

James E. Talmage
Quorum of the Twelve
edited by James P. Harris

Ernest L. Wilkinson
BYU president
edited by Gary James Bergera

A SPECIMEN

Confidence amid Change is set in Adobe Caslon, a revival typeface based on British gunsmith and type designer William Caslon's 1734 London design. The titles and running heads are set in Neue Helvetica, a version of Swiss designer Max Miedinger's original typeface, refined by German type foundry Stempel in 1983 for digital composition. The shaded bars throughout the book represent the timeline of the diaries.